Organisations and the ~~Business Environment~~ nent

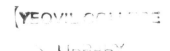

Organisations and the Business Environment

Second edition

David Campbell and Tom Craig

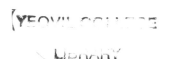

ELSEVIER
BUTTERWORTH
HEINEMANN

AMSTERDAM • BOSTON • HEIDELBERG • LONDON • NEW YORK • OXFORD
PARIS • SAN DIEGO • SAN FRANCISCO • SINGAPORE • SYDNEY • TOKYO

Butterworth-Heinemann is an imprint of Elsevier
The Boulevard, Langford Lane, Kidlington, Oxford, OX5 1GB, UK
30 Corporate Drive, Suite 400, Burlington, MA 01803, USA

First edition 2005
Reprinted 2008

Notice
No responsibility is assumed by the publisher for any injury and/or damage to persons
or property as a matter of products liability, negligence or otherwise, or from any use
or operation of any methods, products, instructions or ideas contained in the material
herein. Because of rapid advances in the medical sciences, in particular, independent
verification of diagnoses and drug dosages should be made

British Library Cataloguing in Publication Data
A catalogue record for this book is available from the British Library

Library of Congress Cataloging-in-Publication Data
A catalog record for this book is available from the Library of Congress

ISBN: 978-0-7506-5829-4

For information on all Butterworth-Heinemann publications
visit our website at books.elsevier.com

Printed and bound in *China*

08 09 10 10 9 8 7 6 5 4 3 2

Working together to grow
libraries in developing countries

www.elsevier.com | www.bookaid.org | www.sabre.org

ELSEVIER   BOOK AID
            International   Sabre Foundation

Contents

Part II The external business macro-environment **121**

Chapter 8 *The political environment* *123*

Acknowledgements

We wish to thank the members of the Caledonian Business School and the Newcastle Business School for their support and counsel during the preparation of this text. Worthy of particular thanks are Elaine Bradley and Shelly Liu of Glasgow Caledonian University and Margaret English at Strathclyde University for their invaluable contributions and encouragement. Also, our thanks to the team at Elsevier and special credit goes to the editorial and production team at Charon Tec Pvt Ltd for their professional service and patience throughout the production of this book.

To my grandchildren Gemma, Fiona and Lewis
TC

Business organisations

CHAPTER 1

Organisations and organisational theories

After studying this chapter, students should be able to describe:

- what an organisation is;
- the ways in which organisational theories differ;
- the organisational and management ideas of the *classical* thinkers;
- the development and principles of *scientific management*;
- the concept of *bureaucracy*;
- the *human relations'* theories and the work of Elton Mayo;
- the essentials of *systems* thinking as it pertains to organisations;
- what is meant by *contingency theory* and how it relates to organisations.

1.1 What is an organisation?

The origins of organisations can be traced back to ancient civilisations where various groupings of individuals, such as armies and civic administrations, were designed as social structures that would facilitate collaborative activities to achieve the desired goals.

The industrial revolution in the nineteenth century triggered rapid economic and manufacturing growth, with emerging businesses radically altering the pattern of working life from individual or family run cottage industries. New methods of running businesses were required and, although all organisations can exhibit similar characteristics, the evolutionary path for individual businesses is determined by such factors as size, diversity, ownership, nature of the business and the complexity of the business environment.

Talcott Parsons (1960)[1] described the development of organisations as the principal mechanism by which things get done in a highly differentiated society and that goals can be achieved that are beyond the reach of individuals.

In studying the nature and functions of organisations, it is worth starting with a working definition and *Buchanan and Huczynski* (2003)[2] suggested the following:

'Organisations are social arrangements for the controlled performance of collective goals.'[2]

This definition, concise though it is, shows us the two most important features of organisations: they are *social arrangements* and they exist to *perform*. We can say the following general things about the organisations:

- They all contain *people* (although it may be argued that some natural groupings of animals in the wild may also be organisations).
- The people in the organisation *perform* a role and their continued membership of the organisation is dependent upon such performance.
- The organisation has a *collective goal* to which all members subscribe.
- All of the roles, taken together, help the organisation achieve its collective goal.
- Different tasks according to their expertise, interest or specialism.
- There is a clearly defined *hierarchy of authority* so that each member of the organisation is aware of where he or she 'fits in'.
- The limits or *borders of an organisation are usually clearly defined.* This means that there is usually no doubt whether a particular person is 'inside' or 'outside' of the organisation.

Question 1.1

According to the definition discussed above, decide whether the following collectives are organisations or not:

- The United Nations
- Chartered Management Institute

- Robbie Williams Fan Club
- IBM Ltd
- Caledonian Business School
- Royal Navy
- Nationwide Building Society
- National Union of Students
- A school of whales.

1.2　Why do organisations exist?

Why is it that people form themselves into organisations in order to carry out business activities? Why do they not simply act alone to fulfil their individual objectives? The answer is that the format of an organisation offers many advantages over the other option which is many people acting alone.

Firstly, organisations facilitate *synergy*. Synergy refers to the benefits that can be gained when people work together rather than apart. Something can be said to be synergistic when the *whole is greater than the sum of the parts*. More popularly, synergy can be expressed as '2 + 2 = 5'. On a simple level, two people *together* lifting heavy logs onto a lorry can achieve far more work than two people lifting logs separately. A rally team of two enables the team to win a race if they work together with one driving and one navigating. If the two were to work separately, then each person would have to drive and navigate at the same time.

Secondly, organisations facilitate the *division of labour*. Our two workers lifting logs are both performing the same task, but the rally team is divided into two separate but complementary jobs – a division of labour. It is quite possible, and may be even preferable, for the navigator to not even hold a driving licence, but if he or she is a good mapreader, the rally team is greatly strengthened. Similarly, the driver does not need to know how to read maps, provided he or she can take instructions from the navigator and drive well. The two specialists working together do not only produce synergy, but they also enable a task to be accomplished that neither member could accomplish alone.

Thirdly, adopting the format of an organisation enables increased performance owing to the establishment of *formal systems of responsibility and authority*. When such systems are implemented, they enable all members to fully understand how roles are divided, and to accept and respect both responsibility and authority. They facilitate synergy and an effective division of labour by co-ordinating activities so that individuals act in concert to the overall benefit of the organisation.

1.3 An overview of organisational theories

Now that we have come to broad understanding of what an organisation is, we turn to a discussion of the various theories that have been put forward to analyse organisations and explain how and why organisations 'work'.

We can all readily appreciate that organisations differ. Some are big and 'bureaucratic' whilst others are small, 'lean and mean'. Furthermore, the way that organisations are managed also varies widely. Some management styles are highly regimented within formal structures whilst others are *laissez faire* and 'laid back'.

These differences have led to a diversity of individuals' experience at work. Academics have sought to help explain the reasons for these differences in management style and how organisations work, through the use of organisational theories. It is impossible to say that 'good management is …' or that 'an organisation should be managed in this way'. It all depends upon the context of the organisation, its purpose and the type of people that work in it. Over the course of the past century, academics have evolved theories which aid our understanding and hence our ability to explain, how organisations 'work'.

The theories can be grouped under four broad convenient headings. They are presented in chronological order and we will examine each in turn:

- classical theories,
- human relations' theories,
- systems theories,
- contingency theories.

1.4 Classical theories

Definition

We use the word *classical* in various ways during normal conversation. For example, it can be used to describe the study of ancient Greek or Roman culture or to denote widely acknowledged works of lasting significance and excellence, such as music by Beethoven or paintings by Van Gogh.

The principles that underpin classical scholarly activities were adopted by the earliest theorists of management in organisations at the start of the twentieth century and their influence continues to the present day. The classical management thinkers emphasised the purpose of organisations and viewed them as formal structures through which a hierarchy of management could achieve organisational goals and objectives. They believed that effective management could be distilled down into rules, guidelines or principles, which, within limits, would be transferable to all managerial contexts.

Broadly speaking, classical theorists focused on an organisation's output and productivity rather than the individuals in the organisation. Thus, many were concerned with the methods by which the human resources could deliver the greatest output at least cost.

An underlying assumption of classical theories is that the human being, as a social and working being is relatively predictable in his or her responses to given situations. This assumption of predictability underlies the work of all of the classical theorists. Put simply, it states that *if* a certain managerial style or set of conditions is applied to the working environment, *then* individuals will respond in a predictable way. The theories we consider later in this chapter make the assumption that man is somewhat a more complex being than the classical thinkers realised.

'Classical' as a title, conceals a broad range of theories. Within this category, there are many important thinkers who have advanced differing techniques and philosophies for managing organisations. We will examine the contributions of the most important thinkers, dividing our discussion into three categories: the work of *Henri Fayol*, the *Scientific Management* school and the concept of the *Bureaucratic* organisation.

Henri Fayol

Fayol (1841–1925) was a French industrialist who spent his entire working life with a coal mining company. His main contribution to organisational theory was his attempt to break down the management job into its component parts. He defined management as follows:

> 'To manage is to forecast and plan, to organise, to command, to co-ordinate and to control.'

His work is best remembered for his '*six activities*' and his '*fourteen principles*' (Table 1.1). He developed these from his own experiences as a manager and he worked them out in his own working life, with beneficial effects.

Table 1.1

Fayol's fourteen principles of management

Principle	Meaning
Division of work	One man, one job; specialise work
Authority	Manager must be able to give orders and be sure they will be carried out
Discipline	Respect and order throughout the workplace
Unity of command	Remove confusion by having one employee report to only one boss
Unity of direction	One boss is responsible for the planning and direction
Subordination of individual interests to the general good of the company	Employees should be prepared to put the company first
Fair pay	Pay should be fair to the employee and acceptable to the organisation
Centralisation	Management authority and responsibility ultimately rests with the centre
Scalar chain	The observance of an orderly hierarchy line of authority from bottom to the top
Order	Housekeeping, tidiness, order in the work environment
Equity	Fairness and a sense of justice
Stability of tenure	As far as possible, provide job security
Initiative	Staff should be encouraged to show initiative
Esprit de corps	Encourage and develop teams and a friendly working environment

Fayol's 'six activities' are those he considered to be the principal areas of concern to an organisation:

- technical activities,
- commercial activities,
- financial activities,
- security activities,
- accounting activities,
- managerial and administrative activities.

The tribute to the influence of Fayol's work is that his *activities* roughly describe the duties of the modern board of directors. We would use different names today, but the tasks are essentially as Fayol described.

Fayol established '*fourteen principles*' that, in his opinion, provided the elements of good organisational management. He himself applied them and found them to work.

Again, when we consider the list, we will see that many of them are still considered today to form the basis of good management practice. Fayol's '*general tenets of management*' can be summarised as follows:

- specialisation promotes efficiency,
- low employee turnover promotes efficiency,
- good morale increases productivity,
- employees should be treated equitably,
- unified goals + co-ordinated efforts,
- authority carries responsibility.

Question 1.2

Find out the composition of a typical board of *executive directors* in a modern company. You will probably arrive at five or six 'job titles'. To start you off, one of them will probably be the marketing director.

Scientific management

Scientific management is so called, not because it is used for managing scientific activities, but rather that it assumes a scientific model of man working in organisations. If quantitative methods are employed to aid management processes, then, it is argued, efficiency gains can be made. For a given work input, more output can be gained when work is organised using measurement, feedback and refinement.

Among the earliest records of attempts to time work and establish *standard times* for production are the attempts of a Frenchman called *Jean Radolphe Perronet* who studied the manufacture of pins to improve efficiency of their manufacture. By the start of the twentieth century, with the industrial revolution in full swing, we can see the impact of Robert Owen's work on layout and method at the New Lanark Mills running in concert with his pioneering work on social and welfare conditions for employees. He is credited with being the first to recognise that fatigue and the working environment could have adverse affects on workers' productivity. By raising the living standards of his workers, via housing, medical care and schooling for children, he was able to attract and retain better employees than his competitors.

We can now look at the pioneering contributors to the school of scientific management: *Frederick Winslow Taylor, Frank and Lilian Gilbreth, Henry Gantt and Charles Bedaux.*

Frederick Winslow Taylor

Frederick Winslow Taylor (1856–1917) was one of the earliest of all the organisational management theorists. He worked for the Bethlehem Steel Company in the USA, and it was here that he developed his theories of scientific management. In 1909, he published his *Principles of Scientific Management* – a treatise on this subject arising from his own experience as an industrialist and the outcomes of his early research. He was the first to propound the idea of applying quantitative methods to management problems. This evolved into '*work study*' – the analysis of work methods and the rate of work. His theories were quite revolutionary in a day when it was believed that increased productivity arose from simply taking on more people and making them work harder.

Taylor introduced the idea of comparing employee performance against a standard. This involved finding the optimum way for a given job to be done and determining the expected 'standard' times for elements of the job. He also emphasised the need to ensure that the workplace ergonomics (i.e. the man–machine interface, layout and lighting) were best suited for the tasks to be performed. The term '*time study*' can be attributed to him as observations of worker performance were made with the use of a stopwatch, measure actual performance against the expected standard. In this way rewards or punishment would be determined by management via a system known as 'piece-rates' – in crude terms the more produced by workers, the more earned or vice versa.

In one notable piece of research, Taylor demonstrated his principles by showing the relationship between work output and the size of labourers' shovels. In a study at the Bethlehem Steel plant in the USA, it is reported that he used a man who was reputed to be a good worker and who placed a high value on monetary reward. The initial size of shovel was capable of carrying an average load of 38 pounds and this resulted in the labourer shifting 25 tonnes of pig iron in a day. When a smaller shovel size was used, the daily load rose to 30 tonnes. A 25 pounds shovel produced even higher daily loads. The worker, in addition enjoying the praise of his observers, was also promised extra-financial reward as an incentive to move more pig iron per shift. The end result was that the work that was formerly done by 500 men could be achieved by just 140 and labourer's wages rose by as much as 60%.

The principles of scientific management can be summarised as follows:

- development of optimum organisation structure via time and motion study and ergonomic design;
- development of scientific methods to replace the old 'rule of thumb' practices;
- scientific selection and training of employees;
- motivation by money.

It should be noted that some criticisms can be made of scientific management techniques and what has been termed '*Taylorism*':

- it ignores the psychological needs of workers,
- the subjective side of work is neglected,
- there is an assumption that money is the *only* motivator,
- adopting a simplistic view of productivity,
- group processes are ignored,
- collective bargaining and trade unions do not have a role.

However, Taylor's legacy lies in the development of *work design, work measurement and production control* which changed the nature of industry with the creation of such functions as *work study, personnel, maintenance and quality control*.

Frank and Lillian Gilbreth

Frank and Lillian Gilbreth were associates of Taylor but, with experience of unionised organisations, they demonstrated less enthusiasm for timing jobs and developed laws of human motion from which developed *the principles of motion economy*. In Frank's early career he was interested in *standardisation* and '*method study*', and an example of his work stemmed from his observations of the variety of methods employed by different bricklayers on construction sites where he worked. He set about establishing a standard work method with a resultant increase in output from 1000 to 2700 bricks per day.

It was Gilbreth who coined the term '*motion study*' to cover their field of research and as a way of distinguishing from those involved in '*time study*'.

Henry Gantt

Henry Gantt is best remembered for his development of the 'Gantt chart'. He argued that time could be used more effectively if tasks in an operation were carefully planned in sequence and resources were apportioned accordingly. This would have the advantage of management having more control over events and it would prevent time 'leaking' in fruitless or unnecessary jobs. Gantt charts are used today in a wide variety of planning and control processes.

The Gantt chart is a project planning tool which helps plan the use of resources within a limited time period. It is constructed with consecutive activities plotted in a horizontal direction with time along the *x*-axis. It offers the advantage that the project manager can see at any one time what should be going on and which activities will follow on from completed activities. With a simple modification, the chart can be made to highlight which activities, if any, are critical. Critical activities are those which directly influence the finishing time of the overall project.

Charles Bedaux

Charles Bedaux introduced the concept of '*rating assessment*' in timing work. He adhered to Gilbreth's introduction of a rest allowance to allow recovery from fatigue. Although crude and poorly received at first, his range of techniques proved significant in the development of work study, particularly that of *value analysis*.

Production assembly line

Rapid developments in technology, machinery and the improvement of materials in the early twentieth century paved the way for the arrival of '*the moving assembly line*'. In particular the internal combustion engine had been invented, leading to the development of the motorcar. Streamlined production was required to meet demand and the first assembly line method of manufacture can probably be attributed to *Sears and Roebuck* in the USA. A famous example of the change to modern assembly line techniques can be found in *Henry Ford's* introduction of '*the moving assembly line*'. Before the changes the productivity measure was that of a car chassis assembled by one man taking about 13 hours, but 8 months later, following the application of *standardisation* and *division of labour* the total labour time had been reduced to 93 minutes per car.

Max Weber

Bureaucracy

The words *bureaucracy* and *bureaucratic* have, over recent years, become understood as being synonymous with 'red tape', 'officialdom' and the general impersonality of large and inefficient organisations. Such a conception of bureaucracy, whilst understandable, is a rather cynical description of some of the negative features of this otherwise highly effective method of organisational management.

The concept of bureaucracy was first put forward by the German academic and sociologist, *Max Weber* (1864–1920). His research, which was translated into English in 1947, sought to establish the reasons why individuals acted in certain ways in organisations and why they obeyed those in authority over them. Put simply, Weber found that people obeyed those in authority over them because of the influence of three types of authority:

- *Traditional authority* is that which subordinates respond to because of their traditions or customs;
- *Charismatic authority* occurs when subordinates respond to the personal qualities of a charismatic ('gifted') leader;
- *Rational–legal authority* is authority brought about solely by a manager's position in an organisation. Implicit in rational–legal authority is that subordinates obey a superior because the superior is in seniority over them in the organisational hierarchy.

Weber, whilst recognising the importance of the first two in some areas of life, was primarily concerned with rational–legal authority in his study of organisations. This form of obedience is the prominent form in modern organisations: Weber termed this *bureaucracy*. He continued to argue that the authority structures in bureaucracies could be a highly efficient organisational form, and that a proliferation of bureaucracies could result in gains in efficiency for organisations and in the country as a whole.

Question 1.3

In which contexts might we encounter traditional and charismatic authority?

According to Weber, bureaucracies could be described by certain characteristics. Underlying these characteristics were the dual themes of administration based on expertise ('rules of experts') and administration based on discipline ('rules of officials'). Laurie Mullins explains these characteristics as follows:[3]

- Tasks of the organisation are allocated as *official duties* among the various positions.

- There is an implied clear-cut *division of labour* and a high level of *specialisation*.
- A *hierarchical authority* applies to the organisation of offices and positions.
- Uniformity of decisions and actions is achieved through formally established systems of *rules and regulations.* Together with a structure of authority this enables the co-ordination of various activities within the organisation.
- An *impersonal* orientation is expected from officials in their dealings with clients and other officials. This is designed to result in rational judgements by officials in the performance of their duties.
- Employment by the organisation is based on *technical qualifications* and constitutes a lifelong career for the officials.

Stewart (1986) summarised the four main features of bureaucracy as follows:

- *Specialisation* applies primarily to the job rather than the job holder. The specialisation of roles 'belongs to' the organisation so that the specialisation can continue if any given specialists leave the employment of the organisation.
- *Hierarchy of authority* stresses a strict demarcation between management and workers. Within each strata of the organisation, there should be clearly defined levels of authority and seniority.
- *System of rules* is intended to engender an efficient and impersonal operation in the organisation. The system of rules should normally be stable and continuous, and changes in the rules should be in exceptional circumstances only.
- *Impersonality* means that the exercise of authority and the extension of privileges should be carried out strictly in accordance with the laid down system of rules. No partiality should be given to any individual on personal grounds.

Critics of bureaucracy argue that rigid hierarchical structures and controls can stifle initiative and actually reduce *effectiveness* in the drive for *efficiency*.

Question 1.4

In what ways might bureaucracy be advantageous to an organisation and in what ways might it be disadvantageous?

1.5 Human relations' theory

Human relations' theory

The objectives of the classical and human relations' theorists are essentially the same – to achieve the maximum organisational efficiency. The difference can be seen in the *modus operandi* by which they propose to bring this about. We saw previously that the classical theorists proposed a rational model that assumes a high degree of human predictability. The human relations' theories proposed that because organisations are composed of humans, focusing on human needs and motivation is the way to bring about optimal organisational output.

Central to human relations' theory is the belief that people are the key resources of an organisation. Harnessing and cultivating their potential and eliciting their willing contribution are therefore the most effective ways of increasing organisational efficiency.

Critics of the human relations' theory claim that it tends to promote employee satisfaction over organisational goals and encourages a soft or paternalistic style of management.

Elton Mayo

The work of *Elton Mayo* (1880–1949) and his experiments at the Hawthorne plant of the Western Electric Company in Chicago are generally thought of as the principal foundations for human relations' theories of management in organisations. Mayo, a Harvard University professor, was primarily concerned with people's experience at work and accordingly, his researches at the Hawthorne plant between 1927 and 1932 focused on the worker rather than on the work itself (which is in contrast to the work of Taylor).

The *Hawthorne studies* centred on the study of individuals and their social relationships at work. Divided into several stages, Mayo and his colleagues varied the conditions under which workers operated and then studied output to analyse the correlation between the two. Social arrangements in the workplace were varied – the numbers of people who worked together, their seating arrangements, etc. – and the work output was measured as each variable in working condition was changed.

The findings suggested that individuals at work produced a higher output when management took into account their social relationships. They found that a feature of people at work is that they form groups. It seemed that people felt more comfortable in groups and this could be used by the organisation to produce greater productivity.

Hawthorne findings

In summary, the findings of the Hawthorne experiments were as follows:

- An individual's identity is strongly associated with his or her group. They should be considered less as individuals and more as members of the group.
- An individual's affiliation and sense of belonging to the group can be more important to him or her than monetary rewards and other working conditions.
- Groups can be formal (set up by the organisation) or informal (chance social groupings). Both can exercise a strong influence over the behaviour of individuals at work.
- Managers and supervisors would do well to take this group behaviour into account when seeking to extract the maximum amount of work from their subordinates.

The lasting influence of Mayo can readily be seen in most of today's organisations. Most employees are organised into teams, groups, task forces, etc. More modern developments have included briefing groups, quality circles and 'buzz' groups. Management have, over the intervening years, made attempts to influence the norms of groups in order to make them act in accordance with the general objectives of the organisation. When this can be achieved, groups can become 'self-policing' and when a high degree of cohesion is achieved; a lower level of supervision will be needed.

Question 1.5

Do you know what briefing groups and quality circles are? If not, find out. You should find them in any good quality management or operations management textbook.

One way in which group thinking has been found to enhance output over recent years is to reconfigure production lines specifically to increase an individual's opportunity for social interaction. Figures 1.1 and 1.2 show one such example of this. In Figure 1.1, the person sitting at station C on the production line has the opportunity to interact meaningfully with only two people: the people at stations B and D. When the line is 'bent round', however (Figure 1.2), the same person has his or her potential interactions increased from two people (B and D) to five people (B, D, H, G and F).

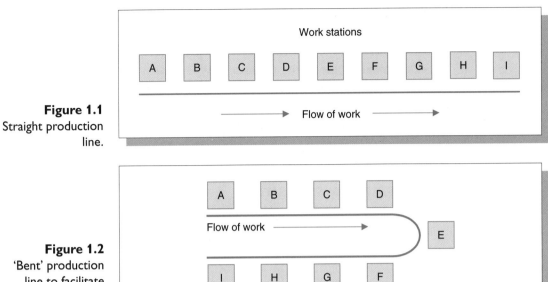

Figure 1.1
Straight production line.

Figure 1.2
'Bent' production line to facilitate more social interaction.

1.6 Systems theories

Definition

The distinguishing feature of systems' theories is that whereas classical theories see organisations in essentially scientific terms, and human relations' theorists view them in terms of the individuals working in them, systems theorists contend that the most realistic view is to see an organisation as a total system. This view, they contend, transcends both of the former theories and takes into account the more holistic context both inside and outside an organisation.

An organisation is an example of what has been termed an *open system*. An open system is one which must necessarily have a high degree of interaction with its environment (Figure 1.3). This is in contrast to a *closed system* – one in which there is no interaction with the external environment (a diver's underwater breathing apparatus, e.g. approximates to a closed system). An open system of any sort has three stages: inputs, conversion and outputs. All three are essential for the normal workings of the system.

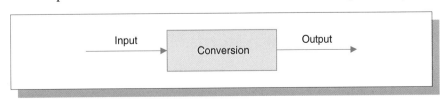

Figure 1.3
An open system.

As such the model includes inputs from the environment, the conversion or transformation of inputs to finished goods, and the output of those finished goods into the environment. This involves an interrelated set of elements functioning as a whole. Interdependent sub-systems, like finance and personnel, work toward *synergy* in an attempt to accomplish an organisational goal that could not otherwise be accomplished by a single sub-system.

Organisations and organisms

The organisation as a body

It may aid our understanding of this concept to consider a simple example. The human body is an example of an open system. It requires several essential inputs, such as air, food, heat, shelter and water. The body converts these in its normal functioning and then produces its outputs, such as energy, work, exhaled air products and excretions. The body is utterly dependent upon its environment – it would not take long for a lack of air to have a profound effect on the body. A further category of system quickly becomes apparent in this example – that of sub-systems in the body. The reasons why the total system of the body can perform the conversions in question are because it contains a nervous system, a renal system, a biochemical respiratory system and many others. Each of these sub-systems has its own inputs, conversions and outputs. They are equally interactive with their own respective environments.

It was the analogy between the biological body and the *body corporate* which first gave rise to a systems understanding of organisations. The concept that both types of bodies contained a number of interrelated and interdependent sub-systems was noticed in 1951 by the biologist *Ludwig von Bertalanffy*. His *General Systems Theory*[5] was further explored and developed by *Miller* and *Rice*, also both biologists, who likened corporate bodies to biological organisms.[6] The complexity of both biological and corporate bodies, and their interrelationships with their environments suggested that management of such systems required an understanding that all parts of the body were essential to normal and productive functioning.

Socio-technical systems

The systems theorists, in the light of their comparing of organisations to organisms, rejected the simplistic views of the classical and human relations' theorists. Classical theories, they argued, emphasised the technical requirements of the organisation and its productivity needs – 'organisations without people'. In contrast, human relations' theories focused too much on the psychology and interaction of people – 'people without organisations'.

In reality, organisations comprise both the technical features of such things as work study (classical theories) *and* the human input emphasised by Mayo. Systems theory thus holds that organisations are *socio-technical systems*. In a socio-technical system, it cannot be said that people are more important than an organisation's technology, structure, work methods or any other visible or tangible feature. Both are equally necessary and, importantly, both are subject to influence from the organisation's external environment (in the context of an open system). A failure of any sub-system in the organisation, be it a human or a technical failure, will harm the normal working of the organisation.

The pursuit of thought in this area led later writers in systems theory (adopting a *holistic* view of organisations) to devise a list of four key variables which, it was suggested, were the major determinants of output:

- people and social groups,
- technology,
- organisational structure,
- external environment.

Readers should note that this list includes both 'social' and 'technical' determinants of organisational performance.

Social groups and technology

The relationships between social groups and their employment of technology were also studied by the systems theorists. The implicit suggestion of classical theories is that technology, if properly applied, is the source of increased productivity and conversely, the human relations' theorists would have said that output is essentially a function of social groupings.

The *Tavistock Institute of Human Relations* in London, working in the 1940s and later, conducted research which showed the difficulties of linking output to just technology *or* social arrangements. One of the most important researches in this regard was the '*long-wall*' study.

Prior to the introduction of mechanisation in British coal mines in the 1940s, miners worked in small teams in a localised area of the seam. The teams developed a high degree of interpersonal cohesion over the years. They worked together on shifts – possibly going for hours without encountering other teams. Members shared out jobs and this resulted in individuals becoming multi-skilled but non-specialised ('jack of all trades, master of none'). As the teams worked on only a small part of the coalface at any one time, this method of working was termed the '*short-wall*' approach.

When mechanisation was introduced, a change in working practices was necessitated wherein:

- a much longer area of the coal seam could be worked on at any one time (the *long-wall* method of working);
- the earlier small teams were disbanded and replaced in a shift with a much larger group, all working together on the long wall;
- shifts became specialised in that, on a three shift system, one shift would work the face, another would clear up the debris and move the coal away from the face and the third would move the wall along the seam to an unworked area;
- shifts, because they involved many more workers together, were supervised.

To the surprise of the pit management, it was found that the introduction of mechanisation and the long-wall methods actually caused a reduction in output. Furthermore, conflicts arose within and between shifts. Absenteeism increased, morale noticeably decreased and shifts frequently blamed others for poor work.

These findings led *Trist, et al.*[7] of the Tavistock Institute to conclude that effective work arose from an interdependence of social conditions *and* technology. It involved taking into account the technology used, its layout, ease of use, etc. *and* the fact that individuals seemed to produce more work in groups in which they felt comfortable.

The problems at the coalface were eventually overcome when the composite long-wall method was introduced. This was an arrangement which allowed small groups to work together and still make efficient use of the new technologies of the time. The long-wall study is seen as a vindication of the socio-technical systems approach taken by systems theorists.

1.7 Contingency theories

Definition

The contingency approach to organisational management had its roots firmly in the systems theory, and in most respects, the two are arguably indistinguishable. The essence of the contingency approach is that the manner in which an organisation should be managed *depends* upon the wide range of variables which may apply to that organisation at any point in time. We can readily appreciate that the environmental conditions, the types of technology employed and the level of human motivation varies over time, according to organisational context. This approach suggests that it is impossible to prescribe any one type of management in all internal and external conditions. It rejects an absolutist approach to behaviour and management and puts forward, in its place, a relativist proposal (we may describe Taylor, Fayol and Mayo as essentially absolutist). The contingency theorists did not reject earlier ideas, in fact they recognised the utility of the philosophies, but only in certain circumstances. Scientific management and the human relations' theories each have their place when the environmental conditions were conducive to their use.

Contingency theory argues that organisational design, management and control structures should be tailored to fit the needs of individual organisations. Factors in organisational design will be dependent upon ownership, the environment, size, technology and the particular nature of the work.

Burns and Stalker

The study by *Burns* and *Stalker* (1966)[8] centred around 20 British companies in what they considered to be five broad environmental conditions, ranging from 'stable' to 'least predictable'. Among this sample of organisations, they also identified two extremes of management practice in the organisations: *mechanistic* and *organic* practice. It was suggested that both of these approaches are equally correct and rational in their appropriate environmental and organisational circumstances.

Mechanistic management systems are rigid in nature. The study showed that these work best in organisations that experience stable environmental conditions. Mullins contends that

- the characteristics of mechanistic management are similar to those of bureaucracy;
- tasks are specialised;
- clearly defined duties and procedures;
- clear hierarchical structure;
- knowledge and expertise centred at the top of the organisation;

- clear instructions and decisions from superiors as methods of control over organisational activity;
- insistence on loyalty of employees to the organisation and to their superiors.

Conversely, it was suggested that *organic* organisations were most appropriate in changeable environmental conditions. The 'surprises' inherent to a changeable business environment necessitated a more flexible and less rigid organisational philosophy than that provided by the inflexibility of a mechanistic organisation. Organic organisations have the following characteristics:

- The importance of special knowledge, skills and experience to the success of the organisation.
- A continual redefinition of tasks as the environment changes.
- A network, rather than a hierarchical structure of control and authority (characterised by an increased importance of cross-functional rather than hierarchical relationships).
- Superior knowledge is not necessarily related to a person's authority in the organisation.
- Communication is more lateral than up-and-down, reflecting an emphasis on information rather than instructions and commands.
- A widespread commitment of employees to the overall tasks and goals of the organisation.
- An emphasis on the contribution of individuals within the organisation.

Burns and Stalker contended that organic organisations were best suited to a changeable business environment, which is of course in contrast to the roles of the mechanistic organisation. It is important to appreciate that there are shades-of-grey between the two mechanistic and organic extremes, and that which is best *depends*, or is *contingent upon* the environmental conditions.

Lawrence and Lorsch

Lawrence and *Lorsch*,[9] worked from Harvard University in the 1960s. They were concerned with two key variables in organisations: structure (of the organisation) and environment. Their study involved examining organisations in relatively unstable, or changeable environments and others in stable ones. Within these organisations, they sought to see which managerial practices were different and which were the same in the two types of environments. They borrowed terms from mathematics to describe differences in management practice.

Differentiation

Differentiation refers to the degree to which management practices, attitudes and behaviour vary (or differ) from manager to manager within the organisation. In particular, the differences refer to:

- the varying orientation to certain organisational goals (e.g. cost reduction is felt more keenly by accountants and production managers than sales people and engineers);
- the varying time perspectives and time orientations (e.g. research and development (R&D) people tend to work on much longer time scales than sales and administrative people);
- the varying degrees of interpersonal orientation (e.g. sales people tend to be more relationship oriented than production people);
- the varying formality of functional department structures across the organisation (e.g. production departments tend to have 'taller' and more complex structures when compared to the relative informality of R&D departments).

Integration

Integration refers to the degree to which management attitudes and practices are common among managers in an organisation and the extent of collaboration that exists between managers. This is the opposite of differentiation.

Conclusions

The Lawrence and Lorsch study analysed the sample of organisations for the degree of integration and differentiation that makes for successful business performance in the different business environments. They arrived at a number of conclusions:

- Companies in highly changeable business environments perform better when there is a high degree of both integration *and* differentiation in the organisation.

- Companies in relatively stable business environments perform better when there is a lesser degree of differentiation but a high degree of integration.
- One drawback of differentiation is that it is harder to resolve conflict in a highly differentiated organisations.
- Conflict resolution is done better in well-performing companies than in their poorly performing competitors.
- In unstable and uncertain environments, integration is more common among mid- and lower levels of management. In more stable environments, the senior levels exhibit more integration.

Again we see that the most appropriate management practices for an organisation *depend* upon its environment. Both differentiation and integration 'work' in their respective contexts.

Assignment 1.1

Choose one of the following statements and discuss its merits with reference to management and organisational theory:

- Good management is about whipping subordinates into submission.
- If you want people to work harder, you have to be nice to them.
- Strict rules, lavish rewards and swift punishments are the key to organisational success.

References

1　Parsons, T. (1960). *Structure and Process in Modern Societies*. Glencoe, IL: Free Press.

2　Buchanan, D.A. and Huczynski, A.A. (2003). *Organisational Behaviour An Introductory Text*, 5th edn. London: Prentice Hall.

3　Mullins, L.J. (2004). *Management and Organisational Behaviour*, 7th edn. London: FT Prentice Hall.

4　Stewart, R. (1986). *The Reality of Management*. London: Pan Books.

5　von Bertalanffy, L. (1951). Problems of general systems theory: a new approach to the unity of science. *Human Biology* **23**(4): 302–312.

6　Miller, E.J. and Rice, A.K. (1967). *Systems of Organisation*. London: Tavistock Publications.

7　Trist, E.L., *et al.* (1963). *Organisational Choice*. London: Tavistock Publications.

8　Burns, T. and Stalker, G.M. (1966). *The Management of Innovation*. London: Tavistock Publications.

9　Lawrence, P.R. and Lorsch, J.W. (1969). *Organisation and Environment*. London: Irwin.

Further reading

Buchanan, D.A. and Huczynski, A.A. (2003). *Organisational Behaviour An Introductory Text*, 5th edn. London: Prentice Hall.

Clegg, S.R., *et al.* (2004). *Managing and Organizations: An Introduction to Theory and Practice*. London: Sage Publications Ltd.

Cole, G.A. (2003). *Management Theory and Practice*, 6th edn. London: Thomson Learning.

Dawson, S. (1996). *Analysing Organisations*. London: Macmillan Press.

Dixon, R. (1991). *Management Theory and Practice*. Oxford: Butterworth Heinemann.

Fayol, H. (1949). *General and Industrial Management*. London: Pitman.

Johns, G. (1996). *Organisational Behaviour. Understanding and Managing Life at Work*, 4th edn. Harper Collins.

Lawrence, P.R. and Lorsch J.W. (1969). *Organisation and Environment*. Irwin.

Mullins, L.J. (2004). *Management and Organisational Behaviour*, 7th edn. London: FT Prentice Hall.

Naylor, J. (2004). *Management*, 2nd edn. Harlow: FT Prentice Hall.

Pettinger, R. (1996). *An Introduction to Organisational Behaviour*. London: Macmillan Press.

Taylor, F.W. (1998). *The Principles of Scientific Management*. Toronto: General Publishing Company Ltd.

Weber, M. (1964). *The Theory of Social and Economic Organization*. London: Collier Macmillan.

Worthington, I. and Britton, C. (2004). *The Business Environment*, 4th edn. Harlow: FT Prentice Hall.

Organisational and business objectives

After studying this chapter, students should be able to describe:

- mission, vision and values of an organisation;
- the purpose of an organisation's mission statement;
- the complex nature of defining business goals and objectives;
- the most important business objective;
- the stakeholders;
- the view that stakeholder coalitions determine the business objectives;
- the view that an organisation's principals essentially determine the business objectives.

2.1 Vision

This is an aspirational view of the desired state of the organisation at a point in the future. The timeframe is dependent on the nature of the organisation and its environment but a typical vision would be set for 3–5 years ahead and reviewed annually in line with actual results and changing circumstances. The vision is in effect a statement of strategic intent that serves to focus the energies of the organisation management towards the setting and achievement of specific goals and objectives. Its aspirational nature means that it is consistently revised, as each set of goals are achieved, and further stretching future situations are established.

2.2 Mission

The *mission* of an organisation is a general expression of the overall purpose of the organisation or, more simply, a broad description of the business it is in – its *raison d'être*. It broadly defines the scope and boundaries of the organisation, which should be in line with the expectations and values of major stakeholders.

Mission statements

Some organisations find it helpful to provide a concise and clear written statement of their broad objectives. Whilst such statements are called different names, most find the term *mission statement* to be the most suitable. They have increased in popularity over recent years, and more and more organisations have come to appreciate their advantages. In particular, recent years have seen an increased realisation that public as well as private sector organisations should establish clearly defined objectives. It has thus become increasingly common for institutions like universities, hospitals and schools to construct mission statements.

Why have a mission statement?

There are a number of advantages to having a clearly set-out and written-down statement of wider objectives:

- It *clearly communicates the objectives* and values of the organisation to the various stakeholders groups. This theoretically prevents people from misunderstanding the purposes of the business.
- In the normal operation of an organisation, it is important that *all members work towards the same ends*. Clearly stated objectives facilitate this, especially if the organisation is decentralised or where the employees tend to work independently of each other. There is great value in all parts of the organisation working together and coherence is encouraged when overall objectives are clearly understood.
- It can serve to *influence the actions and attitudes of employees* in the company. This is important when the company has

clearly defined objectives and the co-operation of employees is necessary to ensure that strategies and plans are implemented.

The rationale for having a mission statement is perhaps encapsulated in the words of the Cheshire cat in Lewis Carroll's *Alice in Wonderland* 'If you don't know where you're going, it doesn't matter which way you go.'

What does a mission statement contain?

The style and content of mission statements, as we might expect, varies enormously. Some are long and detailed whereas others are short and to the point. There are no 'rights' or 'wrongs' of how it should be presented or what it should contain – it all depends upon the organisation and its culture. In practice, mission statements usually contain the following:

- Some *indication of the industry* or business the organisation is mainly concerned with. In many cases this will be obvious from the company name (e.g. Imperial Chemical Industries plc – ICI) but in others, some elucidation may be of value (e.g. the name *GlaxoSmithKline* conceals the fact that the company makes pharmaceuticals and health-care products).
- An indication of the realistic market share or market position the organisation should aim towards. This may be stated as 'we aim to become the leading supplier …' or 'to become a major company in the textiles industry'. Most statements of this type in mission statements are reasonably realistic as management realise that an unreachable objective may demotivate the workforce or bring ridicule from outside observers.
- A brief summary of the *values* and *beliefs* of the organisation. Such a statement may be actual (as it is) or aspirational (as management want it to become). Phrases like 'caring company', 'friendly staff', 'valued employees' and 'working as a team' are examples of the company putting across its values in a mission statement.
- Specific and *highly context-dependent objectives* are sometimes expressed in the mission statement. This type of statement will obviously vary greatly from organisation to organisation and some mission statements contain no expressions of this

type. It may refer to a particular competitive environment or uniquely to the industry in which the organisation competes.

Examples of some mission statements:

Mission statement – British Telecommunications plc

British Telecommunications (BT), as a very large company, expresses its objectives in a relatively brief document which is designed to communicate its objectives to its wide ranging and disparate types of employee and stakeholder. The document is divided into two parts. The first part is its vision and the second, its mission.

Vision
to become the most successful worldwide telecommunications group.

Mission
- *to provide world class telecommunications and information products and services,*
- *to develop and exploit our networks at home and overseas, so that we can*
  - *meet the requirements of our customers,*
  - *sustain growth in the earnings of the group on behalf of our shareholders,*
  - *make a fitting contribution to the community in which we conduct our business.*

Source: BT plc web site.

Mission statement – Easyinternet café

To be the world's leading Internet café that is the cheapest way to get online.

Source: Easyinternet café web site.

Mission statement – Psion plc

Our mission is to grow rapidly and profitably through innovation in mobile Internet. In pursuing this mission, we will deliver value:

- To shareholders through superior returns.
- To customers through solutions and devices that enhance their quality of life and personal effectiveness.
- To staff through a stimulating environment that encourages innovation.

Source: Psion plc web site.

Mission statement – J Sainsbury plc

Our mission is to be the consumer's first choice for food, delivering products of out-standing quality and great service at a competitive cost through working 'faster, simpler and together'.

Source: J Sainsbury plc web site.

Question 2.1

▪ Examine the above examples of mission statements and describe your perceptions of what messages each of the organisations are trying to convey.

2.3 Organisational goals

Goals

Organisational goals represent broad-based intentions that derive from the overall mission, and provide a sense of direction which leads to the achievement of its aspirational (visionary) and challenging position at some point in the future.

The broadly stated goals usually require further sub-division into manageable components (i.e. objectives) which provide the focus for managers who have specific roles and responsibilities to deliver the desired outcomes. The overall objectives are then translated into specific activities that cascade through the organisation to the workforce who actually perform the day-to-day tasks that produce the finished goods and services. Goals can be qualitative or quantitative in nature and provide the key elements in achieving the organisation's vision.

More precise statements in the form of *objectives* cascade from the goals and these are translated into targets, or quantifiable outcomes, for employee activities and tasks the direction is set for the achievement of the vision over the desired timeframe.

Objectives

Objectives are key elements for the organisations success and it is essential that they meet robust criteria. A useful *aide-memoir* for setting effective objectives can be found in the mnemonic *SMART*:

- *Specific* = explicit statement of required outcomes.
- *Measurable* = means of assessing results against plan.
- *Achievable* = within the capabilities of people and resources employed.
- *Realistic* = practical and sensible assessment of capabilities.
- *Time related* = completion date and interim milestone dates where appropriate.

Targets

Business targets are quantified and time-based objectives that define the measurable outputs. They can be expressed in financial or numerical terms.

Objectives: implicit and explicit

The question, '*why does a particular organisation exist?*' or '*what are the objectives of this organisation?*' at first glance, may seem rather straightforward. We may assume, for example, that a private business such as a brewery primarily seeks to make a profit whilst a hospital exists to provide health care. We will see in the course of this chapter that such simplistic definitions sit uncomfortably alongside the complexity of influences that are brought to bear upon an organisation, and that organisations may have many objectives at the same time.

To simplify our discussion, we can seek to divide objectives into two broad categories: those which are expressly stated by an organisation, and those which are not, but which we can safely presume to be the case. We can readily imagine that a large company such as the car manufacturer Nissan, as a private company, exists to make a profit. The company states this publicly: '…*we aim to build profitably the highest quality car sold in Europe.*' Similarly, a hospital trust, such as the University College Hospitals group in London, exists primarily to provide a service that is health care. Again, the trust states this publicly; to '*maintain and develop a local, national and international role as a provider of comprehensive, safe, accessible and high quality care for patients*'. We can consider these objectives to be *explicit*, because they are perhaps obvious and (often) stated publicly by the organisation.

The activities of such organisations suggest to us that their primary objectives, important though they are, are not the only objectives they pursue. Many organisations, for example, seek to be fair and to act responsibly towards their employees and customers in the belief, perhaps, that such sub-objectives support their explicit goals. Such objectives are said to be *implicit* because they are *implied* by the organisation's policies and activities. Implicit objectives do not oppose the primary objective; they usually complement it and help towards its accomplishment.

Question 2.2

Suggest what you consider to be the primary (most important) objectives of the following organisations:

- Microsoft
- easyJet
- Body Shop
- KFC

Case: 'Out of this World'

A new concept in retailing was launched in late 1995 when 2000 individuals united behind a shared vision of shops that would present a direct challenge to destructive consumerism. *The Creative Consumer Co-operative Ltd* (a registered industrial and provident society – a type of co-operative owned by its members – see Chapter 5) was formed and its members invested money to establish shops under the trading name of *Out of this World*. The shops sell the usual wide range of consumer products that you might find in your regular 'conventional' supermarket. What is unique about Out of this World is that it only sells a product when it is satisfied that both the products sold and the producers meet certain ethical or environmental criteria. Based in Newcastle upon Tyne, Out of this World currently has shops in Leeds, Nottingham and Newcastle upon Tyne itself.

Aimed at people who care about the way that products are produced and the behaviour of the producer companies, one the core values Out of the World's core values is *Fair Trade* and it sells a wide range of organic products which sometimes cost a little more than foods prepared from conventional sources. This is due to the extra costs involved in producing some organic products.

The shops themselves are said by the company to be an 'experience' rather than a conventional shopping environment. Each shop has a database which gives shoppers information on suppliers (e.g. in the Third World) and products to assist them in their choices. Shops are designed not only to provide an enjoyable shopping experience, but also an educational one.

All types of products sold in the shops are carefully chosen for their contribution to:

- the promotion of personal health;
- human welfare;

- environmental sustainability;
- fair trade (the name given to trading relationships which do not exploit or take economic advantage over the producer, often in the Third World);
- community and local development;
- animal welfare.

So what are the objectives of Out of this World? In its share prospectus, the company give the following explanation:

Is profit a dirty word? Profit is important to Out of this World. It is not a primary objective but it is an essential condition of success. It is a word that we will use... not as an incentive to personal gain or greed but as the test of the organisation's efficiency and sustainability. Profit, for Out of this World, is a significant aspect of business terminology, not a raison d'être.

It follows from the above explanation that profit is not the primary motive of the company but a necessary prerequisite that enables it to fulfil its primary objective.

In 2002, Out of this World won the award of the UK's 'Best Established Retail Store'.

Source: Out of this World web site, 2004.

Question 2.3

Suggest as clearly as possible what the primary objective of Out of this World might be.

Different types of business objectives

There are a huge number of objectives which businesses may pursue in addition to their primary objectives. Some of these will be *quantitative* in nature and some *qualitative.*

Quantitative objectives are those whose achievement can be measured using numerical or financial criteria. They can be specific and accurately measured. It follows that the successful achievement of quantitative objectives can be easily seen and it is equally visible when they are not achieved. Examples of quantitative objectives might include:

- targets for market share;
- target accounting or financial performance (e.g. profit margins);
- target levels of year-on-year growth;
- target levels of productivity or efficiency;
- number of new product launches (i.e. two new products this year);

- buy a subsidiary in France to exploit European markets;
- to gain a quality accreditation certificate.

Qualitative objectives are more difficult to measure because they are not based on a numerical indicator. This does not mean they are any less important than quantitative objectives – types of objectives will vary from business to business. Examples include:

- to attain a public perception of being a 'good employer';
- to be seen as a responsible 'environmental' or 'green' organisation;
- to improve the quality of management;
- to improve customer satisfaction;
- to improve staff training.

Such objectives are essentially intangible in nature and as such, it is hard to know the exact point at which the objective is satisfactorily realised. If, for example, an organisation wishes to improve its employee skills, we can see that this is a broad qualitative objective. We cannot tell from this by how much it wants to improve them or at what point we will be able to say that the objective will have been accomplished.

2.4 The prime objective

There is one objective which applies to all businesses without exception. It is the highest and the clearest objective, and it is so obvious that it is rarely articulated. It is universally presumed to apply in all cases. The prime objective in business is *to survive* – to stay in business.

The individuals in organisations may differ on some other business objectives. It may be the case, for example, that management wish to increase profitability and that the trade union representing the workers wants a pay increase – potentially conflicting objectives. On this and many other examples, there will be debate over business objectives. Over the issue of survival, however, there is no debate.

If the company does not survive, then:

- employees and management lose their jobs;
- shareholders lose their investment;
- suppliers do not get paid for the goods they have supplied;
- customers must look elsewhere for their supplies;
- the government does not benefit from tax revenues from employees and from tax on profits.

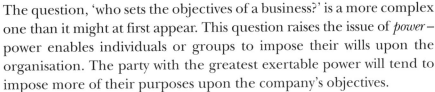

2.5 Who sets business goals and objectives? Two viewpoints

The question, 'who sets the objectives of a business?' is a more complex one than it might at first appear. This question raises the issue of *power* – power enables individuals or groups to impose their wills upon the organisation. The party with the greatest exertable power will tend to impose more of their purposes upon the company's objectives.

There are two broad approaches to the issue of who sets organisational objectives. They are partially in conflict and partly complementary. The first approach, *stakeholder analysis* contends that objectives are arrived at by many interested parties in coalition, whilst the simpler model of *principal–agent analysis* argues that the objectives of a business are to be determined by the company's owners and directors alone. In other texts, this dual approach is described as the *stakeholder–stockholder dichotomy*.

2.6 The integrated journey from mission to vision

The journey from an organisation's mission to the achievement of its vision requires an appropriate structure in which management roles and responsibilities are defined with ownership of the organisation's functions co-ordinated via clearly articulated goals and objectives. The relationship is shown in a simplistic fashion in Figure 2.1. This particular model, on the left-hand side, shows a downward cascade from the mission though roles, responsibilities and specific objectives. To meet the daily ongoing work, these objectives are organised and delegated though a series of activities which in turn are sub-divided into actual tasks (units of work). This example shows a situation where it has been judged that one of the goals will need manageable performance improvements over 3 years. Specific objectives have been set, leading to year-on-year targets.

2.7 Stakeholders

What is a stakeholder?

A stakeholder can be defined as 'any person or party that has an interest in, or affected by, the activities of an organisation, however, strong

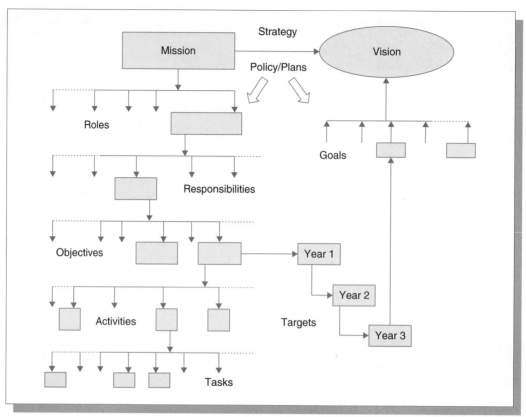

Figure 2.1
Schematic relationships of mission and management activities to achieve vision.

or weak that interest may be. The interests of stakeholders may or may not be primarily financial in nature.

It immediately becomes apparent that many parties, including shareholders, community members and regulators fit into this broad definition. Some stakeholders have an urgent and vital interest in the organisation whilst others have only a slight concern and that from a considerable distance. A broad and general list of possible stakeholders would include the following parties:

- shareholders/owners;
- management;
- employees;
- competitors;
- employees' families and dependants;
- suppliers;
- customers;
- workers' (trade) unions;

- bankers;
- moneylenders other than banks (e.g. some individuals lend cash to businesses);
- communities served by the organisation;
- near geographical neighbours (i.e. 'next-door' neighbours);
- pressure groups and opinion formers;
- financial auditors (in the case of limited companies);
- regulatory authorities (e.g. Health and Safety Executive and regulatory QuANGOs);
- other businesses in the locality (e.g. the local newsagent, pub).

In addition to the above list, there are many parts of the state which may have an interest in an organisation:

- The Inland Revenue collects direct taxes from a private sector business;
- Her Majesty's Customs and Excise collects indirect taxes;
- Local government collects local taxes from businesses within its area;
- The Department of Social Security collects employers' National Insurance contributions and must pay unemployment benefit to individuals if the company becomes insolvent;
- The Department of Trade and Industry;
- The Department for Education and Employment benefits from businesses as both sources of students and employers of its school leavers and graduates.

Hence we see a complex picture of interests emerging. We can also see that not all stakeholders want the same things for any given business organisation. Whilst some stakeholders will be in concurrence, others may profoundly disagree over the objectives of the organisation in question.

Question 2.4

Attempt to generate a list of the specific stakeholders in the following organisations:

- the university or college at which you are studying;
- your local authority;
- a local sole trader such as your local window cleaner;
- mobile telecommunications company.

Stakeholder coalitions

According to the theory of stakeholder analysis, the objectives of a business depend upon the relative strengths of the various stakeholders. The stakeholders who can exert the most powerful influence over the organisation will have most input into the objective-setting of the business. Similarly, stakeholders with little influence, strong though their interest may be, will have little influence over the company's objectives (e.g. the pub which benefits from lunchtime business from a nearby large employer has an intense interest in the large employer, but clearly has little or no influence over it).

According to this theory of objective-setting, the predominant objective of the business will be those of the most powerful shareholders or, the objectives of the most powerful coalition (purposeful grouping) of stakeholders. It is clear that some stakeholders on their own could not bring any meaningful influence upon an organisation, but when they act in concert with other stakeholders, their aggregate influence naturally increases in power.

Whilst it is uncommon for any given stakeholder to want *exactly* the same as any other, they often have sufficient in common to mount a common assault on one small area of objective-setting within an organisation.

A conflict in stakeholder interests – Sellafield nuclear complex

The Sellafield nuclear fuels complex was opened by British Nuclear Fuels in 1957. Situated just north of Whitehaven in West Cumbria, the Sellafield site includes a number of nuclear reprocessing plants, the Calder Hall nuclear power station and the Thermal Oxide Reprocessing Plant (ThORP). The collective plants in the Sellafield complex employ, between them, around 7000 people with another 1000 contractors being continually used on site. Sellafield is Cumbria's largest employer and it is estimated that 30% of all jobs in West Cumbria are dependent, either directly or indirectly, on the complex. These jobs are seen as being particularly important as West Cumbria is an area of high unemployment with a relatively depressed economy.

A stakeholder analysis of the Sellafield situation reveals some interesting conflicts and two opposing stakeholder coalitions.

The 'for' coalition

Some stakeholders feel the plants are of enormous importance and must be protected and, if possible, expanded. The government considers nuclear energy to be a vital part of its overall energy strategy. Electricity can be produced from coal, gas, oil and other sources, but it is considered wise to spread production across as many fuels as possible. This should mean that a drop in the supply of one input would not have too bad an effect on the overall production of electricity in the country. The employees and their unions support the plants as they are a vital source of employment for the communities. The same attitude is taken by the local authorities in the area for similar reasons. Sellafield's customers are spread across the world. Power generators send their used nuclear materials to Sellafield or ThORP and it is returned to them in a form which enables it to be re-used at a cheaper price than sourcing 'virgin' materials. A plant the size of the Sellafield complex necessarily has many suppliers – local engineering companies, catering businesses, laundries, etc. and it follows that they, too, have vested interest in seeing the plant prosper.

The 'against' coalition

Just when you think that the Sellafield complex is an unmitigated blessing, it should be remembered that there are some particularly vocal stakeholders who have misgivings about the plants, some of whom would rather see it closed down completely. Environmental pressure groups argue strongly that nuclear power should not form a part of the UK's energy policy owing to the risks of radiation leaks during use and the problems with disposing of spent nuclear fuel once it has come to the end of its useful life (some nuclear fuels can remain radioactive for 10,000 years). In addition, some health professionals and researchers have suggested that the plants are a source of harmful radiation, both to the workers and to the surrounding population. Evidence has been put forward that may suggest that there is a higher incidence of leukaemia and other serious diseases in the locality of the plants. Concern has also been expressed that radiation from the plant may have teratogenic effects (causing problems in pregnancy and birth defects). The Government of the Republic of Ireland is also concerned about the complex. Ireland is separated from Sellafield by the Irish Sea and some citizens of the Republic believe that harmful effects from the plants may affect parts of their country.

Whilst the controversy over Sellafield has been notable and well publicised, the collective weight of the 'for' coalition has outweighed the 'against'. It seems that the 'against', however, convincing their arguments may be to some people, will have to remain as a vocal but somewhat impotent coalition whilst the economic forces for keeping Sellafield remain as convincing as they are.

Stakeholder 'mapping'

The extent to which any stakeholder is able to influence the objectives of an organisation depends upon two variables: the stakeholders' interest and power.[1]

- stakeholder interest refers to the *willingness* to influence the organisation. In other words, interest concerns the extent to which the stakeholder cares about what the organisation does.

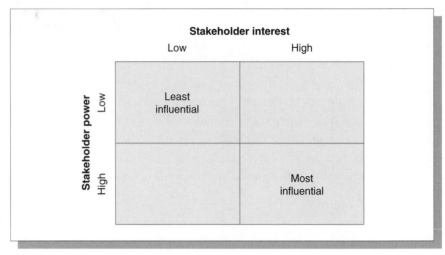

Figure 2.2
The stakeholder
map.

- stakeholder power refers to the *ability* to influence the organisation.
- coalitions of stakeholders can significantly shift the balance of power.

It follows from this that the actual influence that a stakeholder has will depend upon where the stakeholder is positioned with respect to ability to influence and willingness to influence. A stakeholder with both high power and high interest will be more influential than one with low power and low interest. We can map stakeholders by showing the two variables on a grid comprising two intersecting continua (Figure 2.2).

By examining the stakeholders or stakeholder coalitions of any organisation, we can visibly see which stakeholders are the most powerful. We could also use the map, for example, to assess which stakeholder is likely to exert the most influence upon the organisation's objectives. It would enable us to see any potential conflicts which may arise if, for example, we see two conflicting stakeholders in the same area of the map that is two conflicting stakeholders with the same degree of power and interest.

The managing director and the board of directors are examples of stakeholders with both high power and high interest. This is because they not only manage the business but also depend upon it for their jobs. The bar to which employees retire after or during the day's work is an example of a stakeholder with high interest but low power.

Question 2.5

Suggest examples of stakeholders who may fit into each section of the grid. Concentrate on the categories of low interest, low power and low interest, high power.

Two views of stakeholder theory

We might ask the question 'why' should organisations be influenced in their objectives by their various stakeholder groups. We have seen that the stakeholders may vary in their aspirations for the organisation and so managing the various views may be a bit tricky to say the least. There are two approaches that organisations can take in respect of managing stakeholder aspirations (although academic authors have identified a more complex picture).[2]

The *instrumental* view of stakeholder theory says that organisations take stakeholder opinions into account only inasmuch as they are consistent with the objective of profit maximisation (or other conventional indicators of success). Accordingly, it may be that a business modifies its objectives in the light of environmental concerns *but only* because this is the best way of optimising profit or achieving success. If the loyalty or commitment of an important stakeholder group (e.g. customers) is threatened, it is likely that the organisation will modify its objectives because not to do so would threaten to reduce its profits. It follows from the instrumental stakeholder approach that an organisation's values are guided by its stakeholders' opinions – it may not have any inherent moral values of its own except for the over-riding profit motive.

The *normative* view of stakeholder theory takes a 'Kantian' view of business ethics (derived from the German philosopher Immanual Kant, 1724–1804). Kant emphasised the notion of duty and good-will in civil matters and in relationships. Underpinning his ethical philosophy is the notion of respect for the moral duty that one party or person should have towards another. Extending this argument to stakeholder theory, the normative view states that organisations should accommodate stakeholder aspirations not because of what the organisation can 'get out of it' for its own profit, but because it observes its duty to each stakeholder. The normative view sees stakeholders as ends in themselves and not as merely instrumental to the achievement of other ends.

2.8 Agents and principals

The argument that the principals of an organisation are the only significant influences on objective-setting is one of the foundational and fundamental principles of capitalism. The principals of an organisation are those parties that own it – either directly (stockholders) or indirectly (the government in public sector organisations).

This concept is perhaps a simplification of the notion of stakeholder analysis. It suggests that as the owners of a business, the shareholders, are the only party who have a legitimate right to determine its objectives and policies. The agents of an organisation are the directors or those individuals which the principals have placed in charge of the affairs of the organisation. Objectives are conveyed to the agents and once received; the agents do not need to take cognisance of any other concerns in the execution of their duties. Put simply, according to this concept, the principals say to the agents 'I appoint you and pay your remuneration; therefore you will carry out my agenda for the organisation.' The agents, according to this viewpoint, would be acting irresponsibly if they were not to obey their principals.

What are the objectives of agents and principals?

If this theory is to be given credence, then we ought to see in practice the objectives of shareholders taking pre-eminence in commercial organisational objective-setting. The supreme objective of ordinary shareholders is twofold: to receive the *maximum dividend per share* and to enjoy *capital growth* on the market value of the share. Both of these can only be maximised when the business is enjoying a period of high profitability. Hence, the primary objective of the shareholder is for the agents to *maximise profit* above all other objectives. As most shareholders are not in regular contact with the agents, they will usually be indifferent to the concerns of other stakeholders and will directly oppose any stakeholders who wish the company to increase its costs for any reason whatsoever.

The basis of market economics is that individuals will place their money where they believe they will receive the maximum return on it. Most shareholders would consequently be displeased if they heard that the agents of their investment (the directors) were paying too much attention to the desires of other stakeholders in a way that would reduce the return on shareholders' investment. In such circumstances, they may have the right to say '*what do you think you are doing with my money?*'

Agents must manage a much more complex set of variables than their principals. It is the agents' job to balance the many calls upon the business and to take a longer-term view than the shareholders. The shareholder will certainly not enjoy the same level of knowledge on the market conditions of the business and must therefore, to a large extent, *trust* the agents in the vast majority of their decisions and actions. It must be remembered though, that the maximisation of profitability is very much in the agents' interests as well as the shareholders'. A failure to maintain high levels of profitability will usually precipitate a fall in the share price and a lower level of dividends to shareholders. Not only will such actions of directors make them vulnerable to being voted off the Board by the shareholders (thus losing their job), but an unattractive share falls in value and makes the company vulnerable to takeover (which may also mean the agents being replaced). In addition, directors often have a profit-linked element in their reward packages, meaning that a higher profit enables a higher level of remuneration to be achieved.

Assignment 2.1

Select an organisation of your choice, from private, public, or voluntary sector (If you prefer, you can create a fictional organisation). Using the template at Figure 2.1 above, prepare a worked example of the model that includes details for the following elements:

- A brief mission statement.
- Write a vision statement and select one component of it which can be used for the creation of a goal.
- Set a goal that feeds directly to the visionary element.
- Establish the role of the manager who will have ownership of this part of the organisation's strategic intent.
- Identify one of his/her responsibilities directly related to the goal in question.
- Set an objective plus relevant and realistic targets for the current year and each of the three subsequent years.
- Identify a related activity and associated task(s).

References

1   Johnson, G. and Scholes, K. (1993). *Exploring Corporate Strategy, Text and Cases*, 3rd edn. Englewood Cliffs, NJ: Prentice Hall (adapted from Mendelow, A. (1991). *Proceedings of 2nd International Conference on Information Systems*, Cambridge, MA.

2   Donaldson, T. and Preston, L.E. (1995). The stakeholder theory of the corporation: concepts, evidence and implications. *Academy of Management Review* **20**(1): 65–91.

Further reading

Boddy, D. (2002). *Management an Introduction,* 2nd edn. Harlow: FT Prentice Hall.

Johnson, G. and Scholes, K. (2002). *Exploring Corporate Strategy, Text and Cases,* 6th edn. Harlow: FT Prentice Hall.

Mullins, L.J. (2004). *Management and Organisational Behaviour,* 7th edn. London: FT Prentice Hall.

Naylor, J. (2004). *Management,* 2nd edn. Harlow: FT Prentice Hall.

Needle, D. London: *Business in Context,* 4th edn. London: Thomson Learning.

Scott, W.R. (2003). *Organizations Rational, Natural and Open Systems (International),* 5th edn. New Jersey, USA: Prentice Hall.

Useful web sites

Fair Trade Foundation: www.fairtrade.org.uk
Tearfund: www.tearfund.org
Traidcraft: www.traidcraft.co.uk
Cafedirect: www.cafedirect.co.uk

CHAPTER 3

Non-incorporated organisations

After studying this chapter, students should be able to describe:

- what is meant by an *non-incorporated organisation*;
- what is meant by a legal entity or *juristic personality*;
- what is meant by a sole proprietor;
- what are the advantages and disadvantages of holding sole proprietor status;
- what is meant by a *partnership*;
- what are the advantages and disadvantages of holding partnership status?

3.1 Non-incorporated organisations

There are two broad categories of privately owned business organisations, that is, those not owned by the state. The distinction rests upon the status of the organisation in the eyes of the law (the legal status). In this chapter, we will discuss one of these categories, *non-incorporated* organisations, whilst in Chapter 4, we will examine the second category – limited companies or *incorporated* organisations.

The distinction between these categories revolves around the rather odd question: *What is a person?* This question does not refer to the biologist's definition of a person, but the legal definition. In business, a

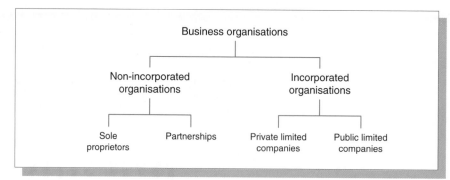

Figure 3.1
Taxonomy of private sector business organisations.

person (or a *legal entity*) may be a biological person, or it can be a collection of people.

We shall see in Chapter 4 that incorporated organisations are unique in that the law primarily recognises the organisation as a legal entity in its own right, and not the employees of it. This is not the case in unincorporated organisations.

What is a 'legal entity'?

In legal and business studies, the concepts of human and legal personality can be different. That which legal people call a *juristic personality* is any party that the law recognises as a single entity ('person'), in that the state will enforce contracts made by that 'person'. A legal entity has certain rights:

- to make contracts;
- to carry out business transaction;
- to own property;
- to employ people;
- to sue and be sued for breach of contract.

In the case of the simplest form of business – the sole proprietor, the law does not recognise the business entity of 'the sole proprietor', but it does recognise the human person who is the sole proprietor.

The issue becomes a little more complex when we consider limited companies (see Chapter 4). The law recognises the company as the legal personality in its own right. Hence, it is the entity of the company which makes contracts. The employees of the company who are empowered to make contracts *on the company's behalf* are called its agents. These are usually senior or specialised employees of the company.

The two major types of business enterprise we shall consider in this chapter are essentially individual 'human' legal entities, and, as we shall see, this has some important implications for the individuals concerned.

3.2 Sole proprietors

What is a sole proprietor?

The sole proprietor or sole trader is the simplest form of business arrangement. Such a person is usually, but not necessarily, a sole person carrying out some sort of business. As there is no legal requirement to declare oneself as a sole trader, nobody knows exactly how many there are, but it is thought that there are well over 1 million such businesses in the UK. There is no formal setting-up procedure for sole traders – they simply begin in business. Furthermore, apart from keeping records for tax purposes, there is no requirement to keep records of any kind.

Most sole proprietors are one-person concerns, but others employ a few staff as helpers. Some, albeit in exceptional circumstances, may employ up to 100 staff. Most 'self-employed' people operate as sole proprietors, common examples of which include:

- trades people (joiners, plasterers, electricians, painters, roofers etc.);
- market stall holders;
- small independent retailers (e.g. fish and chip shops, newsagents, greengrocers etc.);
- 'cottage industry' proprietors (e.g. craft workshops);
- farmers;
- window cleaners.

The nature of the sole proprietor means that setting-up costs are limited to the tools or premises required to carry out normal business activities. Whilst this can be reasonably sizeable (e.g. for a shop or a milk-round), in most cases, it is relatively small. Consider the cost, for example, of setting-up as a window cleaner: the price of a ladder, a mop and a bucket. Many sole proprietors carry out business on an occasional business (e.g. when they have no income from any other source), whereas others spend all of their working lives in this form of business arrangement.

Question 3.1

In addition to the examples given above, can you think of any other businesses which are usually carried out by sole proprietors?

As we might expect, sole proprietors enjoy some advantages from their status in law, and some disadvantages.

Advantages of holding sole proprietor status

■ As there are no legally required setting-up procedures, it *costs nothing* to begin trading as a sole proprietor, apart from the necessary capital costs. It follows that it is also quick, with no approvals or complicated forms to fill in.

■ The sole proprietor, as the owner of the business (or more correctly as the business – the sole proprietor *is* the business), has total claim on all the business's earnings. All *profits and earnings belong directly to him or her.*

■ The owner is 'his own boss' as the only employee of the business. This has several advantages. Firstly, *decisions can be made quickly* as he has nobody else to consult. Secondly, he has *total autonomy* to organise his work as he sees fit. Thirdly, he is *independent* of any other working partner – he can please himself.

■ With the exception of tax returns, there is *no requirement placed upon sole proprietors to submit formal documentation* annually as limited companies must (see Chapter 4). This saves a lot of time and cost that other forms of business entity must spend on book-keeping and auditing. It also means that confidentiality can be preserved – nobody except the tax authorities need ever find out how much the sole proprietor earns or how much he has 'saved for a rainy day'.

Disadvantages of holding sole proprietor status

■ The very nature of the business as a small or one-person concern means that *all of the tasks in the business must be performed by the owner/manager.* Such tasks include the operations (e.g. the window cleaning or the plumbing work), selling and advertising (if appropriate), invoicing and collecting debts, filling in tax documentation and so on. This necessarily puts pressure on the workload of the sole proprietor.

- The *skills and abilities that the business has access to are limited to those of the owner.* If the owner is particularly poor at any skill, the skill deficiencies are to the detriment of the business. This is usually a key consideration as the owner, although he may be proficient in his trade, may be poor at administration, selling or any number of important business functions.

- The work of a sole proprietor is usually *labour intensive.* This means that when the sole proprietor is not working, no money is coming in. This tends to mean that 'luxuries' like holidays, sick days and other reasons for 'time off' may be a rare occurrence, especially if there is pressure to keep working to bring in money.

- The small size of the sole proprietor business means that they usually suffer from *poor economies of scale.* This means that the sole proprietor has little *buying power,* and will consequently pay a higher price per unit of material (e.g. per nail, piece of wood, tin of paint, etc.) than larger businesses who are more likely to buy in bulk.

- A sole proprietor suffers from what is known as *unlimited liability.* This is a major disadvantage of all forms of non-incorporated business. As the sole proprietor is a human legal entity, he does not benefit from *limited liability.* In practice, his means that the owner of the business (the sole proprietor) is liable for any or all of the business's losses from his own personal reserves, without limit.

Unlimited liability – a sad story

Johnny Banana is a sole proprietor who specialises in decorating and plumbing. He accepted a contract to work in a large country mansion, with a focus on redecorating and replumbing in and above the art gallery. The art gallery in the mansion was of international renown and housed several rare Renoir's, Picassos and a few valuable Lowry's.

What the owner of the mansion didn't realise was that Johnny was not very good at his job. On arriving at the house, Johnny decided to start with the plumbing. He re-routed several water and sewage pipes above the gallery and re-housed some channels under the expensive tiled floor. After this, on the second day, Johnny started to repaint the walls on which the expensive paintings were hung.

Things started to go wrong when he removed a Picasso from the wall to paint behind it. Laying it on the floor, he kicked over a can of paint and unfortunately most of it landed on the painting. Whilst furiously trying to wipe the paint off with some rags, one of the pipes above the gallery ruptured allowing sewage to dribble onto one of the Renoir's. Leaving the Picasso to rush to the sewage pipe, he nudged the ladders, toppling over another tin of paint, which also landed on the unfortunate Picasso. By now, the dribbling foul water was causing irreparable damage to the Renoir. The copious expletives uttered by Johnny caused the mansion's owner to enter the gallery.

The two paintings were judged to have been ruined. Johnny was advised that he owed a total of £14 million in respect of the two paintings. As Johnny was a sole proprietor, the entire value of the demand had to be met from his personal reserves. His total worth was comprised of the value of his house: £30,000, and the value of his van: £500. Johnny was declared bankrupt – a situation which meant that he could not take advantage of mortgages or any other loans, thus he lost his home and his business with little prospect of rebuilding either of them again.

3.3 Partnerships

What is a partnership?

The second major form of unincorporated business is the partnership. *The Partnership Act 1890*, defines a partnership as,

> … the relationship which subsists between persons carrying on a business with a view to profit.

This definition is a little unclear and it does leave room for some interpretation. It will therefore come as no surprise to learn that a number of different partnership arrangements have been employed by business people over the years.

A partnership is like a sole proprietor in some respects and unlike it in others. Like a sole proprietor, a partnership is not *incorporated* and therefore suffers from *unlimited liability*. In contrast to the sole proprietor, partnerships are a legally acknowledged and recognised form of business organisation.

By definition, there must be at least two partners in a partnership. There is no legal upper limit, but in practice, they rarely exceed twenty.

Partnership arrangements are occasionally found in the 'trades' (such as electricians or builders), but are more common among professional concerns such as:

- surveyors;
- architects;

- accountants;
- management consultants;
- lawyers and solicitors;
- general practitioners.

Partnership agreements

Partnerships are usually set up by all partners signing a legally bind-ing partnership agreement. This is a simple and cheap procedure, which requires the services of a solicitor or a similarly appointed legal professional.

A legally binding agreement is meant to avoid two possible unpleas-ant situations arising.

- Partners are equal in their positions in the partnership unless the other partners agree to elevate one of their number to the position of senior partner. All profits ensuing from the business of the partnership are equally divisible between all partners (unless it is agreed that senior partners should receive more). Without a legal agreement, there would be nothing to prevent some of the other partners 'ganging-up' on one partner (who they may perceive as having done little work) to not give him his rightful share of the partnership's profits.

- We have already seen that partnerships do not enjoy limited liability. In the event that the partnership has to absorb a loss, the amount must be made good from the personal reserves of the partners. In such a circumstance, some partners may be tempted to say '*I am not a part of this organisation, I was just help-ing out. Therefore I am not liable for any of these losses*'. This would leave the other partners 'carrying the can'. A formal declar-ation of partnership leaves no doubt as to who the partners are, thus preventing this situation from arising.

Advantages of holding partnership status

- The fact that there are more people in a partnership than a sole proprietor means that *more capital can be raised*. This will enable the business to benefit from a higher capacity than a smaller business. It follows that the more partners take part in the venture, the more capital may be invested.

- In common with all non-incorporated business organisations, there is *no need to submit accounts* as limited companies have to. This saves time and costs, particularly the costs of having accounts externally *audited* (a compulsory requirement of limited companies).
- The partners, as the sole owners of the business, are *entitled to distribute all of the profits among themselves*. There are no complicated ownership structures to take account of, which is sometimes the case with incorporated organisations.
- The fact that there are several people in the partnership means that there is likely to be a *breadth of skills and abilities* from which the business can benefit. This is in marked contrast to the predicament of the sole proprietor, who only has his own skills to call upon.
- Organisations which benefit from the labour inputs of more than one person can *divide up tasks between individuals*. This means that there can be a degree of specialisation and no single partner need shoulder too much of the workload. One partner may specialise, for example, in the administration of the business whilst others perform the operational tasks.
- Whilst the business has unlimited liability, the fact that there are more individuals involved means that *any losses can be shared equally* among the partners. This reduced the burden of risk that any single partner must endure.

Disadvantages of holding partnership status

- In common with all non-incorporated organisations, partnerships have *unlimited liability*. Furthermore, the situation of losses can be somewhat more complex than losses for a sole trader as the losses must be borne by all the partners, even if they are caused by the defective actions of just one (although this may be modified by the terms of the partnership agreement).
- The need to set up a *legal partnership agreement* incurs a nominal charge.
- The nature of a partnership in contrast to a sole proprietor means that *decisions must be arrived at by consultation* and

agreement between partners. This usually makes for slower decision-making than in sole trader arrangements, and opens up the possibility of conflict between partners.

- The *individual independence of the sole trader is lost.* An equal partner in a partnership does not of himself have the authority to decide on time off, the types of work carried out, the standards of quality observed and so on. Such decisions must normally be taken in consultation with the other partners.

- The nature of the partnership agreement is such that if one partner leaves the partnership for any reason (e.g. a 'bust-up' or death), then the partnership is automatically dissolved. Most partnerships make a special clause in their agreement to account for this possibility.

Except for the statutory requirements that the business should keep records for tax purposes, a partnership, like the sole proprietor, need not keep or publish any other financial information (unlike limited companies). Due to this, it is possible for partnerships to keep financial details secret (such as the magnitude of their total sales). This feature may be of value in some competitive circumstances.

Whereas most sole proprietors remain as relatively small businesses, some partnerships grow to be of considerable size. The large accountancy-auditing firms are partnerships (such as Price Waterhouse, Spicer and Oppenheim, etc.) as are some multinational surveying and architects' practices.

Assignment 3.1

You have a friend who has just received a bequest of £15,000 from the will of his recently departed grandmother. When you ask him what he intends to do with the money, he informs you that he intends to open a coffee bar and to run it himself. He says that he intends to run it as a sole proprietor but then suggests that you may be interested in joining him as a partner in the venture.

You are required to do the following:

- Advise your friend about the pros and cons of running a coffee bar in the legal form of a sole proprietor.
- Discuss the merits of joining your friend as a partner in the coffee bar business.

Further reading

Cole, G.A. (2004). *Management Theory and Practice*, 6th edn. London: Thomson.

Worthington, I. and Britton, C. (2003). *The Business Environment*, 4th edn. Harlow: FT Prentice Hall.

Useful web sites

The Chartered Management Institute: www.managers.org.uk
UK Government departments' pathway: www.gateway.gov.uk
The Industrial Society: www.indsoc.co.uk

CHAPTER 4

Limited companies

Learning objectives

After studying this chapter, students should be able to describe:

- the different types of incorporation;
- the nature of shares and shareholding;
- the differences between public and private limited companies;
- the legal requirements for limited companies;
- the meaning of limited liability;
- the advantages and disadvantages of limited company status;
- the nature of holding companies;
- the roles of a company's senior officers.

4.1 Introduction

An organisation as a legal entity

In the case of a sole proprietor, we saw in Chapter 3 that the law recognises the human person carrying out business with a view to profit. Similarly, for partnerships, the law recognises the partners as individuals, albeit working together under a legal agreement. The type of organisations we shall consider in this chapter is quite different from those we considered in the previous chapter.

4.2 Corporations

English law recognises three ways in which new corporations can originate either by *charter*, *statute* or by *registration* – and a corporation exists until it is formally dissolved. Corporations have similar rights and privileges as humans and, while companies may be corporations, it should be noted that there are different types of corporation.

Corporation by charter

The crown can create any corporation it chooses, and this route of incorporation is usually used by public bodies, such as a university. As the royal charter does not state the precise details of the legal powers of this type of corporation, any contracts it makes cannot be declared void on the grounds of '*ultra vires*' (i.e. acting beyond one's powers). This is a clear distinction with other types of corporations.

Corporation by statute

Corporations can be created by Acts of Parliament, as evidenced in the case of the boards of nationalised industries and as such corporations' powers are defined by statute they are liable to the rule of '*ultra vires*' and, if necessary, contracts falling into that category may be deemed void.

Corporation by registration

This process applies to companies registered under the *Companies Act* and probably corresponds most closely to the common use of the term '*corporation*'.

4.3 Limited company

A limited company is a separate legal entity created by *incorporation* at *Companies House* that entails the issue of a certificate and company registration number. The registration is in effect the company's ID and although the company name can be changed at any time the registration number can be retained. The profits, losses, assets and liabilities belong to the company which is owned by its members, the *shareholders*, and run by managing directors (MDs). This gives the directors *limited liabilities* and, if the company should fail, the personal assets of the directors are protected. As a company has a life of its own the business can continue to trade despite the death or resignation of any directors or shareholders.

A limited company, or an incorporated organisation, is one wherein the law primarily recognises the organisation as a person and an 'organisational person' acts just like a human person in law (as we saw in Chapter 3):

- to make contracts,
- to carry out business transactions,
- to own property,
- to employ people,
- to sue and be sued for breach of contract.

Hence, when customers, suppliers or employees deal with a limited company, the contracts they make are with the company and not with the employees they deal with. The *juristic personality*, in this case, is a limited company.

Contrast this with *registered unlimited companies* where the company members are liable for all debts incurred by the company. Unlimited companies are classed as 'private' for share trading purposes and as such their shares cannot be offered for sale to the public.

Limited liability

The need for a form of business organisation other than the ones we have so far considered first arose not long after the beginning of industrialisation in the nineteenth century. Clearly, for a business to grow in order to allow it to benefit from economies of scale and meet market demand, more investment would be needed than just a few people could provide. The problem was that investors would be reluctant to invest in business if they could be personally pursued for losses, especially if the investor did not intend to take an active role in managing the business. To answer these disincentives to invest, the idea of *limited liability* was developed.

Limited liability allows many people to invest in a business which is good for the business's growth and development. If the business succeeds, the investors benefit from a share of the business's profits (as a *return* on their *investment*). If, however, the business fails or incurs large losses, the investors will not be liable for anything other than the value of their initial investment. It is said that their liability is limited to the value of the money invested in the business. Of course, business failure means that shareholders lose this money investment, but they would not be pursued for money from their own personal wealth, as is the case in non-incorporated businesses.

How limited liability works

Limited liability, in its simplest sense, works as follows:

- The founders, on behalf of the entity of the company announce that it intends to carry out business activity and that investors are welcomed. The mechanism by which this happens varies from the informal ('do you want to invest in my business idea?') to the highly formal, such as the when a public company (see later in this chapter) publishes a 'prospectus'.
- The value of the business (either its actual or its proposed value) is divided up into small 'chunks', typically of between 25 pennies and £1. Each of these 'chunks' is called a *share*.
- Individuals buy a number of shares in the business and in doing so, become *shareholders*.
- In exchange for the use of individuals' investment, the *agents* (see below) of the company make certain commitments. Pre-eminent among these is that they will manage the company for the benefit of the shareholders and will, to the best of their ability, provide an acceptable financial return on the shareholding.
- The company's agents use the shareholders' money to buy equipment and stock to use in the normal course of business. If the company succeeds, the value of shareholders' funds will grow as demand for the shares drives the share price upwards. If the company fails, the shareholders lose the entire value of their investment.
- Under no circumstances, can shareholders be pursued for more than the value of their shareholding. Parties owed money at the time of company failure can only make claims against the value of the assets of the company.

Limited liability partnerships

A limited liability partnership (LLP) shares many of the features of a normal partnership, but it also offers reduced personal responsibility for business debt. Unlike members of ordinary partnerships, an LLP itself is responsible for any debts that it incurs and not the individual partners.

Agency

A very important concept in the context of limited companies is that of agency. In simple business organisations such as the sole proprietor, it is obvious who has the power to act on behalf of the business – the person who is the business. When the business itself is the juristic personality, it is harder to decide who can act on behalf of the company. The law recognises an important category of human person who is empowered to by the shareholders to act on their behalf in respect of the company – the agents. A company's agents are usually its directors who are empowered to make contracts on behalf of the company. The shareholders to whom the agents report, and are accountable, are called the company's *principals*. The principals, collectively oversee the work of the agents and may replace agents if they feel they are incompetent or are not acting in the principals' best economic interests.

4.4 Shares

At one time, shareholding was the almost total purview of insurance companies, banks and other institutional investors. Changes in the structure of industry in the 1980s, including the privatisation of many former state monopolies (see Chapter 10), made it more likely that many thousands of individual people would hold shares. This meant that as well as buying your water services from *AWG plc* (parent company of *Anglian Water*), you could also hold shares in the company, and hence be one of its owners.

The number of shares that a company issues is known as the *share volume*. Larger companies obviously have larger share volumes than smaller ones due to the larger company value that is divided into shares.

Question 4.1

Find out the share volumes for the following companies. You will find this information in the share pages of a broadsheet newspaper, such as the *Financial Times*:

- Marks and Spencers plc.
- Diageo plc.
- British Telecommunications plc.
- EasyJet plc.
- HBoS plc.

Types of shares

Shares are not all the same. Companies in the UK issue three types of share:

- *Preference shares* give their holders rights that other shareholders do not enjoy. Preference shareholders are usually guaranteed a dividend whatever the financial results of the company. If the company is unable to pay a dividend, it is be carried over to the subsequent year where the shareholder is paid for the 2 years – a principle known as *cumulative dividend payment.* In many cases, preference shareholders are entitled to, in the event that the company is wound up, repayment of their investment in preference to ordinary shareholders. Against the benefits of preference shares is the drawback that dividends are often fixed in advance and do not vary. If the company has a good year, it is possible that the ordinary shareholders will receive more than preference shareholders.

- *Ordinary shares* are by far the most common type. The precise rights of ordinary shareholders depend upon the company's articles of association (see later). In most cases, ordinary shares entitle the holder to attend and vote at the company's Annual General Meeting (AGM). In addition, they may expect a variable dividend, dependent upon the level of profits made in any given financial year. Unlike preference shares, ordinary shares do not carry a right to a dividend. In the event that the company is wound up, ordinary shareholders are usually last in the 'pecking order' and will only receive any cash if there is anything left once all the operational debts have been settled. Ordinary shares carry with them the possibility of high return but also more risk than preference shares. This is due not only because of the variable dividend but also because of the almost certain loss in the event of company failure.

- *Deferred shares* are very rarely used, but are worthy of note. Sometimes issued to the founders or employees of a limited company, they receive dividends only if there is cash available after preference and ordinary shareholders. However, once the other shareholders have been paid, the deferred shareholders may be the beneficiaries of the rest of the profit, divided between them.

- *Share options* are not shares as such, but represent a right to buy shares at a certain pre-determined price. Usually granted to a company's managers and directors, they are designed to act as an incentive to achieve higher productivity and profitability. It may be that an executive director is offered a share option at £1. If the share price is below £1, the director has no financial incentive to exercise his or her share options. If, however, the share price rises to £2 per share, the director can buy shares at £1 and then sell them immediately at £2 (the current market value). In doing so, he or she makes a profit of £1 per share with no risk and no investment (unless the director decides to hold the shares for sometime in anticipation of future rises in share price). Executive share options are described by the number of shares that the executive can buy at the fixed price. Senior directors are usually granted more share options than others.

Shares and control

Shareholders

Shareholders are the people and organisations who ultimate own the company. By owning a part of the 'stock' of the company, they necessarily have an important say in the affairs of the company. The objectives of shareholders, in most cases, can be described as follows:

■ They want to see a return on their investment in the form of a *dividend*. Dividends are paid as a percentage of the profits that the company makes. It follows that the higher the profits, the higher the dividend per share.

■ They want the value of their shares to rise. A shareholder will buy the shares at a certain price and it would be advantageous if a profit could be made when the shares are sold. Growth in the market value of shares is called *capital growth.*

Shareholders, as a group, have control over the company by their voting rights. Each single share endows the owner with a single vote on company affairs, so the weight of a shareholders influence is directly proportional to the number of shares held. Votes can be cast at the *AGM* of the company and at any *Extraordinary General Meetings* (EGMs) that the company may call from time to time.

Both of the central shareholder objectives mentioned above are served by profit-making. It follows that shareholders are principally concerned with the company, not as an employer or a producer of goods, but as a source of profits. This attitude has a knock-on effect on the other controlling influences upon the organisation.

The way in which shares are distributed can determine the overall control of the company. Ordinary shares, as we have seen, give their holders the right to vote on resolutions at company meetings. It follows that the higher the shareholding, the greater the degree of power over the company's affairs. Any single shareholder who holds 51% or more of the company's ordinary (voting) shares has, by definition, absolute control over the company. It may also be the case that a shareholder with a lesser holding has a high degree of power, depending on the structure of the rest of the shareholding. If one single shareholder has, say, 40%, but no other shareholder has more than 1%, it follows that the larger shareholder has a great deal of influence even although he or she may not have overall control.

Companies limited by share and by guarantee

Limited by share

When a company is formed by the investment of share capital, it is said that the company is *limited by share*. This means that, as we have seen, the share capital is the limit of the investors' liability. In the unfortunate event of company failure, the creditors will seek payment from the company's assets, including, if necessary, the share capital. If the company's assets and its share capital runs out before all of the creditors have been paid in full, then it is unfortunate for the creditors.

Case: Railtrack plc

The privatisation of British Rail resulted in separate companies responsible for different aspects of the railways industry. The national rail network infrastructure (i.e. track, signalling, bridges, tunnels and stations) is owned and operated separately from the running of trains. In 1994, ownership and operation of the network were taken over by Railtrack plc and the company was floated on the stock market in 1996 with a share price of £3.80. By 1998, the 515 million issued shares had hit a high value of £17.68 per share. However, the company experienced serious difficulties with huge investment requirements of modernising the ageing network, exacerbated in the aftermath of fatal accidents at Southall in October 1998 and Hatfield in October 2000. Railtrack posted its first loss of £534 million in May 2001, and faced a deepening crisis following another fatal accident at Ladbroke Grove in June 2001. The company requested government funding support of £700 million by December of that year, rising to £1.7 billion by March 2001 but the government refused to put any more money into the struggling company and by the end of October 2001 Railtrack plc was placed into *administration*. The first day of share trading after going into administration showed the Railtrack share price at just £2.24. After initially refusing to offer anything, the government promised to offer compensation of between £2.45 and £2.55 per share, with the first instalment in January 2003. Under the terms of the agreement, the company agreed to abandon plans to sue the government over the decision not to support the funding requirements as the cost and length of the litigation was unlikely to improve the position for shareholders.

Limited by guarantee

A much less common type of limited company is that *limited by guarantee*. It relies not on investors buying shares, but on individuals agreeing to underwrite part of the company's debt if it fails. Companies limited by guarantee are uncommon because unlike those limited by share, they have no way of raising capital from shareholders. The individuals guaranteeing the company do not inject capital but agree to accept some of the liability. In most cases, the amount of money guaranteed by the guarantors is small, sometimes as little as £1. Any profits that the company makes are re-invested in the company, as there is no requirement to pay dividends to shareholders.

Since the guarantors are required to provide money (in the event of failure) for no return, such companies typically tend to be organisations engaged in non-profit making, benevolent or charitable pursuits, such as social clubs, research associations, community businesses or professional bodies. However, a major exception can be found in *Network Rail* which is a private company limited by guarantee, formed to manage and revitalise Britain's railways, in the aftermath of the collapse of *Railtrack plc*.

Example: Network Rail Limited

Network Rail is a private company *limited by guarantee*, responsible for the operation, maintenance and renewal of Britain's rail infrastructure. As a company limited by guarantee, it runs along commercial lines but without shareholders. It aims to make surpluses from its operations, and instead of paying dividends, profits are re-invested in improvements in the infrastructure. Network Rail is run by a board of directors but is owned by *members* who are drawn from two general categories: that is, industry members and public members, selected from a wide range of stakeholder organisations and members of the public. In addition the *Strategic Rail Authority* (SRA) is a member of Network Rail. In total there are 116 members, the majority of whom are public members with similar rights to those of shareholders in a public company, except that they have no financial or economic interest in Network Rail, such as rights to a dividend or any other form of payments. The role of the members is to hold the board accountable for its management of the business and to ensure that Network Rail is managed with high standards of *corporate governance*. The members have a duty to act in the best interests of the company, not their own or the organisations they represent. There is no government guarantee but, in certain circumstances and where Network Rail is unable to raise any further finance, the company can make use of 'stand-by loans' provided by the SRA.

4.5 Public and private limited companies

There are two broad types of limited companies. The distinction rests upon the access to the company's shares.

The *private limited company* is denoted by the term 'Limited' – often abbreviated to 'Ltd' – and is the most common form of limited company (such as Campbell and Craig Limited). The shares in this type of business are held by private individuals who, in many cases, also work for the company (e.g. the MD). The shares in private companies are not generally available to the public. If an individual wishes to buy shares in the company, they must approach a shareholder directly and seek his or her consent to transfer the shares upon payment of an agreed sum. It may be the case that share transfers must be approved by other shareholders in the company as well.

In a *public limited company*, denoted by the term 'plc' (such as British Telecommunications plc). Anybody can buy shares in a plc and such access is the key distinction between a public and a private company, where the public at large do not have general access to the shares. The shares in a public limited company are freely bought and sold through a stock exchange – a central point which manages all public share dealings. In Britain, we have the London Stock Exchange, located near to the Bank of England in the City of London. The London Stock Exchange is one of the world's most important financial institutions and handles more transactions in shares than any other exchange in the world.

It is usually, but not necessarily the case that larger companies tend to be plcs. During the growth of a company, which almost always starts off as a private limited company, successful trading brings the need to make larger investment in the business. By making the privately held shares publicly available, that is, by turning it into a plc, cash can be generated for such purposes. This change in share structure is called floatation, because its shares are 'floated' on the stock exchange. (*Note*: The suffix 'plc' is shown as 'ccc' in Wales.)

4.6 Qualifications for limited liability

The state considers the extension of limited liability to a business, something of a privilege. It is, after all, possible, in the worst circumstances, for a company to cease trading leaving debts unpaid and shareholders out-of-pocket. In exchange for the granting of limited liability status, the law makes certain demands on a company, contravention of which would result in the privilege being withdrawn.

A limited company must:

- upon its inception, file its articles of association at Companies House;
- upon its inception, file its memorandum of association at Companies House;
- annually, without exception, file audited accounts of the business at *Companies House.*

Companies House is an executive agency of the state which is charged with the job of maintaining records on all limited companies. It must retain all records and ensure that all audited accounts are received from each company annually. All information in Companies House is publicly available, so anybody can inspect the articles, memorandum or accounts of any company at their leisure. For companies in England and Wales, Companies House is based in Cardiff and for Scottish companies, it is based in Edinburgh.

The articles of association

This document, which is deposited with the *Registrar of Companies,* sets out the internal procedures of a registered company and particularly includes:

- the identities of the shareholders (if a private limited company);
- the company status as private or public;
- the process for electing directors;
- the names and home addresses of the directors of the company;

- the identity of the company secretary;
- the name of the accountant or accountancy practice who will be the auditors of the company's annual accounts;
- the powers and responsibilities of the above-mentioned directors;
- the rules regarding the calling of meetings of shareholders (which will include the AGM).

Throughout the life of the company, many of these statements will change. The company can modify its articles of association at any time subject to shareholder approval. Alternatively, the company can choose to adhere to one of the *model articles* which form part of the *Companies Acts (1985 and 1989)*.

The memorandum of association

These documents include:

- The trading name that the company intends to adopt or has adopted. This must not be a direct copy of any other company name (e.g. if an existing company is called *J Smith Ltd*, a new company would not be allowed to adopt that name; it could, however, call itself *J D Smith Ltd*).
- The address of the company's head office (called the 'registered office' and whether it is to be registered in England, Scotland or Wales).
- The broad purpose of the company. Most companies intentionally make this reasonably broad to allow them to diversify into other activities if appropriate.
- A statement that the 'members' (shareholders) are claiming limited liability in accordance with the relevant companies legislation.
- The value of the company's share capital.
- The types of shares issued and the numbers of each.
- The distribution of the shares (e.g. 'Mr J Smith, Director, has 30,000 ordinary shares').
- A 'declaration of association' in which the shareholders and agents state their intention to form a company and to take up shares in it.

Again, the memorandum of association can, with shareholder consent, be amended from time-to-time as becomes necessary.

Annual audited accounts

The accounts of a limited company are a record of its financial state at a particular date (the 'year end') and a summary of its financial performance over the previous year. There are strict financial rules which dictate how they should be constructed to prevent misrepresentation and so that comparisons can be fairly made between companies (the *financial reporting standards* (FRSs) and the *statements of standard accounting practice* (SSAPs)). We will examine these statements in some detail in Chapter 11.

The accounts must contain three separate documents:

1. The *profit and loss account* (or income statement) provides a summary of the performance of the business over the year. It gives the company's total sales, a breakdown of its costs, and hence it profit figure. This statement also discloses how much of the profit must be paid in tax and how much is being retained or repaid to the shareholders as dividends.

2. The *balance sheet* is a summary of the company's financial state on the last day of the accounting year (the same day that the profit and loss statement is produced). The statement is called a balance sheet because it contains two 'sides' which, by definition, equal each other. In simple terms, the first side describes where the company has obtained its assets – the amounts from shareholders, from loans, from retained profits, etc. The second side describes what the company has used its assets – how much it has invested in plant and buildings, in stocks, in external investments, in cash at the bank, etc. Hence, it is not 'magic' when the balance sheet balances, unless something has been forgotten, it simply has to.

3. The *cash-flow statement* describes the net cash movements in and out of the company over the course of the financial year. The important feature of the cash-flow statement is that, as its name suggests, it records the inward and outward net movements of cash.

After each of the statements has been prepared, the accounts must be *audited*. This involves an independent firm of accountants coming into the company and checking that all of the information in the accounts is correct. They will look at the company's records behind the accounts to make sure that the accounts represent a true and fair view of the company's financial position on the year-end date.

Once the accounts have been prepared and audited, they must be submitted to Companies House.

4.7 Limited companies: advantages and disadvantages

We have seen that the organisation known as a limited company is significantly more complex than those of the sole proprietor and the partnership. There are several conditions that they must meet. Yet it is the case that the vast majority of businesses in the medium-to-large sectors are limited companies. In this section, we will identify the major advantages and disadvantages of opting for this legal form of business.

Advantages

- By taking on limited company status, the owners of the company can benefit from *limited liability*. No matter what the company's agents do and regardless of the size of the losses made, the shareholders liability (or risk) is limited to the value of his or her shares.
- The fact that most limited companies – even small ones – have several shareholders, means that *more capital is likely to be available* for the business than would be the case for a sole trader or a partnership. If necessary, the company can create new shares for sale to the market as a means of raising extra finance.

Disadvantages

- The setting up and running of a limited company is decidedly more cumbersome than that of an unincorporated business. There are several *legal constraints and procedures*, which must be observed and these invariably involve both cost and expensive management commitment.
- The fact that the business benefits from limited liability may make some organisations *reluctant to lend money* under some circumstances. If a bank knows that any outstanding debts can only be paid from company assets, then a weak asset base may make some lenders wary. This is a particular problem for smaller companies or those that are already in heavy debt.
- In the cases of both sole traders and partnerships, the managers of the business are also its owners. Hence, their investors have total say as to the distribution of profits and can, if they

wish, pay all profits out to themselves. The fact that limited companies are run by shareholders' agents means that investors *are not automatically entitled to all the profits* of the business and may have little say in how the operation is run (unless you are a majority shareholder). Agents rarely pay out all of the profits as dividends because it is the shareholders' longer-term interests to retain some profit for future investment.

4.8 Holding companies

A *holding company* is a special example of a limited company, and as the name implies this is essentially a 'dormant' company whose primary function is to hold, and if necessary, maintain an asset. Typical examples would be share portfolios, intellectual property rights and physical property. The use of a holding company will often make the transfer of the underlying assets much simpler, as a straightforward share transfer in the holding company can be affected rather than transferring title of individual assets.

We have seen that any party which owns 51% or more of a company's shares by definition has control over the owned company. This is because, assuming the shares owned are voting shares, the shareholder can impose his or her will and policies upon the owned company. If more than 51% of the shares were owned by the shareholder, say 100%, this would not give the shareholder any more power, but he or she would obviously be entitled to more payment in terms of dividends.

Company shares can be owned by either individual people or by other organisations. Some companies, however, exist solely to own other companies – by buying a controlling shareholding in the business. These are holding companies.

Holding companies, in one respect, do not do anything directly. Usually based around a single head office, all holding company activity occurs in its *subsidiaries*. The term 'holding' derives from the fact that the head office 'holds' the shares of other companies. The head office may buy and sell entire companies or they may build the companies they own by investing in them and enjoying the dividends from their activities. By virtue of the nature of their business activity, holding companies tend to be larger organisations and many of the UK's most important companies have opted for this form of organisation. Most are also plcs and perhaps understandably, the name of the holding company tends to be less well known, or provides any indication of the companies owned. For example, *Diageo plc* owns many famous brands, such as Guinness, Smirnoff vodka, Johnny Walker whisky and Gordon's gin.

Shareholders who invest in a holding company are actually investing, indirectly in several companies rather than just one. Some investors take the view that this is a lower risk investment than putting money into a single company that does not have the breadth of interests of a holding company.

In all legal respects, holding companies are the very same as any other limited company. They must file their articles and memorandum of association and must produce an annually audited set of accounts, although we might expect their corporate purposes – set out in the memorandum of association – to differ from an 'ordinary' company.

Owned and owning companies: some terminology

Accountants attach different names to companies owned by holding companies, depending upon the percentage of the shares owned. Generally speaking, we refer to the holding as the *parent company* – referring to its role as guardian and senior. For the owned company, accountants use three terms:

1 If the parent owns in excess of 50% of (and therefore has control over) the owned company, the owned company is called a *subsidiary* of the parent.
2 If the parent owns between around 20% and 50% of the owned company, the owned company is called an *associate* of the parent.
3 If the parent owns less than around 20% of the smaller company, the smaller company is called a *related interest* of the parent.

Holding companies and the creation of wealth

The mechanism by which a normal business creates wealth is easily understandable. It produces an output which is of value to the market and in selling products, the company reinvests profits and grows. As holding companies do not themselves produce anything, it must increase in value through the activities of its subsidiaries.

There are two essential ways in which a holding company can increase its wealth:

  ▪ It can extract profits, in the form of dividends, from its subsidiaries. By having majority voting rights, the parent can determine the dividend, which on some occasions may involve overturning the recommendations of the subsidiary's board.
  ▪ It can buy a company for one price, increase its value and sell it off at an increased price. This can sometimes take the form of buying an existing group of companies and gaining a cash

surplus by splitting the group up and selling the member companies individually.

See Chapter 21 for a full description of a typical holding company structure.

4.9 Control and management of limited companies

The internal controls of a limited company are the responsibility of the senior management group (as is the case in all other forms of organisation). The form that this grouping takes varies according to the type of organisation. In small businesses, overall control may be exercised by a single person, but in most organisations, this task is entrusted to a group. In limited companies, this grouping takes the form of a board of directors. The way in which limited companies are managed has been the subject of some discussion over recent years. This area of management thought has been labelled *corporate governance*.

The governance of a limited company is guided by a number of influences, some of which are statutory (i.e. required by law) and some which are advisory (see also Chapter 25). A generalised 'hierarchy' is shown in Figure 4.1.

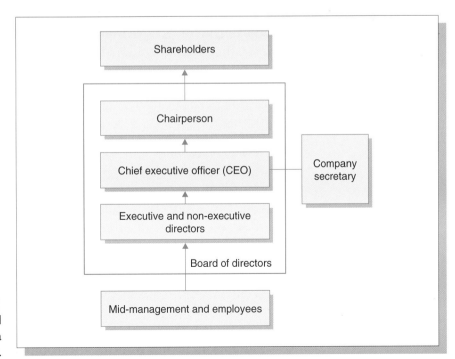

Figure 4.1
The general structure of a limited company.

It becomes clear that there are a number of people and groups involved in controlling the activity in a limited company. We will examine each one in turn.

Directors and managers: what is the difference?

The role of a director in a limited company is quite unique. Directors have responsibilities unique to their office that other managers do not have.

- A manager is responsible only to his or her immediate superior, whilst a director, in addition to being responsible to a superior, is also responsible, *en masse* with the other directors, to the shareholders (in their role as agents).
- A manager's contract is usually 'permanent'. Most directors must offer themselves for re-election every 3 years (depending upon the internal rules of the company). This means that if their performance has not been to the liking of the shareholders, his or her contract is not renewed resulting in the loss of the job.
- A manager is only responsible for the area of work under his or her direct command. Also, any member of the board, in addition to his or her own functional responsibility, is usually made collectively responsible for the total organisation.

The chairperson

The chairperson of a company is technically its most senior employee, but in many cases, his or her role will be primarily presidential (i.e. he or she *presides*) rather than operational. In the USA, this role is reflected in the job title where a chairperson is referred to as the company president. This means that the chairperson, especially in the case of larger companies, will not be involved in the day-to-day decision making of the organisation. The chairperson has two primary roles:

- To *chair the meetings* of the board of the directors, the AGM and any extraordinary meetings that are held. As the chairperson is answerable and accountable to the shareholders *only*, he or she must ensure that at all times, the shareholders' interests are pre-eminent in all company decisions.
- To report to, and if necessary, *liaise with the shareholders* of the company. The chairperson is the 'go-between' who is ultimately answerable to the shareholders on behalf of the company.

The chairperson's statutory requirements include the important task of reporting in a formal document to the shareholders. The Chairman's *Statement* will appear in the front of the company's annual audited accounts and, if the company produces one, also in the 6-monthly interim accounts.

The chief executive officer

The *chief executive officer* (CEO) is sometimes called the MD or *general manager* (GM) and is responsible for actually managing the business. This is in contrast to the job of the chairperson who may assume an overseeing or advisory role but would be unlikely to 'get involved' in the operations of the company. Reporting to the chairperson, the CEO is the *chief steward* of the shareholders' assets and must act in such a way as to achieve maximum return on shareholders' funds.

Among the CEOs duties, the most important duties will be the following:

- to manage the company with the objective of achieving the maximum *financial benefit of the shareholders*;
- to ensure that all aspects of company activity are *within the law*;
- to *sign the annual accounts* of the company as being a 'true and fair view' of the company's finances at the time;
- to *formulate strategies* suitable for the company and to implement them in conjunction with the other members of the board;
- to be *responsible for the resources* of the organisation and to see that all resource allocations are equitable and in the interest of the shareholders;
- to *approve all major investments* made by the company.

Executive and non-executive directors

In addition to the chairperson and the CEO, the board will also have a number of *executive* and *non-executive directors* (NEDs).

Executive directors

Executive directors are full-time employees of the company and report to the CEO who he or she falls into this category. In most companies, each executive director will be charged with oversight of a specific part of the company's activities. In some cases, each director will be responsible for a *function*, such as the marketing function (a marketing director), the financial function (a finance director) or similar. In other cases, for example in the case a company which controls a chain of hotels, each director will be responsible for a hotel. It all depends upon the type and structure of the company in question.

Non-executive directors

NEDs are directors who are not full-time employees of the company, but are expected to provide a strong, independent and objective element to Board discussions. Their involvement can vary from attendance only at board meetings to some degree of involvement as consultants, carrying out special projects for the company. Although NEDs receive a salary for their contributions, it is usually less than their executive colleagues:

- they may have a unique *knowledge or expertise* of the industry or products produced;
- they may have a large number of *business or political contacts* that the company can benefit from;
- they may, by their very presence on the board, bring credibility *to the company* which would be beneficial in their particular industry;
- it may be that an important *stakeholder insists upon the appointment*. A good example of this might be an appointment as NED of a senior employee of the company's bankers;
- companies may appoint NEDs to comply with the Combined Code of *Best Practice in Corporate Governance* (see Chapter 25).

Company secretary

The company secretary is the most senior administrative officer in the company. Whilst the occupant of this office is not usually a director (although it is possible to combine the offices), he or she will usually be privy to all board business. British company law requires that there are at least two offices in a limited company: one director and one company secretary – such is the importance that the law attaches to the job.

The company secretary should not be confused with the traditional view of a secretary as a personal assistant. It is considered to be an important senior management position and it is rewarded with a senior management salary.

The statutory responsibilities of the company secretary include the following:

- he or she is the one who is primarily responsible for the submission of audited accounts – even although it is the directors who sign them;

> ■ he or she is charged with ensuring that the company complies
> with the law in all respects. This includes company law, con-
> tract law and other areas like Health and Safety laws. For this
> reason, many company secretaries have some legal training.

Assignment 4.1

A friend asks your advice about investing in (buying shares in) a company called ABC
plc. In its last corporate report, the following statement was included:

ABC plc has complied with the Combined Code except for the following provisions:

■ *the company's CEO and chair reside in the same person;*
■ *the company has no audit, nominations or remunerations committee;*
■ *the directors do not retire by rotation and all directors are on permanent contracts;*
■ *directors emoluments are not disclosed.*

Advise your friend about the wisdom of such an investment considering the implications
of each of the areas in which it has failed to comply with the Combined Code (see
Chapter 25).

Further reading

Bain, N. and Band, D. (1996). *Winning Ways through Corporate Governance.*
London: Macmillan Press.

Cole, G.A. (2004). *Management Theory and Practice,* 6th edn. London: Thomson.

Solomon, J. and Solomon, A. (2003). *Corporate Governance and Accountability.*
John Wiley & Sons Ltd.

Worthington, I. and Britton, C. (2004). *The Business Environment,* 4th edn.
London: Pitman.

Useful web sites

The Chartered management Institute: www.managers.org.uk
UK Governments departments' pathway: www.gateway.gov.uk
Confederation of British Industry: www.cbi.org.uk

CHAPTER 5

Other business organisations

After studying this chapter, students should be able to describe:

- why some business organisations do not readily fit into the *'incorporated/not-incorporated'* distinction;
- what is meant by a *not-for-profit* organisation;
- the features of *charities*, quasi-autonomous non-governmental organisations (*QuANGOs*) and *public sector organisations* which make them good examples of not-for-profit organisations;
- the purpose of the *National Council for Voluntary Organisations* (NCVO);
- the idea of a *co-operative* and explain how co-operatives work;
- what is meant by *franchising* and describe the features of such a business relationship.

5.1 Introduction

In Chapters 3 and 4 we saw that most business organisations can be divided into two categories: *incorporated* businesses (i.e. limited companies) and *unincorporated* businesses. We shall see in this chapter that some organisations do not readily fit into either of these categories.

5.2 The profit motive

An underlying assumption of the two types of organisation we have considered so far is that they exist *primarily* to make profits. This is not to say that they do not have other important objectives, but that without the prospects of making profit, they could not exist. Profits are used to reinvest in the business to enable it to grow, prosper and to repay the investors. We can easily understand that a motorcar manufacturer does not exist primarily to make cars *per se*, important though that is, but to make cars in order to make money and profits.

Other organisations exist which do not have profit as a primary motive. This is not because they do not need money, but because profits are necessary *only* to enable them to pursue other, more important (to them) objectives. We shall examine three examples of such organisation. For obvious reasons, this category of organisation is said to be in the not-for-profit sector.

What do for-profit and not-for-profit organisations have in common?

These two categories of enterprise share certain common features:

- they all *require revenues* with which to carry out their operations;
- they all *incur expenditure* in the execution of their operations;
- they all *need people* to perform the many and varied duties involved;
- they all *produce a product or service* of some description in that it has an output which its customers or beneficiaries value;
- they all have *consumers* of the organisational output – customers, clients, or individuals (or plants and animals!) they aim to provide the product or service for;
- they must all be *managed* to enable organisational objectives to be achieved.

In many ways, the management and administration of for-profit and not-for-profit organisations will be similar. Hence, management skills and techniques may be largely transferable between the two sectors. In this chapter, we will examine three types of not-for-profit organisations and two 'other' types of business.

The not-for-profit organisations we will look at are:

- charities,
- government organisations,
- QuANGOs.

The 'other' forms of business organisation are:

- co-operatives,
- business franchises.

5.3 Charities

Charities are characterised by their primary objective of a wish to provide a product or service to a specific target group rather than to extract money in exchange for goods and services. Such a product or service is usually, but not always, *charitable* in nature, a term which implies that it is provided from a benevolent motive (the word *charity* is an old English word meaning love).

The beneficiaries of charities are many and varied. We are all familiar with those which seek to provide relief from human suffering, such as Oxfam, Christian Aid and World Vision, but many others exist. Medical charities aim to support sufferers of certain illnesses which include support groups and those which carry out research into diseases, such as the Multiple Sclerosis Society and the Cancer Research Campaign. Other charities include animal protection societies, environmental groups and religious organisations (e.g. churches).

Not-for-profit terminology

Not-for-profit organisations use different terms to describe 'profits' and 'losses'. If a for-profit has excess money left over at the end of an accounting period, it is called a profit because it is assumed to profit (bring benefit to) the owners. Similarly, a shortfall of money is termed a loss, because the owners must endure the loss if reserves are not available to cover it.

Not-for-profit organisations, because they have different ownership arrangements, refer to excess money as *surpluses* and shortfalls as *deficits*. Surpluses are carried over to the subsequent accounting period to be used by the organisation and deficits are expected to be made up from subsequent donations or other cash injections.

Charities and tax

The state recognises the works that charities do and allow them exemption from the taxation that would apply to normal *for-profit* businesses. Tax benefits apply to charities on both donations and in regard to surpluses. Taxpayers who make a commitment to pay regularly to a certain charity may fill in a *covenant* form. The covenant enables the charity to claim back the tax (up to the standard rate) that has already been paid on the money earned by the donor. Secondly, whereas for-profit organisations must pay tax on their profits, this requirement is not made of charities. It is assumed that charity surpluses are not used to benefit the owners, but to be re-used by the charity in the pursuance or its benevolent objectives.

Charities and people

Like their for-profit counterparts, charities can vary in size from the very small to the reasonably large. As such organisations exist primarily for a charitable purpose, they are understandably reluctant to spend large sums on staff remuneration. Whilst some staff in charities enjoy salaries and terms comparable to employees in the for-profit sector, many of the more important people fall into two unique categories:

- Some charities make extensive use of *volunteers*. A volunteer by definition gives his or her time and energies free-of-charge, and they would only do this if they were in broad agreement with the objectives of the charity. Such volunteers may be those who assist in 'doing the books' for a charity, people who help in the local Oxfam shop or the organist at the local parish church.
- Professionals sometimes supply their labour and expertise to charities at a rate of pay below the market rate they would enjoy in the for-profit sector. These may be individuals who use the later part of their careers to invest their efforts in charitable work or skilled people who believe so firmly in the charity's objectives that they are willing to forego monetary reward.

Both of these employee types enable charities to operate on a much lower cost base than for-profit enterprises. Lower operating costs mean that the majority of income can be used for providing the charity for which the organisation exists (Tables 5.1 and 5.2).

Business in the Community

Business in the Community (BITC) is an independent charity set up in the early 1980s, and now has some 700 member companies, with the commitment to continually improve their positive impact on society. BITC also runs the *PerCent Club*, which is an initiative that encourages

Table 5.1

The UK's top ten fund-raising charities, by total income (2002)

Name of charity	Financial year ended 2002 income (pounds in million)
National Trust	251
Cancer Research UK	225
Oxfam	189
Salvation Army	183
British Red Cross Society	160
Barnardo's	142
British Heart Foundation	115
Save the Children	110
RNLI	105
NSPCC	

Source: Keynotes.

Table 5.2

UK's top ten fund-raising charities: FTSE 100 charity givers ranked by percentage of pre-tax profit donated in the year 2002

Company	% of pre-tax profit	Cash (pounds in thousands)	Gifts in kind (pounds in thousands)
Reuters	12.7	6400	13,700
Northern Rock	5.0	14,800	–
Kingfisher	4.6	1400	–
Unilever	3.4	8826	256
Smith & Nephew	3.3	423	182
Legal & General	3.1	1670	52
Rio Tinto	2.8	15,724	620
Shell Transport & Trading	2.3	58,620	–
Cadbury Schweppes	2.0	1094	227
Amersham 2001	2.0	184	8

Source: *The Guardian* giving list/the *PerCent* Club.

companies to donate at least 1% of their pre-tax profit to charity. The PerCent Club also identifies the full value of companies' social investment by including a monetary value of employees' time, skills and resources as well as their cash donations.

NCVO

NCVO is the umbrella body for the voluntary sector in England, with sister councils in Scotland, Wales, and Northern Ireland. NCVO has a growing membership of over 3000 voluntary organisations, ranging from large national bodies to community groups, volunteer bureaux, and development agencies working at a local level.

Research in 2003, commissioned by NCVO, suggested that the definition of charity was not clear to many members of the public. Current English charity law is based on a 400-year old statute that deems organisations carrying out religious, educational or poverty work to be worthy of 'charitable status'. However the law excludes many other organisations that people think of as charities, such as Amnesty International. In 2003, The *Charities Bill Coalition*, which includes NCVO, Amnesty International UK, Cancer Research UK, British Heart Foundation, British Red Cross, NSPCC and many others was established to campaign for statutory measures which would make charitable status dependent on evidence of public benefit.

5.4 Government organisations

Government organisations in the form of central departments and local authorities comprise the administrative part of the state (see Chapter 8 for a detailed discussion of these organisations). As such, they are funded mainly through taxation revenues which are channelled to the organisations by Her Majesty's Treasury. As they are funded by the taxpayer, it is assumed that they exist primarily for the collective taxpayers' benefit. The goods and services provided by such departments are those which, it is argued, cannot or would not be reliably or adequately supplied by the private sector.

Local government is located in town halls, civic centres and county halls, and is intended to manage some government functions at the local level. By having this part of government 'closer to the people', it is assumed that local responsibility and accountability will be greater.

What do government departments and local authorities provide?

The goods and services provided by these organisations fall into two broad categories:

- *Public goods* are goods and services that are provided for the population in general. They tend to be things that are needed by everybody, regardless of the individual's specific need. Among them are:
  - defence,
  - police,
  - transport infrastructure (in the most part).
- *Merit goods* are provided by the state to be taken advantage of as and when the population has need of them. Whilst we all benefit from the protection offered by the police and defence services, we only use merit goods in certain circumstances. Common examples are:
  - health service (used when we are ill);
  - social security and unemployment benefits (e.g. when we are unemployed);
  - education (when we are young or wish to increase our learning in later life).

Question 5.1

There are over 20 central government departments. Find out the names of each of these departments.

You could try the governmental publications section of your university at library or at the web site: www.cabinet-office.gov.uk

Governments as not-for-profit organisations

Neither central nor local government is designed to make a profit in the same way that a private sector company is. The emphasis is therefore not on profits, but rather on achieving value for money and on reducing costs. Each part of government (each department or local authority) is apportioned a budget which is more-or-less fixed for any given financial year. Hence, government ministers and local councillors must provide all the necessary services required of them within the strict cash-limit set (although some services will be charged for).

Increases in efficiency and productivity are generally encouraged by senior politicians, and the effect of such efficiency drives is often felt by individual public-sector employees, such as nurses and teachers.

5.5   QuANGOs

What are QuANGOs?

The word QuANGO stands for *quasi-autonomous non-governmental organisation*. As the name suggests, they have a unique role.

Quasi-autonomous means that the organisations act largely autonomously (under their own supervision). The term *quasi* refers to the fact that whilst on a day-to-day basis they are autonomous, their objectives and operational briefs are set by the government or individuals acting on its behalf. They are entrusted with carrying out certain tasks on behalf of the government but are given a high degree of autonomy in how they actually carry out their duties.

Non-governmental refers to the feature of these organisations that they are not part of the government itself. They do however implement many parts of government policy and spend a lot of government money.

What do QuANGOs do?

The government sets up a QuANGO when it needs to carry out part of the government's policy but does not feel that it should be carried out directly by a government department. It is assumed that appointees to the QuANGO will bring an objective, independent and informed viewpoint over an area. This, it is thought, is preferential to having the area overseen by a government minister who may be seen as carrying out policy for political advantage.

The range and remit of QuANGOs are many and varied. The best-known examples include the British Broadcasting Corporation (BBC) and the regulatory bodies that control the prices of utilities such as gas, electricity and water. Others include the Business and Technical Education Council (BTEC) and many regional development bodies, charged with spending government money in a politically impartial way to encourage industrial investment in the regions. If you are studying in England, the university at which you are studying will be funded in large part by a QuANGO called the HEFCE (Higher Education Funding Council for England) which is charged with spending the higher education budget (a figure of several billion pounds) independently of government for the benefit of the university sector. In Scotland this is covered by the Scottish Higher Education Funding Council (SHEFC). QuANGOs are staffed by specialists in the respective fields, thus bringing an expertise and independent view on their administration and spending.

Criticisms of QuANGOs

Some criticism has been levelled against QuANGOs on the grounds that they spend billions of pounds of taxpayers' money and that they are electorally unaccountable. This means that whereas government ministers remain accountable to Parliament regarding their actions and policies, those that work in QuANGOs do not. The increased use of QuANGOs in the implementation of government policy over recent years has given rise to the somewhat critical term *quangocracy* (rule by QuANGOs). It should be born in mind that such criticisms are prevalent amongst those groups who feel that they have had a 'raw deal' from a QuANGO or who feel that government money should be spent by those who are directly electorally accountable. QuANGOs do however have a number of distinct advantages:

- As QuANGOs are quasi-autonomous, they act largely as they see fit, regardless of which government is in power. If their roles were taken by government ministers, the politicians may be more open to the charge that actions were influenced for party political advantage (e.g. by inordinately increasing the funding to a university in a marginal constituency).
- QuANGOs are generally staffed by individuals who have expertise in the field over which the QuANGO has control. This theoretically means that their performance will be optimal, which may not be the case in the tasks undertaken were carried out by 'generalist' politicians, who may not have expertise in the field (imagine if the BBC was directly controlled by the government).

Evidence to the fact that QuANGOs do not favour an incumbent government can be found when it is remembered that QuANGOs are often critical of government policy. The former head of one QuANGO, the Chief Inspector of Prisons, Judge Stephen Tumim, was at times highly critical of government policy with regard to his area of responsibility. Such criticism could not have conceivably been made if such a task was not delegated to an independent person in that you wouldn't expect a government minister to criticise his own government's prisons policy.

5.6 Co-operatives

What is a co-operative?

After the industrial revolution of the late 1700s, the ownership of business became largely concentrated in the hands of a relatively few industrialists and entrepreneurs. The 'ordinary' people of the day had a number of criticisms of the shops that they bought their goods and services from, and it was thought that by collectively owning a shop they could achieve certain objectives:

- members could enjoy a share of the surpluses made by the shop;
- members could control the quality of goods sold in the shop;
- ownership of the shop would be devolved to those who actually used it.

In response to these concerns, the idea of shared ownership of a business by its customers was introduced in the 1840s in Rochdale, England. The traditional co-operative is both a for-profit and a not-for-profit organisation at the same time. It is for-profit, in that goods and services are sold to its members at a price that includes a 'mark-up' against cost, but if it is not-for-profit, in that all profits are allocated according to the wishes of the co-operative's members and not used to benefit already wealthy shareholders.

In addition to consumer co-operatives like the formation of a shop co-op, producers also found it helpful to join together in the same way. Such producer co-operatives were intended to provide farmers and other small producers of goods and services by pooling their output into a jointly owned business. This gave each small producer the ability to sell produce with the pricing and distribution power of a larger business. Producer co-operatives were and are used to enable members to compete more effectively with larger competitors. Some farming communities adopt this business format to distribute their products. One such co-op, Milk Marque, is a major UK producer of milk.

How do co-operatives work?

We have seen that co-operatives are founded upon the basis that profits should be shared out, not to distant shareholders, but to the members – customers or producers, depending on the type of co-operative. The principle of the co-operative is that at the financial year end, the amount of money that would be paid out in dividends to shareholders if it were a conventional limited company is paid out instead to the co-operative members in proportion with the amount they have spent in the shop or the amount they have produced (and hence the co-operative dividend is proportional to the amount they have contributed to the profits).

Those wishing to form or join a co-operative are asked to buy a share. The value of the share is usually nominal and members rarely buy more than one share (this is because multiple shares do not entitle members to an increased share of the surplus or greater voting power). Each member of the co-operative is entitled to use one vote when voting on matters concerning the management of the business. This control structure ensures that no single member becomes so powerful so as to influence or control the business that may act to the detriment of the majority of members. The cash raised from the share issue is used as the initial capital to obtain premises and stock. Surpluses are then paid to the members as dividends in proportion to their total purchase values or production volumes.

In the earliest days of co-operatives, every purchase by members was logged by an ingenious mechanical device involving a ball, troughs and pulleys. Latterly, this mechanism was updated to the use of trading 'stamps' which were issued in proportion to the value of the purchase. Trading stamps could then be exchanged for goods in the co-operative shop or in some cases, claimed as monetary dividend. Co-ops of the traditional type are rare today, but the principle has been carried on by some companies whose shares are owned by its employees ('employee-owned' or 'workers' co-operative' companies). Some coal mines and bus companies, for example, have been bought from the former owners by their employees and have been subsequently run as employee-owned businesses.

Both consumer and producer co-operatives can be registered as limited companies but they can also opt for registration as *Industrial and Provident Societies* under the Industrial and Provident Societies Acts 1965 to 2002.

5.7 Franchises

What is a franchise?

Suppose you have good idea for a business. You may well gain some start-up capital and, after some time and a good deal of effort, the business becomes a success. The most obvious thing for you then to do is to increase the size of your business by expansion, which will typically involve opening new premises from which to operate a second outlet. As your initial business worked, there is a high probability that the second outlet will be similarly successful. At this point in your business's expansion, you have a choice:

- obtain the necessary capital yourself, open the second outlet and manage it yourself;
- offer the opening of the second and subsequent outlets as franchises.

To franchise a business means to allow somebody else to operate your business idea as their own business. In exchange for his or her use of your successful idea, the franchisee will pay you some money, while he or she manages the outlet and takes on the full financial risk of the outlet. The franchisee will gain the use of your company name, your logo, products, etc. and you, the franchisor, enjoy the financial rewards of the enterprise without doing any of the work or taking any of the risk. The franchisor will usually impose strict conditions upon a franchisee in exchange for the franchise. If the parent business observes a certain way of doing things, a certain code of dress or similar, this will apply to the franchised outlet in order to protect the image of the enterprise as a whole.

As a mechanism of business growth, franchising seems to work best in the area of retailing. This is because 'High Street' presence rests greatly upon brand images and immediately identifiable shop facias. In addition, retail consumers have traditionally placed a premium on buying from a trusted and proven shop or chain of shops.

Question 5.2

Find examples of five well-known franchised operations in the UK.

Pros and cons of franchising

For the franchisor

The advantages of this form of business arrangement are that financial returns can be made from the business idea with little drain on the head-office management resource. In addition, whilst the business is seen to expand, no financial responsibility is assumed by the head-office.

Whilst the franchisor will benefit from a number of payments from the franchisee (typically a signing-on fee, an annual fixed payment and an agreed percentage of sales or profits), these will not amount to the total that would be realised if the new outlet were operated centrally. In exchange for the benefits, the franchisor thus foregoes some financial income and must endure a loss of direct control over the business.

For the franchisee

The franchisee, who is usually a small businessperson, benefits from a ready-made business proposal. This has a number of advantages, not least being that the risk of failure is significantly lower than if he were to launch his own 'cold' idea. In addition, he will probably find that loan capital is more forthcoming from banks and other lending institutions. The franchisor is usually available to give advice and consultancy as an experienced operator in the field. This may be helpful when deciding where to locate and how to arrange to interior of the outlet.

The disadvantages for the franchisee include the fact that the costs of taking and maintaining the franchise are likely to make a sizeable dent in the profits. The franchisor will usually lay down strict rules of conduct, dress and behaviour which, as well as incurring cost for the franchisee, reduces his or her independence as a business manager. Failure to observe the franchiser's rules may well result in the loss of the franchise.

Assignment 5.1

As we have seen above, many UK organisations make substantial donations to charitable causes:

- Suggest reasons why should they choose to do so.
- Including the data for year 2002 shown above, identify the top 10 donors for each of the 5 years till the latest published results.
- Find reasons for changes in their relative positions.

Further reading

Carlton, I. (ed.) (2000). *The Guide to Public Bodies: Quangos*. London: Carlton Publishing and Printing Ltd.

Manley, K. (1994). *Financial Management for Charities and Not for Profit Organisations.* London: ICSA Publishing Ltd.

Ross, C. (ed.) (2004). *Charities Digest 2004.* London: Waterlow Professional Publishing.

Useful web sites

Department of Trade and Industry: www.dti.gov.uk
Oxfam: www.oxfam.org.uk
Tearfund: www.tearfund.org
Office for National Statistics: www.statistics.gov.uk

CHAPTER 6

The location of a business

Learning objectives

After studying this chapter, students should be able to describe:

- what is meant by the various dimensions of business location (micro- and macro-decisions);
- the principal factors that determine where a business is located;
- the relative significance of these factors for some types of industry.

6.1 What is a business location?

This may seem a very straightforward question. The location of a business refers, in this context to its physical location; literally referring to the ground upon which the organisation mainly operates. We can examine this matter on a macro- or a micro-scale, the relevance of which will be different for different types of business.

Macro-decisions are those concerning the location and physical organisation of a business in 'big' terms. For some companies, this will mean determining the countries, or even the continents in which the business will operate. For others, it may refer to which parts of this country the business should operate in. Such matters are generally considered to be *strategic* as they can have a significant effect on the success or failure of the business.

Micro-decisions, as the name suggests, refer to location decisions taken once the macro-decisions have been made. It might be that a company decides to build a factory in Europe (the macro-decision), but it then needs to be decided which European country and which city in the chosen country is most suitable. For smaller companies, micro-decisions would concern the street on which to locate, or even which part of a given street.

Macro-decisions in business location: GlaxoSmithKlinePlc

GlaxoSmithKline was formed in January 2001 as a result of a merger between GlaxoWelcome and SmithKline Beecham. It is headquartered in the UK with operations in the USA. It is one of the industry leaders with an estimated 7% of the world's pharmaceutical market. Prior to this merger, Glaxo had undergone a programme of significant geographical expansion. Whilst its activities had previously been centred on Western Europe and North America due to the buying power of health services and individuals in those regions, several moves were made towards other regions of the world. Some parts of the world were showing signs of growth, both in economic and population terms, and it was seen fit to make investments in such countries to take advantage of these favourable conditions. In consequence, Glaxo established centres in parts of South America, Eastern Europe and China. The micro-decisions, important though they would become, were less important at the outset than just 'being there'.

Micro-decisions in business location: retail outlets

It has been said that there are three important aspects of retailing: location, location and location. Whilst this is an obvious simplification, it underlines the importance of the location decision. A retail outlet must be located where it is most convenient for its customers to reach it whilst also catering for the customers' sensibilities and wants. Such is the importance of the micro-decision in retailing that whilst one part of a street in a city may be ideal for the business, another part of the same street may be useless. This is for two reasons.

Shops cater for a certain type of person (the *demographic profile* of the customer, see Chapter 28) and must be located at a point of easy access for the target customer group. One need look no further than the main high street stores to see that they are located where the target profile group is in high concentration. Shops like Marks and Spencer would usually seek a location that provides easy access to the shop for a strong concentration of quality conscious people, with high levels of disposable income, who are prepared to pay a premium price for quality products and service. In contrast, 'budget' chains like Aldi and Kwik Save are usually located out-of-town centres in suburbs predominantly populated by individuals and families who are principally concerned with prices and optimising their spending power via 'no frills' organisations.

The second aspect of retail location is the *volume of traffic* that will regularly pass the shop. Traffic, in this context, does not mean cars and buses, but the number of individuals in the target market segment who will pass the shop frequently or who will find the shop convenient to get to.

6.2 Factors in business location

With the foregoing in mind, we must now turn our attention to the factors that a business takes into account when deciding where to locate. These factors will be equally applicable for both macro- and micro-location decisions, depending upon the individual business.

There are a number of factors that can help to determine business location. The contribution that each factor has will naturally vary from case to case. The most significant factors are shown in Figure 6.1.

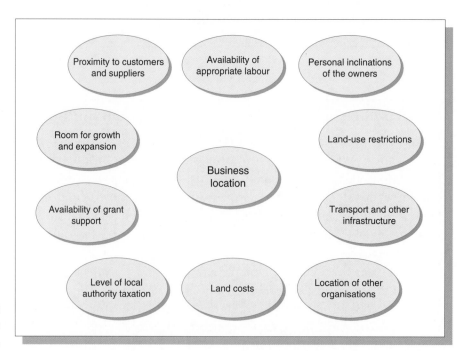

Figure 6.1
Factors that determine business location.

6.3 Proximity to customers and suppliers

If is obvious that the success of a business relies heavily on customers having straightforward access to the business's output. This factor is more important when the nature of the supplier–customer relationship is one which involves frequent personal contact and where customers buy little and often from the business. It becomes less significant as a deciding factor when business is conducted largely on a mail-order or telecommunications basis. Hence, this factor is one of the pre-eminent factors when deciding upon the location of a retail business (shop) but less important when locating a catalogue mail-order business.

It is also a major factor in cases where transportation represents a significant cost to a business when, for example, the products are bulky or perishable in nature. It is common to locate near to the largest concentration of customers in this case or to operate a distribution outlet for the business in close proximity to the customers.

The importance of proximity to customers and suppliers: just-in-time supply

The just-in-time (JIT) manufacturing philosophy is one which, among other things, stresses the sourcing of incoming materials little and often rather than in bulk (we examine JIT in some detail in Chapter 24). The advantage of this for the JIT customer is that low stocks are held and this helps cash flow significantly. In consequence, materials must be supplied to the customer at very short notice and often in relatively small quantities. For this reason, suppliers, particularly those who supply the majority of their output to one big customer, often set up close to the customer. When the large Nissan development began in Tyne and Wear in the early 1980s, the JIT operation at Nissan demanded frequent supply of car components. Many suppliers located new plants close to the Nissan plant and one supplier even installed an internal rail linkage to the Nissan plant over the short distance to the car production line.

Proximity to suppliers (and other inputs)

Proximity to suppliers is the other side of the same coin to proximity to customers. We would consequently expect this factor to assume greater importance when goods are expensive or inconvenient to transport. We usually, for example, find large installations, such as oil refineries on the coast at a point near to the oil-field. This is because the transport costs of oil via pipeline are relatively expensive. Similarly, we typically find fish processors near to the quays at which fish are landed. In this case, the location is decided by the perishability of the product.

Proximity to customers and suppliers – a summary

Proximity to *customers* will be an important factor when:

■ customers buy little and often;
■ a single customer (or small group of customers) buys a large proportion of a business's output;
■ the business operates on a personal contact basis with its customers;
■ the business's goods are perishable or expensive to transport;
■ the business's major customers operate a low stock manufacturing policy (e.g. JIT).

Proximity to *suppliers* will be an important factor when:

■ the business has a large requirement for material (tangible) inputs;
■ the business buys little and often;
■ material inputs to the business are bulky or expensive to transport;
■ there are few choices of suppliers (i.e. supply is highly concentrated);
■ goods inputs to the business are perishable;
■ the business employs a low stock manufacturing policy (e.g. JIT).

The location of other parts of the organisation or similar organisations

Some types of organisation benefit or suffer from close proximity to partner divisions of the same organisation or organisations of similar type ('suffer' in the case of some organisations' proximity to their competitors). We can sometimes observe the various departments or subsidiaries of the same organisation concentrating in one region or town or a 'cluster' of businesses in the same industry. In some decisions, the location of a department will be an obvious decision if there is unused land or buildings on the main company site. For other location decisions, there may be more operational reasons for the location decision. We can observe, for example, a concentration of government departments around Whitehall whilst Teesside has a high concentration of chemical companies.

This factor may assume some importance when:

■ there is the likelihood of a high degree of personal contact between the different sites;
■ there is special 'earmarked' land for a particular type of business or where one part of the organisation has spare capacity (e.g. land) on its site that another part of the same business would be cheaper to occupy than to build a new plant elsewhere;

- it would be of commercial advantage to be located in close proximity to each other (e.g. so that customers can visit more then one shop in one trip to a retail park);
- when transport costs could be reduced by the location (e.g. distribution points may be located near to the manufacturing plant to avoid transport costs).

6.4 Availability of appropriate labour

Labour, as one of an organisation's key inputs, is necessarily an important factor in location. The key consideration here is the availability of *appropriate* labour rather than the availability of labour *per se*.

Some businesses in, for example, heavy industries (e.g. shipbuilders, steelworks, etc.) require relatively large numbers of skilled and semi-skilled workers. Furthermore, in practice, much of this labour is male. It follows that businesses of this type would be located in regions where the key labour input is plentiful. Of course, one could plausibly argue that the employer attracts the key labour input to its vicinity. Other types of business require staff with key intellectual skills, such as science, computing or accountancy. This is one reason for the concentration of banking and finance in the City of London.

In addition to the availability of labour inputs, business location is sometimes influenced by government regulation. Some organisations are guided in their choice of country of location by the degree of regulation of the workforce in the country. In some countries, employers must, by law, make more provisions for employees than in others. Countries with less regulation of the workplace may attract more relocation than those with more. This is one of the reasons why the UK government refused to subscribe to the terms of the Social Chapter of the Treaty on European Union 1992 (Maastricht Agreement) – a charter increasing employee rights in the workplace.

6.5 Access to transport links

For some organisations, the need for transport links assumes great importance in location decisions. In this context, transport infrastructure includes suitable road networks in the vicinity, rail connection, seaports and airports.

This factor is especially important for businesses that rely heavily on the transport of goods to and from their plants. For this reason, most manufacturing industry is centred on areas of the country which are well supplied by motorways and rail-freight termini. Local authorities are aware of the importance of this factor for manufacturers when they seek to encourage companies to invest in their locality. The first step in setting up a local business park is often to upgrade the roads linking the park to the nearest motorway or trunk road.

For some industries, this may be the single most important factor. It is obvious, for example, that shipbuilders must locate on a major waterway as ships cannot be transported overland once completed. Similarly, nuclear power generators are usually located on the coast, as the power generation process requires a large amount of circulating water.

6.6 Access to energy and utilities

All organisations have some requirement for utilities, such as gas, electricity and water. It follows that this is a factor to businesses in the same way as it would be for an individual looking to buy a house. Whilst all main centres of population are well served by the utilities, some outlying areas are not. This is particularly true of gas supplies which are somewhat more expensive to carry to remote areas than electricity.

In addition to utilities, some businesses have a high dependency on modern telecommunications networks. The rapid advances in telecommunications technology in the 1990s have enabled many organisations to develop their activities in parts of the world that would not have been previously possible.

6.7 Costs of land

The cost of land varies significantly across the UK according to the differences between the supply (of land) and its demand. It has historically been the case, for example, that land is more expensive in the south east of England than in say, the far north of Scotland. The reasons for the disparity are not difficult to understand. The higher population density in the London area (see Chapter 11) means that there will be a higher demand for land, which is subject to finite supply (i.e. there is so much and no more). The highland region of Scotland has much lower land prices resulting from supply being plentiful and demand being relatively (compared to London) low.

Some businesses, particularly those involved in manufacturing, have the need for a lot of land. Whereas many service businesses can operate from a small suite of offices, a manufacturer may require land space for warehousing and production in addition to offices. High land costs are thus bound to affect such businesses more than others. For this reason, manufacturers do not tend to locate in areas of very high land cost unless there is some other very compelling reason for doing so.

6.8 Local authority taxation and grants

In order to support local authority services, local government charges residents and businesses in their area with local taxation. The amount charged to each business will depend upon both the level of expenditure of the local authority and the amount of grant money from central government. It follows that not all local authorities charge the same level of local council tax.

Areas with lower local authority taxation will obviously be more attractive to businesses than areas with higher local tax.

Availability of grants

Funding is available from a number of sources to stimulate business activity in certain areas of the country. Assisted areas are selected for their need for industrial investment to offset higher-than-average unemployment. Grants are offered to encourage new business investment, and to encourage existing companies to grow and expand within the same locality. The regions which qualify for grant support are chosen according the levels of unemployment that the areas suffer.

The Department of Trade and Industry (DTI) identifies three categories of assisted area:

- development areas (DAs);
- intermediate areas (IAs) that offer different types of assistance to DAs);
- Northern Ireland (seen as a special case due to its singular problems in attracting businesses to locate into the region).

DAs are mainly those which have suffered from decline in traditional industries, such as mining, shipbuilding, steel and other heavy engineering businesses. Accordingly, DAs are centred on Clydeside, Tyneside, Teesside, South Wales, Merseyside, South Yorkshire and parts of the West Midlands. An IAs, which attract a lower level of grant support, include some outlying areas of the country which have been unable to attract as high a level of investment as more central regions.

With effect from 1 April 2004, the DTI replaced *Regional Selective Assistance* (RSA) and *Enterprise Grants* (EG) in England with a new product called 'Selective Finance for Investment in England' (SFI). The assistance product is delivered by Regional Development Agencies and is aimed at securing growth in productivity, measured by Gross Value Added (GVA) per Full Time Equivalent (FTE) employee compared to the sector and national averages; and higher skills, with the majority of jobs required to be at NVQ level 2 (or equivalent) and above. Most manufacturing businesses are eligible to apply, as are businesses in service industries that supply a national rather than local market. Applicants can be companies, partnerships or sole traders. Grants are not available simply for transferring jobs from one part of the country to another and assistance can be provided to:

RSA can be provided to:

- establish a new business;
- expand, modernise or rationalise an existing business;
- set up research and development facilities;
- enable businesses to take the next step from development to production.

European Commission restrictions apply in some sectors, including steel, coal, synthetic fibre, vehicles, and agricultural products. Restrictions also apply where support for projects would simply displace or reduce existing jobs in similar businesses elsewhere.

Investment in assisted areas is available from sources other than the DTI. Regional quasi-autonomous non-governmental organisations (QuANGOs), such as development agencies, are often instrumental in attracting new business to the areas in which they operate. In addition to non-repayable grants, loans at preferential rates are available from European institutions, such as the European Central Bank and the European Coal and Steel Community.

Example – assistance for business development

Following the demise of traditional industries, such as steel, coal mining and shipbuilding, the UK government provided financial and material inducements to attract foreign technical companies to locate premises in the UK that would help regenerate local economies and provide job opportunities. Large electronics companies like International

Business Machines (IBM) and Motorola were attracted to Scotland and by the 1980s there was a big enough concentration of electronics firms in Scotland's central belt – a 50 mile high-tech corridor stretching from Glasgow to Edinburgh – that earned the nickname 'Silicon Glen'. By 1996, the new electronics sector producing 35% of Europe's personal computers (PCs), 12% of the world's semi-conductors and employed some 55,000 people. However, by the early twenty-first century the sector had gone into sharp decline – a fall of about one-third in 2002 alone.[1]

The root causes can be traced back to the aggressive marketing for foreign investment in the 1980s and 1990s when Original Equipment Manufacturers (OEMs) – builders, on behalf of brand name companies, of high-tech hardware (such as PCs and mobile phones) were attracted to the country. Despite the apparent permanence of their factories and warehouses, these companies proved to be highly cost sensitive with short life-cycle products and low-yielding manufacturing operations that could easily be relocated to more economical parts of the world. By 2003, the government's development agency, Scottish Enterprise, had shifted its policy from attracting OEMs (or relatively simplistic assembly plants) to firms higher up the technological chain, such as software development (Figure 6.2).[2]

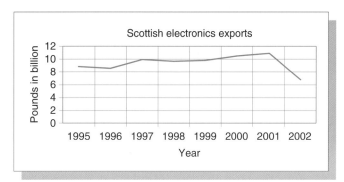

Figure 6.2
Scottish electronics exports[3].

6.9 Restrictions on land use

Restrictions on land use can be imposed by both central and local government. An example of land-use restriction includes the imposition of a 'greenbelt' around a major conurbation. In this case, special planning permission is required for any development in the greenbelt – a measure designed to ensure that cities do not simply continue to expand into surrounding countryside.

Local authorities may also impose restrictions. Some left-leaning local authorities have made their areas 'nuclear-free zones' – a ban on, among other things, businesses based on the use of nuclear technologies. In some cases, the quality of the land itself (i.e. the soil) may be important, as might the quality of drainage, the risks of subsidence, etc.

6.10 Personal preferences of the owners

The personal preferences of business owners regarding location is a particularly important factor when the business is run by an owner–manager. Businesses run in this way are usually relatively small. In most cases, it is common for small businesses to be set up in the region in which the owners and their families are already established. It may be traumatic, for example, to uproot a family, away from friends, schools, etc. for reasons of locating a business in a region which may be in closer proximity to suppliers, customers or whatever.

There may be business as well as personal reasons for 'staying' in a locality with which the owner is familiar. Owners of small businesses tend to build up business contacts over the years, which may be used to advantage when carrying out business activities.

6.11 Room for expansion

As part of their strategic planning, some businesses locate in a specific location because the site in question has land around it which offers the opportunity for future expansion. Such businesses tend to be ambitious and may be relocating as part of a market development strategy (see Chapter 7 for a discussion of market development).

This is one reason why manufacturing businesses tend to be located on the peripheries of towns and cities. By constructing a plant adjacent to 'spare' land, the opportunity remains for new building work to take place if needed without having to demolish other buildings first. Local authorities vary in their willingness to grant permission for business expansion into adjacent land and this is another important factor in some business location decisions (although central government can over-rule a local authority).

Assignment 6.1

Choose a business from the following list:

- a road haulage company,
- a soft-drinks manufacturer,
- a call centre,
- a mail-order company,
- a retail supermarket.

Assume the business is considering relocating or establishing a part of the business to the town or city in which your college or university is located. Prepare a report for the senior managers of the business discussing the advantages and disadvantages of the area for a business of the type in question. This will involve you examining the factors that would be most important to a business of the type you have chosen and then finding out the 'state of play' of these factors in your area.

Once you have researched the issues and written the report, make a final recommendation to the senior management (i.e. should it or should not it relocate into the area?).

Your report should be approximately 2000 words in length.

References

1   news.bbc.co.uk (2003).
2   Business week (2002).
3   Scottish Executive (2003).

Further reading

Birkin, M. *et al.* (2002). *Retail Geography and Intelligent Network planning*. London: John Wiley and sons Ltd.

Burstiner, I. (2001). *How to Start and Run Your Own Retail Business*. London: Citadel Press.

Salvaneschi, L. (ed. Howell, B.) (2002). *Location, Location, Location: How to Select the Best Site for Your Business*, 3rd edn. London: Entrepreneur Press.

Schiller, R. (2001). *Dynamics for Property Location*. London: Routledge.

Useful web sites

Office for National Statistics: www. statistics.gov.uk
Business Link: www.businesslink.gov.uk
Department for Transport: www.dft.gov.uk
Department of Trade and Industry: www.dti.gov.uk

CHAPTER 7

Growth in organisations

After studying this chapter, students should be able to describe:

- Ansoff's generic product–market expansion grid and its contents;
- market, product development and diversification;
- what is meant by internal growth and why it is adopted as a growth strategy;
- the meaning of external growth and why it is adopted as a growth strategy;
- types of mergers and acquisitions (integrations).

7.1 Trends in business growth

A potted history

Prior to the industrial revolution in the late eighteenth century, businesses were locally based and usually very small. Often located around agricultural communities, such businesses were typically engaged in crafts and simple service industries. The dawn of automation and increased urban demographic concentration brought about a completely new climate in the external business environment. For the first time, businesses were able to make much greater quantities of their products and increased demand provided the economic incentive for businesses to gear up for higher production levels. In consequence, the first large businesses appeared, employing hundreds or thousands of people rather than just a few. The nineteenth century witnessed the birth of a large number of businesses that eventually grew into large companies, many of whom are still operating today.

The extent of business growth was limited by problems with communications and transport between the businesses and their suppliers and customers. Developments in the twentieth century, however, reduced these limitations. The invention and refinements in both the internal combustion engine and in air-flight made the transportation of goods and people significantly easier. Running parallel with these developments was the development of modern telecommunications systems. The result was the removal of many of the factors that limited business growth. Consequently, the twentieth century witnessed the emergence of many very large businesses whose economic interests encompassed the world. Today, the business world comprises all sizes of organisations and businesses in all stages of growth and development.

Big is beautiful

It is usually assumed in business that growth is good and that bigger is better than smaller. This view is held for a number of reasons:

- Bigger companies, by increasing their sales, have the opportunity to earn more profits (although not necessarily a higher percentage of profits against sales).
- Bigger companies enjoy a higher market share than smaller companies. Higher market shares allow the larger business to have more of an influence over the market price of a product – an opportunity to increase profit.
- Bigger companies are usually more robust than smaller ones. This means that size renders a business more able to cope with economic trauma, such as a sudden decline in sales or a sudden change in government policy.
- Bigger companies have the opportunity to benefit from increased economies of scale – the reduction of unit costs resulting from increases in size and buying power.

This chapter is concerned with the ways in which businesses seek to gain the advantages of larger size.

7.2 Ansoff's growth and expansion matrix

The American academic *H. Igor Ansoff,*[1] in seeking to distil the complex patterns of business growth into simplified directions, arrived at his product–market expansion matrix. He found that although businesses take many and varied routes to growth, all of these can be simplified to one of four simple generic growth strategies. It is usually shown in the form of a simple two-by-two matrix (Figure 7.1).

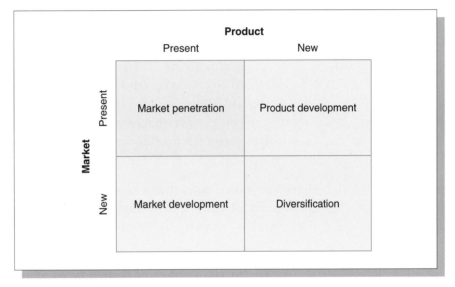

Figure 7.1
The Ansoff's
product–market
expansion matrix

Ansoff's matrix provides a simple but effective focus for considering different options for growth, and provokes debate about whether to find new customers for existing products. According to the matrix, businesses have essentially only four generic mechanisms of growth, but the ways that organisations actually follow the four directions will vary (Table 7.1).

Table 7.1
A summary of Ansoff's product–matrix expansion grid

Market penetration	Same markets	Same products
Market development	New markets	Same products
Product development	Same markets	New products
Diversification	New markets	New products

Market penetration

Business expansion which involves the organisation growing by the use of existing products in existing markets is known as market penetration. It is said that the organisation further penetrates the market which it already serves. It thus involves the organisation increasing its market share – attracting more customers in the market to use the existing products.

Market penetration is an appropriate strategy when:

- the existing market has growth potential and is currently profitable;
- other competitors are leaving the market, thus reducing the competition in supplying the market;
- the company has a great deal of experience in the market which it can take advantage of in understanding what the market wants;
- the company is unable to pursue a strategy involving entering new markets, due to such things as insufficient resources or inadequate knowledge.

There are several ways that a business can attract more market share. The essence of market penetration is to make the business's products more attractive than its competitors' products:

- The business can *reduce the price* of its products. Depending on the price elasticity of demand (see Chapter 17), lower price may attract a higher volume of sales. Price reductions can usually only be maintained over a protracted period of time if it can also reduce its operating costs accordingly.
- *Quality can be improved.* By making products better match the requirements of the customer; the buyers will tend to have more confidence in the products.
- The products can be *differentiated*. By giving the products a unique or distinctive quality, customers may switch brands to the differentiated product.
- Product *distribution can be widened*. By selling the products through more outlets, more customers will be able to access the business's output.
- *Production can be increased* by means of operational investment. Increased output may increase market share if customers are prepared to purchase the extra volume.
- *Advertising* and other marketing promotions, by making more customers aware of the products, can increase market share.

■ A business can increase its market share by *acquisition*. The purchase of a competitor making similar products instantly increases a business's market share.

Market development

Market development is growth by means of placing a business's existing products into new market sectors. It is said that businesses that pursue this option develop new markets for their products. It involves 'transplanting' products into market sectors which are 'new' for the products. By doing this, the business sells more of the product by spreading its output across different market segments.

In this context, new markets can be completely new geographical markets (e.g. a different region or country), or a different segment of the same geographical market (see Chapter 28 for a discussion of market segments). The key to market development is that although markets are increased, products remain essentially unchanged. It follows that the key to successful market development is the transferability of the product. Some products transfer well to other markets, whilst others are specific for one segment only.

It is said that the product is *repositioned* as a player in a new market. An example of market development on a grand scale is the repositioning of the McDonald's fast-food chain from its domestic 'home' in North America to appear as a symbol of western culture in Eastern Europe and Russia.

Product development

Growth by product development occurs when an organisation increases sales in its existing markets by launching new products aimed at the same market segment. In this context, the term 'new products' can mean several things:

■ it can mean completely new products such as when a manufacturer of vacuum cleaners starts producing washing machines;

■ it can mean the development of additional models of existing products, such as television sets with 'standard' viewing features or 'home cinema packages' or integrated 'free to air' facilities;

■ it can mean the creation of different quality versions of the same product, such as the 'lead-in', or basic model of a car, through a series of different specifications (and prices) to the 'top of range' model that offer choices to different groups of purchasers in the market.

The product development approach is common among businesses that feel they understand their customers and can thus supply more of their wants and needs. The principal reasons for pursuing this approach to growth include:

- the company already holds a high share of the market and feels that it could strengthen its position by the launch of new products;
- there is growth potential in the market thus providing the opportunity of a good economic return on the costs of a new product launch;
- changing customer preferences demand new products if they are not to desert the company for a competitor's products;
- as a means of 'keeping up' with competitors who have already launched new products.

There are several ways that product development can be accomplished. Many companies develop new products through their research and development functions (which in some organisations are called 'design' departments). In some cases, organisations increase their product offering by buying a company which currently offers different products to the same customers.

Diversification

Under some business circumstances, organisations elect to make a complete change. Growth by diversification involves approaching new markets with new products. It follows that in most cases, this strategy represents a higher risk of failure than any other of the three we have considered previously, due to the potential lack of knowledge among management about the new situation. Again, this growth strategy can be achieved by the internal development of new products or by the acquisition of a business already in the new market.

Diversification is appropriate when:

- current products and markets no longer provide a financial return that satisfies the shareholders or principals of the organisation;
- the organisation has 'spare resources' after it has pursued its requisite expansion exploiting existing products and markets;

- the organisation wishes to broaden its portfolio of business interests across more than one product/market segment;
- the organisation wishes to make greater use of any existing distribution systems in place, thus diluting fixed costs and increasing returns;
- the organisation wishes to take advantage of any 'downstream opportunities' such as the use of by-products from its core business activities.

Ansoff's general strategies can be achieved in two different ways. We now need to turn to these two mechanisms: internal growth and external growth.

7.3 Internal growth

Internal growth occurs when a business grows by reinvesting its profits back into the same business entity. By buying new plant, equipment and by taking on more people to operate them, the business increases its capacity (the volume of output it can produce). With an increased capacity, the business can meet higher demand and accept a higher market share, thus increasing its financial income. The business usually continues to invest its profits over many years, thus consolidating its position. This method of growth is sometimes referred to as *organic* growth due to its effects on the numbers of people that the business employs.

Internal growth has been the prominent method of growth since modern business began during the industrial revolution. Many of the 'big names' in business today began as relatively humble small businesses, but which wisely invested profits over the years to arrive at their current size.

To rely wholly on internal growth as a means of business expansion has both advantages and disadvantages. The advantages include the possibilities of the building of long-term working relationships which lead to a strong team culture and a sense of security, and even pride in the organisation. Disadvantages include the potential limitations on skills and expertise that may come to light if the organisation continually rejects growth by external means.

7.4 External growth

The second mechanism by which organisations can grow is by external growth. Whereas internal growth occurs by investing profits in the same business, external growth involves using the business's money to invest in other businesses. This is achieved by one of two mechanisms: mergers and acquisitions (M&A).

M&A: what are they?

From time to time, major M&A are reported on the national or international news. For example, the year 2000 started with the £112 billion merger of Britain's the biggest company *Vodafone* with the German conglomerate *Mannesmann*. At the time it was seen as the biggest merger in corporate history but was over-shadowed later that year by the merger of *American Online* and *Time Warner*. Also, by December 2000 *Glaxo Wellcome* and *SmithKline Beecham* were two companies that had grown to their respective sizes via M&A over a number of years. In the year 2000 they merged to form the pharmaceutical giant *GlaxoSmithKline* – valued at £120 billion it is the world's largest drugs company. There is also the interesting case of *Rolls-Royce Motors*, which was part of the *Rolls-Royce* company until its floatation as a separate entity in 1973. The motor company built cars under the *Bentley* brand at its Crewe factory until it was bought by *Vickers plc* in 1980 who subsequently sold it to *Volkswagen* in 1998. Although the motor company had been sold, the rights to the *Rolls-Royce marque* (i.e. the iconic *'Spirit of Ecstasy'*) were retained by the aero engine manufacturer *Rolls-Royce plc* until 1998 when the rights to the marque were granted to the *BMW group*, with whom there had been long history of collaboration on aero engine projects. This gave birth to *Rolls-Royce Motors plc*, although it was agreed that *Volkswagen* would continue to build cars wearing the *Spirit of Ecstasy* marque at Crewe until the end of 2002.

Whilst such 'big money' acquisitions may be less frequent, less grand M&A activity are very common occurrences in most sectors of business.

Mergers

A merger occurs when two separate companies agree, usually by mutual consent, to come together, not unlike in a marriage of two people. Such an arrangement can obviously only come about by the consent of the two companies' respective shareholders. In most cases, the shareholding in one of the companies is simply commuted to shares in the new business entity, albeit possibly at a slightly different share price.

The issues raised by business mergers are similar to those experienced when two people 'merge'. They frequently involve:

- the surrendering of independence previously enjoyed by the two individual businesses;
- the possibility of a clash of cultures as the two businesses realise they have different ways of doing things and of thinking about things (culture is discussed in Chapter 22);
- the shedding of labour as the two participants seek to save money by *economies of scale* (e.g. the merged company will require fewer managers and operations can be combined, thereby eliminating duplication of activities);
- taking on a new identity as a result of the merger which sometimes involves upsetting people who have an understandable affection for their former business identity.

The potential benefits of a successful merger are, however, quite compelling. The *synergies* (i.e. the whole being greater than the sum of the parts) that can result from two parties working together, rather than against each other, can be marked. In addition, the larger size of the organisation means that greater economies of scale can be enjoyed with the resulting reduction in unit costs.

Mergers are usually entered into with a great deal of negotiation and careful thought, because once merged, it soon becomes difficult to demerge. Notwithstanding the undoubted intensity of discussion and negotiation prior to most mergers, the research seems to indicate that the majority are unsuccessful. The management consulting firm McKinsey & Co. made a study in 1986 of mergers involving 200 large businesses. The findings showed that only 23% of the mergers were successful as measured by an improvement in business performance and an increased value to shareholders.

However, recent years have, if anything, seen increased merger activity in some business sectors. In particular Britain's banks and insurance companies have gone through an unprecedented period of consolidation, as they faced up to increased competition from internet-based companies, such as Smile and Egg. At the start of 2000 *The Bank of Scotland* was unsuccessful in its bid for *The National Westminster Bank* which, after a bitter battle, was taken over by *The Royal Bank of Scotland*. *The Bank of Scotland* then became a target for *Halifax*. The merger of *Halifax* and *The Bank of Scotland*, now trading as *HBOS*, is a prime example of the drive towards 'big is beautiful' in this sector as more branches, cash machines and lending power facilitates a better service to customers. The intensification of competition for mortgages and lending customers together with a need to reduce costs has been the main motivator behind the merger activity in the banking sector.

Acquisitions

If a merger is a marriage, an acquisition is a takeover. By purchasing a shareholding (of voting shares) of over 50%, a company can control another and impose its will upon it. There are two broad types of acquisition:

- A *friendly takeover* occurs when the board of the acquired company recommends that the shareholders sell their shares to the acquirer. A company's directors, as agents of the shareholders, are legally required to act in the shareholder's best economic interests. By examining the proposals put forward by the acquirer, the board have come to the conclusion that the acquisition would benefit the shareholders.

- A *hostile takeover* is when the directors of the acquired company do not wish to become part of the acquirer. They believe that the acquisition is not in the best interests of the company or the shareholders and they thus resist the offer and advise shareholders to reject the price offered. However, the directors' legal obligation to act in the best interests of the shareholders sometimes means that if the acquirer offers a price for the shares in excess of the market's expectations for the share price, the directors recommend that shareholders accept the price. This obligation remains the case even although they may personally oppose the takeover. Major hostile takeovers in the last few years have included the £4.9 billion takeover of the *Forte* hotel group by *Granada* in 1995 and the *Argos* catalogue store chain by *GUS plc* in 1998.

The arguments in favour of acquisition are similar to those for mergers. The increase in size gives the acquirer synergies and increased economies of scale. In addition, acquisitions can be selectively made to pursue any of Ansoff's generic growth strategies.

The track record of acquisitions is not particularly impressive as many end in divestment after a failure on the part of the acquirer to successfully manage the strategy of the acquired business. Prof Michael Porter of Harvard Business School conducted a study of merger behaviour among 33 large US-based businesses between 1950 and 1980. He found that 53% of related acquisitions and 74% of unrelated acquisitions were subsequently divested (the terms *related* and *unrelated* are defined later).

Types of M&A

Both M&A ('integrations', meaning 'becoming one') can be divided into sub-categories depending upon the relationship of the two companies involved. These distinctions aid our understanding and are shown in Figure 7.2.

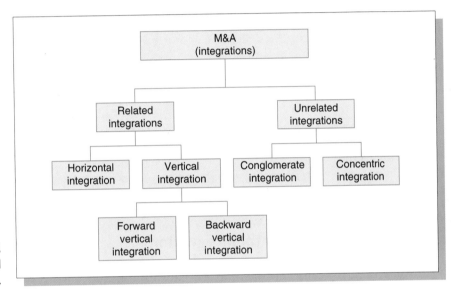

Figure 7.2
Types of merger and integration.

Related integration

M&A are said to be related when the two companies involved in the integration are in the same industry. It is important, however, to define what we mean by 'industry' in this context. In its broadest sense, an industry comprises all parts of the supply chain for a good or service. In the brewing industry, for example, the 'industry' includes brewers, their suppliers of malt, hops, etc., their customers (bars, off licences, etc.) and their competitors. This is shown in the schematic in Figure 7.3.

The form of Figure 7.3 shows us that related integration can occur in one of two directions: horizontally or vertically:

■ Horizontal integration is growth by acquisition of, or merger with a competitor.
■ Vertical integration is acquisition of or merger with a business backwards or forwards of the organisation in the supply chain.

There are thus two vertical directions:
- backward vertical integration – integration with a supplier,
- forward vertical integration – integration with a customer.

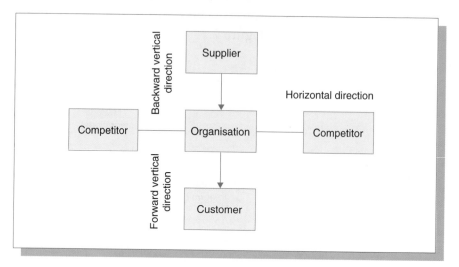

Figure 7.3
Horizontal and vertical integrations.

Horizontal integration

This approach, as we have established, involves two competitors join-ing forces which have previously supplied the same goods and/or ser-vices to the same market. The result of horizontal integration (by merger or acquisition) is thus to increase the concentration of supply. The acquirer immediately gains the market share of the acquired business and thus avoids the arduous task of winning it in open competition which would be the task facing the business if it adopted an internal growth strategy. Ansoff would identify this strategy as an example of mar-ket penetration.

Horizontal integration offers a relatively low risk expansion strategy to an organisation. This is mainly due to the transferability of manage-ment expertise. The main advantages of pursuing this approach rest upon the increased market presence:

■ Economies of scale can be gained as the larger (combined) business can exercise greater buying power over its suppliers. The fact that the business now buys higher quantities of com-mon inputs means that it will be able to negotiate lower unit prices. This will obviously contribute to a lower unit cost for the organisation enabling higher profits to be made.

■ The greater market share may enable the organisation to have a greater control over prices in the market. The closer supply comes to a monopoly, the greater, the control of prices results. If, by enhancing market presence a business can increase or maintain prices, an opportunity clearly exists to increase profit.

Vertical integration

The logic behind vertical integration lies in 'locking in' the forward or backward links in the supply chain.

Backward vertical integration enables an organisation to gain control over one of its suppliers. This offers the following advantages:

■ guaranteeing supply which may be important for some inputs which are subject to shortages;

■ prices to competitors (if competitors are existing customers) can be maintained whilst the integrated organisation gains goods at a preferable transfer price.

Forward vertical integration enables an organisation to gain control over one of its customers. This mechanism of growth offers the following advantages:

■ it guarantees an outlet for the company's output which means the production and sales can be forecast with greater certainty;

■ in controlling the customer, the organisation can ensure that the customer gives priority to inter-group sales. This means that the customer's buying power can be used to favour its group partner at the expense of competitors.

Both strategies, in addition to the advantages above, obviously also serve to increase group sales and hence total profits. They also have the beneficial effect of broadening an organisation's portfolio as new products and markets are brought under the organisation's umbrella.

Unrelated integration

M&A are said to be unrelated when the two companies involved in the process are in different industries. According to Prof Ansoff,[1] this type of business growth can be described as diversification (i.e. new products and new markets).

It follows from our discussion of related integration that the two parties do not compete with each other in any part of their business and that they do not supply or buy from each other. This does not however mean that the two companies have nothing in common. There are two types of unrelated integration depending upon how much the two parties have in common.

Concentric diversification

Some diversifications occur between organisations which are not in the same industry but nevertheless do have something in common in that some skills are transferable between the two companies. Such integrations are said to be concentric.

Companies who pursue concentric diversification see the advantage that they can expand their product and market portfolios without completely 'jumping ship'. This can mean that the integration is less of a risk than a complete move into new products and new markets. Examples of this growth strategy include mergers or acquisitions between businesses which share common technologies, common marketing approaches or manufacturing plants that can be merged together. It might be, for example, that a television manufacturer acquires a manufacturer of audio equipment. Although the two businesses serve different markets, their common core competencies of the design and manufacture of electronic equipment and marketing consumer goods to the retail markets should mean that the acquisition has a higher probability of success.

Conglomerate diversification

In contrast to concentric diversification, conglomerate diversification is characterised by merger or acquisition into a business sector which has no obvious links with existing products or markets. It follows that no organisational competencies or operational expertise is directly transferable between the two businesses. This necessarily introduces a more pronounced element of risk into the integration, but, conversely, it represents the most effective mechanism of widening the total product and market portfolio.

Many of the world's largest and most important holding companies are highly conglomerate diversified (hence they are sometimes called *conglomerates*). Whilst some large companies like Imperial Chemical Industries plc (ICI) are essentially concentrically diversified companies (i.e. entirely in the chemicals sector), others like the UK-based industries Hanson plc and BAT are conglomerates.

Case: Hanson plc

In 1964 Hanson Trust was created in the UK, out of the former Wiles Group, by James Hanson and Gordon White and, as Hanson plc, went on to become one of the world's largest companies with a strategy of growth through acquisition. In the 1970s and 1980s Hanson became a multi-national concern with interests across the world ranging from chemical factories in the US to electricity supply in the UK and gold mines in Australia. Hanson produced cigarettes, batteries, timber, toys, golf clubs, jacuzzis, cod liver oil capsules and cranes.

By the 1990s the environment in which Hanson operated was changing as investors began to look beyond the 'traditional' big conglomerate to companies focused on single sectors. In 1996 it was decided to change the strategy from a diversified industrial conglomerate into a focused heavy building materials business. The distinct businesses of Imperial Tobacco, The Energy Group, and Millennium (the US chemicals business) were de-merged and subsequently became quoted companies in their own right. The companies remaining with Hanson were the major building materials operations of American Red Cross (ARC), Hanson Brick and Cornerstone. From 1997 to 2000 the remaining non-core businesses were sold while considerable money was spent on acquisitions plus substantial capital investment on plant upgrades to build up the existing businesses.

Early in 1999, to highlight the fact that Hanson was now a unified company, the names of all the operating companies were changed as follows: ARC became Hanson Quarry Products Europe; Cornerstone, Hanson Building Materials America and Hanson Brick, Hanson Bricks Europe. The company's business in Southeast Asia became Hanson Pacific.

Acquisitions continued, particularly in the US, and the company was developed into a global player with the acquisition in 2000 of the Australian construction materials business 'Pioneer International'. In January 2002 Hanson created an integrated building materials business in Europe by combining its quarry products and bricks operation.

By early 2004, Hanson was the largest producer of aggregates and the third largest producer of ready mixed concrete in the world. With a worldwide turnover of £4000.5 million and an operating profit of £433.3 million, Hanson had more than 28,000 employees involved in operations in 17 countries across four continents.

Source: Hanson plc web site.

Assignment 7.1

Identify an example of a merger in the last 3 years and compare the merged company's performance with the respective company positions for the 3 years prior to the merger, in terms of:

- shareholder value,
- market share,
- economies of scale (e.g. number of managers, employees, accommodation, etc.).

Assignment 7.2

You have just joined the board of directors of a company involved in the manufacture and distribution of beer. It is a smaller regional brewer which does not own any outlets such as pubs and is a one-site business.

At your first board meeting, the financial director puts forward some proposals on the expansion of the business. 'As a result of our recent successful rights issue', he began, 'we have sufficient funds to pursue a number of possible options'. He went on to explain that he has analysed the possibilities of both an acquisition and a joint venture. 'There are a number of possible acquisition targets', he continued. 'I have had contact with a number of companies. One makes beer in another part of the country to our present location, one makes *Scrumpy*, and another is a farming complex in Kent which produces hops and barley malt whilst another still is a chain of off-licences. The one 'outsider' chance we have is to buy up a paint company in Hull. On the joint venture front, there is scope for a joint licensing agreement with a German lager producer. This would involve us brewing and marketing their lagers over here whilst they would do the same for our range of English real ales over there in Germany'. The financial director concluded that the final option was to put the money on deposit at the bank and let it accumulate interest. 'At least we know the money is safe in the bank', he mused, 'even although we might make a lower return on it'.

You are required to do the following:

- Identify each of the financial director's options according to the growth strategies described in this chapter.
- What factors should the board consider in evaluating each of the options?
- Given that the company is relatively small with a limited management resource, which course of action would seem to be the most appropriate?
- Which options should definitely not be pursued?

Reference

1   Ansoff H. Igor (1988). *Corporate Strategy (revised edition)*. London: Penguin Books.

Further reading

Campbell, D., *et al.* (2002). *Business Strategy, an Introduction*, 2nd edn. Oxford: Butterworth Heinemann.

Cartwright, S. and Cooper, C.L. (1996). *Managing Mergers, Acquisitions and Strategic Alliances*. Oxford: Butterworth Heinemann.

Johnson, G. and Scholes, K. (2002). *Exploring Corporate Strategy*, 6th edn. Harlow: FT Prentice Hall.

von Krogh, G., *et al.* (1993). *The Management of Corporate Acquisitions, International Perspectives*. London: Macmillan.

Useful web sites

Confederation of British Industry: www.cbi.org.uk
Department of Trade and Industry: www.dti.gov.uk
European Commission: http://europa.eu.int/comm/competition
Office for National Statistics: www.statistics.gov.uk
The Competition Commission: www.competition-competition.org.uk

The external business macro-environment

CHAPTER 8

The political environment

Learning objectives

After studying this chapter, students should be able to describe:

- the meaning of the term 'state';
- the composition of the British state at national level;
- the structure and responsibilities of devolved and local government;
- the evolution and objectives of the European Union (EU);
- the institutions of the EU.

8.1 The political 'state'

The actions and policies of political institutions have a profound effect on the way in which businesses operate. All businesses must act within legal and regulatory conditions which are set by the state in which the business is located.

Each autonomous region of the world is comprised of a *state*. The various parts of the state set out the conditions in which both its citizens and businesses exist. Hence, to be a part of the state system carries with it certain *privileges* (or *rights*) and *responsibilities*.

The *privileges* available to members of a state include access to the goods and services that the state provides. For example, we expect to benefit from:

- national security (ensured by the state's provision of armed forces and a nuclear deterrent);

- health provisions (hospitals, etc.);
- educational establishments (schools and universities);
- law and order (police and the judiciary);
- good transport links;
- social security provisions (e.g. child benefit, unemployment benefit).

In exchange for enjoying the state's provisions, citizens must also accept certain *responsibilities*. The principle responsibility of the citizens of a state is a legal one. Citizens' legal responsibilities include our agreement to abide by the laws that the state puts in place. We agree to pay taxes, to obey the laws and to allow others their rights to live peaceably and unmolested. Failure to observe our responsibilities in this area will result in the state bringing a sanction against us (such as fines and imprisonment).

Political philosophers like John Locke (1632–1704) and Thomas Hobbes (1588–1679) proposed the notion of a *social contract* that exists between the government of a state and its people. This concept means that those who observe their responsibilities have a right to enjoy its privileges. Conversely, those who wish to enjoy the benefits of a state must also accept their responsibilities. Continued order in society depends upon the vast majority accepting their responsibilities and the order in a state system would soon become untenable if this were not the case.

8.2 Levels of political influence

The effects of political institutions upon a business come from three quite separate 'levels'. These levels exist in an approximate hierarchy, but it is not the case that each level automatically can claim authority over the lower one. The authority and influence of each level varies between different policy areas and over time (Figure 8.1).

Sub-national political influence arises from the actions and policies of the local authority that exercises power in the immediate vicinity of the business. In the UK, local authorities are subject to national government, based in Westminster. National government determines the policies that affect every business and each local authority. Supranational political influence is political policy that can affect many countries at the same time. For the UK, the principal supranational influence comes from the European Community (EC). The EC has certain powers over the UK state, but in other matters, the national government remains pre-eminent over national affairs.

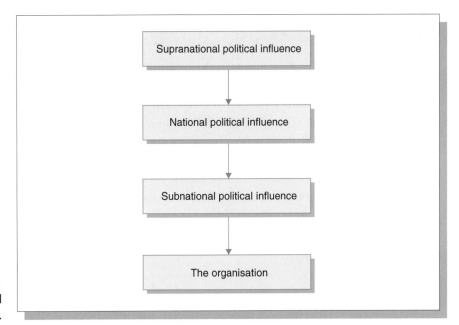

Figure 8.1
Levels of political
influence.

8.3 What is the 'state'?

A state (not to be confused with a 'government') is a self-governing, autonomous geographical region comprising a people with (usually) a common recent history. The state has the right to raise tax revenues from its people and exert the force of law over them. As a concept, a state has four distinct and separate components and states differ in how these 'organs' are set in place and how they are structured. The four organs are present in all cases. The components of a state are as follows:

- *The executive* responsible for overseeing all other parts of the state, for policy-making and for proposing legislation to the legislature.
- *The legislature* responsible for drafting, debating and passing laws which will apply to the people of the state.
- *The judiciary*, an independent (by varying degrees) part of the state, responsible for enforcing both statute laws (passed by the legislature) and common law (law generally accepted but not recorded in statute).
- *The secretariat* responsible for carrying out the administration of the state through a number of departments, authorities and government agencies. (*Note*: Some textbooks subsume the secretariat into the executive.)

8.4 The state at national level in the UK

The state in which the majority of readers of this book will reside or study is correctly called the (or Her Majesty's) United Kingdom of Great Britain and Northern Ireland. This is shortened, for obvious reasons, to the United Kingdom or the UK. It is often the case that the full name is slightly different from the common name. Germany, for example, is formally referred to as the *Bundesrepublik Deutschland* (the People's Republic of Germany). Let us look at the role of the various organs of state, paying particular attention to their composition in the UK.

The executive

The executive is that part of the state which is empowered to oversee all other parts and to make policies and actions that determine its direction. In a democracy, such as the UK, the composition of the executive is determined by those over whom they will exercise power – the people of the country. More commonly called *the government*, the executive has powers, given by the people, to execute policy based on a *manifesto* – a statement put out by a political party in advance of a general election. The period of time that an executive is mandated to serve varies from country to country. In the UK, there is an upper limit of 5 years whilst in the USA, the president (and his or her cabinet) is elected after exactly 4 years.

The UK executive is primarily made up of the prime minister and the members of the cabinet although it also includes a number of ministers below cabinet level. As the senior members of the party commanding a majority in the House of Commons, the cabinet contains the politicians who head each of the government's departments. This facilitates the enactment of policy through the departments.

Democracy

The prevalent system of government in the western world is called *democracy*. The meaning of the word can be seen in its construction from the ancient Greek language. *Demos* means 'the people' and *cratos*, 'rule by'. The clear implication is that government is installed by those over whom it will govern.

Democracy is in contrast to the so-called *authoritarian* forms of government, most notably *aristocracy* and *autocracy*. Aristocracy (*ariston* in the ancient Greek word for 'the best') is a form of government first propounded by the Greek philosopher Plato.

According to the theory of aristocracy, individuals who are superior in intellect and judgement should be identified early in life and trained to govern. In autocracy (*auto* means 'the self'), a single powerful ruler, sometimes a dictator, exercises supreme executive power. In both of these philosophies, the opinions of the people are not sought. In aristocracy, the underlying supposition is that the opinions of the normal citizens are not reliable, or are inferior to those of the informed and intelligent rulers. Autocracy, in practice, is based on the view that the opinions of the people simply do not matter.

The earliest stirrings of democracy were the city states of ancient Greece. Realising that government worked more smoothly with some degree of involvement of the people, the leaders of the day invited the opinions of the men of the state in open forums. The idea was refined in the seventeenth and eighteenth centuries with a number of philosophical theorists, notable amongst whom were the Scotsman John Locke (1632–1704), the English thinker Thomas Hobbes (1588–1679) and the French philosopher Jean Jacques Rousseau (1712–1778). By proposing that the state should be governed by elected commoners (ordinary people) with a number of 'checks and balances' to prevent excessive abuses of power, these philosophers were among the key intellectual architects of modern democratic government.

Modern democracy has a number of features which are found in most democratic states.

- There is an *electoral system* wherein the people elect part (sometimes all) of the legislature and executive.
- There are a number of *competing political parties* with differing agendas, offering alternative political emphases to the voters.
- There is an *independent judiciary* which interprets and enforces the laws passed by the legislature.
- There are usually a number of *groups which legitimately bring pressure on elected representatives* in order to further their own agendas (e.g. the anti-abortion lobby, environmental pressure groups and the press). It follows that a democracy allows, within the bounds of libel law, freedom of speech and expression.

The British system ensures that the government is opposed as a matter of constitution. When the leaders of Her Majesty's loyal opposition oppose the government in the House of Commons and in the media, they are simply doing what is rightly expected of them – providing a potential alternative government and demanding the government defend their policies and actions. This system of checks and balances is designed to prevent an abuse of government power and policy excesses.

The power vested in the executive varies from country to country. The same is true of the role of the chief executive (who in the UK is the prime minister). The nature of democratic government ensures that the head of the executive does not have excessive powers which can be exercised without an endorsement of the legislature. In the UK, the prime minister must gain the support of a majority in Parliament for any changes in legislation, but does have a good deal of power as a result of his or her rights to (albeit with the nominal consent and agreement of the reigning monarch):

- appoint and dismiss the members of the cabinet;
- appoint and dismiss other members of the government below cabinet level;
- appoint senior civil servants and senior bishops in the established church (the Church of England);
- nominate the date of a general election within the term of a 5-year parliamentary session;
- appoint those who chair cabinet committees;
- confer titles and recommend people for honours (e.g. knighthoods, etc.).

In order to remain as prime minister, the incumbent must continue to enjoy the support of his or her party in the House of Commons as without this, he or she would be unable to enact legislation or policy. As part of the democratic system of executive accountability, the prime minister (or a deputy) must answer questions from Members of Parliament (MPs) at 12 noon every Wednesday when Parliament is sitting. The debate takes place in the House of Commons and is an important part of Parliament's control over government. It gives MPs the opportunity to raise issues and find out about the government's plans. It is a half hour session and usually starts with a general question from an MP about the Prime Minister's engagement. Following the answer the MP raises a particular issue of current political significance. The Leader of the Opposition then follows up on this or another topic.

Prime Minister's question time is particularly important for the leaders of the main political parties as it is regarded by some as a key measure of their overall performance.

In other states, the remit if the head of the executive differs slightly. The chief executive in the USA for example (the President), has specific executive powers set out in a written constitution. Among the President's unilateral powers is a right to veto (overturn) legislation passed by the US legislature unless the legislation has been passed by Congress by a two-thirds majority. The British Prime Minister does not have this power, but such a situation would not usually be necessary owing to the fact that he or she is the head of the largest party in the British legislature.

The legislature

The legislature is that part of the state that is responsible for the drafting and passing of laws. In the UK, the composition of the legislature is slightly more complex than in most other modern democracies. Whereas in other countries like the USA, the legislature is entirely elected, the UK has an elected component and two unelected parts that may be considered as quasi-aristocratic. The British legislature therefore has three components.

The House of Commons

The *House of Commons*, at Westminster, is the main parliamentary arena for political encounters, with elected MPs. There are 659 MPs which includes the prime minister and most of the members of the cabinet, each of whom represents a section of the population known as constituencies. The MPs are divided into the *government benches*, and the *opposition benches*; that is, those parties which are not part of the government. The government is formed by the political party that gains a majority of constituency seats through the 'first past the post' election system, and a government can only remain in office for as long as it has the support of a majority in the House of Commons. Although the House of Commons is only a part of the legislature, and has traditionally been regarded as the *lower house*, it has primacy over the non-elected House of Lords. For example, *Bills* concerned solely with taxation and public expenditure ('*money bills*') that have been introduced in the Commons must be passed by the Lords promptly and without amendment. When the two Houses disagree on a *non-money bill*, the Parliaments Act can be invoked to ensure that the will of the elected chamber prevails, as a *constituency*. The life of a Parliament is divided into sessions, each of which usually lasts for 1 year until formally ended (*prorogued*) by the queen, normally in October or November. Parliament has a 'half-term' break of 1 week in February and a longer summer break (*recess*) from July to September. If there has been a general election, sessions may be longer. For example, the session following the 2002 general election ran for more than a year.

The House of Lords

The *House of Lords* is the *upper house* (sometimes referred to as the *second chamber*) of the UK Parliament and consists of the *Lords Spiritual* and the *Lords Temporal.* The Lords Spiritual (*Spiritual Peers*) consist of the Archbishops of Canterbury and York and 24 diocesan bishops of the Church of England. The Church of Scotland, which is Presbyterian, is not represented by spiritual peers, while the Anglican Churches in Wales and Northern Ireland are not established churches and are therefore not, represented either. Three of the 24 seats are always filled according to the order of seniority of consecration (with the exceptions of the Bishops of Gibraltar and of Sodor and Man (the Isle of Man) who are ineligible to sit in the House of Lords). On resigning his *see* a bishop ceases to be peer of Parliament and his seat is taken by the next longest-serving diocesan bishop. (*Note:* Some authorities differ on whether or not Lords Spiritual are actually regarded as peers – see *Debretts Peerage and Baronetage*[1] and *Encyclopaedia Britannica*[2].) The Lords Temporal consists of *hereditary peers, non-hereditary peers* (life peers) and life peers created to help carry out the judicial duties of the House – up to 12 Lords of Appeal in Ordinary (or Law Lords) and a number of Lords of Appeal. Hereditary peerages are automatic by virtue of parentage whereas others are non-hereditary. This latter category includes some retired senior politicians (e.g. Baroness Thatcher) and bishops in the established church (Church of England). Members of the House of Lords receive no salary for their parliamentary work, but they can claim for expenses (up to a maximum daily level) incurred in attending the House. In 1999, in line with the Labour Government's wishes, legislation was passed to reduce the number of hereditary peers. In 2001, the Queen announced her intention to give non-political life peerages to the 15 people recommended by the House of Lords Appointments Commission.

The monarchy

The *monarchy* is the oldest institution of the British state and goes back well over a thousand years. As *Head of State,* the *Queen* is responsible for the summoning, proroguing and dissolving Parliament and giving *Royal Assent* to all legislation passed through the UK Parliament (comprising the Houses of Commons and Lords). Unlike the other two parts of the legislature, the monarchy does not take any part in the debating of legislation, and can be seen to be strictly 'above' the squabbling of party political controversy. Although it does not actually mean very much in practice, the monarchy is said to be 'served' by Parliament, but such an assignation does not actually mean much in practice. The Queen formally appoints important office holders, including the prime minister and other government ministers, judges, officers in the armed forces, governors, diplomats, bishops and some other senior clergy of the Church of England. She also confers peerages, knighthoods and other honours. In international affairs, the Queen, as Head of State, has the power to declare war and make peace, to recognise foreign states, to conclude treaties and take over or give up territory.

The divine right of kings

In modern times, it is taken for granted that the reigning monarch assumes no part in the active policy-making government of the state. The king or queen, as the nominal Head of State is considered an important but impotent member of the legislature as the office of monarch carries with it little power to influence or debate political or legislative issues. This has not always been the case.

In the first half of the second millennium AD, the kings and queens of England, Scotland and Wales (and their medieval predecessors), assumed executive powers. In other words, the monarchy was the unelected power which could execute absolute power over the citizens of the state. The ancient doctrine of the *divine right of kings* held that the monarch, as head of state, was answerable only to God. Whilst the monarch must therefore accept that he or she would be judged by God according to the manner in which they governed, ordinary people, including Parliament, had no right to challenge the decrees of the monarchy. This all changed in the 1640s.

Oliver Cromwell was a senior parliamentarian at this time, who became increasingly concerned at the autocratic manner in which the king of the time, Charles I, was exercising his power. The matter came to a head in 1645 with the conclusion of the *English Civil War* when the parliamentary forces, led by Cromwell, defeated the forces of Charles I at Naseby Field in modern-day Leicestershire.

Believing that the right to govern was gained by a mandate from the people rather than by a monarch accountable only to God (although Cromwell was a Christian and a Puritan), Cromwell consented to the execution of Charles I in Whitehall in 1649. After a period during which the monarchy was abolished (and Britain was consequently a republic), it was restored in 1660 when Charles II was crowned after Cromwell's death. However, the outcome of the civil war had signalled a major readjustment in the English political constitution that the most important policy-making body is the elected part of the state and that the monarchy is effectively subject to it. This remains the case today.

Who can vote?

To vote in parliamentary elections in the UK, an individual must be a British citizen, a citizen of another Commonwealth country or of the Irish Republic, aged 18 years or more, and resident in the UK. He or she must also be included in the register of electors for the constituency, and not subject to any legal incapacity to vote.

Question 8.1

- Which political parties are currently represented in the House of Commons?
- How many MPs did each of these parties have at the last general election, compared with the current position?

How laws are made?

A law begins its life as a draft document called a *Bill*. A Bill can be put forward by the government, by the opposition parties, by ordinary MPs (in a so-called *private member's bill*) or occasionally by a member of the House of Lords. The Bill then passes through the following stages in both Houses of Parliament:

1 First reading, where the Bill is published with no debate.
2 Second reading, where the general merits of the Bill are debated.
3 Committee stage, where the Bill is examined in detail by a cross-party Parliamentary Standing Committee of about 20 members. The Committee can propose amendments to the Bill before it returns to the House.
4 Report stage, where the amended Bill is reported to the House for approval.
5 Third reading, where verbal amendments may be made in debate and the Bill is finally approved by the House.

When the Bill has received its three 'readings' in each House and assuming it has received a voted majority at each reading, it then goes to the monarch. The king or queen must sign the Bill because it has been duly passed by Parliament. Upon receiving *Royal Assent*, the Bill becomes an *Act of Parliament* and eventually passes into British law.

The secretariat

What is the secretariat?

The secretariat or administration of the state is by far the largest of the four 'organs'. It comprises the various government departments and the large part of the economy which is commonly called the *public sector*. This part of the state, which employs, directly or indirectly through government agencies, around 6 million people, serves whichever party is in government (theoretically) without partiality. The work of some departments covers the UK as a whole (e.g. Ministry of Defence). Other departments, such as the Department for Work and Pensions, cover the whole of England, Scotland and Wales but not Northern Ireland, while others such as the Department for Education and Skills are mainly concerned with England and Wales.

Most departments are headed by ministers, but some are non-ministerial departments headed by a permanent office holder and ministers with other duties are accountable to Parliament for them. For example, the Secretary of State for Education and Skills accounts to Parliament for the work of the *Office for Standards in Education* (OFSTED). OFSTED is headed by Her Majesty's Chief Inspector of Schools in England, who is largely independent of the Secretary of State.

Central government departments are staffed largely by *civil servants*, whilst local governments employ *local government officers*. Professionals are well represented in the public sector, notable among whom are health professionals like most doctors and dentists, educators like teachers and university lecturers, public sector accountants and administrators (Figure 8.2).

A *non-departmental public body* (NDPB) is a national or regional public body, that works independently of ministers to whom they are

- Department for Constitutional Affairs
- Department for Culture, Media and Sport
- Department for Education and Skills
- Department for Environment, Food and Rural Affairs
- Department for International Development
- Department for Transport
- Department for Work and Pensions
- Department of Health
- Department of Trade and Industry
- Foreign and Commonwealth Office
- Her Majesty's Customs and Excise
- Her Majesty's Inspectorate of Constabulary
- Her Majesty's Inspector of Prisons
- Her Majesty's Land Registry
- Her Majesty's Treasury
- Home Office
- Ministry of Defence
- Northern Ireland Office
- Privy Council Office
- Public Bodies and Agencies
- Scotland Office
- Wales Office

Figure 8.2
Government
departments.

accountable. There are more than 1000 NDPBs in the UK, which comprise two main types:

- *Executive NDPBs* are those with executive, administrative, commercial or regulatory functions. They carry out set functions within a government framework, but the degree of operational independence is variable. Examples include: the Health and Safety Executive and the Environment Agency.
- *Advisory NDPBs* are those set up by ministers to advise them and their departments on particular matters. Examples include: the Low Pay Commission and the Committee on Standards in Public Life. Some Royal Commissions are also classified as advisory NDPBs.

Question 8.2

Suggest reasons why central government might locate much of its activities in areas other than London.

The secretariat and the executive

We have seen that the actions of the secretariat are determined by the policies of the executive. Cabinet members are placed in charge of government departments, but each department is also staffed by a hierarchy of permanent managers who remain in place as their political 'masters' come and go. The job titles of these senior managers vary from department to department, and each department usually has a senior civil servant in Whitehall in addition to a chief executive who oversees the activities of the department on a day-to-day basis. We can see the relationship between the executive and the secretariat in Figure 8.3.

The judiciary

There would be little point in having a legislature to make law if the state did not also have a means by which it could be powerfully enforced. This is the explicit role of the judiciary. Although the head of the judiciary is a member of the cabinet (the Lord Chancellor, who is also a member of the House of Lords), the part of the state which executes justice is largely independent of the executive and the legislature in practice.

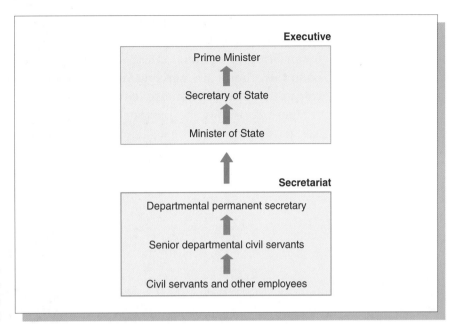

Figure 8.3
Relationship
between executive
and secretariat.

Question 8.3

Find out the following things about judiciary:

- What is the name of the current Lord Chancellor?
- A senior member of the legal system is the *Attorney General*. Find out what this person's role is and how it differs from that of the Lord Chancellor.

The judiciary is composed of the various levels of courts. These vary in significance from the local magistrates' court to the highest court; the House of Lords. Different courts specialise in different types of law and there are strict legal rules which govern, which cases are heard at which courts. They all have in common one thing – the decisions made in them are on behalf of the state. It is thus the state and not the judge which sends a convicted person to prison, because the judge is empowered to act for the people of the state as a whole.

There are two ways in which the judiciary can act on behalf of the state. Firstly, in *civil cases* – disputes between two parties – the judiciary acts as an *umpire*. An umpire or referee ensures that fair play occurs. The state is thus empowered to award damages against an offender in much the same way as a football referee awards a free-kick to the offended team after a foul is committed. Secondly, in *criminal cases*, the judiciary sits as an *executioner*. Criminal cases are those wherein, even although the offence may have been committed against an individual, the offence is sufficiently serious for the state, and not the individual, to bring a case against the accused. The judiciary has a much wider range of measures it can bring to criminal cases, including imprisonment and in some countries, the death penalty. We will examine the composition and role of the judiciary in more detail in Chapter 14.

Figure 8.4 shows the passage of a successfully prosecuted criminal case passing through the legal process. We can see how only the 'deciding' part of the process is the judiciary. The other 'administrative' roles in the judicial process are discharged by the secretariat.

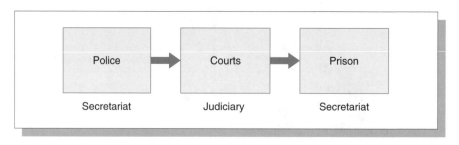

Figure 8.4
The secretariat and
the judiciary.

8.5 Devolved government

The Scottish Parliament

In a referendum held in September 1997, 74% of those who voted endorsed the UK Government's proposals to set up a Scottish Parliament and Executive to administer Scottish affairs, and an additional question saw 64% of the voters in favour of giving the new Parliament tax-varying powers. As a consequence, the Westminster Parliament introduced legislation which led to *the Scotland Act 1998* becoming law in November 1998. Elections to the first Scottish Parliament for almost 300 years were held in May 1999, and it met for the first time in July of that year. The Scottish Parliament's 129 members (MSPs) are elected for a fixed 4-year term via the *Additional Member System* of proportional representation that gives each voter two votes: one for the constituency MSP and the other regional vote for a registered political party or an individual independent candidate. There are 73 single-member constituency seats and 56 seats representing eight regions, based on the European Parliamentary constituencies. Each region returns seven members and these MSPs are allocated so that each party's overall share of seats reflects its share of the regional vote.

Unlike the Westminster Parliament, the Scottish Parliament does not have a second chamber to revise legislation but detailed scrutiny of Bills is carried out in committees or by taking evidence from outside experts. The House of Lords no longer considers Scottish legislation on devolved matters, although it remains the final court of appeal in hearing civil cases from arising from the Scottish Courts (Figure 8.5).

Figure 8.5
Scottish Parliament:
devolved areas of
responsibility.

Areas of responsibility devolved to the Scottish Parliament

- Health
- Education and training
- Local government
- Housing
- Economic development
- Wide range of home affairs, civil and criminal law
- Transport
- The environment
- Agriculture, fisheries and forestry
- Sport, culture and the arts

The Scottish Executive

This is the administrative arm of government in Scotland, and has responsibility for all public bodies whose functions and services have been devolved to it. It is accountable to the Scottish Parliament and headed by the *First Minister*, who is normally the leader of the party with most support in the Parliament.

National Assembly for Wales

The *National Assembly for Wales* was established following the passing of the *Government of Wales Act 1998* by the UK parliament, and the subsequent *National Assembly for Wales (Transfer of Functions) Act 1999* enabled the transfer of the devolved powers and responsibilities from the Secretary of State for Wales to the Assembly. Since then, the powers of the Assembly have been increased via a series of Acts of Parliament.

Within its powers, the Assembly debates and approves legislation which reflects the particular needs of the people of Wales. The elected politicians, who are accountable to the Welsh voters via the ballot box, decide the policies, priorities and the allocation of funds made available to the Assembly by the UK Treasury.

The *Welsh Assembly Government* is responsible for developing and implementing programmes, for all issues that have been devolved to

Wales, via the civil service and a wide range of sponsored bodies. It is led by a First Minister and a Cabinet of eight ministers who are accountable to the Assembly and its committees for their actions. However, Wales remains part of the UK and the Secretary of State for Wales and MPs from Welsh constituencies continue to have seats in the Westminster Parliament.

Northern Ireland Assembly

The *Northern Ireland Assembly* was established as part of the *Good Friday Agreement 1998* (sometimes referred to as the *Belfast Agreement*). The Assembly is the prime source of authority for all devolved responsibilities with full legislative and executive authority. However, following bitter disagreements between the political parties, particularly over the de-commissioning of arms by para-military organisations, the Assembly was unable to conduct effective business and it was suspended on 14 October 2002. The UK Government re-introduced direct rule from Westminster, and responsibility for the direction of the Northern Ireland Departments was assumed by the Secretary of State. (*Note*: At the time of publication this is still the position.)

Regional Assemblies

Voluntary regional chambers have been established in each of the eight English regions outside London (see Figure 8.6), and have adopted the title of '*Regional Assemblies*', but should not be confused with the statutory, elected regional assemblies for which preparatory provisions are set out in the *Regional Assemblies (Preparations) Bill (Bill 3 2002-02).*

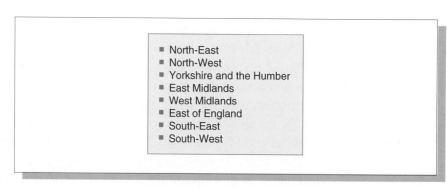

- North-East
- North-West
- Yorkshire and the Humber
- East Midlands
- West Midlands
- East of England
- South-East
- South-West

Figure 8.6
The English Regions.

8.6 Local government

In addition to the influences upon the business sector exerted by the policies and structures of central government, a second 'layer' is also worthy of our study. Each area of the UK is controlled locally by a local authority. The geographical area and population over which a local authority governs varies from region to region and also changes over time, as central government makes changes to this provision.

Whilst central government in the UK has legislative power over all local authorities, it is deemed helpful to devolve some powers to the arm of government at local level to enable it to be 'nearer to the people' in the hope that it will be more responsive to local needs. The fact is that the needs of communities vary across the country and by having a local layer of government; such differences can be accounted for.

Unitary and federal local government

The constitutional basis of local government varies greatly depending upon whether the state operates a unitary or a federal constitution.

A *federal* system is operated in many democratic states including Germany and the USA. A federation of any kind is an agglomeration of independent bodies that have chosen to merge together. In doing so, they allow the federal government certain powers but retain some for themselves. The federal government does not have the right to over-rule individual states in matters which are of local concern. The federal government is therefore a 'servant' of local government and not the other way round. In the USA, for example, the federal government in Washington, headed by the president with two legislative houses (the *House of Representatives* and the *Senate*), is responsible for economic policy, defence, foreign policy and other areas which are best dealt with at the national level. The individual 'states', headed by a *state governor*, retain responsibility for, among other things, education, policing and some local judicial matters (e.g. some states have the death penalty whilst others have not).

A *unitary* local authority system is the converse of the above. According to the constitution of a unitary state, central government exercises, more or less, total executive power over local government organisation. Local authorities in a unitary state must act according to the frameworks set for them by central government. From time to time, central government amends the responsibilities and powers of local government. Over recent years, central UK government has restructured local government by scrapping some authorities whilst instituting others. When a British local authority carries out local education policy it is only because it has been instructed to do so by central government: this duty could be taken away from it or additional duties added to it.

Local government in the UK is based in town halls, civic centres and county halls, depending upon the nature of the area over which the authority governs. The nature of regions controlled by the various types of local authority varies. Some oversee a large area of mainly rural population (e.g. Northumberland County Council), whereas inner-city areas (areas of small geographical area but high population) are controlled by metropolitan or Borough Councils (e.g. Enfield Borough Council is one of the many councils in Greater London).

How is local government controlled?

In a democracy, such as the UK, local government is controlled in the same way as central government – by elected representation. At the local level, representatives are called *councillors* and each one represent a small part of the local region called a *ward*. Councillors are local people who have offered themselves to serve on the local authority and have been duly elected by popular ballot in a local election. Whereas national politicians will generally campaign on national issues (such as national unemployment, the National Health Service and the national economy), local candidates are uniquely concerned about local issues. Typical among these will be local transport infrastructure, local schools and local authority services and spending.

Question 8.4

Find out the following about the local authority in the locality in which you are studying.

- the name of the local authority;
- the political party which controls the authority;
- the name of the leader of the council (the leading councillor in the majority party).

The same system of competing political parties operates, for most councils, at the local level, so most candidates who stand for a seat on the local authority will represent one of the main national political parties. The party which has the majority of local councillors in any given authority is said to have *control* of the council as, by voting as one, their policies cannot be overturned by the opposition of all other councillors.

	Name of representative	Area represented
Central government	MP	A constituency
Local government	Councillor	A ward

Collectively, councillors in a local authority constitute the *executive* of local government. They sit on various council committees which have power over a range of local provisions. In the same way, that executive policy in central government is carried out by a national secretariat, at local level, *local government officers* are responsible for carrying out the decisions of elected councillors.

Representatives and delegates

Astute readers will notice that the word *representative* has been used in this chapter to describe the roles of councillors and MPs. This term is in marked contrast to the role of a *delegate*. Both representatives and delegates operate on behalf of an organisation; the difference lies in the autonomy given to the person in their responsibilities.

A *representative* is appointed on the basis of his or her abilities to represent the organisation or constituency. The importance of appointing the right person is seen when one realises that once appointed to represent, he or she acts in whatever way they see fit. They do not need to refer back to the constituency in order to be instructed how to act. It is said that a representative is mandated to represent the constituency on the basis of his or her pledges at the time of selection. An MP is a representative.

A *delegate* acts on behalf of an organisation or constituency according to a brief. He or she has no authority to act on his on her own volition. Delegates are appointed to attend such things as conferences, where they are instructed how to vote on various issues and what to say on behalf of an organisation. This principle is used in the management practice of delegation, when a manager passes work to a subordinate with a brief as to the subordinates instructions, limits of authority, time limit on the job, etc.

How is local government funded?

Local government is charged with the provision of local services. These are managed at the local level, for the benefit of the local population and must usually be funded in part by local people. The cost of running local services and the administration of local government is met in several ways.

- Some money is allocated to each local authority from *central government funds*, via (in the case of authorities in England and Wales) the Department of the Environment. As central government funds, this money is raised through general taxation.
- The local authority can raise a relatively small amount of money from *fees and charges*. An example of this revenue is the entrance fee at the swimming pool or the amount you pay for the local authority employee to come and clear your drains.

■   Any other money that the local authority needs in addition to that raised from these first two sources must come from *local taxation*. This is money paid directly to the local authority by residents and businesses located within the area covered by the authority. The mechanism by which local revenues are raised has been the subject of much debate over recent years. When the old 'rates' system was replaced with the ill-fated 'community charge' (or *poll tax*) in the late 1980s, political pressure forced central government to scrap it in 1991, introducing in its place the *council tax* – a system where the amount paid depends upon the value of the resident's home.

Each year, a local authority will prepare a spending budget. Similarly, the Department of the Environment will prepare a *standard spending assessment* (SSA), based on the previous year's spending, whilst taking into account any changes to the authority's duties. The local authority budget will work like this (greatly simplified):

	£
Standard spending assessment	XXX
minus central government grant	XXX
minus other sources of local revenue	XXX
Shortfall	XXX

The shortfall, a figure of many millions of pounds, must be made good by local taxation. The figure is divided up by the number of local taxpayers, accounting for 'banding' according to house value, and each home and business receives an invoice for the amount – usually collected as a monthly payment.

Central government in a unitary state, such as the UK, retains the right to 'cap' local authority spending. If the local authority's budget exceeds the SSA, central government can block a local authority's council tax level, insisting it is brought down to a lower amount. Such a move is usually very unpopular with the local authority in question as it must make cuts in services to account for the shortfall in funding (although the council taxpayers are usually more appreciative).

The duties of local government

As the UK is a unitary and not a federalist state, the responsibilities and duties of local government are determined by central government.

Moreover, they change from time to time as different governments implement differing policies regarding local government.

Change in the responsibilities of local government over the years of the Margaret Thatcher and John Major Conservative Governments tended to focus on contracting out certain local authority contracts to private businesses. Such a process, such as the invitation of tenders to provide the authority with its refuse clearing services, was designed to provide the local taxpayer with optimal value for money as the local authority accepts the lowest quote for the contract. Some services are subject to a process called *Compulsory Competitive Tendering* (CCT). This means that services covered by CCT must (in law) be offered to tender to outside contractors although the authority's Direct Labour Organisations (DLOs) may also apply for the tender to supply the service.

The statutory duties (set out in legislation) of local government include at least a partial role in:

- the maintenance of local *transport infrastructure* (e.g. local roads, pavements, etc.);
- the provision of local *education services*, which includes non-grant-maintained schools but not universities;
- *environmental services* (e.g. hygiene and licensing of pubs, clubs, etc.);
- *social services* (care of the less economically unfortunate and others considered as vulnerable);
- collection of household *refuse* and its disposal;
- the provision of local authority *housing* and homes for senior citizens;
- adequate care of *homeless persons*.

8.7 The EU: supranational political influence

A business can experience some degree of influence from political institutions at a level above its national government. Such institutions are ones which affect many countries, and in some cases, all countries. The major supranational influence on UK businesses is the EU, although others do exist (such as the United Nations).

The beginning of the EU

That which we now call the EU began life in 1957 as the European Economic Community (EEC). After the Second World War ended in 1945, there was a general mood among the European nations that the countries should become progressively closer, and that formal links should be instituted to secure a 'friendly', peaceful and prosperous future. The initial idea of the EU almost certainly came from the wartime British Prime Minister, Sir Winston Churchill, who, in 1945, made an important speech on the theme of unity among European nations in the French city of Strasbourg where a plaque now 'marks the spot'. The concept of *European integration* was promulgated by the French Foreign Minister, Robert Schuman, in a speech on 9 May 1950 – a date which has been adopted as the 'birthday' of the EU and celebrated annually as *Europe Day*.

The first successful attempt at European co-operation came in 1952 with the establishment of the European Coal and Steel Community (ECSC) under the *Treaty of Paris, 1951*. The ECSC was set up between France, Italy and the Benelux countries (Belgium, the Netherlands and Luxembourg) although West Germany joined later. It served to abolish trade restrictions between the member countries on coal and steel imports and exports and to co-ordinate production levels and pricing policies.

The success of the ECSC prompted political leaders to investigate the possibility of closer co-operation on a much wider scale. After much negotiation, the various proposals were formalised in *The Treaty of Rome, 1957*, one of the most significant international accords of the twentieth century. Resulting from this legal document, two communities came into existence on 1 January 1958: the EEC and the European Atomic Energy Community (EURATOM). Notwithstanding the seminal influence of Churchill in the vision behind the EEC, the UK declined to participate in both the ECSC and the initial EEC organisation.

The name of the EEC has changed since its inception, causing some confusion among observers. The EEC was the Community of Nations which was primarily concerned with closer economic ties. The changing perceptions and roles of the various parts of the Community prompted the heads of state and government to approve the name to be changed to the EC (dropping the narrower 'economic' part) as part of the *Maastricht Agreement of 1992*. The term EU was later introduced to describe the 'umbrella' organisation of nations which includes the EC, the ECSC and EURATOM. For most purposes, our discussion will use the term EU.

Membership of the EU

The membership of the EU has grown to include more and more European nation states since its beginnings in 1958. Some of the countries that joined subsequent to its formation would not in fact have qualified in 1958 owing to the fact that they were not, at that time, democratic in their form of government. Spain, for example, was effectively a dictatorship until Franco died in November 1975, after which a democratically elected government was installed. Portugal and Greece, similarly, are relatively recent democracies.

The Founder members, in 1958, France, West Germany*, Belgium, the Netherlands, Luxembourg, and Italy were joined by the UK, the Republic of Ireland and Denmark in1972. By 2004, membership of the EU had risen to 25 countries with some 374 million citizens, consequently making it the largest single trading block in the world. (*Note: East and West Germany were re-unified as Germany in 1989.)

Objectives of the EU

The debate

The intensity of political debate which surrounds so many European issues may serve to confuse observers as to the EU's essential objectives. The broad spectrum of political opinion within the member states contains a plethora of varying attitudes regarding how the EU should grow and develop. The two extremes of opinion are as follows:

- The EU member states should eventually converge to become a single federal political state ('the United States of Europe'). There should be a single European currency and each member country should be the same as a USA state, such that the UK would act in essentially the same way as, for example, Texas or California.
- The EU should be disbanded and all overtures to increased European integration should be immediately discontinued. The individual European nation states have long histories and unique peoples. To try to mix such disparate cultures and economies would not only be a coarse and artificial effort, it is also unnecessary and undesirable.

Within these two extremes lie many positions and attitudes to the EU. In reality, the *raison d'être* and objectives of the EU have evolved and changed over the years. Whilst initially, the majority saw the EU primarily as a trading bloc, the debate over recent years has centred on the possibility of moves towards federalisation. Perhaps the only EU objectives which are more or less common to all member states are those which are detailed in the various Treaties and European Acts, although many of these have been the subject of heated debate within the various member states.

European single market

The creation of a single European market was the objective upon which the EEC was founded in 1958. A single market is one which comprises several separate nation states that act, in matters of trade, as though they were the same country. Within any given country, there are no restrictions on trade and the same benefits and restrictions apply to all businesses. Single markets, such as the EU are designed to be advantageous for businesses by allowing them to grow and expand without the limitations of national borders. Whilst allowing businesses to export goods without restriction offers the opportunity of expansion, importing materials without having to pay duties on them reduces the costs of a production process. Both of these features are potentially good for business. The converse of this, of course, is that as well as UK businesses gaining access to markets in other EU states, businesses from other EU states gain access to the UK. For some businesses, this is a threat.

There are several conditions which must be in place before a single trading bloc can be created (trading blocs as a feature of international business are discussed in Chapter 15):

- The abolition of internal tariffs and quotas (tariffs, or duties, are taxes charged on goods upon their importation; quotas are maximum limits placed upon the amounts of imported goods).
- The application of a common external tariff, enabling quotas and tariffs to be uniformly applied to goods imported from countries outside the Union.
- The harmonisation of laws helping or hindering business activity in each member state of the Union.
- The harmonisation of economic conditions in each member state, such as similar monetary conditions and closer fiscal regimes.

European integration

European integration is the process whereby the member states set up common institutions to which they delegate some of their sovereignty so that decisions on specific matters of common interest can be made democratically at European level. It is based upon four founding treaties:

- The *ECSC Treaty*, which was signed in Paris on 23 July 1952 and expired on 23 July 2002.
- The *EURATOM Treaty*, which was signed along with the Treaty of Rome on 25 March 1957.
- The *Treaty of Rome* (often simply referred to as 'The Treaty') which established the EEC.
- The *Treaty of EU*, which was signed in *Maastricht* on 7 February 1992, introduced new forms of co-operation between the member state governments.

The Maastricht Treaty established the EC, and the removal of the word 'economic' from the title of EEC indicated a fundamental change in the Community's approach to the ideals of the EU as a whole, a move away from a single market to a closer political and economic union (e.g. the Treaty made provisions for inter-governmental co-operation in the areas of defence, justice and home affairs). As a consequence a new structure, the so-called 'three pillars' was established for the EU as can be seen in Figure 8.7.

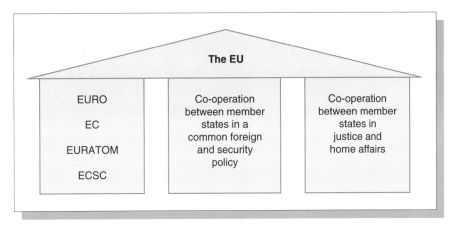

Figure 8.7
The three pillars of
the EU.

The EU describes itself as a family of democratic European countries, committed to working together for peace and prosperity.[3] It is not a state intended to replace existing states and is unique in that member states have set up common institutions to which they delegate some of their sovereignty so that decisions can be made democratically at European level. The EU objectives enshrined in the Maastricht Treaty of 1992 are as follows:

- To promote economic and social progress which is balanced and sustainable, in particular through the creation of an area without internal frontiers, through the strengthening of economic and social cohesion and through the establishment of *Economic and Monetary Union* (EMU), ultimately including a single currency.

■ To assert the European identity on the international scene, in particular through the implementation of a common foreign and security policy including the eventual framing of a common defence policy which might in time lead to a common defence.

■ To strengthen the protection of the rights and interests of the nationals of member states through the introduction of a citizenship of the Union.

■ To develop close co-operation on justice and home affairs.

■ To maintain the *acquis communautaire* (i.e. the entire body of European laws) and build on it with a view to considering to what extent the policies and forms of co-operation introduced by this Treaty may need to be revised with the aim of ensuring the effectiveness of the mechanisms and institutions of the Community.

Economic and Monetary Union

It follows that if EU member states are truly to act in matters of trade as though they were one country, then as well as enjoying trade without tariffs and quotas, they will also share more or less identical economic conditions. This means that they will share identical levels of monetary pressure (i.e. the same interest rates and rates of monetary growth) and exchange rates which do not vary against each other.

Economic and Monetary Union

In 1994 the *European Monetary Institute* (EMI) was established, as the forerunner to the *European Central Bank* (ECB). Its objectives were to help strengthen the co-ordination of monetary policies with a view to ensuring price stability; to make the preparations required for the establishment of the European System of Central Banks (ESCB) and for the conduct of a single monetary policy and the creation of a single currency. At the EU leaders meeting at the Madrid European Council in 1995, it was decided to name the single currency the '*euro*' and that there would be a 3-year transition period between the creation of the euro and the introduction of notes and coins. On 1 January 2002, euro banknotes and coins went into circulation for the 12 EU member states that share the single currency, and became a part of daily life for over 300 million people living in the euro area.

UK Government position on the single currency

Membership of EMU would mean that the UK would adopt the euro as its currency, and UK interest rates would be set by the ECB, on the basis of economic conditions in the euro area as a whole.

The UK Government policy towards EMU, under the Labour Administration of Tony Blair, was originally set out by the Chancellor of the Exchequer, Gordon Brown, in his statement to the UK Parliament on EMU in October 1997. He said that the UK was committed to the principle of joining the single currency and that the policy was founded on these key building blocks:

- A successful single currency within a single European market would in principle be of benefit to Europe and the UK, in terms of trade, transparency of costs and currency stability.
- The constitutional issue is a factor in the UK's decision but it is not an overriding one, so long as membership is in the national interest, the case is clear and unambiguous and there is popular consent.
- The basis for the decision as to whether there is a clear and unambiguous economic case for membership is the Treasury's comprehensive and rigorous assessment of the 'five economic tests'.
- Whenever the decision to enter is taken by the Government, it should be put to a referendum of the British people.

The Labour Government described its decision on EMU membership as a reflection of the belief in what is best for the long-term economic interests of the British people and the performance of the UK economy. If re-elected at the next General Election a decision on entry to EMU would be the people's choice via a referendum following the next General Election, provided that Gordon Brown's 'five economic tests' have been met. The five economic tests:

1 *Convergence*: Are the business cycles and economic structures compatible so that the UK and others could live comfortably with euro interest rates on a permanent basis?

2 *Flexibility*: If problems emerge, is there sufficient flexibility to deal with them?

3 *Investment*: Would joining the EMU create better conditions for firms making long-term decisions to invest in Britain?

4 *Financial services*: What impact would entry into EMU have on the competitive position of the UK's financial services industry, particularly the city's wholesale markets?

5 *Growth, stability and employment*: Will joining the EMU promote higher growth, stability and a lasting increase in jobs?

European Central Bank

The ECB was set up in 1998, under the Treaty of EU. Its main purposes are to introduce and manage the new euro currency, conduct foreign exchange transactions and ensure the smooth operation of payment systems. The ECB is also responsible for framing and implementing the EU's economic and monetary policy. The bank works within the ESCB which covers all member states, although as of 2004, only 12 countries had joined the *euro area*. Those 12 countries, together with the ECB, make up what is called the *Eurosystem*. The ECB is completely independent, with the EU institutions and member state governments obliged not to try to influence the ECB or the national central banks.

One of the Bank's main tasks is to maintain price stability in the euro area and to preserve the purchasing power of the euro.[3] This means keeping inflation under strict control and bank aims to ensure that the year-on-year increases in consumer prices is less than 2%. It does this in two ways:

- Controlling money supply, mainly by setting interest rates throughout the euro area.
- Monitoring price trends and assessing the risk they pose to price stability in the euro area.

Political union

The objective of political union is probably the most controversial of those held by participants in the EU. According to the proponents of political union, once full EMU has been successfully accomplished, then in many respects, the EU is already operating as one country anyway. Full EMU would mean that all EU states would share the same currency, the same central bank controlling monetary policy and previous national borders would become irrelevant as far as they concern the passage of people, trade and capital. It is thus a small step to create a federal European 'super state' much like the models adopted in the USA and some other federal countries like Switzerland.

The federalisation debate has become one of the most fractious over recent years and any number of opinions have been put forward *vis-à-vis* its possibility and desirability. In the UK, there are elements in all of the main political parties that see it as desirable, but the UK has emerged as one of the main voices in the EU who see the loss of sovereignty of the British Parliament as unacceptable. Proponents see federalisation as the logical extension of the many moves to closer co-operation that have taken place over the past 40 years, whereas the opponents see a richness in the diversity of different European histories and cultures that may be lost if they were all submerged into one big super state.

Certainly, the instruments are in place in preparation for political union. We can see that the EU has each of the 'organs' of state and, by devolving more and more power to these organs, political union may become increasingly realistic over time.

Powers and responsibilities of the EU

The powers and responsibilities of the European Parliament have changed and increased, most notably since the *Treaty on EU 1992* (Maastricht). Its principal powers and responsibilities are as follows:

- To generate initiatives for the political and economic development of the EU.
- To supervise and appoint the European Commission and, if necessary, to dismiss it (the Commission is the European secretariat).
- To debate and vote upon initiatives put forward by the Commission.
- To monitor the day-to-day management of the various other parts of the EU.
- To examine petitions and requests addressed to the Parliament by ordinary European citizens; to confirm the accession of new member states to the EU.
- To agree (together with the Commission), and adopt the annual budget of the EU.

Note. The Parliament's Committee on Budgetary Control (*COCOBU*) monitors how the budget is spent, and each year Parliament decides whether to approve the Commission's handling of the budget for the previous financial year. This approval process is technically known as 'granting a discharge'.

The European 'organs of state'

The Treaty of Rome 1957 set in place institutions that would enable the EU to eventually operate as a single federal state. Whilst these establishments have their place in the various stages of the development of the EU, the founders had in mind that they could facilitate the coalescence of nations into a European federal state if the political will of the member states wished this to happen.

The EU's executive

The European executive is called the *Council of Ministers* (or the Council of the EU) and it is the EU's main decision-making body. The Council was set up by the founding treaties in the 1950s and represents the member states. Its meetings are attended by one minister from each of the EU national governments, and because the members of the Council are elected ministers in their respective countries, they empowered to make policy on behalf of their own and other member states. The ministers are accountable to their own National Parliaments and to the citizens represented by that parliament, thereby ensuring the democratic legitimacy of the Council's decisions.

When the Council meets to discuss European financial matters, the finance ministers from each member state assemble (the representative from the UK will be the Chancellor of the Exchequer). On agricultural issues, the Council will comprise the agriculture ministers, on health matters, the health ministers and so on. From time to time, the heads of state or government meet (the Prime Minister, the German Chancellor, the French President, etc.) in a summit. Such meetings tend to be called to discuss high-level strategic matters, such as the development of the EU and political changes in the EU structure, such as moves towards political union. The European heads of state or government meet at least twice a year in the context of the European Council. The presidency of the Council rotates, with each member state assuming oversight for a period of 6 months, supported by the General Secretariat, which prepares and ensures the smooth functioning of the Council's work at all levels. The minister at the Council representing the presiding country assumes the chairman's role in Council meetings. The presidency rota for 2003–2006 is given in Table 8.1.[3]

The European executive has supreme influence over the policies of the EU although it also has a pivotal role in the legislative process. A building is reserved for meetings of the Council in Brussels, although some meetings take place in Luxembourg. The Council is served by a committee called the Committee of Permanent Representatives (COREPER). COREPER comprises the member states' permanent ambassadors to the EU and it prepares the work of the Council in addition to acting on the decisions of the Council, such as setting up committees to make preparations or to study particular matters of interest.

Table 8.1

Rota of terms of EU presidency

Year	Term (6 months)	Country
2003	First	Greece
	Second	Italy
2004	First	Ireland
	Second	The Netherlands
2005	First	Luxembourg
	Second	UK
2006	First	Austria
	Second	Finland

Table 8.2

Vote weightings in the Council of Ministers for each EU member state (at 1 November 2004)

Vote weightings in the EU Council of Ministers	
UK, France, Germany, Italy	29
Spain, Poland	27
The Netherlands	13
Belgium, Czech Republic, Greece, Hungary, Portugal	12
Austria, Sweden	10
Denmark, Ireland, Lithuania, Slovakia, Finland	7
Cyprus, Estonia, Latvia, Luxembourg, Slovenia	4
Malta	3

Source: Europa.[3]

Decisions are passed by the Council on a democratic voting system. However, ministers from different member states carry more or fewer votes depending upon the population they represent (i.e. the population of their country). The number of votes each country can cast is shown in Table 8.2. The most common voting procedure in Council is *qualified majority voting* (QMV), which means that, for a proposal to be adopted, it needs the support of a specified number of votes. A qualified majority is reached if:

- a majority of member states (in some cases a two-thirds majority) approve;
- a minimum of votes is cast in favour, which is 72.3% of the total.

In addition, a member state may ask confirmation that votes in favour represent at least 62% of the total population of the EU. If this is not the case, the decision will not be adopted.

In some particularly sensitive areas, such as the Common Foreign and Security Policy, taxation or immigration policy, Council decisions have to be unanimous – in other words, each member state has the power of veto in these areas.

The EU's legislature

The principle forum for debate in the EU is the *European Parliament*. The Parliament usually sits in Strasbourg, France, although sometimes it meets in Brussels. Its administration (the *General Secretariat*) is based in Luxembourg. Although it is called a Parliament, it does not have the same functions or procedures as the Westminster Parliament in that it does not have sole responsibility for the legislative process within the EU (the EU legislative process is discussed in Chapter 14).

The first elections to the Parliament were in 1979 and its size has grown as new member states have joined the EU over the intervening years. At the end of 2004, the European Parliament comprised 626 *Members of the European Parliament* (MEPs), each of whom was elected for a period of 5 years, and it is forecast that by the end of 2009 this number will have risen to 786,[3] as more countries join the expanding EU (see Table 8.3).

Table 8.3
Number of MEPs per country in EU

Country	1999–2004	2004–2007	2007–2009
Austria	21	18	18
Belgium	25	24	24
Bulgaria	–	–	18
Cyprus	–	6	6
Czech Republic	–	24	24
Denmark	16	14	14
Estonia	–	6	6
Finland	16	14	14
France	87	78	78
Germany	99	99	99
Greece	25	24	24

Table 8.3 (*contd*)

Country	1999–2004	2004–2007	2007–2009
Hungary	–	24	24
Ireland	15	13	13
Italy	87	78	78
Latvia	–	9	9
Lithuania	–	13	13
Luxembourg	6	6	6
Malta	–	5	5
The Netherlands	31	27	27
Poland	–	54	54
Portugal	25	24	24
Romania	–	–	36
Slovakia	–	14	14
Slovenia	–	7	7
Spain	64	54	54
Sweden	22	19	19
UK	87	78	78

Each member represents a constituency, although the size of a European constituency is generally much larger than its domestic equivalent.

Although the members come from different countries, they sit in Europe-wide political groups in the Parliament, rather than national blocks. In this respect, it is like Westminster, in that members sit with their political parties regardless of which part of the EU they represent. The major political groupings in the Parliament are shown at Table 8.4.[3]

Question 8.5

Find out the following:

- The name of the European Parliamentary constituency in which you are studying.
- The name of your MEP.
- The political party to which your MEP belongs.
- The European Parliamentary Party grouping in which your MEP sits.

Table 8.4

Number of seats per political grouping in EU

Political group	Number of seats
European Peoples Party (Christian Democrats) + European democrats	232
Party of the European Socialists	175
European Liberal, Democratic and Reformist Party	52
European United Left/Nordic Green Left	49
Greens/European Free Alliance	44
Union for Europe of the Nations	23
Europe of Democracies and Diversities	18
Non-attached	33

The EU's secretariat

The administrative arm of the EU is the *European Commission* and is based in Brussels, Belgium and in Luxembourg. The Commission is headed by 20 European Commissioners but it also contains around 15,000 officials divided between 30 senior administrative officers called Directors-General. One of the Commissioners is chosen by the member states to occupy the office of President of the European Commission, whose task it then is to guide the policy of the Commission. The 20 Commissioners are appointed by their domestic governments to serve the EU as a host national of their home country. There are two each from France, Germany, Italy, Spain and the UK, and one from each of the other EU countries. The duties of a Commissioner are to the EU and not to their home countries – they are there to serve the EU and not to represent their respective home governments. Each Commissioner is given oversight over an area of EU policy (such as transport, trade, etc.) but decisions are taken on the basis of collective responsibility.

The Commission has three broad areas of responsibility. The primary *raison d'être* of the Commission is to be the 'guardian' of the various European Treaties. In this responsibility, it ensures that each member state fully implements the provisions of each treaty, such as the terms of the Maastricht Treaty 1992. It has powers to impose fines or to initiate proceedings against any country for failure to enact the provisions of a Treaty, referring the country, if necessary, to the European judiciary. Secondly, the Commission has the sole right to initiate legislation. It has the power to bring its influence to bear on each stage of the law-making process in negotiation with the European Parliament, the Council and the Member States. Thirdly, the Commission has the responsibility to issue rules for the implementation of EU Treaties and to administer the financial budgets. The majority of EU expenditure falls within four major funds:

- The European Agricultural Guidance and Guarantee Fund.
- The European Social Fund.
- The European Regional Development Fund.
- The Cohesion Fund.

Each fund is an effective redistribution of the total EU budget, with money raised from each member state as a condition of membership of the Union.

Question 8.6

- Who is the current President of the European Commission?
- What nationality is he or she?
- Britain has two European Commissioners. Who are they?
- What are their areas of oversight?

The European judiciary

There are two courts which comprise the legal arm of the EU: the *European Court of Justice* and the *European Court of First Instance*, which is a relatively recent development, having been established in 1988. Both courts are overseen by 15 independent judges (one from each country) who serve the judiciary for a period of 6 years although the judges in the Court of Justice are assisted by nine advocates-general. Both courts are located in Luxembourg and each, being part of the supranational political structure, has supremacy over national courts.

The European Court of Justice and the Court of First Instance differ in their jurisdictions (i.e. areas of legal responsibility and oversight). The Court of First Instance can only hear trial (or First Instance) cases whereas the Court of Justice can also hear appellate (or appeal) cases, usually from senior national courts. The Court of First Instance hears cases brought by businesses and private citizens of the community and does not have the wider powers of the Court of Justice.

The Court of Justice enforces the Treaties and legislation of the EU. It can find member states guilty of failing to comply with European law and impose fines for contravention. The Court can also give preliminary legal rulings or interpretations of the various European laws when parties are engaged in a dispute as to the extent or meaning of a certain piece of law.

Other EU bodies

In addition to the four main bodies we have so far discussed, there are others of which we should be aware.

The *Court of Auditors* is located in Luxembourg. It acts as the EU's internal auditor and checks that all revenues are collected from member states and that expenditure is incurred in a lawful and regular manner. The Court consists of 15 members appointed with the unanimous decision of the European Council after consultation with the European Parliament. It submits an annual report to the Council and Parliament to confirm that the Commission has correctly managed the Community's budget.

The *Economic and Social Committee* (ESC) is a body of 222 members which sits in Brussels. Its *raison d'être* is to express opinions on matters of business, economics and social affairs, and is consequently composed of those able to comment on such matters – representatives of European employers, employees and other economic stakeholders. It is consulted prior to any major European decision on economic and social matters and may submit opinions on its own initiative. It typically submits about 170 opinions per year. A similar body is the ECSC Consultative Committee, which comprises 108 members and acts in a similar capacity to the ESC in matters concerning the coal and steel industries.

The *Committee of the Regions*, like the ESC, has 222 'permanent' members and an equal number of 'alternate' members who represent local and regional authorities throughout the EU. Both types of members serve 4-year terms on the Committee, which was established in March 1994. The Committee of the Regions must be consulted by the other European institutions in relation to a number of areas concerning regional interests (such as the provision of aid to a region of the UK such as rural South Wales). It is assumed that representatives of the various regions can reliably inform the EU institutions on such matters as local education, youth, culture, public health, etc. The main Committee meets in plenary session five times a year, although its work continues with eight commissions and four sub-commissions.

Assignment 8.1

▪ If you are using this textbook as part of a class or group, organise a debate comprising two sides presenting arguments before an audience (the rest of the class). Eight to ten volunteers should divide into two sides. One team should prepare a case in favour of the contention: *European federalisation would be good for the UK.* The other side should prepare the case against (i.e. that federalisation would be bad for the UK. The debate itself should comprise both sides presenting their cases to an equal time limit (say 20 minutes each), beginning with the case in favour. The class then should have the opportunity to question each team. After a final summing up of both arguments by the two teams, the class should vote on the contention based on the arguments put forward.

▪ Discuss the proposition that local government is unnecessary and a waste of local taxpayers' money. Do you agree that all of its functions could be managed either by private companies or direct from central government?

▪ The Labour Government has stated that it will hold a referendum, after the next general election, on whether the UK should join the 'Euro zone'. Discuss whether this should be a single-issue vote or an integral part of each political party's manifesto with a clear statement of the parties' positions.

References

1   Kidd, W., *et al.* (ed.) (1985). *Debretts Peerage & Baronetage.* Australia: MacMillan Education.

2   Hoiberg, D.H., *et al.* (ed.) (2003). *Encyclopaedia Britannica.* London: Encyclopaedia Britannica (UK) Ltd.

3   Europa web site: www.europa.eu.int/(31 October 2004).

Further reading

Bovaird, T. and Loeffler, E. (ed.) (2003). *Public Management and Governance.* London: Routledge.

El-Agraa, Ali M. (2004). *The European Union – Economics and Policies.* London: FT Prentice Hall.

Fenney, R. (2002). *Essential Local Government.* London: LGC Information.

Gros, D. and Thygesen, N. (1998). *European Monetary Integration. From the European Monetary System to Monetary Union,* 2nd edn. London: FT Prentice Hall.

Hitiris, T. (1998). *European Union Economics,* 4th edn. Harlow: FT Prentice Hall.

McCormick, J. (2002). *Understanding the European Union – A Concise Introduction.* London: Palgrave MacMillan.

Peele, G. (2004). *Governing the UK*, 4th edn. London: Blackwell Publishers.

Pollitt, C. (2003). *The Essential Public Manager (Public Policy & Management)*. London: Open University Press.

Rose, A. and Lawton, A. (1999). *Public Services Management.* Harlow: FT Prentice Hall.

Wilson, G.K. (2002). *Business and Politics. A Comparative Introduction*, 3rd edn. London: Palgrave Macmillan.

Useful web sites

www.directgov.uk/
www.parliament.uk/
www.Scottish.parliament.uk/
www.wales.gov.uk/
www.ni-assembly.gov.uk
www.regions.odpm.gov.uk/

The economic environment 1: macro-economic management

After studying this chapter, students should be able to describe:

- the difference between micro-economics and macro-economics;
- the complex nature of macro-economic decisions;
- the generic types of national economy;
- who manages the national economy;
- the meaning and components of fiscal policy;
- the meaning and the components of monetary policy;
- the role of the central bank in monetary policy;
- the significance of the major macro-economic indicators:
  - economic growth,
  - inflation,
  - interest rates,
  - exchange rates,
  - unemployment,
  - balance of payments.

9.1 The macro-economic environment

Micro- and macro-economics

In Chapters 16 and 17, we will examine micro-economics – the theories behind business costs and revenues, and the theories of product supply and demand. In this chapter, we will consider how the macro-economic environment can influence a business.

The terms 'micro' and 'macro' are both derived from the ancient Greek language. Micro means 'small', so micro-economics is the economics of individual buying and selling decisions and the economics of individual businesses. It addresses the questions concerning the volumes of production of individual businesses and price and wage levels.

Macro-economics, borrowing from the Greek 'macro' for large, is the study of the 'global' or collective decisions that are made by millions of individuals and businesses rather than individual buying and selling decisions. It examines the national and international aspects of economics and how national economic policies affect individual households, consumers and businesses. Macro-economics is also concerned with the ways in which the state manages the economy by using the range of economic 'levers' or 'weapons' at its disposal (Figure 9.1).

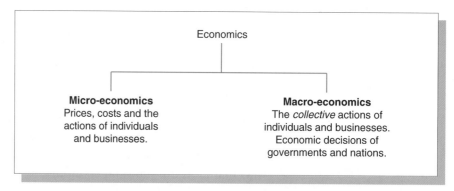

Figure 9.1
Different branches
of economics.

Micro- and macro-economics – an imperfect metaphor

If you look at a picture from a great painter, you can appreciate it on two levels. From a distance you can enjoy the totality of the painting, its spatial arrangements, the configurations of the figures, the blends of light and shade, the colours, and so on. If you then approach the painting and examine it in detail, possibly with a magnifying glass, you can analyse the intricate individual brush strokes, the textures and the individual colour amalgams.

Whilst we mainly see the big picture, we can readily appreciate this would not exist without the intricate, painstaking work invested in each stroke. The quality of the painting comprises both levels of appreciation.

We can view macro-economics as our view of the total painting and micro-economics as our examination of the intricate strokes and textures. Macro-economics concerns the effects of thousands or even millions of individual micro-economic decisions.

The macro-economic 'environment'

Given that macro-economics concerns the 'big picture' of economics, it is reasonable to ask what the components of the macro-economic environment are inasmuch as they can affect business (which, after all, is the subject of this book). The macro-economic environment includes such national and international concerns as:

- levels of tax levied by the government;
- levels of public expenditure (i.e. spending by the state);
- the price of borrowing money (i.e. interest rates);
- the rate of growth of the money supply;
- the size and rate of growth of the economy as a whole;
- the rate of inflation in the national economy and how this compares to other countries;
- the value of currency when it is used to exchange for foreign goods and services;
- the rate of unemployment (i.e. the number of people unemployed compared to the total labour force);
- the pattern of business and capital transactions that a country carries out with foreign countries (expressed in the balance of payments statement).

Changes in the macro-economic environment are very important to both businesses and individuals. This is principally because they can affect their income and (in the case of businesses) profitability. Changes in any of the macro-economic *indicators* (see later) can affect an individual business in either or both of two ways. Let us consider a simple example: an increase is announced in National Insurance (NI) contributions.

- Individuals must pay more NI contributions from their salaries and will therefore have less money to spend in buying the business's products. This means, when taken as a whole, that a downward pressure is exerted on business revenues (although it should be noted that, in reality, the relationships between consumer expenditure, NI contributions, taxation, and pension contributions are quite complex). This is an *indirect influence* on the business from the macro-economic environment. Put simply, by having a lower level of *disposable income,* consumers may delay or cancel plans to make purchases from businesses.

- The company itself will be required to pay more of its profits (in the form of employer's contribution) to the Department of Work and Pensions. This means that there will be less money left over (profit) to reinvest in the future of the business or to pay dividends to shareholders. This is a *direct influence* from the macro-economic environment.

The complexity of the macro-economic environment

Differences of economic opinion

One of the most noticeable features of this area of economics is the considerable disagreement over what are the best courses of action in any set of economic circumstances. Although propositions may have been obtained scientifically, economists can disagree because the facts may be deficient or there may be doubts on causal connections. Also, some propositions may contain hidden value judgements, or indeed unconscious individual bias may affect analysis. For example, you may hear one politician or economist say that interest rates should be increased, whilst others will advocate the opposite view. One businessman may want to see the value of the pound sterling devalued whilst others will argue strongly that it should be maintained or strengthened. Why is there such disagreement amongst the informed on how macro-economic policy should be conducted?

The reason is this: any change in the macro-economic environment will, to a greater or lesser extent, usually work to the advantage of one part of the economy whilst causing harm to another. Some businesses will be pleased with a change whilst others will feel the opposite. A strong pound over time means that a disproportionate amount of spending goes to overseas suppliers because imports will be cheaper to buy while export goods will be more expensive in foreign markets. This results in a widening of the *trade deficit* and a negative contribution to the growth in *gross domestic product* (GDP). The principle of any change 'cutting both ways' applies to all of the components of the macro-economic environment and it is this feature which makes its management so difficult and sometimes controversial.

Let us consider a simple, but vivid, example.

Wednesday 16 September 1992 – 'Black' or 'White'?

Wednesday 16 September 1992 was an important and dramatic day for the UK economy and for British businesses, when massive currency speculation forced the UK government to withdraw from the pound (sterling) from the European Exchange Rate Mechanism (ERM).

The UK had joined the ERM in October 1990 and effectively guaranteed that the British Government would follow economic and monetary policy that would prevent the exchange rate between the pound and other member currencies from fluctuating by more than 6%. The pound entered the ERM at 2.95 Deutschmarks (D-marks) (the official German currency at that time) to the pound, which meant that if the exchange rate ever neared the bottom of its permitted range (i.e. 2.778 D-marks); the government would be obliged to intervene.

From the early 1990s, high German interest rates, which had be set to avoid inflationary effects related to German re-unification, had been causing considerable stress across the whole of the ERM. Following the Danish rejection of the Maastricht Treaty in the spring of 1992, those ERM currencies that were trading close to the bottom of their ERM bands came under speculative attack in the foreign exchange markets. By September of that year, when the French voted to sign the Maastricht Treaty, the currency speculators turned their attention to the Italian Lira and the British pound. On 16 September 1992, the UK Chancellor of the Exchequer, Norman Lamont, announced a rise in the UK interest base rate from 10% to 12% in order to tempt speculators to buy pounds. Despite this, and a promise later the same day to raise rates again to 15%, dealers kept selling pounds. By 7 p.m. that evening, the Chancellor announced that Britain would leave the ERM and base rates would revert to 10%. In the aftermath, the pound fell, reaching a low point below 2.20 D-marks in 1995, before making a sustained recovery to a healthier level of 3.20 D-marks. The effects of the high interest rates helped push Britain into recession as the housing market crashed and a large number of businesses failed. The cost of trying to prop up the value of the pound is estimated to have cost the people of UK £4 billion in reserves.

By any standards, this was a major change in the macro-economic environment. The Labour Party, who were in opposition at that time, saw this change as a bad day for Britain and coined the term 'Black Wednesday' to describe the events of 16 September 1992.

But was this change all bad for UK businesses or was it in part beneficial? Arguably, it was both since the economy benefited in the longer term by allowing interest rates to find their natural level. Also, the lower value of the pound had a great influence on any business that dealt directly or indirectly with foreign suppliers or customers. Exporters, by and large, were pleased with the devaluation because it meant that their goods and services would be cheaper to foreign customers. This is because less foreign currency would need to be exchanged into sterling to meet the British company's asking price, which would be set in sterling because the exporter is a UK company. Exports could be expected to increase – good news for companies like ICI and BAE Systems who are amongst Britain's major exporters. Conversely, the devaluation was bad news for importers. If goods were purchased from Germany, then more pounds would have to be found to exchange for deutschmarks to pay for the German goods. Hence, the price of imported goods like French cars and Japanese consumer goods rose after the devaluation of the pound sterling. Businesses therefore had to either absorb higher costs or else pass the increased cost on to the customer in the form of increased prices – equally undesirable outcomes.

Generic types of national economy

The balance between state control and the market system varies across the world. It is this balance that is a major characteristic of the generic types of national economy. We can view this as a continuum (Figure 9.2).

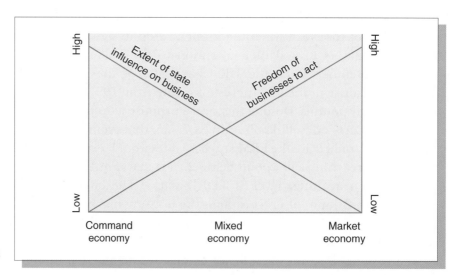

Figure 9.2
Markets continuum.

A *command economy*, in its purest sense, is one wherein all of the commercial activity in a country is controlled directly by the state. There are no private businesses in a command economy and the state ensures an acceptable level of employment and economic activity by its direct control. In a true *market economy*, there is no state control at all – everything in the economy happens through the natural workings of the market mechanism. The state, in a market economy would adopt a completely *laissez-faire* (i.e. the French term for 'let it be') approach, and would allow all business to proceed unregulated. The *mixed economy*, as its position on the continuum suggests, is a mixture of the two. There is a large private business sector and a sizeable state influence which regulates, to a greater or lesser extent, the activities of private business. Mixed economies can vary according to the degree of state influence. Some are very close to the market economy whilst others have higher levels of state intervention.

Question 9.1

- Which type of economy best describes the UK?
- Which countries, either in the past or present, best resemble the command economy?

9.2 Management of the national economy

The management of this important aspect of the country's fortunes is the responsibility of a number of important people employed by the state although their decisions are greatly influenced by the activities of business in general. The principal 'officer', who is empowered by the state to make the most important economic decisions, is the *Chancellor of the Exchequer*. The Chancellor is an elected individual who is accountable to Parliament and who, along with the Foreign Secretary and the Home Secretary, occupies one of the three 'great offices of state' (reporting the Prime Minister). He or she has the power to pull several 'levers' which can influence the general economic climate in which businesses must operate. Each year, the Chancellor sets out the national *Budget*. This is a statement of projected taxation and spending plans for the forthcoming financial or *fiscal* year (from 05 April to 06 April), although the Chancellor can also make any number of other adjustments to the economy throughout the year. It has become the norm in recent years for the Chancellor to issue an Autumn statement on the economy.

A significant change in the management of the national economy occurred in 1997 when the Government introduced legislation that devolved responsibility for the setting of *base interest rates* to the *Bank of England*, with the major objective of controlling the *rate of inflation* via the interest rate mechanism. The rationale behind the change was to remove direct political interference in the economic decision-making process. The legislation provides that if, in extreme circumstances, the national interest demands it, the Government has the power to give instructions to the Bank on interest rates for a limited period.

The *Governor of the Bank of England* is appointed by the Prime Minister and holds a very important and influential position. He or she works closely with the incumbent Chancellor, advising on monetary and financial stability, and exercises control and regulation over the British banking system, which in turn has great influence over the business sector in the country. Under his or her direction, the Bank's *Monetary Policy Committee* (MPC) meets on a monthly basis to examine all the available economic data, analyses a range of domestic and international economic and monetary factors to decide if an adjustment to the base interest rate is required. The Bank also publishes a quarterly inflation report, which provides a detailed analysis of inflation and gives an assessment of the prospects of inflation relative to the inflation target. The annual average interest rates for the years 1998–2004 are shown in Figure 9.3, a period of relative stability and moderate rate levels. It is interesting to compare the rates from recent years with the many fluctuations of rates over time. Of particular note is the record low level of 2% which was in force twice in the 1930s (also 16 times in the nineteenth century!) and the record high of 17% in 1979. The most recent highest figure was 14.88% in October1989.

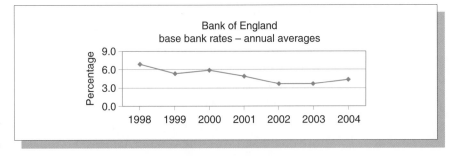

Figure 9.3
Base interest rates.
(*Source*: Bank of
England.)

Question 9.2

■ What is the name of the current Chancellor of the Exchequer?
■ Where is the official residence of the Chancellor?
■ To what political party does he or she belong?
■ Who is the current Governor of the Bank of England?

The *Chief Secretary to the Treasury*, like the Chancellor, holds a Cabinet position (although the Chief Secretary has not always been in the cabinet) and is an elected Member of Parliament. As such, he or she is accountable to Parliament. The Chief Secretary is responsible for regulating government spending through the various government departments and agencies which in turn, influence the level of employment in the public sector. The decisions of the Chief Secretary can have a profound influence on some businesses as they directly affect companies who supply government departments. Such private sector businesses include manufacturers of pharmaceuticals, aircraft, military equipment, paint, construction and many others. In addition, because government spending determines the public sector pay increases of around 6 million people, an influence can be exerted on the demand side of the economy (the spending power of 6 million people is significant when it represents around 25% of the working population). Government spending is also one of the key regulatory influences on the economy as a whole.

The 'markets' as an influence in the macro-economic environment refer to the stock exchanges and other capital markets across the world, principally those in the world's main financial centres of London, New York, Tokyo, Hong Kong and Frankfurt. It would be untrue to suggest that the markets, which deal in millions of international financial transactions every day, actually 'manage' national economies. However, it is the aggregate (i.e. collective) influence of these transactions in shares, bonds and currencies which can profoundly influence or even determine government policy in regard to the macro-economy. The Chancellor and the Governor carefully monitor activity in the markets and sometimes take action in response to trends in the buying and selling of currencies, shares and other 'commodities' by the markets.

9.3 Businesses in the macro-economy

In an ideal world, the conditions in the macro-economic environment would always be favourable to the business sector. Let us examine what these conditions might look like.

Low tax levels (or low *fiscal pressure*) would be the first and most obvious condition. If the government allows businesses and consumers to retain more of their incomes for themselves, it follows that companies could grow and invest and that consumers would spend more money with businesses – another source of business growth. As business growth would be strong, a downward pressure would be exerted on unemployment as businesses took on more people to meet the increased demand from consumers.

Low monetary pressure would act in a similar way to low fiscal pressure. If the banking sector (at the command of the Chancellor and the

Governor) lends money at a low rate of interest then:

■ businesses would pay less on loans used to invest in growth and development, and,

■ consumers could afford higher loans and thus would spend more with businesses.

These factors, taken together, would exert a significant influence on favourable business growth, although we will see later that such conditions may have longer-term effects which might damage businesses.

9.4 Government finances and fiscal policy

Sources of government income

The state has many needs for money. We saw in Chapter 8 that it provides many services through its various departments and the total cash requirement for these is very substantial indeed. Government money is raised through a number of channels. Figure 9.4 shows the percentage value of the main sources of revenue, while Table 9.1 displays the actual monetary values of those sources.

The actual monetary values are shown in Table 9.1.

Figure 9.4
Sources of
government revenue
for fiscal year ended
2003. (*Source*: Office
for National
Statistics.)

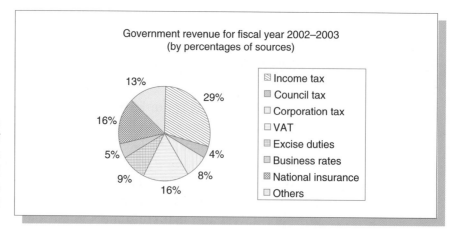

Government revenue for fiscal year 2002–2003
(by percentages of sources)

- ▨ Income tax
- ▤ Council tax
- ☐ Corporation tax
- ☐ VAT
- ▥ Excise duties
- ▦ Business rates
- ▩ National insurance
- ☐ Others

29%
4%
8%
16%
9%
5%
16%
13%

Taxation

The major source of revenue is, as we have seen, taxation. There are two types of taxation: direct and indirect.

Table 9.1

Monetary values of the sources of government revenue (for fiscal year 2003–2003)

Source	£ billions
Income tax	118
Council tax	16
Corporation tax	33
VAT	64
Excise duties	38
Business rates	19
National insurance	65
Others	55
Total revenue	407

Source: Office for National Statistics.

Direct taxation

Direct taxation is tax paid on taxable income. The rates at which tax is payable on income change from time to time and according to how much income is made (higher rates apply to higher incomes). Individuals pay direct tax on their personal incomes whilst businesses pay it on their profits. Direct tax is collected by the Inland Revenue.

Indirect taxation

Indirect taxation is tax levied upon some of the things we buy. It is sometimes called expenditure tax or turnover tax. Unlike direct tax, the payment of indirect tax is, to a certain extent, optional in that if, for example, you choose not to buy alcohol, then you will not pay alcohol tax. The price we pay for many goods and services includes an element of tax which is collected by Her Majesty's Customs and Excise. There are various types of indirect taxation.

  - *Value-added tax* (VAT), which is the most important, involves a fixed percentage being added to the price of a good or service. All goods and services are classified in one of three ways with regard to VAT.
    - *VAT rated:* VAT is levied upon the price of the good or service;
    - *VAT exempt:* goods and services which are not subject to VAT;

– *zero rated:* goods and services which are subject to VAT, but upon which, VAT is not currently applied;
- *Hydrocarbon tax* is the indirect tax levied on some products derived from oil. A substantial percentage of the price of petrol, diesel and industrial solvents (e.g. white spirit) is tax.
- *Tobacco tax* is paid, as the name suggests, on tobacco products like cigarettes and cigars.
- *Alcohol tax* is paid on beer, wine, spirits and liqueurs.
- *Import duties* are taxes paid on some goods imported into the UK. Since the creation of the single European market in 1993, no import duties (sometimes called import *tariffs*) are payable on goods bought and sold between businesses in European Union states. However, if you were to import a car from South Korea or Japan, the UK would require a payment to be made which would be a fixed percentage of the price paid for the car from the far eastern exporter.

Question 9.3

The rates of indirect tax vary from time to time. Find out the following:

- Who determines the rate of VAT?
- The current rate of VAT.
- Three examples of VAT exempt products or services.
- The current level of indirect tax payable on a packet of 20 cigarettes.
- The current level of indirect tax payable on a pint of beer.

Sources other than taxation

Whilst the bulk of government money is gained from taxation, the government receives revenues from some other sources.

- *National insurance* is paid by individuals and employers and is 'earmarked' for use specifically by the Department of Social Security.
- *Rents* from property and land owned by the state.
- *Incomes from licences* which include those granted to extract oil from British coastal waters.
- *Dividends from shares* held by the state.
- *Capital injections* of cash may arise from such things as privatisations of previously state-owned businesses.

Question 9.4

Find out the current:

- basic rate of income tax,
- highest rate of income tax.

Are the current rates historically high or low?

Government expenditure

The government has many calls upon its financial resources. The majority is spent through its various departments, although, in the event of a fiscal deficit, some must be reserved for debt repayment and interest payments (Figure 9.5). The management of fiscal policy presents many problems to the Chancellor. Whilst, on the one hand, he or she wants to provide quality services, such as education, he or she knows that high taxes to pay for them are bad for both businesses and consumers. Hence, the chancellor's decisions on fiscal matters are invariably criticised by somebody. This is often the basis of party political argument.

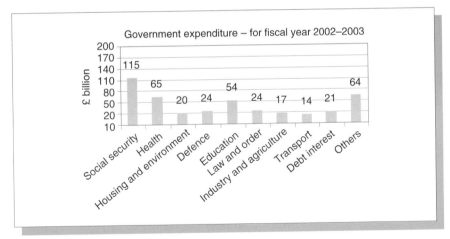

Figure 9.5 Allocation of government spending for fiscal year ended 2003. (*Source*: Office for National Statistics.)

Surpluses and deficits

The fiscal part of macro-economics centres on the government's financial revenues and expenditures. Each financial year, the government receives income from a number of sources (e.g. taxes) and it also spends so much through the various departments and government agencies. Government spending, in some respects, is very much like our normal household situation. Each year, individuals earn certain amounts and spend certain amounts. If they spend less than they earn they are left with a cash surplus. On the other hand, if they spend more than they earn, they must find some way of financing the deficit (e.g. by approaching the bank manager for an overdraft). The same is true of government spending, but on a much grander scale.

If, in any given financial year:

- the government spends *less* than it makes in revenues, the difference is referred to as a *budget* (or fiscal) *surplus*;
- the government spends *more* than it makes in revenues, the difference is referred to as a *budget* (or fiscal) *deficit.*

A fiscal surplus enables funds to be set aside for reserves or tax reductions, whereas a deficit must be financed by borrowing (i.e. the country goes into debt).

The amount of money that the government must borrow in a given fiscal year is called the *public sector borrowing requirement* (PSBR). The PSBR is a monthly, non-seasonally adjusted figure which measures the size of the government's deficit. It comprises three components:

- the central government borrowing requirement;
- the local authority borrowing requirement;
- the public corporation borrowing requirement.

Central government accounts for the largest element of the PSBR. Central government undertakes some borrowing in order to lend funds on to local authorities and public corporations. Local authorities have seen reductions in their fund-raising powers and are increasingly reliant on central government for funding, whilst the privatisation of former public utilities (such as gas and water) has reduced the significance of the *public corporation borrowing requirement* in recent years.

In the event of a fiscal deficit, the PSBR will be a positive figure whilst in the happy event of a fiscal surplus, the PSBR will be negative. It follows, of course, that borrowed money must be repaid. The amount of money that the government puts aside each year for this purpose, the *public sector debt repayment* (PSDR), constitutes a sizeable part of government cash outflow (especially with the interest payments that must be paid on the debt). The borrowing requirement can vary from month to month, but year on year comparisons of the PSBR generally provide a clearer picture of the health of the economy. For example, in the years between 1992 and 1997 there was a series of deficits for each of those years before the country moved into surplus in 1998 and each of the subsequent years until 2003 when a deficit was once more recorded.

An alternative measure of public sector fiscal position is *public sector net borrowing*, which additionally takes account of capital investment. This involves substantial sums of money as can be seen in the financial year 2003–2004, when the government had a net borrowing deficit of £34.8 billion on a net debt level of £394.7 billion. This deficit represented some 33% of GDP, and was an increase of almost 2% over the previous year. However, it was still relatively low when compared to the debt peak of 44% in 1997 – the highest level since the mid 1980s (Figure 9.6).

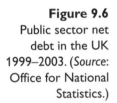

Figure 9.6
Public sector net debt in the UK 1999–2003. (*Source*: Office for National Statistics.)

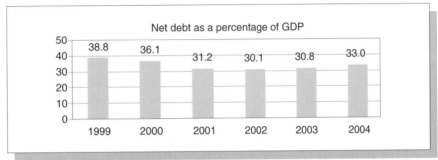

The Labour government's Chancellor of the Exchequer, Gordon Brown, established two fiscal rules to ensure responsible financial management:

- The *golden rule* which states *that*, on average over the economic cycle, the Government should borrow only to invest and not to fund current expenditure. This means that the average surplus on current budget over the cycle should be positive. The surplus on current budget is defined as current income (e.g. taxation) less current expenditure (e.g. social benefits), less capital consumption plus capital taxes.
- The *sustainable investment rule* which states that public sector net debt, as a percentage of GDP will be held, over the economical cycle, at a prudent and stable level. This means that the average surplus on current budget over the cycle should be positive.

9.5 Monetary policy

We have seen that one way in which the government can regulate the economy is by the use of fiscal measures. If the Chancellor increases tax, for example, he will slow down inflation by taking spending power out the economy but at the same time, economic growth may be slowed. Fiscal measures are very powerful tools that can be used to great effect.

The second set of levers that the government can pull to regulate the economy are monetary measures. Whereas fiscal policy concerns the use of taxation and government spending to regulate the economy, monetary policy concerns controlling the *price* and *supply* of money.

The price of money

The price of (borrowed) money, sometimes called the rate of interest, is the price paid to gain the use of somebody else's money. Varying the price of money can be used to powerful effect as a tool to regulate and control activity in the macro-economy. The government views the use of interest rates as a vital instrument in the control of inflation and, as we saw earlier, the Bank of England's MPC has been empowered to set rates it judges to be appropriate to the changing economic environment.

The price of money – a simple example

Bob McRobert wanted to buy a house, but he did not have sufficient funds for the full purchase price of the property. He approached a well-known national building society with the question 'Can I have £70,000 to put towards the price of a house please?' After surveying Bob's financial situation, the manager of the building society branch said, 'Yes, we will let you have a mortgage for that amount, against the security of the house, but you will have to pay the current market price for the money we lend you.'

He continued, 'As long as you have use of our money, and the agreed repayment period is twenty-five years, you will pay 6% interest on the outstanding loan so long as you enjoy its benefit. Over the 25 years of the repayment period, the figure of 6% may go up or down depending on the decisions of the Bank of England's MPC.'

Hence, the mortgage on Bob's house is somebody else's money which must be paid for at the current rate of interest – an example of paying the price for borrowed money.

The price of money therefore only applies to a situation where borrowed money is involved. It follows that whilst individuals and businesses must pay the rate of interest on loans from banks and building societies, so financial institutions must pay interest on money they use which does not belong to them – savers' deposits.

Most students know all about overdrafts and credit card debts which are subject to interest, whilst most businesses make extensive use of the banks' money in the normal conduct of their business. Reducing the interest rate can introduce spending power into the economy (because you are likely to spend more if you have lower pay-back charges), whilst an increase has the opposite effect. Consumers and businesses with large debts (e.g. a family with a large mortgage and a car loan) are particularly sensitive to changes in this type of *monetary pressure*, whereas it has less impact on those who are 'cash-rich'.

Money supply

The money supply is about the amount of money in circulation in the economy. If there is a lot of money in circulation, there will be a higher aggregate spending than if money supply is limited. The issue of money supply is more complicated that it appears when we take into account the fact that the word *money* includes more than just cash. Cash is only a part of the money used by consumers and businesses. Money supply also includes the growth in total credit and changes in the amount of foreign currency that people in the UK make use of.

Measures of money supply growth

The problem with measuring how much money is circulating in the economy and how fast the money supply grows, is that defining 'money' is not as straightforward as it may seem. Money, in its broadest sense is anything that can be exchanged for goods and services. We can, for example, use money from our pockets (notes and coins), cheques from a current account, cheques made out from a deposit account, credit and in some cases, foreign currency. To account for the breadth of definitions, the government uses several measures of money supply growth (Table 9.2 and Figure 9.7).

Table 9.2
Monetary growth measures in the UK

Measure	Broad or narrow	Definition
M0	Narrow	The total value of notes and coins in circulation.
M2	Narrow	M0 plus all 'sight' deposits (e.g. in current accounts).
M4	Broad	M2 plus deposits in savings accounts.
M3H	Very broad	M4 plus foreign currencies held by UK banks and residents.

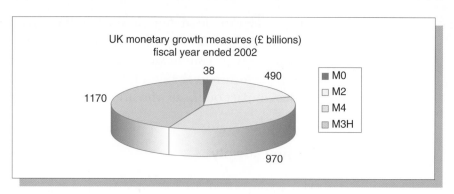

Figure 9.7
UK monetary
growth measures –
fiscal year to 2002.

The broad/narrow distinction refers to the breadth of the types of money included. Clearly, M0, as it only includes actual notes and coins can be seen as a narrow definition. M4 is considered to be broad because it also includes money that does not actually exist in the form of notes and coins. The deposits held in savings accounts are said to be *notional* in that their full paper value does not exist in the form of notes and coins. If everybody withdrew their deposits at the same time, not all depositors could be paid as the banks would run out of notes and coins. The banking system acts upon certain assumptions, one of them being that there will be a certain amount of stability in people's financial situations, causing approximately the same amount of money to be withdrawn as is deposited.

Monetary volume and velocity

In measuring the use of money in the economy, we need to be aware of two important principles, those of the *volume* of money circulating and its *velocity* of circulation.

We can see from Figure 9.8 that money circulates between consumers, businesses and banks. Most consumers usually obtain their cash from a bank, either across the counter or through a cash point. They then spend it with a business in exchange for goods and services. The business then deposits the cash with its bank. They then get more cash from the bank and the cycle goes round again.

If we consider the simplest measure of money, M0, the volume of money in an economy is the total number of notes and coins on circulation. If the government reduces the volume of M0 (i.e. takes cash out of the economy by destroying more notes than it currently prints), then it might be thought that spending would go down, but this is not necessarily the case. Let us imagine a simple example – there is a reduction

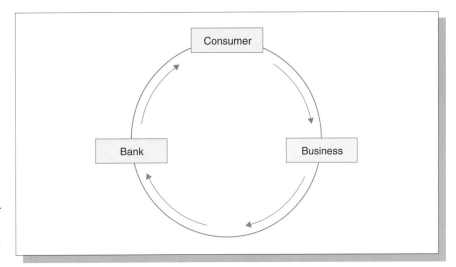

Figure 9.8
The circulation of
money in an
economy
(simplified).

on the volume of M0. We extract our cash from the bank as usual and
we then take our cash and spend it at a major high street retailer. Lots
of other people do the same until the bank gets low on its cash reserves
due to the reduction in volume. In order to avoid running out of cash,
the bank rings the retailer and asks if it can deposit its day's takings earlier than usual. The retailer obliges and delivers its cash (which we spent
earlier in the day) to the bank for recirculation. Hence, the velocity of
money has increased because the volume has been reduced.

Thus, in simple terms, there is an inverse relationship between volume and velocity, that is *if volume is reduced, velocity tends to increase*, and,
if volume is increased, velocity tends to (but does not necessarily) decrease (see
the notes on the *quantity theory of money* in Chapter 10).

This model holds true only up to a point. The picture becomes more
complex when the cycle we encountered above is no longer a closed
system. If extra cash is introduced into the cycle or if cash is taken out of
the cycle, then the volume – velocity relationship may no longer hold.

Cash injections into the money cycle can occur, for example, when:

- Savers spend some of their savings.
- Foreign currency is changed into sterling (effectively a cash
  injection from abroad). This happens, for example, when a UK
  business exports goods.
- The government releases reserves into the economy in the form
  of government spending (e.g. by building hospitals, roads or
  increasing the funding to your university).
- Individuals or businesses borrow money to invest and thus keep
  their cash for immediate spending (borrowed money from a
  bank does not exist as cash).

Cash 'leakages' from the cycle occur when:

- People put cash into the bank as savings rather than spending it.
- People pay tax to the government (money which cannot be recycled immediately).
- People make investments using cash. For example, by buying shares or government bonds.
- Money goes abroad, for example, to pay for imported goods or services, foreign bank deposits or foreign holidays.

Hence, a more accurate money cycle will be as shown in Figure 9.9.

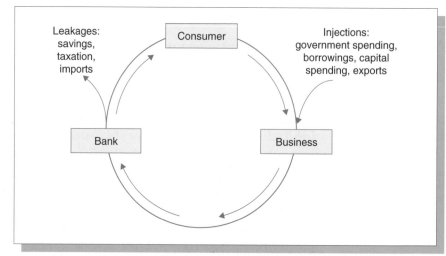

Figure 9.9
Money cycle
showing leakages
and injections.
(*Note:* Leakages and
injections can occur
at any point in the
cycle, not just at the
points shown.)

The Bank of England and monetary policy

The *Bank of England* (BoE) is the central bank for the United Kingdom and is sometimes referred to as the 'Old Lady' of Threadneedle Street, which has been its home in the centre of the UK's financial system since it was founded in 1694. The BoE was nationalised in 1946 and gained independence in 1997. In addition to providing banking services to its customers, the BoE manages the UK's gold and exchange reserves plus the government's stock register.

The prime goal of any central bank is to safeguard the value of the currency in terms of what it will purchase at home and in terms of what other currencies. *Monetary policy* is directed towards the achievement of this goal and the provision of a framework for non-inflationary economic growth. As with most other developed countries, monetary policy operates in the UK mainly through influencing the *price of money*, that is the base interest rate (see Section 9.2 above). In pursuit of the goal of maintaining a stable and efficient monetary and financial framework, the BoE has two core purposes; that of *monetary stability* and *financial stability*.[1]

- ■ *Monetary stability* means stable prices and confidence in the currency. To safeguard the integrity and the value of the currency, the BoE primarily takes action through the conduct of *monetary policy*, which involves maintaining price stability, as defined by the annual inflation target set by the government. High inflation can seriously damage the health of the economy while low inflation (price stability) can help to foster sustainable long-term economic growth. Broadly speaking, the Bank's MPC sets interest rates at a level to ensure that demand in the economy is in line with the country's productive capacity. For example, if rates are set too low demand may exceed supply and lead to the emergence of inflationary pressures so that inflation is accelerating. On the other hand, if rates are set too high, output is likely to be unnecessarily low and economic growth will go into decline.

- ■ *Financial stability* entails detecting and reducing threats to the financial system as a whole. Such threats are detected through the Bank's surveillance and market intelligence functions. They are reduced by strengthening infrastructure and by financial and other operations at home and abroad. Since 1997 the Bank has had responsibility for the financial system, while the *Financial Services Authority* (FSA) supervises individual banks and other financial institutions, including recognised financial exchanges such as the London Stock Exchange. The Bank works closely with HM Treasury and the FSA to ensure a common position on issues that could de-stabilise the financial system as a whole, and co-operates with other central banks and international organisations to improve the international monetary system.

Lender of last resort (LOLR) is a role that can be adopted by the Bank when it is perceived that there is a threat to the stability of the financial system. In such a situation, the Bank may intervene to stand between an intermediary and the market place in order to facilitate payments and settlements, which might not otherwise be completed. In extreme cases, emergency financial support by the Bank might be provided, as the LOLR, but this is only done where failure of one institution could bring down other (otherwise viable) institutions. The LOLR role requires public money and must therefore be carefully justified. It should be noted that this 'safety net' only exists to protect the financial system as a whole and not for the protection of individual institutions or their managers and shareholders.

In summary, the BoE's main functions include:

- acting as the government's bankers (handling the huge public sector finances);
- acting as a central banker to the main clearing banks (e.g. Barclays, National Westminster, etc.);
- managing the country's foreign currency reserves (foreign currency which the country keeps to influence the value of sterling as the need arises);
- managing any debts which the country has with foreign countries or other banks (or of course any surplus which the country may have);
- issuing of notes and coins for general circulation, overseeing the printing and minting of money and the destruction of used notes and coins;
- acting (in exceptional circumstances) as the LOLR;
- implementing monetary policy (varying interest rates and the supply of money – of all types – in the economy).

9.6 Economic 'indicators'

When observers want to assess the strength of a national economy, it is unusual to look at the levels of fiscal or monetary pressure. It is more common to look at other parts of the economy which are largely determined by fiscal and monetary policies. By examining the figures and trends in these 'indicators', the strength of an economy can be assessed.

Economic growth

Growth and inflation

If we were to plot the totals of all business transactions in the UK over a long period of time, we would see that the graph would show a definite upward trend. This is because each year, the total (aggregate) sales in the country are usually greater than in the previous year. There are two causes for such increases.

- Demand in the economy increases. Each year, we spend more than the previous year. This could be due to the fact that we earn more in real terms, or that the prices of goods and services have fallen in real terms, making them more affordable. By becoming richer, we spend more as time passes.

■ Prices have risen over the previous year. Hence, we must spend more just to maintain the same level of business activity and quality of life that we did last year. This is growth resulting from inflation.

A key objective of both government and businesses is that of *non-inflationary growth*. This is growth brought about entirely by increased production and consumption with no element of increased prices causing the year-on-year increase. A key term in measuring growth is that of 'real' growth. Real growth is the rate of increase in the economy's output minus the prevailing rate of inflation over the same period. This, in turn, can be measured by one of two aggregate figures.

■ The GDP is the concept of the total economic activity taking place in UK territory. GDP can be viewed as incomes earned, as expenditures incurred, or as production. It is 'gross' in the sense that it does not deduct the cost of wear and tear, because this is impossible to measure and hard to estimate (Figure 9.10).

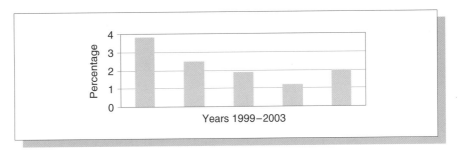

Figure 9.10
GDP growth in the UK. (*Source*: Office for National statistics.)

■ The *gross national income* (GNI) – previously known as *gross national product*, or GNP – is the GDP plus any net overseas income received by UK-based individuals and businesses (after allowing for outgoings). Overseas income includes profits from foreign investments and interest and returns on bank deposits and other financial investments (Figure 9.11).

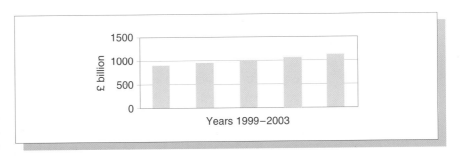

Figure 9.11
GNI growth in the UK. (*Source*: Office for National statistics.)

We can also use GDP and GNI to measure the wealth in a country in the form of the *real income per capita* (i.e. for each person). This is the GDP or GNI divided by the number of people in a country. It is seen as a measure of the increasing or decreasing economic wealth of the population. However, we must be careful not to assess the wealth of a nation purely by looking at the GDP or GNI figure as this tells us little about the actual economic standards of living enjoyed by individual citizens. For example, larger countries tend to have higher total GNIs and therefore *GNI per capita* is a better inter-country comparative measurement. Consider the data in Table 9.3 and note the significant relative differences in the 'league tables' when measuring against GNI or GNI per capita.

Table 9.3
Inter-country comparisons of GNI and GNI per capita

Country	GNI $ billion	Country	GNI per capita $ billion
1 USA	10,019.7	1 USA	35,200
2 Japan	4141.4	2 Switzerland	34,000
3 Germany	1853.4	3 Japan	32,600
4 UK	1426.5	4 Sweden	24,700
5 France	1309.8	5 UK	24,300
6 Italy	1091.8	6 Austria	23,300
7 Mexico	617.2	7 Germany	22,500
8 Spain	583.1	8 France	21,500
9 Switzerland	245.4	9 Italy	18,800
10 Sweden	219.4	10 Spain	14,500

Source: OECD.

Positive and negative growth

The expectations of economic growth are part of our business and societal culture. Most consumers and businesses expect to become richer and more comfortable as they progress through life, not less so. However, it should be noted that there are times when growth is strong and times when it is slow or even when it is negative. Such variations are due in large part to the fact that economic activity is approximately cyclical. There are sustained periods when both spending and investment are high and businesses enjoy growing, buoyant conditions. It seems though, that from time to time, economic activity slows down. Slow economic growth is obviously bad for business. On some occasions, an economy's GDP actually falls against the previous year and this is called negative growth or *recession*. Recession is defined by many economists as at least two consecutive quarters of decline in a nation's GDP.

Whilst the actual value of economic growth is important to domestic consumers and businesses, perhaps more important is the value of the UK's growth compared to that of its main industrial competitors. If, for example, the UK experiences an outstanding year of real growth – say of 10% – but both Germany and France enjoy a rate of 12%, then in international terms, the UK has shrunk in relative terms, against the competitors, by two percentage points. This type of comparative analysis applies to most of the economic indicators.

Inflation

Inflation can be defined as the year-on-year overall (aggregate) rise in prices. It can also be defined as the year-on-year reduction in the value of money, because a one pound coin will be worth less in spending power this year compared to last year by an amount equal to the rate of inflation.

Causes of inflation

The major causes of inflation are two-fold. The two causes can work independently of each other, but it somewhat goes without saying that inflationary pressures are at their most when both factors are at work simultaneously.

- *Cost-push inflation* occurs when the costs to industry are increased. These can be due to increased energy prices, increased import prices (which may be linked with a fall in the value of the domestic currency), increased labour costs or any number of other input price changes. Whilst businesses may be able to absorb cost increases in the short term, any sustained increases in industrial costs must be 'passed on' to the consumers, and eventually leads to retail prices inflation. This effect has been termed *supply-side inflationary pressure.*

- *Demand-led inflation* is brought about by an excess of spending power in the economy over the economy's ability to meet the demand. Producers will tend to increase their prices when they are confident that there is an excess of demand. This type of inflation can be stated simply as 'too much money chasing too few goods' and has two equally obvious causes.

Firstly, demand led inflation can be caused by anything that causes aggregate spending power in the economy to grow. Such factors will include cuts in the rate of tax, cuts in monetary pressure, high wage rises, increases in government spending, falling unemployment, etc. Such changes are said to come from the *demand side* of the economy. Secondly, it can be caused by anything that prevents the business sector from meeting demand, for example higher fiscal and monetary pressure, high wage demands, low investment, etc.

Inflation measurement

In December 2003, the *consumer prices index* (CPI) replaced the *retail prices index* (RPI), or '*headline rate*', as the UK official measurement system for inflation. To calculate the rate of retail inflation, the CPI uses a notional 'basket' of consumer products to monitor prices each month in determining the percentage change in prices over the course of a year. The *RPIX*, or '*underlying rate of inflation*', excludes mortgage interest payments and is still used to calculate state pensions, whereas the CPI is used to calculate income-related benefits. There are other measures of inflation outwith retail prices, such as the rise in industrial costs – '*factory gate prices*' inflation. These are of less direct concern to consumers but tend to be indicative of future movements in the CPI because business cost increases are usually passed on to consumers eventually.

The following chart (Figure 9.12) contrasts the RPI measure with the newer CPI results and shows a low and relatively stable level of UK inflation in recent years. It is interesting to compare these figures with historical data and examine the changes in fortune over the years. For example, since 1948 there have been many fluctuations in the inflation rates for the UK with a record high in 1975, when the average RPI peaked at 26.9% and a record low in 1959 when the average RPI registered 0.6%.

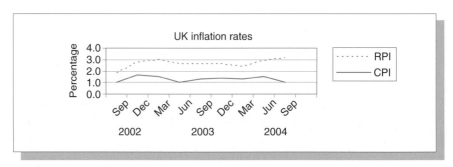

Figure 9.12
CPI in the UK.
(*Source*: Office for
National Statistics.)

Question 9.5

Compare the above results with the government target of 2% for 2004, and discuss the implications for the economic health of the country.

The effects of inflation

The reduction of inflation is an objective which is shared by all businesses and political parties. It is generally accepted that low inflation is good for the majority of people and businesses in an economy. Its management consequently forms a major plank of government economic policy whichever party happens to be in power.

The effects of inflation in an economy are summarised as follows:

- If the UK rate is higher than those of its major competitors, it will, over time, make British businesses less price competitive in international business transactions. This is the most important of the negative effects of inflation.
- It tends to exert an upward pressure on wage demands. This increases company costs, and, through the increased prices to cover the increased labour cost and through increased spending power, it can make inflation worse. This is referred to as a *wage-price inflationary spiral.*
- Variable or erratically increasing prices adds to the uncertainty of the economic environment. This can have a negative effect on business confidence and may delay investment and spending.

Inflation in international trade

Both the UK and France export motor vehicles to other European states (which they both do). Suppose that this year, the price of the French car, say a Peugeot, is £20,000 (in the Euro equivalence). The British built car, say a Rover, also costs £20,000. This price parity means that a car buyer in Belgium would choose between them using non-price criteria (such as appearance, handling, style, 'feel', etc.). The two cars are equally price competitive.

Over the course of the following year, the UK and France experience different rates of inflation. In the UK, the rate is 10%, but in France, it is only 5%. This means that costs in the countries will have increased by these percentages (the respective rates of inflation). If the full effects of these cost increases are passed on to the customers then, for the French Peugeot the new price would be:

$$£20,000 + 5\% = £21,000$$

and for the British Rover, the new price would be:

$$£20,000 + 10\% = £22,000.$$

Hence, the British car is less price competitive because of the higher rate of inflation. Rover's other choice, instead of passing on the price increase, is to set their price equal to the price of the Peugeot and absorb the lower profit margin. Either way, the results for Rover are unpleasant.

Question 9.6

For the following changes in the economic environment, say whether each of the changes is most likely to be inflationary or deflationary.

- A cut in the basic rate of income tax (reduced fiscal pressure).
- An increase in interest rates (increased monetary pressure).
- A decrease in unemployment.
- A cut in government spending (increased fiscal pressure).
- Devaluation of the domestic currency.

Value of currency

The value of a currency refers to its value against other (foreign) currencies. At any point in time, the pound sterling will have a value against all other currencies. The most important exchange rates are those of the countries with which Britain does most business – the euro, the US dollar and the Japanese Yen.

In a small, open economy, like the UK, the exchange rate is the single most important price indicator. It determines what we pay in sterling for our imports and so feeds directly into domestic prices. The exchange rate of the pound is of vital interest to any business in the UK that deals with foreign companies – as a supplier, customer or partner.

Demand for sterling

The value of currency, like any other economic commodity, is determined by the demand for the commodity. An increase in the demand for bananas would cause their market price to rise, and the same is true for currency.

■ *An increase in the demand for British goods and services.* When a UK-based business exports a product (e.g. a car) or a service (e.g. an insurance policy), then foreign currency must be changed into sterling to pay the British company. The demand for sterling goes up and so, therefore, does its value. Customers will only buy British goods if they are more competitive than foreign ones – they are higher quality, cheaper or both. There is therefore an important link between the exchange rate and the competitiveness of British business.

■ *High interest rates.* The amount of interest that international investors can obtain by putting money on deposit will influence the country in which they place their cash. If the British interest rate is higher than it is in other countries then the UK will attract investment capital. Again, the investors (who manage vast sums of money on behalf of banks, insurance companies and other financial institutions) will have to buy sterling in order to place it in UK banks. Hence, its value will increase (Table 9.4).

Table 9.4
The effects of interest rate changes upon bank deposits

Interest rate	Bank deposits	Value of sterling
Increases	Increased	Higher
Decreases	Decreased	Lower

Question 9.7

Find out the current exchange rate of the pound sterling against:

■ the euro,
■ the Japanese yen,
■ the US dollar.

For each one, try to identify the trend – is it on an upward or downward trend against the pound?

The effects of a high or low exchange rate

The matter of exchange rates is quite complicated as we can only say if a high or a low exchange rate is particularly favourable or unfavourable dependent upon the particular circumstances of the business concerned.

In summary though, we can say the following of a *high value of sterling* (relative to other major currencies):

- It will make *exports relatively uncompetitive* (i.e. expensive). This is because more foreign currency will have to be changed into sterling to meet the British asking price. Conversely, a lower value of sterling will make exports more price competitive.
- It will make *imports relatively cheap*. Less sterling will be required to be exchanged to meet the foreign seller's price. Whilst this may be good for company costs, it may not be good for British businesses if foreign goods are cheaper. This will also increase the value of visible imports (see section on balance of payments later in this chapter), which will have the effect of reducing the exchange rate for reasons we will see later. Again, a low exchange rate will have the opposite effect.

An example can be found with oil which is internationally priced in US dollars and means that if the pound rises against the US dollar, the price of oil in sterling is cheaper. The effect on exports is the opposite in that a rising pound means that British exports are more expensive, and therefore less competitive, when the sterling price is converted to a higher price in foreign currency.

The one objective in regard to exchange rates which most businesses do have in common is that they should be relatively stable. We have seen the high or low exchange rates will please some organisations and displease others (depending, for example with whether they are mainly importers or exporters), but very few like to see frequent and erratic fluctuations. Stability of exchange rates increases the certainty of carrying out international business transactions and this tends to increase the volume of business across national borders.

Unemployment

Definition

The UK Office for National Statistics describes unemployment as a count of jobless people who want to work, are available to work, and are actively seeking employment.[2] This is in line with the definition of the *International Labour Office* (ILO) of the United Nations which defines the measure of unemployment as '*those people without a job who were available to start within two weeks of their Labour Force Survey (LFS) interview, and who had either looked for work in the few weeks prior to the interview or were waiting to start a job they had already obtained*.[3] The ILO definition is used internationally so that comparisons between countries can be made, allowing consistent comparisons over time. In the UK, the *claimant count* measures only those people who are claiming unemployment-related benefits (e.g. *Jobseeker's Allowance*). It is always the lower measure because some unemployed people are not entitled to claim benefits or choose not to do so.

When employment is high the gap between unemployment and the claimant count tends to widen as some jobless people who were not previously looking for work start to do so. By actively looking for work, they may become classified as unemployed under the ILO definition, but they will not feature in the claimant count unless they also begin to claim benefits.

Unemployment is measured, like most of the economic indicators, on a monthly basis. Observers often analyse unemployment in terms of its upward or downward trend, rather than the actual figure itself. Governments tend to analyse the level of unemployment as a percentage of the total labour force, often making comparisons with other 'competitor' countries.

Level of unemployment

The level of unemployment is generally taken to be an indicator of the economic health of a country. Rising unemployment, in most cases, is generally assumed to indicate that businesses are shedding jobs or curtailing recruitment – not things that are typical of behaviour in times of rapid economic growth. Whilst the level of unemployment may not be of direct concern to businesses, it could be contended that a large pool of available labour, which can often be bought in at favourable cost (i.e. lower wages) is of some advantage. The negative effects of unemployment, particularly the inclination of the Chancellor to maintain fiscal pressure (to facilitate the payment of unemployment benefits), probably outweigh any benefits the business may enjoy from a wider choice of recruits.

The data shown in Figure 9.13 reveals an ILO measurement for UK unemployment of 4.8% at 30 September 2003, and represented one of the lowest unemployment rates among industrialised countries (see Figure 9.14). Indeed, this was the lowest level recorded since records began in 1984, and was very much in line with the claimant count figure (i.e. people claiming Jobseeker's Allowance) which was at its lowest level since September 1975. The forecast (linear) trend line also reveals continuing downward movement.

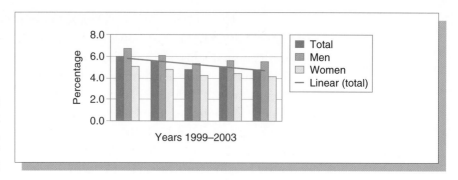

Figure 9.13
UK unemployment
rates 1999–2003.
(*Source*: ILO Labour
Force Survey.)

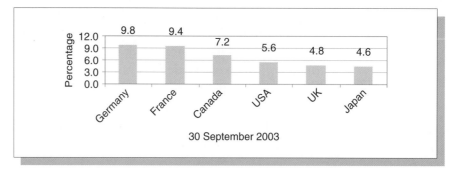

Figure 9.14
Unemployment
international
comparisons.
(*Source*: ILO Labour
Force Survey.)

Types of unemployment

The total unemployment figure is made up from a number of 'types' of unemployed people. The type is linked to the respective cause.

- *Frictional unemployment* is caused by friction in the labour market. In this context, friction means a difficulty in matching jobseekers with employers. It takes some time for peoples' skills to be matched up with employers who are seeking those skills. It may be that there is a shortage of teachers in London, but an excess in Scotland. This is overcome in some cases by migration to areas where the skills are in demand. Frictional unemployment is necessarily temporary in nature, representing a period of transition for jobseekers from one job to the next.

- *Seasonal unemployment* occurs as a result of varying labour demand at different times of the year. The tourism and building industries take on more labour in the summer whilst postal services and retailers increase their labour requirements towards Christmas. As a result of seasonal unemployment, the overall rate can fluctuate over the year.

- *Structural unemployment* arises as a result of changes in the structure of industry and the commercial sector in general.

Recent years have seen the decline in traditional industries like ship-building and mining. Many businesses which once employed thousands of people, simply no longer exist. Unemployment arising from such closures, often regionally concentrated, has been the major contributor to the national unemployment total since 1970.

■ *Cyclical unemployment* is unemployment that arises as a result of cycles in the state of the economy. In times of rapid economic growth, unemployment falls as businesses take on more labour whilst in recession; unemployment will increase as businesses shed labour.

■ *Technological unemployment* is seen by some as being a type of structural unemployment. The increased use of technology in all areas of business life has reduced the need for labour. The increased use of robots, for example, has reduced the need for workers on production lines, whilst the computerisation of banking and accounting systems has reduced the need for book-keepers and clerical staff. Motorcar manufacturers once employed tens of thousands of people to perform simple engineering tasks. Extensive automation of motorcar plants means that they now produce more cars with a fraction of their former labour requirement.

Seasonal, frictional and cyclical causes of unemployment tend to be short term, whilst structural and technological unemployment are more worrying to governments due to their long-term effects.

Effects of unemployment

The effects of unemployment on a community and in the country are complex. In regions of the country that have suffered high rates of unemployment for sustained periods, it seems that the unemployment has engendered effects other than just the personal misery that it can involve. We can consider the effects of unemployment as falling into three categories:

■ The *primary effects* are the experiences of the people being made unemployed and of the businesses that have been forced to close or lose some of their employees. Redundancy or the closure of a large employer can have the effect of reducing the affected people's confidence, increased stress, depression and even despair. The loss of earnings to a family and the enforced idleness can engender a number of social and domestic problems.

■ The *secondary effects* of unemployment arise as a result of the closure of large employers or of a large number of employers in a region. Secondary effects extend to the suppliers to a closed business, its contractors and customers. Suppliers may be forced to close as a result of the closure of the business buying its output. A significant loss of employment in a locality can also have the result of reducing spending power which can lead to the closure of other local businesses such as shops and pubs.

■ The *tertiary effects* include demographic migration away from areas of high unemployment and the deterioration of such localities as a result. Some semi-rural areas in the UK which formerly depended upon employment from mining have suffered declining population and a reduction in local services as a result. Young people tend to leave the locality to gain work and hence local populations get progressively older.

Most governments have come to the conclusion that a situation of 'full employment' is essentially unachievable. Some argue that it is not actually desirable as the spending power created by full employment would potentially be very inflationary (see the discussion on the Phillips curve in Chapter 10). Notwithstanding this, governments often make concerted efforts to reduce unemployment as it is known to have several undesirable effects.

The disadvantages of unemployment to the various affected parties are as follows:

■ The *costs of state assistance* to the unemployed can be very significant, especially in times of recession when unemployment is high and tax revenues are relatively low. The UK government has, over recent years, sought to carefully monitor unemployment assistance as it is not only expensive to the taxpayer, but if over-generous, can also act as a disincentive for the unemployed to return to work. Coupled with the fact that unemployed people do not contribute income tax, the costs to the state can be seen to be significant.

■ Unemployment, especially structural unemployment, can result in a *loss of human skills* to the economy. The closure of many heavy engineering operations signalled an increase in structural unemployment and many skilled workers began to lose their skills through periods of prolonged unemployment. Whilst for some skills this may not be very significant (i.e. those which the economy has decreasing demand for), for others the costs of retraining in these skills may be significant.

■ Unemployment represents an underutilisation of one of the main factors of production. Put simply, human resources add value to goods and services in a business so unemployed people are not being used for this economic purpose. It is thus said to be a *waste of human resources*.

■ There is much debate regarding the *links between unemployment and a number of social disorders* such as increased crime, ill health and deteriorating race relations. Whilst some dispute such links, the majority of observers concede that unemployment is one of the factors that contribute to such disorders. It is argued, for example, that if people are in work, they not only have less time on their hands to be a menace to society, they also have less financial reasons for being so.

Balance of payments and trade

The *balance of payments* statement is a record of a country's transactions with the rest of the world. It records all cash movements in and out of the country, and provides a picture of the net balance of earnings (credits) and payments (debits). A balance of payments surplus arises when credits are greater than debits and a deficit occurs when the debits are greater than credits.

Although the statement is issued monthly, most interest revolves around the annual statement which is the sum of all the monthly statements for a 1-year period.

There are two parts of the balance of payments account. The *current account* records all payments that result from trade in goods and services, whilst the *capital account* records movements of capital for investment purposes and the currency transactions which make trading (shown in the current account) possible. The two parts of the balance of payments statement must therefore, by definition, balance. There tends to be a statistical error resulting from inaccuracies in recording cash movements and this figure is termed the *balancing item*.

The current account

The recording of transactions that arise through normal trading activities are naturally split into two categories: goods (visibles) and services (invisibles).

Visible transactions record trade in physical goods:

- Imports occur when goods enter the UK. British businesses, in paying for the goods, send money overseas, causing a cash outflow from the UK.
- Exports occur when a UK business sells goods to foreign customers. Cash flows into the UK to pay for the exported goods.

The difference between the values of visible imports and exports is called the *balance of trade*. This figure (especially whether it is positive or negative overall) is thought to be a good indicator of the competitiveness of British manufacturing. If the balance of trade is a negative figure for the year, it means that the UK has imported more goods (in value terms) than it has exported. This is taken to mean that for reasons of quality and/or price, foreign goods are more attractive to buyers than British goods although this can also be affected by the value of the currency. The UK government is keen to see increased exports and reduced imports, not least because of what this would say about the desirability of British goods.

Constructing the balance of payments account – two simple rules

The balance of payments account records movements of cash, not goods or services. Hence, the following rules apply when constructing the account:

- All money flowing into the UK, for any reason, is entered as a *positive* figure in the account. The UK has become 'richer' by the amount of money coming into the UK;
- All money flowing out of the UK is entered as a *negative* figure in the account.

It therefore follows, for example, that exports, inward investment and inward bank deposits are entered as a positive figure. Imports, overseas investment by UK companies and money we take on holiday to France are entered as a negative figure. In the UK, balance of payments statement, all figures are entered in pounds sterling. Foreign currencies held in the UK are converted into pounds value at the current exchange rate for the purposes of the statement.

Invisible transactions mainly comprise movements in cash to pay for services. Also included is dividends and interest from investments. When a Spanish shipping company takes out insurance with Lloyd's of London, cash flows into the UK. Conversely, a British student going to study abroad is benefiting from an education service, causing money to flow out of the UK in course fees. The *invisibles balance* is the difference between all invisible inflows and outflows and it can be a positive or negative figure.

Over recent times, Britain has witnessed several years of balance of trade deficits, but this is partly compensated for by relatively healthy invisibles balances (Figure 9.15). The message from such figures would seem to be that Britain is competitive in its supply of services, but less so in its manufacturing sector.

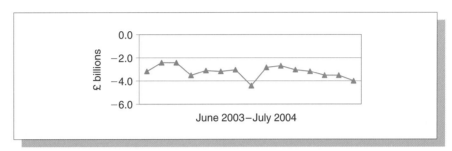

Figure 9.15
UK balance of trade.
(*Source*: Office for
National Statistics.)

The *current balance* records the overall surplus or deficit arising from all trading activities with overseas parties (exports and imports). Calculated simply by adding together the balance of trade (the visibles balance) and the invisibles balance, the current balance is viewed as an indicator of competitiveness and is useful for analysing a country's comparative trading performance.

Regular positive current balances appear to indicate buoyant trading conditions for a country's economy, while frequent deficits may indicate that there are trading difficulties. For example, the currency exchange rates may be more favourable to importers than exporters, or there may be structural problems with certain sectors of industry.

The current account is reported on a quarterly basis and typically the results fluctuate from quarter to quarter. Figure 9.16 shows the end of quarter results for the United Kingdom, over the years from 1998 to 2004, for the current account balance as a percentage of GDP.

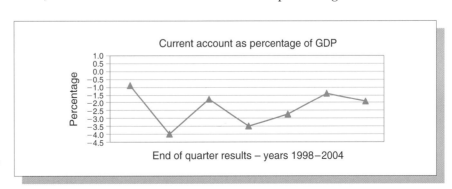

Figure 9.16
UK current balance.
(*Source*: Office for
National Statistics.)

Question 9.8

If the balance of trade is a good indicator of the competitiveness of British manufacturing, describe the significance of the invisibles balance and the current balance overall. Comment on the performance of the UK from Figures 9.15 and 9.16.

The capital account

The capital account is more correctly called the *transactions in external assets and liabilities.* It records financial movements across the national borders which are not linked directly with trading relationships.

The various components of the capital account are predominantly as follows:

- *Foreign investment in the UK* occurs when foreign businesses either buy British business or build plants in the UK to carry out business. Foreign acquisitions include the purchase of Rover Group by BMW whilst Toyota's greenfield investment in Derbyshire is an example of a 'new-build' (these are both discussed in Chapter 15). The inward flow of funds to pay for foreign investments means that this is a positive figure on the statement although positive figure is partly offset by transfers back to the foreign country of returns on the investment.
- *UK investment overseas* represents funds that have left the UK to pay for overseas investments, although the negative outflow figure can be offset by returns to the UK of returns on foreign investments such as dividends. An example of inclusions in this category is UK companies buying shares in overseas companies. If Hanson plc buys a company in North America or if ICI builds a chemical plant in Asia, the values of these investments would be entered as UK investment overseas. On a less grand scale, this entry also includes UK residents who buy holiday homes abroad.
- *Currency transactions* show the movements in sterling as it is exchanged to or from other currencies which occur whenever one currency is exchanged for another. Imports and exports both involve changing money from one currency to another. Bank deposits to and from the UK will also involve a currency transaction.
- *Inward and outward bank deposits* show the values that are moved across the sea for the purposes of banking deposit.

> ▓ *Changes to the 'official reserves'* refers to the BoE's reserves of currency. This is a sum amounting to billions of pounds and is held in both sterling and a range of foreign currencies. It is used, among other things, to influence the exchange rate of sterling.

Question 9.9

For the following items, say:

1   Where they would be entered in the balance of payments account.
2   Whether they would be entered as a positive or negative item.

▓ GlaxoSmithKline, the British pharmaceuticals company, buys a US-based company.
▓ The government of Canada buys submarines from British Ministry of Defence.
▓ Motorola invests £1.5 billion in a microchip factory on Tyneside.
▓ You buy a Japanese Nissan car.

Different parts of the balance of payments statement signify different things. We have seen that the current balance is an indication of the competitiveness of the UK's trading sector. The balance between inward and outward investment is an indicator of the attractiveness of the UK as a place to invest whilst the difference between inward and outward bank deposits is usually influenced by monetary policy over the year.

Assignment 9.1

During the period 1999–2003 the UK enjoyed a period of declining interest rates from around 5% to about 3.5%. At the same time, the annual rate of inflation was stable at about 2%.

Questions

▓ Explain the theoretical link between interest rates and inflation.
▓ Discuss the reasons why inflation might remain stable despite declining interest rates.
▓ What other changes might occur to other economic indicators as a result of falling interest rates.

References

1   Bank of England web site (www.bankofengland.co.uk) October 2004.
2   Office for National Statistics web site (www.statistics.gov.uk) October 2004.
3   International Labour Office web site (www.ilo.org) October 2004.

Further reading

Abel, A.B. and Bernanke, B.S. (2003). *Macroeconomics*, 4th edn. London: Addison Wesley Publishing.

Barro, R. and Sala-i-Martin, X. (2003). *Economic Growth*, 2nd edn. London: MIT Press.

Begg, D. and Ward, D. (2004) *Economics for Business*. London: Higher Education.

Books, I., Weatherstone, J. and Wilkinson, G. (2004). *The International Environment*. Harlow: FT Prentice Hall.

Curwen, P. (1997). *Understanding the UK Economy*, 4th edn. London: Palgrave Macmillan.

Dornbusch, R. and Fischer, S. (2003). *Macroeconomics*, 9th edn. London: McGraw-Hill Education (ISE editions).

McEachern, W.A. (1994). *Macroeconomics. A Contemporary Introduction*, 3rd edn. London: Thomson Publishing.

OECD (2000). *Economics Statistics*. Paris: OECD.

Sloman, J. and Sutcliffe, M. (2004). *Economics for Business*, 3rd edn. Harlow: FT Prentice Hall.

Whitehead, G. (1996). *Economics* (Made Simple Series), 15th edn. Oxford: Butterworth Heinemann.

Useful web sites

UK Government departments' pathway: www.gateway.gov.uk
Department of Trade and Industry: www.dti.gov.uk
Incomes Data Survey: www.incomesdata.co.uk

CHAPTER 10

The economic environment 2: competing economic philosophies

After studying this chapter, students should be able to describe:

- an 'ideal' set of economic circumstances;
- the effects of pulling fiscal and monetary 'levers';
- the broad evolution of economic philosophies;
- the classical economic philosophies of Adam Smith;
- the economic philosophies of John Maynard Keynes;
- the monetarist theories of Milton Friedman.

10.1 A review of economic objectives

The 'Nirvana' scenario

Can you imagine a situation where a government had the national economy exactly as it wanted? Let us look at this ideal 'Nirvana' situation:

- *Interest rates* would be low enough to stimulate industrial investment and consumer spending, but high enough to give savers an acceptable return on their deposits and to support an acceptable exchange rate.
- *Monetary growth rates* would exactly match the rate of inflation.
- *Taxation* levels would be low enough to stimulate investment and consumer spending, but high enough to maintain an acceptable level of public spending.
- *Government spending* would be high enough to provide quality public services, but low enough to enable tax levels to be maintained at acceptable levels.
- *Inflation* would be lower than competitor countries, but high enough to meet the expectations of some stakeholders, such as homebuyers, who like to see the price of their homes appreciating.
- The *foreign exchange value of the currency* would be high enough to avoid excessive costs to importers, but low enough to favour a high level of exports or to necessitate an increase in monetary pressure.
- *Unemployment* would be low enough to obviate the need for government spending on unemployment support, but high enough to enable employers to acquire labour as they needed it.
- The *rate of economic growth* would be high enough to stimulate high levels of business activity, but low enough to offset the threat of inflation.
- The *balance of trade* would be sufficiently in surplus as a result of a high excess of exports over imports, but not so high, so to put too much upward pressure on the foreign exchange value of the currency.
- There would be a sizeable *fiscal surplus*.

We can see that each 'indicator' is finely balanced. Furthermore, as we explore the complex interrelationships between the various factors (see Chapter 9), we can see that a change in any of them precipitates changes in others. The hard fact of economic management is that the 'Nirvana' scenario is impossible. Governments must, it seems, accept some good and some bad at any time in their management of the economy. Any change in the economic environment will have some welcome effects and some unwelcome ones.

Question 10.1

Suggest some advantageous and disadvantageous effects of the following hypothetical changes in economic conditions:

- The Bank of England's Monetary Policy Committee (MPC) announces a cut in interest rates.
- Inflation falls to less than 0.5% a year – the lowest figure ever.
- The pound gains 15% against all other major world currencies.
- The Chancellor announces that value-added tax (VAT) is to be completely scrapped.
- The indirect tax on petrol is trebled.
- Unemployment rises by 25% over the year.
- Britain leaves the European Union (EU).

Pulling economic levers: a summary of causes and effects

We examined the various aspects of macro-economic management in Chapter 9. The senior managers of the economy have two primary economic levers they can 'pull' – the matters of monetary and fiscal policy. Changes in any part of such policies have a 'knock-on' effect in other parts of the economy (Table 10.1).

10.2 A brief history of economic philosophy

Mercantilists

In the sixteenth and seventeenth centuries, *mercantilism* was the name given to the economic philosophy adopted by many merchants and statesmen, which was based upon the belief that a nation's wealth was derived from the accumulation of gold and silver, and that countries without the natural resources of those precious metals could only earn gold and silver by selling more goods than they bought from abroad. The commercial imperatives of this philosophy influenced political leaders to intervene in the market by granting subsidies to help the export of domestic goods, while imposing import tariffs to restrict import trade.

Table 10.1

Effects of pulling monetary and fiscal 'levers'

Lever 'pulled'	Effects of change
Increased monetary pressure	▪ Inflation: downward pressure ▪ Investment: downward pressure ▪ Value of currency: upward pressure ▪ Unemployment: upward pressure ▪ Economic growth: downward pressure
Decreased monetary pressure	▪ Inflation: upward pressure ▪ Investment: upward pressure ▪ Value of currency: downward pressure ▪ Unemployment: downward pressure ▪ Economic growth: upward pressure
Increased fiscal pressure	▪ Inflation: downward pressure ▪ Investment: downward pressure ▪ Public spending: may increase ▪ Unemployment: upward pressure ▪ Economic growth: downward pressure
Decreased fiscal pressure	▪ Inflation: upward pressure ▪ Investment: upward pressure ▪ Public spending: may decrease ▪ Unemployment: upward pressure ▪ Economic growth: downward pressure

Physiocrats

The *Physiocrat* movement in eighteenth century France opposed mercantilist economic philosophy, arguing that it promoted trade at the expense of agriculture. They believed that agriculture was the sole source of wealth and viewed the economy as a circular flow of income and output. The physiocrat philosophy advocated a *laissez-faire* style of government. The term *laissez faire*, French for *let it be*, implies an economic strategy directed by an ideology that business should be 'left alone' as far as possible, to manage itself with government influence only being exerted reluctantly.

The Classical school

Adam Smith (1723–1790)

The Scotsman, *Adam Smith* (1723–1790) has been called 'the father of modern economics'. His now classic work, *An Inquiry into the Nature and Causes of the Wealth of Nations* (shortened to *The Wealth of Nations*), was published in 1776; coincidentally the same year as the initial foundation of the USA. The book, considered a seminal influence on politico-economic systems, was the first major contribution to economics as an intellectual discipline. The book identifies the three factors of production, and the major contributors to a nation's wealth, as land, labour and capital. In Smith's view, the ideal economy is a self-regulating system that automatically satisfies the economic needs of the poor. Smith's philosophy is covered in more detail in Section 10.4 below.

Reverend Thomas R. Malthus (1776–1834)

Arguably one of the most influential works in the study of economics was *Essay on Population*, written by the *Reverend Thomas R. Malthus* (1776–1834) in 1798. This seminal work introduced Malthus' '*Principle of Population*' in which he argued that population tends to increase geometrically while the production of food increase arithmetically (e.g. respectively, 2-4-8-16-32-64, etc. and 2-4-6-8-10-12, etc.). Following this logic population will eventually outstrip the production of food. The force of a rapidly growing population against a limited amount of land would bring diminishing returns to labour and lead to chronically low wages which would seriously depress the standard of living for most of the population. Malthus also challenged the view that a market economy would produce full employment and saw unemployment as direct consequence of too much saving and too little spending in the economy. Malthus based his work on a single country – Great Britain, and was unaware of the impact of the industrial revolution and world-wide developments in food production, and raw materials in addition to advances in birth control. However, while his views (and those of the earlier physiocrats) on overpopulation did not materialise in nineteenth century Britain, they have a certain global resonance in the twenty-first century.

David Ricardo (1772–1823)

David Ricardo (1772–1823) wrote about the distribution of wealth in his *Principles of Political Economy and Taxation*, published in 1817. He described conflict between landowners on one hand and labour and capital on the other. For example, the growth of population and capital pressurises the fixed supply of land, thereby pushing up rents, and depressing profits and wages. Ricardo introduced the concept of *economic rent* which states that: rents are 'price determined' and not 'price determining', and this can be demonstrated with examples of commodities of limited supply, or rarity value, facing increasing demand.

John Stuart Mill (1806–1873)

John Stuart Mill (1806–1873) wrote in his famous book, *Principles of Political Economy*, that the production of wealth is a bitter process that is subject to harsh, unstoppable laws like competition. He defined economics as the practical science of the production and distribution of wealth, and saw a distinct difference between the market's ability to efficiently allocation of resources and its ability to equitably distribute income. Mill was a great believer in the power of competition, yet his ideas helped pave the way towards state intervention on the wide range of issues we recognise today.

The Marginalist school

Marginalist economists emphasised that prices are determined not only by the costs of production but also by the level of demand, which in turn depends upon customer reactions to the goods and services. The marginalist view states that in a free market economy, capital, land and labour (*factors of production*) receive returns equal to their contributions to production. For example, the distribution of income can be justified on the basis that people earn exactly what they or their property contribute to production.

The Marxist school

In the mid-nineteenth century Karl Marx (1818–1883) published *Das Kapital* in which he developed his labour theory of value. This states that a commodity's worth is directly related to the hours of work that have gone into making it, under the normal conditions of production and with the average degree of skill prevalent at the time. Marx contended that value is only created by labour; the worker is entitled to the full fruits of production. However, the workers are denied their fair share of what they produce as the surplus values of rent, interest and profits are stolen from them by the capitalist class. He reckoned that the growth of riches by the capitalist class through the exploitation and increasing impoverishment of the working class masses, and would inevitably lead to revolution and the overthrow of that system. In that sense, Marx saw capitalism as an evolutionary phase in economic development that it would ultimately destroy itself and leave a world free of private property. This has not proved to be the case and the examples of the collapse of communist states in the latter part of the twentieth century would seem to indicate fundamental weaknesses in Marxist economic philosophy.

The Institutionalist school

The Institutionalist school of economic theory regards individual economic behaviour as something that is part of the wider social pattern which is influenced by contemporary lifestyles and values. They are critical of the classical school of thought that indicates that people are primarily motivated by economic self-interest. The institutionalists argue against *laissez-faire* attitudes and maintain that equitable distribution of income requires government controls and social reform.

The Keynesian school

In 1936, John Maynard Keynes published his major work, *The General Theory of Employment, Interest and Money*, in which he contradicts the classical view that in a recession, wages and prices would fall to restore full employment. Keynes argued that infact when people's incomes were depressed by falling prices and wages, it would prevent a revival in spending and only government intervention could revitalise consumer spending. A more detailed account of Keynes' philosophy is presented in Section 10.5, but in broad terms his major contribution to modern economics can be summarised as the need for governments to spend and decrease taxation when private expenditure is insufficient, and likely to lead to recession. Alternatively, if private spending is too high and threatens to boost inflation then government should increase taxation and reduce its spending. To a large extent the Keynesian analytical framework remains at the heart of modern macro-economic analysis.

10.3 Government and economic strategy

Whilst it may be the case that the objectives of economic management remain broadly the same (the 'Nirvana' scenario), governments of different political persuasions do not agree on how to manage the economy to bring about the most favourable outcome. Furthermore, the way that governments have managed the economy has changed over time as different approaches have gone in and out of fashion.

Let us consider a simple example. We saw in Chapter 9 that economic growth is not always as strong as governments would like. Sometimes the rate of growth slows and it can even decrease – a recession. Nobody likes recessions. Unemployment increases therefore DSS (Department of Social Security) spending goes up, tax revenues fall, companies 'go bust', consumers feel 'the pinch' as their disposable incomes decline, and so on. The question is this: how should the government act with regard to economic policy in times of recession? There are a number of possibilities (Table 10.2).

Table 10.2 offers only some of the possibilities open to the Chancellor in times of recession. We can see that each possible action has finely balanced pros and cons, and that any decision made will be both praised and criticised.

Table 10.2

Options in a recession

Action	Advantages	Disadvantages
Do nothing	Saves the bother of worrying about what to do next! Allows a 'natural' development of the economy without government interference.	Government spending and unemployment continue to rise, tax revenues and business confidence continue to fall.
Increase taxes	Offsets the increased spending on unemployment benefits – may avoid or reduce a budget deficit.	May have the effect of making business confidence even lower than it is and of reducing consumers' spending power. Increases unemployment.
Reduce taxes	Stimulate spending and investment. Reduce unemployment.	Inflationary and may bring about a budget deficit.
Increase government spending	Invests in public services, stimulates spending through public sector jobs and projects.	Bound to cause a budget deficit as tax revenues will be falling at the same time. Exert an inflationary pressure.
Reduce interest rates or increase monetary supply	Stimulate spending and investment.	Inflationary and would put downward pressure on the foreign exchange value of the currency.

In practice, economic decisions tend to be made along broadly ideological lines. Politicians tend to have certain underlying beliefs which guide their views on how to manage the economy. In consequence, the economic decisions of any political party in government tend to be relatively predictable, and it is usually possible to trace a common intellectual thread over time.

Traditionally, the divisions in economic philosophy have tended to fall along party political lines. This has been the case in many countries in addition to the UK, a notable example being the changing governments in the USA. Left-of-centre parties, such as the British Labour Party and the Democrats in the USA, have broadly tended to follow one economic philosophy, whilst right-of-centre parties, the UK Conservatives and the USA Republicans, have traditionally adopted a contrary philosophy.

10.4 The 'classical' economic philosophy of Adam Smith

Prof. Adam Smith was born and brought up in the small port of Kirkcaldy, just across the Firth of Forth from Edinburgh. After being educated at the University of Glasgow, Smith held academic positions at Glasgow and Oxford Universities as well as carrying out some work abroad. His contemporaries regarded Smith primarily as a political philosopher, and his early writings were in that area. His first major work, *The Theory of Moral Sentiments*, published in 1759, was essentially a philosophical work.

Smith's economic philosophy

Arising from his earlier work, *The Wealth of Nations* set out Smith's economic theories. Although he was not primarily an economist (one could argue that economics was not defined as an academic discipline prior to Smith), his penetrating and incisive analysis of economic systems in the book has been applauded by countless observers since its initial publication.

The 'invisible hand'

According to Smith, macro-economic systems work best when the individuals and businesses in the economy are allowed to behave according to their own economic best interest. In other words, individuals behave in a way that they believe will bring them the greatest personal wealth, thus increasing their quality of life. If we wish to increase our quality of life, we spend our income to benefit from the goods and services which offer us the best value for money and utility. The collective actions of many such people acting on the same level of self-interest will, Smith argues, ultimately benefit everybody by creating a buoyant economy.

To explain how this works, he put forward his theory of the 'invisible hand'. In a market economy – one in which the government plays only a minimal role – individuals are guided by an invisible hand in pursuing their own self-interest, which, when taken together, leads to the benefit of the economy as a whole:

consumers act in own best interest $\rightarrow$ optimal performance of the total economy.

The invisible hand is a mechanism which links individual economic decisions and the aggregate benefit derived from them. Each of a consumer's decisions is led by the invisible hand which 'mystically' acts to maximise the wealth of the macro-economy as a whole.

The invisible hand idea does not guarantee an equal distribution of wealth or income. It acknowledges that some will be better-off than others. Rather, it states that *given* a nation's social and political conditions, and its relative wealth of resources (financial, material and human), the invisible hand will guarantee an optimal economic well-being of the citizens as a whole.

Smith's assumptions

A key underlying assumption of classical economics is that economic systems work entirely freely. They are not in any way impeded or skewed by government interference; in short, it assumes market economy conditions. It follows that any government interference will in some way undermine or distort the market mechanism, and hence render the nation's wealth sub-optimal. Classicists argue, for example, that government attempts to redistribute wealth in an economy, by 'robbing the rich to give to the poor' or by subsidising certain industries, ultimately work to the disadvantage of the total economy. In markets where demand exceeds supply, prices must be allowed to rise to equilibrium notwithstanding any perceived inequalities of the price rise decision. All changes in market conditions must be allowed to rapidly readjust without government involvement to maintain the efficiency of each market in the economy.

Classical economics in different markets

Classical economics can apply to all parts of the economy, not just the markets for goods and services. The same principles apply in the markets for financial assets and for labour. In the same way that the price for goods and services can rise or fall in line with changing conditions of demand and supply, so can the price of money and the price of labour. Lenders of money are free to increase or decrease their rate of interest on loans in line with the effective demand for loans. The more controversial point is that wage rates, along with prices, can fall as well as rise to meet equilibrium market conditions. Furthermore, just as we might expect the prices of money and goods to respond rapidly to changes in demand, the same is true of labour.

Wage and price flexibility is crucial to the invisible hand concept. It must be possible for wages and prices to be infinitely variable as the forces of demand and supply drive them up and down. Measures such as a statutory minimum wage or interest rate ceilings would undermine the invisible hand's operation. In a market with perfect information, price changes would be brought about as soon as there is a change in the equilibrium; that is, it would readjust immediately. In practice, there is necessarily a time-lag as the market adjusts to new economic circumstances.

Neo-classical economics

A softening of the classical approach

Since Adam Smith's initial theories were published, his ideas have been developed and refined as the macro-economic situation has changed over the years. Whilst the theory has been developing, all classical and neo-classical economists have held two doctrines as axiomatic:

- that people do and should pursue their economic self-interest;
- that market prices will adjust reasonably quickly to balance quantities supplied and demanded.

There has been some dilution of Smith's 'pure theory' in order to accommodate the complexities of the political environment. It is simply impractical, given the powerful stakeholder coalitions in most democracies, to have literally no government involvement in the workings of an economy; so much of the debate has centred on *how much* involvement there should be. Neo-classicists argue that whilst some government involvement may be necessary (say to redistribute a small percentage of the wealth to obviate extremes of poverty); it should be kept to an absolute minimum.

The *'laissez-faire'* school

In recent years, this neo-classical approach to macro-economic management has been dubbed the *laissez-faire* approach. The prominent political proponent of this idea in the 1980s was Prime Minister Margaret Thatcher, strongly influenced by her close political allies, Sir Keith Joseph and Enoch Powell. The politico-economic doctrines which became known as *Thatcherism* are primarily characterised by a neo-classical economic approach to the management of the economy. In the USA, President Ronald Reagan also employed a *laissez-faire* approach to a lesser extent. However, the macro-economy in both of these countries already had a sizeable public sector, so the objective of those latter-day neo-classical economics was to reduce as far as possible the influence of the state over commercial activity.

Traditionally, the neo-classical economic philosophy has been embraced by right-of-centre political parties. The British Conservative Party, for example, has had a number of policies which clearly mark it out as broadly neo-classicist. Its underlying view is that the tax levels should be reduced and its huge privatisation programme of the 1980s is testimony to this. While in opposition during the years of the Thatcher Conservative government, the Labour Party (a left-of-centre party) strongly criticised those particular Conservative policies, and whilst some of its opposition can be put down to the fact that it is constitutionally bound to oppose the government, the underlying reason is that left-of-centre parties traditionally espouse a contrary economic philosophy to neo-classicism (Keynesianism, see Section 10.5), one which favours relatively more government influence.

However, when the Labour Party, under Tony Blair's leadership (and its re-branded image of *New Labour*) became the government following the 1997 election, there was no reversal of the privatisation programme. Nor did income tax dramatically rise, although the level of indirect taxation did significantly rise. Also, as we saw in Chapter 9 one of the Labour government's first major economic decisions was to pass control of interest rates to the Bank of England, with the prime aim of controlling inflationary pressures – the rationale being to distance political ideology from sound and prudent economic management. We therefore find that the Labour government, with Tony Blair as Prime Minister and Gordon Brown as Chancellor of the Exchequer, provides an interesting mix of economic philosophies and policies worthy of study.

Classical economics and business cycles

In Chapter 9, we examined the effects of cycles upon business activity and consumer spending. The fact that economic downturns are an unpleasant experience for all parts of the economy might tempt us to think that government should take any measures possible to reduce the impact of recession. Classical economists say that even when recessions occur, governments should not be tempted to intervene.

Recessions, according to classicists, are times of readjustment in demand, supply and prices in an economy. They can be seen as an opportunity for the economy to lose uncompetitive companies and to gain efficiency by shedding surplus labour along with other superfluous costs. Such a process of 'purging the dross' ultimately strengthens a country's economy. Downward troughs in an economic cycle also serve to defeat inflation, as the downward pressure on wages and prices takes effect.

Criticisms of classical economics

Most economists agree, even non-classicists, that Smith's economic theories can work-in theory. The problems with it have mainly arisen because of the political restrictions on an economy, preventing businesses and consumers from trading in true market economy conditions. Classicists would argue that if a classical economic system is allowed to run its course, it would eventually benefit almost everybody in society. However, some stakeholders have prevented this from happening owing to their contrary economic and political persuasions. This section is concerned with the criticisms of Smith and the reasons why it has broadly failed to be implemented in a true market economy setting.

It overlooks the necessity of a state sector

The social and political changes that have taken place since the work of Adam Smith have signalled significant changes in citizens' expectations. It is broadly assumed, across the political spectrum, that certain public and merit goods are not only desirable, but necessary. Such things include the state provision of national defences, education, health services and many others. The costs of such services necessitate the state making tax demands of individuals and businesses. Furthermore, direct state influence on business, through such things as grants and indirect taxes, have further moved the economy away from a market situation to mixed economy status.

It ignores inequalities in society

Classical economics is an economic theory. It is used by politicians, but it cannot be said to be a politico-economic theory *per se*. In consequence, it has been modified by neo-classicists to include the main elements, but with many concessions made to make it more politically palatable. Critics have said that Smith's ideas are unworkable and even uncaring because they offer no direct solution to economic inequality. Smith, writing in 1776, was doubtless used to seeing a great deal of poverty in society but assumed that by the country as a whole growing richer, the poor would indirectly benefit through increased employment, etc.

Political sensitivities bear upon this issue in the present day. When the Conservative government privatised the utilities in the 1980s – a gesture underpinned by a neo-classical economic ideology – it was criticised by the opposition parties owing to the perceived risks of the removal of price protections enjoyed by the less economically fortunate. The government sought to address this criticism by appointing regulators (see Chapter 19). One of the roles of the utilities' regulators is to determine pricing levels such that competition is encouraged and pricing is 'fair'.

It underestimates the time-lag in price and wage adjustment

The limitations on the speed of information travel means that a change in the state of supply or demand is not immediately disseminated to all players in any given market. Whereas in a perfect market, price and wage adjustments would be immediate, the imperfections in markets usually mean that a time-lag occurs between a change in supply and demand, and the concomitant price adjustment.

Question 10.2

How effective is the use the bank base rate mechanism been as the major weapon against inflation?

10.5 The economic philosophy of John Maynard Keynes

Who was Prof. Keynes?

If it has ever been suggested that academics are closeted in their ivory towers with no influence on the real world, then the lifework on Keynes (usually pronounced 'kanes') is testimony to the fact that one man's work can significantly influence the economic activity of two entire First World continents for a generation. His economic doctrines were not only highly influential; they were practised for over 40 years in the world's major economies.

Prof. John Maynard Keynes (1883–1946) was an Englishman and a Cambridge academic. He set out his economic ideas most clearly in his noted work, *The General Theory of Employment, Interest and Money*, first published in 1936 – one of several books which Keynes published. The point at which his seminal book was written is salient to its contents – after the experience of the First World War which was immensely costly in both human and monetary terms, and in the middle of the Great Depression – a time of great economic slow-down when national unemployment reached around 20% of the working population.

In addition to his academic writings, Keynes also acted as an important advisor to several politico-economic initiatives. His economic projections were used by the UK Government in both First and Second World Wars, but his most notable 'non-academic' achievement was probably his input to the *Bretton Woods* conference on international *exchange rates* in 1944. As well as having a profound influence on the world's exchange rate systems, the Bretton Woods conference also established the *World Bank* and the *International Monetary Fund* (IMF). His well-publicised membership of the esoteric '*Bloomsbury group*' in the 1920s and 1930s brought him into close contact with some of the most notable artists and philosophers of his day.

His economic doctrines were not considered by governments when his *General Theory* was first published. After the Second World War, his ideas came to the fore and were, for almost 40 years, considered to be almost axiomatic.

Keynes' economic doctrines

Keynes' economic ideology (termed *Keynesianism*) is in stark contrast to the classical doctrine of Adam Smith. Whereas Smith argued that government should adopt a 'hands-off' approach with regard to economic regulation, the very essence of Keynesianism is a belief that the government has a crucial role to play in the management and regulation of the macro-economy.

It is probable that uppermost in Keynes' mind, in writing *The General Theory*, was the economic problems facing the country in the Great Depression. Seeing the misery caused by the severe downturn in an economic cycle, he proposed that rather than allowing markets to rule the economy, with its unpleasant effects in times of recession, the government should adopt a much greater role in its management. Whilst the primary purpose of government influence should be to reduce the intensity of economic downturns, Keynes continued in *The General Theory* to describe a much wider economic philosophy embracing all aspects of macro-economics.

Keynes recognised that one of Smith's most important assumptions, namely, that wages and prices respond rapidly to changes in supply and demand, is not usually the case in imperfect markets. He contended that it is simply a fact that there would be long periods of time when prices and wages would be out of equilibrium with actual market conditions. Hence, whereas a downturn in the demand for labour ought to signal a reduction in the price of labour (lower wages), the existence of unemployment was testimony to the fact that labour was overpriced – a disequilibrium. If demand for labour falls but its price remains the same, it is inevitable that unemployment will result. The same is true of the prices of goods and services – time-lags between changes in supply and demand, and the response of the market price rendered Smith's theories, in the opinion of Keynes, unworkable.

The problem of unemployment

According to Keynes, unemployment was a double evil. It had two highly negative effects:

- it was a source of great misery to its sufferers;
- it significantly reduced the spending power (and hence the total level of demand) in the economy.

So not only is unemployment bad for the individual, but a high rate of unemployment is bad for the economy because unemployed people do not have the spending power necessary to maintain a buoyant economy. In times of recession, unemployment is also one of the main features which holds an economy back from recovery.

Keynes argued that if unemployment could be held to a minimum or even eliminated, then the result would be a robust economy with continually high spending power, which in turn would benefit the citizens.

The Keynesian role of the government

According to Keynes, a classical economic approach could not guarantee a high level of employment. On the contrary, in a classical system, unemployment is likely to fluctuate in sympathy with wages and prices as market prices continually change according to market forces. Prof. Keynes argued that due to its sheer size and its huge spending power, the state should use its economic muscle to maintain employment and hence aggregate spending power.

When an economic cycle was in a 'boom' unemployment would be naturally low and hence the state need only assume a supervisory or 'back-seat' role. However, at the point at which the economy begins to show signs of slow-down in preparation for a recession, the government should increase its spending to maintain a high aggregate level of demand in the economy. This may take the form of such things as capital investments (such as road building) or revenue expenditures (such as increased industrial grants or procurement; say of ships or equipment for the health service).

By maintaining demand in the economy, employers would have no need to shed labour. No upturn in unemployment means no reduction in spending power. No reduction in spending power means no recession.

Astute readers will have realised that increased government spending has obvious implications for the budget situation and fiscal policy. A feature of Keynesianism is a belief that short-term fiscal deficits brought about by spending to obviate recessions would soon be repaid by revenues from taxes from individuals and businesses benefiting from the avoidance of recession.

Criticisms of Keynesianism

Like classical economics, Keynesianism has its critics. Economists have the advantage, in assessing this philosophy, of having seen it in action. This gives the opportunity of seeing how the economy responds, over the longer term, when Keynesian principles are applied. The criticisms centre around the implications of Keynesianism for inflation and for the long-term competitiveness of the economy, once it has been practised for some period of time.

It sees unemployment as the pre-eminent economic indicator

Critics argue that the Keynesian focus on unemployment as the major determinant of demand is too simplistic. The effects of high levels of unemployment upon other economic indicators are significant. Working in 1958, 20 years after the publication of *The General Theory*, A.W. Phillips discovered that there was an inverse relationship between unemployment and inflation over a longer time period. In other words:

- the lower the rate of unemployment, the higher the inflationary pressures;
- the higher the rate of unemployment, the lower the inflationary pressures.

It follows from Phillips' work, that the price of high or full employment may be high inflation. Similarly, low or reducing unemployment will usually be deflationary.

According to the Phillips curve, a level of employment to the left of the point at which the line intersects the zero inflation line will be inflationary. Unemployment can be set at a point at which there will be no inflationary pressure in the economy and a figure of unemployment to the right of the intersection will actually be deflationary.

Critics of Keynesianism argue from Phillips' work that maintaining employment at high levels regardless of other conditions in the economy will precipitate inflation. The question then must be asked, 'Which is worse, high inflation resulting from low unemployment, or a recession resulting from a fall in aggregate demand?' This question is something of an imponderable and arguably rests in the purview of politicians rather than economists.

It discourages competition and thus acts against competitiveness

Critics of Keynesianism believe that a high level of government intervention in the economy prevents markets from operating efficiently.

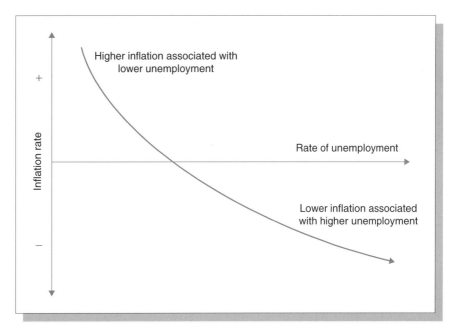

Higher inflation associated with
lower unemployment

+

Inflation rate

Rate of unemployment

Lower inflation associated
with higher unemployment

−

Figure 10.1
The Phillips curve.

In order to maintain employment in the economy, it may be the case that the government 'bails out' a large employer which would otherwise become insolvent and close. The effect of such support over time is an economy comprising many inefficient businesses which could not effectively compete were it not for government assistance. Such a state of affairs does not encourage increased efficiency, and may even positively encourage complacency and wasteful bureaucracy.

Similarly, whereas classical economists see recessions as a vehicle for disposing of uncompetitive competitors, a Keynesian system which minimises the effects of economic downturns would not facilitate the demise of such businesses. Such a short-termist approach measure, say the critics, makes for an inefficient business sector.

It increases the size of government

There is something of a debate amongst politicians and economists about how much of a nation's wealth the government should account for. The UK is typical of most western nations, whose state sector accounts for around 45% of national wealth.

In order to have the financial ability to influence the economy through Keynesian policies, the state sector must be at least a certain size. Consequently, governments which have exercised a Keynesian approach over a period of time tend to be larger than otherwise. Ofcourse, this is a predictable criticism of Keynesianism by classicists.

In the opinion of some, the ideal is to have a small state sector which allows businesses to operate with a minimum of state 'interference'. In order to have the financial 'clout' to be able to spend to obviate recession, the state must levy sufficient in tax and other revenue earners and, accordingly, exert its influence through spending.

This issue is a matter of intense political debate. The political right wing tends to contend that government should be smaller in order to pursue a neo-classical economic philosophy while the left argued that the state has a responsibility to maintain a certain level of spending in order to provide services and influence. Rather than stating such objectives explicitly, the underlying economic persuasion is often shown up by proposed policies, such as 'less government' or 'improved social services', respectively.

Question 10.3

What is meant by full employment?

10.6 The economic philosophy of Milton Friedman

Who is Prof. Friedman?

Milton Friedman (1912) was probably the most influential economist of the latter third of the twentieth century. His ideas began to assume greater prominence among academics and politicians after Keynesianism began to be questioned with its apparent inflationary effects. He was appointed Professor of Economics at the University of Chicago, Illinois in 1946. His published works have reflected his *laissez-faire* approach to economic theory. In *Capitalism and Freedom* (1962), Friedman argued for the decentralisation and replacement of traditional welfare services. Other books have expatiated his theories of monetarism, such as *A Monetary History of the United States 1867–1960* (1963) and *Monetary Trends of the United States and the United Kingdom* (1981). Prof. Friedman led the economic research of what became known as the '*Chicago school*' of economic thought and was awarded the Nobel Prize for economics in 1976.

Friedman's economic doctrines

Monetarism

Friedman's major contribution to economic thought was through his development of what has become known as *monetarism* or 'new classical' economics. He and his colleagues at the University of Chicago, working from the 1950s onwards, concluded that economic management should be primarily geared to the control of inflation. Having had the benefit of observing Keynesianism in action for some years, the monetarists believed that the fiscal management which characterises Keynes' philosophy were not only inflationary but acted against the best long-term interests of the economy.

The essence of monetarism is a belief that the best way to regulate the economy is by the careful use of monetary rather than fiscal instruments, particularly the use of monetary supply as a means of controlling inflation. In practice, such an emphasis is coupled with a belief that the state should assume a less influential role with regard to its fiscal policy (i.e. that it should adopt a *laissez-faire* approach). According to most monetarists, economic management should be 'hands-off' except for a minimal influence in order to implement monetary policy. In this respect, monetarists eschew Keynes and his 'big government' notions, preferring instead to identify with a neo-classical approach.

The quantity theory of money

The intellectual basis of monetarism goes back to an economic formula first put forward early in the twentieth century. Known as the *quantity theory of money*, it is expressed as follows:

$$MV = PQ$$

where, M is the rate of monetary growth (i.e. the *nominal money supply*), V is the velocity of circulation of money in the economy, P is the price of goods and services, Q is the total quantity of goods and services sold in the economy.

Put simply, this theory shows a direct causal relationship between the rate of monetary growth (M) and the price of goods and services (P; the growth in which is inflation). It follows from this relationship that a restriction in the rate of monetary growth should enable inflation to be controlled, with all the benefits that low inflation affords. If, for example, the government or central bank (whichever has the responsibility for monetary policy) wishes to limit the annual rate of inflation to 3%, then it should restrict the main indicators of monetary growth to approximately the same figure. For M0 (see Chapter 9), this restriction is straightforward as cash minting and printing can be controlled directly. For other elements of monetary growth, for example, bank deposits and loans, monetary measures such as the varying of interest rates can be used to restrict the money supply.

The monetarists' use of this theory led to them being labelled, quite reasonably, as 'neo-quantity theorists'.

Assumptions of the quantity theory

In order for monetary growth to be used as a means of controlling inflation, two important assumptions must be made. Both are linked to the mathematical form of the equation itself. The first assumption is that the velocity of circulation (V) is relatively constant notwithstanding any changes in the money supply. The second is that the aggregate quantity of goods and services produced by an economy (Q) will not expand in sympathy with any increases in prices. The importance of these assumptions can be shown by rearranging the equation.

If $MV = PQ$, then it follows that (by simple rearrangement):

$$P = \frac{MV}{Q}$$

or

$$P = \frac{V}{Q} \times M.$$

If we wish to control the growth in P (inflation) by varying M, then there should be no (or almost no) change in V or Q; that is, they must, together, form a constant. If the term V/Q can be shown to be constant, then we can say that:

$$P \propto M$$

or

$$P = kM$$

where k is constant and equals V/Q.

The quantity theory of money no longer holds if either *V* or *Q* varies when there is a change in either of the other two (*P* or *M*). Economist *Michael Stewart* discusses these assumptions as follows:

> 'What the quantity theory does is to assert a particular causal relationship. Put crudely, it says that *V* does not change very much (or changes in a steady and predictable way), and therefore there is a close correlation between *M* and *PQ*; and that it is changes in *M* that causes changes in *PQ*, and not the other way round.'
>
> He continues, ... the fact that increases in *M* generate increases in *PQ* is not the end of the matter: the question now arises of how far the increase in *PQ* takes the form of an increase in *P*, and how far of *Q*. In other words, how far does an increase in the money supply lead to a rise in output [Q], and how far does it simply lead to a rise in prices? At its very simplest, the monetarist theory says that it cannot lead to a rise in output because the normal condition of the economy is one of full utilization of resources and hence maximum output; therefore it simply leads to a rise in prices.[1]
>
> *Source*: Reproduced with the permission of Penguin Books Ltd.

Hence, the monetarist theory rests upon the assumptions that velocity of circulation adapts slowly and predictably, and that the economy is operating at more-or-less full capacity (thus eliminating the possibility of a rapid change in *Q*). In some circumstances, these assumptions hold true, but in others (such as when there is spare manufacturing capacity in the economy), circumstances are less predictable.

Monetarism and unemployment

Like the classicists, monetarists believe in the idea of a self-regulating economy. This means that if left alone (except for the implementation of monetary policy), wages and prices will adjust to find their natural equilibrium. Hence, when all wages are in equilibrium, supply balances demand in the labour market and there will be what the monetarists term a *natural rate* of unemployment. The monetarists' natural rate is quite different from Keynes' notion of full unemployment. Monetarists accept that when supply in the labour market exceeds demand, and wages consequently fall, some people will prefer not to work, believing their labour to be worth more than the low wages on offer. This, in a sense, is voluntary unemployment as potential workers elect not to work, considering the wages on offer to be unworthy of their time and effort.

Whilst such a natural level is unfortunate if historically high, the government should not be tempted to intervene to reduce unemployment by 'artificially' increasing wages (such as by the imposition of a statutory minimum wage). Such interference would lead to inflation – the very thing that a government is trying to purge from the economy.

Governments which have pursued monetary policy have attempted to reduce unemployment by effectively making it as unpleasant as possible. By reducing the level of unemployment benefit and state support, the motivation to accept a job on low wages is increased. Reductions in unemployment benefits thus meet two economic objectives in concurrence with monetarist theory: to encourage people to accept work and as part of a neo-classical wish to minimise state influence.

Assignment 10.1

1 Select one of these former utilities:
   - Telecommunications
   - Gas
   - Water
   - Electricity.
   and conduct research that will help you answer these questions:
   - How much money did the government receive from the privatisation floatation?
   - How did the government claim to use the cash raised?
   - What has been the impact of the size of the workforce?
   - How has its structure changed (if at all)?
   - Who are the competitors in its sector?
   - Why did the Labour government not re-nationalise the company?
2 Monetarist theorists argue that government imposition of a statutory minimum wage would stimulate inflation and subsequently lead to increased unemployment levels. Discuss the actual impact on the UK economy since the implementation of the *National Minimum Wage Act 1998*.

Reference

1   Stewart, M. (1991). *Keynes and After (Penguin Economics)*, 3rd edn. London: Penguin Books Limited.

Further reading

Aspromourgos, T. (1995). *On the Origins of Classical Economics.* London: Routledge.

Begg, D., *et al.* (2002). *Economics,* 7th edn. London: McGraw Hill.

Friedman, M. (2002). *Capitalism and Freedom.* USA: University of Chicago Press.

Kenway, P. (1993). *From Keynesianism to Monetarism. The Evolution of UK Macroeconomic Models.* London: Routledge.

Keynes, J.M. (1997). *The General Theory of Employment, Interest, & Money.* London: Prometheus Books, UK.

Laidler, D. (1991). *The Golden Age of the Quantity Theory.* Princeton, NJ: Princeton University Press.

Malthus, T. (2002). *Essay on the Principle of Population.* Washington: Indypublish.com

Marx, K. and Engels, F. (ed.) (1999). *Das Kapital,* New edition. London: Gateway Editions.

Mill, J.S. and Sher, G. (ed.) (2001). *Utilitarianism,* 2nd edn. New York: Hackett Publishing Co Inc.

Moggridge, D.E. (1995). *Maynard Keynes. An Economist's Biography.* London: Routledge.

Riccardo, D. (1996). *Principles of Political Economy and Taxation.* London: Prometheus Book, UK.

Rider, C. (1995). *An Introduction to Economic History.* London: Thomson Publishing.

Smith, A. (1982). *An Inquiry into the Nature & Causes of the Wealth of Nations,* vols 1 and 2. Indianaplois, IN: Liberty Fund.

Smith, A. (1984). *The Theory of Moral Sentiments.* Indianapolis, IN: Liberty Fund.

Smith, A. (2003). *The Wealth of Nations.* London: Bantam Classics.

Stewart, M. (1991). *Keynes and After (Penguin Economics),* 3rd edn. London: Penguin Books Limited.

Useful web sites

Office for National Statistics: www.statistics.gov.uk
UK Governments' departments: www.gateway.gov.uk
The Economist: www.economist.com
The Financial Times: www.ft.com

CHAPTER 11

The sociological environment

Learning objectives

After studying this chapter, students should be able to describe:

- the nature of the sociological environment;
- the nature of demography and how it can affect organisations;
- the relationship between education and organisation skill requirements;
- the changing patterns of employment;
- the impact of societal values, attitudes and behaviours;
- the fashions and trends in opinion and preferences that can affect organisations.

11.1 What is the sociological environment?

In one sense, sociological influence on an organisation can come from any internal or external source involving *people*. This clearly includes a wide variety of possible stakeholder influences, such as customers, employees, suppliers, opinion leaders and trade unions.

The sociological environmental presents two important facets which are relevant to business:

- the features of the population, including its size, distribution, composition and changes (demography);
- the opinions, beliefs, cultural norms and preferences of the population.

We will examine these two components in turn.

11.2 Demography

What is demography?

Demography is the study of human population dynamics. The scope of the subject includes:

- the size of the population in the country (or a region) as a whole;
- growth or decline in the population (birth and death rates);
- the composition of the population by geographic location and distribution;
- the composition of the population by skill and education level;
- the composition of the population by concentration and density;
- the composition of the population by age and gender profile;
- the composition of population by its economic activity (e.g. the size and structure of the working population);
- changes in the population distribution by migration.

Why is demography important to business?

The size, composition and distribution of the population are not just a matter of academic interest. Businesses take account of demography in a number of areas of activity. Its importance is linked to both the demand and supply sides of the market 'equation'.

On the demand side, demography informs a business as to how it should organise its location or the distribution of its products. A business is more likely to locate its distribution outlets where there is a high concentration of the key segment of its market. We examined the factors that inform business location in Chapter 6 when we learned that for some businesses, the concentration of specific types of people is the key determinant of where business is set up. For retail outlets (shops), for example, the number of 'targeted' people (i.e. those within the market segment boundaries, see Chapter 28) within convenient travelling distance of the shop is of prime importance to the success or failure of the business.

On the supply side, an organisation will take account of demography in its access to key inputs. Perhaps the most obvious input in this regard is that of the supply of labour. All businesses must be aware of demography in their search for appropriate labour. One of the key reasons, for example, why motorcar manufacturers establish their sites around large centres of population is due to their need for several thousand employees of all types of skill. Clearly, such a demand for labour could not be so easily met in a rural area of lower population density.

Population

'Population' simply refers to the number of people that inhabit a given geographic area. In terms of global demography, the world's total population has shown a significant increase.

Total world population is estimated to have been around 300 million in the year 1000 AD. Between the turn of the first millennium AD and the beginning of the industrial revolution in 1750, it grew relatively slowly to 728 million. Changes in migration, bringing about areas of high demographic concentration since then, have precipitated a significant acceleration in population growth. For example, by 1900 the world population had grown to an estimated 978 million, accelerating to 3000 million (3 billion) by 1962 and reaching 6.1 billion by 2001. Forecasts by the United Nations indicate that the world's population will reach 8.5 billion by the year 2025. Such a marked population increase has given rise to the coining of the phrase 'population explosion'. The concerns associated with such a population explosion include worries about food supply, the implications for the redistribution of wealth and the potential effects on the environment (see Malthus in Chapter 10).

In contrast to the rapid increase in the population as a whole, the populations in most of the world's wealthiest countries have remained relatively manageable. This means that the key areas of growth are the poorer and less-developed regions like Africa, India, South and Central America (the Third World). In any country, the determinant of population growth is the disparity between the birth and death rates. In developed countries, the death rate has fallen with advances in such things as medical knowledge and healthier living conditions. However, stable population is more or less maintained because the number of births per year has also fallen as couples have greater access to contraception, are less concerned about infant mortality and more certain of prosperity in old age.

The UK population increased by some 65%, from 38.2 million in 1901 to 58.8 million in 2001.[1] However, the rate of growth has slowed over time, with the period between 1951 and 2001 showing an overall growth of just 17%, which is much smaller than the population growth averages for many other developed countries. For example, over the same period the average growth for European Union (EU) Europe was 23% while the USA and Australia recorded average growths of 80% and 133%, respectively,[2] where there are considerable migration influences.

The rate of increase has slowed over time and the population is actually expected to begin to decline mid-way through the twenty-first century (Figure 11.1).

In every year since 1901, with the exception of 1976, there have been more births than deaths in the UK and this natural change is one of the two main components that determine population size and change, the other being migration.

The projected population of the UK, for each of the decades from 2001 to 2051 is shown in more detail in Table 11.1.

The twentieth century has witnessed some quite marked annual fluctuations in the number of births in the UK; the highest number of 1.1 million was recorded for 1920 while 1970 recorded the lowest number of 657,000. The 1930s saw the UK experience a severe economic downturn (the 'depression'), followed by the Second World War (1939–1945) and the subsequent years, till around 1950, showed a marked downturn in the birth rate – which is defined as the number of live births per thousand

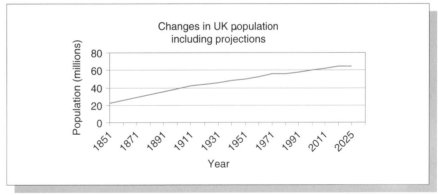

Figure 11.1
Changes in the UK population including 2000-based projections for 2011–2025. (*Source*: Office for National Statistics.)

Table 11.1
Projected population (thousands) of the UK and constituent countries 2001–2051

Years	2001	2011	2021	2031	2041	2051
UK	58,837	60,524	62,386	63,656	63,922	63,672
England	49,181	50,859	52,725	54,140	54,735	–
Scotland	5064	4983	4895	4735	4484	–
Wales	2903	2947	2997	3012	2980	–
Northern Ireland	1689	1735	1769	1768	1723	–

Source: National Statistics Population Trends, Winter 2002, No. 110.

of the population. Rising prosperity throughout the 1960s signalled a significant rise in what has become known as the 'baby boom' before falling away again in the 1970s. Interestingly, the 1960s 'baby boom' produced more females than males and can be correlated with the slight increase in the number of births in the 1980s and 1990s.

There was no significant trend in the number of UK deaths in the first half of the twentieth century, although there were evident annual increases at the time of the two world wars, and the significant peak of 715,200 deaths in 1918, at the time of an influenza pandemic. From the 1950s we can see smaller fluctuations and a slight rise in the number of deaths per year until a peak of 675,600 in 1979 when numbers started to fall. This decline is projected to gradually halt in the early 2010s (Figure 11.2).[3]

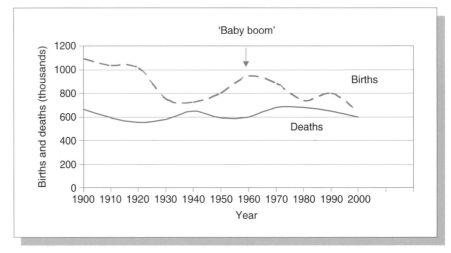

Figure 11.2
Births and deaths in the UK. (*Source*: National Office for Statistics.)

It should be noted that almost 60% of the projected 4.3 million increase shown in Table 11.1 is attributable to the assumed level of net inward migration. The remainder is due to a projected natural increase (i.e. more births than deaths) as can be seen in Table 11.2, which details the projected components of UK population change, for each of the 5-year period from 2001 to 2026.

The projected trends in births and deaths mean that the UK population can be expected to experience natural decline from the 2030s onwards. However, according to the projected migration, the size of the UK population is not expected to decrease until the second half of the twenty-first century.

Question 11.1

Suggest reasons why the birth and death rates have declined in the UK.

Table 11.2
Projected components of UK population change (thousands), 2001–2026
(annual averages)

Years	2001–2006	2006–2011	2011–2016	2016–2021	2021–2026
Population at start of period (thousands)	58,837	59,657	60,524	61,459	62,386
Live births (thousands)	675	683	698	709	705
Deaths (thousands)	613	609	611	624	651
Net natural change (thousands)	62	73	87	85	54
Net migration (thousands)	102	100	100	100	100
Overall change (thousands)	164	173	187	185	154
Population at end of period (thousands)	59,657	60,524	61,459	62,386	63,156

Source: National Statistics Population Trends, Winter 2002, No. 110.

Age distribution of the UK population

In the past 50 years, the decline in birth and death rates (defined as the number per thousand in a given year) has seen a considerable ageing of the UK population. For example, over the period the proportion of the population aged less than 16 years has decreased from 24% to 20% while the population aged 60 years and over has increased from 16% to 21%. The ageing of the population reflects longer life expectancy, and the average (mean) age is expected to rise from 39.1 years in 2001 to 42.4 years of age in 2026 (Figure 11.3).[2] Behind these statistics lie some interesting facts:

- Life expectancy at birth, based on the mortality rates at 2001, is expected to rise from 75 to 79 years in 2026 for men and from 80 to 83 years for women. Also, the number of people over 75 years of age is expected to increase from about 4.4 million in 2001 to 8.3 million by 2040.
- For the first time in history, by 2001, people over the age of 60 years (21%) formed a larger part of the population than people under 16 years of age.
- In terms of population ratio, males in the UK outnumbered females until the late 1940s, after which females became the majority. There are fewer males than females at all ages over 21 years (Table 11.3).

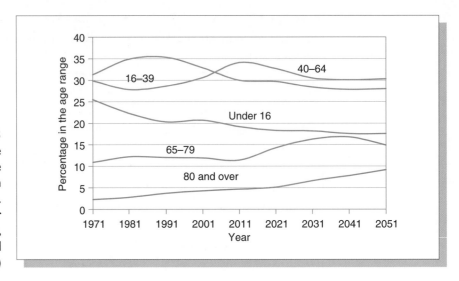

Figure 11.3
Age range
distribution of the
UK population
(1971–2051).
(*Source*: Office for
National Statistics,
Census 2000-based
projections.)

Table 11.3

UK population by age and gender (annual percentages)

	Under 16	16–24	25–34	35–44	45–54	55–64	65–74	75+
Males								
1901	34	20	16	12	9	6	3	1
1931	26	18	16	13	12	9	5	2
1961	25	14	13	14	14	11	6	3
1991	21	14	16	14	12	10	8	5
2000	21	11	16	16	13	10	8	5
2011	18	12	13	15	15	12	9	6
2025	18	10	13	13	13	14	10	9
Females								
1901	31	20	16	12	9	6	4	2
1931	23	17	16	14	12	9	6	2
1961	22	13	12	13	14	12	9	5
1991	19	12	15	13	11	10	9	9
2000	19	10	14	15	13	10	9	9
2011	17	11	12	14	14	12	9	9
2025	17	10	13	13	12	14	11	11

Source: Office for National Statistics.

These trends have a number of implications including some important ones for the state. The disparities that are forecast between these age groups indicate that the numbers available to take part in the workforce may fall whilst the numbers of older people will increase. The number of people of state pensionable age, at 2004, is projected to increase from 10.8 to 12 million by 2011 before easing to a gentler rate of increase to 12.2 million by 2021. However, a faster increase is then likely to resume with longer-term projections suggesting the number of people of pensionable age reaching a peak of 15 million around 2040.[2]

This is expected to become a significant problem as the older population will require more health care and pensions whilst those available to pay for these provisions through tax will become fewer – one reason why the government may have to take these provisions outside the public sector.

Population density

The population density refers to the number of inhabitants per unit area of land (usually expressed in *persons per square kilometre*). In more common parlance, this means how 'tightly' people are packed together. We can analyse this both across the different parts of the UK and by comparing the UK with other countries (Table 11.4).

The UK itself has a very wide distribution of population by density, with an overall average of about 250 people per kilometre. This average

Table 11.4
Population densities of selected EU countries[4]

Country	Population density (persons per square kilometre)
UK	239
Germany	235
France	108
Belgium	337
The Netherlands	464
Ireland	52
Finland	17
EU average	117

Source: World population profile, 1998.

conceals very broad disparities as the four UK countries have quite distinctive density profiles (Figure 11.4). Scotland is the least densely populated with 65 people resident per square kilometre; next comes Northern Ireland with 125; then Wales with 141 and England with 380. Indeed, nearly 84% of the total UK population lives in England.

Figure 11.4
Population density in the UK. (*Source*: Office for National Statistics, General Register for Scotland, Northern Ireland Statistics and Research Agency.)

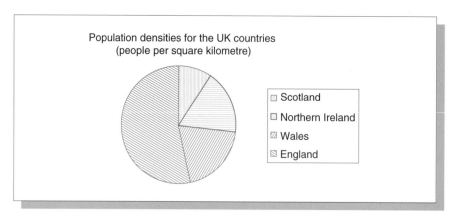

A closer examination of the national averages reveals further disparities. The area of highest density (Greater London) has a density of over 500 times that of the area of lowest density (the highland region of Scotland). Greater London contains 4400 people per square kilometre whilst the highlands of Scotland average only eight people in the equivalent area (but a much higher concentration of sheep, salmon, otters, etc.).

The bulk of the UK population is concentrated in seven major *conurbations* or centres of particularly high density:

- Greater London and the South East.
- West Midlands (Birmingham).
- South and West Yorkshire (Leeds, Bradford).
- North West and Merseyside (Greater Manchester, Liverpool).
- Tyne, Wear and Tees (Newcastle and Sunderland).
- Scottish Central Lowlands (Glasgow and Edinburgh).
- South Wales (Cardiff and Swansea).

It is not surprising from such a distribution of density that we find most businesses and social facilities to be similarly distributed. Hence, the centre of the UK's financial and service industry is in London whilst the West Midlands is particularly known for its high proportion of manufacturing industry. Similarly, facilities like hospitals and universities also show a higher concentration in these conurbations.

The population, skills and education

The success or failure of businesses depends in large part on the availability of people with appropriate levels of skills and education. The demographic trends in this respect contain some good news and some not-so-good news for the UK in comparison to its international competitors.

The UK has witnessed a marked increase in enrolments in further and higher education and, accordingly, an increase in the number of students pursuing study beyond the age of 16 years. Figure 11.5 shows this increase

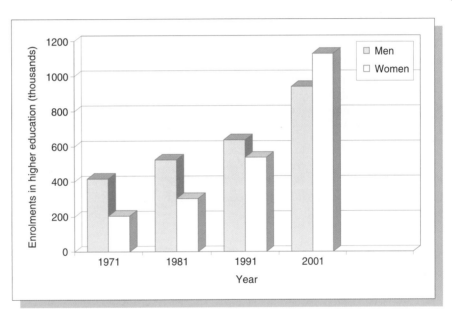

Figure 11.5 Students in higher education at the end of December each year. (*Source*: Department for Education and Skills; National Assembly for Wales; Scottish Executive; Northern Ireland Department for Employment and Learning.)

in one form of post school education – higher education. (*Note:* The numbers here include home and overseas students.) Between 1971 and 2001, the number of enrolments by men on all undergraduate courses more than doubled but for women the increase was even more dramatic, with nearly five times as many enrolments on undergraduate courses. By the end of 2001 there were 2.1 million students in higher education, 55% of whom were women. Trends of this nature are considered to be very encouraging for business in the UK. In short, it can be taken to mean that the UK is becoming better educated and more highly skilled. However, the upward trend conceals within it some not-so-good indicators, for example a decline in the number of applications to study science and engineering in higher education. This trend has triggered some of the UK's major employers of scientists to run science workshops in schools to attempt to stimulate pupils' interest in science with a view to increasing the number of quality science graduates in future years.

Question 11.2

Suggest reasons for the relatively large increase in the number of women in higher education.

The changes in the educational level of the population are not, however, restricted to higher education. Notwithstanding the increase in higher education enrolments, graduates still form a relatively small proportion of the population (Table 11.5). *Note*: GCE = General Certificate of Education, GSCE = General Certificate of Secondary Education.

Table 11.5

Highest education qualifications in the UK – percentages by gender and age, Spring 2001

	Degree or equivalent	Further/higher education (below degree)	GCE A-level or equivalent	GCSE grades A–C or equivalent	Other qualifications	No qualifications
Males						
16–24	8	4	30	34	10	15
25–34	22	8	26	20	15	9
35–44	19	8	30	16	14	12
45–54	19	9	33	11	13	16
55–64	13	7	31	8	14	25
All males	17	7	30	18	13	15
Females						
16–24	8	4	30	37	8	13
25–34	20	9	18	29	13	10
35–44	15	11	15	29	14	15
45–54	12	11	12	20	17	26
55–59	7	10	10	17	20	37
All females	14	9	17	27	14	18

Source: Department for Education and Skills from the Labour Force Survey.

In recent years there has been a focus on *lifelong learning* and many adults continue their education, either for personal satisfaction, enjoyment or to develop new skills for career development. Enrolment rates for adult education are generally higher for women than men (Figure 11.6).

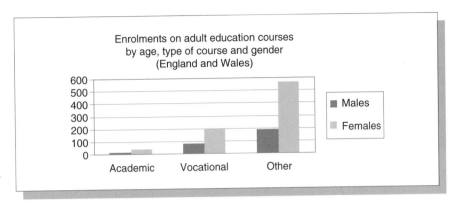

Figure 11.6
Enrolments on adult education courses at November 2000. (*Source*: Department for Education and Skills; National Assembly for Wales.)

The working population

The size of the working population in a country is important for two reasons:

- Labour, as a factor of production is one of the determinants of the country's ability to add value to goods and services, thus affecting the prosperity of the country.
- The number of people either in work or available to work determines how much money the government can raise in tax revenues. This, in turn, influences the quality of life and the ability of the state to provide public and merit goods and services.

We might expect the size of the working population to roughly reflect the size of the population as a whole and whilst this is broadly true, a number of factors have introduced complications in the relationship between the two, and a key feature is the *participation rate*, which identifies the proportion of the population who actually work.

Economic activity

People are considered to be *economically active* (or in the *labour force*) if they are over 16 years of age, but less than 59 years for women or 64 years for men, and are either in work or actively looking for work.[5]

The balance of men and women who are economically active has shifted significantly since the mid-1980s, with the economic activity rate for men falling by 5–84% by 2003, while that for women rose by 17–73% for the same period. As the economically active includes those people who are unemployed, the rates are less likely to be affected by the economic cycle than employment rates (Figure 11.7).

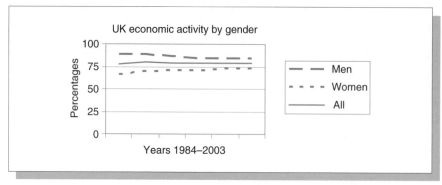

Figure 11.7
UK economic
activity rates by
gender. (*Source*:
Office for National
Statistics.)

Ageing labour force

The average age of people in the labour force has been gradually increased over the last 15 years from 37.5 to 39 years with a continuing upward trend. The fact that the UK's residents are living longer means that there are more old (i.e. retired and therefore economically inactive) people in the population. When this is combined with a more-or-less falling birth rate, the result is a complicated picture with, as we have seen, some potentially worrying consequences, particularly with regard to the declining the number of people available to meet employment requirements, and the generation of sufficient revenues to meet rising pension and social welfare commitments.

Patterns of employment

Structural change

The UK economy has experienced structural change in the last 40 years with a decline in the manufacturing sector and an increase in service industries. In 1981, one in three male employee jobs were in manufacturing but this had fallen to one in five by 2002. The proportion of female employee jobs in the manufacturing sector has also fallen, from just under one in five to one in ten.

Over that period, the largest increase for both male and female jobs was in the financial and business services, which by 2002 accounted for one in five of both male and female jobs.[6] By comparison, over that period the proportion of both male and female jobs in sectors, such as Health, Education and Public Administration has remained broadly stable.

Working hours

Traditionally, employees in the UK have worked longer hours per week than their European counterparts, and although the *Working Time Regulations 1998* limits the working week to a maximum of 48 hours (with scope for some exemptions) it has not yet reversed the trend and the average hours worked per week by British workers still tend to be higher than most of their European counterparts (Table 11.6).

Table 11.6
Average hours worked per week for selected European countries

	Males	Females
UK	45.2	40.7
France	40.2	38.6
Germany	40.5	39.4
Italy	39.7	36.3
Belgium	39.1	36.9
EU average	41.2	39.0

Source: Office for National Statistics, Social Trends, 2001.

Flexible working

There are more females than males in the UK population[1] and the increasing rate of female participation in the labour force, combined with changing patterns of family life and social values, has encouraged employers to offer degrees of flexibility in working patterns in order to attract and retain good employees. By Spring of 2001, around 20% of UK full-time and 23% part-time employees were able to adopt some type of flexible working arrangement, with women more likely than men to have flexible working patterns.

Question 11.3

What types of flexible working patterns are currently in use in the UK?

11.3 Fashions and trends in society

In addition to changes in the size and structure of the population (demography), it is also true that populations change in their preferences.

In some cases, fashions and trends are linked to demographic trends (such as an increased demand for baby clothes during a period of increased birth rate), but at other times, preferences change, seemingly 'by themselves'. Some types of preferences seem to change often whilst others show a consistent increase or decrease over time. This is the nub of the difference between fashions and trends:

- A *fashion* is generally taken to mean a relatively temporary increase in preference. Fashions may also be roughly cyclical and are difficult to predict.
- A *trend* is a longer-term change in consumer preference. Consumers sometimes demonstrate a long-term increase or decrease in their preferences.

It is important to appreciate that fashions and trends do not refer just to products. Opinions, beliefs and forms of behaviour are also subject to change. In some areas of opinion, such as political polling, opinion changes form the basis of entire industries. Some areas of human preference are notoriously fickle, such as many things associated with health. Take, for example, the concerns over unhealthy eating habits and obesity which prompted *McDonald's* to introduce a new range of 'green' products in 2004. This was supported by heavy investment in a publicity campaign, designed to influence public opinion and promote a positive image of the brand.

Question 11.4

Fashions and trends can apply to product preferences. Suggest three product types that are currently in fashion and three that are currently showing a trend in increased popularity.

Income and affluence

Household disposable income per head of population, adjusted for inflation, more than doubled between 1971 and 2002, with subsequent expenditure in household expenditure. By 2002, total household expenditure was approximately £600 billion, more than double the 1971 level, in real terms and over three and half times the level recorded for 1951 (Figure 11.8).

How people choose to spend their income has changed over time; reflecting changes in society, consumer preferences and the growth of choices available to the consumer. For example, expenditure on tobacco fell by 40% between 1971 and 1999 but has remained fairly stable since

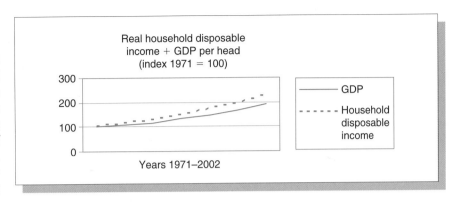

Figure 11.8
Real household
disposable
income + gross
domestic product
(GDP) per head of
population.
(*Source*: Office for
National Statistics.)

then, while UK tourist expenditure abroad increased by almost 600% and financial services by 500% in the same period. Interestingly, the overall expenditure on food increased by only 37% although the combination of increasing real wages and lower real (after inflation) prices brought about a plethora of changes in the food supply industry. In the early 1970s, the first supermarkets in the UK were known for their 'pile 'em high, sell 'em cheap' philosophy with the general belief that price was the most important buying decider for customers. Increased buying power coupled with cheaper food real prices has precipitated a general trend in higher quality foods, more choice and a much wider range of food products.

A similar trend can be seen in other consumer products (Table 11.7). Note the relative proportional changes in real terms of typical items of average household expenditure between 1971 and 2000. The downward trend identified for alcohol is, like food, the result of increasing real spending power and a reduction or stabilisation in the real price of alcoholic beverages. The case of food is reflected in the alcohol markets – more choice, more exotic products, more competition and an insistence on higher quality.

The higher levels of disposable income have allowed people to spend on lifestyle products and services. Increased spending on service items, such as holidays and entertainment, and durable goods, such as cars, mobile telephones, personal computers and domestic appliances has resulted in proportionally less being spent on essential non-durable items, such as food, fuel and power.

Lifestyle changes associated with the UK's age profiles, attitudes to marriage and family circumstances have not been lost on the marketing world who have been quick to target products at growing areas of affluence. For example, there are a significant number of affluent pensioners, many of whom are still relatively young, following the spate of 'early retirements' from downsized organisations in the 1990s, giving rise to the acronym 'woops', that is, well-off older people. At the other end of the spectrum we find 'dinkies', that is, double incomes no kids.

Table 11.7

UK household expenditure at constant 1995 prices (indices: 1971 = 100)

	1981	1991	1999	2000	Pounds in billion (current prices)
Household goods	134	211	294	306	145.3
Rent, water and sewerage charges	121	140	155	157	82.0
Transport and communication	104	116	133	137	58.3
Clothing and footwear	144	214	312	328	57.8
Alcohol	128	135	143	144	34.5
Recreational and cultural activities	142	184	234	228	29.3
Financial services	135	348	443	467	26.9
Fuel and power	119	145	138	141	31.2
Tobacco	89	72	60	60	15.1
Other services	131	211	284	296	73.9
Less expenditure by foreign tourists, etc.	152	187	238	237	−14.7
Household expenditure abroad	193	298	586	648	31.6
All household expenditure	121	167	211	220	594.8

Source: Office for National Statistics.

11.4 Changes in social values, attitudes and expectations

Over time, the population collectively adjusts it values and adopts attitudes which are generally adopted and then manifest themselves in a variety of norms and behaviours. Unlike changes resulting from economic stimuli, values and attitudinal changes tend to be less predictable due to their more complicated causation.

Attitudes to debt

Attitudes to debt in the UK have changed considerably over the last couple of generations. Prior to Second World War the prevalent view among the majority of the population (i.e. the working classes) was that debt was a 'bad thing' and that if you could not afford it you did without. Stability and growth of working opportunities, with the security of regular incomes, and government relaxation of credit controls, over the last 30 years has encouraged an upward trend in borrowing which is now seen as quite normal and the level of debt in the UK by 2004 is the highest ever recorded. By July 2004, the amount of money owed by consumers in the UK had, for the first time, passed the £1 trillion mark, and the Bank of England reported that about 80% of UK personal debt was in the form of loans secured against homes, such as mortgages and re-mortgages.

The level of debt has been accompanied with a dramatic rise in the number of people seeking help with debt problems form advisory agencies, such as *Citizen's Advice* and the *Consumer Credit Counselling Service*. The *National Consumer Council* estimated that about 6 million families were struggling to keep up with credit commitments at a time when borrowing was continuing to rise. The main cause of concern is that increases in interest rates could force heavily indebted consumers into deep trouble, as most debt owed is secured against properties. Increased property values have seen a massive rise in *mortgage equity withdrawals*, which describes borrowing secured on dwellings but not invested in the housing market.[5] However, some economists, argue against the view that the UK is sitting on a 'debt time-bomb' as the increase in borrowing has been more than matched by an increase in real terms in financial assets over the past 10 years or so.

The impact for business is highly significant with manufacturers and retailers able to capitalise on the spending power of the country, albeit based on a debt mountain (Figure 11.9).

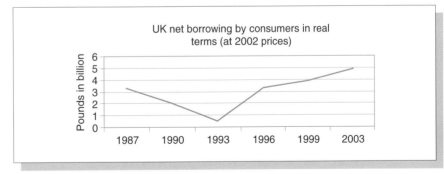

Figure 11.9
UK net borrowing by consumers. (*Source*: Bank of England; Office for National Statistics.)

Ecological concerns

An area of public opinion which has gathered prominence in recent years has been concern over the earth's environment. However, over time, there can be wide variations in the collective opinion of the population and the respective weight of opinion for specific issues.

Between 1997 and 2001, the level of concern about traffic issues (congestion, fumes, noise) rose from 37% to 52% and concerns about air pollution rose from 30% to 41% over that same period. Often the relative positions fluctuate dependent on prevailing conditions. For example, the report in 1996 which identified a link between *Bovine Spongiform Encephalopathy* (BSE) and *Creutzfeldt-Jakob Disease* (CJD) promoted food chain concerns about methods of livestock breeding and processing to the top of the agenda at that time. Similarly, the *Braer* oil tanker which ran aground in Shetland in 1993, spilling 850,000 tonnes of crude oil, heightened concerns about pollution.

A survey by the Department for the Environment, Food and Rural Affairs (Defra)[7] revealed the environmental issues of most concern to the UK population in 2001 (Figure 11.10).

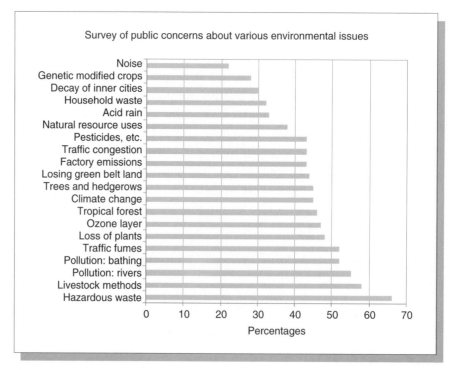

Figure 11.10
Public concerns
about various
environmental
issues. (*Source*:
Defra.)

Other selected areas of opinion

The large numbers of changes that have occurred over recent decades in demography and in economic prosperity have precipitated many changes in attitude and opinions in their wake. When we add in factors such as global communications which make us all much more aware of the world, we can see that there are many potential influences upon our attitudes and actions.

Many people have become much more health conscious than they were (or than their parents were). Things that 50 years ago would not even been heard about can now change customer buying patterns in quite drastic ways. A large number of people have taken to activities like jogging and aerobics whilst 'unhealthy' products, such as those containing high levels of polysaturated fats have been on the decline. The number of adults in Great Britain who smoke cigarettes declined from 45% of the population in 1974 to 26% in 2002, and 68% of smokers surveyed in 2002 said that they would like to stop smoking altogether.[8]

Some may argue that we have also become increasingly isolated we tend to spend more of our leisure time watching television and playing computer games and less time than we used to in more social pursuits. This is beneficial for television advertisers but some have expressed concern that such trends may pose an eventual threat to the cohesion of society. In addition, car ownership has continued to rise, with the average number of households across the UK having access to more than one car growing by almost 5% between 1991 and 2001 to 71.5%.

Changing leisure pursuits are also in evidence in the ways in which we choose to take our holidays. Whereas at one time the typical family holiday comprised a week at the nearest sea-side resort to the family home, increased prosperity and increased leisure time have signalled the growth of important industries. In 1970, UK residents took a total of 4.2 million foreign holidays. By 2001, this figure had increased to over 38 million – good news for the airline and holiday industries, not such good news for hotel owners in Bognor, Bridlington, Blackpool and Bexhill.

Assignment 11.1

- The next 50 years are expected to witness a rise in the number of retired people and a relative decline in the number of younger people. Discuss the implications of these changes for the National Health Service (NHS), the university system and government's finances.
- Identify changes in social values, attitudes and consumer expectations over the last 15 years and discuss how they might impact upon manufacturers and retailers.

References

1 *UK Census 2001.*
2 *National Statistics Social Trends.* No. 32, 2002 edition.
3 *UK 2002-Based National Population Projections, 2004 to 2051.* Government Actuary's Department.

4   McDevitt, T.M. (1999). *World Population Profile: 1998*. Washington, DC: US Government Printing Office.

5   *National Statistics Social Trends*. No. 34, 2004 edition.

6   *Short-term Turnover and Employment Survey* (2002). Office for National Statistics.

7   *Survey of Public Attitudes to Quality of Life and to the Environment* (2001). Department for Environment, Food and Rural Affairs.

8   *General Household Survey, Living in Britain* (2002). Office for National Statistics.

Further reading

Dixon, S. (2003). *Labour Market Trends (implications of population ageing for the labour market)*, vol. 111, No. 2. ISSN: 1361-4819.

Haralambos, M., *et al.* (2004). *Sociology Themes and Perspectives*, 6th edn. London: Collins Educational.

Kerslake, P. (2002). *Life in 2020*. Auckland: New Zealand Management.

Peterson, P.G. (2002). *The Shape of Things to Come: Global ageing in the Twenty-First Century. Journal of International Affairs* (Fall edition, 2002). New York.

Watson, T. (2003). *The Sociology of Work*, 4th edn. London: Routledge, an imprint of Taylor & Francis Books.

Weeks, J.R. (1994). *Population. An Introduction to Concepts and Issues*, 5th edn. London: Thomson.

Useful web sites

National Statistics: www.statistics.gov.uk
Government Actuary's Department: www.gad.gov.uk
General Register Office for Scotland: www.gro-scotland.gov.uk
National Assembly for Wales: www.wales.gov.uk/keypub
Northern Ireland Statistics Research Agency: www.nisra.gov.uk
Home Office Immigration and Asylum Statistics: www.homeoffice.gov.uk/rds
United Nations Population Information Network: www.un.org/popin
The Commonwealth: www.thecommonwealth.org

CHAPTER 12

The technological environment

After studying this chapter, students should be able to describe:

- the advantages that technology offers to an organisation;
- how a business uses technology;
- what is meant by information technology (IT) and how IT is used by a business;
- what is meant by operational technology and how it has affected business activity;
- how technology has influenced product research and design.

12.1 Business and technology

The growth of technology

The growth and expansion of technology has been one of the key characteristics of the twentieth century. Although the scientific heritage goes back many hundreds of years, the development and application of technology and its effects on social and business life, has been enormous since the early years of this century. In the year 1900, the world was very different than it is today. It was a world that had never conceived of flight, television, antibiotics, anaesthetics or computers, and in which the telephone and the motorcar were in their infancy.

Such a massive set of changing circumstances has had a profound effect on almost every part of personal and business life. Technological change has brought about the possibility of global communications, inter-planetary transport, the worldwide development of businesses and the greatly increased speed (manufacturing and distribution), and quality of manufactured products. In this chapter, we will consider the ways in which businesses use technology and how its development has changed organisational life and may continue to do so in the future.

What advantages does technology offer a business?

The starting point of our discussion is to examine the benefits that the various types of technology have brought to business.

Technology can help a business to *reduce costs*. One of the most obvious ways in which this has been done is to replace manual tasks with automation. Much of the work that was previously performed by armies of line workers in a factory or by teams of clerical workers in an office can now be carried out by machines of various types.

Technology offers the business an opportunity to *increase quality* through the removal of human error, and the introduction of more consistent procedures. The reduction of errors by increased automation offers the possibility of greater customer confidence and lower costs through reduced error corrections.

Technology enables business to make significant *increases in productivity*. Productivity refers to the business's ability to produce output with a specific level of resource. The employment of technology renders the business more efficient – machines can work longer hours with no breaks; they never 'ring in sick' nor go to the bathroom. In short, more work output can be produced for the same cost, or less, than if the work was performed by humans.

Technology can help businesses to accelerate processes. The more rapid transmission of information coupled with the mechanisation of many tasks means that decisions can be made faster and goods can be produced more rapidly than previously.

Technology facilitates the making of *better and more accurate decisions*. We know from our own experience at home that we are more informed about complex issues than ever before through such media as radio, television and other electronic means of communications. In business, the rapidity and accuracy of information transmission has enabled managers to have possession of the information they need to make informed decisions.

How does a business use technology?

The ways in which technology has pervaded business life is not dissimilar to how we encounter it in our personal lives. We use it in the kitchen, in our cars, for entertainment, to communicate, in education and in countless other areas of life. It is thus a difficult task to distil the effects of technology on business into a few key areas.

One way of subdividing technology in business is to categorise it by its use. Although the technology used in different parts of organisational life may be similar, we can nevertheless consider technologies as essentially separate according to where it is employed within the organisation. Accordingly, we can identify three ways in which businesses use technology:

- communications and information management;
- operations (e.g. in manufacturing);
- product design and in research.

In the remainder of this chapter, we will examine these three broad areas of technological usage.

12.2 Information technology

What is IT?

IT is a term which encompasses many new types of technology and pervades an even wider range of applications in business. We can define IT as:

> technology that is dedicated to the generation, transmission, storage, organisation or management of information.

We can immediately appreciate that such a definition can include a lot of things. We might use a calculator, for example, to generate information and then use a computer to manage it. Then we might use a telecommunications network to transit the information. All of these technological vehicles are part of IT.

There have been a number of trends in this area of technology. The key trends are towards:

- increasing speed of processing and transmission;
- increased accuracy and more 'user-friendly' forms of information;

◾ miniaturisation (i.e. the components used in IT become smaller).

When taken together, it would not be an exaggeration to say that IT has transformed many areas of home and business life. Information and its technology have grown to become the core activity of a number of very large industries as well as having a substantial impact on almost all of us.

Why is information important?

Information has a number of important functions, both in business and in our domestic lives. The communication of information is a major factor in maintaining cohesion in society and a vital factor in the normal functioning of business and the state.

Firstly, information facilitates *control*. When we examine control systems in Chapter 22, we will see that information is needed throughout the process to communicate standards and to provide feedback.

Secondly, and linked to the use of information for control, is the use of information to *influence attitudes and actions*. The influence upon actions can be either instructive (prescriptive) or restrictive. The former influences what we do, or should do, and the latter, what we do not do, or what we believe we should not do.

Thirdly, information is essential to enable those in business to *make decisions*. Intelligent decision-making rests upon the notion that those who make decisions are in possession of all relevant information. Organisations often put formal communications channels in place for this purpose although in many cases, decisions are taken using information gathered by more informal means (e.g. by word of mouth).

Fourthly, information is used to *educate and to entertain*. The book you are currently reading is an example of educational communication whilst one of the purposes of television is to entertain.

How is IT used in business?

The applications of IT in business are many and varied. In one sense, IT is used in all areas of business, but it has found particular use in a few key areas.

Firstly, IT is used in *administration*. Included in this area of application are:

◾ office uses, such as word processing and graphic design;
◾ numerical analysis by the use of spreadsheets;

- accountancy uses, such as computerised report generation and electronic ledger compilation;
- banking uses, such as electronic funds transfer;
- salary and personnel administration.

Secondly, IT is used in *business communications*. This category includes:

- television and radio communications;
- telephone and fax systems;
- electronic mail (e-mail);
- satellite systems;
- the Internet.

Thirdly, IT is used in *information gathering*. This area may make use of other types of IT such as communications systems. This category includes:

- library information systems;
- databases (computerised systems which contain a lot of information in a readily accessible form);
- electronic point-of-sale (EPOS) systems which enable a business to rapidly accumulate information on its sales.

The 'ingredients' of IT

Although as we have seen, the uses of IT in business are many and varied, there are two key 'ingredients'; two core areas of technology that comprise IT systems. These two ingredients are computers and telecommunications technologies.

IT and computers

Computers form such a significant part of organisational life that it is difficult to imagine how organisations ever coped without them. Furthermore, nowhere is the progress of technology more marked than in the speed of innovation in this area. In addition to the importance of computers to business, they have come to form an important element in many other parts of life as well, from usage in our motorcars and video recorders to controlling medical equipment and burglar-alarm systems.

We use the term *computer* in more than one way. The most usual meaning of the term is to describe a programmable device which is designed to perform a wide range of data-processing tasks. However, we also speak of computers controlling equipment, parts of cars and in domestic appliances like microwave ovens. The part that both types of computer share is called a *processor*. In most appliances, the processor is a small semi-conductor chip, and is therefore called a *microprocessor*. The ways in which processors are used leads us to distinguish between two essential types:

- *Programmable processors* are found in devices that we would recognise as computers. They can be programmed to perform many different tasks.
- *Embedded processors* are sometimes called *dedicated* processors and cannot be reprogrammed. They are designed to perform a predetermined task and are embedded in an appliance as a mechanism of control. They have no useful purpose if they are removed from the appliance for which they are designed.

Both types of processor are accompanied by components that support the processor's designed purpose. A programmable processor is surrounded by components that assist the processor (usually called a central processing unit (CPU)) in its purpose. This includes memory that can both be written to (such as random access memory (RAM), and storage memory such as a hard or floppy disk), and memory that cannot be written to and is permanent (read only memory (ROM)). It will also include mechanisms of both inputting data to the CPU and a means by which outputs from the CPU can be read. A dedicated processor will not usually contain memory but will provide input and output capabilities although these may be inaccessible to the user.

Computers (using programmable processors) are often subdivided into types by their size. Three types have traditionally been identified:

- *Mainframe computers* are very large and have a central processor that can support many users at the same time. Each user is located at a terminal which is linked to the main CPU; terminals may be located either locally (e.g. in the same building) or remotely via telecommunications links. Remote terminals may be located anywhere in the world. Mainframes usually demand specialist personnel to manage them and are typically housed in rooms which are subject to controlled environmental conditions. Large computers of this type are used by organisations that have the need to process large amounts of data simultaneously such as banks, universities and insurance companies.
- *Minicomputers* are smaller than mainframes but can nevertheless be of a considerable size and power. They work on the same principles as a mainframe except that can support a lower number of users. Minicomputers are used in organisations that have a need for several rather than many users simultaneously such as office complexes or scientific laboratories.

■ *Microcomputers* are stand-alone machines. They have a CPU that can only be accessed from one input device: that is, one keyboard, a floppy disk drive or similar. For this reason, micro-computers are always 'stand-alone' machines. They contain their own data storage capability, usually in the form of an 'on board' hard disk and have output devices in the form of monitors and printer terminals. The use of a microcomputer gives the user autonomy that other computer types do not. This, coupled with their growing ease of use and reducing price (in real terms) has made this the key growth area in computer usage.

In some organisations, microcomputers are connected together in the form of a *local area network* (LAN). A LAN is used to connect stand-alone microcomputers together in an office locality. The central point of the LAN is a *file server* from which users access programmes and information. The file server can also be used as a point for interconnecting users for the use of e-mail and as a link to external information sources such as the Internet.

IT and telecommunications

If computers in their various forms are responsible for managing information, then telecommunications systems are responsible for transmitting information. Like all other areas of technology, telecommunications has been the subject of rapid innovation and change in recent decades.

The word *telecommunication* means communication over a distance (the prefix *tele* means 'distance' and appears in other words where *tele* means the same thing: *tele*phone, *tele*kinesis, *tele*pathy, *tele*vision, etc.). At its simplest, there are only two ways in which information can be electronically transmitted from one place to another:

■ along physical wires or optoelectronic links,
■ through the air by means of electromagnetic transmission.

The innovation underlying the key developments in telecommunications is that of a widespread switch from old analogue transmission to modern digital information. This has resulted in much faster and more accurate telecommunications and, importantly, has facilitated the connection of computers (which are also based on digital technology) together over a distance.

There are a number of key trends in respect of business and telecommunications. An increase in real incomes coupled with a fall (in real terms) of the prices of telecommunications services has stimulated much higher usage and ownership of telecommunications appliances. Whilst the telephone has been a feature of some domestic homes for many years, ownership has increased quite markedly since over the past three decades. Other developments are much more recent:

- The *facsimile* or fax, a device for transmitting images became popular in the 1980s replacing the telex, which involved communicating a typed message. Faxes are now a part of every office in organisations in the First World.

- The *mobile telephone* (and mobile fax) also came to the fore in the 1980s. Initially the domain of senior executives and travelling sales representatives, mobile telephony has rapidly achieved universal adoption by people from all walks of life, of all ages and gender. The early years of the twenty-first century have witnessed significant advances with telephony and computing technologies combining to provide a phenomenal range of telecommunication services via sophisticated handheld wireless devices with Internet connectivity.

- *E-mail* (electronic mail) refers to the exchange of messages, usually text, between users who have access to the same computer system or who are connected via a network such as the Internet. Files of sound, video or graphics can be attached to this electronic communications medium and, as a 24 hours a day global service, messages can be stored for later retrieval if a user is not logged on at the time of transmission.

- The *Internet* is a worldwide computer network that connects many smaller networks together and allows all of the computers to exchange information with each other. To do this requires a set of common protocols (rules) for communication. These protocols are called TCP/IP (Transmission Control Protocol/Internet Protocol). The worldwide online population is expanding at a fast rate and is likely to in excess of 1.2 billion users by 2006, according to forecasts by Computer Industry Almanac Inc.[1]

McFarlan and McKenney

The extent to which organisations use and rely on technology in their normal operations varies widely. In attempting to understand these variations, Professors F. Warren McFarlan and James L. McKenney[2] developed a grid comprising two intersecting continua. The *y* continuum describes the organisation's *current* dependence, and the strategic importance of IT and systems in normal operations. The *x* continuum (the horizontal) describes the *future* dependence that the organisation is likely to have on IT given the nature of the industry, customer requirements and competitor behaviour.

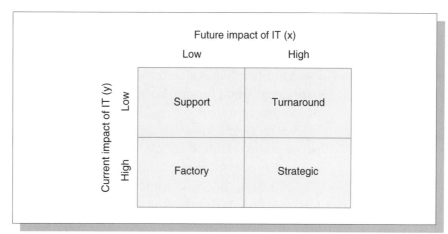

Figure 12.1
McFarlan and
McKenney's IT grid.

When it is constructed, McFarlan and McKenney's grid is like that in Figure 12.1.

For some organisations, IT is of *strategic* importance. This is said to be the case when the organisation's dependence on its information systems is already very high and when its future is also expected to be much highly impacted by developments in IT. Accordingly, the head of IT may well be a member of the organisation's board of directors. Examples of organisation for which IT is strategic include banks, insurance companies and telecommunications companies. It will usually be the case that the business simply cannot operate if the information systems (on computer) 'go down'.

For other organisations, dependence on their IT systems is currently relatively low, but changes in the environment means that IT will eventually become very important. These are organisations in the *turnaround* category of the grid. Most of the major supermarket multiples have just recently undergone this stage by moving from a state where IT was used to help control stock, and assist with accounting to the current state where IT systems are crucial for the logging of sales and many other parts of the retailing process. Supermarkets have, however, some significant investments still to make in IT, such as fully implementing systems to facilitate electronic funds transfer at the point of sale and in stock ordering (although many chains are well down this road). For turnaround organisations, IT is expected to become strategic in the medium term.

Organisations which McFarlan and McKenney describe as *factory* currently have a high dependence on IT for their competitive performance, but future developments in IT are not expected to significantly add to their ability to compete in markets. Some airlines fall into this category where there is a high dependence on IT systems for booking and recording of passengers but where future changes in IT are not expected to increase their competitive edge.

Finally, McFarlan and McKenney identify a category which they refer to as *support*. These are organisations whose current use of IT does not significantly contribute to their ability to compete, and where IT is not expected to affect competitive performance in the future. Such organisation may find IT useful for support purposes such as accounting, word processing and work scheduling, but have not found IT to be a source of leverage over competitors. Organisations in this category may be those performing relatively simple services or manufacturing businesses in low-technology sectors of industry. A company involved in landscape gardening may find a personal computer useful, but its competitive edge will be primarily down to the care and skills of its designers and gardeners. Furthermore, it is unlikely that landscape gardening will ever become so impacted by IT that it becomes a matter of competitive importance.

12.3 Operations technology

Introduction

In the 1970s and 1980s, business and engineering students learned of technologies called CAD and CAM. These were acronyms for *computer-aided design* and *computer-aided manufacturing*, respectively. At the time, CAD and CAM represented a new way of gaining the advantages of technology in their operations departments. In the 1990s, however, the use of computer technology in operations has become so widespread that CAD and CAM have become the norm rather than the exception. It is only a few businesses that have not, at least in a small way, automated parts of their operations department since the advent of a range of new operational technologies.

Broadly speaking, operational technology borrows heavily from the areas and types of IT that we have already encountered. In addition though, operations departments also employ technology based on innovations in electrical, electronic and mechanical engineering which have combined to automate many of the tasks that were previously performed manually.

IT in operations

Almost all types of organisation (with the possible exception of monasteries) have found computer systems to be of immense value in their operations systems. The university or college at which you are studying most likely manages its student recruitment, marks and awards on a database system: an innovation that means that at the touch of a button, all the information about you can be accessed immediately and displayed on a computer monitor.

In other operational contexts, computer systems are used in all parts of the process. Just-in-time (JIT) manufacturers (see Chapter 24) use computer linkages with their suppliers to directly order the appropriate amount of incoming raw material (RM). Systems also exist for scheduling jobs or batches through a production facility in the most optimal way. Production managers usually have a computer terminal on their desks which enables them to find out up-to-the minute's information on their department, such as the batch schedule, the levels of RM and finished goods (FG) stocks or what is currently happening on the 'shop floor'.

Some computer systems offer a comprehensive approach to managing the operations function. Manufacturing processes based on assembly (e.g. cars, electrical goods, etc.) sometimes employ a system called MRP II, the manufacturing resource planning. The 'II' indicates that MRP II replaces a previous regime called MRP, materials requirement planning, a system which only took into account the stock requirements of a job or batch. Once the 'order book' has been inputted, MRP II calculates not only the precise stock requirements for a job or batch, but also the best way to schedule work through manufacturing to enable all orders to be met with the minimum of slack and delay. The system can be modified so that the computer actually orders the precise amount of RM stocks, thus saving the organisation time and money previously needed for a purchasing manager to perform the ordering task (see Chapter 26).

One area of business that has benefited significantly from innovations in IT is the supermarket. Whilst the most obvious and visible change has been the recording of sales by the use of bar codes (as opposed to the assistant typing in the individual prices), other developments have been equally important. EPOS systems have enabled managers to gain immediate information on product sales which guides decisions on such things as product discounting and stock ordering. EPOS systems can also generate 'checkout savers'; that is, discounts vouchers which are generated in response to specific purchases and paid for by competitors to the brand purchased (e.g. a purchase of a six pack of Coca Cola may generate a checkout saver for a six pack of Pepsi).

Engineering technology

Although highly dependent upon IT, innovations in engineering are worthy of separate consideration. We need look no further than our own homes to see the advances in engineering and how they have changed our lives. Most of us have appliances such as washing machines, televisions, hi-fi's, microwave ovens and dishwashers, and we can testify as to the extent to which they have made our lives easier.

In business, the automation and mechanisation of procedures has engendered similarly beneficial results. Some of the earliest mechanised procedures involving ravelling cotton and wool in the eighteenth century have given way in the latter part of the twentieth century to a situation, wherein automation has reached new heights of refinement and accuracy. The work that was previously done by hundreds of human workers has, in many workplaces, been replaced with machines that work with greater accuracy and quality than humans and with greater productivity at lower cost.

The complexity of factory automation varies widely. Some machines are designed to perform relatively simple, repetitive tasks, such as paint jets continually spraying paint at products passing on a single conveyor line. There has, however, been a marked trend in the increasingly complex tasks that machines are made to undertake. More advanced machines make use of microprocessor technology in the forms of both programmable and embedded processors. In the engineering business, *computer numerically controlled* (CNC) technology has been used for many years. CNC machines are machine tools which use coded computer information to produce batches of precisely matched components from such things as CNC lathes and milling machines.

Among the more complex automations are those used in industries like motor manufacture and the production of silicon chips and printed circuits. Machines used in these processes must usually be capable of not only exceptionally minute movements but also of intricate movements through three dimensions. Nissan Motors in Sunderland reports that it uses,

> a family of more than 200 robots provid[ing] an automation level in excess of 80%. Six high-speed tri-axis transfer presses – one 5000 tonne, two 3200 tonne and three 2700 tonne machines – means the Sunderland plant has the highest concentration of these advanced presses in Europe.

12.4 Technology in research and design

We must be careful not to define the term *technology* too tightly. We may tend to think of technology purely in terms of electronics and sophisticated machinery, but the term as it relates to business also includes a wide range of chemical technologies and those associated with the understanding of the world and its materials. Specialist staff that work in research, development and design, such as scientists and specialist engineers are confronted with an even more complex set of technologies with which they must often 'juggle' to benefit the products and processes of the organisations for which they work.

There is scope in this text for only a small sample of examples of the areas of technology that are involved in the various aspects of research and design (in addition to IT and engineering technology which we have already encountered):

- Chemical technology refers to the technology used by chemists in developing new compounds, chemical products and chemical intermediates.
- Biochemical, bio-molecular and pharmaceutical technology relates to chemistry as it applies to life. Technological developments in this area have affected the lives of literally billions of people for the better.
- Gene and genetic technology is one of those areas of research that is perhaps at the leading edge of science. By understanding the genetic 'code' of animal and plant life, knowledge is gained into other areas such as the causes of disease, deformity and the ways in which these can be corrected.
- Materials technology includes such things as metallurgy (the study of metals), ceramics and how these can be used in business products. The implications of materials technology extend to many sectors of business include motors, brushes, shipping, aircraft, rocketry, surgery and clothes.
- Process technology concerns the technology involved in industrial (particularly manufacturing) processes. It borrows heavily from other areas of technology depending upon the industry and type of process in question.
- Aerodynamic technology is important to organisations engaged in the design and manufacture of such products as motorcars, aircraft, missiles and bikes of various types. It concerns the flow of air through, past and over product shapes with the objective of reducing fuel consumption and increasing efficiency (have you ever wondered why many cars are more-or-less the same shape?).
- Acoustic and audio technologies are used by any business engaged in sound. Examples include manufacturers of audio equipment and companies involved in the staging of concerts or concert hall design.

The progress of technology in most of the above areas is just as rapid as it has been in IT. We need look no further than changes in medicine and in pharmaceuticals to see the rate of progress in the wider technological environment.

Assignment 12.1

How would you answer a company's managing director who says that he has sacked his research and development staff because, 'they cost too much money. We can get by with the products we have already got?'

References

1   Computer Industry Almanac Inc: www.c-i-a.com/ September 2004.
2   McFarlan, F. Warren *et al.* (1997) *Corporate Information Strategy and Management*, 6th edn. London: McGraw-Hill Education (ISE editions).

Further reading

Avison, D. and Fitzgerald, G. (2002). *Information Systems Development: Methodologies, Techniques and Tools*, 2nd edn. London: McGraw-Hill.

Bailey, J. (1993). *Managing People and Technological Change*. London: Pitman.

Barrett, P. and Baldry, D. (2003). *Facilities Management*. London: Blackwell Science (UK).

Chaffey, D. *et al.* (2002). *Business Information Systems: Technology, Development and Management in E-business*. London: FT Prentice Hall.

Harry, M. (1994). *Information Systems in Business*. London: Pitman.

McLoughlin, I. and Clark, J. (1994). *Technological Change at Work*, 2nd edn. Milton Keynes: Open University Press.

Peppard, J. (1993). *IT Strategy for Business*. London: Pitman

Zorkoczy, P. and Heap, N. (1994). *Information Technology*. London: Pitman.

Useful web sites

British Automation and Robot Association: www.bara.org.uk
Department of Trade and Industry: www.dti.gov.uk
Retail Systems: www.retailsystems.com

CHAPTER 13

The ecological environment

After studying this chapter, students should be able to describe:

- the influence of environmental concerns on organisations;
- the nature of environmental management;
- the competing demands of economic growth and greater environmental protection;
- the concepts of ecological footprint and ecological degradation;
- the concept of sustainable development.

13.1 A changing cultural and societal environment

A significant change has taken place in business over the past 20 years or so. Whereas at one time, for-profit organisations operated on the principle that, as Milton Friedman said, 'the business of business is business', recent developments have focused on the wider social responsibility of organisations which may not directly be in the pursuit of purely profit aims. The change centres on the question of the extent to which the business has some degree of responsibility to the other members (corporate and individual) of society and the extent to which a business should account for the opinions of the wider public.

In once sense, this change in thinking is testimony to the power of an organisation's stakeholders. In purely economic terms, shareholders have traditionally viewed profitability as the only legitimate objective business, but this has been modified in the light of a number of key concerns among the wider stakeholder community. The increased concerns have encompassed a wide variety of issues and most readers will be able to list many of them from their own experience. In this chapter, we deal with the concerns over the physical (natural) environment.

Sociologists may argue over how this cultural change was initially brought about. Certainly our awareness of wider issues has been heightened by the spectacular rise in global communications. The events in a famine-stricken country are brought directly into our living rooms through television, whilst scientists ruminate, before millions of viewers about the effects of global warming and acid rain. Pictures are broadcast of de-forestation, flooding and drought, presenting us with graphic illustrations of some people's concerns. Coupled with these features has been an increasing sense that business and government have a responsibility to hear the concerns of interested parties and that stakeholders collectively, can 'make a difference'. Notable organisations that actively pursue environmental issue include *the National Trust*, *Greenpeace* and *Friends of the Earth*.

13.2 Business and environmental responsibility

As we have seen, there is an implicit assumption that for-profit businesses exist primarily to make a profit before all else. However, given that a business benefits from society (e.g. from its provision of skilled employees and customers) the question arises as to how much businesses should take account of wider social issues in their policies and decisions.

All organisations have environmental impacts, with heavy industry producing the most visible emissions, including some that are regulated under environmental legislation. However, other organisations, such as offices and retail outlets also have an impact on the environment. They all use resources dispose of waste and produce 'greenhouse gases' from the energy used in lighting, heating and transport.

In practice, the social responsiveness of an organisation depends upon its various stakeholder influences and the personalities and convictions of its management, much as it might do for an individual. Some individuals take great care to buy goods with minimal packaging, to recycle all their glass, paper, etc. and to avoid animal products which have been produced through alleged 'cruelty' to the animal. Others adopt an altogether more indifferent or cavalier approach to wider environmental and ethical issues, not giving a moment's thought to such matters.

It is important to appreciate, however, that many of the environmental issues of concern are covered by a wide range of (mainly) statute laws. There are therefore some issues that are not open to interpretation by individual businesses: a 'minimum' standard of corporate behaviour is provided by the legal underpinning. In this context, laws cover such things as industrial pollution, fish catches in the sea. Such a regulatory regime clearly reduces the scope of an organisation to be guilty of environmental damage, but in large part still leaves some room for debate and voluntary restraint over and above the legal minimum.

13.3 The nature of environmental management

Resource issues

There can be no doubt that the Earth contains only a finite amount of material. The supply of oil, coal, minerals, etc. is therefore not inexhaustible. It is also the case therefore, as time passes and as we use up resources, that fewer and fewer reserves are left to extract.

The problem of diminishing resources has two prominent causes. Firstly, the economic growth across the world over the past century or so has meant that resources have been used in order to produce goods which are in turn used by consumers. By their very nature, manufactured goods require a material input which must be obtained, ultimately from the Earth. Similarly, industrial growth needs energy to turn raw materials into manufactured goods, another requirement for the Earth's resources. Secondly, the growth in population (one of the main causes of increased economic growth) has accelerated the consumption of resources. At the turn of the nineteenth century, the world population was not a cause for concern but as it has grown the rate of resource consumption has also accelerated particularly in the developed and, more recently, in the fast developing economies of China and India.

Different 'worlds'

The terms First and Third World are used a great deal by groups concerned about environmental and ethical matters.

The *First World* is generally taken to mean the sector of the world comprising the wealthy industrialised nations of Western Europe, North America, the Pacific Rim (e.g. Japan),

Australia and New Zealand. The temperate climates and stable democratic government in these countries has over time, provided a business climate which encourages industrial investment, increasing wealth and a high quality of life for its citizens.

The *Second World* is less industrialised than the First World, but still enjoys some degree of industrial development. Comprising Eastern Europe, the former USSR and some regions of Asia and South America. In many cases, Second World countries fall behind First World countries due to centralised economic planning and a state regime that does not encourage private industrial investment.

The *Third World* comprises predominantly most of Africa, and parts of South America and Asia. Such countries are characterised by a low income per capita resulting from relatively poor agricultural output and low industrial development. Third World economies tend to be simple in nature with a currency of low exchange value. In practice, Third World countries often have high levels of debt and high inflation accompanied by a lower standard of living than those in other parts of the world.

Energy resources

In the context of our current discussion, energy is taken to mean the materials that are used to make energy. These are (principally):

- oil,
- natural gas,
- coal,
- nuclear materials.

The first three of these (oil, gas and coal) are known as fossil fuels, due to their having an organic origin (formerly living matter). Materials used in nuclear power generation, on the other hand, are minerals that are mined. There is some confusion as to the precise quantity of energy resources left in the Earth, mainly because oil companies, who spend a lot of time and money prospecting, frequently come across new oil fields which can supply future demands. In consequence, estimates of future reserves are continually being revised.

Opinion is split as to how concerned we should be about energy reserves. Some contend that because they are bound to run out eventually, we should be making investments now to find alternative sources of renewable energy. Others say that because the problem of running out is not immediate, there is no need to be too concerned for the foreseeable future (i.e. for the next century). The economics of the energy business make it difficult to allocate too much money to the development of renewable sources (sources which do not use up finite resources, such as solar, wind and wave power). Like all businesses, they must provide a return to their shareholders, so the incurrence of excessive development costs would make the companies less attractive to investors. Notwithstanding this, there has been an increased level of interest in renewable energy among some parts of the academic community.

The fuels which cause the most concern are those which are in shortest supply, which, as may be expected, are also those in greatest usage (oil, gas and coal).[1] Estimates of the 'number of years' left of these fuels are shown in Figures 13.1 to 13.4. However, it should be noted that estimates can vary according to the source of the information and the assumptions made regarding the level of consumption and price.

Of course, in addition to the 'world' estimates in Figures 13.2 and 13.3, the UK has its own oil and gas reserves, mainly in the shallow continental shelf waters in the North Sea and to a lesser extent, the Atlantic. It is difficult to estimate how much is left to be extracted in British waters as there are fields still to be fully exploited, and developments in technology are enabling exploration in much deeper waters with greater viability of extraction. Some estimates suggest that 48% of the UK's oil reserves and 37% of the UK's gas had been extracted by

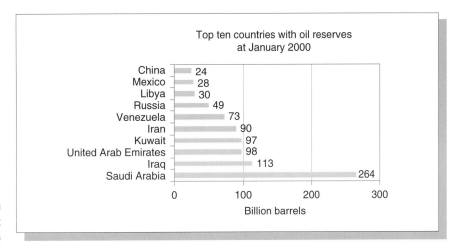

Figure 13.1
Oil reserves: top ten countries. (*Source*: United Nations.)

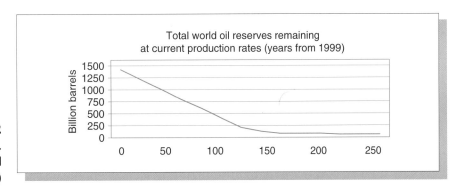

Figure 13.2
World oil reserves. (*Source*: United Nations.)

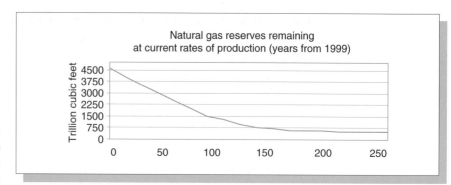

Figure 13.3
World natural gas
resources. (*Source*:
United Nations.)

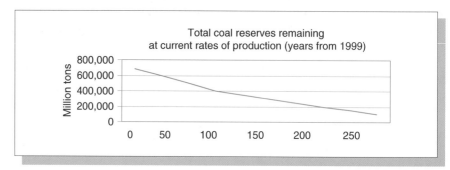

Figure 13.4
World coal
reserves. (*Source*:
United Nations.)

2002, while the more pessimistic estimates suggest a rather more serious picture with perhaps as much as 73% of oil reserves being exhausted and as much as 60% of gas.

It is interesting to note that nuclear fuels, possibly the most controversial form of energy, are also the most abundant. At the end of 2001 it was estimated that there were 4.5 million tonnes of Uranium in the world, most of which is located in Eastern Europe and Asia. Nuclear generators would also be keen to point out that whereas fossil fuels contribute to pollution in the process of power generation, nuclear fuels do not. This is not to say that the storage and disposal of used nuclear fuel is without serious problems.

Mineral and forestry resources

Minerals are those materials which form the bases of many important manufactured products. Prominent minerals are metal ores (from which metals are extracted), materials used in building (e.g. lime, silicates, etc.) and chemicals. The importance of these materials as industrial inputs is beyond dispute and various parties have expressed concern over these reserves.

It is equally difficult to arrive at accurate estimates at the actual world reserves of many minerals as it is for energy reserves. Whilst it is obvious that reserves are finite, known reserves for some materials actually rise over time as more are discovered in different parts of the planet. Notwithstanding this, extraction is usually expensive, especially if the mining takes place in remote parts of the Earth. For reasons of this cost and their finiteness, recycling of some materials has become increasingly common. Whilst recycling is possible for materials like metals, it is not possible for many non-metallic resources, such as talc and gypsum.

Forestry attracts similar concern to minerals. Most of us will have heard of concern over the equatorial rain forests. These are vast areas of natural hard-wood forests which are important for two reasons. They not only provide a natural habitat for a huge range of plants and animals but the trees themselves collectively play an important part in the Earth's ecosystem. Over recent decades, the equatorial forests have been subject to clearance at a rate faster than they can regrow. On a more local level, moves have been made to increase tree coverage in many non-equatorial parts of the world, including in the UK. This is an attempt partly to redress a potential ecological imbalance and partly to support *sustainability*. This is a term applied to forestry that is replaced at least as rapidly as it is harvested.

What is an ecosystem?

The initial observation that all life on Earth exists in a type of balance was made by Prof Arthur Tansley in 1936. We should understand that the concept is very complicated. For our purposes, we can define an ecosystem as follows:

An ecosystem is a self-sustaining complex of interdependent organisms (both animals and plants) and a range of physical environmental factors which exists within a sustainable equilibrium.

The key themes of an ecosystem are that animals and plants are interdependent with each other and with their environment. This means that each organism is dependent upon and is turn, depended on for the normal continuance of life. Each species of organism, as well as being interdependent on other life, is in equilibrium with 'external' environmental factors, such as chemical nutrients and energy from the Sun. The totality of the ecosystem takes account of all organisms on Earth and even influences beyond the Earth, that is energy from the Sun. In practice, to make the study of ecosystems easier, they are subdivided into regional ecosystems such as that which exists in a desert, in a rain forest or even in the duck-pond in the local park. Eventually, all of these 'mini' ecosystems are part of the global picture and none exist truly in isolation.

The delicate balance of an ecosystem can be upset when any single part of it is interfered with. For example, an increase in the intensity of the Sun may cause plants to disappear in some areas of the world. In turn, herbivorous (plant-eating) animals that eat the plants will also die out. Next, the carnivorous (meat-eating) animals that eat the herbivores will die out. The fact that such animals do not live on the land will, in turn, make the deficiency of plants even worse – there will be no animal waste and decomposing animal matter to feed the soil on which the plants grow. The 'knock-on' effects of any disturbance in any part of an ecosystem demonstrate the complexity of the balance.

Extinction and over-fishing

A discussion of species extinction and stock shortage involves extending our definition of 'resources' beyond material resources in the Earth. Concern over these matters rests upon the supposition that a balance of species on the Earth is an essential requirement to maintain the stability of the Earth's ecosystem. From time to time, we see on television a report on a species in one part of the Earth that is in danger of extinction. Such reports can generate strong feelings among viewers and have been known to influence business practice, such as advertising campaigns.

One of the more topical and close-to-home 'life-stock' issues pertains to fish in the seas in and around Europe. Although few of the major species of fish are threatened with global extinction, their numbers in some key localised regions has given cause for concern. The decline in fish stocks can be seen by examining some simple figures. In 1970, it was estimated that the North Sea contained 263,000 tonnes of breeding cod and 403,000 tonnes of breeding haddock. By 1990, both of these had been reduced to around 64,000 tonnes each.

The problems of over-fishing have been of concern for some time. It is estimated that fish stocks in the Baltic Sea (in Northern Europe) are now so depleted that fishing must completely stop immediately if stocks are not to be irreparably damaged. The European Union (EU), in partial response to this problem, has introduced quotas – maximum limits placed upon member states' catches per year. There is some evidence that reductions in quotas does allow stocks to recover. Fishing for herring in the North Sea was banned between 1978 and 1982, allowing breeding stocks to recover and in 2003, 30% of reported fish stocks around the UK were assessed to be within safe biological limits, with spawning levels sufficient to allow a good probability of stock replenishment. However, a body of scientific opinion, notably the *International Council for the Exploration of the Sea* (ICES), argued that spawning rates were not sufficiently robust and that exploitation rates had been too high and consequently the fishing rate should be substantially reduced in order to permit the stocks to fully recover (Figure 13.5).

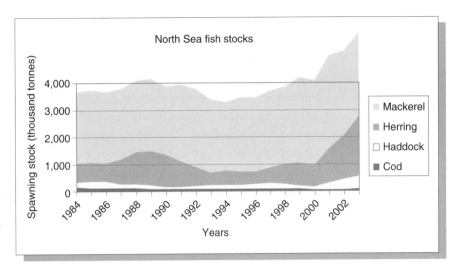

Figure 13.5
North Sea fish stocks plus North-east Atlantic mackerel: 1984–2003. (*Source*: Department for Environment, Food and Rural Affairs.)

Pollution issues

As economic growth, population and consumption have increased over the course of the twentieth century, so the waste arising from the consumption has increased. Physical waste, by definition, unless it can be reused, is defined as pollution. The concerns over pollution are twofold:

- Some concern exists that *certain pollution exists at all*. This occurs when the pollution represents a visual 'eye-sore' (e.g. slag-heaps) or when it is potentially hazardous (e.g. nuclear waste).
- The second area concerns the *effects of pollution on other things*. It is thought, for example, that pollution is a major contributor to global warming, ozone depletion and ecological imbalance. On a more local level, rubbish put into a land fill may pollute local water courses.

Refuse and waste

Physical refuse and waste is an unfortunate result of almost all consumption. Industry produces waste, whether it is in the form of empty containers or piles of burnt coal from a power station. Consumers produce waste from households in the form of used packaging, etc.

The problems from refuse arise mainly from decisions concerning its treatment or disposal. The simple choices of burn it or store it are both equally undesirable in their own ways. Burning thousands of tonnes of refuse each year would itself be a major contributor to atmospheric pollution whilst storing it makes significant demands on space. The favoured method in the UK is to use refuse as a form of land fill; that is, a process of burying refuse and then covering with a layer of topsoil. In other countries, refuse is systematically dumped into shallow sections of coastal sea waters. The result of this is that new 'islands' of rubbish are eventually created.

Some forms of refuse that cannot be stored must be burned. This includes clinical waste (e.g. human tissues, pharmaceuticals and used medical consumables like hypodermic needles) and some industrial by-products. The process of incineration of such materials also presents its own unique problems. It is often the case that such materials release toxic or pungent chemicals on incineration which as well as constituting an atmospheric pollutant is unpopular with local residents.

One form of waste which is of unique concern is spent material from nuclear power generation. Notwithstanding the benefits of nuclear power, nuclear waste has two major drawbacks:

- It is associated with the causation of several serious health hazards. Notable among these are concerns over fears that nuclear waste is:
  - carcinogenic, causing cancers;
  - teratogenic, causing birth defects;
  - mutagenic, causing genetic defects in sex cells.
- It remains a health hazard for a very long time. Some forms of nuclear waste can remain radioactive for as long as 20,000 years.

Although some nuclear fuels can be reprocessed and used again, it follows that all nuclear materials must eventually be stored as waste. Some pressure groups have led vocal campaigns to reduce or eliminate the use of nuclear fuels, mainly for the reasons outlined above.

Industrial pollution

Whilst in one respect the causes of pollution rest with increased consumption as populations have increased, some sectors of industry are viewed by many as being particularly culpable of environmental irresponsibility. The most frequently criticised sector is the chemicals industry. There are two principle causes of 'industrial' pollution.

Firstly, and by far the most important are the *intentional emissions* (by design) that some chemical plants produce as a result of the chemical processes carried out. It is an unavoidable fact that most chemical reactions produce by-products which are of no commercial interest to the business, and these are usually discharged from the plant. Gaseous waste is discharged into the atmosphere whilst liquid waste is often discharged into local water systems (e.g. rivers). The precise method of disposal of industrial by-products will, of course depend on the chemical nature of the material. Local authorities grant permission for some materials to be discharged and so a certain amount of policing occurs.

The second type of industrial pollution is that which happens *by accident*. Although by volume, spillages and leaks account for less than that produced by emissions, they are often more serious in the short-term owing to a high concentration of a chemical 'nasty' in a localised area. The concern over such accidents is heightened by the facts that they are invariably well publicised and that they can wreak havoc to local environments, and in some circumstances, can affect human life in the locality.

Industrial accidents: two notable chemical cases

Union Carbide, Bhopal, India

Union Carbide Corp. (UCar) is a multi-national chemicals group based in the USA. Like its major international competitors, UCar is very widely spread geographically, owning as it does, plants and outlets in many countries throughout the world. The UCar plant in Bhopal, a town in northern India, was just one of its plants in the Asian continent.

The Bhopal plant was geared up to make a pesticide called *Sevin*. This product contained several chemicals, a major constituent being a highly toxic material called methyl isocyanate (MIC). The MIC used to make Sevin was stored on the Bhopal site.

An accident occurred on 3 December 1984, when water entered a tank containing MIC. This caused a rupture of the MIC container and a cloud of the toxic gas leaked out into the atmosphere. The prevailing wind at the time unfortunately carried the cloud across the town of Bhopal. Within a few hours, the gas had killed 2600 local people and its effects left an estimated 300,000 people with long-term respiratory problems. By 1991 it was estimated that one person per day was still dying in Bhopal as a result of the MIC leakage.

The Exxon Valdez oil spill, Alaska

Exxon is one of the world's largest companies. As a multi-national oil company, it operates all over the world and in the UK, is usually known by its *Esso* brand name.

Like all major oil companies, Exxon ships massive quantities of crude oil around the world in large tankers. One of its ships, the Exxon Valdez was involved in an accident in March 1989. The tanker ran aground in a particularly environmentally sensitive waterway in Alaska and spilled its load of crude oil into the surrounding sea. The 11 million gallons of crude oil caused significant damage to the wildlife in and around 1100 miles of coastline in Prince William Sound. Fatalities of the spill were half a million birds, 5500 sea otters in addition to the loss of fish and flora in the sound. Ecologists surveying the scene considered it one of the worst industrial accidents ever as far as its environmental implications were concerned.

'Global' effects of pollution

Whilst the above concerns about pollution are prevalent, there is more concern about the effects of pollution of the global ecosystem than the others, although all factors in this category are more or less inter-linked. It has been suggested that the aggregate effects of all sources of pollution are having an effect on the ecosystem of the Earth as a whole. Experts differ on the extent of the threat, there seems to be an increasing convergence of opinion on some matters.

The 'global threat' causing most concern is that of *global warming*. According to holders of this concern, the effects of continual build-up of certain pollutants in the atmosphere cause the Earth's atmosphere to act a bit like a greenhouse (it has been labelled '*the greenhouse effect*'). This means that whilst the Sun's rays enter the atmosphere and heat the Earth, some of them are prevented from leaking away into space by pollutants in the atmosphere. The effect of this is that the average temperatures on the ground rise over time. The main pollutant causing this effect is thought to be carbon dioxide (CO_2), a gas produced by burning fossil fuels, such as coal, gas and petrol, and by animal life itself in the form of exhaled air. If the average temperature on the Earth rises then, it is believed, a major climatic change will result over the longer term. Although the problem of global warming is (as its name suggests) global, its effects may be felt at a local level. Adverse effects of such a change would include rising sea levels as polar ice caps melt. This would have the effect of increasingly the area of desert in equatorial regions and of flooding large areas of low-lying land, such as parts of Holland and areas of England like Lincolnshire and East Anglia. Crop production would be reduced and a number of health problems would be in greater evidence.

A second effect of global proportion is that of *ozone depletion*. The ozone layer is a thin layer of tri-atomic oxygen molecules high in the Earth's atmosphere. Its effects include the ability to deflect harmful (e.g. carcinogenic) ultraviolet (UV) solar rays away from the Earth. British research societies, which monitor the ozone layer, report that the problem of the disappearing ozone layer is most marked around the poles, but that the trend is very much towards expansion of these holes.

An increased incidence of UV rays on the Earth, as well as adding to global warming, also represents a hazard to health owing to the ability of UV rays to increase the risk of skin cancers in susceptible people. Pollutants thought to contribute to ozone depletion include CO_2, but most particularly a group of chemicals called *chlorinated fluoro-carbons* (CFCs). Traditionally, CFCs were used as propellants in aerosols, as refrigerants and as industrial gases (e.g. for inflating foam plastics). The concern over the effects of CFCs has meant that in most applications, they have been replaced. It is thought, however, that the effects of CFCs on the ozone layer will continue to be negative for some time after their complete removal (owing to the nature of the chemical reaction they bring about).

Under the *Montreal Protocol* (1987), CFC production in the developed world after 1996 was only permitted to supply the basic domestic needs of less-developed countries, plus a very small allowance for essential use (e.g. laboratory and pharmaceutical purposes) and since the peak year of 1988 there has been a reduction of some 95% of CFCs as weighted according to the ozone depletion potential of each compound.

The third major concern, although lesser in significance, is over '*acid*' *rain*. The increased concentration of gases resulting from fossil fuel combustion, particularly CO_2 and sulphur dioxide is predominantly to 'blame' for this effect. Sulphur dioxide, emitted from coal power stations, rises and reacts with water in the atmosphere to form precipitated sulphurous acid. The acid causes damage to plants and water systems when it eventually falls as rain. UK sulphur dioxide emissions, a major cause of acid rain, fell by 69% between 1990 and 2000.

Global temperatures have increased by 0.6°C over the last century.[2]

Indeed, 1998 was the hottest year since records began in 1860 and 9 of the 10 hottest years on record were during 1990–2002.

Climate change and greenhouse gases[3]

A balance between energy coming in from the Sun in the form of visible radiation (sunlight) and energy constantly being emitted from the Earth to space determines the temperature of the Earth. Some of the outgoing radiation is absorbed by naturally occurring greenhouse gases, including water vapour, creating a natural greenhouse effect which tends to keep the surface of the Earth around 33°C warmer than it would be in the absence of these greenhouse gases and it helps to sustain life.

Since the beginning of Industrial Revolution (around 1750), concentrations of the long-lived greenhouse gases in the atmosphere – CO_2, methane (CH_4), and nitrous oxide (N_2O) – have risen as a consequence of human activities. At the same time changes in global climate have occurred and work by an international body of scientists to establish causal links has detected a strong human signal.

The Intergovernmental Panel on Climate Change, in its 1991 report, concluded that based on current climate model predictions we can expect a rise in global temperatures of between 1.4 and 5.8°C by the end of the twenty-first century (and that sea levels will rise by between 0.09 and 0.88 metres. The implications for the UK could be up to a 3.5° increase in the annual temperature by 2080. Such a rate of warming would be without precedent in the last 10,000 years.

Although CO_2 is less potent than the other greenhouse gases on an equal mass basis, the quantity of emissions is so large that remains the main contributor to global warming. The UK contributes about 2% to the global man-made emissions of CO_2, which are estimated to range between 6.2 and 6.9 billion tonnes carbon per annum.

In December 1997, the parties to the Framework Convention on Climate Change adopted the Kyoto Protocol. Under this protocol, the UK agreed to reduce emissions of a 'basket' of six greenhouse gases – CO_2, CH_4, N_2O, hydroflurocarbons (HFCs), perflurocarbons (PFCs) and sulphur hexafluoride (SF_6) – by 12.5% below 1990 levels by the first commitment period of 2008–2012. The UK Government also has a domestic goal to cut CO_2 emissions by 20% below 1990 levels by 2010.

Implementation of the Kyoto Protocol, requiring ratification by at least 55 parties, was halted in March 2001 when the USA officially announced opposition to it, calling it 'an unfair and ineffective means of addressing global climate change concerns'. However, the EU ratified the Protocol in May 2002 and Russia signed the law to ratify the Kyoto treaty in October 2004 paving the way for the international agreement to reduce greenhouse gas emissions to come into force in February 2005.

Source: Department for Environment, Food and Rural Affairs.

13.4 Environmental management

Historically, economic development and growth has been portrayed as beneficial and important to the quality of life in general. Consequently, processes and practices designed to increase production and consumption have generally been encouraged, even though the detrimental effects on the environment have long been recognised. *Environmental management* is concerned with reconciling the need for economic growth with the demand for greater environmental protection and reduced levels of *ecological degradation*. Ecological degradation can be described as the rate at which limited natural resources are being depleted. The concept of scarcity and choice is not new but the way in which human needs are met without compromising the future is a practical challenge for society and all organisations.

Ecological footprint

Modern urban areas cannot sustain themselves with the resources from their own physical areas, but instead draw upon resources and products from a widespread area to be able to maintain their daily needs and consumption patterns. Wackernagel and Rees (1996)[4] refer to this environmental impact of urban areas as a city's '*ecological footprint*', which they define as '*a measure of the 'load' imposed by a given population on nature. It represents the land area necessary to sustain current levels of resource consumption and waste discharge by that population*'. Rather than ask how many people can the Earth support, ecological footprint analysis asks how much land do people require to support themselves – in other words it is not the number of heads that is important but the size of the feet! The average ecological footprint of a modern city dweller is reckoned to be about 12 acres, but that figure can vary quite widely dependent on the density of the population in a given location. For example, according to a *World Wildlife Fund* (WWF) study in 2004,[5] it takes 5.35 hectares of land to keep the average Scot fed, watered and mobile for a year. Although Scotland compares well with the UK overall, it has a bigger ecological footprint than the average for Western Europe and the study concluded that for Scotland to be sustainable it needed to aim for a footprint of just 1.9 hectare, which would balance the amount of land with resources consumed.

Activities which reduce an individual's ecological footprint include:

- buying products from local suppliers,
- recycling,
- avoiding unnecessary car journeys,
- using energy efficiently,
- using electricity from renewable sources,
- avoiding consumption of unnecessary products.

Reducing the individual's ecological footprint means becoming a more conscious consumer, thereby reducing the global environmental impact and working towards a sustainable community.

Sustainable development

The need for collective responsibility has been recognised throughout the world and is referred to as *sustainable development*. The term has been increasingly used since the 1987 World Commission on Environment and Development's report on 'Our Common Future'.[6] It is a philosophy that allows for present generations to meet their own needs without compromising the ability of successive generations to meet their own needs. It has to be accepted that it is difficult to find a balance in reconciling the range of conflicting interests, particularly as there is relatively limited information on the dynamics of economic development and its impact on the natural environment.

13.5 Responses to the concerns

So far in this chapter, we have examined the various concerns that people have over environmental matters as they relate to business. In this section, we look at the ways in which the interested parties have responded to these concerns.

Political responses

Government legislation

The most obvious way that government can respond to people's concerns about environment and ethics is by legislating (making laws). Businesses in the UK are affected by a range of environmental laws from both Westminster and from the EU (although it should be borne in mind that Westminster Acts tend to be in response to European Directives).

The most influential Acts over recent years have been the *Environmental Protection Act 1990* (EPA) and the *Environmental Protection Act 1995*, which regulate environmental pollution into land, water and air. Other important environmental legislation include the *Water Act 2003* and the *Water Resources (EIA) Regulations 2003* which require Environmental Impact Assessment (EIA) to be carried out for water management projects for agriculture, including irrigation, where it is deemed that the effects of the project on the environment are likely to be significant and where planning permission is not required.

The EPA includes the concept of *integrated pollution control* (IPC) which aims to:

- prevent pollution happening (as opposed to clearing up the mess afterwards);
- ensure that business act in such a way that minimises risk to human health and to the environment;
- encourage the adoption by businesses of the best environmental processes (i.e. those which will cause the least harm to the environment);

- assess how much pollution the environment can take without causing irreparable damage;
- ensure that the polluter pays for any clear up.

The Waste Management and Licensing Regulations 1994 were introduced into English law in response to an EU directive. This set of regulations distinguishes between waste disposal and waste management. They seek to encourage businesses to manage their waste more responsibly so as not to harm the environment or increase human health risk. Specifically, the Regulations seek to encourage businesses to:

- prevent or reduce waste production;
- develop products that will not cause harm to the environment;
- to develop techniques for effectively disposing of dangerous substances and materials;
- consider recycling all or part of their waste;
- explore the possibility of using waste as a source of energy.

Responsibility for the enforcement of environmental laws is the responsibility of a QuANGO called the *Environment Agency*. This has the responsibility to monitor activity as it may threaten the environment and to bring charges against offenders according to the provisions of the various environmental laws.

EU influence

The EU has put forward a number of measures in an attempt to influence business and consumer activity in respect of social responsibility. Its methods of persuasion include both legislation and codes of practice. In 1993, an *eco-label* was introduced but was not fully endorsed by the UK and the Department of the Environment Transport and the Regions (DETR) decided to withdraw from the scheme and lobby EU members to establish an integrated product policy.

On the legislation front, Directives have been passed which concern, for example, Europe-wide emissions, manufacturing practices and pollution control. One of the most publicised measures over recent years has been the European law that insists upon the fitting of catalytic converters to all new cars sold in the EU. These are devices fitted to car exhausts that reduce exhaust fume emissions by recirculating part of the emission back into the engine.

Environmental sustainability is encouraged by EU policy frameworks. The *5th EC Environmental Action Programme, 1993* prescribed policies to encourage responsible practice in a number of key areas of business; manufacturing, energy, transport, agriculture and tourism. In agriculture, for example, the framework prescribes a decrease in the use of chemicals, the protection of biodiversity (the breadth of animal and plant life) and natural habitats. In manufacturing, the framework prescribes the reduction of waste, pollution prevention and control, and research into refuse and recycling technology.

The Brundtland Report

Environmental sustainability was the subject of the *Brundtland Report* of 1987. Chaired by the Norwegian Prime Minister (Mrs Brundtland), the Committee reported on ways in which business could consume the world's resources in such a way that allows them to be replenished at the same rate at which they are used. Its broad investigation included aspects of the implications of population growth, resource conservation, food supplies, ecosystem preservation and urban development. The Brundtland Committee proposed a number of key recommendations including:

- recognising people's right to a healthy environment and to protection from environmental deterioration;
- the preservation of environmental resources, ecosystems and biological diversity for future generations;
- the assessment of the environmental effects of economic and business activity;
- the provision of information on the environmental effects of economic activity and resource consumption;
- international co-operation on the use of resources that cross national borders;
- the implementation of environmental protection measures;
- the planning of how environmental (behaviour) standards will be set and put into practice;
- working out responses to environmental 'disasters';
- the limiting of general environmental damage.

Local Agenda 21

One of the most influential governmental responses to environmental concern has been the Local Agenda 21 (LA21) initiative. This initiative arose out of the 'Earth Summit', held in Rio de Janeiro, Brazil, in 1992. Its *raison d'être* is to provide principles for the implementation of environmental conservation measures at the local level. LA21 was thus designed to be carried out by local authorities and although it is wide in its scope, has been criticised by environmental lobbyists as allowing too much interpretation at local level. The implementation of LA21 varies according to the views of local citizens, local organisations and private enterprises in the locality. The timetable set out at Rio specified that a programme for local action should be in place by 1996 on six broad policy areas:

- energy,
- recycling,
- pollution monitoring and minimisation,
- transport and planning,
- environmental protection and enhancement,
- health.

In the UK, many local authorities have failed to meet the 1996 target for these policy proposals. One of the problems expressed by local authorities in respect of LA21 is that no new financial resources were made available to them for its implementation.

Corporate (business) responses

As we have seen, much of the activity of business in respect of corporate responsibility is underpinned by law. The question is thus to ask what organisations do to address environmental concerns over and above the legal minimum.

Many businesses have appreciated that an *appearance* of social responsibility is good for business. Very few businesses exist for charitable purposes only and so it is generally understood that commercial businesses adapt their behaviour with a view to increasing customers' confidence in both the company and its products. For example, chemical companies have made a number of non-mandatory changes including the phasing out of CFC production and the introduction of processes to profitably use by-products as a means of partly reducing waste. Supermarkets have changed their stocking policies to include a range of eco-friendly products, such as special washing powders, free-range meat and egg products, and unbleached paper products.

Marketing practices

One of the most important ways in which organisations have responded to concern is by making changes in its marketing activities. All aspects of the marketing process can be affected by environmental concern. Examples include:

- changes in product design and R&D have resulted in products being designed to increase energy efficiency, to be eco-friendly and to use materials from sustainable sources (e.g. by using wood from sustainable forest areas);
- using product packaging that is less lavish than it might be and an increase in the use of materials that can be recycled;
- informing consumers of the background of a product by a creative use of labelling, such as the 'keep Britain tidy' logo, the use of the recyclable logo, or stating explicitly that the product is made using renewable energy sources;
- supporting environmental projects and sponsorship of 'green' activities by groups, such as the National Trust;
- demonstrating that the organisation has been accredited for having attained *ISO 14001* standard in *environmental management system* (EMS).

One model put forward for 'green' marketing is that of the 'four Ss'. When we examine marketing in Chapter 28, we will see that a conventional marketing process comprises four Ps. The four Ss place a different emphasis on marketing activity:

- satisfaction of customer needs and wants;
- safety of products and the production processes;
- social acceptability of the products, their production and of the behaviour of the business;
- sustainability of the products and production processes in respect of materials used and the method of production.

Case: Saving natural resources and saving money

The Cosmopolitan Hotels Group highlighted their environmental responsibility, in 2003, by taking steps to conserve natural resources when they commissioned a survey by water conservation specialists, McCann Associates. As a result of the survey the group was able to dramatically reduce water usage at three of their Scottish Hotels, with annual savings of some £50,000.

The study covered three of the Group's hotels, the Dean Park, the Normandy and Erskine Bridge Hotels and began with a thorough analysis of water consumption behaviour at each location.

At the first hotel, a leak from a faulty valve was discovered and a repair was implemented within 24 hours, with a projected saving of £31,000 on the annual water bill. Water conservation equipment at the second hotel will reduce water usage by approximately 20%, worth £8000 per year on the water bill. The third hotel was losing water via cistern overflows and the main storage tank. Repairs were made which eliminated the waste of water. This reduction of water waste along with water conservation equipment fitted at the hotel indicates a saving of 30% in water usage – a combined saving of £10,000 per year.

It is staggering to calculate that if the hotel group had not acted in 2003, they would have incurred unnecessary water costs of £250,000 by 2007, as well as the waste of valuable water resources.

This demonstrates an example of how environmental management and the balance sheet can work in perfect harmony.

Source: Reproduced with the kind permission of McCann Associates.

Conforming to standards

A voluntary standard that helps organisations develop an EMS is ISO 14001. This international standard sets requirements for environmental policy, environmental objectives, implementation, control and continuous improvement. By conforming to ISO 14001 organisations assure stakeholders that they have a robust and effective EMS. Prior to the establishment of the international agreed standard, the British Standards Institution had the BS 7750 in EMSs. In the same way that BS 5750 specifies systems for the assurance of product quality, BS 7750 requires a conforming organisation to comply with standards with regard to its responsibility to the environment.

Organisations that conform to the standard undergo the following procedures:

- undertaking a preliminary environmental review of the organisation's processes and outputs;
- documenting the organisation's environmental policy (which is usually the subject of some consultation and debate);
- setting out an appropriate management structure to implement the environmental policy;
- keeping records and registers of wider environmental regulations and their effects;
- establishing specific objectives and targets which must provide for continual environmental improvement;
- formulating an appropriate environmental management programme including a description of the procedures adopted to achieve the targets;
- writing an environmental management manual and accompanying documentation;

- keeping records to show that the procedures are being consistently followed;
- establishing a system whereby environment management systems are regularly audited (checked) for conformance to the system adopted;
- periodically assessing that targets and procedures are appropriate and modifying them as is required to meet the aim of continual improvement.

The award of the ISO 14001 accreditation enables an organisation to demonstrate to its stakeholders that it takes its environmental responsibilities seriously and that it is acting consistently in respect of its environmental management programme.

Changing corporate behaviour

Some organisations formalise their responses to environmental concerns of their stakeholders by modifying or re-writing their *mission statements*. They may include phrases such as, '... to make positive contributions to sustainable development', or '... to actively pursue the most efficient uses of energy'. The Body Shop's mission statement begins with the words, 'to dedicate our business to the pursuit of social and environmental change', and continues, 'to passionately campaign for the protection of the environment, human and civil right, and against animal testing within the cosmetics and toiletries industry'.

These sentiments are further emphasised in the Body Shop's published *trading principles* (see below). Such a top-level expression of commitment is designed to influence behaviour throughout the organisation and to signal to stakeholders the organisation's desire to respond to concerns.

The Body Shop: trading principles

- We aim to ensure human and civil rights, as set out in the *Universal Declaration of Human Rights*, are respected throughout our business activities.
- We will support long-term sustainable relationships with communities in need. We will use environmentally sustainable resources wherever technically and economically viable.
- We will support animal protection throughout our business activities and in many ways.
- We will ensure our accountability and demonstrate our compliance with these principles.

EU Eco-Management and Audit Scheme

Eco-Management and Audit Scheme (EMAS) is a voluntary scheme which incorporates and builds on the ISO 14001 standard, but which also requires participants to publish independent validated reports on performance. Registered companies can use the EMAS logo and make validated 'green' claims about their products, services and activities. It is compatible with the UK Code of Practice on Green Claims and with ISO 14021 which is the standard for environmental claims and labeling.

Consumer responses

Consumers are the cause of most of the other changes – governments and organisations care largely because consumers (ordinary people) care. Popular opinion is thus the engine of change.

Product preferences

The most obvious way in which consumers respond to their concerns is to change the choices of the types of products they buy. A number of changing buyer preferences includes the following:

- a trend towards smaller cars and more efficient car engines;
- increasing sales of organic produce and free-range meat products;
- increasing sales of products with reduced levels of packaging;
- buying lower-packaging 'refills' of products which are used to replenish permanent containers;
- deliberately avoiding buying products from companies who are believed to be guilty of environmental or ethical irresponsibility (boycotting).

Recycling

Many consumers have established the practice of segregating their refuse between that which is recyclable and that which is not. Tins, glass, paper, cloth and some plastics can be recycled and used again, thus requiring less 'virgin' material to be used in future manufacturing. Recycling centres are frequently set up by local authorities (e.g. adjacent to municipal rubbish tips) and in supermarket car parks.

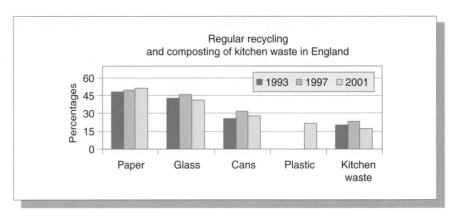

Figure 13.6
Recycling levels in
England. (*Source*:
Department for
Environment, Food
and Rural Affairs.)

Although the UK currently recycles less consumer waste than some other countries, such as Germany and the USA, the LA21 initiative is expected to increase recycling levels in most countries over the longer term (Figure 13.6).

Pressure groups

Individual members of the population in a democracy, like the UK, can seek to have their views represented through the electoral system by voting for political parties who have a manifesto that accords with their sense of values and priorities. However, this may be insufficient for some particular issues or causes and may lead to the formation of specific voluntary like-minded people to try influence ('lobby') government and corporate thinking and actions. Prominent groups for environmental issues include Greenpeace and Friends of the Earth. Occasionally the demarcation between lobbying and active politics becomes blurred and there an example of a pressure group evolving into a professional political party can be found with the Green Party.

Assignment 13.1

If you are using this textbook as part of a class or group, organise a debate comprising two sides presenting arguments before an audience (the rest of the class). Eight to ten volunteers should divide into two sides. One team should prepare a case in favour of the contention:

The business of business is business.

or alternatively,

Stakeholders should only be considered by a business insofar as their demands are consistent with the maximisation of profit.

The other side should prepare the case against. The debate itself should comprise both sides presenting their cases to an equal time limit (say 20 minutes each), beginning with the case in favour. The class then should have the opportunity to question each team. After a final summing up of both arguments by the two teams, the class should vote on the contention based on the arguments put forward.

References

1   *Worldwide Look at Reserves and Production* (2002). *Oil and Gas Journal* **100**(52): 114–115.
2   DTI, 2002.
3   *The Environment in Your Pocket* (2002). Department for Environment, Food and Rural Affairs.
4   Wackernagel, M. and Rees, W. (1996). *Our Ecological Footprint, Reducing Human Impact on the Earth.* Canada: New Society Publishers.
5   World Commission on Environment and Development. *Our Common Future* (1987).
6   World Wildlife Fund. *Scotland's Ecological Footprint* (2004).

Further reading

Cline, W.R. (1992). *The Economics of Global Warming.* London: Longman.
Daly, H.E. and Townsend, K.N. (eds) (1992). *Valuing the Earth. Economics, Ecology, Ethics.* Cambridge, MA, USA: MIT Press.
Drummond, J. and Bain, W. (1994). *Managing Business Ethics.* Oxford: Butterworth Heinemann.
Hanley, N., *et al.* (2001). *An Introduction to Environmental Economics.* London: FT Prentice Hall.
Houghton, J. (2004). *Global Warming: the Complete Briefing.* London: FT Prentice Hall.
Nordhaus, W.D. (1994). *Managing the Global Commons. The Economics of Climate Change.* Cambridge, MA, USA: MIT Press.
Pearce, D. and Barbier, E.B. (2000). *Blueprint for a Sustainable Economy.* New York: Earthscan.

Perman, R. and Common, M., *et al.* (2003). *Natural Resource and Environmental Economics*. London: FT Prentice Hall.

Shrivastava, P. (1995). *Greening Business. Sustaining the Corporation and the Environment*. London: Thomson Publishing.

Taylor, B., Hutchinson, C. and Tapper, R. (eds) (1994). *Environmental Management Handbook*. London: Pitman.

Welford, R. (1993). *Environmental Management and Business Strategy*. London: Pitman.

Useful web sites

Centre for Environment, Fisheries & Aquaculture Science (CEFAS): www.cefas.co.uk

Department for the Environment and Rural Affairs: www.defra.gov.uk/environment/

Department of Trade and Industry: www.dti.gov.uk/energy/

Energy Balances of OECD Countries, International Energy Agency: www.iea.org

International Society for Environmental Protection: www.cedar. univvie.ac.at/

Greenpeace: www.greenpeace.org

Friends of the Earth: www.foe.co.uk

Environmental Change Institute: www.ukcip.org.uk

The legal environment

After studying this chapter, students should be able to describe:

- the nature of law and legal rules;
- the nature of and difference between civil law and criminal law;
- the nature of and difference between common law and statute law;
- the purpose and structure of the British and European Union (EU) judiciaries;
- the types of EU law and the EU legislative process;
- the key areas of business law and the relevant legislation.

14.1 What is law?

When we consider how legal matters affect businesses and other organisations, we should consider it to be essentially a part of the political environment. However, its complexities and importance necessitate a more detailed discussion. This is the objective of this chapter.

Definition and purpose of law

A system of rules

In any society, the complex interrelationships between legally responsible parties, such as people and companies, need to be regulated. It is generally understood that limits must be placed upon activities to prevent miscreants and other irresponsible people from abusing their freedom in a democratic state. Such acceptation leads to the enforcement of 'rules'. However, not all rules carry the same weight. A distinction needs to be drawn between legal rules and other types of rules. We sometimes use the term 'rules' to describe norms of behaviour in society. We may consider ourselves to be breaking 'social rules' if we act in an antisocial manner, such as dressing in an unconventional way, or if we are rude or insulting to others. Within organisations, rules are imposed to facilitate normal functioning and may take the form of rigid procedures and limits of behaviour, such as a rule that receipts must be provided to support all expense claims.

Legal rules are different from social and other rules. They are characterised by the fact that they are enforceable by the judiciary which acts on behalf of the state. So whereas the *de facto* rule 'do not swear in the office' is not enforceable by the state, the rule 'do not steal cars' is. It is a matter of legal and philosophical debate at which degree of seriousness a rule becomes enforceable in law by the state. The rule 'do not walk on the grass' in a public park may, for example, be a rule which some individuals feel should be enforceable in law where others may consider it a matter of utter inconsequence.

As the law is primarily designed to *serve* the citizens of a state, it is reasonable to expect that legal rules should vary according to differing national customs and societal expectations. In traditional Islamic law for example, adultery is considered to be illegal (breaking a legal rule) as it is in contravention of the Qu'ran (Koran). In consequence, the act, if discovered, is (theoretically) punishable by the Islamic state. In contrast, the sensibilities of citizens in western nations like the UK renders adultery an act which may contravene most people's social or ethical code, but is not considered to be punishable by the state. This is not to say that adultery may not lead to indirect legal action in the event that the offended spouse elected to seek a divorce.

The purpose of law

Legal rules serve essentially the same purpose as other types of rules. It does not take a lot of imagination to conceive of the chaos that would arise if football was deprived of its rules and the same is true of society at large. Laws serve three broad purposes:

- to *permit* individuals to engage in lawful activities without apprehension or molestation by others;
- to *restrict* unlawful or otherwise disturbing individuals and behaviour;

■ to *constrain* individuals to comply with legally required activities, such as the payment of taxes.

The normal functioning of society rests upon the assumption that the majority of people agree to comply with the law, in the same way that the normal functioning of a football match relies upon each player complying with the rules. It follows that the majority must view the laws that affect them as reasonable and fair – a situation theoretically guaranteed by having a democratically elected legislature.

Important distinctions in law

When we consider the general area of laws and legal rules, we must be aware of two important ways of dividing law. The first concerns the seriousness of offences and the second concerns the source of law (Figure 14.1).

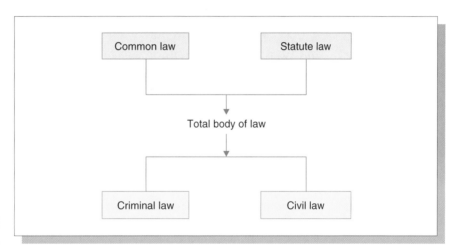

Figure 14.1
Sources and
categories of law.

Civil law and criminal law

At their simplest, matters of civil law and criminal law can be distinguished according to the perceived seriousness of the offences. Civil and criminal law are two distinct areas of legal practice and are overseen by separate parts of the judiciary.

In matters of *civil law*, individuals can bring other individuals (or legal entities, such as companies) to the judiciary in order to have disputes settled. A civil matter is one in which a legal entity feels that they have a legitimate grievance against another, but the 'offence' is a matter which is not serious enough for the state to bring the case to a criminal court.

The nature of the 'offence' is not considered to be a threat to society as a whole. In civil cases, the judiciary therefore acts as an umpire, ensuring that wrongs are redressed and that fairness is enforced. Once a civil court has made a judgement, the ruling carries the authority of the state.

Some of the most common civil disputes concern matters of *tort*. The Law of Torts concerns legal wrongs against an individual which gives the plaintiff (the party that brings the complaint – see later) a right of civil action for damages, but which do not arise over matters of breach of contract or trust. It is a broad expectation in society that individuals should have the right to pursue their lives without personal offence to their persons, property, etc. and to enjoy their possessions and property without unreasonable intrusion by others. Tort concerns such things as trespass, nuisance, negligence and defamation of character. It gives individuals the right of legal redress when they have been offended against in these matters.

A *criminal case* is one in which the offence is viewed as being of sufficient seriousness that, even although it may be an individual that has been 'wronged' the case against the alleged offender is brought by the state (or *the Crown*) in the form of the *Crown Prosecution Service* (CPS) for England and Wales. In Scotland, the *Crown Office and Procurator Fiscal Service* is the sole public prosecution authority, with responsibility for making decisions about, and bringing prosecutions for, almost all criminal offences, statutory (devolved and reserved) and non-statutory (common law).

In criminal cases, the successful prosecution of an offender is assumed to be in the interest of the state and society as a whole rather than just the individual who may have been offended against. In contrast to the judiciary acting as an umpire (as in matters of civil law), the Courts act as an executioner in criminal cases in that it has power to execute (carry out) punishment.

Civil law and criminal law – simple (fictional) example

The author has a next-door neighbour who decides to remove the fence separating the two adjoining gardens. In erecting his new fence, the next-door neighbour 'steals' half a metre of the author's garden by fixing the fence in a new position within the former boundaries of the author's garden. After pointing out the misplacement of the new fence, the neighbour refuses to replace his fence. The author takes the matter to his solicitor who recommends that he brings a civil case against the neighbour. In this case, the author has been offended against, but not in such a serious manner that the state would entertain bringing a case against the neighbour. Apart from the neighbour's theft of a small piece of land, he is a law-abiding, tax-paying citizen. The law acts as umpire, looking at the two conflicting cases and awarding 'victory' to the party who has been offended.

After a sharp exchange of opinions over the newly replaced garden fence, the next-door neighbour produces a gun and proceeds to shoot the author. By fortunate happenstance, the bullet penetrates the author's leg, which, whilst painful, is not a life-threatening wound. After the police had been summoned to the scene and reported back, the CPS decides to bring a criminal case against the neighbour. The state considers a shooting to be of sufficient seriousness that it (the state) should bring the case against the neighbour, even although it is the author who has been shot.

The legal system employs different terminology to describe the various people and processes involved in these two areas of law (Table 14.1).

Table 14.1
Criminal and civil law terminology

Criminal law	Civil law
Cases are referred to as *R v. Smith* (or the Crown v. Smith)	Cases are referred as *Smith v. Jones* (two private parties in dispute)
The *Crown* initiates the proceedings	The *plaintiff* initiates the proceedings
The Crown *prosecutes*	The plaintiff *sues*
The *accused* is prosecuted	The person sued is the *defendant*
The accused is *convicted* of a crime	The defendant is found *liable*
If convicted, the accused is *punished* or *penalised*	If found liable, the defendant is required to *remedy* or to *make reparations*

Statute law and common law

The difference between statute and common law is their respective origins. We saw in Chapter 8 that some laws are made in the state's legislature which in the UK comprises Parliament (the Houses of Commons and Lords) and the monarchy. Laws produced by this mechanism are called statute laws. As Acts of Parliament, they are written down *in statute* in documents called legislation or statutory instruments.

In contrast, common laws, which are no less enforceable than statute laws, are not written down as such. Common laws, which comprise the majority of laws in most modern democracies, are the result of (in the case of UK common laws) over 800 years of legal interpretation by the learned members of the judiciary. Unlike statute law, common law tends to evolve and change over time as members of the judiciary reinterpret ancient *forms of action* in the light of changing social and legal environments. It is generally understood, for example, that murder is highly antisocial behaviour. For this reason, it need not be enshrined in statute – it is a matter of common law. When murder was first punishable by the British judiciary in the dark recesses of medieval history, the most frequent mechanism of the crime was probably by the use of bare hands, clubs or bows and arrows. When however, the gun was invented, the judiciary would extrapolate the spirit of the common law of murder and find gun murderers guilty in the same way as those who had killed by more primitive methods. If murder was the subject of statute law, the statute would have to be revised by the legislature to account for the introduction of a new means of carrying out the offence. Under common law, the fact that murder had been punished in earlier legal cases meant that the judiciary merely had to refer to these, and adapt the law to account for a new means of carrying out the crime.

This brings us to an important principle in common law – that of *judicial precedent*. According to this principle, current cases in matters of common law can be assessed in the light of previously decided cases. If, for example, a case concerned a civil matter where two people disagree over whether a tree should be chopped down, they could scour the annals of previously decided cases and, upon finding a precedent, could appeal to that precedent to decide their disagreement.

14.2 The judiciary

Distinctions in the judiciary

The British judiciary, comprising the complicated system of courts, is divided up according to two broad distinctions. It is thus important that we appreciate the difference between *trial* and *appellate* courts, and between *civil* and *criminal* courts.

Trial and appellate courts

The distinction between trial and appellate courts is straightforward. Trial courts hear cases 'at first instance' or first time around. Appellate courts (or appeal courts) are able to hear cases on appeal that have previously been heard in trial courts. Both trial and appellate courts are used in both civil and criminal cases.

The rules which govern the progress of cases from trial to appellate courts can be very complicated. It is by no means an automatic right for anybody who loses a trial to appeal. Furthermore, the grounds on which appeals are permitted are equally complex. Appeals are usually allowable if, for example, new evidence comes to light that was not available at the time of the initial trial. The basis of jurisprudence in the UK, that is that a person is innocent until proven guilty, means that the appeals procedure is available in order to give people every opportunity to demonstrate that they are not guilty.

Civil courts and criminal courts

These two areas of law demand very different legal procedures. This is due to the respective content of civil and criminal cases. Different skills are required by professionals who operate in these two legal areas and this necessitates that they be separated by the courts system.

In order to demonstrate that either a civil or criminal offence has been committed, evidence is offered. The ways in which evidence is heard and weighed varies according to the area of law and the court in which it is heard. It must be the case, for example, that the weight of evidence required to convict an alleged murderer must be greater than that required to settle a civil case concerning an allegedly broken employment contract. Hence, whilst some types of evidence may be perfectly acceptable in civil cases, the same evidence may not be admissible in a serious criminal case. The judiciary is thus divided into courts intended for different legal purposes.

Structure of the courts system

A general structure of the courts system is shown in Figure 14.2. Some textbooks incorrectly represent the court structure as a hierarchy indicating that some courts have automatic seniority over others. This is not the case as there are complicated rules which govern the passage of a case through the various types and levels of courts.

The House of Lords

The House of Lords is the most senior court in England and Wales. Its legal purpose is appellate only; that is, it only hears appeals and is not a trial court. Its appeals come almost entirely from the Court of Appeal, but can, under certain circumstances, be referred from the High Court.

Cases in the House of Lords are heard by five 'Law Lords' more formally known as *Lords of Appeal in Ordinary*. The seniority of the Lords of

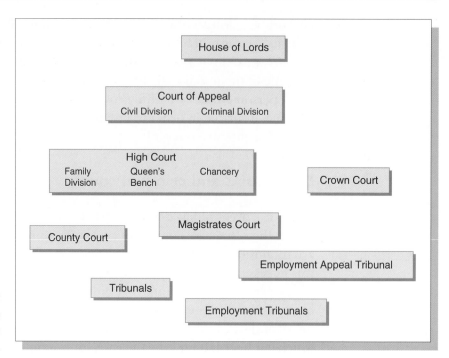

Figure 14.2
The system of the
civil courts in
England and Wales.

Appeal means that they have final jurisdiction over both civil and criminal appeals. Their workload is low compared to other branches of the courts system – usually around 100 cases a year. Appeals only reach the House of Lords in special circumstances, when all other judicial appeals have been exhausted and the qualifications for a case to be heard by the Lords are stringent. In addition to the considerable cost of bringing an appeal to the Lords, the Law Lords will only hear an appeal if it is considered to be 'of general public importance'. This means that there must be a significant degree of doubt regarding the operation of the rule of law in regard to the case. Such cases are few, hence the relatively low workload of the Lords compared to other courts.

The Court of Appeal

The Court of Appeal, which, as its name suggests is appellate only, is divided into two divisions: the civil division which hears civil appeals, and the criminal division, which accordingly hears criminal appeals.

The civil division hears appeal cases which have been referred by the High Court and County Court. Presiding over the civil division only is the country's senior civil judge who carries the title *Master of the Rolls*. The criminal division hears cases that have been referred by the Crown

Court and take the form of appeals against sentence or conviction. It is headed by the *Lord Chief Justice* who is also considered to be Britain's most senior judge (who is considered to be senior to the Master of the Rolls). Both civil and criminal cases are heard in the court by (normally) three judges called *Lord Justices of Appeal*. Civil cases are heard only by Lord Justices of Appeal whilst criminal cases are heard by judges drawn from among the Lord Chief Justice, the Lord Justices of Appeal and the Judges of the High Court.

Question 14.1

Who are the current Master of the Rolls and the current Lord Chief Justice?

The High Court

The High Court has the most complicated structure of any of the courts and has both trial and appellate functions. It contains three divisions:

- *The Family Division* deals with matrimonial disputes (e.g. divorces), the wardship of children and matters of adoption.
- The *Queen's Bench* deals with the main areas of common law, such as the law of contract.
- The *Chancery* division is concerned mainly with property, corporate (business) and tax matters.

Each division is concerned with first instance (trial) cases, but in the form of a Divisional Court, can also hear appeals. The Divisional Court of the Queen's Bench division, for example, has appellate function inasmuch as it exercises 'supervisory jurisdiction' over the quality and legality of decision-making in inferior courts and tribunals.

Crown Courts

These courts, which are located on major towns and cities, have trial and appellate functions, but their area of jurisdiction is purely criminal, that is they does not hear civil law cases. Most of the Crown Courts' work is first instance concerning serious criminal offences, such as murder, physical and sexual assaults, and property offences resulting in a high value of loss or damage. The normal method of trial is by a judge sitting with a jury. The jury – a committee of selected members of the public – hears evidence from both prosecution and defence counsels (legally qualified professionals) and decides, on the balance of evidence if guilt has been demonstrated beyond reasonable doubt. In the event of a guilty verdict being returned, the judge delivers a sentence consistent with the seriousness of the crime. A lesser part of the purpose of a Crown Court is to hear appellate cases referred from Magistrates' Courts.

Magistrates' Courts

Magistrates' Courts are presided over by magistrates or Justices of the Peace – lay persons of notable local standing who usually have no legal qualification. They are advised on legal matters by a legal specialist called the Justice's Clerk. The jurisdiction of the Magistrates' Court is purely first instance and in practice, is almost exclusively criminal with a small civil jurisdiction over such matters as liquor licensing. Their normal case load comprises less serious criminal cases – more serious cases are tried at the Crown Court.

County Courts

County Courts have a purely civil jurisdiction, similar to that of the High Court. Whereas the High Court deals with any value of civil claim, the County Court is concerned with smaller claims – usually up to a value of around £5000.

Other courts

Whilst the vast majority of legal cases are heard at one of the above courts, others do exist for occasional or special purposes, such as industrial tribunals and matters concerning the constitution of the state. These include the *Judicial Committee of the Privy Council* which tries some Admiralty cases and a number of *Administrative Tribunals* which have a range of jurisdictions, such as employment disputes and social security entitlements.

Scottish legal system

Scots Law and the Scottish Legal System have a long history, dating back to the middle ages. Scots Law shares many of the statutory provisions of the law of England and Wales, but Scots civil law remains substantially based on Scots common law rather than statute, and Scots civil law contains elements that have origins in Roman Law rather than English Common Law traditions.

Criminal justice

The criminal justice procedure for Scotland is divided into two distinct areas:

  ▪ *Solemn* – the most serious cases involving trial on indictment before a judge or sheriff sitting without a jury;
  ▪ *Summary* – less serious offences involving a trial before a sheriff, stipendiary magistrate or justice of the peace, sitting alone.

The *High Court of Justiciary* is the country's supreme criminal court, handling the most serious crimes, and is the final court of appeal for criminal cases. The High Court is peripatetic, sitting in cities and towns as required. It comprises the Lord Justice General, the Lord Justice Clerk and another 30 judges, known as Lords Commissioners of Justiciary, who are all appointed by the Queen. Judges can preside over both criminal and civil courts. All criminal prosecutions are brought in the name of the Lord Advocate and prosecuted by the appointed Advocate Deputee.

There are 49 *Sheriff Courts*, each overseen by a Sheriff Principal. These courts have limited sentencing powers of up to 3 years imprisonment and/or an unlimited fine in solemn cases, and up to 6 months imprisonment and/or £5000 fine for summary cases. If the court decides that its sentencing powers are insufficient for a particular case it can remit the case to the High Court.

District Courts sit in each local authority area under summary jurisdiction only and who are presided over by *Justices of the Peace* (lay magistrates) who sit alone or in threes with a qualified legal assessor as convenor or clerk of the court. They deal with many cases of breach of the peace, drunkenness, minor assaults, petty theft, and offences under the *Civic Government Act (Scotland) 1982*.

Civil justice

The Court of Session is Scotland's supreme civil court and can trace its history back to the sixteenth century. It sits in Parliament House in Edinburgh as a court of first instance and a court of appeal. Decisions of this court can be appealed to the House of Lords. The court is headed by the Lord President, assisted by the Lord Justice Clerk and comprises 32 judges who are designated *Senators of the College of Justice* or *Lords of Council and Session.* To hear cases, the court is divided into an Outer House and an Inner House. The Outer House consists of 19 Lords Ordinary sitting alone or, in certain cases, with a jury. They hear cases at first instance on a wide range of matters, including cases based on *delict* (tort) and contract, commercial cases and judicial review. Designated judges deal with intellectual property disputes. The Inner House is effectively the appeal court although it does have a small range of first instance business.

14.3 EU law

In addition to the complexities of the English legal system, a study of the legal environment would be incomplete without examining how European legal institutions and instruments can affect UK businesses and individuals. The European legal system is of importance to the UK because the UK is a member of the EU. Upon joining the EU in 1972 (when the EU was called the EEC or European Economic Community), the UK became (voluntarily) subject to both primary and secondary European legislation and in doing so, effectively surrendered part of its sovereignty over legal matters. In most matters, European law is superior to domestic law in that rulings in the European judiciary take precedence over rulings in UK courts and laws passed by the EU must have their effect on individuals and businesses in the UK.

Types of European law

European laws are divided into two main types: *primary* and *secondary* legal instruments.

The *primary* legislation of the EU is the *Treaty of Rome, 1957.* This is a lengthy legal document which was drawn up as the time of the EU's inception and was the document which legally created the EU. The term *primary* is applied to the Treaty of Rome because all other legal instruments of the EU are subject to it. It sets out the structure of the EU and many of the pivotal legal matters that characterise the EU, such as equal pay for men and women for equal jobs. From time to time, the Treaty of Rome is amended as new ideas come to the fore that member states believe should form part of the EU's primary law. The most notable recent example of such an amendment is the *Treaty on European*

Union 1992 (Maastricht Agreement), in which the member states agreed to pursue closer political and economic union, eventually leading to, among other things, a common European currency (see Chapter 8).

Secondary European law is subordinate to the primary Treaty of Rome. As such, no secondary legal instrument can in any way contravene any part of the primary law. There are three types of secondary EU law:

- *European Regulations* are said to be directly applicable to in each member state as they enter national law without being debated and passed by national parliaments. Hence, when a Regulation is passed, it becomes law in each member state and has precedence over any conflicting provisions of domestic (i.e. national) legislation.
- *European Directives*, like regulations, are binding upon each member state, but their mechanism of implementation is different. Whereas regulations pass into national law automatically, directives are required to be passed into national law after they have first been debated by national parliaments. Hence, a European Directive is implemented in UK law as an Act of the British Parliament. All parts of the provisions of a Directive must pass into national law and there is usually a period of time within which it must be enacted.
- *European Decisions* are narrower in scope that both Directives and Regulations as they are specific to certain member states only. A Decision may be binding upon just one member state as a means of corrective action in, for example, one area of national policy. Decisions are binding upon the 'targeted' state from the date on which the addressee is notified of the Decision.

The EU legislative process

The procedures by which European law is made are significantly more complicated than that for laws made by the UK legislature. This is partly because of the complex structure of the EU and partly due to the wide consultation and amendment procedures that must be undertaken before any law is enacted.

Membership of the EU necessarily means that member states surrender part of their sovereignty over legal matters to the Union. This does not however mean that individual member states simply surrender European law-making to centralised authorities – each state takes an active part in the legislative process alongside their fellow members.

The central European institutions also play an important role as they are empowered to do so (by Treaty) by the governments of the member states.

There are four stages in the EU legislative process:

- The *proposal procedure* involves the ideas for new laws being proposed, together with a draft of the provisions and limits of the proposed law. This task falls to the Commission only, as it acts upon its right of initiative. In some areas of legislation, the Council must be advised and the Council has the power to overturn a proposed law at the proposal stage.

- The *formulation stage* occurs after the proposal has been accepted in principle by the Council. The task of actually drafting the law falls to the European Commissioner with oversight of the area within which the law will operate (e.g. trade, transport, etc.). He or she may consult widely with experts in the field at this stage in order to ensure that all necessary provisions are covered. Once drafted, the law returns to the European Commission (the 20 Commissioners) where a simple majority is required to enable the draft to go forward to the next stage. As a newly created 'Commission proposal', the document goes to the Council (a right guaranteed by the principle of 'compulsory consultation'), together with a detailed explanation of the grounds for the proposal.

- The *consultation stage* is the third procedure in the law's passage. Several EU bodies must be apprised of the proposal. Whilst the Council, as the executive body has the final say, the European Parliament must also be allowed to debate it. The Parliament, acting on behalf of the citizen's of the EU, submits a formal written opinion to the Commission and the Council together with any amendment recommendations. The European and Social Consultative Committee is also invited to express an opinion which again, is delivered to the Commission and the Council. The Commission may, on the advice of the various opinions, decide to amend the proposal before passing it again back to the Council.

- The fourth and final procedure in the formation of a European law is the *enactment stage*. The final (and possibly amended) proposal, once in the possession of the Council, is scrutinised by specialist working parties on behalf of the Council and then by the Council of Permanent Representatives (COREPER). Once these committees are satisfied with the proposal, it goes before a full session of the appropriate committee of the ministerial European Council. Once adopted by the Council, it is signed by the President of the Council. The proposal becomes a law and is published in all nine official European languages in the *Official Journal of the European Communities.*

The EU judiciary

We learned in Chapter 8 that the European judiciary comprises two courts, both based in Luxembourg.

The European Court of Justice

The European Court of Justice is overseen by 15 independent judges – one from each member state, one of whom is appointed as president. They are assisted in their duties by nine senior legal officials called advocates-general, who also serve terms of 6 years. It is Europe's most senior court and assumes supremacy over all national senior courts and has both trial and appellate functions. In addition, the Court of Justice has a special role in the independent enforcement of EU treaties and legislation. The EU describes the Court's judicial functions as follows:[1]

- Actions for failure to fulfil obligations under the (EU's) Treaties. These are civil actions brought (usually) by the European Commission against a member state.
- Actions for annulment against the Council or Commission.
- Actions on grounds of failure to act (against the Council or Commission in the event that either body fails to fulfil its responsibilities).
- Claims for damages against the Community.
- References from national courts for preliminary rulings to clarify the meaning and scope of Community law (the Court's appellate function).

The Court of Justice combines several legal functions in one whole.

- It is a *criminal court* in that it can impose fines upon other parts of the EU, such as the Commission, for failing to discharge its responsibilities.
- It is a *civil court* in that it can settle claims for damages. A key part of this role is the interpretation of a legal document called

the *Brussels Convention on the Enforcement of Judgements in Civil and Commercial Matters.*

■ It is a *constitutional court* in that it can review and settle disputes between Community institutions or review the legality of legislative instruments (a constitutional court is one which has powers to decide the legality of the structure of the EU).

■ It is a *labour court* and an *industrial tribunal* in that it can settle cases concerning the freedom of movement of workers in the Union, social security matters and equal opportunities issues.

The European Court of First Instance

The European Court of First Instance, as its name suggests, is concerned with trial cases only and has no appellate jurisdiction. It is a more recent development than the Court of Justice; having been set up in October 1988 (the Court of Justice was instituted at the same time as the EEC itself). Like its neighbour, the Court of First Instance consists of 15 judges.

Its areas of jurisdiction include the following:

■ actions relating to the various Staff Regulations of the European Communities (the EC, the ECSC and EURATOM);

■ competition law (relating to rules of business competition in member states);

■ coal and steel disputes;

■ all direct actions brought by citizens and businesses against Community institutions except in anti-dumping matters.

14.4 Business law

The legal regulation of business in the UK has increased over recent years. Whilst some aspects of law that affect business are ancient, such as the ancient common laws concerning contract, others have arisen from such factors as employees' increased expectations from employers and the UK's supranational influences, particularly the EU. The result of increased regulation is a complex legal environment which some have argued imposes an inconvenient cost burden upon businesses. There is an active political debate regarding the extent to which business should be regulated, particularly with regard to the regulation of employment policies and employers' obligations towards employees. The political right have tended to oppose greatly increased regulation whilst the European left has tended to espouse a contrary philosophy.

All areas of law that we have considered can affect business – both civil and criminal laws apply to business. Furthermore, the tranche of laws that we need to consider includes both common laws and statute legislation. Recent trends have seen an increase in statutory legislation. In considering this area of law, we will discuss it as it affects the various aspects of business practice. No discussion of this nature can possibly be exhaustive, but it is hoped that readers will gain an appreciation of the types of law that can influence and regulate business practice.

Company law

This area of law affects the legal status of limited companies and hence has no direct bearing on unincorporated organisations, such as sole proprietors and partnerships. The conditions placed upon limited companies and their prescribed legal *modus operandi* are enshrined in a raft of Companies Acts – statutes of Parliament.

Company law has tended to evolve and change as the activities and situations which needed to be legislated for changed over time. The earliest pieces of company law were introduced in the nineteenth century. The *Companies Act 1844*, the *Limited Liability Act 1855* and the *Joint Stock Companies Act 1856* established the notion of a non-human business entity comprising many investors and members and introduced the important concept of limited liability (see Chapter 4).

A new Companies Act is passed by Parliament when it feels the need to update the law to account for changes in business activity or in the business environment. Each one builds upon the provisions of the previous Acts, but unless it is a *consolidated* Act, does not replace or repeal earlier Acts. The interpretation of Companies Acts is made rather more complex by a number of important common law precedents – decided cases which amend the meanings of the Acts.

The tranche of company law is necessary because of the privileges and responsibilities associated with holding limited liability. Accordingly, all limited company activities are regulated by either statute or common law including:

- the constitution and nature of limited companies and limited liability;
- rules governing the issuing of shares and responsibilities towards shareholders;

■ responsibilities of directors and the company secretary;

■ procedures in the unfortunate event of insolvency.

Contract law

Businesses use contracts in a wide variety of contexts. Examples include employees' contracts of employment and sales and purchases being subject to contracts of sale and supply. Contracts, which are a matter of common law, contain four legal components. The law cannot enforce a contract unless all four components are evident. The four components are as follows:

■ There must be an *offer*. This is a declaration that the offering party intends to be legally bound by the terms of the offer. The offer may be in writing, or, importantly in the case of some contracts, the offer may be verbal (spoken rather than written). In some cases, an offer may be implied by conduct. The law accepts many types of offer, but in all cases, they must be clear and unambiguous. An offer can be cancelled at any point up to the time that it is accepted.

■ There must be an *acceptance* of the offer. The acceptance of the offer must also be clear and unambiguous and must be on the same terms as the offer (i.e. it does not contain any amendments or additions). The combination of an offer and an acceptance constitutes an *agreement*, but this is not yet a contract.

■ There must be *consideration* – the legal term for payment. It should be understood that payment need not necessarily be financial; it can be an exchange or swap of payment in kind.

■ There must be an *intention to create legal relations*. This is an agreement to be legally bound by the contract. This is the key difference between informal agreements and contracts. In order to create a legally binding agreement, both parties in the contract must have legal *capacity* – that is, they must be entities which are legally able to make contracts, such as individual people or businesses. In the case of a limited company, the company has legal capacity whilst for non-incorporated businesses; the proprietor is recognised as having capacity.

The law recognises contract as a matter of civil law. A plaintiff who believes that he or she has been unfairly treated under a contract must usually demonstrate that one of the components of the contract is defective or that the other party has failed to honour it in terms of the substance of the offer or acceptance.

The law, personnel and employment

The area of laws as they affect the employment and management of people cover a wide range of activities and practices. Included in this category are laws which cover:

- terms and conditions of employment;
- sex and racial discrimination;
- employment of ex-offenders;
- employment of disabled workers;
- maternity rights;
- equal pay for 'equal jobs';
- dismissal and redundancy.

Some of the most important pieces of employment legislation are discussed below.

The most significant piece of employment law in recent years is the *Employment Protection (Consolidation) Act, 1978*, a wide ranging piece of legislation that provides that, among other things, employees be furnished with written terms and conditions of employment within 2 months of starting. This document should contain the general details of the employment agreement, such as the identity of the two parties, rate of pay, holiday entitlements, job title, etc. Other important employment law issues are discussed below.

Discrimination

Sex and race discrimination are covered in law by three Acts of Parliament. The *Sex Discrimination Acts 1975* and *1986*, the *Equal Pay Act 1970* and the *Race Relations Act 1976*. The overall effect of these laws renders it unlawful to discriminate against anybody on sex or race grounds in respect of selection, redundancy, pay, promotion, training and dismissal.

Employment of ex-offenders

Practices relating to the employment of ex-offenders are covered by the *Rehabilitation of Offenders Act 1974*. This Act is designed to enable ex-offenders to gain employment by selectively declaring their previous prison sentences. In terms of declaring their offences when applying for jobs:

- sentences up to 6 months become 'spent' after 7 years (i.e. there is no requirement to declare the sentence on applications 7 years after release);
- sentences between 6 months and 30 months are spent after 10 years;
- sentences over 30 months are never spent.

Some types of occupation are excepted from the provisions of this Act. These are jobs which are by nature sensitive to any previous criminal involvement and include doctors, teachers and accountants.

Employment of disabled persons

The law attempts to facilitate fair treatment for disabled workers in three pieces of legislation. The *Disabled Persons Acts* of *1944* and *1958* impose a 'quota' on organisations which states that employers of over 20 employees must employ registered disabled people at a rate of 3% of the workforce. Further provisions are added by the *Disability Discrimination Act 1995* (DDA) and the *Companies Act 1985* which provides that companies of more than 250 employees must include a formal statement in their annual reports (i.e. annual accounts) describing how they have acted towards disabled people over the year under review. The DDA came into force in increments from 1996 and the final rights of access came into force in October 2004.

Maternity

Maternity rights are provided by the *Trade Union Reform and Employment Rights Act 1993*. Women are permitted to take time off work, mostly at the employer's expense, to give birth and be with a child for as long as 29 weeks after birth and still retain the right to return to work. A number of qualifying conditions apply for maternity leave, such as length of service, level of pay and hours per week worked (some types of leave, such as time off for ante-natal care are not dependent on length of service). Pay during the time off takes the form of a percentage of salary for a fixed number of weeks (depending upon the length of previous service) followed by a lesser sum called *statutory maternity pay* (SMP).

Termination of employment

The various pieces of employment legislation place limits upon the conditions under which employees may be forced to leave employment. It goes without saying that legal complications would not be expected when an employee voluntary leaves a job (unless the employee is subject to a fixed term under a special contract). The law makes provisions to protect both employers' and employees' rights. The anti-discrimination laws apply to unfair dismissal and redundancy in the same way as they do for recruitment and promotion. It is consequently illegal to select people for redundancy on the grounds of race, gender, trade union membership (or non-membership) or the revelation of a spent conviction (or on grounds of pregnancy although exceptions do exist for this).

The *Employment Protection (Consolidation) Act 1978*, which we encountered above, makes provisions for both unfair dismissal and redundancy. Section 54 of the Act states that, 'every employee shall have the right not to be unfairly dismissed by his employer.' The grounds for unfair dismissal include those mentioned above (on grounds of race, gender, etc.). Redundancy is covered by Section 81 of the Act. It is stated that, '*every employee who is dismissed by reason of redundancy shall receive from his employer a redundancy payment*'. Redundancy occurs when the employer's need for a particular employee's labour is discontinued or reduced. The level of redundancy payment upon redundancy is dependent upon the employee's age, length of service with the employer, and level of weekly wage.

The law and trade unions

The regulation by law of trade unions was one of the key planks of the Conservative legislative programmes throughout the 1980s. During the so-called 'winter of discontent' (a phrase borrowed from Shakespeare) of 1978–1979, the UK was subjected to a large number of strikes by trade unions seeking improved pay and conditions. In some areas of life, these disputes caused a great deal of inconvenience to the public. When the Conservative Margaret Thatcher succeeded Labour's James Callaghan as prime minister in 1979, a reform of trade unions assumed a prominent place in her thinking. In practice, this meant reducing unions' power over employers to cause disruption to assist businesses to maintain normal activity for as much time as possible.

Accordingly, a number of Acts of Parliament were passed which gradually limited the activities of trade unions. Over time, laws in this area gradually increased the regulation of unions. The major laws in this respect are described below.

The Employment Act 1980 had two major provisions:

- the banning of secondary picketing (the practice of union action by employees not in dispute with their employer in sympathy with a set of employees that are);
- the banning of a closed shop unless it is supported by 80% of the workforce (a closed shop is an organisation in which trade union membership is compulsory for all employees – quite common for some organisations prior to this Act).

The Employment Act 1982 provided that trade unions themselves could be subject to fines and prosecuted if they were found to be in breach in the law, including, of course, *the Employment Act 1980*.

The Trade Union Act 1984 addressed issues of democratic control in internal union matters. Included in the provisions of this were the following:

- an insistence that any political contributions made by unions (e.g. to the Labour Party) must be mandated every 10 years by a secret ballot of the members;
- full-time executives employed by a union must be re-elected by secret ballot every 5 years;
- that any proposed strike action by the union be mandated by a secret ballot of the union's membership which could take place at the workplace. This was designed to prevent 'wildcat' strikes where a shop steward calls employees out on strike without a vote.

The *Employment Act 1988* included two major provisions:

- it strengthened the rights of union members who disagreed with the actions of their union;
- it added to the provisions of the Trade Union Act, 1984 by insisting that secret strike ballots should be conducted by post (postal ballot) rather than at the workplace.

The *Employment Act 1990* made the unions themselves legally responsible for any unofficial actions (i.e. against the provisions of previous Acts) of their members. In addition, the Act provided that employers could not discriminate against anybody on the grounds of trade union membership or non-membership.

In 1992, all of the above laws were brought together in a new consolidated Act of Parliament. The *Trade Union and Labour Relations*

(Consolidation) Act 1992 (TULCRA) covers the same provisions as the above Acts.

The law, sales and consumers

The most significant consumer laws

Consumer law is primarily designed to protect the interests of consumers (of products and services) against the unfair actions of business in making transactions. The existing set of laws in this area is both civil and criminal in nature.

The *Competition Act 1998* absorbed the main legislation of the *Competition Act 1980* (which had increased the anti-competitive practices provisions of the *Fair Trading Act 1973) plus* several other pieces of legislation, notably the *Resale Prices Act 1976* and the *Restrictive Trade Practices Act 1976*.

The *Enterprise Act 2002* made major reforms to competition law and consumer law enforcement in the UK. It criminalised individual participation in *cartels*, streamlined appeals mechanisms and established new procedures for tackling trading practices that harm consumers. The provisions of the Act work alongside the *Competition Act 1998*, and largely replace the provisions of the *Fair Trading Act 1973*.

The *Trade Descriptions Act 1968* has provisions to protect consumers from producers or sellers that deliberately mis-describe goods and services in an attempt to persuade consumers to buy. Under the provisions of the Act, sellers may be found guilty of a criminal offence for:

- making a false description of goods offered for sale;
- making a false description of services offered for sale;
- making a false statement of price.

Penalties for contravention of the Act include fines and imprisonment. The emphasis of the Act is on practices that mislead consumers and in consequence, the Act provides that advertisements and other sales presentations must be truthful. Claims that prices have been reduced must similarly be accurate. Goods and services must be on sale for 28 consecutive days at the higher price before a seller can claim that the price has been reduced to the lower, more attractive price.

The *Consumer Protection Act 1987* concerns the liability of sellers arising from the sale of defective goods and services. This is a piece of civil law under which, a plaintiff must demonstrate beyond reasonable doubt that a loss or injury has 'product liability' caused by the producer's (or in some case, the seller's) defective goods or services. As this Act was introduced as part of the implementation of an EU Directive (85/374), its provisions apply to sellers and producers throughout the EU. It also contains provisions for taking actions on producers outside the EU if necessary.

There are a number of defences that a seller or producer can put forward against a civil case under this Act. Under Section 4, these include defences based upon the contention:

- that the defendant did not actually supply the allegedly defective product;
- that the defect did not exist at the time the product was sold (e.g. a fault that develops in a car through the negligence of the owner rather than through bad workmanship);
- that a defect is attributable to a requirement to comply with other existing laws;
- that the level of scientific or technical knowledge at the time of the product's supply was not sufficiently advanced for the defect to be recognised (a rather controversial provision in the case of products, such as pharmaceuticals).

The *Sale of Goods Act 1979* protects consumers by imposing restrictions upon the contracts of sale used by sellers. It imposes three conditions of sale upon all sellers:

- that the goods sold must match the description of the goods presented to the consumer (Section 13 of the Act);
- that the goods supplied must be of '*merchantable quality*' (Section 14 of the Act);
- that the goods supplied must be fit for the purpose indicated to the consumer by the seller (also Section 14 of the Act).

It is worth noting that the terms 'merchantable quality' and 'fitness for the purpose' have been the subject of some debate. Such terms are usually interpreted in the light of the nature of the product. The *Sale and Supply of Goods (Amendment) Act 1995* amended the term merchantable quality to *satisfactory quality*. The terms of the Sale of Goods Act 1979 were extended to services in addition to goods under the *Supply of Goods and Services Act 1982*. This means that consumers of services (e.g. house and car repairs) have the same rights as consumers of goods.

The *Unfair Contract Terms Act 1977* and more recently, the unfair terms in *Consumer Contracts Regulations 1994* prohibit the use of clauses or statements in sales contracts that seek to circumvent the terms of any of the other pieces of consumer protection law. A seller is committing a criminal offence under these Acts if unfair 'exclusion' clauses are inserted which seek to deny a consumer his or her consumer rights. These Acts therefore rule out the use of statements such as 'no refunds given' when such refunds may be required by consumers under the terms of other consumer Acts.

More specific consumer laws

Other pieces of consumer protection legislation address specific areas of the relationship between consumers and business. These include:

- The *Consumer Credit Act 1974* regulates businesses that provide credit facilities to consumers. Its provisions include the requirement that lenders state the annual percentage rate (APR) of the loans and to limit, in some cases, the amounts that consumers can borrow.
- The *Weights and Measures Act 1985* requires manufacturers to use suitably reliable equipment when packaging goods which specify a weight or volume (e.g. a 50-gram bar of chocolate of a 5-litre tin of paint). The goods must not weigh less than the amount specified or comprise a lower volume (as appropriate).

The law, factories and offices

The regulation of activities in offices and factories is a long-standing feature of the business legal environment. The *raison d'être* of this area of law is to provide legal protection from harm for employees whilst they are actually at work.

Early legislation

The earliest significant laws in this area were in the nineteenth century – the various Factory Reform Acts. In the modern era, the most significant laws are the *Factories Act 1961* and the *Offices, Shops and Railway Premises Act 1963*. These Acts broke new ground at the time by placing the majority of the responsibility for health and safety in the workplace onto the employers. This was not to say that employees did not need to be mindful of potential hazards, but that once the employees had fulfilled their obligations, such as wearing the requisite protective clothing, etc., responsibility for accidents rested with the employer. The *Fire*

Precautions Act 1971 extended the general principles of the two earlier Acts to issues concerning fire safety. Two years later, the *Fire Precautions Act 1973* made it a legal requirement for all premises to carry a valid fire certificate showing that it conforms to the requirements of the local fire authorities. Such requirements may include the provision of suitably marked fire escapes, appropriate fire extinguishers placed in key locations, limits on the numbers of people allowed into the premises at any time and the training of certain employees in emergency evacuation procedures.

Health and Safety at Work Act 1974

The *Health and Safety at Work Act 1974* (HASAWA) was a key development in health and safety policy. The provisions of this Act were strongly influenced by the Robens Committee of Enquiry on Health and Safety at Work. The provisions of the Act brought together the contents of earlier laws whilst expanding them to apply to all places of work except domestic employment. Among its most important provisions are descriptions of the roles of both employers and employees in ensuring health and safety in the workplace.

Section 2 of HASAWA states that: 'It is the duty of an employer to ensure, so far as is reasonably practicable, the health, safety and welfare of all his employees.' In particular, this involves:

- The provision of a working environment and equipment that is both safe and appropriate to the work in question. There should also be an appropriate level of maintenance of such equipment.
- The provision of safe access into and exit from the working premises.
- Minimising the risks associated with working procedures.
- Training employees in procedures with a view to reducing the risk of injury.
- Providing adequate levels of supervision.
- The provision of adequate facilities at work to ensure the welfare of employees whilst at work.

In addition to prescribing (albeit in rather general terms) the duties of the employer, HASAWA also sets out the requirements made of employees. Accordingly, employees are made responsible for:

- taking reasonable care at work, both of their own health and safety and of those with whom they work;

> ▨ co-operating with the employer to facilitate the employer's conformance to his duties under health and safety legislation.

Trade unions are also apportioned some responsibility under HASAWA. They were given the right to appoint a health and safety representative on a business site to engage in discussions with employers, on behalf of union members in health and safety matters.

HASAWA is enforced in the UK by the *Health and Safety Executive* (HSE) – a government body established by the Act. The HSE employs inspectors who visit and inspect employers' premises for compliance with the terms of the Act. Continued failure to comply with HASAWA is a criminal offence which is punishable with a fine or imprisonment.

Recent developments

There are a number of legislative influences that have come to bear upon business workplaces since HASAWA. The UK's membership of the EU has brought with a number of directives. Most notably, an *Approved Code of Practice* became effective on 11 January 1993 together with a set of regulations known as the *Management of Health and Safety at Work Regulations* (MHSW).

Meanwhile, the UK Parliament passed the *Control of Substances Hazardous to Health Regulations 1989* (COSHH). This is a set of regulations that tightens the law pertaining to the handling of materials in the workplace and thus COSHH particularly affects those businesses that are engaged in areas like chemicals and engineering. Its provisions also technically apply to all substances used including office chemicals like correction fluid. COSHH provides that all substances used in a business be appropriately labelled, stored and used so as to minimise the risk of harm or injury.

Assignments 14.1

▨ After his secretary became pregnant, the chief executive officer (CEO) of a small engineering company decided to dismiss her. He told a friend, 'I can't afford to give her time off for ante-natal appointments and maternity leave. Money is tight enough as it is. Better to get rid of her now and replace her with someone who is likely to stay for a few years without disruptions such as this.' Advise the CEO of the legal implications of his decision.

■ You have bought a mechanical alarm clock from a major high street retailer and on getting it home; you find that it has no internal workings. Naturally you take the clock back but you are surprised to hear the shop manager say that you bought the clock in good faith and the lack of internal components is a matter you should take up with the clock manufacturer, not the shop. In what respects are the shop acting illegally and what recourse to law might you legitimately make to have the dispute settled?

Reference

1   Borchardt, Dr Klaus-Dieter (1994). *The ABC of Community Law*, 4th edn. Luxembourg Office for Official Publications of the European Communities. Brussels and Luxembourg: ECSC-EC-EAEC.

Further reading

Abbott, K. and Pendlebury, N. (2002). *Business Law*, 7th edn. London: Thomson Learning.

Deards, E. and Hargreaves, S. (2004). *European Law Textbook*. Oxford: University Press.

Judge, S. (1995). *Business Law*. London: Macmillan Press.

Keenan, D. and Riches, S. (2004). *Business Law*, 7th edn. London: Longman.

Lewis, D. and Sargeant, M. (ed.) (2004). *Essentials of Employment Law*, 8th edn. London: CIPD.

MacIntyre, E. (2004). *Business Law*. London: Longman.

Owens, K. (2001). *Law for Non-law Students*. London: Cavendish Publishing Ltd.

Smith, D. and Lawson, R.D. (1996) *Business Law for Business and Marketing Students*. Oxford: Butterworth-Heinemann.

Useful web sites

Department for Constitutional Affairs: www.dca.gov.uk
Eurolegal Services: www.eurolegal.org/
Scottish Legal system: www.scotland.gov.uk

CHAPTER 15

The international business environment

Learning objectives

After studying this chapter, students should be able to describe:

- the factors that have contributed to the internationalisation of business;
- the motivations behind increased internationalisation;
- the various internationalisation entry strategies;
- the major features and operation of multinational companies (MNCs);
- how governments influence MNCs and international business.

15.1 The internationalisation of business

One of the most striking features of business growth in the latter half of the twentieth century has been an increase in growth across national borders. At its simplest the need to buy and sell across borders is motivated by the fact that no country is entirely self-sufficient. Increased business activity and growth has stimulated increased demand for goods, services and factors of production. In the event that such commodities cannot be satisfied from within national borders, foreign suppliers are sought to meet the demand.

Various favourable factors came together in the years following the Second World War which served to greatly intensify the internationalisation of business. These are discussed in the following section. Today, the millions of international trading relationships across the world mean that international business affects, in one way or another, almost every individual and organisation. This may be either directly through such things as imports or exports, or indirectly through the use of foreign currency or foreign goods and services (e.g. French cars, Japanese computer equipment or Brazilian coffee).

Factors that have stimulated increased internationalisation

How then can we explain the growth in business across national borders? Like many phenomena in business, it has several contributory factors. Some of the most important are discussed below.

The communications 'revolution'

The twentieth century has been distinguished by a number of outstanding innovations in communications technology. Since the industrial revolution in the late eighteenth century, the pace of change has accelerated as new technologies have been developed. Whereas previously the fastest method of reliable communication was the galloping horse, information travelling at the speed of light can now circulate the earth several times in less than 1 second. Furthermore, in addition to the enormous speeding up of communications, an unprecedented number of people all over the world now have access to channels of advanced means of communication. Communications can thus reach many more people than ever before at almost instantaneous speed. The changes in communications technology have been so marked that the term the 'communications revolution' has been coined to describe it.

Over recent years, communications technology has grown in line with developments in computer technology and satellite transmission capabilities. The 'digitisation' of all First World telephone systems in the late 1980s and early 1990s enabled telephony to be combined with computers and the communication revolution continued apace into the twenty-first century with '3G' (third generation) mobiles combining the easy access and flexibility of mobile telephony with the power of the Internet. New generations of telecommunications' users are fast developing applications for the sophisticated communication technology. For example, witness the growth and establishment of e-mail and mobile telephony as the natural way of life, as evidenced by the dramatic rise in text messaging and music downloads.

The absence of a fixed-line infrastructure is a particular advantage in boosting the growth of modern telecommunications in Third World countries with major implications for trade and economic development.

The mass media, particularly the medium of television has also enjoyed expansion coupled with reductions in the real price (i.e. after inflation) of technology. This has offered business the opportunity to advertise and communicate with billions of people worldwide in a way that was not possible earlier. The growth of 'global' brands, such as *Coca Cola* and the *Big Mac* is due in part to the promotions made possible by mass communications.

Question 15.1

It has been said that the three most seminal innovations of the twentieth century have been antibiotics, flight and the semi-conductor. What evidence is there to support this statement?

Suggestion: This may take the form of a class debate with one side arguing that the above contention is too simplistic and the other side showing how each of these developments has led on to many other innovations.

Improved transport and related infrastructure

In a similar vein to advances in electronic communication, physical transport of goods has become faster and more reliable through innovations in both vehicular transport and in the infrastructure it uses. The growth and improvements in motorcar technology has signalled a huge growth in independent transport whilst the construction of fast motorway systems has made transport by road faster and safer. However, increasing volumes of traffic with consequent time-consuming congestion have stimulated a trend in the transferral of freight haulage from the roads to the rail network. The rapid loading and unloading of ships together with electronic inventory management in shipping services have increased the usefulness of shipping as a means of goods passage between countries. Airline activity has continued to grow at a fast rate, with the revenue of £13.5 billion generated by UK airlines in 2003. This demonstrated a rise of 6.3% over the previous year and indicated a positive upward trend following the global reduction in long-haul air travel between 2001 and 2003, in the aftermath of 11th September 2001. Also, during that period, the long-haul, business travel oriented airlines experienced significant reductions in business as a result of effects of the outbreak of foot-and-mouth disease in the UK and the *SARS (severe acute respiratory syndrome)* in Asia. Meanwhile the short-haul leisure market continued to expand, driven by the dramatic rise and consolidation in the low-cost airline sector. Growth of the low-cost airlines has been greatly facilitated by penetration of Internet bookings, albeit to the detriment of seat-only charter flights. It is estimated that between 2004 and 2008, the number of UK passengers travelling both into and out of the UK will increase by 13.3%,[1] although that estimated may have to be revised downwards if aviation fuel prices continue to rise and affect the cost of travel.

The net effect of all of these changes is that the movement of people and goods is now much faster and more reliable than ever before. Whereas at one time, a car travelling from Glasgow to London would take a day, having to go along A-grade roads and through many towns, a modern car can make the journey in around 5 hours entirely by high-speed roads – mainly motorway. The modernisation of road and rail links has been a feature of all industrialised countries.

Market homogenisation

According to Prof. Theodore Levitt, a noted American academic, '*the world's needs and wants have become irrevocably homogenised*'.[2] By homogenisation, Levitt means that increasingly, consumers in different countries want the very same products, without any 'tweaking' to account for regional variations in taste or fashion. It is argued that everybody wants the same global brands, such as Levi jeans, Marlboro, Coca Cola and McDonald's. Whilst in some countries, the desire for a brand may be due to the fact that it has some status attached to it (such as Western clothes brands in the Third World), in other cases, everybody wants a certain product simply because it is the best available. A company producing a product which is demanded in many or even all parts of the world (i.e. for which demand is homogenised) will have an obvious incentive to internationalise in order to take full advantage of the global demand.

Examples of products which lend themselves to a globally homogeneous demand include:

- some food and soft-drink brands (e.g. Coca Cola, Big Mac);
- consumer electronics (e.g. Intel personal computer chips and general television designs);
- computer software (e.g. Microsoft Windows, FoxPro, Word-Perfect, etc.);
- pharmaceuticals (e.g. best-selling prescription drugs like Zantac and the antidepressant Prozac);
- defence equipment and aircraft (where the incentive is to have the most up-to-date equipment);

- clothing fashions (e.g. Levi jeans and French ladies' fashions);
- perfumes (e.g. Chanel and Yves Saint-Laurent);
- some alcohol and tobacco brands (e.g. Marlboro, Heineken and some brands of Scotch whisky).

However, there is clearly room for national variations in product or brand design, so it is not the case that *every* product has homogeneous demand. The Findus frozen food brand (owned by Nestlé), for example, produces Fish Fingers for the UK market, but frozen Boeuf Bourgignon for the French. Some companies are successful at making adjustments to their products to make them more acceptable to regional or national tastes and sensibilities.

Question 15.2

- Why have we witnessed growth in homogeneous markets?
- Why do you think it is the case that 'everybody' wants American cola, French perfumes and British pharmaceuticals?

Political stability

The latter half of the twentieth century has been characterised by, among other things, an unprecedented level of concord between the major First World industrialised nations. Whereas Britain and France spent centuries at or near to war over a number of issues, the two are now considered to be the close allies. Similarly, the Germans, Italians and Austrians, erstwhile aggressors, are now prosperous nations which enjoy friendly relations with all other First World countries.

On the domestic front, it has also transpired that industrialised nations have enjoyed 50 years or more (in the UK, many years more) of stable democratic government. In such political structures, we take for granted things that earlier generations could not. It is almost unthinkable, for example, that Britain would go to war against one of its First World partners or that the UK Government would be threatened by insurrection.

Political stability favours business prosperity owing to the presence of certainty. Businesses know that if they make a substantial investment in a politically stable country that the investment is as 'safe' as it can be. Of course, not all parts of the world enjoy such stability, and less stable countries tend to be characterised by lower levels of business prosperity.

One of the major objectives of some supranational political institutions is to maintain and increase political stability, which in turn encourages business activity. The European Union (EU) is an obvious example, but organisations such as the United Nations also help towards this end.

15.2 Motivations behind internationalisation

The reasons *why* companies pursue international strategies obviously differ from business to business. In attempting to distil the many motivations down to a few simplified ones, we can identify three major factors.

Market 'push' motivations

Market push refers to the motivation to seek business from foreign markets because of constraints in the domestic ones. A company which has successfully traded in the UK for decades may seek to expand overseas due to adverse changes in its traditional UK markets. The business is 'pushed' abroad by unfavourable conditions at home.

Examples of market push motivations include the following:

- *Maturity or decline* in the domestic market. The product life cycle, which is described in more detail in Chapter 28, says that all products are subject to growth, maturity and eventually decline. It may be the case that a product entering maturity in one country (thus stopping the growth the company has previously enjoyed), can be offset by growth in hitherto untapped foreign markets. In some cases, the domestic market will reach maturity because 'everybody who wants one has got one', whereas for other products, there may be a trend away from buying a certain type of product (e.g. tobacco products).

- *Increased regulation* in the domestic market. Governments that impose 'excessive' regulation (which is a matter of perspective) on businesses will tend, overall, to encourage businesses to seek to invest in areas where regulation is less. Regulation of business, for example, by imposing employment laws, health and safety rules, etc. invariably entails cost increases, so it is in some business's interests to seek to expand in countries where regulation is less strict. The 'opt-out' that the UK negotiated from the social charter of the Maastricht Treaty of 1992 means that UK labour is in some ways less regulated than most other EU states and this reduced the incentive for some companies to seek to internationalise away from the UK (see also Chapter 8).

- *High labour costs* (and other factor costs) may be linked to regulation of business but may also be a function of the standard of living enjoyed by workers in a country. If labour costs in a domestic market rise to the point where it is no longer economically attractive to stay, the business may seek to expand to a country where labour can be bought at more favourable rates.
- *Inappropriately skilled labour* may be a factor for businesses which cannot find an adequate level of skilling in the domestic labour force of their home countries. Whilst training is an obvious remedy for inappropriate skills, it is thought to be the case that certain countries are somehow inherently better at some skills than others. Companies may look abroad to invest if they suspect that the skills of the local labour force will not be adequate over the longer term.
- *High fiscal pressure* may encourage a business to seek international expansion if it must pay what it considers to be excessive taxes in a domestic economy. The same may be true in episodes of prolonged monetary pressure.
- *Political or economic instability* will be a powerful push factor. We have seen that businesses, just like individuals, like certainty and security. Rapid or unpredictable changes in the political or economic environment may not create conditions wherein a business would be happy to remain.

Market 'pull' motivations

Whilst market push motivations encourage a business to look elsewhere, market pull factors, predictably, are those features of a country which are attractive to businesses. They 'pull' businesses into the country because they possess attractive features to businesses which are considering expanding internationally. Essentially, pull factors will be the opposites of push factors. Countries will be attractive to businesses if:

- there is growth potential in the country's market;
- there is increasing spending power and prosperity (e.g. in 'newly industrialised' nations, like some in the Far East);
- fiscal and monetary pressure is low (the growth of Hong Kong as a centre of inward investment is due in large part to these factors);
- the market for the company's products is undersupplied in the foreign country;

- the country possesses highly skilled workers;
- labour costs (and the costs of other factors of production) are comparatively low;
- there is a more stable political system than the business's home country.

Pull factors are all relative to the home country. It is not, for example, whether a foreign country has highly skilled labour and low tax rates, but whether it has *higher* skills and *lower* taxes than the company's home country.

Portfolio as a motivator

The nature of a business portfolio, as we saw when we considered holding companies (Chapter 4) and external unrelated growth (Chapter 8) is linked to the notion of spreading opportunity and risk. For some 'polycentric' (many-centred) companies, international expansion is sought simply as a method of guaranteeing the company has a meaningful presence in a variety of national markets. Whilst market pull factors will guide such a company vis-à-vis its choice of locations, one of the primary strategic motives will be to ensure its base is sufficiently well spread to enable it to withstand economic shock and to benefit from growth in different national markets.

One of the features of international business is its unpredictability. The fact is that if a company operates in several national environments, it has more variables to watch than if it operates in just the UK. A downturn in the demand for the company's products in Singapore will have less impact on the company as a whole if the Singapore sales account for only a small percentage of its international total.

15.3 Internationalisation strategies

Having looked at *why* companies seek to internationalise, we now come to the question '*how?*' A business has a choice of several methods by which it can extend its business interests beyond its immediate national borders.

The entry strategy (entry into international markets) adopted by an organisation will depend upon several factors:

- The company's *objectives* in becoming internationalised. The entry strategy must match its purposes. A company seeking to dominate the world automotive (car) market would need to adopt a much more aggressive internationalisation strategy than a local paint company which merely wanted to increase its sales volume.

▦ The *resources available* for the international expansion. It makes sense that a business must 'cut its cloth' to match its budgets. Some entry strategies are necessarily more resource intensive than others.

▦ To a certain extent, the strategy chosen will depend upon the *types of products and markets* the company is involved in. Businesses which involve massive amounts of capital expenditure (e.g. oil companies) will need to serve several national markets in order to generate sufficient revenue to repay its capital costs. Similarly, the nature of some perishable food products would preclude their being exported in a conventional way and a more direct investment approach may be more suitable.

The major entry strategies are:

▦ exporting,
▦ international franchising,
▦ international licensing,
▦ international (strategic) alliances,
▦ foreign direct investment (FDI).

All of the above strategies are discussed below.

Exporting

The most straightforward internationalisation strategy is to take the company's products and sell them to foreign customers by means of export. For a UK-based company, the products are made in the UK and then sent by carrier to foreign customers who then pay the UK company in sterling on normal payment terms.

In an organisation's history, exporting is usually the first foray it makes into international markets. It is usually the cheapest and most convenient of the entry strategies we shall consider.

As export sales involve the exchange of money from one currency to another, the competitiveness of British exports depends heavily upon the exchange rate of sterling. A low value of sterling will make British exports more price competitive whereas a high value will make them less. We saw in Chapter 9 that, as well as being very dependent upon the exchange rate, exports are one of the major determinants of it.

Britain's traditional export markets were the British Commonwealth countries, such as Canada, Australia and India. Over recent decades however, Britain's exports have increasingly gone to Europe, particularly the other EU states like France and Germany. The EU accounts for around half of the UK's total exports. This change is partly due to the fact that Europe is nearer than most of the far-flung Commonwealth nations and partly due to the economic advantages of EU membership, particularly the absence of trade barriers to imports and exports across the national borders of EU states.

Example: Export contracts

Imagine the scenario. A ship leaves dock at Humberside laden with cars from a British manufacturer. Heading for Holland, the ship unfortunately sinks exactly half-way across the North Sea. The question is this: *whose loss is this – the exporter's or the importer's?* The answer is that it depends upon the terms of the export contract. The fact that carriage of goods over long distances involves many potential risks means that it must be made absolutely clear at what point ownership of the goods changes hands. Hence, export contracts vary according to the point at which this change of ownership takes place.

- *Ex-works* contracts specify the gate of the exporting company as the point of change. The importer effectively collects the goods from the exporter and assumes responsibility for them all the way to the overseas site. Payment becomes due at the point of pick-up. The seller's responsibilities are limited to assisting the importer with the necessary documentation for the export of the goods.
- *Free-on-rail (FOR)* contracts specify that the exporter assumes responsibility for the carriage of the goods to the nearest rail terminal to the seller's premises. From the train station to the importer's premises, the goods belong to the buyer.
- *Free-alongside ship (FAS)* contracts specify that the goods shall change hands once the exporter has delivered them to the docks and places them ready for loading onto the ship. The importer (buyer) assumes responsibility for the goods from the transfer of the goods onto the ship to the destination.
- *Free-on-board (FOB)* contracts go a few metres further than FAS. The exporter assumes ownership of the goods up to and including the placement of the goods on the outgoing ship.
- *Ex-ship* contracts specify that ownership changes hands at a foreign port of the importer's choice. The payment of shipping and insurance charges by the exporter has obvious implications for the cost of the shipment to the importer.
- *Cost, insurance, freight (CIF)* contracts specify that the exporter assumes responsibility for the shipment all the way to the importer's site in the foreign country.

The export contract chosen will be a point of mutual agreement between the importer and exporter. It follows that the nearer the importer's site ownership changes hands, the more expensive will be the price of the shipment.

There are a number of advantages to using exporting as an entry strategy:

- It enables a business to benefit from international trade with *no significant overseas investment* and at relatively little setting-up or organising cost. The use of foreign agents or distributors usually frees the exporter of such responsibilities.
- The exporter's *risk is limited to the value of the shipment.* Compared to direct investment, when a great deal of investment may be at risk by changes in the foreign country's environment, exporting can be an attractive option.
- The fact that little or no set-up cost is involved in exporting means that an organisation can *attack several foreign markets within a limited budget.* The business can thus benefit from a wide geographical coverage.

There are also some features of exporting that may make it inappropriate for some businesses:

- *Transport and carriage can be problematic* for some types of goods. This problem is exacerbated when the distance is great or when the goods are of a fragile or perishable nature. The costs of transport and insurance can also add costs to exports that can render them price uncompetitive compared to domestic products in the foreign country.
- *Collecting due payment can be a problem* when the customer is in a different country. Legal complications can sometimes result if customers default on payment or if payment is late. Legal instruments are usually put in place using a bank in the importer's country to minimise the risks of non or late payment.
- Exported goods, when entering foreign countries, are sometimes *subject to tariff charges or other restrictions.* Payment of taxes to a host government by the importer has obvious implications for pricing whilst some goods are subject to limitations on the quantities imported. Such protectionist measures mean that exporters have many more factors to consider in exporting than if they were to restrict their activities to domestic business only.
- The number of foreign interests that an exporter has means that the company must be *aware of the business environments of more countries than just its own.* Changes in the internal environment of a country with which the organisation does business can affect the performance of the company. An exporter has an interest in the political, economical and sociological environments of all of the countries it exports to. This significantly complicates the operation of an exporter's business (although this can said to be a drawback of most entry strategies – not just exporting).

International licensing and franchising

Licensing and franchising across international borders, whilst being different in approach, both offer the same benefit: the gaining of international coverage and income with no direct investment.

When we examined the concept of franchise in Chapter 5, we saw that it was a way that a business with a transferable business idea can expand by renting the right to use the idea to a franchisee. Expansion by franchise is thus an expansion option which offers the franchisor the opportunity to gain income at little or no extra investment or risk to himself. Since moving to foreign markets inevitably contains an element of risk which may not be so marked if expansion were to be restricted to the domestic market, some companies have opted for international franchising as a means of internationalisation. Franchising is a strategy that has been widely employed by some famous global brands such as *KFC* and *McDonalds*.

Question 15.3

What are the potential risks that might be associated with a franchising operation:

■ from the viewpoint of the franchisor?
■ from the viewpoint of the franchisee?

Illustrate your response with some company examples.

Licensing is similar in some ways to franchising in that it involves a licensee paying a licensor a fee for the use of a business idea – usually a piece of intellectual property. A licence is a permit granted to a licensee to manufacture or market (or both) a product belonging to a licensor. In international business, a licence will usually afford the licensor the sole rights to use the intellectual property within a certain national market. Whereas franchising involves the use of a business identity, licensing typically involves the use of a brand name, a formulation or a recipe by an existing business.

The benefits to the two parties involved in a licensing agreement are similar to those enjoyed by those in a franchising agreement. The licensor receives low-risk income and increased international exposure of the product. The licensee gains the use of a product which enjoys current success, offering an increased chance of successful business performance.

Licensing is used in a number of sectors of business. Perhaps the best-known example is that of brewing. British consumers seem to attach some value to foreign beer brands and brewers take advantage of this by buying licences to brew certain brands in the UK under licence. One such example of a licensed brand is *Miller Genuine Draft lager*, where the licensor is a North American company, and the licensee is the UK company *Scottish Courage* (the brewing division of Scottish and Newcastle plc).

It is also used in some scientific industries where a local manufacturer in a foreign country may produce a specialist paint or plastic for the foreign country's market.

International alliances and joint ventures

An alliance of two parties, as the name suggests, is a relationship entered into voluntarily and in which both parties retain their full independence. Of course strategic alliances can be used as a basis for business co-operation on a national as well as an international level, and we must not imagine that such relationships are exclusive to international business. Thompson and Strickland have defined a strategic alliance as two businesses working together by:

> ... joint research efforts, technology sharing, joint use of production facilities, marketing one another's products, or joining forces to manufacture components or assemble finished product.[3]

Alliances and joint ventures are both quite different concepts to that of a merger (see Chapter 7), where two companies become 'one'. Alliances tend to be ongoing and even semi-permanent, whereas joint ventures tend to be entered into for a particular 'venture' only, such as several construction companies working together on a large civil engineering project. These types of business relationship borrow a term from biology – it is said that they are *symbiotic* – beneficial to both parties.

International alliances are often entered into as a means of gaining access to foreign markets via the contacts of the partner business in the foreign country. Such relationships often involve *reciprocation* – allowing the foreign partner to similarly use the home country contacts. They can also be used for joint projects where expertise or equipment is shared as a vehicle for meeting both partners' business objectives.

In practice, alliances tend to be relatively short term in nature. This is partly due to the fact that many are entered into for specific projects only and partly because there is sometimes a certain amount of distrust between alliance partners.

Foreign 'direct' investment

A foreign direct investment (FDI) as the name suggests, involves a business actually making a financial investment in another country. This sets it apart from all other entry strategies which all involve conducting cross-border business from a home country base. Due to the fact that a financial investment is made abroad, it is usually the case that FDI occurs only when the organisation is very sure that its investment is right, and that it will be 'safe'. There are two broad types of FDI – an existing foreign company can be acquired or a new plant can be built in the foreign country.

Foreign acquisitions

Holding companies often keep an eye open for companies which are appropriate for addition to the group. This often involves purchasing all or part of a foreign business. Shares are bought in the usual ways – via a stock exchange for public companies or in discussion with the owners for private companies. Some British companies are well known for their international acquisition strategies, notable among which is Hanson plc, which has acquired many businesses all over the world, with a distinct focus on North America (see Chapter 7).

'Greenfield' development

For companies that wish to invest in a certain country but cannot find an appropriate acquisition, it is not uncommon for a new site to be developed and built upon. It is usually the case that 'greenfield developments' of this kind are more expensive and they also carry a greater risk of failure that acquisition, owing to the fact that an acquisition would, have an established customer base. Notable greenfield developments in the UK include those in specialised industries where a new site offers the investor an opportunity to gain premises which precisely match the company's requirements. Such investments have been made in the automotive industry (e.g. Honda, Nissan and Toyota) and in electronics (e.g. Fujitsu, Samsung and Siemens).

Whilst it is obvious that FDI exposes a company to higher levels of risk than the other entry strategies, the advantages are potentially significant. It is often entered into when export volumes have built up to such an extent that it becomes more economic to manufacture in the foreign country rather than to export to it. By manufacturing and selling within the foreign country, the company also circumvents ('gets round') the restrictions that exporters sometimes face, such as taxes placed upon imported items and limits set by host governments on the numbers of certain imported goods.

FDI case 1: Toyota – a greenfield development in the UK

Toyota is Japan's largest motor manufacture and it occupies the third position (by volume) in the world. In 1991, Toyota's worldwide output amounted to 4.75 million vehicles with a financial turnover of over £30 billion. Operating in 150 countries, the company has 29 manufacturing plants in 22 countries, sells its vehicles through over 7000 dealerships and employs more than 100,000 people.

In the early 1960s, Toyota made its first incursions into the European market by exporting cars to Denmark. Its growth in the EU since then has been substantial. By 1992, Toyota was selling vehicles in 22 European countries through 3500 dealerships.

The market potential for sales in the EU, as one of the legs of the 'triad' (the Far East, North America and Europe) proved too tempting to miss for Toyota, and in 1989, it announced plans to make a direct investment in a manufacturing plant in the EU. After much discussion, the company chose two sites in the UK and one in Belgium. Toyota's initial investments in the UK – at Burnaston in Derbyshire and at Deeside, North Wales – amounted to £840 million. Its investment at Diest, Belgium, was in a European parts centre and came to £26 million. Construction of the two UK plants commenced in 1990, and the first

British Toyotas left the production line in December 1992.

Unlike other Japanese motor companies that have invested in the UK, Toyota did not develop a single 'super-site'. The plant in North Wales is dedicated to the production of engines whilst the company's plant in Derbyshire produces passenger cars for the European market using Deeside produced engines.

In common with other manufacturers who have made sizeable inward investments into the EU, Toyota's objective in its direct investment manoeuvre was to overcome the import restrictions which the EU places upon imports from outside its borders. By producing from within the EU, the cars produced are British as far as sales to other EU states are concerned – not Japanese. Of course, direct investment also means that transport costs to other EU states from the UK are significantly less than they would be coming from Japan.

On 30 July 1999, *Toyota (GB) Ltd* became a plc and by September that year, the *Toyota Motor Corporation* (TMC) had listed on both the London and the New York stock exchanges and took full ownership of Toyota (GB) plc.

TMC's commitment to its European operations was further emphasised when the Corporation opened a £10 million car design plant in Cote d'Azur, France to strengthen European influence on new cars. By September 2004 TMC had posted record sales and raised its European sales target figure to 900,000 units. Also, that year TMC invested £18 million in a new production plant, for the Toyota Yaris model, in Valenciennes, France in order to better respond to European parts demand.

Source: TMC.

FDI case 2: Philip Morris – foreign acquisitions in the former communist states of central and eastern Europe

Philip Morris International Inc. (part of the *Altria Group Inc,* since 2003) is the world's largest and most profitable tobacco company. The company produces seven of the top 20 best-selling international cigarette brands, including *Malboro,* the global brand leader, and *Chesterfield, Lark and L&M.*

The Altira Group also owns some internationally renowned companies that are not tobacco based such as Kraft Foods, Jacobs, Suchard and Nabisco. The group has overall ownership of some 3000 brands that are household names throughout the world.

Philip Morris International Inc. was formerly based in Rye Brook USA but moved its headquarters to Lausanne in Switzerland in 2001, perhaps emphasising its global focus. The company employs around 155,000 people in its worldwide operations and its products sell in over 170 countries.

Over recent years, the company has pursued a strategy of direct investment in the tobacco industries of the former communist countries of central and eastern Europe. Central Europe's cigarette consumption is around 600 billion cigarettes per year, which, unlike demand in some parts of the world, is relatively stable (i.e. it is not in decline). The decentralisation of the economies in these states has provided investment opportunities for western companies who, for such reasons as above, wish to gain a market presence in these parts of the world. Philip Morris has had links, through licensing agreements, with companies in central and eastern Europe for over 20 years, so the demise of communism in these countries offered a unique opportunity for expansion (by means of FDI) into these national markets.

Some of its major acquisitions in former communist states of central and eastern Europe include the following:

- Tabak A.S. – Czech Republic.
- Klaipeda State Tobacco Company – Lithuania.
- Krasnodar Tobacco Factory – Russia.
- Almaty Tobacco Kombinat – Kazakhstan.
- Kharkov Tobacco Factory – Ukraine.

Source: Philip Morris Inc. Lausanne.

Question 15.4

What factors could contribute to the strategic reasoning which lies behind Philip Morris's tobacco investments in the former communist states of central and eastern Europe?

It may be helpful to look at 'market push', 'market pull' and portfolio factors in arriving at your conclusions.

15.4 Multinational companies

What is a MNC?

Many of the companies we have discussed in this chapter so far are what we may call *multinationals*. A working definition of a MNC is as follows: *a company which has direct investments in more than one (usually many) different countries.*

For the reasons we have seen in Section 15.1 of this chapter, the growth in multi-nationalisation has been very marked over the past 50 years. The competitive pressures which have built up in international markets coupled with a general relaxation in exchange controls have meant that MNCs have become an important feature of the international business environment. It is thought that MNCs account for over a quarter of the world's economic output.

It follows from the above definition that most MNCs are very large organisations. The head office of a MNC may operate hundreds of divisions or subsidiary companies in as many countries around the world. The turnover of the MNC may well exceed the gross domestic profit (GDP) of many of the countries in which it operates. Many of the best-known corporate household names are MNCs (Table 15.1).

Table 15.1
Some well-known MNCs

UK multinationals investing abroad	Foreign nationals investing in the UK
Hanson	Nissan (Japan)
ICI	BASF (Germany)
BP	Michelin (France)
GlaxoSmithKline	Philips (Holland)
RTZ Corporation	Nestlé (Switzerland)
BAT Industries	General Motors (USA)

The operation of MNCs

The geographical distribution of a MNC offers several potential benefits:

- When a company operates in many countries, it has the opportunity to *locate activities in the country to which they are best suited*. The MNC can take advantage of variations in the business environments of the different countries. It may choose, for example, to locate design and development in a country where skilled technical people are plentiful, such as the UK, but to manufacture products where labour is cheaper, such as the Far East. Marketing communications will usually be based in a country with an advanced communications network, such as the UK or the USA.
- *Opportunity and risk can be spread* over many businesses in many countries. The breadth of portfolio renders the MNC more robust in the event of shocks in regional markets.
- MNCs can *take advantage of legal and fiscal differences in the different countries* in which they operate. By employing a creative use of internal transfer pricing, the MNC can significantly reduce its overall tax burden and thus increase net profits. Accountants can, up to a point, make high profits shown in countries which enjoy a low level of corporation tax and lower profits in higher-tax countries.

The head office of an MNC often operates as a holding company (see Chapter 4). Accordingly, the head office administration of the company usually comprises a small part of the total company operation. The size and importance of a large multinational places an increased significance to the role of the board of directors. The strategies pursued by a large MNC can bring about effects in many parts of the world and can even influence government policies. The senior directors of MNCs tend to be particularly adroit people, many of whom hold several other non-executive directorships, owing to the demand for directors of such a high calibre.

MNCs and governments

When we consider government and business, we usually think of the ways that businesses are influenced by governments. However, the size and economic importance of very large companies means that they can bring their influence to bear upon the governments of the countries in which they operate. Traditionally, national governments have had something of a 'love–hate' relationship with some of the world's major MNCs. Clearly, they can be of enormous benefit to the countries in which they operate in their provision of jobs, their payment of tax revenues and their contribution to GDP, exports, etc. Similarly, their size and their importance to a country can mean that they also have significant influence upon governments. Critics argue that not only is excessive business influence upon government anti-democratic (because it is the government and not large businesses which are elected to govern), but also that such influence is usually representative of certain economic opinions only.

Multinationalisation and globalisation

Some people have confused the terms multinational business and globalised business. Whilst with very large organisations it is often difficult to tell which category they are in, it is generally held that there is a difference. A company is said to be a global business when its multinational expansion has reached the point where it carries out activities in all major parts of the earth rather than a selected few centres abroad. Accompanying this expansion is a change in its corporate culture when the business loses its national bias. In other words, it no longer 'feels like' a Japanese company or a British company – its breadth means that it feels like and is seen as a global business. A global company's head office (e.g. in London) does not see the business as divided into 'home' and 'overseas', but as one company of many parts encompassing the world.

15.5 Governments and international business

We saw in Chapter 9 that cross-border business transactions can directly determine some of the economic 'indicators' in a country, such as the exchange rate. Indirectly, international business can affect domestic unemployment, inflation and the rate of economic growth. It is therefore not surprising that governments take an active interest in the activities of internationalised businesses.

Governments have the ability to influence international business across its borders by implementing a range of measures that are primarily designed to act in the interests of domestic (home) businesses. They can also be used to further the political ends of a governing party or to act against the business interests of a foreign state.

The most important objective of governments with regard to international business is to stimulate business activities that will result in a positive entry in the balance of payments statement (see Chapter 9). This includes:

- exports,
- inward investment,
- inward bank deposits,
- a net surplus on cash transactions.

Similarly, it would, in most cases, wish to minimise imports and other transactions which would exert a downward pressure on the value of the currency, although there are offsetting factors that make it favourable for British businesses to invest abroad.

Common political measures used to influence international business are explained below.

Import tariffs

An import tariff or *import duty* is a form of indirect taxation (see Chapter 9). It is a percentage of the price of an imported good added on and collected (in the UK) by Her Majesty's (HM) Customs and Excise. The percentage added varies according to the category of goods. Such a tax on imported goods serves two purposes:

- it is a source of revenue for the treasury,
- it provides a price disincentive for importers.

Increasing the price of imported goods is partly designed to protect domestic businesses which may be disadvantaged if too many foreign goods were imported. It also helps to support the value of sterling.

An example of the imposition of import tariffs, concerns motorcars. The UK imposes an import duty of 10% of the purchase price on imported motor vehicles when the source of the import is outside the EU. Hence, if a car is bought from Japan for £20,000, the import duty on it would be £2000, making the actual import cost £22,000. Some goods attract lower rates of duty and others are totally exempt.

Import quotas

A quota is a maximum limit set by a government for the import of certain goods. It will usually be an annual total and can be expressed either as a number (e.g. an import quota of 15 million tonnes per year of chemical X), or as a percentage of total products sold. Percentage quotas might be expressed as 'no more than 15% of all widgets sold in the UK shall be imported from outside the EU'. It follows that for percentage quotas, the actual number will vary from year to year as the total varies.

An example of an import quota set by the UK Government refers to car imports. The UK traditionally imposed an import quota of around 10% on cars imported from Japan, which meant that no more than 10% of all new cars sold annually in the UK could be imported from Japan, although the actual number could vary year on year. However, restrictions on the import of Japanese cars into the EU were largely lifted in 2000.

Governments have a wide range of restrictions on imports that can be applied such as the imposition of minimum technical specifications. For example, products may have to conform to particular safety standards concerning their method manufacture and or intended use. The case of USA motorcar exhaust emission standards provides a good example where foreign manufacturers wishing to export their vehicles to the US can be faced with additional cost to bring the vehicles up to the required standard, thereby weakening their cost competitiveness.

Exchange controls

Governments can restrict the volumes of trade across its borders by imposing limits on the amount of foreign currency that can be exchanged within a given time period. This sanction is invariably used to restrict the amount of foreign currency that can be bought. As currency must be bought to purchase foreign goods, exchange controls are an effective restriction on imports.

In addition to the effect of lower imports, exchange controls will also have a positive effect on the capital account of the balance of payments statement. However, as a mechanism of protectionism it is rarely used as it is viewed as being against the principles of international free trade and perhaps a little unfair. It would be inconsistent, for example, for state A to complain of unfair discrimination with regard to business in state B if state A were to impose exchange controls against state B. In consequence, exchange controls have become increasingly rare between developed industrial countries.

Encouraging exports

Due to the benefits to a domestic economy of exports, governments often set in place measures to actively encourage export activity. Whilst the most important determinants of export value are factors in the domestic economy as a whole, such as manufacturing investment, specific measures can encourage increased exporting.

Exports, like most other business transactions, are sold on credit. This means that goods are sent out and then the supplier must wait for payment to come through. Most domestic transactions are sold on credit periods of 30–90 days whereas export business can often involve credit periods of up to 180 days. Capital projects such as the exporting of civil engineering consultancy can involve much longer credit periods – in some cases, up to 5 years.

The major governmental body which assists exporters with their export risks is the *Export Credits Guarantee Department* (ECGD). The ECGD was set up in 1919 and since 1930, has helped exporters of invisibles in addition to visibles exporters (see the section of the balance of payments in Chapter 9 for a discussion of these terms). Its purpose is to provide a special type of insurance against two main areas of risk:

- the creditworthiness of overseas buyers (i.e. covering the risks of non or late payment of debts);
- the economic and political risks arising from events in overseas countries.

Prior to 1991, the ECGD insured both short-term (credit terms of less than 2 years) and long-term (more than 2 years credit) export business. In 1991, the short-term debt insurance role of the ECGD was sold by the Government to the NCM Group, a Dutch insurance company. The ECGD retains the responsibility for insuring debt involving over 2 years' credit.

In addition to its 'hard' financial support for exporters provided by the ECGD, the government also encourages and recognises export performance in non-financial ways. The *Queen's Award for Export Achievement* is an award given to companies whose exports have shown growth or consistency. It applies to all sizes of business and winners receive permission to use the Award's logo on their letterheads and livery.

Inward investment policy

In addition to exports, inward investment is also entered as a positive figure on the balance of payments statement and hence exerts an upward pressure on the value of the currency. Most countries wish to encourage inward investment as it provides jobs, tax revenues and increases GDP. In some cases, inward investments can also contribute to the UK's exports, which, as we have seen, help to support the value of sterling. In order to encourage inward investment, it is in the government's interest to maintain relatively low fiscal and monetary pressure and to not allow the value of the domestic currency to rise to an uncompetitive level. In addition, governments sometimes provide grant support in the same way that it might for any company setting up in certain parts of the country. For large inward investments, negotiations between company and government can occur at a very senior level, with assistance packages individually designed to best meet the investor's aspirations.

International sanctions and embargoes

From time to time, governments see fit to impose severe restrictions on trading with certain countries. These can either be on a unilateral basis (i.e. one country prevents its domestic businesses from dealing with parties from the affected country), or on a multilateral basis. Multilateral sanctions are agreed by many countries together, where a ban is imposed from buying from or selling to businesses in the sanctioned country.

Sanctions can be partial or total and may run for many years. One such example can be found a longstanding row between the EU and the USA over trade in bananas, which was resolved in 2001. The dispute centred on US complaints that concessions offered by the EU to African, Caribbean and Pacific banana exporters harmed the interests of US multinationals that grow bananas in Latin America. The *World Trade Organisation* (WTO) (see below) upheld the US position, on two occasions, and called upon the EU authorities to change their importing procedures. However, in the absence of any alterations acceptable to the US, the Clinton administration in 1999 (with WTO approval) imposed sanctions on a range of EU products worth $191.4 million. The dispute threatened to undermine the dispute settlement authority of the WTO until agreement was finally reached in April 2001. The agreement paved the way for the implementation of an EU importing system for bananas by 2006, based upon a WTO-compatible tariff-only. Under the terms of the agreement the EU would continue to import bananas, during the transition period, based on historic reference periods measuring previous export patterns from producer countries and the USA would suspend its sanctions on July 1, 2001.

From time to time sanctions or embargoes are designed to achieve political rather than business objectives. In some cases, they are imposed as a means of punishment whilst in others, it is hoped that the sanctions will precipitate a change in certain political practices (such as the cessation of the alleged development of weapons of mass destruction in Iraq or an end to human rights abuses). The sanctions on Iraq proved to be ineffective to the US and its allies and ultimately led to the war in 2003.

It goes without saying that businesses affected by governmental sanctions do not like such measures, much as they may agree with the political objectives.

15.6 Single markets and trading blocs

An international single market is one wherein business transactions can be carried out across borders as though they were not there. The UK as a country has a single market because no limitations apply to companies in one part of the country trading with another. A company in England selling to a customer in Scotland need not worry about tariffs, quotas or other protectionist measures because both countries are part of the same UK. In an international single market, the member state agrees to allow free movement of goods, services and sometimes, personnel between them. In this respect, a single market acts as if it was one country. These agreements are sometimes referred to as *customs unions* – agreements between countries to reduce or eliminate customs restrictions pertaining to the import and export of goods and services.

The 'singularity' of a trading bloc varies. Some allow completely free movements whereas others retain some restrictions in order to offer some protection to domestic businesses. In any event, such arrangements act as a stimulant to international business.

The EU

In Chapter 8 we saw how the EU had grown to be a community of twenty five nation states by 2004. The Single European Act 1986 which was signed by all member states set the conditions whereby a single market could be achieved – a common market. Described as 'an area without internal frontiers in which the free movement of goods, persons, services and capital is ensured in accordance with the provisions of this Treaty (The Treaty of Rome 1957)', the European single market came into being at the beginning of 1993. In addition to the single market, the EU also imposes a *common external tariff* (CET) upon all imports into any EU state. The CET means that all countries in the trading bloc impose the same rate of duty on all goods imported from outside the EU. Plans to bring the various EU national economies into closer concurrence, such as stabilising exchange rates, harmonising tax levels and safety standards are expected to render the single market more effective.

North American Free Trade Area and other trading blocs

Western Europe's attempt to generate a single market (the EU) has been emulated by countries in other parts of the world. The potential of a trading bloc in Western Europe is matched both by the *North American Free Trade Area* (NAFTA) and by a proposed trading area in the Asia Pacific region. This would include Japan, Australia and the 'Tigers' (such as South Korea, Taiwan and Thailand). The NAFTA area comprises 370 million people and approximately 30% of the world's economic output whilst the Asia Pacific area would contain more people (2.3 billion) but with a lower percentage of world trade at approximately 20% (although this is expected to grow significantly in the future). It is said that the EU, NAFTA and Asia Pacific together comprise the 'triad' of the world's economy – three powerful economic centres containing the vast majority of the world's production and consumption.

The World Trade Organization (WHO) and GATT

Trading agreements exist on the global as well as the regional level. The most prominent agreements in this category are the *General Agreement on Tariffs and Trade* (GATT) and its successor, the *World Trade Organization* (WTO).

The GATT agreement began life as the Havana Charter 1948 when 23 countries acted as signatories to what they hoped would become an International Trading Organisation (ITO). As negotiations progressed, it became clear that such a worldwide trading bloc was too ambitious and so a general agreement was arrived at. The main points of the agreement were as follows:

- *tariffs* should not be increased above current levels;
- *quotas* should be reduced and eventually abolished;

■ each signatory was a '*most favoured nation* (MFN)'. This meant that trading privileges extended by one member nation to another must be widened to include all of the others. This principle is so important that it is the first article of the GATT which governs trade in goods. MFN is also a priority in the *General Agreement on Trade in Services* (GATS – Article 2) and the *Agreement on Trade Related Aspects of Intellectual Property Rights* (TRIPS – Article 4);[4]

■ the general agreement recognised that other trading blocks may exist, such as the EU and NAFTA, but these were encouraged to be outward-looking rather than insular as far as trading restrictions were concerned.

The WTO replaced GATT as an international organisation in January 1995, but the General Agreement still exits as the WTO's umbrella treaty for trade in goods, updated as a result of the Uruguay Round negotiations 1986–1995. With a membership of 146 countries by April 2003, the WTO has much wider scope than its predecessor in that it encompasses trade in services, investment and intellectual property. Members of the WTO are required to supply a range of trade statistics and the organisation has a speedy trades dispute settlement mechanism that encourages parties to go for arbitration rather than resorting to their own domestic trade policies.

Assignment 15.1

A major far-eastern motor manufacturer is seeking to gain a 'foothold' in the substantial European car market.

Yoe are required to do the following:

■ Outline the options open to the manufacturer in seeking to achieve its objectives.
■ Discuss the pros and cons of the two main options; those of exporting to the EU or of directly investing in a car manufacturing plant somewhere in the EU.
■ Presuming that the company adopts an FDI strategy, discuss the criteria that the company should consider when deciding which European country to build the plant in.

References

1   Keynote report, 2004.
2   Levitt, T. (1983). *The Globalization of Markets.* Harvard Business Review. May/June, 1983.

3   Thompson, A.A. and Strickland, A.J. (1995). *Strategic Management.* London: Irwin.

4   The World Trade Organization (2003). *Understanding the WTO*, 3rd edn. Lausanne, Switzerland: WTO Information and Media Relations Division.

Further reading

Brooks, I., *et al.* (2004). *The International Business Environment.* Harlow: FT Prentice Hall.

Chryssochoidis, G. Millar, C. and Clegg, J. (1996). *Internationalization Strategies.* London: Macmillan. Daniels, J.D. and Radebaugh, L.H. (1995). *International Business: Environments and Operations,* 7th edn. New York: Addison Wesley.

Griffiths, A. and Wall, S. (2001). *Applied Economics,* 9th edn. London: FT Prentice Hall.

Ohmae, K. (1992). *The Borderless World.* London: Penguin.

Piggott, J. and Cook, M. (2001). *International Business Economics: A European Perspective,* 2nd edn. London: Addison-Wesley-Longman.

Sloman, J. (2003). *Economics,* 5th edn. London: FT Prentice Hall.

Taggart, J.H. and McDermott, M.C. (1993). *The Essence of International Business.* London: Prentice Hall.

Useful web sites

Department of trade and Industry: www.dti.gov.uk
EU Business: www.eubusiness.com
International Monetary Fund: www.imf.org
Keynotes: www.keynote.co.uk
World Trade Organisation: www.wto.org/
Organisation for Economic Co-operation and Development: www.oecd.org/

PART III

The external business micro-environment

The market system: prices and costs

After studying this chapter, students should be able to describe:

- the meaning of the terms 'market' and 'market system';
- the difference between goods and services;
- the difference between prices and costs;
- the various types of cost;
- the purpose and meaning of price;
- the various types of revenue and how they are arrived at;
- how prices, costs and revenues can be used to determine the break-even point;
- how prices, costs and revenues can be used to determine the point at which profit is maximised.

16.1 What is the market system?

The 'market'

If you or I want to buy some food, we naturally head for a food shop. Why is this? As we know that at a food shop, there is a business that is willing to part with the goods we need in exchange for our money. Similarly, if I want to sell my car, I may put an advert in the local paper in the hope that I can attract interested buyers who will buy the car from me. People who want to buy second-hand cars may well look in the classified section of the local paper.

We can thus readily arrive at a simple definition of the term *market: a market is a place where buyers and sellers come together*. We use the term market in many contexts in everyday conversation. The job market consists of buyers (of labour) who advertise in papers, jobcentres, etc. and sellers (suppliers of labour – employees and potential employees) who access those sources knowing that they can 'meet' buyers in those pages. The food market exists in your local supermarket as sellers set up a business and buyers go to the shop for the sole purpose of buying food.

The word 'place' in the above definition may or may not mean a physical location. In some markets, it may do (e.g. the quayside market in Newcastle-upon-Tyne, the fish market in Billingsgate), but in many cases, it means a non-physical 'location', which may be in the media, through word of mouth or, increasingly, through computer communications. We speak, for example, of the chemicals market, which consists of thousands of buyers and sellers all over the world who, through a plethora of interrelationships, make themselves known to one another.

Goods and services

Markets are concerned with buyers and sellers of goods and services. The term 'goods and services' is used frequently in this text and is taken to mean the various types of product that are exchanged in business.

A *product*, in its most general sense, is the output of an organisation that is, offered for use or consumption by the buyer. We can immediately see that the nature of organisational outputs varies enormously and it is here that we use our 'goods and services' distinction:

- *Goods* are generally taken to means products that can be touched and seen. They are classified by economists and the government (for recording purposes) as *visible products*. Examples include foods, cars, chemicals, pharmaceuticals and electronic goods. It follows that goods are things we can *own*.
- *Services* are products that can not be touched, but are things that are done for our benefit and are classed as invisible products. Examples include insurance services, trades people like plasterers and mechanics, health provision and legal advice. Services are things that we *use* or *have done* rather than own.

Question 16.1

For each of the following organisations listed below:

- Scottish and Newcastle plc – brewing.
- Tesco – supermarkets.
- GlaxoSmithKline – pharmaceuticals.
- Vodafone – telecommunications.
- British Airports Authority – airports.
- Glasgow Caledonian University – higher education establishment.

state

1 the main product offered to the market.
2 if the product is a 'good' or a 'service'.
3 the buyer of the organisation's product.

The market price

Every time you make a purchase, say of a food item at your local ASDA, you are (probably unconsciously) attesting to the efficiency of the market system. ASDA offers its baked beans for sale at a certain price, say 45 pennies a tin. You go to ASDA because you know it sells baked beans. You look at the price of 45 pennies and you have a choice. You can either say:

- 'no, 45 pennies is too high a price' (result: no sale takes place), or you can say;
- 'yes, I am willing to pay 45 pennies to enjoy the benefit of these beans' (result: sale takes place).

If you decide that 45 pennies is too high a price, you may look elsewhere for your beans. You may try a cheaper supermarket such as Kwik Save or Netto or you may decide to buy peas instead.

On the other side of the market relationship, ASDA will be asking itself some questions. If the sales on baked beans (at a price of 45 pennies) are high, it will conclude one of the following:

- the price of baked beans is about right. We will leave it as it is, or;
- the price for baked beans may be too low. We may be able to increase it slightly and make even more money from the sale of this product.

Conversely, if sales of baked beans are low, it may conclude that the price of baked beans is too high. In such a situation, the most obvious thing to do is to reduce the price and see if the total sales rise.

The market system is thus composed of millions of individual buying and selling decisions. In this chapter, and in Chapter 17, we will examine the features of the various parts of the buying and selling decisions that, in their totality, make businesses 'tick' and national economies 'work'.

Prices and costs: what is the difference?

In common language, we tend to use the terms 'price' and 'cost' interchangeably. In strict business and economic terms, there is a clear difference. Put simply: *the seller's price is the buyer's cost.*

In the above example, we saw that the *price* of a tin of baked beans was 45 pennies. When ASDA bought the beans from its supplier (e.g. Heinz), it would incur a *cost* by buying it. The cost to ASDA would be some amount less than its asking price so that by selling the beans, it could make a profit. To you, the buyer of the beans, the ASDA's price of 45 pennies becomes a cost (to you) of the same amount.

Hence, a business will often speak of its costs to mean the total amount of money needed to operate the business. It will use the prices charged for its products to (hopefully) cover the costs it had incurred.

16.2 A closer look at business costs

Types of costs

When examining business costs, a business first identifies the monetary value of the *total costs* that the business has incurred and then it attempts to see how the total cost is made up.

The first component of the total cost is the *fixed cost*. Fixed costs are those which do not vary with an organisation's output. In other words, they must be paid even if the business does not make or do anything. Examples of fixed costs in most businesses include (Figure 16.1):

- rent on the factory, land, offices, etc.
- local authority taxation;
- some staff/employee costs;
- water rates (if it is not metered);
- repayments on any loans that the business may have.

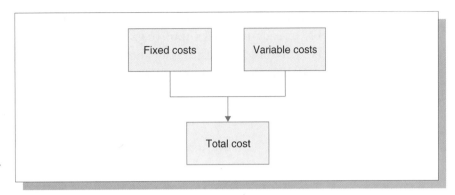

Figure 16.1
Composition of
total cost.

The second component of total cost is the *variable cost*. Variable costs are those which do vary with organisational output: if the business makes nothing, it incurs no variable costs. Examples include:

- raw material costs;
- some labour costs (those employed on a piece-rate basis);
- energy costs (e.g. needed to operate machines);
- transportation costs.

Hence we arrive at a very simple mathematical definition of total cost:

total cost = fixed cost + variable cost   or $TC = FC + VC$.

In examining costs, economists tend to distinguish between what are termed *short-run* and *long-run* costs. In the short-run, it is assumed that production inputs like rent on property are fixed in that the company cannot immediately terminate the use of the property, and thus reduce its costs of the rent. It is thus considered as a short-run fixed cost. In the long-run, however, the fixed costs can be reduced by giving up use of the property (or selling a machine, building, etc.). What was a short-run fixed cost can thus become a long-run variable cost.

Most calculations in micro-economics are based on the short-run basis. When we enter a discussion of economics in the longer run, it can get very complicated as all fixed costs can become variable eventually (i.e. in the very long-run).

Average and marginal costs

Economists, in analysing the costs of a business use the terms average and marginal costs to get a better understanding of how costs are incurred by a business. Let us first define the terms.

The *average cost* of a business describes is the cost, on average, attributable to each unit of output (e.g. each can of beer, washing machine, car, etc.). Whilst businesses may know some costs, (e.g. the material cost) of each item it makes (but in practice even this is often unknown), it can allocate fixed costs to an item by performing a simple calculation. We find the average cost by dividing the total cost by the output in units or quantity.

$$\text{average cost} = \frac{\text{total cost}}{\text{quantity}} \quad \text{or} \quad AC = \frac{TC}{Q}.$$

The *marginal cost* is the total cost incurred by the business for each extra unit of output it produces. Initially, we would expect the marginal cost to fall as output (quantity) increases. This is because each extra unit produced 'dilutes' the fixed costs by that little bit more and although the variable cost attributable to each unit may remain relatively constant, the total cost per unit incurred is likely to fall.

When output rises past a certain level, however, the marginal cost usually starts to rise. At the point at which it starts to increase, the business is beginning to increase its total costs faster that it can recover them through simply producing more units. This is due to short-run diseconomies of scale that creep into a business through having to, say, purchase a new machine to make more units. The point at which marginal cost is at its lowest is, therefore the point at which production is at its most efficient.

Marginal cost is defined as:

$$\text{marginal cost} = \frac{\text{change in total cost}}{\text{change in quantity}} \quad \text{or} \quad MC = \frac{\Delta_{TC}}{\Delta_{Q}}$$

where the symbol Δ (delta) denotes a change in, so Δ_{TC} means the change in total cost.

The costs schedule

The best way to understand how these costs all fit together is to construct a table (Table 16.1). You are given the following information.

Using the information and equations we have already learned, we can now fill in the rest of this table. Fixed costs, by definition will stay the same for all quantities produced. Total cost can be obtained by adding together the fixed and variable costs. Average cost can be obtained by dividing the total cost by the quantity. Marginal cost, in this case, can be calculated by subtracting the previous total cost from the current one. The completed table is thus shown as Table 16.2.

Table 16.1

Costs schedule

Quantity	Fixed cost	Variable cost	Total cost	Average cost	Marginal cost
0	20	0			
1		10			
2		16			
3		22			
4		36			
5		60			
6		100			

Table 16.2

Completed costs schedule

Quantity	Fixed cost	Variable cost	Total cost $(= FC + VC)$	Average cost $(= TC/Q)$	Marginal cost $(= \Delta_{TC}/\Delta_Q)$
0	20	0	20	0	–
					10
1	20	10	30	30	
					6
2	20	16	36	18	
					6
3	20	22	42	14	
					14
4	20	36	56	14	
					24
5	20	60	80	16	
					40
6	20	100	120	20	

Note that we enter marginal cost in-between the lines of other figures. This is because marginal cost describes the difference between the two sets of values in the line (total cost and quantity). It also reminds us that when we come to plot marginal costs, we plot the values between the other values on the *x*-axis.

If we now plot this data on a graph, we arrive at an important principle.

The point 'x' in Figure 16.2 is important. Levels of output to the left of point x mean that average cost is falling with increased output, so it makes business sense to produce at those quantities. To the right of point x, average costs start to rise. Hence, the point at which the marginal cost line intersects the average cost line represents the most efficient short-run output level of the business. In this example it is about 3.5 units.

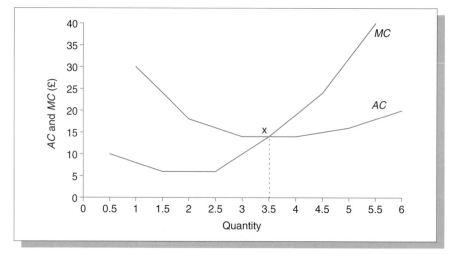

Figure 16.2
Average cost (*AC*)
and marginal cost
(*MC*) against
quantity (short-run).

Question 16.2

Complete the following table and plot the graph. Establish the most efficient level of output.

Quantity	Fixed cost	Variable cost	Total cost	Average cost	Marginal cost
0	15,000	0			
1000		15,000			
2000		24,000			
3000		33,000			
4000		54,000			
5000		90,000			
6000		150,000			

Hint: When plotting marginal cost, plot the numbers between the points of average cost. This is because marginal cost figures represents the difference between the two total cost figures from which average cost is calculated.

16.3 A closer look at business prices

The purpose of the price

The price that a business charges for its goods and services has a number of purposes.

It is a means of *covering the costs* that the business has incurred in bringing the product to the market. Such costs may typically include the cost of the materials in the product, the costs of labour, rent on premises, transport costs, marketing or advertising costs, packaging costs, etc. In this respect, the price charged ensures that the seller does not make a trading loss.

It is a means of gaining wealth and of *making a profit* if the price charged includes a net surplus over all costs incurred. Profits are used to reinvest in the business (e.g. buying more equipment) and to pay the owners of the business a return, such as the giving of dividends on shares.

Profit

We use the term 'profit' in a number of ways in ordinary conversation. In economic terms, the profit is the surplus a business is left with once a price has been achieved in a business transaction and all the costs have been paid.

It can represent the cash surplus on one business transaction, in which case we express it as:

$$\text{profit} = \text{price} - \text{total cost} \quad \text{or} \quad \pi = P - TC.$$

It can also represent the total surplus made by a business over a period of time. This would be expressed as:

$$\text{profit} = \text{total revenue} - \text{total cost} \quad \text{or} \quad \pi = TR - TC.$$

for the time period in question.

The price can sometimes be a *signal to the buyer*. A buyer often makes the assumption that 'you get what you pay for'. In this regard, a low price will communicate certain features of the product to the buyer (e.g. cheap and cheerful, functional, basic, etc.) whereas a high price will have the opposite effect (e.g. quality, premium, luxurious, etc.).

Revenue

The term revenue is sometimes referred to as sales value, turnover, or income. It is the total sales for a business over a period of time and is expressed as:

$$\text{total revenue} = \text{price} \times \text{quantity sold} \quad \text{or} \quad TR = P \times Q.$$

Hence, if the price of a good is £2 and, over the course of a month, the business sells 1000 units, then its revenue for the month is £2 × 1000 = £2000. If sales are consistent over a year, the quantity for the year would be 12,000 and revenue, £24,000.

Average and marginal revenues

In the same way that we calculated average and marginal costs, there is also value in calculating the same for revenues.

Average revenue (*AR*) is the revenue that a business earns from each unit at any given level of output:

$$\text{average revenue} = \frac{\text{total revenue}}{\text{quantity}} \quad \text{or} \quad AR = \frac{TR}{Q}.$$

We should note at this point that we have seen the term TR/Q before. By rearranging the equation we used to calculate total revenue, we can see that the equation:

$$TR = P \times Q$$

can be rearranged as,

$$Q = \frac{TR}{P}$$

or

$$P = \frac{TR}{Q}.$$

As $TR/Q = P$, it follows that if,

$$AR = \frac{TR}{Q}$$

then, because both P and $AR = TR/Q$, it must be the case that,

$$AR = P.$$

So for our purposes (making some assumptions), we can describe the average revenue as price.

Rearranging simple mathematical equations

There are two types of simple equations. The first type involves a plus or a minus and the second type involves a multiplication or division.

Equations which are of the type:

$$a = b - c$$

can be expressed correctly in three ways:

$$a = b - c \quad \text{or} \quad b = a + c \quad \text{or} \quad c = b - a.$$

Equations that are of the type:

$$a = b \times c \text{ (sometimes expressed as } a = bc)$$

can be expressed correctly in three ways:

$$a = bc \quad \text{or} \quad b = \frac{a}{c} \quad \text{or} \quad c = \frac{a}{b}.$$

You can check if your rearrangement is correct by making a, b and c equal 1, 2 and 3, to see if the equation works.

Marginal revenue (*MR*) is the additional revenue earned by selling one extra unit of output. This figure can be found by calculating as follows:

$$\text{marginal revenue} = \frac{\text{change in total revenue}}{\text{change in quantity}} \quad \text{or} \quad MR = \frac{\Delta_{TR}}{\Delta_Q}.$$

A feature of prices is that the more of an item there is on the market, the lower the price of that item will be. If there was only one motorcar for sale in the whole country, it would attract a hefty price. Similarly, if there were more than a billion for sale in the UK, sellers could hardly give them away, they would certainly go for a very low price. We would thus expect both the price per unit (average revenue) and marginal revenue to fall as quantity rises.

We can see how this works by looking at a schedule as follows (Table 16.3).

By using the equations we encountered above, we can fill the table in (Table 16.4).

We can now plot this data as a graph (Figure 16.3).

Table 16.3
Schedule of prices

Quantity	Price	Average revenue	Total revenue	Marginal revenue
1	100			
2	90			
3	80			
4	70			
5	60			
6	50			

Table 16.4
Schedule of prices and revenues

Quantity	Price	Average revenue $(= P)$	Total revenue $(= PQ)$	Marginal revenue $(= \Delta_{TR}/\Delta_Q)$
1	100	100	100	–
				80
2	90	90	180	
				60
3	80	80	240	
				40
4	70	70	280	
				20
5	60	60	300	
				0
6	50	50	300	

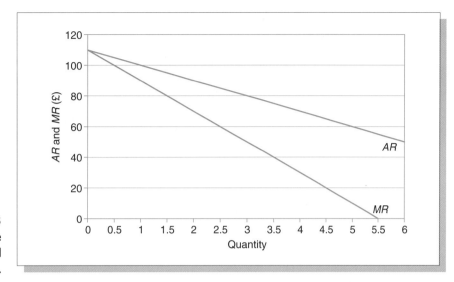

Figure 16.3
Average revenue
(AR) and marginal
revenue (MR).

Simple economic equations: a summary

- Total cost = fixed cost + variable cost
  or $TC = FC + VC$
- Average cost = total cost/quantity
  or $AC = TC/Q$
- Marginal cost = change in total cost/change in quantity
  or $MC = \Delta TC/\Delta Q$
- Profit = total revenue − total cost
  or $\pi = TR - TC$
- Profit (on a single item) = price − total cost
  or $\pi = P - TC$
- Revenue = price × quantity
  or $TR = P \times Q$
- Average revenue = total revenue/quantity
  or $AR = TR/Q$
- Marginal revenue = change in total revenue/change in quantity
  or $MR = \Delta TR/\Delta Q$

16.4 Using prices and costs in business

We may well ask what the purpose is of the foregoing discussion on the various aspects of prices and costs. We will examine two of the most important uses of what we have learned.

Break-even point

By understanding the information we have so far discussed, we can introduce the concept of break-even point – the quantity beyond which the business's revenues exceed its total costs. We can intuitively see that if a business has no output, it is still incurring its fixed costs, such as rent and local authority taxation. Using the equation $\pi = TR - TC$, it is clear that if $TR = 0$ (because nothing is being sold) and TC (which is partly fixed cost) is a positive figure, then π would be a negative figure, that is a loss.

The break-even graph in Figure 16.4 is explained as follows. At zero output, the business incurs the full burden of fixed cost, but no variable cost. There is, of course, no revenue. The loss on operations is the value of the fixed costs.

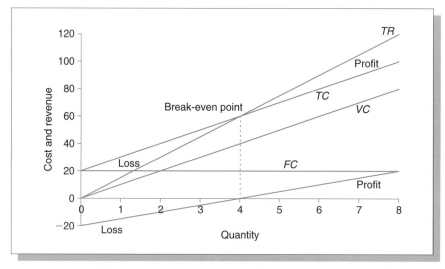

Figure 16.4
Break-even point.

As output rises, the business begins to incur variable costs and hence total cost rises parallel to variable costs (because total cost equals variable cost plus fixed cost, which remains constant). Revenue rises at a faster rate than costs due to the price being in excess of costs with a view to more then covering variable costs. For simplification purposes, the total revenue line makes the assumption in this case that an increase in quantity does not produce a reduction in price. We know this to be something of a simplification, but it enables us to understand the principle of break even.

At the break-even point, output reaches a level at which the total revenue earned from all units produced overtakes total cost. Production below the quantity at break-even point incurs an overall loss to the business whereas at levels above it, an overall profit is made.

Profit maximisation

We can use the theory discussed above to answer the question: what is the optimal output of a business at which profit is maximised? Using the information we have already learned, we can calculate the output of maximum profit in two ways by plotting:

- total cost and total revenue on the same graph;
- marginal cost and marginal revenue on the same graph.

The *total cost and total revenue* approach is as follows. Let us remind ourselves of the behaviour of these two variables. Total costs will be the fixed cost at zero quantity, and will then grow increasingly slowly as the increased quantity dilutes the fixed costs. Eventually, however, total costs will rise with increasing output as the business experiences diseconomies of scale in the short-run. It follows that the shape of the total cost curve will assume a sigmoidal (s-shaped) form. For total revenue, we may expect revenues to grow rapidly as a function of quantity at first, but as the market price for the good falls with increased quantity, the total revenue against quantity will level off.

Using some appropriate figures should aid our understanding (Table 16.5).

Table 16.5
Schedule of total costs, revenues and profit

Quantity	Total cost (= FC + VC)	Total revenue (= PQ)	Total profit (= TR − TC)
0	100	0	−100
1	150	100	−50
2	180	180	0
3	210	240	30
4	280	280	0
5	400	300	−100
6	600	300	−300

We can now plot the graph shown in Figure 16.5.

We can see that the total profit curve reaches its highest at quantity of three units, but by plotting the other two curves as well, we can see why

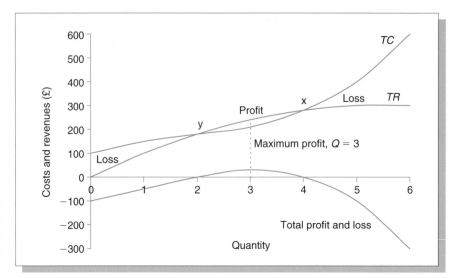

Figure 16.5
Profit maximisation
using total revenue
(*TR*) and total
cost (*TC*).

it is the case. To the left of point y, output levels have not yet provided sufficient revenues to outweigh total costs (which at this stage are mainly fixed costs). Between point y and point x, revenues exceed costs and this is the area of profit. Output of anything between y and x (which in this case is between 2 and 4 units) would yield a profit, but it is at 3 units that the gap between the total revenue and total cost is at its widest; hence the point of profit maximisation. To the right of point x, the two factors of short-run diseconomies of scale (on costs) and reduced price per unit (on revenues), makes for a nasty combination. The curves grow further apart as costs rise and revenues fall.

The *marginal cost and marginal revenue* approach rests upon the following principles. We know that the marginal cost is the cost incurred by producing one more unit of output and that marginal revenue is the extra revenue gained by selling that one more unit of output. We can intuitively understand that if a business incurs more cost than it makes in extra revenue by making one extra unit, then it is unprofitable to make that unit. Using the same figures as in Table 16.5, we can calculate the average and marginal costs and benefits (Table 16.6).

If we now plot marginal revenue and marginal cost against quantity (Figure 16.6), we can see how this approach works. We note immediately that the two lines (*MC* and *MR*) intersect at a quantity of three units, the same quantity as profit was maximised in Figure 16.5. This is not an accident as it is natural that profit should be maximised at this point.

Table 16.6
Schedule of the average and marginal costs, and benefits

Quality	Total cost	Average cost	Marginal cost	Total revenue	Average revenue	Marginal revenue
0	100	0	–	0		
					100	100
1	150	150	50	100		
					90	80
2	180	90	30	180		
					80	60
3	210	70	30	240		
					70	40
4	280	70	70	280		
					60	20
5	400	80	120	300		
					50	0
6	600	100	200	300	–	–

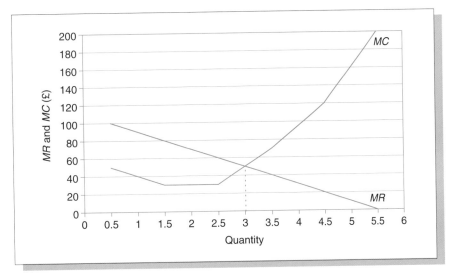

Figure 16.6
Profit maximisation
from marginal
revenue (*MR*) and
marginal cost (*MC*).

Assignment 16.1

The Turtonian band of fly-fishing rods is produced by the Turton Company Limited, a small company in Skelmersdale, Lancashire. The company's owner, Nigel Turton, has given you some data about the company's prices and costs, and he wants you to calculate the following information for him:

- The most efficient output of production.
- The company's break-even quantity point.
- The output level at which Turton's profit is maximised.

The data you are given is this:

- Company's short-run fixed costs: £2000 per year.

Quality	Variable cost at the level of quality	Price per rod at the quality
0	0	–
10	300	130
20	400	126
30	600	122
40	900	118
50	1300	114
60	1800	110
70	2400	106
80	3100	102
90	3900	98
100	4800	94
110	5800	90
120	6900	86

Further reading

For further reading associated with this chapter, see the list at the end of Chapter 17.

The market system: supply and demand

After studying this chapter, students should be able to describe:

- the features and determinants of demand;
- what is meant by the demand schedule and the demand curve;
- the features and determinants of supply;
- what is meant by the supply schedule and the supply curve;
- the mechanisms of price determination and disequilibrium;
- the principles of price and income elasticities of demand;
- the principles of cross elasticity of demand;
- the features of factor markets, particularly the labour market.

17.1 Demand

Demand and effective demand

Whenever we express an interest in purchasing a good or service, we are indicating a demand. Note though, that it is possible to demand a product without actually buying it. You may demand a new motorcar, but for various reasons (e.g. poverty), you are unable to express your demand in the form of a purchase. It is for this reason that economists distinguish desire for a product with its *effective* demand. Producers of goods and services are less concerned with how badly you desire their products, and more with how many you will actually buy and at what price.

Effective demand, as distinct from demand, has three components:

- the actual *quantity demanded* of a good or service,
- the *time period* over which the quantity is demanded,
- the *price* at which the quantity will be demanded over the time period.

Effective demand thus takes into account the customer's ability to buy, not just the desire – however intense that may be. We may say, therefore, that the total demand for product A is 10,000 units a month if the price is 45 pennies per unit. Thus all three components must be in place before the demand can be said to be effective.

The determinants of demand

In seeking to answer the question *why* the demand for a product is as it is, we must explore the reasons behind consumer choices. We can intuitively appreciate that demand for goods and services varies, both according to the type of product and over time. There are five broad variables which determine the demand for any given product:

- the financial ability to pay;
- changing tastes and fashions (i.e. changing preferences);
- the prices of other, related products;
- the consumer's perceptions of what will happen in the future;
- the type of product it is.

We will examine each in turn.

Ability to pay

The ability to pay for goods and services will obviously have a huge influence on demand. If consumers have a lot of spending power (or disposable income), demand for most products will rise. Conversely, if consumers are 'hard up', demand will tend to fall. The power of consumer spending will depend, among other things upon macro-economic features such as:

- the level of wage or income increases,
- tax rates,

- interest rates,
- employment and unemployment levels in the country.

Consumer preferences

The second determinant of demand is the changing face of consumer preferences. If financial issues determine the consumer's ability to buy, preferences concern the consumer's *willingness* to buy. It is obvious that people change over time in what they want to buy. It may be that one type of product is in demand 1 year, but not the next. Preference can be influenced in several ways:

- It can be subject to *fashion*, as is the case with clothes, some forms of art, furniture, music and many other things.
- It may be influenced by increasing or decreasing *trends*, such as a decline in the consumption of cigarettes or an increase in the use of condoms.
- It may be influenced by *advertising*, where a producer persuades people to increase consumption of its products.
- Some goods are subject to *seasonal variation* in demand. We might, for example, expect more ice cream to be sold in hot weather whilst we would collectively demand more duffel coats in the winter.
- Consumption is sometimes informed by *expert opinion*. If an eminent doctor announces that the use of sun-lamps contributes to skin cancer, we might expect a downturn in demand for the purchase and hire of sun-lamps. Conversely, announcements about the cholesterol-reducing properties of bran fibre and red grape juice would tend to stimulate demand for these items.

Prices of other products

The third determinant of demand is the price of other products. This concerns the nature of a product in question and how it relates to other products. A product can be related to other products in one of two ways: it can be a *complementary* or *substitute* product:

- *Complementary products* are related inasmuch as you will need to buy product A if you buy product B. It follows that an increase in demand for product A will stimulate an increase in the demand for product B. For example, if you buy a petrol-driven car, you will need to buy petrol for it. An increase in the number of cars sold will tend to also increase the volume of petrol sold by oil companies. Cars and petrol are therefore said to be complementary goods. A second example might be video recorders and videotapes.

◼ *Substitute products* are related in as much as you will *not need* product A if you buy product B. This is because product A performs essentially the same function as product B. Hence, an increase in the demand for product A will cause a decrease in the demand for product B. If, for example, there is an increase in the demand for butter, we would expect a reduction in the demand for margarine. Similarly, if the price of coffee increases due to a bad Brazilian harvest, we might expect more tea to be demanded in place of (as a substitute for) the more expensive coffee.

Question 17.1

How many pairs of products can you think of that are either complements or substitutes? Try to think of at least four pairs for each category.

Consumers' perception of what will happen in the future

The fourth determinant of demand is the consumers' perceptions of the future. If the consumers of a product collectively believe that there will be a future shortage of the product, then demand will increase in the short term. Conversely, if they believe that the price will come down, they will delay purchases thus reducing short-term demand.

Levels of consumer income and the nature of the product

The fifth demand is determined by the nature of the product itself. There is a link between the demand for different products and other variables, such as personal income. A comparison between the quantity demanded of goods compared to personal income shows three broad types of product (Figures 17.1–17.3).

A *normal good* is one wherein demand increases with income – the more you earn, the more you buy. Examples of normal goods are

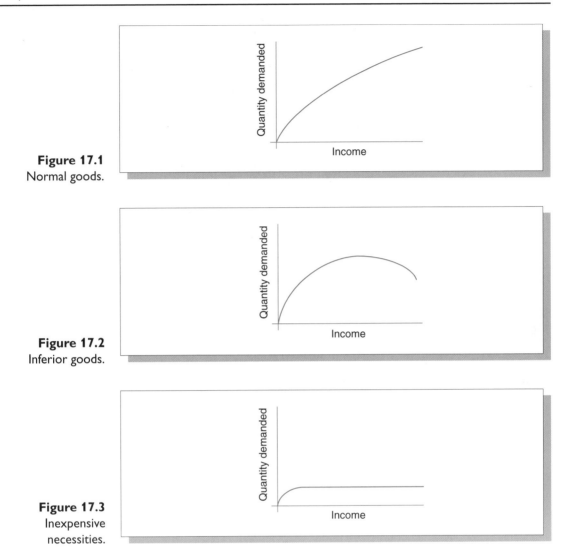

Figure 17.1
Normal goods.

Figure 17.2
Inferior goods.

Figure 17.3
Inexpensive
necessities.

legion; with rising income we will tend to buy more bottles of wine, more holidays, more houses (i.e. we would move more often), etc.

Inferior goods show increased use with rising income, but only up to a point. When a certain level of income is reached, people switch to superior products and hence demand for inferior products declines. Examples of inferior goods would include the cheaper food brands and the use of 'cash-only' supermarkets. In some parts of the country, the use of the bus as a commuter vehicle would be an inferior good as higher income groups switch to private cars to get to and from work.

Inexpensive necessities show an initial increase in demand with income, but there comes a point at a very low level of income where consumption remains constant whatever the income. Examples include salt, sugar and bread. However, much you earn, your demand for salt remains the same.

The demand schedule

In seeking to understand the demand for a product during a time period, we must analyse how the quantity demanded is related to the product's price. We do this by means of a simple table called the *demand schedule*.

The general rule of demand is that there will usually be an inverse relationship between the price and the quantity demanded. In other words:

- the higher the price, the lower the quantity demanded;
- the lower the price, the higher the quantity demanded.

We can illustrate this with a simple example. Product P has the following demand schedule shown in Table 17.1. The quantity refers to the number of units that would be bought by the market in a given time period if the price was set at the figure on the left. Hence, if the price per unit was £100, one unit would be demanded by the market. If, however, the price was set at £40, the market in total would buy five units.

Table 17.1
Demand schedule

Price (£)	Quantity demanded
100	1
82	2
66	3
52	4
40	5
30	6
22	7
18	8
16	9

The demand curve

We can now plot the demand schedule to see on a graph how the quantity demanded of a good or service relates to its price. Figure 17.4 shows the demand curve for the data in Table 17.1. The top left to bottom right slope is typical of the shape of a demand curve. At the top left, the price is high but the quantity demanded is low. At the bottom right, the opposite is the case – low price, high quantity.

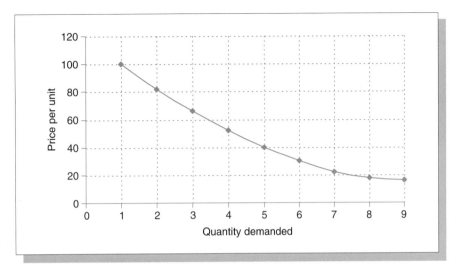

Figure 17.4
Demand curve.

Calculating revenue from the demand curve

Once we have drawn the demand curve, we can use it to calculate the business's potential revenue at any given point along it. We learned in the last chapter that:

$$\text{total revenue } (TR) = \text{price } (P) \times \text{quantity } (Q).$$

At any point on the demand curve, we can calculate the revenue generated at that point simply by multiplying the figure on the quantity axis by that on the price axis. Figure 17.5 uses the data in Table 17.1.

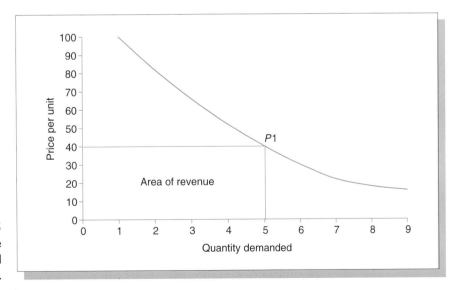

Figure 17.5
Calculating revenue
from the demand
curve.

At point P1, the revenue generated will be £40 × 5 = £200. We can perform this calculation at any point along the demand curve to work out the price and quantity that will yield the most revenue.

Question 17.2

CoolFire is a fashionable brand of Alcopop and you like it due to its dual qualities as an occasional refreshment and as a rapid intoxicant. You earn a professional salary of £30,000 a year. How many 500-millilitre bottles of CoolFire would you buy *per month*, if the price per bottle was as follows? Fill in the table:

Price per 500-millilitre bottle	Number you would buy per month
90 pennies	
£1.30	
£1.65	
£1.95	
£2.60	
£2.90	
£3.20	

If possible, add your figures to those of others (e.g. the members of your class) to get the demand for CoolFire for a bigger group.

Plot the demand curve (when doing this, find the line of best fit rather than just joining the dots).

Answer the following questions:

■ How many bottles of CoolFire would be demanded if the price was £3.50?
■ How many bottles of CoolFire would be demanded if the price was £1.85?

Extension and contraction of demand

The various points along the market demand curve represent the alternative possible price–quantity situations that the total market will accept. If the actual price *P* of product, whose demand curve is shown in Figure 17.4 above, is £52, then we can see that 4 units would be demanded over the time period in question. If the price changes, then the price–quantity situation will move along the existing demand curve. Different terms are used to describe this movement, depending upon its direction:

- A move *up and to the left* will result in fewer units being demanded at a higher price – a *contraction* of demand.
- A move *down and to the right* will result in more being demanded at a lower price – an *extension* of demand.

Let us say that point *x* in Figure 17.6 represents the price–quantity position now. If the price comes down, say to a new price of £30, the quantity demanded would increase to 6 units (point *z*). As the higher quantity is the result, it is said that demand has extended. In the event of a move to a higher price (say to point *y*), the quantity demanded would be reduced, hence the term contraction.

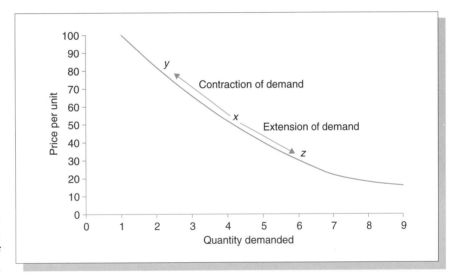

Figure 17.6
Extension and contraction of demand.

Shifts in the demand curve

Under some circumstances, the demand curve itself can move. This happens when more or less quantity is demanded at every price. An example will aid our understanding.

Table 17.2 represents the demand for potatoes in Mr Marrow's small fruit and vegetable shop (a small 'market'). We can now show this schedule as a graph (Figure 17.7).

Table 17.2
Demand for potatoes in Mr Marrow's shop

Price per pound weight (pennies)	Number of pounds weight demanded per week
10	1000
15	850
20	700
25	550
30	400

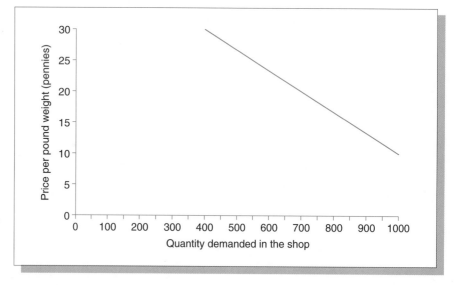

Figure 17.7
Demand curve for potatoes in Mr Marrow's shop.

Demand shift scenario 1

Now suppose (hypothetically) that the Department of Health unexpectedly announces that potatoes can act as an aphrodisiac and prevent the development of serious diseases like cancer. This would signal an increase in the demand for potatoes. Since people would want to eat more potatoes, we would expect them to demand more potatoes whatever the price. This means that whereas some consumers may only have been prepared to pay 15 pennies for a pound of potatoes, the realisation that they were so good for you would mean that they would be prepared to pay 20 pennies in order to secure the benefits of these miraculous tuberous vegetables. In such a circumstance, we would expect a new demand schedule to apply.

Table 17.3

Demand schedule for potatoes in Mr Marrow's shop before and after the medical announcement

Price per pound (pennies)	Number of pounds before the announcement	Weight demanded per week after the announcement
10	1000	1200
15	850	1050
20	700	900
25	550	750
30	400	600

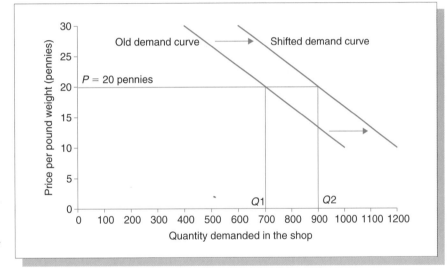

Figure 17.8
Demand curve shift for potatoes in Mr Marrow's shop as a result of the announcement.

Table 17.3 refers to the same shop as does Table 17.2. If we now plot the two demand curves (Figure 17.8), we can see that the curve has shifted as a result of the announcement.

If we take the example of the situation where the price of potatoes was 20 pennies per pound, we can see that (using the old demand curve) the shop would have sold 700 pounds weight per week ($Q1$) before the announcement. After the announcement, it can now sell 900 pounds weight ($Q2$) at that price. This, of course, also represents an increase in revenue for the shop:

Before the announcement:

$$TR = P \times Q$$
$$= 20 \times 700$$
$$= 14,000 \text{ pennies} = £140.$$

After the announcement:

$$TR = 20 \times 900$$
$$= 18,000 \text{ pennies} = £180.$$

The shop in question, in the light of the announcement, theoretically has a happy choice. It can both keep the price the same and sell more potatoes (thus increasing its revenue), or else it can sell the same quantity, but at an increased price (having a similar effect on revenue). Using the demand curve, we can work out how much it could charge for its potatoes if it kept the quantity sold the same (Figure 17.9).

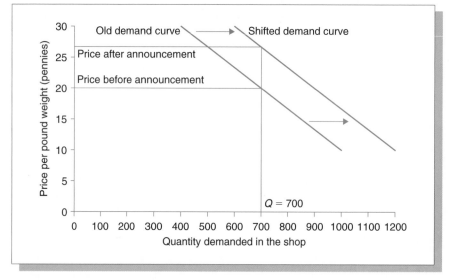

Figure 17.9
Price after announcement at 700 pounds quantity of potatoes per week in Mr Marrow's shop.

Whereas previously, the market would pay 20 pennies for a total quantity of 700 pounds per week, the shop can now achieve a price of 26 pennies for the same quantity. Again, the shop will enjoy an increase in revenue:

Before: $20 \times 700 = 14,000$ pennies $= £140$.
After: $26 \times 700 = 18,200$ pennies $= £182$.

A rightward shift in the demand curve can be brought about by anything that causes more of the product to be demanded at every price. Such situations include, as well as the example we have considered, a fall in the price of complementary goods or a rise in the price of a substitute product.

Demand shift scenario 2

Now suppose that instead of the previous announcement, the Department of Health actually announces (equally hypothetically) that potatoes are bad for you. Suppose that scientists working on potato biochemistry say that they are linked with male impotence and that they can cause rheumatism and haemorrhoids!

In the case of this announcement, we would expect the demand for potatoes to fall at every price. The demand curve would shift down and to the left. This means that instead of selling 700 pounds per week at a price of 20 pennies, Mr Marrow's shop could now only sell say 500 pounds per week (Figure 17.10).

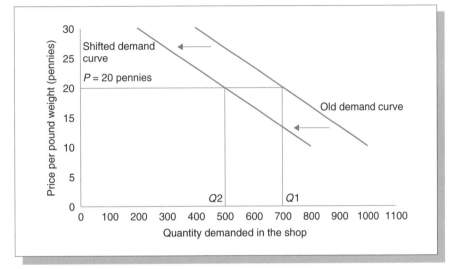

Figure 17.10
Shift in demand after potato health warning, Mr Marrow's shop.

If the price was initially 20 pennies per pound, we know that 700 pounds per week would be demanded ($Q1$). However, the demand for potatoes would reduce if there was a health scare on them. Hence, at 20 pennies, the quantity demanded would fall to 500 pounds per week ($Q2$).

Question 17.3

Which way do you think the demand curve would shift (up right or down left), if the following happened?

- The third world rice harvest failed.
- A new 'cut-price' supermarket opened 400 yards from Mr Marrow's shop.

Question 17.4

Blueberries boost for health
In September 2004, The ITV show *This Morning*, highlighted the results of research by the *USDA* into the health benefits of *blueberries*. The research confirmed that a serving of wild

blueberries delivers more antioxidant power than 20 different fruits and berries, including strawberries, raspberries, cranberries and prunes. Antioxidants are important because of their potential to protect against Alzheimer's disease, cancer and heart disease. Within 24 hours of the broadcast, supermarkets throughout the UK reported a massive upsurge in demand for blueberries and that all stocks had been completely sold out:

- What do you think happened to the demand curve for competitor fresh food products, such as strawberries and raspberries, after the TV broadcast?
- What would happen to the market price for competitor fresh food products, given that the short-term supply curve would remain unchanged?

17.2 Supply

What is supply?

There are two sides to the market system. Having examined the demand side, we turn to supply.

Supply refers to the quantity that producers would want to provide for the market at a given price. In general terms, the higher the price a producer can charge for a product, the more that producers will tend to produce of that product. Conversely, a low market price will tend to stimulate a lower quantity of production. The underlying presupposition behind supply decisions by businesses is that businesses essentially seek to maximise revenues and profits. This presupposition is workable in most situations.

What causes supply?

The decision to supply goods and services to a market depends upon several factors. The quantity of a product supplied will thus depend upon the following factors:

- The *price* which the producer can obtain for the product.
- The *prices of other goods*. If, for example, a competitor is producing a substitute product which is expected to be cheaper, this may deter some producers from supplying the market.
- The *costs of producing the product*, which will, in turn, depend upon the wider economic environment, such as labour costs, tax rates, etc.

- *Changes in technology* may reduce the costs of production and stimulate a higher level of supply to the market.
- *Seasonal variations.* Producers of traditionally seasonal products will produce goods in anticipation of increased demand. Ice cream manufacturers will increase production in the early summer months on the assumption that the summer weather will precipitate a higher demand.

The supply schedule

A supply schedule is constructed in the same way as a demand schedule (Table 17.4). Information might be gathered about producers collectively on how many units they would supply to the market over a range of possible prices. Equally, supply schedule can also be constructed for an individual supplier, just as a demand schedule can apply to an individual consumer. The bigger the sample of suppliers represented in the supply schedule, the more informative and meaningful the schedule will be for predicting the nature of the market relationships for that product.

Table 17.4
Demand and supply schedules for potatoes in Mr Marrow's shop

Price	Supply quantity, pounds per week	Demand quantity, pounds per week
10	400	1000
15	550	850
20	700	700
25	850	550
30	1000	400

If we return to our earlier example of the potato, the supplier (in this case, Mr Marrow the shopkeeper) makes the decision on how many potatoes to supply depending upon how much money he can get for them. If the market price is high, he may forego stocking carrots and other vegetables to sell more potatoes instead. If the price is low, he would be inclined to dedicate less of his shelf space to potatoes and more to other products which might be expected to yield more profits. The following supply schedule describes the quantity of potatoes that Mr Marrow's shop would offer for sale at each price.

The supply curve

Once we have researched the supply of potatoes for this shop, we can now plot the supply curve from the supply schedule (Figure 17.11 and Table 17.5). We can see from this graph that it is the converse of the demand curve. At the bottom left, low quantities would be supplied because of the low price. At the top left, higher volumes would be supplied because higher prices are achievable. We described the variable on the demand curve as having an *inverse* relationship with each other. On a supply curve, price and quantity, rising together are said to have a *positive* relationship.

Figure 17.11
Supply curve for potatoes in Mr Marrow's shop.

Table 17.5
Supply curve for potatoes – Mr Marrow's fruit and vegetable shop

Price per pound (pennies)	Quantity supplied (pounds) per week
10	400
15	550
20	700
25	850
30	1000

Extension, contraction and shifts in supply

In the same way that we can express changes in price and quantity by moving up or down the demand curve, we can do the same for supply

(Figure 17.12). Supply is extended when the price–quantity situation moves up and to the right (more quantity at higher price). It is contracted when it moves down and to the left (less quantity, lower price).

Similarly, anything that causes more or less to be supplied at every price (such as a good or bad harvest), will cause a shift in the supply curve (Figure 17.13).

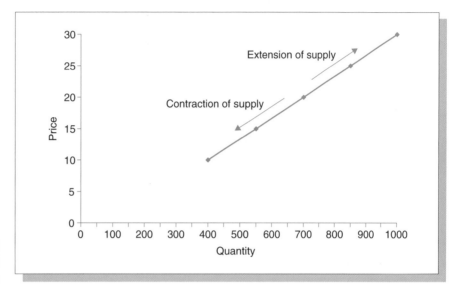

Figure 17.12
Contraction and
extension of supply.

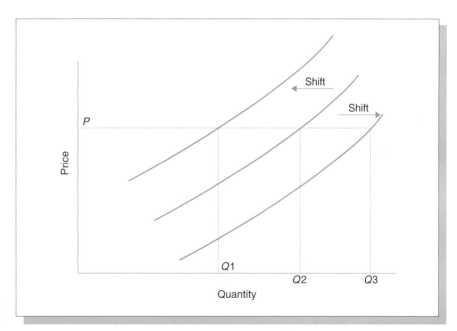

Figure 17.13
Shifts is supply.

If $Q2$ is the initial quantity supplied at price P, then:

- a leftward shift would reduce $Q2$ to $Q1$ at the same price – less supply at every price;
- a rightward shift would increase $Q2$ to $Q3$ at the same price – more supply at every price.

Supply shifts are brought about by changes in the internal or external environment of the suppliers. To show how this might work, a rightward shift (more supply at every price) could be caused by:

- Decreases in the costs of production. If the supplier can get labour or materials at lower cost, it can produce more for the same cost.
- A fall in the price of other goods. If suppliers receive less revenue by producing some goods, they will tend to produce other goods instead. For example, if the price of baked beans falls, food suppliers may produce more peas. This would signal a rightward shift in the supply curve for peas.
- Technological improvement both reduces the costs of production and can increase production capacity.

Question 17.5

Consider the supply of bus services by bus operators. If more bus services are supplied at every price:

- Which way would the supply curve for bus services shift?
- What might cause this increase in supply at every price?

17.3 Price determination

So far in this chapter, we have looked at the demand side (the quantity that would be demanded over a range of prices) and the supply side (the quantity that would be supplied over a range of prices). The problem is that we do not yet know what the actual price of a good or service will be. Both the demand and supply curves represent a number of possible price–quantity situations, but we do not know at what price the product will actually sell.

The equilibrium point

By comparing a product's supply and demand curves on the same graph, we can see that there is one price that both parties (producers and buyers) 'agree' on. This is the point at which both the suppliers and the consumers agree. The noted Cambridge economist *Alfred Marshall* described the supply and demand curves as two blades of a pair of scissors. Neither blade on its own is enough to 'cut a price'. They must both be present and known before the price can be determined.

We can see how this works by looking again at the supply and demand curves for potatoes at the fruit and vegetable shop we considered earlier (Figures 17.4 and 17.11). If we look at these two curves together, we can see that at a price of 20 pennies and a quantity of 700 pounds per week, the curves intersect. This intersection is called the *equilibrium point* (Figure 17.14).

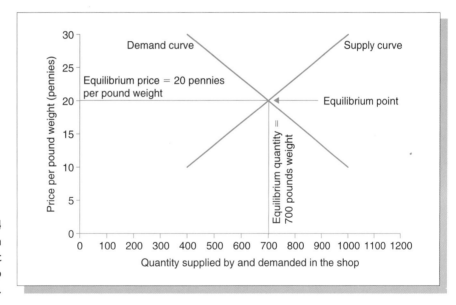

Figure 17.14
The equilibrium point, potatoes at Mr Marrow's shop (per week).

Disequilibriums

The term *equilibrium* is used in this context for a very deliberate reason. The reason for this is that whenever the equilibrium is disturbed, the market price will always tend to return to this point.

If the supply and demand curves remain approximately in position over a long period of time, the equilibrium price and quantity are likely

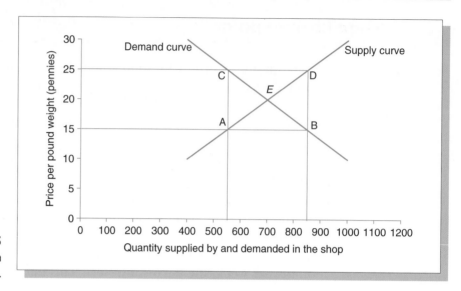

Figure 17.15
Disequilibrium
positions.

to similarly remain in a stable position. A condition called *disequilibrium* can occur when for one reason or another, a price or quantity situation exists which is away from the intersection point of the two curves. The ways in which this can happen are shown in Figure 17.15. The demand and supply curves are those we have previously considered for potato sales in Mr Marrow's small fruit and vegetable shop.

We have seen previously that the equilibrium point is at a price of 20 pennies per pound at a quantity of 700 pounds per week. By examining Figure 17.15, we can see how two types of disequilibrium can arise.

Disequilibrium type 1: demand exceeds supply

On Figure 17.15, we can see that the price of 15 pennies intersects the supply curve at $Q = 550$ pounds per week (point A) and the demand curve at $Q = 850$ pounds per week (point B). This means that at $P = 15$ pennies, 850 pounds per week are demanded, but only 550 pounds are supplied. Hence, there is an excess of demand oversupply of 300 pounds per week (the distance between the curves at the price in question).

It follows that if, for any reason the price of potatoes is 15 pennies, there will be a situation of undersupply, or a shortage. In most market situations, the supply side (in this case Mr Marrow, the shop owner) will sense that there is more demand for potatoes than he can supply (e.g. he may sell out of his week's supply of potatoes by Wednesday). His reasonable course of action under such circumstances would be to increase his price, which of course would result in a reduction in quantity sold. Hence, the market situation would approach the established equilibrium position at a price of 20 pennies.

Disequilibrium type 2: supply exceeds demand

The position of supply exceeding demand can be seen in Figure 17.15 by the points C and D. If the price of potatoes was 25 pennies then 550 pounds per week would be demanded (point C) and 850 pounds per week would be supplied (point D). This represents an oversupply of 300 pounds per week – the distance between the two curves at the $P = 25$ pennies price. Again we see that a substantial disequilibrium exists. In this case, the shop would be left with a glut of potatoes at the end of the week. In order to get rid of the excess potatoes, the supplier is likely to reduce the price of the potatoes thus encouraging buyers to increase their quantity of purchase. The natural tendency is thus for the market situation to re-equilibrate.

Changes in the equilibrium point

The equilibrium point is not 'cast in stone' and from time to time, it moves. There are two situations that can cause this (Figures 17.16–17.19):

- a shift in the demand curve causes an extension or contraction in supply,
- a shift in the supply curve causes an extension or contraction in demand.

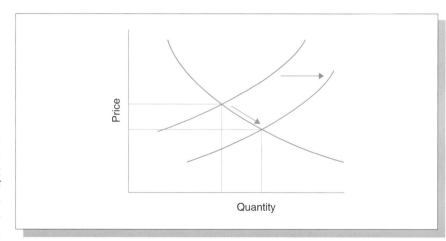

Figure 17.16
Rightward shift in supply curve causing extension of demand – lower price, higher quantity.

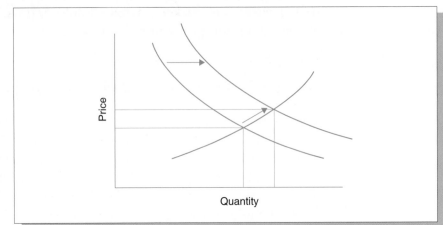

Figure 17.17
Rightward shift in demand causing extension of supply – higher price, higher quantity.

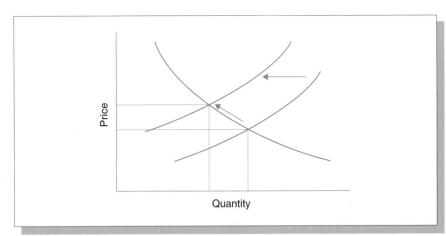

Figure 17.18
Leftward shift in supply curve causing contraction of demand – higher price, lower quantity.

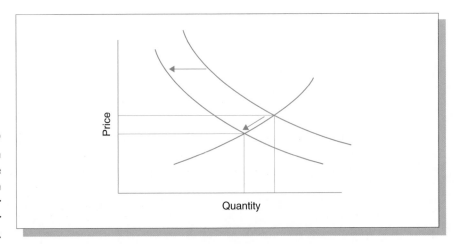

Figure 17.19
Leftward shift in demand curve causing contraction in supply – lower price, lower quantity.

17.4 The price elasticity of demand

Defining price elasticity of demand

Suppose that a company sales director wishes to increase the value of her sales of company products. She has an idea: to reduce the price of the goods in the hope that by doing so, more of the company's products will be demanded by the market. She decides to put the idea to the accountant who, being financially minded, asks the question, 'would your proposed reduction in price result in higher or lower total revenues (TR)?' Clearly, if the price reduction is not more than made up for in increased quantities sold, the reduction is of questionable economic and business sense. The accountant may well ask the sales director to return to her office and examine the demand curve for the products to seek an answer to the query. The sales director can answer the accountant's question straightaway if she knows the *price elasticity of demand* for the product in question.

We have seen that on a demand curve, the revenue earned at different points on the curve can vary as the figures for price and quantity change. We can intuitively appreciate that the relationship between price and quantity will be determined by the nature of the curve itself, that is, its slope (gradient) and shape.

The price elasticity of demand measures the relationship between price, quantity and TR. It can be calculated mathematically as:

$$Ep = \frac{\Delta q/q}{\Delta p/p}$$

or, by simple mathematical rearrangement, as:

$$Ep = \frac{\Delta q}{\Delta p} \times \frac{p}{q}$$

where Ep is the coefficient of price elasticity of demand, Δp is the change in price, Δq is the change in quantity resulting from the change in price, p is the price prior to the change and q is the quantity demanded prior to the change in price.

For some calculations, it is easier to use the formula expressed as:

$$Ep = \frac{\text{percentage change in quantity demanded}}{\text{percentage change in price}}$$

When the equation is calculated for any given change in price, you will arrive at a number for *Ep*. We can use this number to tell us the price elasticity of demand for the product:

- *Ep* is <-1 or >1, we say that the product in question has price elastic demand.
- *Ep* is <-1 or 1, we say that the product in question has price inelastic demand.
- *Ep* equals exactly ±1, we say that the product has a unitary price elasticity of demand.

The sign (positive or negative) of *Ep* is usually ignored. In practice, it invariably turns out to be negative, but this is not important in the context of this discussion. For other types of elasticity (see cross elasticity, Section 17.6), the sign is very important.

Example: The sales director's decision

The sales director we encountered above is contemplating reducing the price on two of her products. One of them, a premium brand of frozen dessert currently sells for £2 per unit. By examining the demand curve for the product, she calculated that if she were to reduce the price by 10% to £1.80, she could increase sales from 5000 units per month to 6000.

The other product she is considering is an over-the-counter pharmaceutical. A month's pack of the drug currently sells for £5. She calculates from the demand curve that a 10% price reduction to £4.50 would increase units sold from 10,000 per month to 10,100.

In order to answer the accountant, she calculates the price elasticity of demand for the two products:

	Premium dessert (£)	Pharmaceutical (£)
p	2	5
Δp	−0.2 (i.e. 20 pennies)	−0.5 (i.e. 50 pennies)
q	5000	10,000
Δq	1000 (i.e. 6000–5000)	100

Hence, using the equation:

$$Ep = \frac{\Delta q}{q} \times \frac{\Delta p}{p}$$

Premium dessert:

$$Ep = \frac{1000/5000}{-0.2/2} = \frac{0.2}{-0.1} = -2$$

A price elasticity of -2 is > -1 and is therefore price elastic.
Pharmaceutical:

$$Ep = \frac{100/10,000}{-0.5/5} = \frac{0.01}{-0.1} = -0.1$$

A price elasticity of -0.1 is < -1 and is therefore price inelastic.
The sales director returns to the accountant with the figures she has calculated. The accountant, after surveying the figures says, 'we will go ahead with your proposed price reduction on the dessert but not on the pharmaceutical. In fact, I might even increase the price on the drug.'

Price elasticity and the nature of the product

Whether the demand for a product is price elastic or inelastic depends in large part on the nature of the product itself. Products which have a price elastic demand have a demand quantity which is relatively dependent upon (or responsive to) price. This means that a reduction in price produces a proportionately greater increase in quantity and hence revenue (because $TR = P \times Q$). This tends to be true of products which are considered to be non-essential in nature or which your buying decision rests largely upon its price. You might, for example, opt to buy smoked salmon for the weekend, if it is on special offer at the supermarket when you would not normally buy it due to its elevated price.

Products which have a price inelastic demand are ones you would buy with relatively little regard to price. In other words, they are items that you place a high value upon, ones that you feel you need rather than want or ones which have such a low price anyway that a slight increase does not seem to matter. These are consequently typically necessities, staple goods or products you associate with well-being and health. This category also includes goods and services which are potentially addictive in nature, such as tobacco and narcotics. To illustrate using an extreme case, if you are suffering from excruciating toothache, you are likely to ask the pharmacist for the best or most effective analgesic rather than the cheapest. This is because your buying decision is based upon the performance of the product rather than its price.

Question 17.6

Based on the nature of the following products, say whether you think their price elasticity is most likely to elastic or inelastic. Each refers to the general category of goods and not individual brands within the category:

- toilet paper,
- motorcars,
- pain-killing drugs,
- a textbook which you are instructed by your lecturer to buy,
- caviar,
- malt whisky.

Perfect elasticity and inelasticity

We have seen that elasticity and inelasticity refer to the relationship between price and quantity. In the case of a product whose demand is price inelastic, we expect to see quantity varying proportionately less than price, whilst we would expect the opposite for a product with a price elastic demand. When we take these two ideas to their possible extremes, we arrive at two 'perfect' situations:

- For perfectly demand price *elastic products*, we would expect there to be no change in price regardless of the quantity demanded.
- For perfectly demand price *inelastic products*, we would expect there to be no change in quantity demanded regardless of the price charged.

These two extremes are shown in Figures 17.20 and 17.21.

Figure 17.20
Perfectly elastic
demand curve.

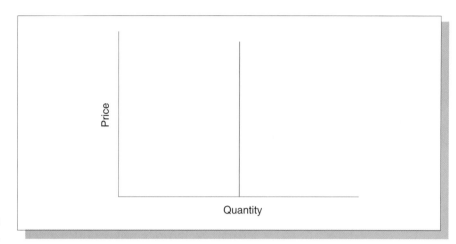

Figure 17.21
Perfectly inelastic
demand curve.

Price elasticity and revenue

The conclusions that we can draw concerning the relationship to a product's price elasticity and movements in revenue follow logically from what we have already learned. It rests upon the simple mathematical relationship $TR = P \times Q$.

For a product with price elastic demand, a reduction in price will produce a proportionately greater increase in quantity, thus more than off-setting the price reduction. Ep, being by definition, more than 1, means that the percentage change in Q will be greater than the percentage change in P.

We can see how this works by inserting notional figures. Product A sells say 5000 units per day at a price of £1. The revenue is thus ($TR = P \times Q$), £1 × 5000 = £5000. We then reduce the price of product A to 90 pennies, a reduction of 10%. As the demand for product A is known to be price elastic, we expect a proportionately greater increase in Q than the reduction in P, say a 20% increase to 6000 units per day, or:

$$Ep = \frac{\text{percentage change in } Q}{\text{percentage change in } P} = \frac{20}{-10} = -2\%$$

After the change, the revenue earned per day will have risen from £5000 to 90 pennies × 6000 units = £5400 – an increase in revenue of £400.

For demand price inelastic products, the converse must be the case. The Ep of <1 means that a price change is not offset by a proportionate change in quantity. Again, an example may clarify the point. Product B also sells 5000 units per day at £1, making total daily revenue of £5000. After a price reduction of 10% to 90 pennies, sales rose by only

5% to 5250 – a figure which does not compensate for the reduction in price. Hence, with a price elasticity of $(5/-10) = -0.5\%$, the new revenue becomes 90 pennies $\times$ 5250 = £4725 – a reduction in daily revenue of £275.

We can thus draw two conclusions:

■ Products which have a price elasticity of demand are relatively *responsive* to price changes:
  – a decrease in price will produce an increase in revenue,
  – an increase in price will produce a decrease in revenue.
■ Products which are price inelastic for demand are relatively *unresponsive* to price changes:
  – a decrease in price will produce a decrease in revenue,
  – an increase in price will produce an increase in revenue.

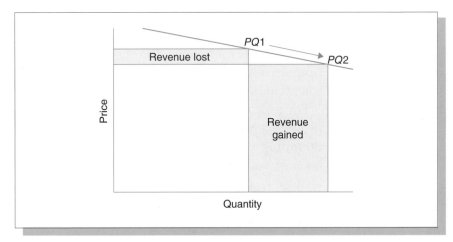

Figure 17.22 Revenue changes on a price elastic demand curve.

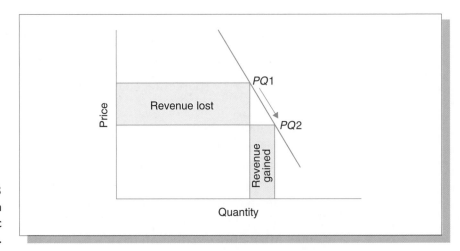

Figure 17.23 Revenue changes on a price inelastic demand curve.

Figures 17.22 and 17.23 show how this works on the respective demand curves.

The price reduction in Figure 17.22 results in a larger 'block' of revenue gained than lost. This is shown by the shallow gradient arising from the elastic nature of the demand. The opposite is true of the inelastic demand curve of Figure 17.23. The price reduction results in a larger 'block' of revenue lost than gained. Although only price reductions are shown on the graphs, readers will appreciate that increases in price simply elicit the opposite response as that described.

Question 17.7

For the following situations, calculate the price elasticity of demand. For each one, say whether the demand is elastic, inelastic or unitary (*Hint*: Use the equation $Ep = (\Delta q/q)/(\Delta p/p)$:

Original price (£)	Price change (£)	Original quantity (units per month)	Quantity resulting from price change (units/month)
5	−1	1000	2000
600	−60	30,000	32,000
20	−1	10,000	10,500
5.40	−0.2	400	400
400	20	2000	1800

Question 17.8

For the following market situations, calculate the price elasticity of demand. For each one, say whether the demand is elastic, inelastic or unitary (*Hint*: Use the equation Ep = percentage change in quantity demanded/percentage change in price.):

Price change (%)	Quantity change (%)
−2	1
−5	7
8	−8
7	−5

Price elasticities at different points along a demand curve

A feature of demand is that the price elasticity of demand can, in some cases, vary along the length of a given demand curve. If the demand curve is linear (such as some of those we have considered above), the demand will become increasingly price inelastic as demand is extended from left to right. We can see how this works by constructing a simple example. The data in Table 17.6 can be plotted graphically as in Figure 17.24.

At all points to the left of $Q = 5.5$, the positive marginal revenue is testimony to the fact that demand is elastic. We learned earlier that elastic demand is characterised by a decrease in price resulting in increased revenue. A positive figure for marginal revenue shows that the demand it describes must be elastic.

At $Q = 5.5$, TR is at its greatest. This is the point of transition on this curve between elasticity and inelasticity. An incremental (very small)

Table 17.6

Price elasticities at different points

Q	1		2		3		4		5		6		7		8		9		10
P	10		9		8		7		6		5		4		3		2		1
TR	10		18		24		28		30		30		28		24		18		10
MR		8		6		4		2		0		−2		−4		−6		−8	

MR: marginal revenue.

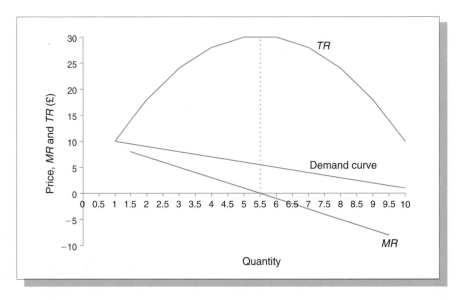

Figure 17.24
How elasticity varies along a demand curve. MR: marginal revenue.

change in price has brings about no change in TR (at the plateau between $Q = 5$ and $Q = 6$).

At points to the right of $Q = 5.5$, the marginal revenue becomes negative. This means that a decrease in price (a downward move on the price axis) results in a fall in revenue – inelastic demand.

Question 17.9

What would a demand curve look like whose elasticity of demand remains the same along its entire length?

17.5 Income elasticity of demand

The concept of elasticity can be applied to more areas of economics than just price and quantity demanded. The same principles, for example, can be applied to the supply side (the elasticity of supply). In this section, we also consider the relationship between individuals' income and their quantity demanded of certain products.

It is patently obvious that as our incomes vary, so does our demand for certain products. During our austere student years, we tend to make economies on such things as food and accommodation as a matter of necessity. Once we graduate and our incomes accordingly increase, we tend to increase our expenditures on these goods and many more besides (such as cars, holidays, etc.). There is clearly a link, then, between income and quantity demanded for some goods. We can analyse the nature of this demand in the same way that we did for prices by looking at the notion of income elasticity.

The equation for calculating the coefficient of income elasticity (Ei) involves substituting price for income in the equations we have previously encountered:

$$Ei = \frac{\Delta q/q}{\Delta y/y}$$

or

$$Ei = \frac{\Delta q}{\Delta y} \times \frac{y}{q}$$

or

$$Ei = \frac{\text{percentage change in quantity demanded}}{\text{percentage change in income}}$$

where *Ei* is the income elasticity of demand, Δy is the change in income, Δq is the change in quantity demanded resulting from the change in income, *y* is the income prior to the change and *q* is the quantity demanded prior to the change in income.

The rules about the outcome for the coefficient and elasticity hold true for income elasticity:

■ *Ei* is >1, we say that the product in question is income elastic.
■ *Ei* is <1, we say that the product in question is income inelastic.
■ *Ei* equals exactly 1, we say that the product has a unitary income elasticity of demand.

The same product features apply to elasticity and inelasticity of income as for price. There are clearly some types of product that we must all buy regardless of income. These are necessities and have an income inelastic demand. Conversely, for some goods, our consumption will be more responsive to our income. These tend to be things we consider to be non-essential goods, for which, demand is income elastic. Although question 11 examines income elasticity for an individual, readers should be aware the economists usually examine this principle in the form of *aggregate demand*. Aggregate demand concerns the effects on quantities purchased as the national average income rises or falls.

Question 17.10

You are a business graduate earning £20,000 when, one happy day, your boss calls you in and says that she is so pleased with your performance and that she is awarding you a £10,000 pay rise to £30,000 per year. As a result of your 50% increase in income, how will your spending patterns change?

The following table shows your supposed purchases of certain goods and services last year when your salary was £20,000. Estimate your purchases of the same items for the forthcoming year on your higher income:

Last year	This year
Holidays	1
Toilet rolls	52
Pairs of jeans	2
Cans of beer	500
Restaurant meals	10

If possible, add your figures to those of others, such as the members of your class. This will give a figure for the larger indicative market of your class. For each product above, calculate the product's income elasticity of demand. (*Hint*: Use the equation Ei = percentage change in quantity/percentage change in income.) The change in income obviously remains constant at +50% whilst you can calculate the percentage change in quantity as $((\Delta q/q) \times 100)$.

17.6 Cross elasticity of demand

In addition to using the concept of elasticity to examine the nature of the relationships between price and quantity demanded, and income and quantity demanded, we can apply it to the relationship between two separate products. We know that varying the price of a product will have a bearing upon its quantity demanded depending upon its price elasticity, but we do not know whether such a price adjustment will have a bearing upon the sales of other products. Cross elasticity of demand gives us the answer to this question.

The cross elasticity of demand that exists between two separate products can be calculated using the equation:

$$Ec = \frac{\Delta q_A / q_A}{\Delta p_B / p_B}$$

which can also be expressed as:

$$Ec = \frac{\Delta q_A / \Delta p_B}{p_B / q_A}$$

or

$$Ec = \frac{\text{percentage change in the quantity demanded of product A}}{\text{percentage price change in product B}}$$

where Ec is the cross elasticity between products A and B, Δq_A is the change in quantity demanded of product A, q_A is the original quantity demanded of product A, prior to the change, Δp_B is the change in price of product B, p_B is the price of product B prior to the change.

Earlier in this chapter, we encountered the idea of related products. You will recall that there are two ways in which products can be related – they can be complementary to, or substitutes of each other. It is, of course, possible for two products to not be related at all (e.g. naval submarines and lollipops).

The figure calculated as *Ec* has two significances:

■ Its sign, either positive or negative tells us the manner in which the two products are related:
  – a negative *Ec* means the two products are complementary,
  – a positive *Ec* means the two products are substitutes.
■ Its magnitude tells us the degree to which they are related:
  – a relatively large negative figure tells us the two are strongly related as complements,
  – a relatively small negative figure tells us the two are weakly related as complements,
  – a relatively large positive figure tells us the two are strongly related as substitutes,
  – a relatively small positive figure tells us the two are weakly related as substitutes.

Demand for complementary goods will rise in sympathy with each other, for example, a rise in car ownership will produce a rise in the demand for petrol. It follows that an increase in the price of cars which will signal a reduction in quantity demanded for cars will, by association, produce a proportionate reduction in the quantity demanded for petrol. We see therefore that a reduction in the price of cars produces an increase in the quantity demand for petrol. Hence, the equation for *Ec* contains a positive figure and a negative figure, which, when divided, always give a negative answer.

Demand for substitute goods will change in opposition to each other. A reduction in the price of butter will encourage consumers of margarine to switch from margarine to butter. This will signal a reduction in demand for margarine, hence both the price of butter and demand for margarine go in the same direction – in this case downwards. Two like signs, either two negatives or two positives, when divided by each other, make a positive; hence a positive *Ec* demonstrates a substitutionary relationship.

Question 17.11

For the following situations, calculate the cross elasticity of demand. For each one state the manner in which they are related and comment on the strength of the relationship:

■ The price of product B is cut by 2% in order to increase sales. The quantity demanded of product A falls by 5%.

■ The price of product B is increased by 10% to cover increased operating costs. The quantity of product A demanded decreases by 4%.

■ The price of product B is decreased by 5%. The quantity demanded of product A decreases by 8%.

Perform the same tasks upon the following:

	Original price of A (£)	Change in the price of A	Original quantity of B	Change in the quantity of B (£)
1	10	−2	5000	−3000
2	25	+2.5	17,000	115,000
3	56	−5.6	60,000	+500
4	100	+10	1,000,000	+100

17.7 A factor supply and demand market system – the labour market

Supply and demand of labour

So far in this chapter, we have considered micro-economic theories as they relate to the supply and demand of conventional goods and services. The same theory can be applied equally to other sectors of commercial transaction. One such area is the supply and demand in the markets of the *factors of production*. A factor of production is an organisational input which is necessary to produce an output of goods or services. Individuals (private citizens) may buy goods and services because they wish to enjoy them. This motivation to buy contrasts with that of factors, which are purchased by organisations as a matter of necessity to facilitate their normal functioning.

Factors of production

Factors of production are organisational inputs which are necessary in order to enable the organisation to produce its output.

The factors of production are:

- land and buildings,
- plant and equipment,
- materials and energy for consumption or processing,
- labour.

One of the factors of production is labour. Whereas in many commercial situations, individuals represent the demand side and businesses represent the supply side, the opposite is usually the case in the labour market.

Have you ever wondered why certain things are true of the labour market? A 20-year-old snooker player can earn more in a single championship match than a nurse earns in a year. Similarly, a university lecturer earning perhaps £35,000–40,000 a year earns three times as much as a checkout operator at the local supermarket. On top of all these peculiarities, the chairmen of some of Britain's companies earn well over £1 million per year whilst somewhere between two and three million people in the UK are unemployed. A skilled manual worker in a European Union country will typically earn in the region of £50–70 per day whereas in India, the daily rate is nearer to 60 pennies.

To some people such features of the labour market might appear unfair, but we must remember in studying economics, that the market for labour is like any other market. Nobody would suggest that all goods and services should have the same price, and we intuitively understand why some products remain unsold after the Christmas rush owing to a lack of demand for them.

The supply side of the labour market comprises the sellers of labour – those who have the necessary skills and are available to work. For any given occupation, more people will tend to opt for a job which pays a higher wage rate. Lower numbers will offer themselves for lower-paid jobs. This explains the traditional shape of the supply curve in this context. The demand side consists of anybody who wishes to buy labour, employers such as businesses and public sector organisations.

The same shaped demand and supply curve exists for the labour market as for those in the markets for goods and services.

Market price of labour

The general form of the supply and demand curves for labour will be familiar, except that the *y*-axis is the wage rate and not price (wages are

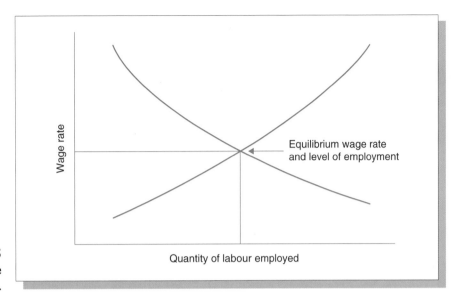

Wage rate

Equilibrium wage rate
and level of employment

Quantity of labour employed

Figure 17.25
Equilibrium wage
rate for a given job.

the 'price' of labour), and the *x*-axis is numbers employed and not quantity. The general form is shown in Figure 17.25.

The supply and demand conditions will be unique for each job and hence the equilibrium point (the market wage) is similarly unique for each job. For a job with a plentiful supply of labour, the position of the supply curve will be to the right of one for which labour is scarcer. Hence, more will be employed but at a lower wage rate.

The supply and demand curves for labour can shift in the same way as they can for goods and services. The demand curve may shift if, for example, a new technology is introduced which requires a certain type of labour or there is a decline in demand for traditional labour, such as shipyard welders. The supply for a particular type of labour may shift with changes in population or certain university courses going in or out of 'fashion'. Any of these changes will create a new equilibrium point and hence a new wage rate for the occupation.

Disequilibrium in the labour market

The workings of the labour markets as free markets rests upon the assumption that wage rates are allowed to rise and fall as the two curves shift over time. Disequilibrium can occur, as in the case with any other markets, when one of two situations applies:

■   A time lag occurs between a supply or demand shift and the re-establishment of the equilibrium.

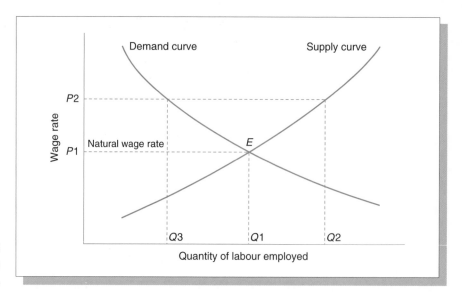

Figure 17.26
Disequilibrium in
the labour market.

▨   When for some reason, there are artificial constraints placed
upon the wage rate which prevents it from moving in response
to changing supply or demand conditions.

We have already learned that disequilibrium result in either over or
under supply of the commodity in question (in this case, labour). In
the case of the labour market, the most common disequilibrium is
oversupply. The scenario is shown in Figure 17.26.

Assignment 17.1

Mr Marrow sells more than potatoes in his fruit and vegetable shop. The following
information applies to his sales of Brussels sprouts:

Price (pennies)	Supply quantity (pounds per week)	Demand quantity (pounds per week)
5	500	1400
15	650	900
25	800	550
35	950	300
45	1100	150

The price $P1$ and quantity $Q1$ in Figure 17.26 show the equilibrium values of the labour market for the job in question (which could be any job). The oversupply is shown by supply equal to $Q2$, but with demand for labour equal to $Q1$. In this situation, there is an oversupply of labour of $Q2 - Q1$. The situation may have arisen as a result of a shift in either curve but due to such things as trade union pressure, the wage rate does not re-equilibrate. Labour is thus overpriced, resulting in oversupply – a condition more commonly referred to as unemployment.

Question 17.12

- On the same graph, draw the demand and supply curves.
- Derive the equilibrium point.
- Calculate the revenue at the equilibrium.
- Calculate the price elasticity of demand between $p = 5$ and $p = 15$ pennies.
- Calculate the price elasticity of demand between $p = 35$ and $p = 45$ pennies.

Demand for Brussels sprouts increases as the result of a bad cabbage harvest. Demand increases by 200 pounds weight per week at every price:

- Draw the new demand curve onto the same graph.
- Derive the new equilibrium point.
- Calculate the revenue at the new equilibrium.
- What quantity would Mr Marrow sell if he kept the price at the old equilibrium.
- Calculate the price at which Mr Marrow would maximise his revenue at the new level of demand.

Further reading

Begg, D., Fischer, S. and Dornbusch, R. (2002). *Economics*, 7th edn. New York: McGraw Hill.

Bosworth, D., *et al.* (1996). *Economics of the Labour Market*. London: FT Prentice Hall.

Dobson, S., Maddala, G.S. and Miller, E. (1995). *Microeconomics*. New York: McGraw Hill.

Ekelund, R. (2000). *Economics, Tudy Guide*. London: Addison Wesley.

Ferguson, P.R., Rothschild, R. and Ferguson, G.J. (1993). *Business Economics*. London: Macmillan Press.

Harrison, B., Smith, C. and Davies, B. (1992). *Introductory Economics*. London: Palgrave Macmillan.

Harvey, J. (1998). *Modern Economics. An Introduction for Business and Professional Students*, 7th edn. London: Palgrave Macmillan.

Harvey, J. (1999). *Mastering Economics*, 5th edn. London: Palgrave Macmillan.

Miller, R.L. and Fisher, R.P.H. (1995). *Microeconomics: Price Theory in Practice*. London: Longman.

Sloman, J. and Sutcliffe, M. (2004). *Economics for Business*, 3rd edn. London: FT Prentice Hall.

Sutcliffe, M. (1994). *Essential Elements of Business Economics*. London: Letts Educational.

Whitehead, G. (1996). *Economics Made Simple*, 15th edn. Oxford: Butterworth Heinemann.

CHAPTER 18

Industry and market structures

Learning objectives

After studying this chapter, students should be able to describe:

- what is meant by the terms 'market' and 'market structure';
- what factors determine market structure;
- what is meant by monopoly, oligopoly and perfect competition;
- the pros and cons of some of these market structures.

18.1 Introduction to industries and markets

We have seen in earlier chapters that there are two sides to the market system: buyers and sellers. In this chapter, we take a closer look at how these two sides are organised and structured. The market system can be shown by a simple diagram like that in Figure 18.1.

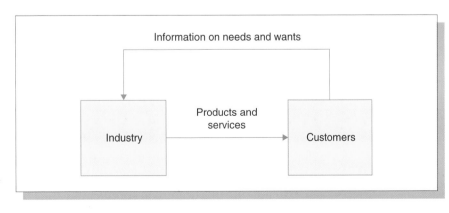

Figure 18.1
A schematic of the market system.

We can see from Figure 18.1 that there is a two-way relationship between the two sides of the system. An industry generates products (goods and services) to supply to the customers. Similarly, the industry producing the goods relies on accurate information from the buyers. Information is gathered by monitoring the demand for products and by listening to comments made on product quality and usefulness.

18.2 Market structures

The features of the relationship between the two sides of the market are determined by two important variables. It is these variables that determine which side is the most powerful in any given relationship:

- the number and selling power of sellers of a specific product;
- the number and buying power of buyers of a specific product.

The number of sellers

The markets for some products comprise literally thousands of suppliers. For others, it is just a few suppliers in the entire world, or even just one. If, for example, you want to buy potatoes in the UK, you have the choice of buying from thousands of shops or, if you are a shopkeeper, you can buy from a large number of farms or potato producers. On the other hand, if you want to buy an anti-human immunodeficiency virus (anti-HIV) drug to combat the symptoms of the acquired immune deficiency syndrome (AIDS) condition, you would have to trade with *GlaxoSmithKline plc,* the patent owner and dominant world producer of the main drug, although considerable social and political pressures are growing on a global scale to force the supply or allow the manufacture (under licence) of low cost generic versions of such drugs.

The number of suppliers and how they are organised leads us to an important concept' that of *concentration of supply.* In a market with very few suppliers, it is said that supply is concentrated in the hands of just a few large suppliers. In extreme cases, supply can be totally concentrated with just one supplier. The example of potato production demonstrates the opposite case, a very low concentration of supply.

The number of suppliers that a buyer can go to for an essentially similar or identical product will have a significant influence on how the supplier behaves. Producers in markets with a high supply concentration are able to have more power over buyers than those with lower concentrations. In the case of a dominant supplier like the HIV situation, previously mentioned, the company (GlaxoSmithKline plc) is able to charge a relatively high price for it because of its high concentration of supply. A large number of producers who each compete for customers' business are at a pricing disadvantage because of the customers' ability to simply 'shop around' for cheaper prices or better service. An example of this latter situation exists in some high streets which have a large number of similar shops, such as the electrical shops in London's Tottenham Court Road or the Asian restaurants in the Rushholme district of Manchester or some areas of other major cities. Suppliers find themselves having to offer incentives to attract customers, such as lower prices, better product or service quality.

The number of buyers

The demand side of the market system can be analysed in the same way as for the supply side. In the market for some products, buyers are very concentrated to the point where in some cases; there may be just one buyer of a product (a condition known as *monopsony*). For other products, the market contains many buyers, possible tens of millions of people.

A condition of high buyer concentration puts the buyers in a more powerful position over suppliers than those in a state of low buyer concentration. Two examples will demonstrate this point.

High buyer concentration: Swan Hunter's shipyard

In the market for large shipping, there are relatively few buyers. Whilst the number of suppliers of ships has been significantly reduced over recent decades, the importance of single orders from the very few buyers to the remaining shipyards is often a matter of survival. In the case of the Swan Hunter's shipyard in Wallsend, North Tyneside, the major buyer of its ships has traditionally been the British Ministry of Defence.

In the first part of 1993, the Ministry of Defence was preparing to place a large order for a helicopter landing ship and Swan Hunter, along with other yards, prepared its bid to undertake the work. In the May of that year, it was announced that the work was to go the Vicker's yard in Barrow, Cumbria. The loss of an order from its only significant customer meant that Swan Hunter had literally no orders. This necessitated a large number of immediate redundancies and the eventual closure of the yard – a loss of 2500 jobs in an area of high unemployment.

The case of Swan Hunter shows the difficulties of suppliers depending upon a market with very few or even one buyer. At best, the supplier is in a weak bargaining position with regard to pricing, and at worst, the monopsonist (single buyer) can precipitate the failure of the supplier.

Low buyer concentration: clothes-washing detergents

The market for domestic detergents (as opposed to detergents for industrial purposes) is an interesting one. The demand side comprises potentially almost everybody, as we all wear clothes and therefore have a need to wash them. Hence, there are tens of millions of clothes-washing detergent customers in the UK.

The supply side is quite different from the demand side. We have already encountered the concept of concentration of supply and the supply of washing powders is very concentrated indeed. Two very large producers, between them, control over 90% of the market. The two companies compete vigorously for an increased share of the large but unconcentrated demand side. Individual washing powder customers like you and me have little power over the powerful suppliers in as much as we are not in a position to dictate prices or other terms of supply. We are able to choose between brands, but cannot directly influence the powerful suppliers.

18.3 Industry structures

In attempting to understand the way in which markets are structured, we usually divide markets up according to the number of suppliers there are of a product into a given market. This is not to say that the number of customers is unimportant, but that in practice, a concentration of demand is much less common than a concentration of supply. In most cases, we can assume that demand is relatively unconcentrated, and that market conditions are determined much more by the degree of concentration of the supply side.

The degree of supply concentration can be shown by the use of a simple continuum Figure 18.2. At the two extremes, monopoly is the case of a single supplier and perfect competition is the case of an infinite number of suppliers (*zero concentration of supply*). At the various points along the continuum lie the varying degrees of concentration between the two extremes (markets which are, to a greater or lesser extent, *oligopolistic*).

In the remainder of this chapter, we will examine the various types of supply concentration and their implications for the relationships between suppliers and buyers.

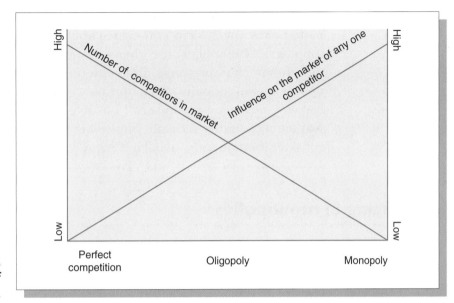

Figure 18.2
Continuum of
market structures.

18.4 Monopoly

What is a monopoly?

A true *monopoly* is said to exist when the supply of a product into a market is totally concentrated in the hands of a single supplier. Note though that it is possible for there to be more than one supplier of a product, but only one supplier of the product into a given market. In other words, monopoly exists when a supplier faces no effective competition in its market and consequently has pricing power in the market. We shall see in Chapter 19 that the legal definition of a monopoly is somewhat broader than this description.

Prior to the widespread privatisation programmes of the 1980s and 1990s (see Chapter 19); many of the utilities (e.g. gas, electricity, telecommunications) were state-run monopolies. This meant that consumers had no choice who to purchase their gas from; they could buy from the erstwhile Gas Board or go without gas. In this case, the 'market' in which there was no competition was a very large one, the entire country. On a smaller scale, monopolies can exist in much smaller markets. It may be, for example, that a certain milkman has a monopoly on 'doorstep' milk deliveries in one area of a town or city. There are obviously many milk-round businesses in a large city, but for the few streets in question (the 'market' in this context), there is only one supplier.

An obvious question to ask at this point is why certain markets are monopolies whereas most others are not (i.e. most markets have many suppliers). Monopolies arise when for some reason; would be competitors are somehow prevented from entering the market to offer competition to the monopolist. Such hurdles to market entry are called entry barriers. There are a number of possible entry barriers which render market entry either difficult, impossible or undesirable, and we shall consider them in some detail in Chapter 20.

Pricing in monopolies

In theory, a monopolist is in a very powerful competitive position. As the only supplier of a product, and unaffected by the pricing of competitors' products, the monopolist is able to charge any price for the supply of its goods. It is effectively able to say to the demand side, 'buy from us or go without'. It said, therefore, that a monopolist is a *price setter*. In theory, then, monopolists should be able to make exceedingly high profits.

In practice, it is not this simple. Monopolists that can actually make excessive profits are very rare. An effective ceiling is put on prices by one or two mechanisms:

- *Regulatory restrictions*   When price limits are imposed upon the monopolist by a government body or a piece of legislation.
- *Product-linked restrictions*   Products with a relatively high price elasticity of demand will simply experience a reduction in demand with higher prices. This will obviously result in a reduction in revenue. Monopolists trading in products with a highly price inelastic demand will, of course, be in a much more potentially profitable position.

Given that a true monopolist is a price setter, we can see that it may be possible for suppliers to be in this position even although competitors may exist. If a supplier in a competitive market (i.e. one with more than one supplier) has sufficient market share to dictate market prices then the supplier is said to be a *virtual monopolist* because it dominates the market supply. In a virtual monopoly market, smaller competitors are forced to set their prices roughly in line with their much larger competitor (the virtual monopolist is referred to as a *price leader*). They become price followers which results in their profits being more-or-less determined by the virtual monopolist.

Are monopolies good or bad?

We must be careful not to judge monopoly as being necessarily good or bad. However, the prevailing political tide in recent years has been to encourage competition in markets by splitting large monopolists up thus enabling the parts to compete against each other. One of the key objectives of the Conservative Government's privatisation programme (see Chapter 19) was to dismantle state monopolies to introduce competition into such markets as electricity and telecommunications. When businesses are forced to compete, their natural inclination is to reduce costs and increase quality in order to gain market share. This is clearly in the interest of the consumer.

The pros and cons of monopoly can be summarised as follows.

Advantages of monopoly

- Large companies (such as monopolists), tend to be stable and are often able to withstand changes in the economic environment. This is an effective guarantee of ongoing supply.
- If there is only one supplier, potentially wasteful duplication of some activities, such as research and development is avoided.
- The high prices that the monopolist may charge can be used to generate high profits. These, in turn, can be invested to improve product quality and service to the customer.
- Large companies, such as some monopolists enjoy increased economies of scale. This leads to lower unit costs. Whilst this is of advantage to the monopolist, increased profits can lead to increased investment, improved products, better service and sometimes, lower prices.

Disadvantages of monopoly

- If the monopolist charges excessively high prices, the effect on customers can be unpleasant, especially if the monopolist supplies an important product, such as gas, electricity or telecommunications.
- Lack of competition can sometimes make the monopolist 'flabby' and inefficient. This may have the effect of further increasing prices as the monopolist attempts to cover higher

costs. This was one of the major criticisms of former state-run monopolies, such as utility providers.

- The customer is deprived of choice of supplier and hence has no choice of product.
- The total concentration of supply means that if the monopolist cannot supply for any reason (e.g. industrial disputes) then there is no alternative supply to the demand side.

18.5 Monopolistic competition

A variation on the theme of monopoly is *monopolistic competition*, which is said to exist when products have a monopolistic market share in a relatively small part of the market; that is, a small segment of the total market. When many products each occupy their own 'little monopoly', then they do not directly compete with each other even although the products may be very similar.

A typical way of achieving a situation of monopolistic competition is *product differentiation*. This is the practice of making the product unique to enable it to be more acceptable to a specific segment or *niche* in the market. A highly differentiated product which has a high market share in a relatively small market segment enjoys the possibility of commanding a premium ('price setting') price, the same characteristic as a monopolist.

One of the most important mechanisms of achieving differentiation is by product branding. By aggressively promoting a brand, producers of consumer goods attempt to build loyalty to the brand to the exclusion of others. By engendering a brand with unique product qualities (e.g. superior washing power, unique taste or texture), customers remain loyal and thus do not switch to other brands which offer different product benefits. Key technological innovations can also serve the purpose (such as a new format for music recording). As with all monopoly situations, the company's objective is to separate its products to such an extent that the customer has just the one effective choice of product within the sector. The idea of removing customer choice within the sector is the key to monopolistic competition. If a company can develop a product to such an extent that customers automatically think of their product, then they have succeeded in this regard.

The competition arises from this scenario because it is the sectors themselves which compete for business. Sellers will attempt to achieve customer loyalty within their sector. If this can be achieved, then their repeat orders will be assured.

18.6 Oligopoly

An *oligopoly* is the next most concentrated type of market supply after monopoly. In an oligopoly, the majority of supply comes from a relatively small number or relatively large producers.

Within the category of market structure called oligopoly, there is a wide variation of concentration ratios. In some markets, the concentration can rest with as few as two significant suppliers (a situation known as *duopoly*). In other cases, there may be many more companies (say up to twenty) who, between them, control market supply.

Two examples will serve to illustrate the point.

Oligopoly

Example 1: Clothes-washing detergents

The UK market for clothes-washing detergents is dominated by two major companies: the US-based multinational Proctor and Gamble (P&G) and Lever Faberge, part of the Unilever group. The two companies account for around 86% of the detergent market value, with the remainder shared between smaller brands and *own labels*. Therefore it is effectively a *duopolistic market* (Table 18.1).

Table 18.1
Clothes-washing detergents brand shares

	Value of sales (pounds in million)	Brand share (%)
P&G	420	51
Ariel	173	21
Bold	107	13
Daz	66	8
Fairy	66	8
Dreft	8	1
Lever Faberge	288	35
Persil	235	28
Surf	50	6
Lux/stergene	3	–
Others/own labels	115	14

Source: Mintel.

Table 18.2
The leading UK grocery retailers 2001/2002

	Company	Number of stores	Market shares (%)
1	Tesco	1981	21.7
2	J Sainsbury	493	14.3
3	ASDA	258	11.9
4	Safeway	481	8.6
5	Somerfield	1269	4.3

Source: National Statistics/Mintel.

Example 2: Food retailing
The food market in the UK is very large; the annual food sales for the year 2002 amounted to £99.6 billion. Supply into the market is largely concentrated with the five largest producers accounting for just over 60% of the total market (less concentrated than the washing powder market). The remainder of the market is held and fought over by smaller chains and independent 'corner shops', such as *Lidl* or *Spar* (Table 18.2).

Pricing in an oligopoly

Unlike monopolists, big players in oligopolistic markets are rarely powerful enough to be price setters. This means that they are not able to increase their prices to achieve higher profits, because customers are able to simply switch to competitors. If you noticed that prices have risen in your regular supermarket, you will be inclined to switch suppliers to another shop. It follows that oligopolists are approximately interdependent upon each other in as much as their prices are usually roughly the same.

Price interdependence works by binding all oligopolists, more-or-less, to the market price. Whilst any competitor could theoretically increase or decrease its price, in practice unilateral price changes are rare.

If a competitor 'breaks ranks' and *increases* its prices, customers will tend to change suppliers. The price increases will thus tend to result in a fall in revenues for the company in question. The company thus has every incentive to reduce its prices back to their original level.

If a competitor unilaterally *reduces* its prices, then a series of events is set in train which adversely affects all of the competitors in the oligopoly. It is called a downward price spiral:

- competitor unilaterally reduces its prices;
- customers switch to the cheaper supplier;
- competitors lose market share to the cheaper supplier;
- competitors reduce their prices to parity with the cheapest competitor;
- customers tend return to their regular supplier (although their temporary switch of supplier may result in less loyal buyer behaviour).

The result of the unilateral price reduction decision by one supplier is that all the competitors end up making lower revenues and hence lower profits. Of course, such wholesale price reductions are very welcome to the customers.

As a result of this price interdependence, oligopolists tend to be very careful when it comes to pricing. Price wars benefit none of the competitors in the longer term and competition tends to occur in *non-price* areas. The pricing tensions that exist in oligopolies usually ensure that prices remain relatively stable.

Competition in an oligopoly

The price interdependence that oligopolists experience means that they must compete with each other for market share on bases other than price. This gives rise to the idea of *non-price* competition. Non-price competition involves the competitors attempting to gain ground on each other by the use of a wide range of measures. Some are designed to increase customer loyalty (i.e. repeat purchases from a supplier) and others are designed to encourage customers to switch suppliers.

The precise non-price measures taken will depend upon the industry and the things that customers value. If the business can give the customers more value (or perceived value), both customer loyalty and increased market share objectives can be served.

Examples of non-price measures include:

- more outlets in key locations;
- more attractive outlets (e.g. in retailing);
- better or more professional service;
- loyalty incentives, such as loyalty cards (in supermarkets) or money off next purchase;

- increases in quality of products and service;
- advertising and other marketing promotions;
- increases in product range offered;
- longer guarantees or warranties, etc.

We can see that many of the markets we come across regularly show evidence of these non-price competition measures. This is because most markets are oligopolistic and so find this the most appropriate competitive strategy. The market for washing powder, for example, is noted for its high dependency on advertising and claims of superior product performance rather than using price to encourage consumers to switch brands.

18.7 Perfect competition

At the other end of the market structure continuum to monopoly is *perfect competition*. Whereas monopoly represents a situation of total concentration of supply, perfect competition is a situation where both the supply and demand sides have zero concentration.

It follows that if there is no concentration of supply, there must be a very large number of suppliers such that no single supplier has the ability to influence the market price.

In its 'pure' form, perfect competition has several distinguishing characteristics:

- a very large number of sellers, each of which occupies a tiny or insignificant market share;
- a very large number of buyers;
- a product which is incapable of being differentiated and where all sellers sell an identical product;
- all buyers have identical cost structures – they all pay the same for materials, rent, labour, etc.;
- no single buyer or seller is of sufficient size to influence price;
- there are no innovations or 'secrets' which may give one buyer or seller an advantage over another;
- there are no entry or exit barriers associated with competing in the market.

Like monopoly, 'true' perfect competition is virtually unknown in practice – it represents the extreme at which there is no concentration of supply or demand at all. Some markets, however, exhibit very low supply and demand concentrations and so approximate to perfect competition. Examples include the market for fruit and vegetables in a large town or city market square or the market for bed and breakfast accommodation in a large city.

Owing to the features of perfect competition, the market price for any given product is arrived at purely through the economic forces of supply and demand. As no buyer or seller is big enough to set the price, each supplier must take the market price; they are said to be *price takers*. This tends to lead to medium or low profits for the supplier and relative price stability for the buyer.

Assignment 18.1

At the beginning of 2004, the Bradford-based supermarket chain, William Morrison, was positioned sixth in the UK 'league table' of leading grocery retailers. Later that year, after a lengthy takeover campaign, against fierce competition from other major players in the supermarket business, Morrison's assumed control of the Safeway supermarket chain.

Tasks:

- What was the effect of the safeway acquisition on Morrison's share of the grocery retail market, and position in the 'league table'?
- Obtain data on the share prices for Morrison's and their main competitors over the 12 months following the takeover. Plot the data on a simple graph and establish the share price patterns and trends for the companies. Suggest reasons for any variances in the relative values.

Further reading

Begg, D., Fischer, S. and Dornbusch, R. (2002). *Economics*, 7th edn. New York: McGraw Hill.

Dobson, S., Maddala, G.S. and Miller, E. (1995). *Microeconomics*. New York: McGraw Hill.

Harrison, B., Smith, C. and Davies, B. (1992). *Introductory Economics*. London: Palgrave Macmillan.

Harvey, J. (1998). *Modern Economics. An Introduction for Business and Professional Students*, 7th edn. London: Palgrave Macmillan.

Sloman, J. and Sutcliffe M. (2004). *Economics for Business*, 3rd edn. London: FT Prentice Hall.

Sutcliffe, M. (1994). *Essential Elements of Business Economics*. London: DP Publications.

Useful web sites

Office of Fair Trading: www.oft.gov.uk/business/mergers

Market reports: http://reports.mintel.com

Financial reports: http://money.guardian.co.uk

CHAPTER 19

Government and market structures

After studying this chapter, students should be able to describe:

- how and why the state influences markets and market structures;
- the key pieces of legislation that affect market and industry structures;
- how regulatory quasi-autonomous non-governmental organisations (QuANGOs) affect market and industry structures;
- what is meant by nationalisation and privatisation, and describe the pros and cons of each.

19.1 Government influence on markets

The matter of whether and how many governments should influence the workings of markets is controversial. Some believe that markets work best, that is, to everybody's eventual benefit, if they are left alone to find their own level. Others believe that it is an important duty of government to affect the workings of markets to ensure that excessive profits are not made and that individual consumers are protected from high prices and undersupply.

In one sense, this debate goes to the heart of political ideology. The political right have traditionally leaned more to the 'leave markets alone' position whilst the political left have traditionally argued more for an 'interventionist' approach to markets and industries. In Chapter 10, we saw that both of these positions can be traced back to a key intellectual 'architect' – a seminal economic philosopher who shaped the two broad strands of thought.

In most modern states, such as the UK, the broadly held opinion is that there is a need for some government influence on markets; the debate is rather on how much and to what extent government should be involved in this.

Why might government want to influence market structures?

If we accept that most governments see some need to influence the operation of markets, we then should ask what the objectives of such influence might be. There are a number of possible objectives:

- to increase competition (and thus give consumers more choice);
- to protect consumers (e.g. from monopoly pricing);
- make business more competitive and productive;
- to increase the competitiveness of UK businesses abroad (e.g. by forcing businesses to reduce their costs in response to increased competition);
- to make efficient use of a nation's scarce resources (e.g. oil and gas reserves, human resources, etc.).

It is generally assumed that one of the purposes of government is to protect its citizens. This duty is in part discharged by ensuring that the citizen's economic interests are not damaged by excessive prices and that there is no undersupply of some key goods and services. In addition, governments usually wish to stimulate business productivity, higher product quality and lower business costs. Many of these objectives can be served by government measures that encourage competition in markets.

How does government influence markets and market structure?

The objectives discussed above can be achieved by governments using a number of measures which are designed to influence market structures:

- introducing legislation that prescribes and limits certain types of business activity;

- setting up regulatory bodies, which are given the power to impose restrictions upon businesses;
- selling and buying businesses to and from the private sector – the processes of privatisation and nationalisation.

In the remainder of this chapter, we will examine these three instruments of government influence.

19.2 Legislation and market structures

UK legislation

In Chapter 14 of this book, we looked at the various areas of law that apply to businesses. We must, however, be careful to draw a distinction between business law in general, and competition and market laws in particular. Competition law is designed to directly influence competition in business and this is typically achieved by influencing market structure.

The Competition Act 1998

In the UK, the *Competition Act 1998,* which came into force on 1 March 2000, was designed to ensure that businesses compete on a fair and level basis. It also brought UK competition policy into line with *European Union Law,* as defined in *Treaty of European Union 1992,* signed at *Maastricht.* This treaty changed the name of the *European Economic Community* (EEC) to simply the *European Community* (EC). The *EC Treaty* came into force on 1 November 1993.

Under the Competition Act 1998, a monopoly is defined as a situation wherein a single supplier has in excess of 25% of the supply into a market. This would seem to be at variance to the 'economist's definition' we encountered in Chapter 18. However, given that we also learned that we can define a monopolist as a *price setter,* the Act takes the view that any single supplier with more than a quarter of the total market supply has sufficient dominance to significantly influence price and market conditions – a *virtual* monopoly. Clearly, this is potentially against the interests of the consumer.

Restrictive practices are forbidden under the provisions of the Act. If a situation occurs where two or more large competitors 'collude' on prices (i.e. make a formal or informal agreement to set an artificially high price), then the colluders are effectively acting as a monopoly. Customers are deprived of their ability to 'shop around' to get better prices and service from different competitors in the market.

Mergers and acquisitions are also covered by the Act. We saw in Chapter 8 that these are mechanisms by which business grow and expand – by buying or merging with others to increase their size. Given that a monopoly is defined under the Act as being a business commanding in excess of 25% of market supply, the Act gives the state the power to block an acquisition or merger which will result in the combined business having in excess of a 25% share (a virtual monopoly) of supply. This power is, however discretionary; not all cases need to be reviewed; it is usually at the discretion of the Secretary of State for Trade and Industry.

The Competition Act 1998 absorbed the main legislation of the *Competition Act 1980* (which had increased the anti-competitive practices provisions of the *Fair Trading Act 1973) plus* several other pieces of legislation, notably the *Resale Prices Act 1976* and the *Restrictive Trade Practices Act 1976.* The 1998 Act makes provision for strengthening competition through two principal prohibitions, based on the prohibition:

- on anti-competitive agreements (Article 81);
- of abuse of dominant position in a market (Article 82).

The Competition Act 1998, which was amended on 1 May 2004 to empower the *Office of Fair Trading* (OFT) (see below) to investigate and impose penalties on undertakings breaching the prohibitions on anti-competitive behaviour, should be viewed in tandem with the *Enterprise Act 2002.*

The Enterprise Act 2002

The *Enterprise Act 2002* made major reforms to competition law and consumer law enforcement in the UK, including the removal of government ministers from most decisions on mergers, criminalising individual participation in *cartels* (see below), streamlined appeals mechanisms and establishing new procedures for tackling trading practices that harm consumers. The provisions of the Act work alongside the Competition Act 1998, and largely replace the Fair Trading Act 1973.

19.3 Regulatory bodies

The government's second mechanism of influencing market structures is to set in place a variety of regulatory bodies. These bodies, as their name suggests, regulate industries on behalf of the government and consumers to ensure that consumer and competitive concerns are not overlooked. In most cases, such regulatory authorities are independent of government and are established as QuANGOs (see Chapter 5) to ensure impartiality. They are usually staffed by people who understand their areas of oversight more thoroughly than politicians – a measure designed to ensure that the best people are in place to make important decisions that protect consumers but do not unnecessarily penalise the businesses in question.

The main bodies that have a bearing on markets and market structures are the OFT, the *Competition Commission* (CC) and the regulatory bodies set up to monitor the various utilities.

The OFT

The *Enterprise Act 2002* established the OFT as an independent statutory body with responsible for making markets work well for consumers, via the promotion and protection of consumer interests throughout the UK, while ensuring that businesses are fair and competitive. The OFT takes its powers from consumer and competition legislation and has three main operational areas:

- competition enforcement (CE),
- consumer regulation enforcement,
- markets and policies initiatives.

The CE division of the OFT plays a key role in enforcing EC and UK competition laws, stopping *cartels* and other forms of damaging anti-competitive agreements. The CE division also aims to stop any abuse of a dominant market position and promotes a strong competitive culture, via education programmes, across a wide range of markets.

A *cartel* is an agreement between businesses not to compete with each other and is usually verbal and often informal. Agreements can cover a variety of areas, such as price or output levels, credit terms, geographic areas of supply or which customers each will supply. Cartels can occur in almost industry, and can involve goods or services in manufacturing, retail or distribution, but some sectors are more susceptible than others perhaps because of the nature of the business or the environment. For example, where there are few competitors, little differentiation in the products, the economy is in recession or there is excess capacity in the industry.

Under the Competition Act 1998, and Article 81 of the EC Treaty 1992, cartels are prohibited and any business found to be a member of a cartel can be fined up to 10% of its worldwide turnover. In addition, the Enterprise Act 2002 makes it a criminal offence for individuals to dishonestly take part in the most serious types of cartels. Anyone convicted of the offence could receive a maximum of 5 years imprisonment and/or an unlimited fine.

The CC

The *CC* was established by the Competition Act 1998 on 1 April 1999 to replace the *Monopolies and Mergers Commission* (MMC). The CC is an executive *non-department public body* (NDPB), independent from government, though wholly funded by the *Department of Trade and Industry* (DTI). Its prime function is conduct in-depth inquiries into mergers, markets and the regulation of the major regulated industries. Inquiries are undertaken in response to references made to the CC by other authorities – usually the OFT or, in certain circumstances, by the Secretary of State, or the regulators under sector-specific legislative provisions relating to regulated industries (the CC has no power to conduct inquiries on its own initiative).

The Enterprise Act 2002 introduced a regime for the assessment of mergers and markets in the UK and, in most merger and market references; the CC is responsible for making decisions on the competition questions and for making and implementing decisions on appropriate

Figure 19.1
The CC's mission statement (reproduced courtesy of the CC).

The CC: mission statement

In becoming a world class competition authority, the Commission's activities will contribute:

- to an increase in the level of of competition in the UK economy;
- to the UK's economic performance and productivity in the international economy, where competitive pressures are becoming increasingly global.

Its contribution will also make markets work well for consumers. In many cases consumers will benefit from:

- lower prices,
- a wider range of choice,
- more innovation,
- higher quality products and services.

remedies. This contrasts with the old legislative regime where the MMC was only empowered to make recommendations to the Secretary of State for Trade and Industry.

The CC consists of approximately 50 members, who are appointed by the State for Trade and Industry for 8-year terms, following open competition. Appointments are made on the basis of individual experience, ability and diversity of background and not as representatives of particular organisations, interests or political parties. There are specialist panels for utilities (gas and electricity), telecommunications, water and newspapers.

Utilities' regulatory bodies

Some markets attract particular regulation unique to themselves. When the utilities were privatised in the 1980s (e.g. telecommunications, gas, electricity, etc.), supply passed from the state sector to the private sector. In some cases, this meant that rather than having a state-run monopoly, there was a privately run monopoly (or, at least a highly concentrated supply by the new private-sector suppliers). In other privatisations, the privatisation process was accompanied by the creation of competition between the various parts of the privatised businesses.

Either way, Parliament at the time deemed it necessary to maintain some level of public control over the pricing and supply of utilities, even though they were now privately owned (i.e. by shareholders). In consequence, the utilities' regulators (or 'watchdogs') were given powers to determine prices for the products as well as controlling the number and type of competitors in each market. The reasons for such a high level of regulation are due to the fact that:

- in many cases, the *privatised businesses were monopolists*, or at least that they were big businesses with high market shares;
- *utilities are supremely important* to the well-being of people in the country. They are quite different in significance to other products like luxury goods and even foods.

Each utility has its own independent regulatory body. Like the CC, the utility regulators are QuANGOs.

The principle ones are:

OFCOM – Office of the Regulator for UK Communication Industries, with responsibilities across television, radio, telecommunications and wireless communication services.

OFGEM – Office of the Regulator for Gas and Electricity Markets.
OFGEM (NI) – Office of the Regulator for Gas and Electricity Markets (Northern Ireland).
ORR – Office of Rail Regulation.
FSA – Financial Services Authority.
OFSTED – Office for Standards in Education.

19.4 Privatisation and nationalisation

The issue of who owns business is one of the main determinants of market structure. The selling-off of formerly state-owned businesses was one of the key policy areas of the Conservative governments of the 1980s and 1990s.

Privatisation is the selling of state-owned assets to private individuals. It is called *privatisation* because ownership of the business passes from the public sector (the state) to the private sector (individuals and private businesses). In privatising a business, the government issues shares to the estimated value of the business and these are then sold through the usual channels of the Stock Exchange. If more than 50% of the issued shares are sold to the public, then state control over the business is lost.

Nationalisation is the very opposite of privatisation. A business is nationalised when the state takes control of a business that was previously in the private sector. The nationalised business will be run by the government as part of a government department, government agency or state-controlled company (e.g. the erstwhile British Coal). This sometimes involves the creation of a state-run monopoly.

A brief history of privatisation and nationalisation

The salad days of nationalisation were the years following the Second World War. Having led the coalition government during the war, the Conservative Prime Minister Winston Churchill (1874–1965) was defeated by Labour in the general election of 1945. The war had taken a toll on the country and the electorate saw a need for a wide-ranging economic and social regeneration programme.

The new Labour Prime Minister, Clement Attlee (1883–1967), set about the task. In addition to significant investment in rebuilding the country's infrastructure (assisted by the United States' *Marshall Plan*), a priority of Attlee's government was to directly manage the country's key industries. Prior to the war, most utilities were operated by private companies, in many cases covering a small area of the country only. In the climate of national regeneration, certain industries were seen as being strategically important to the country's redevelopment. The business categories in the nationalisation programme included the utilities, coal, rail and some heavy engineering businesses, such as shipping and steel. Over the following decades, other businesses were taken into state ownership, including airlines, motor manufacturing and defence equipment producers, such as some military hardware companies and producers of ordinance.

The vast majority of nationalised businesses remained in the public sector until the new Conservative government was formed by Margaret Thatcher in 1979. One of the main thrusts of Conservative policy during the 1980s and 1990s was to privatise the previously nationalised businesses. In consequence, one by one, the government monopolies and other state-owned companies were broken up and sold off to the private sector. By the turn of the decade (in 1990), the government had divested itself of the majority of its direct interests in industry. Privatisation was not without its critics. The opposition parties of the time continually argued against each privatisation, believing that such businesses should remain under state control.

The principal conservative privatisations in the 1980s

Date privatised	Company	Value (£)
1979*	British Petroleum plc	7.4 billion
1981*	British Aerospace plc	513 million
1982	Amersham International plc	71 million
1982	National Freight Corp. plc	54 million
1984*	British Telecommunications plc	3.9 billion
1986	British Gas plc	5.4 billion
1987	British Airways plc	900 million
1987	Rolls Royce plc	1.08 billion
1987	British Airports Authority plc	1.3 billion
1988	British Steel plc	2.5 billion
1989	Water authorities	5.3 billion

*First share issue where other followed in later years. *Source: Education Guardian,* 4 June 1991.

The debate over privatisation and nationalisation

The debate on privatisation and nationalisation cuts to the core of political ideology (see Chapter 10). The divide in the debate falls approximately along party political lines. The political right (the UK Conservative Party) have traditionally believed in a free-market approach to managing the economy whilst the left of centre (the UK Labour Party) have traditionally espoused the belief that strategic industries should be under state control.

Prior to the election of Tony Blair as Labour Party leader, Labour's Policy with regard to state ownership was summarised in the much-discussed 'clause four' of the Labour Party Constitution, which stated:

> To secure for the workers by hand or by brain the full fruits of their industry and the most equitable distribution thereof that may be possible upon the basis of the common ownership of the means of production, distribution and exchange, and the best obtainable system of popular administration and control of each industry or service.

Although the wording of this clause four was later replaced, it was the guiding philosophy underpinning Labour's opposition to the privatisation programme of the 'Thatcher years'. The Conservatives, in marked contrast, were guided by the philosophical underpinnings of the *laissez-faire* school of economic thought mainly attributable to the classical economic school of Adam Smith and the monetarist theories of Prof. Milton Friedman of the University of Chicago (see Chapter 10).

It follows that any discussion of the pros and cons of privatisation and nationalisation must necessarily be incomplete without an enquiry into the underlying philosophies of the two policies. Such a discussion is beyond the scope of this text and so a general examination will suffice. There are strong arguments, in theory and practice, both for and against state ownership of some businesses.

The case for nationalisation

Those who argue for nationalisation have tended to subscribe to the following arguments:

- It allows the government to exercise control over strategically vital areas of industry. Some industries, particularly the utilities, are arguably too important to be left to the 'vagaries' of market forces and the pursuit of profits by their owners. It also means that market supply can be guaranteed by government regardless of the movements of market forces.

- By controlling strategic industries, the government is in a position to exercise a wider influence on business activity and consumers' spending in the country. The use of intelligent pricing of key utilities can be used as one of the economic 'levers' used to regulate the economy. Items like energy, communications and transport constitute a significant proportion of both business and domestic expenditure and by selectively increasing or reducing the prices of such commodities; the government can influence the wider economy. If, for example, the government wishes to stimulate the economy, it could use lower utilities prices as one of the ways of achieving this objective. The converse would be the case if it wanted to slow economic growth.

- Direct control over key industries allows government to ensure that some goods and services are provided which could not be profitably provided by the private sector. Some areas of provision appear not to be able to be provided at a profit and so would not be attractive to private investors. This includes rural bus services and the majority of health provision.

- Nationalisation provides government with the opportunity of 'bailing out' companies who could not survive without government assistance. In doing so, it can thus keep such businesses afloat. This is seen as being appropriate when the business is a particularly important employer (such as a large employer in an area of high unemployment) or when the business produces a particularly important product. It ought to be stressed that this is one of the most controversial uses of nationalisation and controversy usually surrounds such an investment of taxpayers' money.

- It provides the government with a means of ensuring that key services are equalised throughout the country. Those in favour of nationalisation argue, for example, that the outlying and rural regions may suffer because it is uneconomic to offer the same level of service (gas, electricity, etc.) to those living in the major cities.

The case against nationalisation

The opponents of nationalisation have gained much 'ammunition' from the fact that many important businesses were previously nationalised and so we can learn by observing how they worked in practice. The following arguments are typical against nationalisation:

- In many cases, nationalisation resulted in state-run monopolies. This was previously the case in each of the utilities. It follows that any of the arguments against monopolies in general are applicable in this context (see Chapter 18), such as a lack of competitive pressure and a restriction in consumer choice.
- In practice, many of the previously nationalised businesses were considered to be 'flabby' and inefficient. Critics argue that without the commercial pressures upon private companies, nationalised businesses were often overstaffed and over-bureaucratic. Management in the businesses could always count on the Treasury (i.e. the taxpayer) to 'bail out' any losses and provide such subsidies as became necessary.
- Again, following on from the previous point, state-run businesses actually ended up costing the Treasury money rather the contributing to it. This obviously is a potentially undesirable situation as it can put pressure on other areas of government finance.

The case for privatisation

The underpinnings of the case for privatisation are based within the belief that market systems should be allowed to work more-or-less without governmental interference. It follows that the main proponents of privatisation are on the political right-wing who tend to espouse the economic theories of such thinkers as Adam Smith and Milton Friedman (see Chapter 10).

The proponents of privatisation argue that it has several advantages:

- In many cases, privatisations involved the breaking-up of a state-run monopoly. It follows that in doing so, competition is being introduced into previously monopolistic markets. As we have seen (Chapter 18), an increase in competition tends to result in lower prices and higher quality which is of benefit to consumers.
- The actual sale (by means of share issue) of government assets generates revenues to the Treasury. Receipts can be used by the government for other worthwhile state purposes, such as tax cuts or possible investment in government services, such as health, education or infrastructure.

■ Any subsidies that were previously granted to a business when it was nationalised is saved (by the state) when it is privatised. Any losses are borne by the shareholders rather then by the taxpayer (although it should be borne in mind that in some privatisations, the government 'wrote-off' the debt of the business at the time of the sell-off – effectively a subsidy from the taxpayer).

■ The state will receive tax revenues from the privatised businesses whenever they report taxable profits. In this regard, privatised businesses are just like any other private company.

■ Privatisations are good for the City of London and for the Stock Exchange in particular. An inflow of investments from overseas in privatised businesses will have a potentially beneficial effect on the capital account of the UK balance of payments account.

The case against privatisation

Those who argue against privatisation are often the same people who argue in favour of nationalisation. In contrast to the free-market ideologues who vigorously support privatisation, opponents tend to espouse a left-wing political ideology which has traditionally believed in a higher level of state influence on the business sector.

The principal opponents of privatisation argue as follows:

■ It necessarily reduces the size of the public sector and thus may reduce the government's ability to influence the level of economic activity in the country.

■ It involves 'selling the family silver.' This is taken to mean that the state sells off its valuable assets which at best is a pity and at worse is betraying the trust of those who invested in the 'silver' (formerly state-owned assets) in the first place.

■ Privatised businesses are necessarily concerned with profits in addition to maintaining standards of service. A risk is thus introduced that the profit-seeking companies may overlook some customer groups who it would not be profitable to supply (such as rural communities with gas or bus services).

■ In some cases, privatisations have involved the state losing direct control over potentially strategically vital industries, which include some defence equipment manufacturers and electricity generators. There may be times of national emergency when these may be (according to some) best controlled by the state but privatisations have made this legally impossible.

- Some have raised questions as to whether privatisation has actually achieved its objectives of increased competition. In some cases a state-run monopoly has simply become a privatised monopoly (or a virtual monopoly). Oft-quoted examples of this include British Gas and British Telecommunications (BT) although recent policy changes in these sectors are expected to increase competition to a certain extent.
- Criticisms have been raised about the high levels of profits that some privatised utilities have made. BT, for example, is capable of making over £3 billion each year in pre-tax profits. Critics argue that instead of making high profits, such companies should charge lower prices to their customers. Similar arguments have been advanced against the allegedly excessive salaries of directors in privatised companies.

Clearly, the arguments both for and against both privatisation and nationalisation can be compelling. In practice, one's conclusions may be guided more by one's political leanings than by a rational and objective analysis of the arguments.

Assignment 19.1

1 In 2004 the Bradford-based supermarket retailer William Morrison Group acquired the Safeway supermarket chain. Your tasks are to:
   - Discover what conditions, if any, were applied by the CC in sanctioning the takeover.
   - Discuss the compatibility of this decision with the CC's mission statement, shown above.
2 Over recent years, the CC has made several important decisions that have influenced the structures of certain industries. Choose a case upon which the CC has blocked a merger or acquisition and find out the following:
   - The market structure of the industry in which the two affected businesses were players;
   - The reasons why the merger or acquisition was proposed.
Suggest the reasons why the CC blocked the proposed merger or acquisition.

Further reading

Armstrong, M., Cowan, S. and Vickers, J. (1994). *Regulatory Reform. Economic Analysis and British Experience.* Cambridge, MA: MIT Press.

Beesley, M.E. (1992). *Privatisation, Regulation and Deregulation*. London: Routledge.

Clark, A. (1999). *Organisations, Competition and the Business Environment*. London: FT Prentice Hall.

Clarke, T. and Pitelis, C. (eds) (1995). *The Political Economy of Privatisation*. London: Routledge.

Griffiths, A. and Wall, S. (eds) (2004). *Applied Economics*, 10th edn. London: FT Prentice Hall.

Martin, S. and Parker, S. (1997). *The Impact of Privatisation: Ownership and Corporate Performance in the UK*. London: Routledge.

Useful web sites

Department of Trade and Industry: http://www.dti.gov.uk
Financial Services Authority: http://www.fsa.gov.uk/
HMSO: http://www.hmso.gov.uk/acts
Office of Gas and Electricity Markets: www.ofgas.gov.uk
Office of the Regulator for Communications: http://www.ofcom.gov.org.uk/
Office for the Regulator for Rail: http://rail-reg.gov.uk/
UK Competition Commission: http://www.competition-commission.org.uk/

CHAPTER 20

Comparing industries and organisations

After studying this chapter, students should be able to describe:

- a model that explains differences in company and industry profitability;
- what is meant by the bargaining power of buyers and suppliers;
- what substitute products are and how the threat of substitutes can affect profitability;
- how the threat of new entrants into a market can affect profitability;
- how the intensity of competitive rivalry can affect profitability.

20.1 Introduction

The profits that businesses achieve vary greatly, both from industry to industry and between competitors within industries. Some industries consistently return outstanding financial results, announcing high dividends and pleasing shareholders whereas in other industries, there are tiny profits or even losses. Companies involved in electronics, pharmaceuticals or computer software often make substantial profits, whereas those in coal-mining, shipbuilding or textiles generally make lower profits.

Even within a given industry, some companies make high profits whilst other companies struggle through, year after year trying to break even or sustaining losses. This chapter attempts to analyse why these variations exist and the implications of these features for the strategies of companies in the industry context.

20.2 Five forces of industry profitability

An influential American academic, Prof. Michael E. Porter of Harvard Business School (1980) developed a framework for analysing the nature and extent of competition within an industry. He argued that there are *five competitive forces* which determine the degree of competition within an industry (see Figure 20.1).

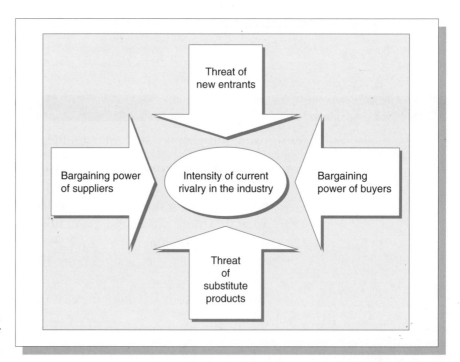

Figure 20.1
Michael Porter's five forces of competition.

We can see from the diagram that the central force is that of the rivalry between existing competitors. This is quite intentional, as the profitability of an industry will depend largely upon this single factor. If competition is intense in an industry then there will be a downward pressure on the profitability of each player in the industry. This is because intense competition necessitates cutting prices to retain and gain business or incurring additional costs of supporting a product in the market place. Conversely, light competition, or none at all, will enable competitors to make higher profits (the extreme of which, as we have seen, is a monopoly).

This central force has, in turn, four major determinants. It is these which determine the intensity of the competitive rivalry in an industry. We will examine the four 'peripheral' forces and then come to the one central force.

20.3 Bargaining power of suppliers

Suppliers are those individuals and enterprises that provide the organisation with its inputs. Examples of inputs include:

- materials and operational inputs, including stocks, land, buildings, etc.;
- human resources (e.g. employees);
- finances (e.g. from banks in the form of loans).

If an organisation is forced to pay a comparatively high price for these inputs, there will be a downward pressure on the potential profitability of the company. If, conversely, the organisation can secure the inputs at a favourable price, the opportunity exists for money to be saved which can increase profits. There are several situations that can affect this force.

- The *market structure* of the industry has a powerful effect. The nearer the organisation tends towards monopsony (see Chapter 18), then the weaker the supplier will be. The structures of supplier and buyer bases can vary widely. Some industries have few very large buyers who buy from a highly fragmented supplier base, whereas others have many small buyers who source from a highly concentrated supplier base. Supplying power results from a large supplier selling its output to a small company or when the supplier has a unique product with a price inelastic demand.
- Of course, input need not just be of materials; it can be uniquely qualified *personnel* which cost a great deal of money to secure. Trade unions may also increase the price of labour inputs (powerful suppliers of organised labour) when they insist on a certain level of pay in exchange for continued supply of human resource co-operation. If the organisation has a high dependency on employees with rare skills, it follows that a higher price will be attached to this particular input (e.g. highly qualified scientists or uniquely experienced computer programmers).
- The *cost of finance* and its availability may also affect profitability and may even have a bearing on a company's survival.

Large companies will generally find it easier to secure long-term loans, debenture capital, etc. than smaller ones. The concentrated nature of the banking industry means that this can be a significant factor for all industries to a greater or lesser extent. The interest rates at which loans are agreed (which can seriously influence net profits) will depend upon the bank's estimation of the risk of loan default and this will vary from company to company and from industry to industry.

A company will tend to have power over its suppliers, and hence will be able to gain savings on unit cost, if:

- it is a large organisation which can consequently buy in large quantity;
- it is a monopsonist (or near monopsonist) of a certain input;
- the organisation consumes a large proportion of a supplier's output;
- it has a highly fragmented supplier base;
- it uses commodity and undifferentiated material inputs;
- it has a low labour requirement relative to its sales turnover;
- it requires relatively unskilled labour;
- it has an non-unionised labour force;
- it has a labour force with non-transferable skills (who are thus 'locked in' to the employer);
- it is able to sustain debt at negligible risk of default;
- it has low financial gearing (see Chapter 29).

The converse of the above will tend to reduce the organisation's power over its suppliers.

20.4 Bargaining power of buyers

The power of an organisation over its buyers reflects exactly the previous discussion on the power of suppliers. It follows logically that if a company has pricing power over its customers then it can inflate prices and increase revenue, and, by maintaining costs at existing levels, can increase profits. If a company sells a product which is an important input to a customer's operation *and* it is difficult to obtain elsewhere, then it follows that the supplier will have power in its approach to pricing.

The issue of market structure is as pertinent with regard to this force as it is to the issue of bargaining power of suppliers – it is simply the converse. When the buying power is concentrated then one would expect this to exert a downward pressure on the profitability of suppliers into the market, especially if the supplier base is highly fragmented. There are many good examples of this situation in the UK. As the retail supply of food and DIY goods have become increasingly oligopolistic, suppliers to the retailers have suffered a noticeable reduction in prices chargeable to the retailers coupled with other unfavourable terms of supply such as longer credit periods and demands for shortened lead times. On a more mundane level we can readily appreciate that as a customer of British Telecommunications (BT) plc, the author is a very weak buyer. His annual phone bill of around £350 is negligible to the company (with its annual turnover of over £18 billion) and he would get a short response if he alone were to request a reduction in unit price from the supplier of telephone services. This means that the bill must be paid exactly as BT prescribe or else go without the benefit of a BT telephone.

20.5 Threat of new entrants

A key pressure on profitability arises from a company's competitors. It usually follows that the fewer competitors a business has, the greater the opportunities will be to make higher profits. It goes without saying that new entrants will seek to join an industry that can achieve high profits. What potential new entrants may not realise is that the reason *why* an industry is so profitable might be precisely because it is very hard to enter. Conversely, those industries which have a high turnover of 'joiners' and 'leavers' will tend to return relatively modest profits. The key determinant of the number of competitors is the 'height' of *entry barriers* which present obstacles to would-be competitors who wish to enter the industry.

As a rule of thumb we can say that low entry barriers will encourage new entrants and high entry barriers will deter them. Hence, industries which are hard to enter are generally those which have few competitors (and hence a lower degree of competitive rivalry).

Entry barriers can take several forms. Which are the most important ones will depend upon the sector of industry in question:

- The most important entry barrier in most industries is the *capital requirement*. This can vary from just a few pounds to enter the window-cleaning market (the price of some second-hand ladders, a bucket and a mop) to tens of billions of pounds, which is the price of entering the petrochemicals refinement industry.
- *Legal permission* or *government licences* can be another barrier to entry. Some industries are protected by government legislation in as much as competitors must gain a licence to operate within

the sector in question. For reasons of ensuring quality in critical sectors and sometimes for reasons of national security, the government will demand that certain exacting criteria are met before a company will be allowed to operate. As well as being a long and inconvenient process, gaining such approval can be costly and in this respect, it can also be considered as a capital requirement of market entry. In some sectors of industry, the weight of *government legislation* can represent a significant investment and source of great inconvenience to new entrants. Laws regarding pollution, health and safety and employment of individuals can be restrictive and expensive, especially in areas like the chemical industry. In addition, suppliers of the utilities must observe strict pricing limits which are imposed by regulatory bodies (see Chapter 19). These pricing structures put pressure on costs and profitability, and these can be a disincentive for companies to enter the industry.

■ Some companies enjoy a *unique access to supply or distribution channels*. When this is the case, new entrants simply cannot do business in the sector. The reasons for unique access to inputs or output channels may be as the result of government restrictions or may have arisen by forward or backward vertical acquisition of an existing player in the industry (see Chapter 7).

■ *Intellectual assets* (or intellectual resources) and unique competencies may represent an entry barrier to would-be competitors in some business sectors. If an organisation possesses certain intellectual assets which are difficult or impossible to obtain or circumvent, then a significant hurdle exists to new entrants. In this context, intellectual assets can be taken to mean such things as:
  – licences;
  – patents;
  – brand names, logos, registered trade-marks and registered designs;
  – uniquely qualified personnel and 'know how';
  – formulations and recipes.

20.6 Threat of substitute products

Substitute products are those that can be used instead of those produced by a given organisation. For example, we might frequently substitute margarine for butter or switch between different brands of margarine.

A company whose products can easily be substituted for others will naturally find that price increases are more likely to lead customers into having their wants and needs met by substitutes. There are two general types of substitutes:

- *Direct substitutes* are substitutes of essentially the same kind. If you go to the local DIY 'shed' and you find that Dulux white gloss paint is too expensive, you might consider buying Crown paint or the retailer's own brand – both more-or-less direct substitutes. Substitution by a direct substitute requires no change in the operation in question – you apply the paint in the same way whichever brand you are using. Direct substitutes in, for example, the pharmaceuticals industry includes the widely available analgesic (pain-killing) drugs like aspirin, paracetamol and ibuprofen. All of these drugs are available in different substitute forms.
- *Indirect substitutes* are products which are different but which can, under certain circumstances, perform the same role. Over recent years, we have seen more and more parts in cars made out of plastics whereas at one time, internal parts such as dashboards would have been made from metal or wood. Hence, plastic is an indirect substitute for metal in some circumstances. Similarly, margarine is an indirect substitute for butter, in contrast to substituting one brand of butter for another (which would be an example of direct substitution).

Downward pressures on profitability will arise if a company's products are easily substitutable, especially if there are many equivalent direct substitutes (sometimes called *counter* products like two brands of aspirin). The use of indirect substitution in industrial processes usually requires some redesign or adjustment of the process on which it is used. For this reason, indirect substitution sometimes offers less of a threat than direct.

The key manoeuvre to make products or services less substitutable is to *differentiate*. A differentiated product, in this context, is one which is perceived by consumers as being so different from other, similar products, that by substituting it for a counter, the consumer would be losing a key quality. The bases upon which products are differentiated are numerous. Typical examples in the well-known retail sector include claims of higher quality, a distinctive flavour or strongly defined image or a well-trusted brand to which consumers have become loyal. Marketing people often seek to establish a *unique selling proposition* (USP), a distinctive product feature which separates their product from others.

20.7 Rivalry between existing competitors

The intensity of competition varies greatly from industry to industry. Some industries are comprised of competitors who are friendly and genial to one another whereas others are characterised by aggression, mutual suspicion and dislike. The way in which competitors behave towards one another can have a significant bearing on the profitability of companies in the industry. We must remember that it is the other four forces which largely determine the strength of this force.

It is important to note that the intensity of competition is not usually related to the actual size of the industry (i.e. the *number* of competitors). Rather, it is related to:

- the position of the industry on the industry growth cycle (competitive intensity reaches a maximum at the maturity stage);
- the structure of the industry (i.e. the degree of concentration of supply);
- the price elasticity of demand of the products supplied by the industry;
- the extent of differentiation of products supplied by the different competitors (differentiation reduces substitutability and hence competition);
- the pressures exerted by the other four of Porter's forces.

Companies within an industry can compete with each other in two general ways.

- *Price competition* involves using price to attract buyers. This invariably means *price leadership*, the practice of unilaterally (usually) reducing price in order to increase market share. Such practice results in a short-term gain in business at reduced profit margins, but other competitors may follow the leader downwards in price to win back their lost market share. The result of course is that all players in the industry make lower margins and it is not uncommon for the smaller and weaker competitors to go out of business through not being able to absorb the losses in revenue. Price competition is very rare in oligopolistic industries as competitors usually recognise their mutual price interdependence.
- *Non-price competition* occurs when competitors seek to gain market share by means other than price adjustment. Non-price instruments include product differentiation, new product launches and a whole battery of above, and below line promotions

(see Chapter 28). Of course, these manoeuvres are expensive in themselves. Oligopolists can spend as much as 6% of total turnover on marketing promotions whilst some chemical companies spend as much as 12% of total sales on research and development (R&D), continually attempting to gain competitive advantage through new product introductions.

Lower profits are made in industries in which competition is intense, whether on a price or non-price basis.

A summary of Porter's five forces and profitability is given in Table 20.1.

Table 20.1
Porter's five forces and profitability: a summary

Force	Upward pressure on profitability	Downward pressure on profitability
Bargaining power of suppliers	Weak suppliers	Strong suppliers
Bargaining power of buyers	Weak buyers	Strong buyers
Threat of new entrants	High entry barriers	Low entry barriers
Threats from substitute products	Few possible substitutes	Many possible substitutes
Competitive rivalry	Little rivalry	Intense rivalry

20.8   Case study: Some simple comparisons

We will now investigate two industries: the British pharmaceuticals industry and the British paint industry. Pharmaceutical companies are primarily concerned with the design and manufacture of chemical compounds which bring about therapeutic, stabilising or prophylactic (preventative) effects upon the bodies of individuals (drugs). Paint companies are defined as those concerned with the production of paints, liquid surface coatings, powder coatings and varnishes.

As an overview, let us look at a summary of some of the financial results within these industries for the year ending 2002.

Table 20.2 shows examples of company profitability in pharmaceuticals and paints.

We can see immediately that there is a difference in profitability between the two sectors: it would appear that pharmaceuticals companies earn higher profits than paint companies. The results reported here are typical of the pharmaceuticals sector. It is rare when a company in this sector makes less than 20% return on sales. Paint companies

Table 20.2
Examples of company profitability in pharmaceuticals and paint.

Company	Sector	Turnover	Trading profit as percentage of sales
GlaxoSmithKline plc	Pharmaceuticals	£18 billion	31.3
ICI paints	Paints	£2163 million	9.4

Note: Trading profit is taken to mean profit before interest, tax and extraordinary items.

might dream of these levels of profit. The industry average profit margin in the paint industry is usually between 5% and 8%. A key strategic enquiry is to ask why these disparities exist.

Porter's five forces: the British pharmaceutical industry

The UK is a very strong player in the global pharmaceutical industry. It boasts the largest pharmaceuticals' company in the world (Glaxo SmithKline) and four out of the world's ten best-selling drugs (including the 'number one' spot). Directly employing around 65,000 people in Britain, with 'feeder industries' employing many more, the UK industry is a large net exporter of drugs, accounting for a trade surplus in this sector of well over £1 billion (i.e. of exports over imports). Growth in the pharmaceuticals sector has rarely been below 10% per year and return on sales is invariably of the order of 20% or higher (often much higher). Around 42% of the total workforce in the pharmaceutical industry is employed within R&D.

The UK pharmaceuticals industry as a whole is fragmented, although the past decade has seen considerable corporate activity which has resulted even more powerful leading players, such as GlaxoSmithKline plc, AstraZeneca plc and Pfizer Ltd. However, the market is still able to support numerous small, independent manufacturers.

Force 1: Bargaining power of suppliers

Drug companies tend to be large due to the capital investment necessary to get up and running in the first place (GlaxoSmithKline, in the year to 2003, had total worldwide sales of £18.5 billion and a trading profit of £6.5 billion). This factor alone gives the companies in the sector buying power due to economies of scale as large companies regularly buying in bulk can negotiate cheaper unit prices with their regular suppliers.

Drug companies' strength in regard to this force is further reinforced by the added value of the product itself. Essentially, a drug is a chemical product made by the reactions of other, simpler chemicals. The drug company buys in relatively cheap (unit priced) chemicals, and by their complex chemical processing, adds value to them to produce the final product. The commodity nature of the raw materials also means that supplies could be obtained from several possible suppliers – no single supplier is distinctive enough to exert a threat to a pharmaceutical company. The cost of raw materials bought by a pharmaceuticals company usually represents a relatively small proportion of the total cost structure of the business. Suppliers have little power over a pharmaceutical company.

Force 2: Bargaining power of buyers

Most drugs have highly price inelastic demand. For some drugs, the coefficient of elasticity will be almost perfectly inelastic. We must begin by asking who the buyers of drugs are. There are three broad categories:

- direct sales to National Health Service (NHS) pharmacies;
- prescription sales from retail pharmacies (where the doctor prescribes the drug);
- 'over-the-counter' (OTC) sales of non-prescribed drugs to members of the public.

The simple fact is that none of these customer groups are much price sensitive when it comes to the purchase of drugs.

The NHS is a part of the government and recent years have seen many advances in the complexity of medical treatment in the NHS. Such developments have required more complex pharmaceutical preparations which have necessarily meant higher drugs bills for the NHS. The purchase of prescribed pharmaceuticals in the UK is done on behalf of patients by the relevant health service, and are then prescribed to patients by qualified doctors and dispensed to them by pharmacists. The vast majority of pharmaceuticals are effectively 'bought' by the NHS, which negotiates an overall profit margin with its suppliers in a centralised fashion under the *Pharmaceutical Price Regulation Scheme* (PPRS). The PPRS is a voluntary scheme agreed between the industry and the NHS that effectively caps company profit levels on drugs to the NHS. The scheme, which is negotiated between industry representatives and the government every 5 to 6 years, controls the maximum profit that companies can make on their NHS sales but does not control the prices of individual drugs. The scheme does not apply to generic medicines or private prescriptions, generic pricing being controlled through the *Drug Tariff.*

In spite of the new deal under the PPRS, expenditure on prescribed pharmaceuticals is expected to rise as a result of the pressures of an ageing and increasingly infirm population, expending possibilities of treatment and growth in the private sector. The spending on *Prescription-Only Medicines* (POMs) in the UK is forecast to reach £11.25 billion by the end of 2005 (see Figure 20.2).

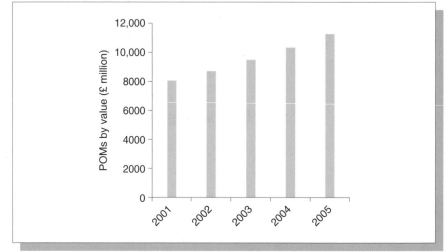

Figure 20.2 Forecast UK market for POMs by value (pounds in million). (*Source*: Keynotes.)

The increased spending over time is in large part due to the expectation of the NHS patient that every and all necessary drugs for a patient's treatment will be supplied free of charge and when needed. The government in the form of the NHS may be unwilling to risk the unpopularity of refusing medication to a patient on the grounds that the price of the drug is too high (there are, however, efforts to reduce the NHS drugs bill).

The doctors who prescribe drugs are professional people who have the well-being of their patients as their highest professional objective. They will therefore tend to prescribe the most appropriate medicament regardless of the price (the doctor may not even know the price). As, in the UK, there is a fixed charge for prescriptions, the actual cost to the NHS of the drug (over and above the prescription charge), will usually be of little concern to the patient. Recent changes in the status of general practitioner (GP) practices (assuming 'fund-holder' status) may be modifying GPs' approaches to drug prescription.

The relief of pain and discomfort, and the desire to be cured are extremely strong motivators for individual consumers. Put simply, individuals are usually prepared to pay a high price, if necessary, for the means to ensure the continuity of life or for the relief of pain. Highly differentiated drugs for the treatment of life-threatening illnesses can command a particularly high price.

In essence, purchasers of drugs buy them because they *need* them, and this explains the highly price inelastic nature of the demand. When the choice is 'Pay the asking price or suffer' (or 'Pay the asking price or see your patients suffer'), the choice becomes something of an academic one. We all know what it is like to be in pain, whether it is toothache, migraine or something more serious. In such unfortunate circumstances, we will have experienced an intense need for a medicament, usually with little regard for the price. This fact in itself exerts an upward pressure on profitability for the drug companies.

Force 3: Threats of new entrants

The entry barriers that apply to the pharmaceutical industry are very high.

- The *capital costs* of setting up a pharmaceutical plant are very large. The complexity of the chemical processes and the technology that must be installed mean that minimum capital investment is of the order of hundreds of millions of pounds. GlaxoSmithKline, the world's largest pharmaceuticals company, has assets of around £5 billion – a lot of money to find for would-be new entrants.
- *R&D* costs, both of introducing new products, and of maintaining the market share of existing ones are very high. Spending on new product development, longer term research and related activities is typically around 16% of total sales – a figure significantly higher than other sectors of the chemical industry. We have already encounteredGlaxoSmithKline, which employs 7000 scientists and spends well over £1 billion a year in this activity. R&D personnel in this area of science must be highly qualified and highly skilled (and consequently highly paid). In addition, new drugs in the UK must gain an individual entry in the 'official' listing of drugs – the *British pharmacopoeia*. It is estimated that the full cost of bringing a new drug to the market is of the order of £90 million and can take up to 12 years.
- A great deal of *expertise* is necessary in order both to develop pharmaceutical products and to make them safely and efficiently in a factory. A company tends to learn and develop its procedures over time, and to modify and improve things over years and decades.
- The *selling process* for drugs is very expensive, predominantly because the customer base is so diverse. Competitors in the industry employ a large number of representatives, who, due to

the nature of the products and the initial customers (doctors and pharmacists), must be individuals well versed in bio-chemistry and medicine. In consequence, the majority of these representatives are science graduates or qualified nurses. Whilst it may be said that all sales representatives are expensive, with their salaries, expenses and cars, it may be said that pharmaceutical sales representatives cost more than most. More are needed per area of territory (compared to other industries), as a sales call is usually to just one doctor (or one practice) and there are a lot of doctors to call on.

- Intellectual resources play an important role in the pharma-ceuticals industry. Many drugs have *brand names* that patients and doctors have learned to respect over time. New entrants would have to overcome this barrier in order to ensure their new products are prescribed in preference to established products. Some drugs have international *patents* that prevent competitors from manufacturing a counter or similar product.

The clear conclusion that can be drawn from this discussion is that the entry barriers in the pharmaceuticals industry are exceedingly high. These represent a strong deterrent to would-be new entrants to the industry, and they serve to maintain the market in its existing form and structure. The fact there has not been a serious new entrant into this industry for many years is testimony to the height of these barriers. This is a source of upward pressure on potential profitability.

Force 4: Threats from substitute products

There are few substitutes to pharmaceuticals, when considered as a general group of products. The very low price elasticity of demand reflects the difficulty (or inability) to substitute. One might argue that 'alternative' medicines, and such practices as acupuncture, homeopathy and others may be substitutes, but these are practised in a minority of cases of illness. The clear fact is that it is very hard to effectively substitute a drug. This is a source of upward pressure on potential profitability for pharmaceutical companies.

Within the sector itself, companies can, to a certain extent, substitute each others' products. Each drug has what is called a *generic* name. This describes the chemical nature of the product. Some companies attach brand names to generics in an attempt to differentiate them in their favour (e.g. the generic drug paracetamol (or *para-acetyl amino phenol*), is sold under such brand names as Anadin paracetamol,

Panadol and Hedex). The most common way by which companies avoid the threat of generics is to patent the formulation, but this only applies to new products,

Force 5: Intensity of competition between existing competitors

The intensity of rivalry varies in the pharmaceuticals sector according to product type. In the OTC market, competition among some products (e.g. analgesics or painkillers) is quite intense. This results in lower profits than in the prescription medicines market. The area of least intense competition is that of pharmaceuticals protected by patent. This is because competition is not possible due to legal barriers.

The contributory effect of the other four forces means that competition in this industry is much less intense than in most other industries. Most serious competitors in the industry make reasonable profits, which tend to mean that the *need* to step up the rivalry is usually absent.

Summary

All five forces, to a greater or lesser extent, act in favour of the industry. Some, such as the threat of new entrants act strongly in favour of companies in the sector. This is what Porter himself would call a 'five star' industry. We would rightly expect it to return high profits.

Profitability differences in the same industry sector

There can be substantial differences in profit between companies in the same sector. For example, before the merger of Glaxo Wellcome and SmithKline Beecham in 2001, to form the new company of GlaxoSmith Kline plc, the two companies had typically declared annual profits of around 31% profit and 25%, respectively. What could be the difference between two companies in the same sector that would in such a difference in profit?

The two companies differed in the range of products they produced. The majority of Glaxo Wellcome's products were within the prescription pharmaceuticals market – many protected by patent. SmithKline Beecham had a powerful presence in this sector but also had sizeable interests in the OTC market with its brands *Phensic, Tums, Night Nurse, Ribena, Nicorette, Horlicks, Locozade, Macleans* and *Hedex* (to name but a few). It is this difference (the breadth of their respective product ranges) that is the key to the differences in profitability. SmithKline Beecham's significant participation in the OTC market meant that profits were lower owing to competition in this sector. Glaxo Wellcome's concentration in the prescription medicine's market reduced the ability of competitors to substitute its products.

Glaxo Wellcome produced a number of important prescription medicines. Two of them, *Zantac* and *Retrovir*, among the most profitable drugs in the world owing the significant demand for both of them, and their protection by international patent (making demand very price inelastic). For more than 20 years, Zantac has been the major drug for treating gastrointestinal ulcers, while Retrovir has been the world's major treatment, to date, for the symptoms of human immunodeficiency virus (HIV) and acquired immune deficiency syndrome (AIDS). Both of these products eliminate the legal threat of direct substitution and make indirect substitution difficult. The fact that the two drugs accounted for a large proportion of the company's output (Zantac: 28%; Retrovir: *ca.* 12%) meant that this factor (a reduced threat of substitution, one of Porter's five forces) was *the* principal cause of Glaxo Wellcome's superior performance. It should be borne in mind, however, that although its profitability was higher, Glaxo Wellcome's portfolio was narrower than SmithKline Beecham's making it potentially less able to withstand threats to any of its major products. In particular, the patent expiry of its two major products would put Glaxo Wellcome's profitability at risk unless replacements could be found.

The answer to competition between these two players was resolved in January 2001 when they merged into one giant company called GlaxoSmithKline (GSK). GSK now has an estimated 7% of the world's pharmaceutical market and is quoted on the London and New York Stock Exchanges. The 2003 results for GSK showed an annual growth of 5% in total pharmaceutical turnover to a value of £18 billion.

Porter's five forces: the UK paint industry

The total UK paint industry is worth around £1.5 billion (compare with the NHS expenditure of around £3.5 billion on drugs) and can be seen as a fragmented industry with more than 250 small to medium sized companies. Although there are more competitors than in the pharmaceuticals industry, sales are much lower. Most of the paint companies are small businesses (typically with annual total sales of under £10 million and employing fewer than 100 people players) and the market is dominated by two main brands: the *ICI*-owned *Dulux* paints and *AzkoNobel*-owned *Crown* paints. Dulux has historically had the larger market share but Crown has narrowed the gap in recent years. The third largest paint manufacturer is the Kalon Group plc, who is mainly concerned with *own-label* paints and has seen steady growth in their market share in recent years. This has been a consequence of packaging and marketing on the same lines as premium brand products, such as the *B&Q* range of *New England* and *Tate* paints with exclusive colour charts and heavy television advertising.

Force 1: Bargaining power of suppliers

The raw materials from which paint is made are largely sourced from a number of large chemical intermediate manufacturers who supply many other industries besides the paint industry. Many of these suppliers are multinationals whose sales to paint companies represent a relatively small percentage of their total sales. This suggests that the suppliers might be able to exert some power over the paint companies and whilst this is true in part, the power is partly offset by the oligopolistic nature of the supply industry. Furthermore, most raw materials in the paint industry are relatively undifferentiated (e.g. white spirit), and paint companies may have a choice of as many as five companies from whom they can buy.

Force 2: Bargaining power of buyers

The markets for paint products include trades people (via trade distributors), the DIY retailers, local authorities and a whole range of industrial concerns. For relatively undifferentiated paint products, such as decorative paints, the principal outlets are the retailers and trade distributors: both of which are relatively concentrated. The large paint companies, who have a large proportion of their outputs going to this area, have had to endure a downward pressure on prices resulting from the high buying power of the large DIY 'sheds' (e.g. B&Q, Homebase, Wickes, etc.). Differentiated products supplied into more fragmented markets can maintain higher margins but these products have lower volumes than the decorative 'white gloss' markets.

Force 3: Threats from new entrants

The capital costs of entering the paint industry are relatively low – typically under £10,000, presuming reconditioned equipment is purchased and a minimum amount of raw material stocks. A chemistry graduate with a few years experience in the industry would have sufficient know-how to operate a small paint company so the intellectual resources requirement is not prohibitive. There is some mandatory legislation that applies to the industry, but these are not expensive for small companies. Formulations for paint products are widely available from raw material suppliers (e.g. the formulations for a simple white gloss or emulsion paint are decades old, and can be obtained from any resin or pigment supplier. Most paint chemists could scribble such a formulation down on the back of an envelope.).

Force 4: Threats from substitute products

The fact that there are over 250 UK manufacturers of paint, all producing essentially similar products means that there are many direct substitutes for most paint products. Some differentiated products (e.g. anti-graffiti paints) have fewer substitutes and these usually command a price premium. The non-essential nature of the product (compared to pharmaceuticals) means that there are a number of indirect substitutes such as tiling, cladding, plastic coating, polyvinyl chloride (PVC) plastisol and in some cases, wallpaper. In addition, architects are skilled at designing buildings which do need to be painted at all, such as by using non-corroding metals such as aluminium.

Force 5: Intensity of competition between existing competitors

There is necessarily some degree of competition in the paint industry. It is a very mature industry (i.e. the total demand for paint grows either slowly or not at all) and in consequence, growth can only be achieved at the expense of a competitor's market share. Price competition is rare, largely due to the fact that margins are already relatively low (but price reductions are occasionally brought about by powerful buyers). Competitive advantage is often brought about by advertising and a range of below-line promotions, and most companies also provide free on-site technical service to customers.

Summary

We can see that paint companies face something of a 'mixed bag' with regard to Prof. Porter's five forces. There is no single force which acts strongly in favour of the individual paint manufacturer and some (e.g. threats from new entrants) act strongly against the industry. We would consequently expect competitors in the industry to return low to medium profits.

Assignment 20.1

Arthur Knightley has decided to set up a company called Genes R Us Limited. He will specialise in manufacture of designer denim wear for the teenage market, using his own designs. From his own observations he believes that there is a niche market for low price fashionable clothes, particularly for females in the 14–17 years age group. His strategy is based upon short shelf-lives for his products with new designs or modifications ready for the retail market every 6–9 months.

Questions 20.1

- Which entry barriers is the company likely to encounter in seeking to enter this market?
- Use Porter's five-force model to explain the type of competitive position that such a business might encounter if the entry barriers could somehow be dealt with.
- What levels of profitability might the company expect to return (you should be able to derive from your five-forces analysis)?

Further reading

Ansoff, I. (1987). *Corporate Strategy*. London: Penguin.

Johnson, G. and Scholes, K. (2003). *Exploring Corporate Strategy*, 6th edn. Harlow: FT Prentice Hall.

Porter, M.E. (1980). *Competitive Strategy: Techniques for Analysing Industries and Competitors*. New York: Free Press.

Porter, M.E. (1985). *Competitive Advantage: Creating and Sustaining Superior Performance*. New York: Free Press.

Useful web sites

The Competition Commission and the Treasury Site: www.open.gov.uk
The Competition Commission of the European Union:
www.europa.eu.int/comm/competiton/

PART IV

Business management

CHAPTER 21

Organisation structure

Learning objectives

After studying this chapter, students should be able to describe:

- what is meant by organisation structure;
- management issues in organisation structure;
- the main factors that influence the structural design;
- centralisation, decentralisation, span of control, unity of command and delegation;
- the flexible firm;
- the advantages and disadvantages of different types of organisation structure.

21.1 Why do we have structures?

In order to achieve their goals and objectives, organisations need to arrange the work into manageable segments and align the segments so that individual efforts are co-ordinated for optimum organisational effectiveness. These alignments form the organisation structure and this chapter describes various models of structure, and examines the advantages and disadvantages of adopting particular structures.

21.2 What is structure?

Organisation structures have been the subject of much interest by management scholars over the years, and, as we saw in Chapter 1, Taylor[1] described the need for '*structures of control*' while Max Weber's view of bureaucracies[2] called for '*authority structures*'. The rapid growth

of organisations and the increasing complexity and their environments stimulated the contingency school of management theory which
studied the relationship of the environment and structure. The *contingency*[3] approach concludes that organisations are most effective when
their *structures are appropriately designed to match the relationships of the particular nature of the business, the external environmental factors, and the market conditions.*

According to Henry Minzberg,[4] an organisation's structure is '*the sum
total of the ways in which it divides its labour into distinct tasks and then achieves
co-ordination between them*'. In other words structure represents the *pattern of relationships of the workforce and their relative positions in the organisation.* The structure provides the *framework for order and control, whereby the
organisation's activities can be planned, organised, directed and monitored.*

21.3 Management issues in organisation structure

Line and staff employees

The first management consideration is to examine how employees are
distinguished from each other in terms of how they 'fit in' to a typical
organisational structure – the issue of line and staff employees. Different
specialist divisions and departments within an organisation contain a
predominance of either line or staff employees.

Line employees are those that are directly responsible for achieving
the organisation's objectives. Line employees are therefore found in
departments that are responsible for producing, selling or servicing
the organisation's products (e.g. in operations, marketing and after-
sales servicing).

Staff employees are responsible for supporting the line employees in
their tasks. Staff are therefore found in departments that advise, support
or provide expertise, such as personnel, research and development
and finance.

The line and staff distinction can be best understood by the use of an
example. A business producing cars is known for its car-making activities. Its primary objective is to produce and market cars in order to
make profit. The company needs its staff functions *because of* its line
functions. The personnel and finance functions would have no purpose at all unless they were in support of the company's primary (car-
making) activities, which is performed by the line employees. Nissan is

not known primarily for the quality of its finance function (important though this is), but for the output of its line employees, its cars.

Span of control

The *span of control*, sometimes called the span of management, is a simple concept which describes the number of subordinates that directly report to a single manager. Some managers oversee large teams of subordinates (a wide span of control) whereas others manage just one or two subordinates, a narrow span. It follows that the span of control will have a large influence upon the structure of an organisation.

Historically, there have been attempts to establish formulae that would establish the optimum span of control, by writers, such as V.A. Graicunas[5] and L.F. Urwick,[6] but modern organisational experiences show that there is no definitive span of control that can be universally applied. It is simply not possible to say that a manager must have *x* subordinates and no more or less: it obviously depends upon the managerial context. It is, however, important that the span is appropriate to the manager's skills and brief, and the nature of the subordinates. If the span is too broad, the manager will have too many subordinates and his or her ability to oversee their activities will be reduced. If the span is too narrow, the organisation is paying a manager who is effectively underemployed: a waste of money and human resources.

The optimum span of control in any given context will depend upon a number of factors:

- the skills of the manager in question;
- the ability of the subordinates to work without regular oversight;
- the complexity of the work undertaken;
- the variety of the work undertaken;
- the extent of any automation and the type of technology involved;
- the stability (susceptibility to change) of the organisation;
- the health and safety situation of tasks undertaken by the subordinates;
- how much the organisation can afford to pay for management.

Hence, a highly skilled manager overseeing a team of competent 'self-policing' subordinates may have a very broad span whereas (to take the extreme) an inept manager overseeing a team of poorly motivated subordinates in a dangerous environment will require a very short span.

Delegation

A second management issue in structure is the extent to which work is delegated downwards through the organisational structure. *Delegation* is the mechanism by which managers pass on work to subordinates. This enables the burden of work to be shared and it also relieves a manager of tasks, thus freeing him or her up to carry out jobs more suited to his or her skills.

The implicit rules or guidelines of delegation are not as straightforward as they might at first appear. In Chapter 22, we examine the notion of matching authority and responsibility. In this context, we will see that when a manager delegates work to a subordinate (over which, by definition, the manager has authority), then it is the manager and not the subordinate who is ultimately held responsible for the outcome of the delegated act. The manager may in turn, of course, hold the subordinate responsible for that area of authority delegated, but it is in the manager's interest to ensure that sufficient instruction is given to enable the subordinate to correctly carry out the delegated task.

A subordinate to which a task is delegated is formally referred to as a *delegate*, although this term is rarely used in business. The principle of matching authority and responsibility means that the delegate is empowered to act only in accordance to his or her specific brief. If the delegate acts outside of the brief (or set of instructions), the process breaks down as the subordinate is assuming authority which he or she has not been granted by the manager.

There are a number of advantages and disadvantages of delegation, from the point of view of the organisation.

Advantages

- It relieves the manager of some of his or her workload, and can therefore be a major time management aid.
- It helps to develop the skills of the subordinate, thus making him or her more useful to the organisation.
- It may serve to motivate the subordinate by granting a greater degree of responsibility.

Disadvantages

- A risk is taken that the subordinate may not be 'up to the job' and may consequently make errors.

■ Successful completion of a delegated task relies upon the communication of the instructions to the subordinate. It thus relies upon appropriate skills in this area on the part of the manager.

■ The manager may be reluctant to delegate owing to the risks associated with it. Some managers adopt the attitude that 'if you want a job done, you have got to do it yourself'. This clearly depends upon the personality of the manager.

21.4 Structure design

The design of organisation structure is the process by which managers decide upon a particular kind of structure and, if we consider the contingency approach, the choice of design will reflect each organisation's specific situation. The determinants of a relevant structural configuration for an organisation will derive from the following elements:

■ mission of the organisation (i.e. nature of the business and its goals);

■ size and complexity (e.g. global conglomerate, multi-locations, wide range of products, etc.);

■ internal environment (e.g. capital or labour intensive business, leading edge technology, etc.);

■ external environment (e.g. relatively stable or dynamic and volatile?);

■ culture (i.e. values, beliefs, customs and practice);

■ people (e.g. the mix of skills, competencies, motivations, etc.);

■ nature of the work (e.g. specialist functions, project or batch manufacturing, etc.);

■ activities (i.e. the fundamental tasks that deliver the products or services).

It should be noted that this is not necessarily a simple process as the individual factors are highly variable and in a dynamic situation the weight attracted to each can have a considerable impact on the appropriateness of the structural design. For example, an organisation that is operating in a relatively stable environment, such as the Civil Service, may be well suited to a *mechanistic* format with a rigid structure of clearly delineated management levels of authority and narrow spans of control. On the other hand, such a structure would be severely restrictive to an organisation trying to compete in fast moving or highly competitive technological sector that would require to *organic* in nature, with a high degree of flexibility and devolution that facilitates decision-making by employees close to the customer interface (Figure 21.1).

Figure 21.1
Characteristics
of mechanistic
and organic
organisations.

Characteristics of mechanistic organisations	**Characteristics of organic organisations**
▪ High degree of specialisation ▪ Rigid departmentalism ▪ Clear chain of command ▪ Narrow spans of control ▪ Centralisation ▪ High degree of formalisation	▪ Cross-functional teams ▪ Cross-hierarchical teams ▪ Free flow of information ▪ Wide spans of control ▪ Decentralisation ▪ Low formalisation

21.5 Centralised and decentralised organisations

Definitions

A key structural consideration is the extent to which the organisation is decentralised. Like all aspects of organisational structure, the degree of decentralisation will depend upon the nature, purpose and size of the organisation.

Centralised organisations are characterised by power and decision-making concentrated in a single powerful 'centre'. The centre may be a single individual or a head office. No major decision-making power is devolved to any other part of the organisation.

Advantages of centralisation

▪ It enables managers in the centre to maintain a tight level of control. The risks of problems occurring in the parts of the organisation are thus potentially reduced.

▪ It avoids the potential problems of introducing complex and expensive organisational structures.

▪ Standardised procedures are uniformly applied throughout the organisation.

▪ Communications are quicker and cheaper when the entire organisation is located close together.

▪ The risks associated with delegation are avoided.

Disadvantages of centralisation

■ A centralised structure is best suited to a stable environment and is generally incompatible with effective management in a dynamic, highly competitive environment.

■ The centre's need for bureaucratic controls of efficiency can inhibit the overall effectiveness of the organisation;

■ It restricts the ability of local managers to use their knowledge of local circumstances to adapt their area of activity the optimum benefit of the organisation.

■ Customer responsiveness is at risk with local managers limited in their authority to make decisions at the customer interface.

■ Centralised control can have a detrimental effect on management development by stifling local initiative.

■ Senior managers can be overburdened with relatively minor operational issues at the expense of their strategic roles.

■ It can lead to a surfeit of functional specialists at the 'centre', adding to the overhead costs of the business.

Decentralised organisations are characterised by, to varying degrees, devolution of power from the centre to its peripheral parts. The 'parts' of an organisation to which power is devolved may be distinct divisions, departments, subsidiary companies (for holding companies), strategic business units (SBUs), or profit and cost centres.

Like many things in business, the varying degrees of decentralisation can be shown as a continuum. At one extreme, fully centralised structures are those which have no evidence of any delegated power to any other part of the organisation. At the other extremity, fully decentralised organisations are characterised by power entirely devolved to its peripheral parts. Between the two extremes lie the various possible 'real-life' cases. Many organisations are partly decentralised and these could be shown as lying at various points along the continuum.

What determines the extent of decentralisation?

The fact that organisations exist in many states of decentralisation means that no single approach is the best in all cases – the ideal degree of decentralisation for an organisation has a number of determining factors (Figure 21.2):

■ *The mission or objectives of the organisation.* Businesses which are relatively unambitious in terms of growth may remain

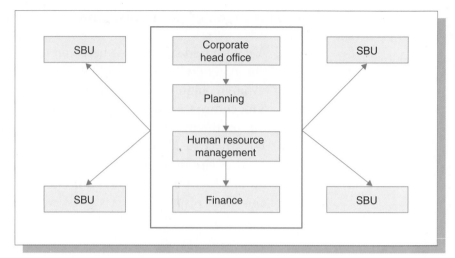

Figure 21.2
Example of a
decentralised
organisation.

centralised. Companies seeking to serve many markets or wishing to grow in other ways will tend to become increasingly decentralised.

- *The growth of organisations.* Control from a centre becomes increasingly difficult as size increases.
- *The nature and type of the organisation.* Sole proprietors will tend to be highly centralised but multinational and holding companies will tend to be more decentralised.
- *The output that the organisation provides and its markets.* Clearly, a business which distributes products nationally or internationally will be more decentralised than a corner shop. Similarly, products like petrochemicals will tend to be produced by companies which are more decentralised than producers of local products (e.g. Grassmere gingerbread or Edinburgh rock) will be more centralised.
- *The management style used in the organisation.* Some managers like to keep their eye on all activities in an organisation whereas others are happy to delegate to decentralised divisions or departments. This, of course, will be highly dependent on other factors, such as size.

Advantages of decentralisation

- It means the organisation can engage in a wider range of activities and can operate in many locations at once.
- It enables increased specialisation in the decentralised parts (e.g. those who 'know best' about a certain market, a specific product line or a specific range of activities).

- It can reduce the time taken to make key decisions. If power is devolved, decisions can be made by managers in the decentralised parts without the need to refer to the centres every time a decision needs to be made.
- The devolution of power serves to develop and improve the skills of managers: a feature which may also serve to motivate them.

Disadvantages of decentralisation

- Optimum advantage may not be made of the organisation's finance and human resources.
- Scope for mutual ventures and developing synergies between units can be severely limited.
- SBUs may find themselves in competition with each other.
- Business unit managers may have insufficient support from the centre.

Examples of decentralised organisations

Most organisations are decentralised to some extent. Some, however, exhibit a high degree of decentralisation:

- Multinational companies (where the parts are located in different locations of the world).
- Holding companies (the parts are subsidiary companies).
- Her Majesty's Government (the parts are government departments).
- Some large private limited companies.

21.6 Divisionalised organisations

In the case of a divisionalised organisation, the business is subdivided into managed units or *divisions*, each of which is concerned with discrete functions, such as production, sales, service or serving a market sector. Divisions are based upon the grouping together of people with a shared specialism. By acting together within a specialism, it is argued that synergies can be obtained both with and between divisions. There are four common methods of divisionalisation:

1 by functional specialism (typically operations, human resource management (HRM), marketing, finance, resource and development (R&D));

2 by geographical concentration (where divisions are regionally located and have specialised knowledge of local market conditions);

3 by product specialism (where divisions, usually within multi-product companies, have detailed knowledge of their particular product area);

4 by customer focus (where the company orientates itself by divisions dedicated to serving particular customer types, for example retail customers, industrial customers).

At first glance this may appear similar to a decentralised organisation but the corporate headquarters (HQ) treats each division in much the same as they would for an SBU. Also, the HQ will contain functional departments, such as Planning, HRM and Finance to support the divisions and each HQ department may have a degree of control over their respective functional areas (Figure 21.3).

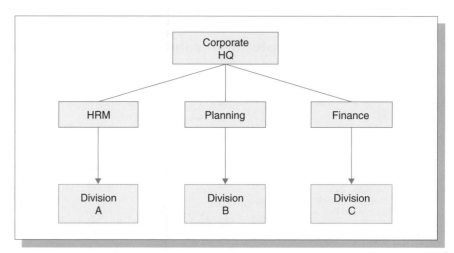

Figure 21.3
Example of a divisionalised organisation.

Advantages of divisionalised organisations

- A uniform approach to managing activities can be taken with functional support from HQ.
- Each division can deliver discrete operations.
- Clearly defined areas of responsibility.

Disadvantages of divisionalised organisations

- Functional control from HQ may prevent the development of appropriate processes suited to local conditions.
- Individual divisions may operate in a 'maverick' style which could be counter the corporate aims and objectives.

21.7 Models of organisation structure

When we examine the manner in which organisations arrange themselves internally, we are necessarily doing so in fairly general terms. This is because each organisation will assume a structure unique to itself in order for it to optimally operate within its environment. The way in which it organises its line and staff employees, its usual span of control and the extent to which it is decentralised, will all have an important influence on the actual structure.

Whilst it is true that there are as many different organisational structures as there are organisations, our task in studying this area is to look for groupings and general types which are most common, and that will help us to understand the principles involved.

One of the commonest ways of dividing structures is as follows:

- those based on hierarchical relationships;
- those which are not.

The key distinction between them is the extent to which the organisation observes the principle of the *unity of command.*

The unity of command

This is a very simple principle which states simply that any given person in an organisation should report upwards to only one superior or, 'one person, one boss'. To some people, this may appear a rather obvious and common-sense approach to management, but as we shall see, it is not universally observed.

Unity of command offers some key advantages. The most obvious of these is that it avoids any confusion on the part of the subordinate as to who to take orders from. Its disadvantages include the possibility that 'taking orders' from one boss may extinguish the subordinate's flair and creativity. The lack of observance of the principle of unity of command is the basis of non-hierarchical organisational structures.

Structure: the 'shape' of a business

The structure of an organisation indicates the 'shape' of the business, and is often described in terms of 'height', 'width' or complexity.

Height refers to the *number of layers* that exist within the structure. The guide to how high an organisational structure should be depends upon the complexity of the tasks that a proposed strategy entails. A small, single-site manufacture will typically be involved in competing in one industry, sometimes with a single product type. This scenario is much less complex than a multinational chemical company that competes in many national markets, in several product types and with a high dependency on research and legal regulations. Essentially, height facilitates the engagement of specialist managers in the middle of an organisation who can oversee and direct its many and varied activities. Not all organisations have this requirement and it would be more appropriate for such organisations to have a flatter structure.

Tall and short structures

Tall structures, involving more layers of specialist managers, enable the organisation to co-ordinate a wider range of activities across different product and market sectors. It is more difficult for senior management to control and is more expensive in terms of management overhead costs (Figure 21.4).

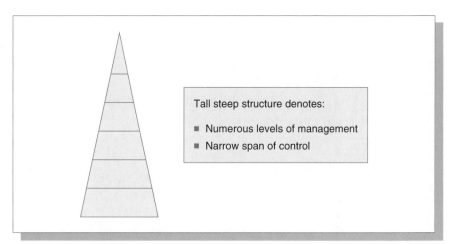

Figure 21.4
Example of a tall
steep structure.

Short structures involve fewer management layers, enabling a greater degree of senior management control, and are economical to operate.

Traditionally short structures were seen as most suitable for smaller organisations engaged in few products or market sectors, but the drive for cost efficiencies, facilitated by technological advances in recent years, has seen significant changes in the number of layers of management, even in the world's largest companies. The term '*de-layering*' has become a permanent addition to the manager's vocabulary, and flatter organisations are seen to encourage greater teamwork, co-operation and customer orientation (Figure 21.5).

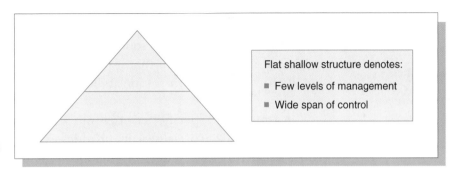

Figure 21.5
Example of a flat
shallow structure.

Hierarchical structures

The basis of the different forms of hierarchical structures is the strict observance of the principle of the unity of command. A line of command can consequently be traced from all members up (or down) through the ranks of the organisation to or from the chief executive or chairman. Members are usually divided into divisions or departments which are charged with a certain area of responsibility.

The various forms of hierarchical structure are distinguished from each other according to how the parts of the organisation are separated. The most common forms are:

- organisation by specialism (functional structure);
- organisation by geographical concentration (geographical structure);
- organisation by customer focus (customer structure);
- organisation by product type (product structure).

Each type of structure shares the same generalised 'shape' (see Figure 21.6). The general form is sometimes referred to as an 'M-form' structure, owing to its supposed similarity to the shape of the letter.

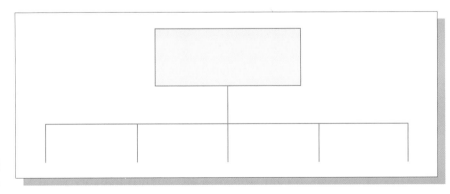

Figure 21.6
'M-form' structure.

Functional structure

A *functional* structure closely follows the 'classical' school of thought in organisational structure in that it provides the first steps in determining the formality of roles, responsibilities, control and co-ordination of activities.

The grouping of specific activities into separate departments, on the basis of technical or specialist skills, provides scope for economies of scale and is a structure well suited to companies with narrow product ranges.

Specialists are typically divided into five key functional areas:

- finance and accountancy;
- marketing and sales;
- human resources;
- technical (e.g. research and development, engineering);
- operations (e.g. manufacturing).

Functional structures tend to be employed by organisations based on a single site, such as a small to medium sized companies or single-site subsidiaries of larger organisations. It is a structure well suited for businesses engaged in manufacturing. On the negative side, the inflexible nature of such a structure creates difficulties when trying to trade different products and services in different markets. Also, as an organisation grows in size and complexity, there can be considerable problems co-ordinating the different functions.

Geographical structure

Geographical structure is appropriate when an organisation needs primarily to provide a local coverage of all of its functions to a specific region of the country or the world. Large multinationals frequently structure themselves in this way to facilitate a faster and more regionally appropriate response to customer needs. It may be, for example, that a large multinational has a division which concentrates on North America, another on Europe, another on East Asia, and so on.

Smaller companies may use the idea of geographical structure on a less grand scale. It may be the case, for example, that a UK-based company operates regional offices as a basis for sales activity and product distribution. On this scale, the company may have an office to cover Scotland, another for the South East, another for the Midlands, and so on.

Geographical structure offers the advantage of keeping the organisation near to its customers and in doing so, providing the 'feel' of a local company even although it may be based far away. It also means that managers based in the geographical regions will be nearer to the customers to hear what they want to buy and to design and distribute products accordingly. As a result, such structures usually represent decentralised activities with senior functional managers at HQ who provide direction and support for the local managers.

Geographical markets clearly differ in their tastes and preferences and this structure provides for a local response to such variations.

Customer-based structure

A customer-based structure is similar in philosophy to a geographical structure in that it recognises that the organisation must structure itself to meet the needs of specific customer groups. Again, this type of approach tends to be more appropriate for larger concerns, although smaller companies often operate it in part.

When the customer base serviced by a company is broad and it comprises several different customer types, this structure offers some advantages. It is self evident that retail customers (i.e. the public) require a different approach to industrial customers. Accordingly, some organisations operate separate divisions to service each customer segment, for example retail, industrial, local government, etc. Larger personal computer companies may find such a structure to be useful where one division may service business customers, other universities and educational establishments, other retailers, other mail-order customers, and so on. The advantage of such a structure is that each type of customer is catered for on his or her particular terms.

Product-based structure

Product-based structures are suitable for companies that operate within several different product areas (i.e. different product types) where each area requires some degree of specialisation in its management. It is usually the case that expertise is not very transferable from one product type to another, so managers remain as specialists in their area; within their own product-based division.

This type of structure is in evidence in larger chemical companies. Many large chemical companies are involved in several types of chemical which each require a high degree of specialist skill in research, selling and strategy. Companies like the German company Hoechst or the UK's ICI are primarily structured in this way. Within their broad chemical expertise are the various specialities (separate divisions), such as plastics, pharmaceuticals, agro-chemicals, intermediates, etc. It is quite possible for a research chemist or a salesperson to be very good at plastics but to know nothing about pharmaceuticals; hence the wisdom of the product-based structure.

Non-hierarchical structures

We have already learned that some organisations do not observe the principle of the unity of command in such a strict way as hierarchically structured organisations. The thinking behind non-hierarchical structures is to 'free' employees from the rigidity of reporting to one boss to facilitate a more creative and flexible approach to work. The most common form of non-hierarchical structure is the *matrix structure.*

Matrix structure

A matrix structure is actually something of a hybrid (see below), in that it contains both an approximate hierarchy and a strong non-hierarchical element. Employees will usually have a nominal 'boss', but the bulk of their time at work will be spent in cross-functional teams. In the team-working, employees work closely with a team leader who is not their line manager and in this respect, they can be said to have two people to whom they 'report'. Some more complex matrix structures involve employees working in several teams at once, thus 'confusing' reporting lines even more.

This potential confusion is the reason why some businesses have elected not to adopt a matrix structure. James Ross, Former Chief Executive of the multinational telecommunications company, Cable and Wireless, has said:

> 'We rejected matrix management, if by [that] you mean that every person has two bosses ... I have operated within that sort of a system and it is theoretically perfect. Practically, it is expensive ... It leads to slow decision-making and confusion of accountability'.

Matrix structures are, however, useful in organisations that must carry out a range of relatively diverse tasks and which require staff to be especially flexible. It would rarely be employed in small or simple businesses whose tasks were mainly repetitive and predictable. The cross-functional teams in a matrix structure are typically short to medium term in their constitution, often formed and then reformed according to the project needs of the organisation. Accordingly, staff will often end up working alongside a larger number of colleagues than in purely hierarchical structures.

When shown diagrammatically, matrix structures are usually shown as a 'net' of interconnecting lines of reporting (Figure 21.7). Such a representation is necessarily oversimplified as it implies that any given employee only has two reporting lines: one to his nominally hierarchical line manager and one to a team leader. In practice, an employee may report to more than one team leader – a state that cannot be shown on a net diagram.

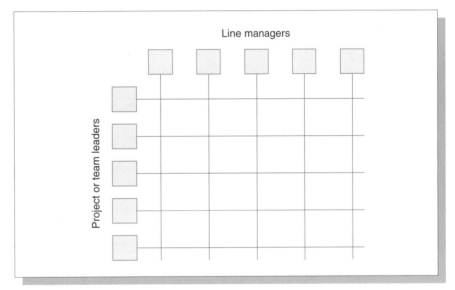

Figure 21.7
The matrix
structure.

Matrix structures are found in many organisational contexts. An example close to home for many readers is the structure of some university business schools. Academic staff are based in specialised divisions, such as management, marketing, accountancy, human resources and so on. Within the division, lecturers have a line manager called a division leader. From the division, lecturers are appointed to work in course teams alongside specialists from other divisions and in doing so, have an additional reporting line to the course leader. This means that in practice, staff often see more of the course leader and other lecturers on the course than they do of their own line manager (the division leader). As lecturers teach on several courses, the cross-functional team (actually a cross-divisional team) become a 'second home' to the lecturers involved. The composition of each course team changes at the beginning of each academic year as staff are shuffled as division leaders see fit. A typical business school matrix structure is (imperfectly) represented in Figure 21.8.

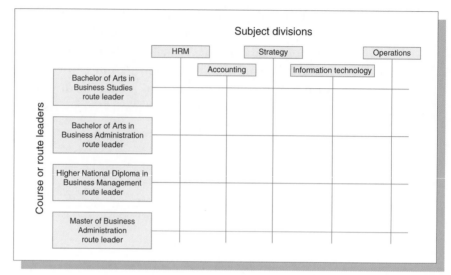

Figure 21.8
Example of a matrix structure in a university business school.

Matrix 'type' structures can also feature in otherwise hierarchically structured organisations. On occasions and to meet a specific project objective, staff are seconded to project teams which involve staff from a range of specialisms. A major chemical company recently set up a team of specialists to look into the possibility of setting up a particular set of operational philosophies called world-class manufacturing. The team comprised staff seconded from their respective departments for a period of 1 year, each of whom possessed knowledge important to the team: a scientist, an accountant, an operations manager and a human resources manager.

Hybrid structure

When we consider the distinctions we have discussed above, we should be aware that it is quite possible for more than one to be evident in an organisation. We have already seen that an otherwise hierarchical organisation can use elements of matrix management in their structures. Similarly, hierarchical structures can use more than one of the 'types' (product, functional, etc.) within the total corporate structure. Figure 21.9 shows how this may be the case for a typical large business operating in several geographical regions and selling more than one product type.

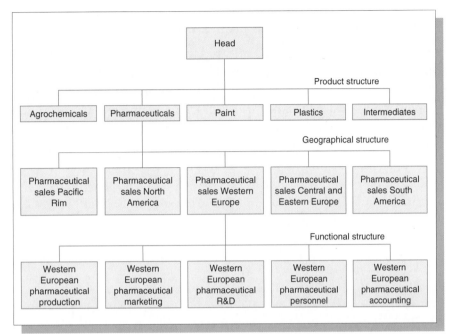

Figure 21.9
Example of a hybrid organisational structure.

21.8 Holding company structures

The head office of a holding company is usually relatively small compared to the size of the rest of the company. It will be staffed by the group's senior directors, accountants, strategists and often, legal people (Figure 21.10).

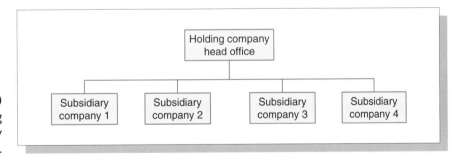

Figure 21.10
Typical holding company structures.

The way in which subsidiaries fit into the group and the fact that they are kept quite separate from other group companies means that they can be excised and sold with no effects on any other company in the group. Similarly, new acquisitions can be 'tagged on' to the structure.

Scottish & Newcastle plc:[7] a typical holding company structure

Scottish & Newcastle (S&N) plc is a large company that operates through directly owned brewing subsidiaries in the UK, France, Belgium and Finland, and owns 50% of a joint venture with Carlsberg Breweries covering Russia, Ukraine, the Baltic Countries, Lithuania and Kazakhstan. Across all these businesses, its international brand exports business and functions. S&N employs *ca.* 20,000 people. In some high-growth markets S&N has also entered into partnerships with local companies, either by taking strategic stakes or participating in joint ventures. The group has three divisions: *beer*, operating a number of breweries in the UK, Eire, Sweden, Belgium, South Africa and China; *retail* with a chain of public houses in the UK and *leisure* with holiday centres, hotels and children's activity centres (Figure 21.11).

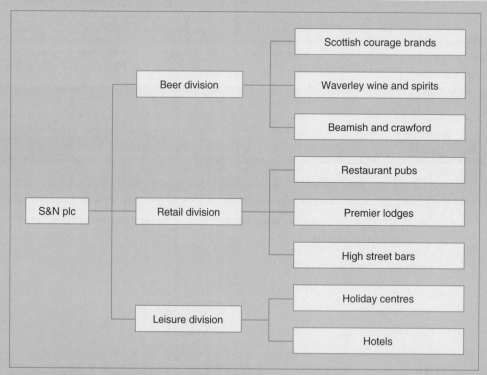

Figure 21.11
Structure of S&N plc at December 2003.

The composition of S&N is fluid and dynamic dependent on the strategic direction of the company as witnessed, for example, by the sale of its Center Parcs holiday business, Pontin's holiday centres and the sale of the Theakston brewery and some 1400 pubs in the UK during 2003, while acquiring HP Bulmer – the Hereford based cider maker and developing a new hotel in Swansea.

Why adopt a holding company structure?

There are several reasons for adopting a holding company structure:

- By having a business that has interests in more than one product and market sector, the holding company is said to have a *broader portfolio* of business interests. A business that only operates in one sector, say a paint company is vulnerable if there is a drop in the paint market. For a company which owns businesses in many sectors, a drop-off in one sector will offer a lesser threat to the group as a whole. Spreading opportunity and risk is this way is one of the strategic objectives of a holding company.

- The fact that subsidiaries are kept as separate businesses by the parent (i.e. they are not all brought together under one 'roof') *the parent can easily dispose of or acquire companies*. The emphasis of the group can be quickly adjusted by buying or selling companies as market conditions dictate.

- The control of many companies from a single head office provides the parent with a *ready-made decentralised structure*. By giving the management of each subsidiary a certain degree of autonomy, the parent can benefit from the company without committing parent management time to the company.

- The value to shareholders of the subsidiary company can be increased by the investment of parent company management skills to its operation. This is not only beneficial to the parent's shareholders but also the employees of the subsidiary.

21.9 The flexible firm

The *flexible firm* is a term used to describe an organisation that has a loose-knit structure that is capable of adaptation to allow fast response to new and changing customer and market place requirements. Employees in such an organisation are expected to adopt *multi-skilled* roles, and are trained to perform a variety of tasks. They are therefore capable of moving between different functions, as the situation demands.

Core-periphery organisations

Recent trends in the utilisation of labour resources have seen organisations '*down-sizing*' their payrolls to a *core* of permanent employees who execute the fundamental activities of the organisation. This allows the organisation flexibility in managing fluctuations in its labour requirements by hiring casual, part-time or contract workers on an ad hoc basis.

'Shamrock' organisations

Charles Handy used the term '*shamrock*'[8] to describe a '*core-periphery*' arrangement in which an organisation utilises its labour resources in three elements: each denoted as the leaf of a shamrock. Firstly there is the *core* of permanent professionals, technicians or managers who take their identity and purpose from their work and, in effect, 'are the organisation'. Secondly there is '*contractual fringe*' that is comprised of self-employed professionals or technicians (perhaps ex-employees) who are hired by the organisation to perform their specialist tasks and thirdly there is the '*flexible workforce*' who carries out temporary or part-time work.

Organisation charts

The organisation chart is a generalised schematic representation of the formal structure of an organisation that provides an illustration of the formal reporting relationships and allocation of work between functions. The presentational styles of charts vary from organisation to organisation, particularly in the degree of detail provided, but the basic elements of a practical chart will include the following:

- *Chain of command*: clear lines of the relationship of authority and responsibility, linking the relevant positions and shown in boxes on the chart.
- *Unity of command*: the single flow of authority down the hierarchical pyramid.
- *Span of management*: the number of direct reports per manager.
- *Departmentalisation*: the division and grouping of activities, with functional relationships identified.

Question 21.1

What are the difficulties in creating and maintaining a truly representative organisation chart?

Assignment 21.1

Buildatronic plc manufactures and assembles products for the electronics industry. It was founded 25 years ago and has grown from a family owned concern to its current plc status with a workforce of almost 1000 employees.

The company has traditionally been organised hierarchically according to function, which suited its original batch manufacture style of production. However, the major source of profit growth over the last 5 years has been as a direct result of diversifying and adding to the product range. The company has been moving from high volume, low profit margin products to more sophisticated low volume; high profit margin customised 'total solution contracts'. This, in turn, has dramatically changed their traditional customer base of small to medium enterprises (SMEs) in the local area to include major conglomerates throughout the UK.

On the downside, the success with these types of contracts in a highly competitive market, has been putting considerable strain on the operations department, where delivery dates for routine batch orders are now regularly late and employee relations have deteriorated in recent months.

Nevertheless, the quality of their products and service at the top end of the range has been attracting interest from overseas and the Chief Executive Officer (CEO) is keen to develop export trade, particularly in the emerging markets of Eastern Europe. Discussions have already taken place regarding the establishment of a manufacturing presence in one or more countries.

The CEO is aware that the traditional structure is proving to be a hindrance and, after attending a management seminar, believes that inter-functional co-operation could be greatly improved by the implementation of a partial matrix structure in the organisation. The main argument is that a matrix organisation and cross-functional team-working would provide flexibility and enhanced performance to the organisation.

The senior management team are divided in their support for such a change and some alternatives views have been expressed. The CEO has therefore decided to seek the expert services of an external consultant, and in that role, you are asked to prepare a report that addresses the following issues:

- The limitations of the existing hierarchical structure.
- The advantages and disadvantages of a matrix structure.
- How might they gain some of the benefits of a matrix structure without fully restructuring the organisation?
- Should consideration be given to adopting any other forms of structure? For example, geographical.

References

1   Taylor, F.W. (1998). *The Principles of Scientific Management.* Toronto: Dover.

2   Weber. (1964). *The Theory of Social and Economic Organisation.* USA: Macmillan.

3   Lawrence, P.R. and Lorsch, J.W. (1969). *Organisation and Environment.* USA: RD Irwin.

4   Minzberg, H. (1979). *The Structuring of Organisations – a Synthesis of the Research.* London: Prentice-Hall.

5   Graicunas, V.A. 2004. In: Cole, G.A. (ed.). *Management Theory and Practice,* 6th edn. London: Thomson.

6   Urwick, L.F. (1955). *The Elements of Administration.* London: Pitman.

7   www.scottish-newcastle.com (accessed 12/12/04).

8   Handy, C. (1989). *The Age of Unreason.* London: Business Books.

Further reading

Armstrong, M. (1999). *Managing Activities.* London: CIPD.

Campbell, D., Stonehouse, G. and Houston, B. (2001). *Business Strategy an Introduction.* Oxford: Butterworth Heinemann.

Chandler, A.D. (1962). *Strategy and Structure.* Boston, MA: MIT Press.

Cole, G.A. (2004). *Management Theory and Practice,* 6th edn. London: Thomson.

Mullins, L.J. (2005). *Management and Organisational Behaviour,* 7th ed. London: Prentice-Hall.

CHAPTER 22

Organisation culture: leadership, power and control

Learning objectives

After studying this chapter, students should be able to describe:

- the things that influence activity inside an organisation;
- the nature of power, influence, authority and responsibility;
- the nature and types of leadership in organisations;
- the principle of control and the nature of control in organisations;
- the nature and meaning of corporate culture;
- the determination of culture and its importance in organisations;
- the essentials of Charles Handy's culture typologies.

22.1 The influences on activity inside an organisation

Why do people in an organisation act and think in the way that they do? Activity in organisations varies enormously. In some organisations, people rush around under continual stress whilst in others; the pace of life is much more relaxed. Compare for example, the nature of work in your local fast-food retailer (e.g. *KFC* or *Burger King*) with the academic staff of a university. In the fast-food outlet, staff are trained in a few essential skills, they tend to engage in mainly repetitive tasks and they work within strictly defined limits. In the university, staff have a broader range of skills, their job involves a great diversity of experiences and their work is interpreted, with equal legitimacy, in a wide range of differing approaches.

Such a contrast in peoples' experience of work depends in large part on four features of the organisation:

1 the nature of power and authority;
2 the nature of leadership employed;
3 the types of control;
4 the forms of corporate culture prevalent within it.

These features of an organisation are inextricably linked to each other in that they partly determine each other.

22.2 Power and authority in organisations

Power, influence and authority

In attempting to define the term power, it may be helpful to look at what it is not. Power is not the same as authority:

- Power is a person's *ability* to do or act, for example to allocate resources or to control situations.
- Influence is the process of *exercising* power.
- Authority is a person's legitimate right to influence others.

We can see that there may well be a difference between a person having the ability to influence and their having a right to do so. *Ability* to influence can occur in any moral or organisational context, whereas a *legitimate right* tends to be within the context of a moral or legal framework. Authority, therefore is invested in a person by a superior body, be that the state, an organisation or God. We accept the authority of a judge in a court of law because he or she has the authority of the state – a judge has the right, on behalf of the state to cast judgement upon you. Conversely, we would probably accept the power of a maniacal criminal wielding a gun in a dark back-alley – not because of his legitimate right to control you (he has no such right), but because of his there-and-then ability (i.e. power derived from the possession of a gun).

Of course in one respect, our agreement to obey a person may result from either power or authority (or both) and it is here that the demarcation lines between the two can become blurred. We might readily appreciate, for example that a policeman has authority and a terrorist exercises power, but what is the source of the influence of a trade-union leader over an employer or a religious cult leader over some gullible followers? It is here that we must introduce the concept of responsibility.

Acceptance of authority

Chester Barnard (1938)[1] stated that there are least three aspects to authority: *legitimacy, credibility and position.* A command is legitimate if it stems from a proper position in the hierarchy. However, position can be abused and, if it is, that authority loses credibility. Even if a command is legitimate from a credible source, it will only be obeyed if it is understood and seen as *compatible* with the organisation's interests and not incompatible with the receiver's personal interests or values. It also has to be within the *competence* and *capacity* of the person receiving the command.

Authority and responsibility

We have seen that authority is a person's right, from a legitimate source, to influence others. In practice, authority can be distinguished from power as the former is matched with an equal degree of responsibility. If authority is a person's legitimate right to influence or command others, responsibility is the person's degree of accountability or answerability for that over which they have authority. It is possible for authority and responsibility to be either matched or mis-matched:

- Responsibility matches authority when the person is accountable for precisely the area over which he or she has authority.
- Responsibility and authority are mis-matched when one of two situations exists:
  - A person has a greater responsibility than he or she has authority over. This is unfair to the manager who will be held accountable for things outside the area over which he or she has control.
  - A person has a greater authority than he or she has responsibility for, this is unfair to the subordinates and may result in unrestrained power and overbearing authoritarianism.

The principle of matching authority and responsibility has a number of important implications. Personnel professionals use the principle when designing jobs and allocating people to positions of responsibility. It is used as a basis for personnel appraisal as people are assessed according to their degree of authority and responsibility. If both are matched, then an individual charged with an area of responsibility *and* given the appropriate authority may be either:

- praised for the favourable accomplishments of the charge or
- penalised for the unfavourable performance of the charge.

Either way, when authority and responsibility are balanced or matched, the manager cannot say 'don't blame me; I didn't have the authority to manage the area of responsibility you allocated to me'. This principle of accountability is carried across to many other areas of life, including politics. A senior politician, such as the prime minister is invested with a great deal of authority, and accordingly, a great deal of responsibility. In consequence, if the prime minister's government fails to perform well, he or she can be voted out of office and replaced.

Types of power

Both power and authority have in common the ability to influence the behaviour of others. In this section, we leave behind our discussion of the legitimacy of such ability and turn to the generic sources of a person's ability to influence another. This ability hinges upon the question; what makes one person obey another?

Different authors have used different names to describe the types of power and authority. We shall consider two complementary classifications.

J.K. Galbraith

Prof. *John Kenneth Galbraith* (1985),[2] the noted American economist and political thinker suggested that power can arise from three sources and proposed names to describe each one:

- *Condign power* is influence exerted over another by offering an unpleasant alternative to obedience. This might take the form of 'perform this task or else...', or 'if you do not do this, you will be punished'. Of course, the alternative to obedience need not necessarily be punishment; it might be withdrawal of privileges, social ostracism, dismissal or banishment. The qualification for exercising power is access to the means of punishment.

- *Compensatory power*, as its name suggests, is the opposite of condign power. This type of power works by offering a reward for obedience. If condign power is the stick, then this is the carrot. It might take the form, 'if you perform this task, I will give you…' In order to wield compensatory power, one must have access to the means of reward, such as money, privileges or social status.
- *Conditioned power* is influence exerted upon people who have been previously conditioned to obey. This type of obedience (e.g. to conform to norms of societal behaviour), occurs because people have, by their previous experiences and taught values, come to accept certain authorities without question. A leader who employs this means of power must appeal to people's sense of conditioning and need not use condign or compensatory methods of control.

Example of power and legitimate authority

The Managing Director of a large organisation has considerable power and influence over the direction of the organisation and its employees. For example, he or she is able to exercise various types of powers, such as condign power where employees who do not conform to the prescribed standards, can be disciplined in a variety of ways from reprimands through to dismissal from the company.

Also, the use of compensatory power is intended to demonstrate that, by conforming to work expectations, employees can benefit from monetary compensation (e.g. salary increases, bonuses or promotions).

Conditioned power also has a significant bearing in that employees with a *work ethic* background will accept that they have a duty to work and obey legitimate orders.

Such a complex set of compelling factors is not at all uncommon in organisational life – very few managers or leaders lean on just one type of power.

The authority to exercise *legitimate power*, through the issuing of orders and expectation of obedience, is relative to organisational rank. For example, take the case of a chief executive who has had the ultimate power in a particular organisation. In that formal position as an employee of the organisation that individual will have had extensive legitimate powers, such as authorising multi-million pound transactions, hiring, promoting and dismissing employees. However, once formal ties with the organisation whatsoever, say by retirement or resignation, that individual will no longer have any organisational power or authority whatsoever. He or she may not even be able to enter the office building again without security clearance by current employees.

A. Etzioni

A similar and complementary view of types of power is given by *Etzioni* (1975)[3] – a model which, it may be argued, is simpler in its approach than Galbraith's. It is a model which does not recognise influence arising from a person's preconditioning:

- *Coercive power* is power that relies upon the use of threats, of unpleasant sanctions or force. In other words this is the use of physical or tangible power as the prime motivational instrument to achieve objectives. In this respect, it is similar to what Galbraith calls condign power.
- *Remunerative power* involves gaining influence through the manipulation of rewards and other material resources – approximately equivalent to Galbraith's compensatory power. In the workplace this can be translated as *reward power* with pay or non-pay incentives for contributions.
- *Normative power* is compensatory in nature but relies upon intangible rewards rather than material benefits. Examples of such rewards include the conferment of esteem, status and prestige. Galbraith would include this as a type of compensatory power.

Negative power

This is the ability to stop things happening and is usually manifest in organisations with low morale or incongruent employee and organisational goals. For example, employees who mistrust their managers or feel a sense of grievance with certain 'legitimate' management actions may decide to react negatively by a variety of means, such as non-cooperation or deliberate sabotage.

22.3 Leadership in organisations

What is leadership?

Leadership is an interpersonal influence directed toward the achievement of a goal or goals. *Kevin Freiberg* (2001),[4] describes leadership as a dynamic relationship based on mutual influence and common purpose between leaders and collaborators in which both are moved to higher levels of motivation and moral development. This definition is significant in that it identifies three vital elements of leadership: *relationship* which is the connection between people, *mutual* which means shared in common and *collaborators* who co-operate or work together.

At its simplest, leadership is the quality evident in a leader. A leader can be defined as *an individual who knows where he or she is going and is able to persuade others to go along as well.* There are consequently two dimensions to leadership; the *conceptual* and the *interpersonal*. It follows of course, from this definition that a person with just clear objectives but no abilities to take others is not a leader. The same can be said for someone with powers of persuasion but no objectives for the followers.

The *conceptual* qualities in a leader are those which enable him or her to identify and resolve clear objectives and a route to accomplish the objectives. Of course the objective in mind may be in any sphere of life; in politics, in business, in matters of religion or in one of many other areas. Furthermore, the objective may vary from a great long-term cause to a trifling short-term ploy. Winston Churchill identified clear objectives during the Second World War whilst the biggest boy in a gang of thugs may generate clear objectives regarding aggression towards rival football fans.

The *interpersonal* aspect of leadership is that quality that persuades others to adopt the same objectives as the leader and to follow him or her towards them. We have already identified the types of power that can be used to facilitate this compliance. Some leaders bring about compliance by promising reward once the objective is accomplished, others, punishment for failure to follow and yet others rely on followers' preconditioning to follow. The effects are more or less the same – people following a leader.

Leadership styles

We find leaders in several contexts in and around organisations. We would obviously expect the senior management to lead the staff in the strategic directions identified for the organisation, but leaders are found at lower levels as well. Managers who oversee the work of a shift in the factory or the research in a laboratory are leaders, as are shop stewards and other trade union officials. However, the way in which each of these leaders actually leads will differ, and for good reasons. Clearly, the style of leadership depends in large part on the personality of the leader but in addition, leadership style will be influenced by the nature of the followers and the context of the leader–follower relationship. As in most things in business, we cannot say that any particular style is right or wrong (or good or bad); it is more a case of appropriate or inappropriate in its specific context.

Leadership styles are often shown in the simplified form of a complex continuum based upon the work of Tannenbaum and Schmidt[5] (Figure 22.1).

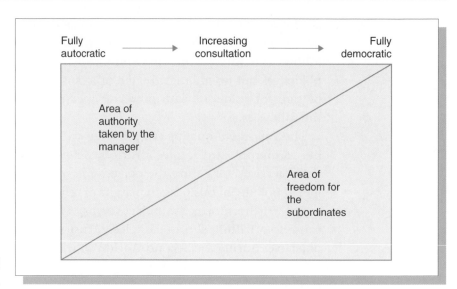

Figure 22.1
Management and
leadership styles.

The two extremes of the continuum are as follows:

■ Fully autocratic leadership is the style in which the leader makes
a decision with no consultation at all with those affected by the
decision and announces it as a *fait accompli* to the followers.

■ Fully participative or democratic leadership is the style demonstrated by a leader fully involving the followers in the making
of a decision. The team members are encouraged to 'chip-in'
to the debate and the leader acts entirely upon the consensus
of the group.

Between the two extremes are any numbers of variations. Leaders tend
to the autocratic end of the continuum when there is a high *power distance* between leader and follower, when, typically, the followers' opinions
are likely to be unfavourable to the decision (such as the leadership of
prison wardens over prisoners). More democratic and participative leadership occurs in situations with a lower power distance when, typically,
the followers' views are seen as being intrinsically valuable or when their
willing agreement is essential once the decision is taken.

Definition: power distance

This is a term attributed to *Hickson and Pugh* (1995),[6] both British writers on organisations.
They use the term to describe 'how removed subordinates feel from superiors in a social
meaning of the word "distance". In a high power distance culture, inequality is accepted…
in a low power distance culture, inequalities and overt status symbols are minimised and
subordinates expect to be consulted and to share decisions with approachable managers'.

Types of leader

Leaders, as we have seen, are in evidence in many areas of life. A working distinction between the various types rests upon the context of the leadership and the nature of the leader. There are five general types.

Charisma originated in theology referring to a talent given by God as a free gift or favour was first used to describe political leadership by Max Weber (1964).[7] The *Charismatic leader's* influence arises principally from the leader's personal charisma or personality. This is typically an unusual combination of attractive personal qualities or traits. Such charisma may include outstanding oratorical or literary skills, high intellect, a powerful 'presence', a pleasing appearance and many others. Phenomena associated with such leadership include:

- followers full-heartedly, perhaps blindly, trust the correctness of the leader's beliefs;
- followers feel affection and willingly obey the leader;
- followers feel an emotional involvement in the mission into which they are led.

A charismatic leader can be morally good or evil and some historical figures that have been considered as charismatic include Adolf Hitler, Martin Luther King and John F. Kennedy.

The *traditional* leader assumes a leadership position due to birth. This category thus includes monarchs, tribal chiefs and, in some cases, managers in long-standing family businesses. Early leadership theories were content theories that focused on 'what' is an effective leader not on 'how' to effectively lead. This *trait approach* assumes that certain physical, social and personal characteristics are inherent in leaders, and therefore sets of traits and characteristics can used to identify the right people to become leaders. For example, *physical* traits may include features, such as height, age and athleticism, with *social* features including being educated at the 'right' school, while *personality* traits may include assertiveness, self-confidence and emotional stability. *Task-related* characteristics include initiative, results-oriented and acceptance of authority. Trait theory has not been able to identify a set of traits that will consistently distinguish leaders from followers and although it posits key traits for successful leaders it makes no judgement as to whether these traits are inherent to individuals or whether they can be developed through education and training.

Situational leadership is the ability to adapt leadership style to match the demands of the situation and/or people. Dr Paul Hersey and Ken Blanchard[8] identified four styles for situational leadership as

Telling, Selling, Participating and Delegating, and described situational leadership as based upon interplay between *task behaviour, relationship behaviour* and *follower readiness*:

- *Task behaviour*: the extent to which the leader tells people what to do, how to do it, when to do it, where to do it and who's to do it.
- *Relationship behaviour*: the extent to which the leader *communicates, listens, clarifies, supports or facilitates*.
- *Follower readiness*: the extent to which the person being led is confident, motivated and competent to deliver the task in hand.

In certain situations individuals might assume a leadership role when a unique set of circumstances thrust him or her to the fore. Examples might include an otherwise ordinary person who takes command in the chaos following a road accident or a fire. Situational leaders tend to take command when, for some reason, a vacuum is left in the usual leadership structure – perhaps in times of crisis or when a specific skill is required, such as first aid or some specialist technical knowledge. It follows that situational leaders may only lead for a relatively short period of time, whilst the specific circumstances persist.

Contingency theories state that successful leaders must be able to identify clues in an environment and adapt their leader behaviour to meet the needs of their followers and of the particular situation. Even with good diagnostic skills, leaders may not be effective unless they can adapt their leadership style to meet the demands of their environment. Fred E. Fiedler's *contingency theory*[9] postulates that there is no best way for managers to lead. Situations will create different leadership style requirements for a manager. The solution to a managerial situation is contingent on the factors that impinge on the situation. For example, in a highly routine (*mechanistic*) environment where repetitive tasks are the norm, a certain leadership style may result the best performance but the same leadership style may not work in a very dynamic environment.

Action centred leadership

John Adair developed his *three circles*[10] approach to leadership at the Royal Military Academy at Sandhurst during the 1970s. He found that effective leaders pay attention to three areas of need for members of the team: those relating to the task, to the team itself and to individual members of the team (Figure 22.2).

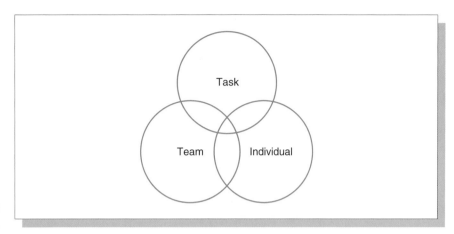

Figure 22.2
Three circles model.

At any time, the emphasis on each circle may vary, but all are inter-dependent and so the leader must watch all three:

- *Task needs* include setting a clear goal and objectives, and organisation and management of the process.
- *Team needs* are things like effective interaction, support, shared work and communication within the team and with other teams.
- *Individual needs* will vary from person to person, but the effective leader will pay attention to, and deal with, how each person is behaving and feeling.

Adair's model of *action centred leadership* (ACL) is important as it looks at effective leadership from the point of view of those being led. Also, because it is quite basic it is easy to understand and apply, providing a sound foundation for learning early in a leadership career.

The *appointed* leader gains his or her influence as the result of an appointment. Appointed leaders are found in bureaucratic or hierarchical organisations and their power rests upon their appointed position within the organisation. Hence, managers and supervisors in organisations are good examples of this leadership type.

The *functional* leader gains influence by intentionally adopting a form of behaviour that has subsequently made him or her a leader. It might be that an individual has observed the traits of other leaders and has reached a position of influence by emulating the same traits. A functional leader is thus in the position of leadership because of what they do rather than what they are (compare this with, e.g. the charismatic leader). Functional leaders, or those that aspire to functional leadership, are sometimes found in politics. There may be a general acceptance that political leaders dress in a certain way, speak in a certain way and 'carry themselves' in a certain way. Politicians seeking high office thus act accordingly to gain such office.

Question 22.1

Which of the above leadership types do you think best describes the following?

- Tony Blair,
- Mahatma Gandhi,
- Sir Alex Ferguson,
- Nelson Mandela,
- Margaret Thatcher,
- Sir Richard Branson.

22.4 Control in organisations

The principle of control

The notion of control pervades most parts of life, it is a far wider concept than just control in organisations. In all cases, a *control system* has four essential components (Figure 22.3):

- *Set performance standards,* the units by which the standard is measured will depend entirely upon the context of the control system.
- *Measure of actual performance* to allow the actual performance to be compared with the standard previously set.
- *Comparison of actual performance with plan* to facilitate the actual performance moving closer to the standard and eventually match it precisely.

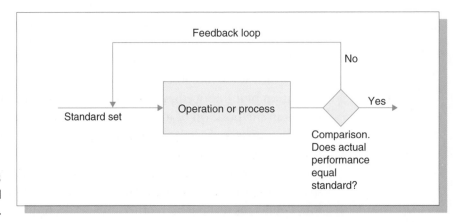

Figure 22.3
A simple control system.

      ■ *A feedback mechanism* to take action (where necessary) to move closer to the standard, or develop opportunities revealed by the data.

Forms and types of control

      ■ *Feed forward* used at the input stage of the process when managers can anticipate potential problems. For example, clearly defining specifications with suppliers to avoid quality problems with raw materials.

      ■ *Concurrent*, immediate feedback at the transformation stage of inputs to outputs.

      ■ *Feedback* provides 'after the fact' data that can be used for future planning. For example, customer reaction to products is used to ensure corrective action for future production (Figure 22.4).

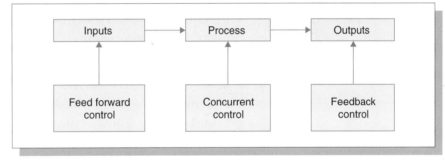

Figure 22.4
Relationships
of control forms
and types.

The nature of management control

In Chapter 1 we examined the major theories of management in organisations. All of these should be viewed essentially as attempts to gain the most effective system of control over the various activities of the organisation. In the case of *F.W. Taylor*, for example, the outputs of a man's day's work can, Taylor propounds, be *controlled* according to the conditions under which the work takes place and the reward structures put in place. This is an attempt to impose management objectives upon workers. The work of *Mayo* and his human relations theories were centred on the use of the work environment and groups to *control* operational outputs and to increase human efficiency. The work of *Henry Gantt* was centred on the *control* of sequential activities to ensure that organisational objectives could be satisfactorily met on time and within resource constraints.

The nature of control measures in an organisation will depend greatly upon the organisation's environmental situation and its culture (see later in this chapter). Some will adopt a 'tight' regime where activities are controlled by frequent checks and low deviation tolerances whereas others will favour a 'loose' control regime. Loose or 'flexible' control allows more freedom of action within set limits where work is allowed to assume certain fluidity. It is, of course, possible for both of these regimes to be present in the same organisation as different work conditions dictate.

Question 22.2

Suggest work situations where it would be most appropriate to adopt a tight control regime and some where a loose approach would be most beneficial.

The mechanisms of management control

In attempting to identify the ways in which organisational control is actually exerted, *Stewart* (1991)[11] proposes that there are three different ways:

- The first control mechanism is direct control by the use of *direct orders, direct supervision, strict rules and regulations*. This method is more acceptable where the employees are poorly skilled, during training and during times of crisis. It would not be acceptable to situations wherein the employees expected to take a part in decision-making or where a 'loose' or 'flexible' culture is most appropriate.
- Secondly, according to Stewart, control can be exercised through the use of *standardisation and specialisation*. Particularly relevant to a *bureaucratic* culture, this type of control rests upon the prerequisite that the work undertaken is of a standard nature and that employees act within predetermined standard guidelines. It can be used to effect in organisations using repetitive procedures (such as workers on a production line) or where managers have so much authority and no more. An example of this may be the limited autonomy given to a franchisee – ability to act provided he or she does not change the appearance of the shop, the nature of the product, etc.
- The third control mechanism is control through *influencing the way that individuals think about what they should do*. Such an 'intrinsic' method of control is probably the hardest to achieve but equally, it is probably the most effective. Unkindly labelled

'thought control', this method is widely used in organisations as individuals gradually acclimatise to behavioural and cultural norms wherein it is instinctively understood that certain forms of behaviour would be unacceptable.

According to *Mullins,*[12] control can be cultivated in organisations by such things as, for example:

- selective recruitment (only recruiting those who will think and act in the desired fashion);
- specific training and socialisation;
- through the use of peer pressure (peers' and colleagues' combined pressure to conform).

Again, we can readily see that each mechanism is highly context dependent; that is, the method adopted will depend upon the work being undertaken and the type of people involved.

22.5 Corporate culture

What is corporate culture?

Culture, along with the nature of control, is a key determinant of activity in business. Furthermore, the culture of an organisation is very closely linked to the control mechanisms set in place by the board of directors – they influence each other.

The culture of an organisation is easy to experience but harder to define. Consider the following:

Edgar Schein (1985)[13] described organisational culture as 'the deeper level of basic assumptions and beliefs that are shared by an organisation, that operate unconsciously and define in a basic taken-for-granted fashion an organisation's view of itself and its environment'. He believed that a distinctive culture develops as people work together and share experiences which shape their views on behaviour and expectations. A succinct and pragmatic definition of culture was offered by *Deal and Kennedy* (1982)[14] who described it as '*the way things are done around here*', while *Ralph Stacey* (1996)[15] provides a reasonably comprehensive definition as '*The culture of any group of people is that set of beliefs, customs, practices and ways of thinking that they have come to share with each other through being and working together. It is a set of assumptions people simply accept without question as they interact with each other. At the visible level the culture of a group of people takes the form of ritual behaviour, symbols, myths, stories, sounds and artefacts*'.

A number of adjectives have been used to describe culture, where each one tells only part of the story. It is the shared beliefs, the 'smell', the 'feel', the 'morale', the personality and the character of the organisation. Culture varies greatly between organisations. Some organisations are 'warm' and 'genial' whereas others are competitive, 'hard' and unfriendly. It is important that we do not become judgmental over certain types of culture – each type may be appropriate in its own organisational and environmental context.

What are the determinants of corporate culture?

The parallel between the personality of an organisation and the personality of a person is one which is of some value. The personality of an adult human is the product of a plethora of influences including his or her genetic make-up, the influences of his or her parents, teachers and peers. The desire to emulate role-models and the ethical or religious framework with which the person has been imbued also has a powerful effect.

The net effect of the various influences on an organisation similarly, over time, forges its culture. Any list would be bound to be incomplete, but following are some of the most important:

- The *philosophy of the organisation's founders* can be influential, even although the organisation may be relatively old. The lasting influence of Joseph Rowntree upon the confectionery manufacturer or a religious leader upon a sect is testimony to this.
- The *nature of the activities in the business*. The culture of a university will tangibly differ from that of a coal-mine or the floor of a heavy engineering *company*.
- The *nature of the interpersonal relationships* and the degree of camaraderie in the organisation. In some organisations, the staff find a natural rapport whereas in others, this is not the case. This is, of course, largely a function of the nature of the personalities in the organisation.
- The *management style* adopted and the types of control mechanism. We saw earlier in this chapter that some organisations adopt a 'tight' control regime and others a looser arrangement. Similarly, management style varies from a dictatorial and autocratic approach to one which is more consensual and democratic.
- Any *influences from the external environment* which can affect the employees' perceptions of their job-security or personal

economic and social outlook. In times of recession, for example, the 'feel' in an organisation will be different from that in more buoyant economic conditions.

Edgar Schein suggested that it is useful to consider organisational culture in three layers:

1   *Values*: often written down as statements about the organisation's mission or objectives, but can be vague, such as 'environmentally friendly'.
2   *Beliefs*: more specific than value statements but focused issues that people can discuss, such as not trading with certain foreign countries on ethical or moral grounds.
3   *Taken-for-granted assumptions*: the real core of an organisation's culture. They are the aspects of organisational life that people find difficult to identify and explain, and are known as the organisational *paradigm*.

The *paradigm* of an organisation is the set of assumptions held relatively in common and taken for granted in that organisation and will be manifest in norms and forms of acceptable thought and behaviour in that organisation.

British Telecommunications plc: an attempt to influence culture

British Telecommunications plc (BT) is one of the growing number of companies who attempt to proactively influence its internal culture rather than allow it to develop of its own accord. The company's five 'values' are communicated to all new employees, available on the company's intranet site and posted throughout BT premises in the prominent view of all employees.

The five values are:

■   *Trustworthy*: we do what we say we will.
■   *Helpful*: we work as one team.
■   *Inspiring*: we create new possibilities.
■   *Straightforward*: we make things clear.
■   *Heart*: we believe in what we do.

Encouragement to 'live the values' is reinforced via the company's recognition scheme whereby any employee can recommend individuals or teams for a tangible (but non-financial) award for notable behaviours that exemplify the values.

                                                                With the permission of BT

Why is culture important?

The diversity of peoples' experience at work suggests that culture does have some significant influences upon a number of facets of organisational life. Some people love their work and find that 'work is more fun than fun'. Others dread the thought of work and find every day stressful and almost intolerable. A good deal of such differences is down to culture. Culture is important because:

- It can affect the degree of employee *motivation.*
- It can affect the *staff turnover* (the rate at which individuals join and leave the organisation).
- It can affect the *morale and goodwill* of employees, which may determine the willingness of employees to 'go the extra mile' from time-to-time as required.
- The fact that culture affects motivation and morale means that it can also have an effect on *productivity and efficiency.*
- It can affect the *quality* of work produced.
- It can have an affect on *employee relations* (the relationship between workers' unions and management).
- It can affect *absenteeism and punctuality.*

Types of culture

We have already seen that each organisation has its own unique culture, but is it possible to sort types of culture into separate categories? A noted writer in the field of culture, *Charles Handy* (1989),[16] proposed that corporate cultures can be divided into four broad categories:

A *power culture* is one that is centred on a single powerful individual. The individual in question will engender his or her own personality to the organisation and, by the dictation of systems and control mechanisms will forge the organisation's culture. Whilst power cultures are common among small companies which may have a dominant owner-manager, there are also some notable examples among large organisations. Examples of this latter category include the cases of Ryanair (Michael O'Leary) and Virgin (Richard Branson). A power culture (which has a lot of influence vested in the one powerful person) is usually characterised by quick decision-making, but this same feature can render the organisation unstable if the person in question is unable to continue in service. The investment of a lot of power in one individual can also have the negative effect of poor delegation and inadequate management development.

A *role culture* is characterised by a regime in which functional specialists carry out functions according to predetermined roles. Role cultures work best in organisations which operate in relatively stable environments. Examples can be found in larger bureaucracies, such as the civil service. The organisation is comprised of many people performing specific roles which are broadly inflexible. Management's purpose in a role culture is concerned with ensuring the roles are carried out efficiently and within defined parameters which is in contrast to the often continually changing management briefs in a power culture.

A *task culture* is based upon a number of people with similar skills being drawn together. The focus of the organisation or grouping is upon a specific task or tasks, and the nature of the task can change over time. Companies with a strong emphasis on research and development (R&D) and professional accountancy practices often have evidence of a task culture. In R&D, many similarly skilled minds may come together to 'crack a certain nut' or overcome a specific problem. Task cultures occur across multi-disciplinary teams in matrix organisations where a team is charged with a project or in a refugee camp where medics, engineers and others work together in a missionary capacity.

A *person culture* is one which exists for the benefit of its members and this has a strong bearing on the 'feel' of the organisation. It is in strong evidence in professional and learned societies, in co-operatives and in communes of various sorts.

The 'artefacts' of culture

Artefacts are things that 'give away' certain features of an organisation. In archaeology, artefacts like pots, toys, tools, etc. give us information about what it was like living in a former age. A human person similarly has certain manifestations which inform observers about their personality. It may be the clothes they wear, their manner of speech, the way in which they interact with others, etc. In the same way, cultural artefacts give an indication to outsiders or newcomers of the nature of the climate inside an organisation.

The first artefact and one which is amongst the most telling are the *symbols* that the organisation uses. Whilst symbols may refer to company logos, the physical appearance of the offices, it may also be the layout of the plant. If, for example, the reception is small and grubby with the receptionist sitting behind an ancient hatch, this gives a very different signal to observers to a reception which is nicely decorated, well-lit, and altogether more welcoming. Similarly, if the R&D department is located in a series of badly maintained portacabins apart from the main plant, this gives an indication of how the organisation views research.

Secondly, *slogans and sayings* can tell us about the culture. These may be positive ones that the organisation's management seek to spread, such as the BT values statements (e.g. '*we work as one team*'), or perhaps the attitude of the workforce could be perceived as cynical or even subversive, with regular usage of sayings like '*if it was not for the customers this would be a great job*'.

The third artefact is the form or *forms of language* that are prevalent within the organisation. Just as you can tell a great deal about a person by listening to them talk, so the ways in which members of the organisation speak to each other and speak to outsiders tells us something about the organisational culture. Compare, for example, the formality of a military situation, where individuals are addressed according to their rank, to an open plan office of 'equals', where a great deal more informality will be in evidence. The latter situation may contain people known by affectionate nicknames and it will usually be the case that everybody is on 'first-name' terms with everybody else.

Fourthly, we can analyse an organisation's culture by its *rituals and routines*. Some companies observe ritualised procedures, such as sending all managers of a certain level to a conference, to an outward bound weekend or similar. It may be that people below the level in question will aspire to the particular management level and associate their presence at the ritualised occasion with 'having arrived'. Rituals also concern honouring the past and honouring longevity of service. The presentation of a gold watch after 25 years service to the organisation is one example. Employees may refer to there being so many years until they receive their gold watch – not for the value of the watch, but for what the watch says about their service to the company. Routines, as their name suggests are more mundane and frequent than the organisation's more elaborate rituals. Nevertheless, the routines observed within an organisation can tell us a great deal about its culture.

Fifthly, an important artefact is *how the culture treats newcomers* to the organisation. This parallels, on the human person level, the impression you get of a person when you first meet. Some people are visibly warm and generous whereas others appear to be more austere and 'businesslike'. A new employee, in seeking to 'find his feet' in a new job, may find the new colleagues to be open, generous and helpful. Conversely, the new employee may find them resentful at his presence and decidedly unwilling to help him or her to adjust, particularly if the new employee was appointed in preference to internal candidates.

The final major artefact of culture are the various *stories* of 'heroes and villains' in organisations that are re-iterated over the years, perhaps elevating them to mythical proportions, may be indicative of the values attributed to certain types of behaviour. For example, a 'hero' may be made of a long-serving and loyal employee ('a company person') who worked extremely long hours without complaint, and would get to work no matter the hardship of, say, extreme weather conditions or illness. This might serve to reinforce the organisation's value of the '*work ethic*'. On the other hand, stories that are told with some humour about a lazy 'villain' who knew all the work avoidance tricks in the book might indicate an environment in which such attitudes are condoned. The culture of the organisation will determine which stories are propagated and remembered long after the events in question.

Assignment 22.1

Upon the retirement of his predecessor, Jim Bean took over as the Governor of Her Majesty (HM) Prison Parkbench, a high security establishment of prisoners considered to be 'criminally insane' and of high risk to the public. Jim's background was as a senior academic at a well-known university and consequently, he was accustomed to the culture and management styles used in higher education establishments. On his first day in the governor's chair, Jim announced that he intended to manage the prisoners in the same way that he used to manage his lecturers. This meant that he would give them autonomy, freedom, trust and discretion in how they spent their time and with whom they associate. Within a month, the prisoners had taken advantage of their new freedom by dismantling their cells and by digging up the recreation field. Prison warders found the period difficult owing to their increased sense of vulnerability with the new management regime. Jim Bean was fired by the Director of the Prison Service owing to his 'highly inappropriate management style'.

You are required to do following:

- Contrast some of the features of the cultures of a prison and a university.
- Compare the leadership styles that are best suited to managing in the two types of institution.
- Describe the types of power that a prison governor might be able to exert over the prisoners.
- Explain where Jim went wrong in his management of the prison.

References

1 Barnard, C. (1938). *The Functions of the Executive.* Oxford: University Press.
2 Galbraith, J.K. (1985). *The Anatomy of Power.* London: Corgi Books.
3 Etzioni, A. (1975). *A Comparative Analysis of Complex Organisations*, 2nd edn, revised edn. New York: Free Press.

4   Freiberg, K. (2001). *Nuts! Southwest Airline's Crazy Recipe for Business and Personal Success.* London: Texere Publishing.

5   Tannenbaum , R. and Schmidt, W.H. (May/June 1973). Harvard Business Review.

6   Hickson D.J. and Pugh D.S. (1995). *Management Worldwide.* London: Penguin.

7   Weber, M. (1964). *The Theory of Social and Economic Organization.* London: Collier Macmillan.

8   Hersey, P. and Blanchard, K.H. (1972). *Management of Organisational Behaviour.* London: Prentice Hall.

9   Fiedler, F.E. (1967). *A Theory of Leadership Effectiveness.* London: McGraw-Hill.

10   Adair, J. (1979). *Action Centred Leadership.* London: Gower Publishing.

11   Stewart, R. (1991). *Managing Today and Tomorrow.* London: Macmillan.

12   Mullins, L.J. (2005). *Management and Organisational Behaviour,* 7th edn. London: FT Prentice Hall.

13   Schein, E.H. (2004). *Organizational Culture and Leadership,* 3rd edn. London: Pfeiffer Wiley.

14   Deal, T.E. and Kennedy, A.A. (1982). *Corporate Cultures.* New York: Addison Wesley.

15   Stacey, R. (1996). *Strategic Management and Organisational Dynamics,* 2nd edn. London: Pitman.

16   Handy, C.B. (1989). *The Age of Unreason.* Boston, MA: Harvard Business School Press.

Further reading

Anthony, P. (1994). *Managing Culture.* Milton Keynes: Open University Press.

Boddy, D. (2002). *Management: An Introduction.* Harlow: FT Prentice Hall.

Brown, A. (1995). *Organisational Culture.* London: Pitman.

Hofstede, G. (1997). *Cultures and Organizations.* London: McGraw-Hill.

Lukes, S. (1974). *Power: A Radical View.* London: Macmillan.

Moss Kanter, R. (1984). *The Change Masters.* London: Unwin.

Robbins, S.P. (2003). *Organizational Behaviour,* 10th edn. NJ, USA: Prentice Hall.

Taffinder, P. (1995). *The New Leaders. Styles and Strategies for Success.* London: Kogan Page.

CHAPTER 23

Change in organisations

After studying this chapter, students should be able to describe:

■ the external environmental factors that can influence change;
■ the motivations for change within organisations;
■ the types of change that take place in organisations;
■ the various attitudes to change that are evident among employees;
■ a range of models that explain how to analyse and manage change.

23.1 Motivations to change

Change has been a feature of organisational life for as long as organisations have existed, but the pace of change has accelerated to a significant extent over recent years. Changes in external environment have brought about the need for organisations to adapt their internal attitudes, strategies, structures and operations to meet the demands of new external conditions. Hence, the study of internal change has increased both in academic circles and in organisations themselves.

Reactive and proactive change

The first distinction we need to understand in this area is that of the two principal sources of impetus to change.

Reactive change is change forced upon an organisation arising from a need to react to a change in the organisation's environment. This can apply to an individual as well as an organisation, for example, you must change your lifestyle if your main source of income is suddenly reduced or discontinued. There are a number of environmental changes that can precipitate reactive change, but they usually have in common an element of necessity, of being unexpected or an element of surprise.

Proactive change, in diametric opposition to reactive change, is planned in advance, usually with a particular objective in mind. Whilst proactive change may be as an indirect consequence of changes in the environment, it is essentially change because the organisation wants, or internally feels the need to change. To relate this to the individual, you might proactively improve your educational qualifications in order to increase your job prospects.

Analysing environmental factors

Every organisation exists within its own internal environment and is influenced by its external environment. The business environment is subject to many changes and the complexity of these environmental influences upon an organisation will vary significantly from case to case. It is therefore necessary for organisations to understand how the changes in the external environment might differentially affect them. Some organisations pass from decade to decade with little change in their environments whilst others must cope with daily or hourly changes which must be addressed.

The stability/complexity grid provides a useful tool for managers to assess the nature of the organisation's environment (Figure 23.1).

Stability, in the context of this grid, refers to *how often* and *by how much* the external environment changes. In a stable environment, there is little external change from year to year whereas in an unstable situation, the environment may change significantly and often. Needless to say, an unstable environment requires more frequent internal change than a stable one.

Complexity refers to the number of potential external influences upon an organisation. In a simple environment, the organisation will have few material influences upon it. In a complex environment, it will have many possible influences which must be monitored.

The nature of the external environment will have a strong influence on the effectiveness of the organisation's management practices. For example, *mechanistic* systems with rigid vertical relationships are best suited to relatively stable environments, whereas *organic* systems, with their flexibility and horizontal networks, are more suited to dynamic

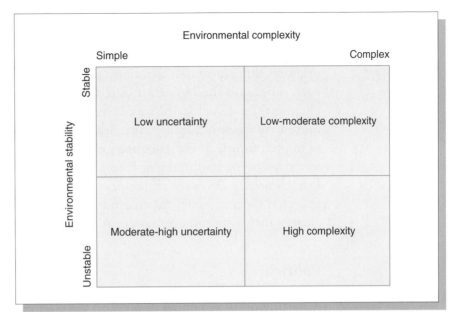

Figure 23.1
The stability/
complexity grid.

and changeable environmental conditions (see also Chapter 1). This is of particular significance in the case of organisations that experience a fundamental change of status, such as *privatisation* when former *nationalised* organisations experience new ownership, in the form of shareholders, and are exposed to competitive market conditions. The change from relatively stable to dynamic environments will necessitate radical changes to structures, practices and culture.

Question 23.1

Generate a list of organisations (including some organisations who have gone through privatisation programmes) which exist in the four broad types of environment identified in the grid in Figure 23.1.

Impetus from the external environment (PESTEL analysis)

The activities of competitors, suppliers and customers will often mean that an organisation will have to implement changes. Customers who change their requirements, competitors who merge or acquire within the industry may require an organisation to modify its structure, culture or other internal features to survive and compete.

The *PESTEL* model offers a useful analytical framework to identify and examine the environmental influences of *political, economic, sociological, technological, ecological and legal* factors on an organisation. (*Note:* Variants on this analytical framework can be found in some texts as *PEST, PESTLE* or *SLEPT* analyses). It should be emphasised that while it is useful to examine the individual elements, they have close relationships with each other and the impact of one may be the result of earlier activity elsewhere. For example, the social conditions that motivated the *suffragette* movement in early 20th century Britain that campaigned for the right of women to vote in Parliamentary elections stimulated political action which led to the required legislation. Subsequent legislation, such as *the Equal Pay Act (1970)* and *the Sex Discrimination Acts (1975 + 1986)* reflected the socio-political environment and compelled employers to change their conditions of service for female employees.

Political

A starting point in analysing political factors might be to examine the stability of the government and therefore its ability to implement its policies. In the UK, for example, the Labour party came to power in 1997 with a landslide majority and was re-elected for a second term in 2001 with another landslide majority. This followed 18 years of Conservative Government and in both instances the size of each party's majorities in the House of Commons was sufficient to ensure a longevity that enabled the respective governments to implement their polices and introduce new legislation. Contrast this with the instability of Harold Wilson's minority Labour Government of 1974 when compromises were needed to obtain support of the other parties. It follows that organisations require knowledge of the political agenda and how they will be affected by government actions. It should also be noted that while some elements of the political environment will act against a company others will work in its favour. For example, an increase in corporation tax will add to an organisation's costs and may lead to a reduction of the workforce while tax incentives for research and development could boost future competitiveness and growth for some industries.

Economic

In the economic environment, changes in fiscal and monetary pressures can manifest themselves differentially across business sectors and bring about the need for varying degrees of organisational change. For example, reductions in interest rates can encourage house purchases and provide a stimulus to the building trade, but that same reduction can encourage greater debt levels via borrowing and may have a negative impact on savings and investments in the banking and finance sectors. Organisations concerned with imports or exports will be affected by exchange rates and trade tariffs while the amount of disposable income – influenced by employment levels, taxation, interest rates and inflation – will impact upon consumer spending, thereby affecting the demand patterns for an organisation's products or services.

Sociological

Sociological influences, particularly changes in the country's demographic profile such as the declining birth rate, an ageing population and the gender balance of people available for work, combined with changing social values and norms are key drivers for organisational change. For example, organisations may have to change working practices to allow flexible work schedules in order to attract and retain employees who have to combine work and domestic responsibilities. Reductions in the number of people available for work, together with their geographic concentration and density, can lead to skill shortages in certain occupations and locations. This can pressurise organisations into seeking technological solutions, such as automation or perhaps moving the operations to a new locality where labour is available. A new locality can of course mean a change to another country where there is less employment legislation and/or labour costs are lower.

Technological

The nature and pace of technological developments in recent years have been of profound significance for organisations with the result that an almost continual programme of technological change has become the norm for many of them. Organisations who wish to remain competitive, or cost efficient, have had to become skilled in adapting to the impact of new technology for all aspects of their activities, whether in their core activities, such as production and distribution, or in support functions, such as human resource management and accounting. Significant programmes of investment in research and development by market leaders and innovators can have dramatic impact. The speed of technology transfer from concept to implementation is of particular importance with rates of obsolescence being accelerated and the life cycle of many products shortened. It follows therefore that new developments in one industry may destroy the viability of another.

Ecological

Global concerns have highlighted the problem of reconciling the perceived need for economic growth with demand for greater environmental protection and reduced levels of ecological degradation, that is, the rate at which limited resources are being depleted. Also, there are serious concerns over the effects of global warming, pollution, waste disposal and energy consumption. Legislation has been introduced in many of these areas but over recent years we have also seen the development of the philosophy of sustainable development which allows for present generations to meet their own needs without compromising the ability of successive generations to meet their own needs. An important consideration for modern businesses, alongside profitability and growth, is that of corporate social responsibility where the key drivers of corporate environmental responsiveness include government intervention, external pressure groups, self-regulation and market forces. It is the latter which may be the most effective determinant of change for many organisations in that by achieving an enhanced market image and improving resource efficiency they can gain a competitive advantage. Consumer preferences can be seen in such areas as increased sales of organic and free-range products, recyclable packaging, and energy-efficient car engines. In some cases, consumers will boycott products where the companies are believed to be environmentally irresponsible.

Legal

Organisations are subject to a wide range of business laws and regulations, covering areas such as employment, competition, health and safety, and trading standards. For many organisations, legislation will be the major driver for changes to their culture and systems. For example, major features of the Management of Health and Safety at Work Regulations (1992) compel employers (with more than five employees) to conduct risk assessments by competent people and maintain permanent records. They must ensure that all of their employees have appropriate safety training and that preventative and protective measures, with specific emergency procedures are in place. Also, the workplace and conditions of work must be suitable for the equipment employed. This legislation has forced changes that might not otherwise have been contemplated by some companies, particularly in the building trades.

Example of a politico-legal impetus for internal change

The *European Working Time Directive* is a health and safety measure promulgated under Article 118a of the *Treaty of Rome* and was implemented in the UK on 1st October 1998. Prior to this legislation, the UK had no explicit restrictions on the working time of employees. In particular employees had no statutory right to paid holiday leave, nor was there a universal limit on the number of hours that could be worked per week. It is worth noting however that the UK has established a certain degree of control on working hours through health and safety legislation for specific hours of employment, case law and implied contract law.

The Working Time Regulations set:

- a limit on average weekly working time to 48 hours (although individuals can choose to work longer);
- a limit on night workers' average normal daily working time to 8 hours;
- a requirement to offer health assessments to night workers;
- minimum daily and weekly rest periods; rest breaks at work; paid annual leave.

The regulations apply to workers other than genuinely self-employed, and those working in transport, offshore work, junior doctors, emergency workers and the armed forces.

Implications for organisations:

Employees' hours of employment are controlled by express and implied terms and conditions, course of conduct and through trade unions. It is an implied term of an employee's contract of employment that the employer provides a safe system of work. A safe system would include reference to the number of hours which the employee is expected to work.

To ensure compliance with the *Working Time Regulations,* employers need to examine, and adjust where necessary, areas such as shift patterns, night work, rest periods, holidays, young workers, health assessments and record keeping. Meeting the regulations is down to whoever pays the employee.

The terms may in some areas be amended by collective or workforce agreements, and where employees are denied these rights they can seek redress through an *Employment Tribunal.*

Impetus from the internal environment

An organisation's internal environment, the subject of part one of this book, can also offer reasons to change. It is frequently the case, however, that a need to change stimulated by an internal weakness or imbalance is precipitated by a change in the external environment.

Hence, internal stimuli are usually an indirect consequence of an external environmental influence.

An internal analysis of an organisation usually takes the form of a survey of its strengths and weaknesses. In seeking to correct or address its weaknesses, the organisation must undergo some change.

The areas which would usually be the subject of review in an internal analysis are as follows:

- *Structures*: appropriateness of existing structure, overall 'shape' of structure, degree of decentralisation, etc.
- *Technology*: adequacy of the technology for current and projected needs. Also, competence to deal with technological changes.
- *Systems*: effectiveness of mechanisms that monitor and control all key activities, for example, quality, management accounting, administration, etc.
- *Culture*: comprehension of the organisation's culture and its appropriateness for the current and changing environment.
- *Human resources*: having the right number of employees in the right place at the right time with the right skills mix.
- *Financial*: knowledge of cash-flow position, profit and loss position, debt and credit position, etc.
- *Marketing*: customer awareness, competitor knowledge, strength of brands, product quality, effectiveness of promotions, etc.
- *Intellectual*: effectiveness of patents, licences, brands, key intellectual personnel, customers' perceptions, etc.

There are a number of strategic planning tools to enable managers formulate competitive strategies in line with their business environments. One of the most commonly used is a simple structured approach known as *SWOT (strength, weakness, opportunities and threats) analysis*[1] which is concerned with the analysis of an organisation's internal and external environment with the aim of identifying internal strengths in order to take advantage of its external opportunities and avoid external (and possible internal) threats, while addressing its weaknesses.

Strengths can be seen as internal positive attributes that add value and weaknesses are internal negative features that militate against the organisation's ability to achieve its goals. Identified *opportunities* are external factors that could be advantageous for the organisation if it has the resource and competence capabilities to pursue. On the other hand, *threats* are factors that can adversely affect the ability of the organisation to progress or indeed survive.[2]

The relationship of critical variables in the external and internal environments may require distinct strategic choices for an organisation.

The TOWS matrix is conceptual framework for systematic analysis that facilitates matching the external threats and opportunities with the internal weaknesses and strengths of the organisation.[3] It may be that an organisation can utilise its particular strengths to combat threats or take advantage of certain opportunities. On the other hand, an organisation might consider strategies that attempt to minimise both weaknesses and threats. For example, cutting back on operations in the hope of making the necessary changes to overcome the weaknesses, or perhaps merging with another company that has the requisite strengths (Figure 23.2).

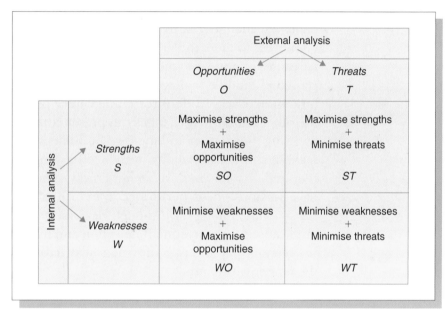

Figure 23.2
TOWS matrix.

23.2 Types of change

When we consider organisational change, we must ask the question '*which aspects of the organisation are we seeking to change?*' We have seen the complexity of the stimuli to change, but managers of a business must ask themselves *how* and *what* to change to enable the organisation to cope with such internal and external influences.

Structural changes

In response to changes in the environment, it is sometimes necessary to modify the structure of the organisation. This may simply be a case of changing reporting systems (e.g. moving one department to be under the authority of a different manager), or it may be more sweeping. The degree of structural change depends upon the extent of change in the organisation's environment. Over recent years, structural change has typically taken the form of 'flattening' the organisation, that is, reducing the number of layers of management, or *de-layering*. This has been greatly facilitated by advances in information technology that has enhanced the ability of managers to have wider spans of control and negated the need for physical proximity to their subordinates.

Significant issues arise when an organisation is de-layered and fundamental changes may be required in the roles and responsibilities of employees to meet the organisation's objectives. This can give particular cause for concern among those who would have traditionally been classed as 'middle managers' who may see the changes reducing their power and status while threatening career progression prospects. On the other hand, such changes can present opportunities for managers by giving them larger and more responsible roles with greater decision making and accountability in their own domains. Employees may be required to *multi-task* and cover a variety of tasks that previously would have previously been performed by individual specialists (contrast with the *Scientific Management* model, described in Chapter 1). This has implications for recruitment, selection and training, or retraining, and the relevant pay and reward systems may have to be changed to match the new environment.

Other reasons to bring about structural changes include reorganisations following acquisitions and mergers. The fact that structural change is sometimes accompanied by staff redeployments and redundancies means that it can be source of stress to employees. An employee being asked to move to different parts of the organisation, possibly to relocate to another part of the country or to learn new skills tends to mean that managing the change is problematic, even though changing the structure on paper is relatively straightforward.

Technological change

There are few more precipitous changes that have occurred in organisations than the introduction and continual updating of technology. As a force, technology has revolutionised many workplaces, often dispensing with thousands of jobs where labour intensive operations have been replaced with automated or robotic processes. Production processes in many industries have been transformed and automated by *computer-aided design* (CAD) and *computer-aided manufacturing* (CAM). This has speeded design processes, radically changed working practices and improved the efficiency of production (see also Chapter 12).

The integration of computer technology, digital telecommunications and the Internet have transformed existing business activities and created new ones. Technological changes can be seen in all areas of organisations' *value chains* – from the *primary activities*, that is, those that are concerned with the creation or delivery of products or services, to the *support activities* that exist to help improve the effectiveness or efficiency of the primary activities. For example, the use of *bar-codes* for *Electronic Point of Sale* (EPOS) has greatly improved inventory management, while *Electronic Funds Transfer at Point of Sale* (EFTPOS) has had major implications for the retailing industry with customers able to purchase goods by credit or debit card and funds immediately transferred from their banks to the stores. A new type of business can be seen in the *call centre* industry where the rapid rise of different types of centre has been a direct result of new technology that enables business to be conducted without the constraints of distance or time zones.

The accelerating rate technological developments, in areas such as the miniaturisation of components, super-conductors, optronics and artificial intelligence, will ensure that change will continue to be a permanent feature of organisational life.

Systems change

Changes in internal systems will often follow naturally from changes in structure and technology. In this context, systems refer to procedures and 'ways of doing things' in the organisation.

As the environment changes, changes may be necessitated in many internal systems, for example:

- reporting procedures and lines of authority;
- control systems (e.g. budgetary control systems);
- financial reporting systems;
- quality systems (e.g. quality assurance measures or inspection procedures);
- information systems, such as access to information from computers and telecommunications links;
- paperwork systems (e.g. paper-form design and changes to circulation lists).

The fact that system changes usually mean a change of 'doing' rather than 'thinking' normally means that such changes are brought about relatively painlessly.

Cultural change

To change the culture of an organisation is often necessary if the organisation is to successfully cope with changes in the external environment. For example, changes in the competitive environment sometimes mean that businesses must progress from being an 'old-fashioned bureaucracy' to a modern 'lean and mean' organisation. The difference between cultural change and all of the others is that this type of change involves changing people – not just systems, technology, etc. It follows that cultural change is the hardest to bring about.

Whereas other changes can be forced upon an organisation in a relatively short time, changing a 'personality' will invariably take much longer. If an organisation can change its structure in a few months, it may well take several years for the culture to catch up. For some employees, a cultural readjustment may be painful as, after many years, they have to change the way they think and act within the organisation.

23.3 Attitudes to change

Burns and Stalker – the context of attitudes to change

We can intuitively understand that some organisations will change more readily than others. Some appear to accept changes as a matter of course whilst others demonstrate stubbornness and inertia. These variations have been partly explained by two of the theorists we encountered in Chapter 1, Burns and Stalker.

Burns and Stalker contributed to the body of organisational theory which became known as contingency theory. They identified two generic forms of organisation depending upon their cultures, structures and systems. *Mechanistic* organisations are characterised by high levels of formality, hierarchical structures and an insistence upon regimented procedures. In contrast, *organic* organisational types tend to demonstrate a higher level of informality with a higher likelihood of a network structure and lateral rather than vertical communication links. The authors saw mechanistic and organic type organisations as two extremities of a continuum, along which, differing degrees of the two could be observable. Furthermore, within larger organisations, both types could be present.

These distinctions have a bearing upon attitudes to change owing to their particular characteristics. Mechanistic type organisations tend to be, by design, 'machine like' in their *modus operandi*. The increased use of bureaucracy and formality tends to mean, in most cases, that change is relatively difficult to implement. Organic type organisations tend to encourage a more entrepreneurial and risk-taking approach and such organisations may well attract individuals who are more inclined to accept change both in the nature of their jobs and in the organisation itself.

Organisations have acknowledged this theory by seeking to adopt a more organic culture as part of the change process. Organisations which were previously bureaucratic and mechanistic have attempted to 'free up' the organisation by reducing the formality and delineation in the workplace. In this respect, they are adopting a more organic culture.

Inertial attitudes

In examining an organisation's resistance to change, organisational theorists borrow a term from physics – inertia. Physicists use the word inertia to describe the force needed to be applied to a body to overcome its resistance to a change in state. It obviously takes a greater force to produce movement in a broken-down car than it does to a football. However, once the initial inertia has been overcome, maintaining its movement is easier. The same is true of organisations. The hard part is beginning the process, but once the process has begun, 'steering' the change, difficult though that may be, is usually relatively easier that overcoming the inertia.

In order to begin the change process, management must overcome the attitudes among people within the organisation that would possibly represent a resistance to the onset of change. We can examine such attitudes as follows:

- *Lack of understanding* about the nature and objectives of the change.
- *Lack of trust* of management's motives and competence.
- *Self-interest* and fear of personal loss – a belief that the change process will result in a deterioration of one's personal conditions, for example, by redundancy.
- *Uncertainty* – an understandable apprehension where employees fear the unknown outcomes of the change (e.g. the change may

necessitate moving house, moving from a job in which they feel competent, etc.).

■ *Social loss* – a fear that the change will result in the break-up of informal groups in the workplace and that they may lose contact with friends or trusted colleagues.

Question 23.2

For each of the inertial attitudes listed above, suggest how management, if possible, may effectively address and overcome each attitude.

Force-field analysis

A noted thinker in the area of change management was Kurt Lewin.[4] In 1951, Lewin proposed the model of a force-field where the state of change in an organisation can be understood in terms of an equilibrium position. The equilibrium is held in place by one set of forces applying pressure for change and opposing and restraining forces which apply pressure to remain with the status quo (Figure 23.3).

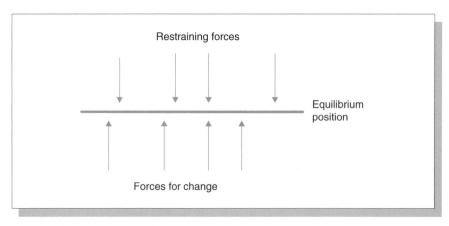

Figure 23.3
Lewin's force-field model.

According to Lewin's force-field model, the pressure for organisational change must be brought about by the pressures for change exceeding the restraining pressures. There are patently two ways in which this can be accomplished:

■ by a build-up in the strength of the for-change forces up to the point that they exceed the restraining forces;

■ by a reduction in the strength of the restraining forces such that the for-change forces gain supremacy without increasing in strength.

According to Lewin, an attempt to implement change by enabling the for-change forces to 'push harder' will, as the diagram suggests, simply result in the restraining forces digging in to retain the status quo – a conflict resulting in no change. Hence, the proclivity to see the process as a war (where the for-change forces must 'win') should be resisted. A preferable stratagem to overcome inertia is for the for-change proponents to work on reducing the strength of the restraining forces rather than to attempt to overcome them. This is accomplished not by attempting to persuade restraining forces of the arguments for change but by for-change proponents gaining an appreciation of the reasons behind the restraining forces. By a process of addressing misgivings and respecting fears and uncertainties, change, argues Lewin, can be more successfully implemented.

23.4 Managing change

The matter of how to manage change has been one of the most well researched and most discussed issues in management circles over recent years. There is consequently much that we could examine in this section. We will discuss some of the most appropriate ideas at this level, but students seeking a more detailed study should access some of the texts listed at the end of this chapter.

There are some principles in relation to change management that are considered as organisational 'best practice', and these are discussed below.

A simple prescription

One of the simplest models for managing change is to assume a hierarchical 'if not, then …' approach. This approach assumes that certain managerial practices are preferable to others. In this respect it is an oversimplification inasmuch as it is self-evident that the most appropriate management approach will be highly context dependent. Figure 23.4 shows the process starting with consultation (with those affected by the change), which, ideally, will be sufficient to carry through the proposals. Other stages become necessary if inertia cannot be overcome by previous attempts. The process ends with coercion when all other attempts have failed – the process of forcing through a change by coercing those affected whether they like it or not.

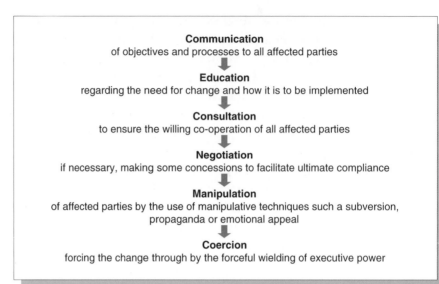

Figure 23.4
A simple
management of
change process.

Useful models

As in many other aspects of management, the use of well-conceived models can help us to understand otherwise complex things. Although others exist, a review of two models which help to explain the management of change process will be of value.

Kurt Lewin's three-step model

Lewin contended that change involved three distinct stages. Each stage required managing in a different way and each was essential to the overall management of a change process. His model is shown in Figure 23.5.

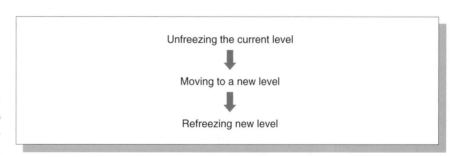

Figure 23.5
Lewin's three-step
model of under-
standing change.

Unfreezing the current level involves abandoning old practices and beliefs before new practices are introduced in order to prevent confusion. It also involves creating a cultural climate of change to the point that individuals expect and will accept the imminent changes.

Moving to the new level involves implementing the change once the old attitudes have been unfrozen. This is the change process itself and involves the management procedures we have previously identified.

The third stage, *refreezing*, involves cementing the new culture and practices into the organisation's culture to prevent employees from falling back into old practices. It follows that refreezing may involve some resolve on the part of management. The new point of equilibrium (as described by the force-field model) must be supported by putting support mechanisms in place which enable employees to feel happy with the new position.

The 'champion of change' model

This model suggests that change can be effectively implemented when led by an individual or group who leads and 'champions' the entire change process. To have a champion not only ensures the process is led (as opposed to being allowed to drift), but also provides a focal point to the process in the form of a visible person. The presence of the champion also provides a visible leadership symbol and a constant reminder of the ongoing momentum of the change process. Figure 23.6 shows the varying degrees of involvement over time of the key groups of people in an organisation if a champion approach is used.

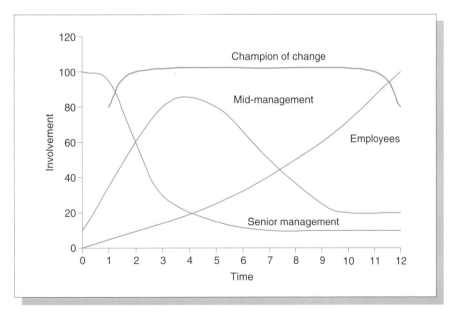

Figure 23.6
The champion of change model.

Any change clearly starts with the impetus and unequivocal support of senior management, hence their high initial involvement. Early in the process, the champion is appointed by the senior management who 'pass on the baton' to him or her. The champion cannot implement any changes without the support of the organisation's mid-managers so this group is involved in order to carry the changes through. It then falls to the mid-managers to communicate the message of change to the workforce who are the people who will be the group most affected by the change. As the mid-managers and workforce become increasingly involved in the change, the senior management role declines and the same is true of mid-managers as the workforce begin to change in their attitudes and actions. Throughout the entire process, the champion is involved in all of the groups to ensure they are properly informed and guided. The champion's role finally declines once the workforce has fully implemented the change.

Assignment 23.1

- How would you respond to a manager who says the best way to implement change in an organisation is to punish employees who fail to change quickly enough to a new regime?
- Discuss the possible barriers to change in a retail company attempting to implement a new system of electronic stock control and a computerised checkout system in its shops.

References

1   Pangiotou, G. (2003). *Bringing SWOT into focus.* Business Strategy Review, vol. 14, issue 2, pp. 8–10.

2   Ansoff, H.I. (1988). *Corporate Strategy* (revised edition). London: Penguin Books.

3   Weihrich, H. and Koontz, H. (1994). *Management: a Global Perspective*, 10th edn. London: McGraw-Hill Education.

4   Lewin, K. (1967). *Field Theory in Social Science: Selected Theoretical Papers.* London: Tavistock.

Further reading

Campbell, D., Stonehouse, G. and Houston, B. (2002). *Business Strategy – An Introduction*, 2nd edn. Oxford: Butterworth Heinemann.

Handy, C. (1996). *Beyond Certainty: The Changing Worlds of Organizations*. Boston, MA: Harvard Business School Press.

Jarrett, M. and Bowman, C. (1996). *Management in Practice. A Framework for Managing Organisational Change*. Oxford: Butterworth Heinemann.

Morgan, G. and Sturdy, A. (1996). *The Dynamics of Organisational Change*. London: Macmillan.

Johnson, G. and Scholes, K. (2003). *Exploring Corporate Strategy*, 6th edn. Harlow: Prentice Hall.

Storey, J. (ed.) (1996). *Blackwell Cases in Human Resource & Change Management*. Oxford: Blackwell.

Weiss, J.W. (1996). *Organizational Behavior & Change: Managing Diversity, Cross-Cultural Dynamics & Ethics*. St Paul, MMN: West.

Worthington, I. and Britton, C. (2003). *The Business Environment*, 4th edn. Harlow: FT Prentice Hall.

Quality management and operational philosophies

Learning objectives

After studying this chapter, students should be able to describe:

- what is meant by quality and why it is important;
- quality systems and standards;
- what is meant by the cost of quality;
- types of quality regimes employed by business operations;
- the purpose of statistical process control (SPC);
- the philosophies of total quality management (TQM) and Six Sigma;
- the features and benefits of just-in-time (JIT).

24.1 Quality

What is quality?

When we discuss quality, we must immediately dispense with the common understanding of the word. When we mention quality in the operations function, we do not refer to any notions of luxury, superiority or premium. If we say, for example, that a Rolls Royce is a quality car, we usually mean that it is a premium car or a luxury car. It is, however, quite possible for an eastern European car or a budget Chinese moped to be of equal quality to the Rolls Royce when we use the word in its precise business context.

Some of the most noted thinkers in the field have described quality in respect to 'excellence' or more accurately 'perceived excellence'. Although quality means many things to different people, in general we can consider quality as *meeting customer needs or expectations.* Hence, strictly speaking, it is quite possible for a product which is designed to be in 'budget' – and which then meets the customer's low expectations – to actually be a high-quality product. An example might be a cheap plastic disposable cigarette lighter, which works consistently for its short life span, and therefore can be described as a quality product in that context. In Table 24.1, we summarise some of the most widely used definitions.

Table 24.1
Some definitions of quality[1]

Quality champion	Definition of quality
W. Edwards Deming	Quality should be aimed at meeting the needs of the consumer, present and future.
Joseph M. Juran	Quality is fitness for purpose for which the product is intended.
Philip B. Crosby	Quality is conformance to requirements (either customer requirements or the specification predetermined for it).
Armand Feigenbaum	The total composite product and service characteristics of marketing, engineering, manufacture, and maintenance through which the product and service in use will meet the expectation of the customer.
John Oakland	Quality is meeting customer requirements.

A vital aspect of quality is that customer requirements should be clearly defined, and agreed between customer and supplier. This requires an explicit statement of what the customer expects from the supplier for the price paid and vice versa. Consider the position of customers who are inconvenienced and disappointed, not because of the specific features of the product or service, but because their expectations have not been met. Differing perceptions of the customer and supplier, perhaps originating form a simple communication misunderstanding, can result in a poor quality experience with resultant complaints, loss of business, refunds, etc. There is also the aspect of consistency in quality where products and services should be right first time and every subsequent time. We can therefore develop John Oakland's definition a little further and say that:

Quality is meeting customers' agreed requirements first time, every time.

The customer's influence on quality and performance

The most important factors that impact on any organisation's operations strategy are those set by the customers. The purpose of any operations function is to manage the value adding activities inside the business in such a way that customer requirements are met in full.

What 'matters' to the customer will, of course, vary from market to market. For each element of product and service that is of concern to a customer, organisations will have an internal response that facilitates the satisfaction of the customer concern. The most successful organisations are those that can most effectively configure their operations to meet the customer requirements. Table 24.2 gives some examples of this relationship.

The list in Table 24.2 is a useful as a starting point to identifying the wide-ranging issues which must be addressed by manufacturing companies and service sector organisations in the quest to become leaders in

Table 24.2
Factors affecting the operating performance characteristics of an organisation

What matters to customers in selecting a product purchase	How a business responds to the customer demand
Low price	Producing at low price
High quality products	Building quality into processes and products
Fast delivery	Short manufacturing time, fast distribution or from finished goods stock
Product reliability	Building reliability into products and delivering dependable service
Leading edge technologies	Emphasis on R&D, keeping abreast of latest developments
Wide product choice	Flexibility to change and wide product mix
Responsive to changes in customer requirements	Flexibility in volume and delivery, quick response times to change

their own markets. Many 'winning' organisations, those that have a competitive advantage in their industry have arrived at the conclusion that one area of concern in operations is more important than any other quality.

The importance of quality

The quality of products, that is, how well they meet customers' expectations is very important in all types of organisation. This is for two broad reasons:

- good quality wins orders, stimulates demand, and retains customer confidence and loyalty;
- poor quality loses orders, erodes demand, and damages customer confidence in the organisation and its products.

Whilst the benefits of high quality are perhaps self-evident, the problems created by poor confidence require some elucidation. One of the reasons why so many organisations have viewed the issue of quality with increased seriousness is a belief that poor quality costs money.

Costs of poor quality sources

With reliable data, managers are able to analyse the 'waste' activities and prioritise action that will provide the best returns. Some of the main sources of the costs of poor quality:

- Appraisal costs are included in the cost of poor quality category as they represent activities undertaken to ensure that (basic) work has been done to the required standard. While it may be argued that such checks are necessary (e.g. with a trainee employee or health and safety) because of the degree and impact of risk or the potential cost of failure it has to be recognised that there is a price to be paid for the lack of confidence, that the work was indeed carried out correctly by the responsible individuals. A company policy that allows inspection to take a large share of quality costs often creates an unquestioning acceptance of the inevitability of quality failure, and such a policy is likely to be very expensive.
- At worst, poor quality products cannot be sold to the customers (for some products such sales may actually be illegal). In this case, the business incurs the *cost of the stock* plus the costs incurred

in producing the product. In cases where 'off-specification' products (sometimes called *seconds*) can be re-worked, costs are incurred in putting stocks back through the factory.

■ Costs are incurred in *correcting faults under warranty* or guarantee. If the materials or construction is not capable of the performance expected by the customer, the product may fail necessitating repair or compensation from the supplying organisation.

■ Probably the highest potential cost of poor quality is the *cost of losing customer confidence.* In competitive markets (i.e. those in which there are many suppliers), it does not take much to put customers off repeat purchases from poor quality suppliers. We all have stories about bad experiences we had with a certain make of washing machine, motorcar or restaurant. Often, bad reputation spreads by word of mouth, so a bad experience not only precludes the disgruntled customer from repeat purchases, but also from those informed of the problem. Conversely, of course, good quality brings about repeat purchases, recommendations and hence intensified customer loyalty.

Quality costing

The accounting process of budget control (see Chapter 29) identifies the costs of the basic work in an organisation but does not normally detail the quality cost elements in the financial returns. The aim of *quality costing* is to identify and analyse the level of quality costs to an organisation under the following three categories:

■ P – Prevention,
■ A – Appraisal (inspection),
■ F – Failure.

This is a management process, known as *PAF analysis,* that uses financial data to determine the proportions of the running costs which can be attributed to 'quality' against groups of activities. By classifying elements of work activities into the relevant (PAF) categories, and allocating the relevant costs, managers are able to see how much is spent on *value-added work* and the *cost of poor quality.* Table 24.3 provides some definitions of the PAF categories.

The following equations can be used to categorise the costs of quality:

$$\text{value-added work} = \text{basic work} + \text{prevention}$$
$$\text{cost of poor quality} = \text{failure} + \text{appraisal}$$
$$\text{total cost of work} = \text{value-added} + \text{cost of poor quality}$$

Table 24.3
Categories of quality costing

Prevention	Costs of activities undertaken to prevent defects in the end result.	For example, training, planning, QA (Quality Assurance), procedures, measurements, role clarity.
Appraisal	Costs incurred with inspections to determine if materials, products or services conform to requirements.	For example, proof reading, vendor rating, quality audits' pre-delivery inspection.
Failure	Costs associated with items that failed to meet the agreed requirements.	For example, re-work, scrap, complaints, downgrading products ('seconds'), waste (time, materials).

It should be noted that poor quality costs very often arise far from their root cause elsewhere in the organisation. For example, a complaint from a customer may be stimulated by an invoice for a faulty or incorrect product, late delivery or some other deviation from the customer's requirements. The cost (in time) of dealing the complaint will initially fall to the accounts people, although the failure may be quite some way back in the quality chain.

24.2 Quality regimes

Quality in operations is imparted using one or more of several possible systems, or *regimes*. The choice of an appropriate regime depends upon the nature of the operations function, and the attitude of the organisation to its particular competitive environment.

In this section, we shall examine some of the major initiatives in quality regimes for operations.

Quality control: post-production

A traditional view of quality control (QC) in UK organisations for many years was that it could only be achieved by inspecting, checking or testing products at the end of the process. QC is thus tagged onto the end as the final hurdle which must be 'jumped' before products are cleared for delivery to customers. Each product will have a specification set for it and staff in QC will check the products to ensure that they meet the basic specification.

The amount or number of products tested in QC will vary according to the type of product. Sometimes, QC will check every single product produced, typically when the production output is low (e.g. the output of one ship). For processes producing thousands of nuts and bolts, however, testing every single product simply is not possible. In this case, a statistically significant *sample* will be taken from each batch for testing.

Although QC at the final stage of the operations process may prevent sub-standard products reaching the customers, it is too late to prevent the failure costs of time, money and materials. As Deming put it *'Defects are not free. Somebody makes them and gets paid for making them.'*[2]

QC: in-process inspections

This regime, as its name suggests, adds extra safeguards to final QC in that the product is tested for conformance to specification at certain points in the process itself. This may include testing materials at the inbound logistics stage to make sure raw materials conform to requirements in addition to key points in the process.

The thinking behind this regime is to root out any problems at the earliest possible stage, just as you would wish to know if you have a disease as early as you possibly could. There is clearly no point in continuing with a batch which you know will fail final QC when it gets there. Whilst there is necessarily a higher cost associated with more testing (such as employing more testers), organisations that employ this regime argue that more is saved by catching poor quality early than is incurred in extra testing.

What happens after QC?

When work-in-progress stocks reach a QC point, whether it is in-process or at the end of the process, there are clearly two possible outcomes of the tests performed: the product is within specification (pass) or it is not (fail). If the stock passes the tests, then there is no problem; it can proceed to the next stage of production or go into finished goods stock ready to go to the customer. If, however, the test is failed (and is hence 'off-specification' or 'off-spec.'), there are a number of possible routes the stock can take. The most appropriate will, of course, depend upon the nature of the product.

- Some products that fail at the end of the process can be *sold off cheaply* to customers as 'off-spec.' products (sometimes called *seconds*). Not all products lend themselves to this type of rescue, but typical examples include clothes with mis-stitched seams and mis-shaped chocolates. The products will still offer some benefit to the customer, even although they are not 'perfect' (an odd-shaped chocolate still tastes acceptable, even although it could not be sold at the normal price).

- Some products can be taken back into the production and *reworked* to bring them back within QC specification. A paint that is not precisely the right colour when it reaches QC can usually be re-tinted to meet the precise colour required. Similarly, a computer with one defective circuit can be returned to production to have the one circuit replaced.
- Other products which fail QC must simply be *disposed of.* Disposal is obviously the option of last resort, and is only taken when there is no scope for rework or selling on cheaply. Typical candidates for disposal would be products such as beer or food with a fatal contaminant or anything that would be unsafe to sell on or to rework.

Quality assurance

Quality assurance (QA) systems do not necessarily replace conventional QC regimes; rather they attempt to reduce the need for QC by assuring quality in advance. This means that quality is '*designed in*' to products and processes in order to reduce the chances of things going wrong once they get into production. This is something of a shift in philosophy away from QC. QC more-or-less accepts that a certain failure rate will occur whereas QA aims at prevention not detection; that is, it attempts to *create good quality* rather than control poor quality. Quality is assured in advance by ensuring that all materials and processes involved in the manufacturing procedure conform to the following key quality criteria:

- *Quality of design* is a measure of how well the product or service has been designed to achieve its stated purpose, and the most important feature of the design, with respect to achieving quality is that of the specification.
- *Quality of conformance to design* starts from the premise that you cannot inspect quality into products or services. A high level of checking at the end of the process often indicates attempts to 'inspect in' quality which adds to costs and decreases viability. The area of conformance to design is concerned with the quality performance of the actual operations, and therefore requires effective recording and analysis of performance data.

The QA regime must therefore account for the following:

- *Design*: Products and services must be designed with quality in mind. This means that research and design professionals,

design in features which will meet the customers' expectations. Product features will not be over or under specified
and each part of it will be testable (if appropriate) during the
products production.

- *Materials*: It must be appropriate to the process. Again, they
  must not be under or over specified (i.e. too bad or too good
  for the product) and must be consistently of the appropriate
  quality.
- *Suppliers*: They will be chosen for their reliability and consistency to supply in addition to the quality of the materials
  themselves.
- *Plant and machinery*: It must be procured and maintained to
  operate within stricter tolerances than might otherwise be the
  case. By having machines that the organisation knows it can
  rely on, the worry that a defect in plant may be responsible for
  poor product quality is removed.
- *Human resources* (HR): Whilst human error is always a potential source of poor quality, the risk of this happening can be
  reduced by appropriate training, development, HR planning
  and by reducing the impact of human error by technologically-
  based safeguards.
- *Operational procedures*: The procedures must provide a framework which is consistent with good quality. If, for example,
  production is organised so that there is room for slovenly
  practice, that will tend to act against good quality. Clearly, the
  way that operational procedures are planned, managed and
  carried out will have a significant influence on the quality of
  the output.

Performance measurement

Performance measurement systems measure the inputs and outputs to an
operation in order to determine how well, or badly, they are used by
the operation. Performance measurement is important to all parts of an
organisation but it is especially important to operations management
because of the direct impact that operations make on the business in
terms of efficiency and effectiveness. Traditional measurement systems
can be criticised for their emphasis on the single measure of cost
whereas modern quality manufacturing techniques, with the change of
focus from management to customer, require examination of processes
as well as outcomes.

Poka-yoke (mistake proofing)

The *Poka-yoke* (or mistake proofing) system was invented by Shigeo Shingo, who also created the *single-minute exchange of die* (SMED) system in which set-up times are reduced from hours to minutes. The term poka-yoke refers to a checklist (of the operation) that will prompt the operator if something is missed or performed out of sequence. Shingo advocates *Zero QC* as the ideal production system in which no defects are produced, and which requires poka-yoke and *source inspections.*

In poka-yoke, defects are examined, the production system stopped and feedback given so that the root causes of the problems can be identified and prevented from recurring. Source inspections involve examination of errors before they become defects and corrective action is taken.

$$\text{errors and defects} = \text{cause and effect}$$

The action may involve stopping the system for correction or an automatic adjustment of the error condition.

Statistical process control

SPC is concerned with *continuous process improvements.* There is variation in the characteristics of all materials, services and people, and therefore there is an inherent variability in every transformation process. Using a collection of statistical tools, SPC measures the performance of processes and facilitates analyses from which decisions on quality correction can be implemented (if necessary) as the products or services are being produced, rather than when they are completed. Common SPC tools are *process control charts, run charts, flow charts* and *frequency histograms.*

Process capability uses SPC techniques to determine the consistency and repeatability of processes. It focuses on whether and how the process delivers what the customer expects.

Kaizen (continuous improvement)

Kaizen is a culturally embedded concept of *continuous improvement*, pioneered by Japanese companies. It concentrates on *small gradual changes involving all employees in every area of the business*, and builds on premise that there is no such thing as top quality since all quality is relative to customer expectations. For example, companies who manage to achieve a level of customer satisfaction at a point in time will see competitors seeking to exceed that level in aiming for 'excellence' rather than 'mere satisfaction'; of course, even trying to achieve customer satisfaction is a major problem for many companies.

The word 'kaizen' is a derivation from two Japanese sources: *kai* means change and *zen* means for the better.

According to Masaaki Imai (1986)[3] the philosophy is '*the single most important concept in Japanese management – the key to Japanese competitive success.*'

Kaizen is process-oriented change, involving operators continuously searching for better ways to do their jobs. It is important that every employee strives for improvement and so an acceptance of kaizen by the *organisational culture* is a vital element.

The PDCA cycle

The concept of the *PDCA* (planning, doing, checking and acting) *cycle* was originally developed by Walter Shewart, the pioneering statistician who developed SPC at the Bell Laboratories in the USA during the 1930s. It is often referred to as the *Shewart Cycle* or the *Deming Wheel*, following its promotion as an effective continuous improvement tool by W. Edwards Deming from the 1950s. PDCA cycle is basically a checklist of those four stages to be addressed in facilitating progress from 'problem-faced' to 'problem-solved' situations (Figure 24.1):

- *Plan*: starts with collecting data, defining the problem and establishing a strategy, or plan to achieve the desired outcome.
- *Do*: trial the changes, on a small scale.

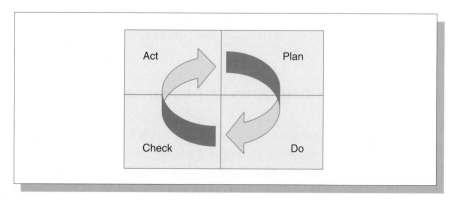

Figure 24.1
The PDCA cycle.

-   *Check*: monitor the improvement via the collection and analysis of data to if the changes are working.
-   *Act*: analyse and hold the gains, if successful or remedy the changes if unsuccessful.

In a culture of continuous improvement the PDCA cycle is not a static vehicle but on reaching the 'Act' (problem-solved) stage, attention again moves to the 'plan' stage to address the next problem situation.

24.3 Total quality management

TQM is a holistic approach which provides awareness of the *customer–supplier relationship* and *continuous improvement* effort in all departments and functions. Whereas other quality regimes have been concentrated on the operations function with the focus of conformance to specifications, the philosophy of TQM applies to the entire business, and is therefore embedded into the culture and structures of the organisation.

A simple definition of TQM can be found by examining the basic elements of actual title:

-   *Total:* every body in the organisation is involved.
-   *Quality:* meeting agreed customer requirements, first time, every time.
-   *Management:* it is a leadership responsibility.

There are many approaches to TQM, with organisations adapting to suit their particular situations but, whatever the approach; the following guiding principles underpin effective implementation (Table 24.4).

A model for TQM

Quality will not happen of its own accord and has to be managed. TQM is about balancing all resources (people, systems and technology) to optimum effect so as to maximise customer satisfaction. TQM promotes improvement through people, using systems and technology to support what they do. The old route to quality in the western world was through systems, with an emphasis on structures and procedures to control quality rather than improve it. This was generally inadequate because the systems were usually imposed upon people, rather than developed with them. The technological route was promoted as the way to eliminate human error by mechanisation, but often failed by neglecting the human element. It is easy to make mistakes faster when

Table 24.4
Guiding principles of TQM

Philosophy	*Prevention not detection*: investment in the prevention of failures in quality protects the customer and produces dividends in the form of reduced costs of waste, errors, re-work and inspection.
Approach	*Management led*: initiative must come from management, encouraging by example and guidance throughout the organisation.
Scale	*Everyone responsible for quality*: creating the climate in which people are willing to take responsibility themselves rather reliance on 'the quality department' – quality cannot be inspected in.
Measurement	*Cost of quality*: measure the three costs of quality elements – prevention, appraisal and failure.
Standard	*Right first time*: it is costly to compromise on quality and therefore the aim is for 'zero defects'.
Scope	*Company-wide*: there are opportunities for quality improvement in every part of the organisation.
Theme	*Continuous improvement*: there is no instant solution and lasting improvement takes sustained effort over years.

automation tackles symptoms rather than the fundamental problems, and consequently the systems and technology routes are high cost. The low cost route starts from the assumption that people are not simply costs to be reduced and minimised assets but assets to invest in and develop.

A relatively simple framework was developed by Prof. John Oakland (1993)[4] which describes the main features and relationships of TQM as shown in Figure 24.2.

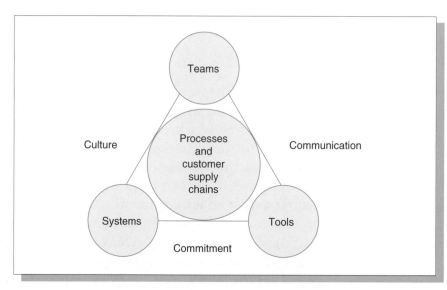

Figure 24.2
Adaptation of Oakland's model of TQM.

At the heart of the model are processes and customer supplier chains that recognise the importance of meeting customer requirements.

Quality chains

The term *customer* does not just refer to the end customer; it also recognises that organisation and the external 'paying' customer but also within the organisation with the *internal customer supplier chain*. For example, there are people working in some organisations that never see the actual finished products or services but will be involved in some part of the overall process, such as taking the initial order, receiving stores or handling the invoice. Each operator in the chain is therefore both a customer and a supplier, with each having the responsibility of meeting their respective customer's requirements.

Value is added at each stage until the final product is paid for by the external customer. Alternatively, failure to meet requirements in any part of the quality chain can have a multiplier effect and create problems elsewhere in the organisation (see quality costing in a subsection under Section 24.1). The effects of a failure in any link in the chain, perhaps by one person or one piece of equipment not meeting requirements will usually find its way to the external customer interface.

Quality systems

To achieve consistency in work processes a company must be organised so that the required standards are known and understood by all employees. This organisation requires management systems to plan, monitor and control all activities. For many organisations this is achieved by setting out objectives through their quality policy and use of a fully documented quality system such as *ISO 9000* (see below). The use of such a system ensures a consistent level of quality which, in turn, promotes customer confidence. In addition, such systems help the organisation to manage internal and external operations in a cost-effective way.

Service level agreements

Service level agreements (SLAs) are agreements with suppliers that define the service to be delivered with explicit and mutually determined responsibilities and priorities clearly articulated. SLAs are in effect contractual obligations (often clauses or a section of a contract) and can be used where a business's ability to meet its customer requirements is dependent upon the supplier (see also *JIT* in Section 24.6).

Typical SLAs will include:

- the service to be provided,
- the standards of service,
- the timetable for delivery,
- the respective responsibilities of supplier and customer,
- provisions for regulatory and legal compliance,
- monitoring and reporting mechanisms,
- escalation procedure in the event of slippage,
- disputes procedure,
- review process.

Many organisations have developed internal SLAs to clarify the parameters of service between departments for their internal customer supplier chains.

Quality standards

Quality standards provide a framework for the development and measurement of quality systems, and effectively establish the specifications for business capability in managing quality. The first UK standard was known as *BS 5750* and that provided the basis for the current international standard of *ISO 9000*, which is the main set of international standards applying to the management of quality systems, or what the organisation does to:

- fulfil the customers' requirements,
- enhance customer satisfaction,
- apply regulatory requirements,
- implement continuous performance improvement.

It includes *ISO 9001* which is the *internationally agreed key standard* for *quality management systems*. Businesses can be certified against this standard when they meet its requirements.

Additionally, the *ISO 14000* set of standards is primarily concerned with '*environmental management*', or what the organisation does to:

- minimise harmful effects on the environment caused by its activities,
- achieve continual improvement of its environmental performance.

Table 24.5
Some QA standards for operations management

ISO standard	Areas covered by standard
ISO 9001	Quality of all aspects of operations and product design
ISO 9002	Quality in all aspects of operations
ISO 9003	Quality in final product inspection only

The vast majority of ISO standards are quite specific to particular processes or materials. For example, some of the QA standards for operations management are shown in Table 24.5.

However, the standards that have earned ISO 9000 and ISO 14000 worldwide reputations are known as '*generic management system standards*', which means that the same standards can be applied to any organisation, regardless of size, in any sector (i.e. private, public or voluntary) and, indeed, whether the 'product' is actually a service.

ISO 9000 defines quality in terms of conformance to requirements and provides a basis for developing QC systems and their respective measurements against the standard. It is not a substitute for total quality with its emphasis on continuous improvement and the involvement of the entire workforce.

Compliance with an ISO standard must be proven to a suitably accredited body of independent inspectors who inspect the organisation's systems to test whether internal quality procedures are actually and consistently being followed. The organisation seeking ISO 9000 accreditation will produce documentation setting out how they will perform each part of the operational process. Once written down in this way, the company will be judged by the assessors according to how consistently it observes the procedures in practice. Once granted, the assessors can call upon the organisation at any time (without warning) to check that procedures are still being followed.

Accreditation is indicated by the award of the ISO certification logo which can be shown on company stationery, vehicles, etc. to indicate the organisation's QA. The seal of approval for assured quality is of great significance in competitive advantage terms, as the organisation seeks to increase its customers, confidence.

Tools and techniques of quality

The quality system provides a framework for recording and dealing with quality problems. However, simply asking staff not to take responsibility for solving their own quality problems is usually not enough. Employees often must be trained and educated so that they can identify problems and deal with them effectively. Many organisations now train staff in basic problem-solving tools and other quality techniques, encouraging them to become proactive in quality improvement activities such as *quality circles* or *quality improvement teams*.

Teams and the organisation

In most modern manufacturing and service companies, work processes are complex in nature and are often beyond the control of any one individual. A *team* approach therefore offers a number of advantages, particularly through the synergy of different but complementary different skills and expertise. Team-workings can also help develop skills and knowledge, and is often more satisfying for the individuals involved in improving morale, participation and decision-making.

TQM and culture

We have seen that for most organisations, the adoption of TQM will require a shift in the corporate culture. Its introduction may prove to be problematic unless the concept is fully taken on board by all members of the organisation. For this reason, in many cases, it takes some time to implement in its 'purest' form. The culture of TQM requires several key changes in attitudes and behaviour (Table 24.6).

Table 24.6
Cultural changes in thinking for TQM

From	To
Reactive management (reacting to problems and circumstances)	Proactive management and forward planning
Inspection (QC)	Prevention (QA)
'Acceptable' quality ('that's good enough')	Zero defects ('right first time, on time, every time')
Placing the blame for a problem	Solving the problem, regardless of blame
Low cost *or* quality	Low cost *and* quality
Good quality costs more	Good quality actually costs less

24.4 Six Sigma

The evolution of quality management continues from TQM to *Six Sigma*, both of which share common origins in the teachings of the great quality gurus like Deming and Juran. Six Sigma was initially pioneered by *Motorola* and *Allied Signal*, and has since been adopted by thousands of companies around the world. It is a holistic philosophy that take its name from the Greek letter 'sigma' which is the symbol used in statistical notation to represent the *standard deviation* of a population (standard deviation is the indicator of the amount of variation or inconsistency in any group of items or processes). The full title of Six Sigma is therefore built upon the statistically derived performance target that a process must not produce more than 3.4 defects per million opportunities – a Six Sigma opportunity is defined as anything outside of customer specifications. It should be noted however that, for many organisations, Six Sigma simply means a measure of quality that strives for near perfection. This is obviously a hugely demanding standard for most organisations and it is interesting to make a comparison with Crosby's philosophy of 'zero defects'.

Six Sigma can therefore be described as a comprehensive and flexible system for achieving, sustaining and maximising business success. It is driven by close understanding of customer needs, disciplined use of facts, data, statistical analysis, and diligent attention to managing, improving and reinventing business processes. Like TQM, it demands leadership commitment with a consistent simple message for all employees reinforcing clear no nonsense ambitious goals.

The fundamental objective of the Six Sigma methodology is the implementation of a measurement-based strategy that focuses on process improvement, and variation reduction through the application of *improvement projects* and the use of two sub-methodologies:

- *DMAIC* (define, measure, analyse, improve, control) which is an improvement system for existing processes falling below specification and requiring incremental improvement.
- *DMADV* (define, measure, analyse, design, verify) which is an improvement system used to develop new processes or products at Six Sigma quality levels. It can also be applied if a current process requires more than just incremental improvement.

24.5 The strategic significance of operations

We will see in Chapter 26 that 'operations' is that part of the organisation which is primarily concerned with 'making' or 'producing' the product or service. If follows that the operations department is the most important function in a business: a car manufacturer does not exist to report on financial performance or to manage its personnel, it exists to make cars and by doing so, money. All other functions such as personnel and finance must therefore be in support of the operations function.

Furthermore, operations can be said to be the most important function because it provides the output which the customer actually pays for and uses. Poor HR policies or poor financial reporting would rarely, in themselves, make customers stop buying from a business, but poor products or bad service certainly would. So we can arrive at a generally accepted principle:

- *good operations department* = competitive business,
- *bad operations department* = unhealthy and uncompetitive business.

What then makes one company's operations department better than others? Or, put another way, in what ways can the operations function add to or take away from the success of the business as a whole? We can answer this by looking at several 'success factors' (which, of course, can also be 'failure factors'):

- *Quality* is the most important success factor for any organisation, as it is central to every aspect of operations. In this context, quality means fitness for the job, which means that materials used must be right at each stage of the process. Materials bought in for the process must be of the right quality; low quality and the product will be sub-standard, too high a quality, and the organisation will be paying more than necessary for its inputs. The same principle applies to the quality of the final product output.
- *Material used* is a vital success factor in the transformation process. It is clearly essential that the materials taken into, and used by an operations process must be correct and of appropriate specification for the process. The appropriateness of materials will have a great bearing upon the final product.
- *Lead time* is the time taken between an order being received and the delivery of the final product to the customer. It follows that companies with shorter lead times have an advantage over those who are slower. The lead time obviously depends upon such things as how the organisation manages its orders, its queues in process and the efficiency of its procedures.

- *Distribution* is extremely important for organisational success. This refers not only to such things as the number, and locations of outlets and depots, but also the method and efficiency of transport of finished goods to the customer. Reliable distribution can win orders whereas unreliability in this area can soon erode customers' confidence in an organisation's ability to supply on time.
- *Cost* incurred by the operations function is the final success factor, but perhaps the most important of all. In most organisations, the operations function is by necessity the 'biggest spender' of company money. There are many ways in which the operations department can and do incur costs, and successful businesses have ways of keeping them under tight control:
  - raw materials and other material inputs;
  - wages, salaries and personnel costs;
  - fixed costs (e.g. rent, rates, insurance);
  - energy costs (e.g. electricity to power processes and machines);
  - investment costs (e.g. new plant and equipment);
  - packaging and distribution costs;
  - maintenance costs of equipment.

The adoption of a quality philosophy in operations is concerned with gaining and maintaining competitive advantage. A culture of quality is has a focus on the achievement of superior operational performance.

24.6 Just-in-time

The original concept of *JIT* was developed in the *Toyota Motor company*, by *Taiichi Ohno*, who saw it as not just a set of techniques but as a philosophy composed of three key elements:

- minimising waste in all forms,
- maintaining respect for all workers,
- continually improving processes and systems.

It can therefore be seen that JIT complements TQM philosophy and, arguably, cannot work effectively out with a quality management regime.

JIT systems are essentially directed towards ensuring that supplies of materials arrive in the right quantities exactly as and when required by the operatives, literally 'just in time'.

What is waste?

The focus of JIT is waste. JIT thus aims to eliminate waste in all the forms in which it occurs in an operational process. By doing this, JIT cuts the costs involved in operations and thus increases an organisation's profitability.

Waste arises from any stock or activity that costs the organisation money but does not add value or generate income. Examples include:

■ Any stock that is not actually being processed (and to which value is therefore not being added). This includes all raw materials, all finished goods and any work-in-progress, that is queuing between production processes.

■ Stocks that have failed a quality test, either in-process or at final QC.

■ Machine 'down-time,' that is production time lost through machines not being operable for any reason, such as breakdown or through tooling up or tooling down between batches.

■ The time and stock involved in producing unsold or unsaleable stocks.

The core themes of JIT

The core themes of JIT address the cultural climate necessary for its successful implementation. In the same way that TQM requires a conducive culture, JIT must also have the support and understanding of all employees (especially, of course, in the operations function):

■ *Simplicity* – All procedures in operations should be kept as simple as possible. This does not mean that complicated things should be made artificially simple, but that nothing should be more complex than it needs to be. Overcomplicating procedures means that more costs are incurred than needs to be the case.

■ *Visibility* – Waste can only be eliminated when it can be seen. In practice, this means that all systems and workplaces should be functional and tidy. It also implies that waste can conceal potential problems (e.g. high stock levels can be used as a buffer to hide poor production planning).

■ *Continuous* – JIT is not a 'fad', it is part of the ongoing success of the organisation, and indeed, the success of the organisation may depend upon JIT.

■ *Involvement* – Even although JIT may be centred on the oper-ations function, everybody in the organisation must be com-mitted to it and involved with it.

JIT and operational practices

When we considered TQM, we saw that it, too, had some key under-lying 'absolutes' which underlie its implementation in practice. The core themes of JIT and the focus on the issue of waste set out the philosoph-ical underpinnings of JIT. The main features of JIT in practice can be summarised by the segments in the 'JIT cycle', as shown in Figure 24.3. The key operational features of JIT are discussed below.

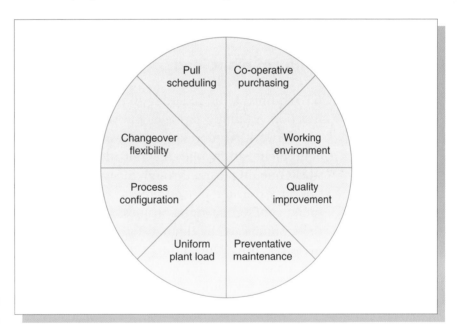

Figure 24.3
The JIT cycle.

Environment

This refers to the management of space and the working areas. Tidiness and order are considered to be important features of a JIT system: 'a place for everything and everything in its place'. Similarly, all informa-tion and paperwork systems need to be transparent and orderly.

Quality

JIT takes the same view of quality as Six Sigma and TQM. As poor qual-ity costs money, it is obviously a source of waste. For this reason, many organisations that operate JIT also observe principles of QA, Six Sigma or TQM. Prevention is better and cheaper than cure.

Preventative maintenance

Given that one form of waste is machine down-time due to breakdown, JIT emphasises maintaining plant and equipment proactively rather than waiting for something to go wrong. This parallels with having a car regularly serviced to keep it in good order as opposed to waiting until the radiator springs a leak on a cold wet night when you are in a hurry to get somewhere. In consequence, JIT observes regular and thorough maintenance schedules on all equipment. Furthermore, all employees are encouraged to immediately report any irregularities in machine operation (such as a 'funny noise').

Uniform plant load

JIT requires skilful planning of the workload through that operations function. A 'lumpy' passage of work can result in periods of underwork or overwork. Underloading of work results in both employees and equipment 'sitting idle' (i.e. not adding value). Overloading results in stocks queuing to get through the various stages in operations and possibly an extension of lead times (possibly leading to an erosion of customer confidence in the business to supply its needs on time). Both of these situations, in their different ways, cost money and introduce waste (i.e. non value adding activity).

In consequence, JIT seeks to even out the flow of work through the operations function. Whilst the pattern on customer orders may make this objective difficult to achieve at times, production planners attempt to smooth out workload as far as possible to eliminate 'lumpiness'.

Process configuration

Process configuration refers to the manner in which processes in a production facility are physically laid out. There are two general ways in which factories can be laid out:

- *Process-based configurations*, where plant is arranged according to the type of process. Batches pass from process area to process area depending on the station which is able to receive the batch at the earliest time.
- *Product-based configuration*, where plant is arranged according to the type of product being produced.

Figures 24.4 and 24.5 show typical routes for three batches under the two regimes.

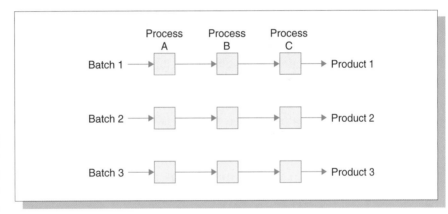

Figure 24.4
Possible route for three batches (1, 2 and 3) through three processes (A, B and C) under a process-based configuration.

Figure 24.5
Simplified route for the three batches through a product-based configuration.

In keeping with the JIT core theme of simplicity, most JIT operations attempt to avoid clutter and confusion. In theory, JIT prescribes that a business uses whichever configuration provides the most visibility and simplicity. In practice, the majority opt for a more or less product-based layout. This offers the possibility of more precise line balancing (see Chapter 28), thus reducing work-in-progress queuing between stations.

Changeover flexibility

We have seen that one of the sources of waste is the time taken to tool-up and tool-down between jobs or batches. It follows that a key way of reducing such waste is to make such changes faster and easier. The parallel is sometimes drawn in this area between the time, it takes for a motorist to change a wheel by the side of a road to a team changing a wheel on Michael Schumacher's Formula One racing car. One takes 20 minutes;

the other less than 8 seconds. The point being that when employees are sufficiently trained and motivated, changeover times can be significantly reduced.

This factor is of importance when designing an operational process. By designing-in a facility for rapid and flexible product-to-product changeover, down-time can be reduced and hence waste avoided.

Pull scheduling

We have seen that one of the sources of waste is stock to which value is not being added – raw materials and finished goods stock. Pull scheduling avoids the creation of such stocks. Under this regime, nothing happens in an operations function until a customer 'pulls' stock through it in the form of ordered stock. This represents a significant change of thinking for many businesses that, when orders are light, will 'make for stock': making finished goods stock for anticipated future orders.

The process of 'pulling' extends backwards through the operations function by a system the Japanese have termed *kanban*. A kanban (the Japanese for 'card') is a signal from one workstation to another to provide goods for the next stage of working. In a JIT operation, work is forbidden unless a kanban is obtained from a forward station, from the customer, to despatch and backwards through the operation. The final kanban is a signal to the supplier to provide the necessary raw material stocks to fulfil the customer's order.

Kanban works as a trigger to start production activity. A simple kanban system is as follows:

■ a customer places an order (a kanban to the despatch department);
■ the despatch department kanbans the final stage of production to supply goods to fulfil the customer order;
■ the final stage of production kanbans the second last stage to supply goods so that the final stage can finish the process to provide the goods requested by despatch;
■ each workstation kanbans the one before it to supply goods in the appropriate state of assembly until the purchasing department kanbans the supplier.

It follows from the kanban principle that providing there are no delays in any of the stages, the lead time for an order is the same as the time it takes to produce it. Such a system requires a very well organised operations function and a very special relationship with the suppliers.

Co-operative purchasing

The kanban principle means that JIT operations make special demands upon their suppliers. They require suppliers to deliver stock:

- immediately or within a very short time period,
- to the point on the production line at which it will be used,
- in the precise quantity to meet customer orders,
- to a consistent quality and often to the buyer's design.

Such demands necessitate a special relationship with a supplier. JIT manufacturers achieve this by cultivating long-term and co-operative relationships with suppliers. The conventional supplier–buyer relationship is based on achieving the maximum amount of concession from the other. This means that suppliers seek to supply at quantities that are convenient for it at as high a price as possible whereas buyers seek to buy at the lowest possible price.

In a co-operative purchasing environment, a buyer (the JIT manufacturer) recognises that the ability to the company to operate its JIT system relies upon reliable supply. In consequence, partnerships tend to be built up wherein suppliers are rewarded with long-term supply contracts, agreed pricing structures and regular communication with the JIT customer. In many cases, the supplier's flexibility is also rewarded with a slightly higher price, that is, reflecting the supplier's higher stockholding and transport costs (see also SLAs in Section 24.3).

The benefits and drawbacks of JIT

JIT offers a number of potential benefits

Firstly, the reduced stockholding reduces the working capital needed to run the business. Working capital is money tied up in stocks, cash-in-hand or in debtors (money owed to the business). Stock is therefore a way of tying up money which cannot be used for other purposes such as investment. A lower working capital not only provides the opportunity for higher profitability, but also increases liquidity (see Chapter 11).

Secondly, JIT provides an opportunity to reduce the costs of the operations department. JIT's focus on reducing stocks, preventing breakdown and on reducing changeover time all help to reduce costs and thus increase profitability.

Thirdly, under JIT, all products are made to the requirements of the customer. This provides increased flexibility as a customer can order the precise quantity needed and to the required specification (i.e. the customer does not merely have to choose from existing finished goods stock).

Potential drawbacks include the possibility of higher unit costs arising from the requirements made of suppliers. Additionally, the fact that finished goods stocks are not held renders the business vulnerable if for any reason the order cannot be fulfilled (such as through machine breakdown or supplier failure).

JIT is therefore best suited to stable conditions where there is predictable customer demand for the finished products and there is a clearly defined material flow. On the other hand, where conditions are complex and demand is uncertain another system called *Manufacturing Resource Planning* (MRP II) can prove to be more effective (see Chapter 26).

Assignment 24.1

Kar-Komponents Ltd uses a batch-process system to manufacture standardised parts that are sold to car accessory retail outlets. Traditionally, the company has worked on a low price, no frills strategy and boasts a reputation for the speed of its order completion. Quality had never been a serious issue for the company but over the last 18 months the number of complaints and returned faulty products has risen dramatically. Nevertheless, most of their customers have been reasonably appeased, with replacements and compensatory goodwill payments. However, they have a disturbing downward trend in market share and, in an attempt to 'stop the rot' and prevent faulty products getting to the customers, some of the best technicians have been re-deployed to QC inspections. This has revealed a very high level of sub-standard units but even so, many faulty products are escaping the 'final safety net' and being shipped to customers. As they offer a 'no quibble' replacement policy, the senior managers feel that it is better to take the risk of supplying potentially faulty products than miss contract delivery dates. Any complaints from major customers are given priority treatment and a senior manager personally oversees the remedial action. The finance manger has reported that unit costs are rising at an unprecedented rate and that urgent cost reductions are essential:

1 Discuss the advantages and disadvantages of this company's manufacturing and competitive strategies.
2 Suggest ways in which they might improve the quality of their products.

References

1   Campbell, D. *et al.* (2001). *Business Strategy an Introduction.* Oxford: Butterworth Heinemann.

2   Deming, W.E. (2000). *Out of the Crisis.* New York: The MIT press.

3   Imai, M. (1991). *Kaizen Key to Japan's Success.* New York: McGraw Hill Education.

4   Oakland, J. (2003). *Total Quality Management: Text with Cases,* 3rd edn. Oxford: Butterworth Heinemann.

Further reading

Brown, S. Blackmon, K. *et al.* (2001). *Operations Management.* Oxford: Butterworth Heinemann.

Crosby, P.B. (1996). *Quality is Still Free.* New York: McGraw Hill.

Hoyle, D. (1994). *ISO 9000 Quality Systems Handbook.* Butterworth Heinemann.

Juran, J.M. (1998). *Quality Handbook,* 5th edn. New York: McGraw Hill.

Oakland, J. (2003). *Total Quality Management: Text with Cases,* 3rd edn. Oxford: Butterworth Heinemann.

Pande, P.S. *et al.* (2000). *The Six Sigma Way.* New York: McGraw-Hill.

Slack, N. *et al.* (2003). *Operations Management,* 4th edn. London: FT Prentice Hall.

Stamatis, D.H. (2003). *Six Sigma Fundamentals.* New York: Productivity Press Inc.

Wickens, P. (1987). *The Road to Nissan.* London: Palgrave Macmillan.

Wilson, G., Cairns, N., McBride, P. and Bell, D. (1994). *Managing Quality.* Butterworth Heinemann.

Useful web sites

British Standards Institute: www.bsi-global.com
Business Link: www.businesslink.gov.uk/
European Foundation for Quality Management: www.iso.org/

CHAPTER 25

Corporate governance and business ethics

Learning objectives

After studying this chapter, students should be able to describe:

- the nature of corporate governance;
- the main features of the Combined Code of corporate governance;
- the nature of corporate social responsibility;
- the nature and range of ethical concerns;
- the Ethical decision models;
- the potential costs poor business ethics;
- the potential benefits of positive business ethics.

25.1 What is corporate governance?

Corporate governance is the process whereby people in power direct, monitor and lead corporations and thereby create, modify or destroy the structures and systems under which they operate.

There are different international models of corporate governance. For example, the European model, as operated in Germany, requires large public corporations to have two-tiered boards – a supervisory board and a management board. The latter is accountable to the former which has employee, shareholder and third-party representatives. This structure ensures that companies are legally accountable to both their shareholders and their employees. There are strengths in this model inasmuch as it has strong governance procedures, while sustaining long-term business growth and stability. On the other hand, it is quite vulnerable to global economic pressures.

In the UK, with a single-tired board system of executive and non-executive directors (NEDs), the prime legal responsibility of plc boards (see Chapter 4) is to their shareholders, although they also have certain statutory obligations to their employees, customers and suppliers. The UK model of corporate governance is designed to provide a dynamic market orientation with fluid capital resources and is mainly concerned with corporate profits rather than long-term investment. Public sector organisations in the UK are likely to have some form of employee involvement with their management boards.

25.2 The need for sound corporate governance

In the late 1980s and early 1990s, there were a number of well-publicised corporate 'scandals', where, it was alleged, some senior managers abused their power to further their own ends or to conduct illegal accounting activities. The most notable cases involved Robert Maxwell and his alleged use of pension money to fund the business, the demise of Polly Peck plc, followed by the arrest and subsequent escape of its chairman, Asil Nadir and the Guinness 'scandal' where a number of senior directors were convicted of false accounting. At the end of the 20th century further scandals emerged with the collapse of companies such as *BCCI*, *Worldcom* and *Enron*, with the loss of billions of dollars for shareholders and thousands of jobs lost worldwide.

Case: Enron

In just 15 years, Enron grew from nowhere to become America's seventh largest company, employing 21,000 people in more than 40 countries. However in October 2001, we witnessed one of the biggest crashes in corporate history. The story began against the background of energy deregulation in the USA and the removal of government controls on that could produce energy and how it was sold. In 1985 two American companies, Houston Natural Gas and Inter-North merged and Enron was born. Enron's basic strategy was to profit from trading futures in gas contracts – buying and selling tomorrow's gas at a fixed price today. This enabled companies to 'hedge' against the risk of upward price movements. By the 1990s Enron had become a massive player in the USA energy-related products' markets, at its peak controlling almost 25% of all gas business, while extending its operations to include other commodities, such as coal and steel. The dot.com boom in 2000 provided

Enron with the opportunity to be among the first energy companies to begin trading through the Internet. They provided a free service that attracted a great deal of business, in a 2-year period the value of products bought and sold online was reported by Enron at $880 billion (£618 billion). Enron's 2000 annual report showed a 40% increase in income over a 3-year period and the share price rose to a high of $90 per share. However the company's growth was increasingly dependent upon its dubious accounting practices as Enron's real revenue was being disguised by a sophisticated system of theoretically independent 'special partnerships' that allowed Enron to make investments and shift the debt off its books, thereby declaring potential income as a buffer against future losses. The company was able to raise investment against its own assets and stock and, by maintaining the impression of a highly successful company via lies about its profits and concealment of debt, the share price was kept high. On 14 August 2001, the Chief Executive Officer (CEO), Jeff Skilling suddenly resigned, citing personal reasons, but investors suspected that all was not well and millions of shares were sold so that by the end of the month each share was worth less than $40. Meanwhile the depth of Enron's problems was becoming apparent to its auditors, Andersen, who was at that time one of the world's top five accountancy firms. The directors at Enron were advised that they would have to change the way they were accounting for its special partnerships, even though it was later shown that Andersen had previously approved the partnerships in question (i.e. Raptor and Condor). Around this time, staff at Andersen started shredding documents relating to their transactions with Enron, actions that would see the company being found guilty of obstructing justice in June 2002. Throughout October and November 2001, Enron struggled to cope with its enormous debt, burden was almost taken over by a much smaller rival, Dynergy, and finally filed for bankruptcy in December 2001. In just 3 months Enron had gone from being a company claiming assets worth almost $62 billion to bankruptcy and a share price of less than $1, and a series of legal actions against the company directors.

25.3 Corporate governance in the UK

Cadbury Committee

The *Cadbury Committee*, chaired by *Sir Adrian Cadbury* was commissioned in 1991 to look into the 'best practices' in corporate governance. The central concern of the Committee was the degree of power, which was considered as essentially unaccountable, vested in the board of directors and in particular the division of responsibilities between chairmen and chief executives. The committee reported in May 1992 with the following recommendations to redress the main concerns:

- There should be a greater usage of *NEDs*. These appointments should be independent of the company and have no financial or business stake in it.
- There should be *regular board meetings* to retain full and effective control over the activities of the company and to monitor its management.
- *Responsibilities and duties at board level should be divided* to ensure that no single person has an over-concentration of power. The independent element of the NEDs should help to accomplish this.
- There should be a *restriction of 3 years* on the contracts of executive directors which would not be renewed without shareholders' approval.
- There should be a *full disclosure of the emoluments* (total earnings) of each director.
- The company should establish three *sub-committees* of the board which would be staffed or overseen mainly by NEDs:
  - an *audit committee* to examine the internal affairs of the company;
  - a *remunerations committee* to recommend levels of directors' pay;
  - a *nominations committee* to recommend appointments to the board.
- There should be a formal statement in the audited annual accounts that the *business is a going concern*, with financial figures and evidence to back-up this claim as appropriate.
- There should be a *separation of the roles of chairperson and chief executive*, that is, these two pivotal positions should not be held by the same person (as is the case in some smaller companies).

The Cadbury Committee did not propose that these recommendation be made statutory (i.e. enshrined in company law), rather that they should be followed voluntarily. However, it has become almost mandatory for all listed public companies, as the London Stock Exchange has recommended their compliance or to formally state the extent to which they do not comply in their annual report. The Cadbury Report has been very influential in reshaping corporate governance over the past few years. In 1995, *the Greenbury Report* examined directors' pay and in 1998, *the Hampel Committee's* study of corporate governance led to the *Combined Code* of best practice in *corporate governance.*

The aim of the Code is to generally improve standards and encourage transparency to facilitate pertinent shareholder questions.

Compliance with the Combined Code for Corporate Governance
J Sainsbury plc: statement of compliance

J Sainsbury plc, the well-known multiple grocery retailer is, like most large plcs, concerned to comply, and to be seen to comply, with all matters of 'good practice' in corporate behaviour. The company holds the leading market share in food and non-food grocery supplies with sales of £15.3 billion through its 498 stores (2003). In the company's annual report for 2003, it is stated that that *'the company is committed to high standards of corporate governance in its business and has complied throughout the period under review with all the provisions of the Combined Code on Corporate Governance. The Remuneration, Nomination and Audit Committees have written terms of reference which define their authorities, duties and membership. These committees are made up exclusively of the NEDs, other than the Group Chief Executive's membership of the Nomination Committee'.*

Source: J Sainsbury plc, Annual Report, 2002.

Principles of corporate governance

Private sector

The main principles of corporate governance for organisations, arising from the reports of Cadbury, Hampel and Greenbury are as follows:

- to have separate roles of chairman and chief executive;
- the structure of boards to have executive and NEDs;
- to have risk management approach;
- to move towards a stakeholder approach;
- to demonstrate transparency, openness and fairness;
- to be fully accountable for actions.

Public sector

The *Nolan committee* (1995), which examined concerns standards of conduct of public office holders in the UK, identified the following *seven principles of public life*:

- selflessness,
- integrity,
- objectivity,
- accountability,
- openness,
- honesty,
- leadership.

British Telecommunications plc: NEDs

British Telecommunications (BT) plc is one of Britain's biggest companies, with a group turnover of £18.5 billion for the year ended 31 March 2004. Its Board at that time comprised:

- Sir Christopher Bland: Chairman (part-time)
- Ben Verwaayen: Chief Executive
- Dr Paul Reynolds: Chief Executive BT Wholesale
- Andy Green: Chief Executive BT Global Services
- Pierre Danon: Chief Executive BT Retail
- Ian Livingstone: Group Financial Director

In addition there are seven NEDs who are considered by the Board to be independent, meeting the criteria of the *Combined Code*.

- Sir Anthony Greener: Deputy Chairman. Other appointment, Chairman of the University for Industry and the Qualifications and Curriculum Authority (formerly, chairman of Diageo).
- Louis R Hughes: Other appointment, non-executive chairman of Maxager Technology Inc. (USA) (formerly, president and chief executive of Lockheed Martin Corporation).
- Maartenvan den Bergh: Other appointment, chairman of Lloyds TSB Group (formerly, president of the Royal Dutch Petroleum Company).
- John Nelson: Other appointment, deputy chairman of Kingfisher (formerly, chairman of Credit Suisse First Boston Europe).
- Executive director of Independent News & Media (formerly, Lord Privy Seal, Leader of the House of Lords).
- Carl G Symon: Other appointment, NED of Rolls-Royce plc (formerly, chairman and chief executive officer of IBM UK).
- Clayton Brendish: Other appointment, non-executive chairman of Beacon Investment Fund (formerly, executive deputy chairman of CMG).

Note: each of these individuals has other appointments with a variety of organisations.

The Chairman and the NEDs regularly meet without the executive directors and, at least annually, the NEDs meet, without the Chairman, to review his performance. To meet best corporate governance practice, the company has established Audit, Remuneration and Nominating Committees of which the first two are entirely composed of independent NEDs.

Source: BT Annual Report, 2003.

25.4 Impact of corporate governance principles in the UK

Corporate governance in the UK is conducted under the notion of 'comply' or 'explain' and, in the main; the development of the principles into practice has been reactive and led by private sector businesses. There is increased commitment to non-financial reporting (e.g. reporting of actions for sustainability).

Impact of corporate governance principles in the UK

In the main, development of corporate governance in the UK has been led by private sector businesses and is generally enacted under the notion of 'comply' or 'explain'. The Higg's Report (2003) raised concerns about the quality of board members and board composition in relation to gender, age, competency, and professional commitments. There is evidence of an increased commitment to non-financial reporting (e.g. reporting of actions connected with sustainability).

25.5 Business ethics

The nature of ethics in business

The ethical debate is slightly more complicated than the environmental one. Whilst there is a broad agreement that 'something should be done' about the environment, there is a wider spectrum of opinion in matters of ethics and morals. Some First World consumers actively campaign for higher ethical standards whilst others adopt the opinion, either stated or unstated, that whilst global warming may in time affect them, the plight of the Third World or the experiences of farm animals do not. This approach, slightly cynically labelled the '*I'm alright Jack*' philosophy, is present, to a greater or lesser extent in all First World societies. The issue is also complicated by the plethora of different religious and cultural convictions held by individuals in the various parts of the world.

The study of business ethics can be described as the systematic analysis of moral matters pertaining to business, industry or related activities, institutions or practices and beliefs. Basically, we are discussing what is right or wrong, not necessarily what is legal. The variety of opinions held over ethical issues can be attributed to the wide spectrum of systems of belief that people hold. Some individuals have a deep sense of concern for almost all ethical issues, some focus on one area of concern (e.g. animal use by business or Third World issues), whilst others don't seem too concerned about any of it. There are many issues that are not of major concern but are strongly held by some consumers in some societies, for example, for a specific religious reason.

Business and social responsibility

We might expect, therefore, a wide range of opinions and practices amongst businesses to their wider role in society. We can divide business responses to social responsibility by considering four broad categories.

- Some businesses are actively *socially obstructive*. This description can be applied to organisations that actively resist any pressures or attempts to modify pure business objectives in the light of social concern. Such organisations may resist attempts to make them abide even to the minimum legal standards of behaviour – behaviour which may be followed by denial and an attempt to keep 'interfering' bodies out of their business. Some have argued that tobacco manufacturers fall into this category as in order to protect their sales of cigarettes, they may effectively deny that tobacco causes as much harm as some health professionals have indicated.

- Some businesses observe no more than their minimum *social obligations*. This description can be applied to organisations that are prepared to abide by whatever restrictions are placed upon them by governments, in other words, the legal minimum. They are unwilling to give credence to any pressure or lobby groups which, in the opinion of the organisation, do not have any statutory influence over them.

■ The third group is *socially responsive*. These organisations submit to minimum legal standards for corporate behaviour towards society and the environment, but go further than socially obligated organisations. The difference is that socially responsive organisations will do more to address people's concerns, if pressurised to do so by stakeholders such as pressure groups.

■ The final group comprises those organisations which seek to make a *social contribution*. This description can be applied to organisations that willingly do all they reasonably can to extend their social and environmental involvement. In this sense, such organisations seek to make a positive contribution to the communities they serve, to help protect the natural environment and to avoid any unethical business practices. Some social contribution organisations may exist primarily for the purpose of promoting social responsibility and ethical business practice.

25.6 The nature of ethical concerns

Ethical issues arising from the nature of markets

One of the problems with the nature of markets is that they are concerned with rationing. We learned in Chapter 16 that the market mechanism serves to bring buyers and sellers together at a price that provides an economic return to sellers whilst at the same time satisfying the needs of the buyers as a collective group. One of the problems with this approach is that a market price necessarily prohibits some individual consumers from enjoying the benefits of the product. The market system thus inevitably results in inequalities. Some consumers have a great deal more than the 'average' consumer whilst others have much less. In many areas of life and business, we freely accept this in that we realise that we cannot all afford certain items like BMW motorcars. In other cases, however, the nature of markets results in inequalities that appear to some to be a little unfair.

Part of the inequality of both the demand and supply sides of the market system arises due to the fact that factors of production are not evenly distributed. Some countries and regions of the world, for example, have inherently better land, better resource reserves and national cultures that are apparently more conducive to business success than others. In consequence, it is an unavoidable fact that some countries are richer and more economically powerful than others.

Countries that are wealthy, those in the First World, have the opportunity to exert influence over poorer countries who have weaker currencies and sometimes intense economic problems. Concern has arisen over some business practices that rest upon this disparity of wealth and currency value. The award of a contract or a sale from a First World based company to a Third World supplier results in an inflow of 'hard' (high exchange value) currency, and this represents an opportunity for powerful First World multinationals to 'exploit' the weaker Third World producers (using the 'bargaining power of buyers and suppliers' we encountered in Chapter 20 with Porter's five force model). This can result in the producer acting unethically to meet the order (such as by employing child labour) or by otherwise acting irresponsibly. Alleged irresponsibility arises when, for example, food crops which could provide food for local people are replaced with 'cash-crops' to sell abroad to gain foreign currency.

Ethical issues arising from the responsibility of business to society

The second area from which ethical concern arises is in the way in which businesses respond to the opinions of their external stakeholders in society. In Chapter 2 we learned that an organisation has a wide range of potential stakeholders, often with conflicting aspirations for the organisation. The manner in which an organisation should respond to its stakeholders is often a matter of controversy. We also learned in Chapter 2 that there are two models to explain the organisation, stakeholder relationship.[1] The normative model suggests that an organisation responds to its stakeholders because they have legitimate rights over the affairs of the organisation and that the organisation sees stakeholders as ends in themselves. Conversely, the instrumental approach argues that organisations observe stakeholder aspirations only inasmuch as they are consistent with maximising profits.

There is often a tension between the wishes of shareholders who have an economic interest in the business's profits, and the wishes of 'community' stakeholders who tend to exhort the business to behave in a more 'responsible' way even though this may result in sub-optimal profits.

Underpinning the idea that businesses should behave responsibly towards society is the belief that businesses, like individual people, are *citizens* of society. Citizens are members of society who have both rights to benefits from society and responsibilities towards it. It is self-evident that businesses benefit from society as a supplier of labour and customers. Accordingly, advocates of the normative model subscribe to the belief that businesses have a moral and ethical responsibility to behave as responsible citizens. In many situations, serving the social responsibilities (to society) of a business may result in short-term costs, but it is nevertheless believed that ignoring its responsibilities can result in long-term losses (the instrumental model).

Predictably then, an organisation interprets its responsibility to its stakeholders in a variety of ways. Concerns which are often considered in this area of business ethics include the following:

- The extent to which a business is involved in the communities in which it is involved.
- Honesty, truthfulness and fairness in marketing activities such as advertising and the statements and images used in marketing communications.
- The use of animals in product testing (although for some products, animal testing is required by law).
- Agricultural practices such as intensive methods of crop growing and the 'battery' farming of some animals (particularly chickens and pigs).
- The degree of safety built into product design and manufacture (e.g. the extent to which suspect meat is used in human food products).
- The extent to which a business accepts its alleged responsibilities arising from mishaps, spillages negligence and leaks (e.g. oil spills, pollution leakages and compensation claims from employees suffering bad health as a result of asbestos or coal dust).
- The amount of money that the company donates each year to charitable causes (this is shown in the company's annual accounts).

Ethical issues arising from the internal and industry practices of business

In addition to an organisation's responsibilities to its external stakeholders, it also has responsibilities towards those inside the organisation and in its micro-environment, its employees, suppliers, customers, etc. Again, much of this area of business practice is regulated by law (see Chapter 13) but some issues are open to debate and interpretation by individual businesses. It is, for example, illegal to discriminate against anybody on the basis of gender or race, whilst safety in the workplace is covered by a raft of laws including the Health and Safety at Work Act 1974 (described in Chapter 13).

Common concerns in this area of ethics include:

- The way in which a powerful company treats its customers, for example, honouring the spirit (in addition to the 'letter') of warranties and the quality of after-sales service.
- The way in which a powerful company treats its suppliers, such as the payment of bills on time and honouring verbal agreements to take stock over a period of time.
- The number of women and members of ethnic minorities in senior positions in the company (some organisations actively try to engage women and minorities at all levels in the organisation).
- The number of disabled workers in the organisation over and above the legal quotas for such and their positions within the organisation.
- The organisation's loyalty to its employees in difficult economic conditions (i.e. how hard it tries to *not* make employees redundant in difficult trading climates).

Responses to the concerns

In addition to legislation and the issuing of voluntary codes of practice, governments and other political institutions have undertaken a programme of gentle and not-so-gentle persuasion. The objective of such tactics is to try to make business behaviour more responsible without the need to impose the burden of legislation. In many matters of environmental concern, we have seen that legislative and regulatory frameworks exist that influence the behaviour of businesses. In ethical matters, such frameworks are much more problematic: how do you legislate that businesses should be 'nice' or 'ethical?'

In consequence, governments and other political bodies have attempted to influence ethical business behaviour by exhortation and persuasion. There is, of course, a difference of opinion on many issues and this gives rise to an element of debate in the country as a whole in respect of such matters as animal experiments. Politicians have been known to agree on some areas of ethical business on such things as the way in which large businesses treat their smaller suppliers and the time taken to pay invoices. On many issues, however, the differences of opinion that exist mean that individuals are often left to make their own minds up with regard to ethical issues.

Some organisations go a step further than modifying their mission statement by issuing a *code of business ethics*. This is a document which states how the organisation intends to act towards its stakeholders. Many of the UK's largest companies have issued such a document including British Airways, Barclays and Lloyds Banks, Whitbread, British Aerospace, Phillips Petroleum and United Biscuits. The *Institute of Business Ethics* in London is a body promoting, among other things, such codes of ethics. Its patrons include senior religious leaders in the UK including the Archbishop of Canterbury and the Chief Rabbi and its council includes some leading businesspeople. The Institute recommends that organisations issue statements in respect of ethical practice regarding:

- relations with customers,
- relations with shareholders and other investors,
- relations with employees,
- relations with suppliers,
- relations with the government and the local community,
- the environment,
- taxation,
- relations with competitors,
- issues relating to international business,
- behaviour in relation to mergers and take-overs,
- ethical issues concerning directors and managers,
- compliance and verification.

Another way in which organisations have changed their practices in the light of concerns is by the compilation of *social accounts*. This is a document which is compiled and published voluntarily by an organisation, unlike its financial accounts which are required by law. Social accounting or social auditing is the recording of the impact the organisation has made upon its stakeholders. The objective of such an exercise is to test how well or badly the organisation has measured up to its mission statement and/or code of business ethics. Organisations that pursue this option tend to have the audit carried out by an independent body in much the same way as, a financial audit is carried out by independent auditors. Social accounts are relatively new to the world of business ethics. Early adopters included several alternative-trading organisations (ATOs – businesses which exist to pursue ethical purposes like 'fair' Third World trade) although the idea may be gradually catching on with more conventional business organisations.

In addition to the broad measures mentioned above, many organisations have taken specific measures in particular parts of their activity. Some businesses involving non-essential animal experiments have discontinued such activities to reflect customer concerns.

25.7 Ethical decision models

As we have seen, ethical issues can arise in varied and complex manners, with different individuals trying to apply different values and solutions to very real-ethical dilemmas. The following summary provides outline descriptions of some common types of decision models:

- *Utilitarian*: this type of process is aimed at producing the greatest good for the greatest number of people.
- *Morale rights*: this approach maintains and protects the fundamental rights and privileges of the people affected by the decision.
- *Justice*: the justice decision model aims to distribute benefits (and penalties) among stakeholders in a fair, equitable or impartial way.

Assignment 25.1

- Suggest potential benefits that can accrue to an organisation that actively pursues positive ethical standards.
- Suggest potential costs to an organisation that could arise from its poor ethical standards.

Reference

1   Donaldson, T. and Preston, L.E. (1995). The stakeholder theory of the corporation: concepts, evidence and implications. *Academy of Management Review*, **20**(1): 65–91.

Further reading

Bradburn, R. (2001). *Understanding Business Ethics*. London: Thomson Learning.

Buchholtz, C. (2003). *Business and Society, Ethics, and Stakeholder Management*, 5th edn. Ohio, USA: Thomson South-Western.

Cannon, T. (1994). *Corporate Responsibility. Issues in Business Ethics, Governance, Roles and Responsibilities*. London: Pitman.

Chryssides, G. and Kaler, J. (1996). *Essentials of Business Ethics*. New York: McGraw Hill.

McInerny, P. and Rainbolt, P. (1994). *Ethics*. London: Harper Collins.

Murray, D. (1996). *Ethics in Organisations*. Kogan Page.

Post, J.E. *et al.* (2001). *Business and Society: Corporate Strategy, Public Policy, Ethics*, 10th edn. London: McGraw Hill.

Weiss, J.W. (1994). *Business Ethics. A Managerial, Stakeholder Approach*. Thomson Publishing.

Winstanley, D. and Woodall, J. (2000). *Ethical Issues in Human Resource Management*. London: MacMillan Business.

Useful web sites

Corporate governance codes: www.eccg.org.codes/
Institute of Business Ethics: www.ibe.org.uk
The Higgs Report (2003), The Cadbury Report (1992), Greenbury Report (1995), Hampel Report (1998): www.dti.gov.uk

CHAPTER 26

Operations management and manufacturing

Learning objectives

After studying this chapter, students should be able to describe:

- the nature of operations in business;
- the significance of the value chain;
- the types and costs of stock;
- the processes involved in purchasing and in the management of inbound logistics;
- the common types of manufacturing system;
- the processes involved in distribution and outbound logistics.

26.1 Operations management

Introduction

Operations management is perhaps the most important function of any organisation. This is because of its crucial role in the success or otherwise of the business. Let us first define this function: *Operations management is directly responsible for the planning, direction and control of the fundamental activities necessary for the organisation to achieve its objectives.* These activities will be to make, sell or provide products or services.

We can note immediately that this 'direct responsibility' is what distinguishes operations from other functions. In a car manufacturer, the operations function is that part of the business which makes the cars.

Without this part of the business, it makes little sense to have a finance function, human resource management (HRM) function, or any other – important though those functions are. Other functions exist to support operations; without which, they would have no reason to be (see the distinction between line and staff employees under Section 21.3).

It is perhaps appropriate to consider some examples:

Type of organisation	Operations function
Manufacturing company	Factory
Newcastle United Football Club	Newcastle United Football Team
Restaurant	Kitchen and waiters
University	Lecturers and researchers

An example close to home to most readers will be the university. A university employs many people apart from lecturers, such as administrators, finance managers, clerical staff, site services staff (e.g. car park attendants, gardeners, etc.) and technical staff. However, the university exists primarily to educate students and to research – only academic staff (lecturers) can do this. All other parts of a university exist to support academic staff in their important duties.

Value chain

The business of organisations can be regarded as systems which transform inputs (resources, materials, etc.) into outputs (goods and services). The activities of an organisation can then be identified in a sequence of activities known as the *value chain*.[1] The activities within the chain may be classified into *primary activities* and *support activities*. *Primary activities* are those which *directly add value* to the final product. *Support activities* do not directly add value themselves but *indirectly add value* by supporting the effective execution of primary activities. A summary of the items in the value chain is shown at Table 26.1 and Figure 26.1.

Different types of organisations will have different value chains. For example, the value chain of Dixons, the electrical goods retailer, does not include the design and manufacture of the products it sells. Marks and Spencer's value chain does include some design but does not include manufacturing. Similarly, not all of an organisation's activities are of equal importance in adding value to its products. Those which are of greatest importance can be considered as *core activities* and are often closely associated to *core competences*. Thus in a fashion house like Calvin

Table 26.1

A summary of the items in the value chain

Primary activities	
Inbound logistics	Receipt, handling and storage of materials (inputs). Stock control and distribution of inputs into final product.
Operations	Transformation of inputs into final product.
Outbound logistics	Storage and distribution of FG.
Marketing and sales	Making the product available to the market and persuading people to buy.
Service	Installation and after sales support.
Support activities	
Procurement	Purchasing of resources.
Technology development	Product, process and resource development.
Infrastructure	Planning, finance, information systems, management.
Human resource management	Recruitment, selection, training, reward and motivation.

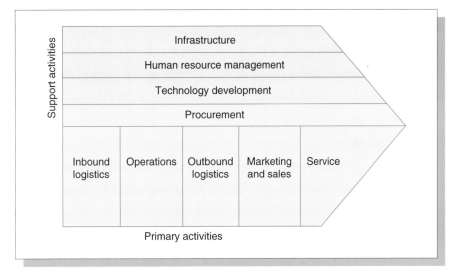

Figure 26.1
The value chain
(after Porter, 1985).

Klein, design activities are of the greatest importance in adding value and the organisation's core competences are concentrated in this area.

Value analysis helps to identify where most value is added and where there is potential to add greater value by changing the way in which activities are configured and by improving the way in which they are co-ordinated.

It is important to note that a company's value chain does not exist in isolation. There will be direct links between inbound logistics of the company and the outbound logistics of its suppliers. This linkage of value chains is sometimes called the *value system* or *total supply chain*. Linkages with suppliers are known as *upstream* linkages while those with distributors and customers are *downstream* linkages (Figure 26.2).

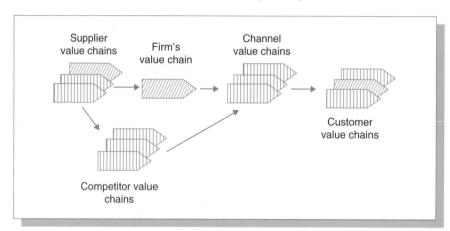

Figure 26.2
The value system.

One of the most notable features of value analysis is that it recognises that an organisation is much more than a random collection of machinery, money and people. These resources are of no value unless they are organised into structures, routines and systems that ensure that the products or services that are valued by the final customer are the ones that are produced. The firm must assess how the resources are utilised and linked to competitive advantage.

26.2 Production management

Production management is concerned with the procurement, deployment and use of resources to manufacture products for distribution and sale to customers. Raw materials (RMs), or purchased parts, (inputs) are transformed into finished goods (FGs) (outputs) and production management is responsible for the techniques and methods that are utilised by the workforce. It is also central to the achievement of quality standards, targets and punctual delivery of orders within budget parameters.

Manufacturing as an example of operations

We have seen that manufacturing is one example of an operations function. However, owing to its complexity and importance, the majority of thinking in the operations sphere has been focused in the area of manufacturing. It is for this reason that the majority of this chapter is concerned with manufacturing, although it should be borne in mind that many of the principles we will discuss are transferable to non-manufacturing operational contexts (e.g. university, bank, restaurant, etc.).

Manufacturing is a process involving the passage of physical goods through an organisation from buying materials in, to distribution of the FG to the customer, and all that happens in-between. A generalised representation of the manufacturing process is shown below:

Purchasing
↓
Goods inward and RMs storage
↓
Manufacturing
↓
FG storage and distribution

Stock

Types of stock

An important part of manufacturing must be introduced at this point: the actual material involved in the process – referred to as *stock* or *inventory*. Stock is divided into three types, depending upon where it is in the transformation process:

- RMs or purchased parts are stocks in their 'raw' state. RMs are those goods that are purchased, before they undergo any processing within the manufacturing process.
- *Work-in-progress* (WIP) is the name given to stocks that are actually being worked on in the manufacturing process.
- FG stocks are those which have passed through the process and are ready for distribution to the customers.

Costs of stock

Central to all stock purchasing and management is the fact that stock of all kinds costs money. We can appreciate the nub of this issue by relating it to our own personal stocks, such as stocks of food. It is a singularly pleasurable experience to open the fridge door to find it packed with immediately consumable fresh foods; cheeses, pâtés, cold meats, fresh juices and many others. It is obvious, however, that such luxuriant stocking costs money. Whilst, with a full fridge, you are prepared for any eventuality, such as friends calling unexpectedly, you must accept the variety of costs that accompany such stock levels.

This has been an issue that has much exercised the minds of the business and academic elite over the past two decades – to find the level of stock that will facilitate normal business functioning without incurring excessive costs for the 'luxury' of excess stocks.

The costs of stock to a business (many of which are equally applicable to the stock of food in your fridge) are as follows:

- The *price paid for the stock* is the most obvious cost. Whenever stock is bought in, money must be paid out for it, thus reducing the amount of money left 'in the kitty'. It follows that stock has an 'opportunity cost' – by buying stock, you have less money to spend on other things and you are foregoing interest on the money that you could earn if the money paid for the stock was deposited in the bank or otherwise invested.
- The *cost of stock storage* has several constituents; the purchase or rental cost of space required to store it, the insurance paid on the stock and its storage space, and wages to staff who are paid to manage the stock.
- The *risk associated with stock storage* is the third cost. If you overstock on food, you run the risk that some of it may 'go off', and in the same way, some business stocks can become obsolescent or become subject to theft or damage.

Operations in everyday life

The author decides to cook. Not being very ambitious, he decides to make a shepherd's pie. Opening his fridge, freezer and larder, the author realises that he has none of the required ingredients. In consequence, he goes to the local supermarket to buy the ingredients in (the purchasing stage). After carefully selecting half a kilo of mince, an onion and some potatoes, he returns home to unpack the goods. Unpacking the food (RMs) on the kitchen bench, he checks the mince for gristle, the onion for bad bits and the potatoes for damage or black bits (goods inward and inspection). The ingredients are then put away until dinnertime (RMs storage).

When the time comes to prepare, the author retrieves the ingredients from the storage units (e.g. fridge) and begins the cooking process by chopping up the onion and frying the mince (the manufacturing or production process). There are obviously several stages in this process, such as boiling, frying and finally baking or grilling. The ingredients, whilst undergoing the process are WIP stocks.

Finally, the shepherd's pie is finished. The author takes the masterpiece from the oven and serves it upon to plates and carries them through to the dining room table for consumption (distribution – no FG storage in this case).

The example of making a shepherd's pie illustrates the principles. In practice, however, the processes involved in operations are rather more complicated. We will examine each stage in turn.

26.3 Purchasing and inbound logistics

Purchasing management

Purchasing management is sometimes referred to as *supplies management*, or by rather grand-sounding names, such as *procurement,* or *inbound logistics.* Essentially, it is about buying materials in to facilitate the normal working of the subsequent manufacturing process.

The job of the purchasing manager is thus to buy the right materials or parts:

- of the right quality,
- in the right quantity,
- at the right price,
- from the right supplier,
- with the right delivery arrangements,
- to arrive at the right time,
- with the right payment or credit terms.

The purchasing manager clearly has an important job as getting any part of the purchasing process wrong can be very damaging to the overall operations process. An inept purchasing manager may, for example, order the wrong materials to arrive too late or possibly forget to order them at all. In either case, the manufacturing process is severely adversely affected. Similarly, a purchasing manager who pays too much for incoming materials will increase operational costs and thus reduce profits.

In a typical UK manufacturing business, the purchasing manager spends around 65% of the company's total income. This means that if the business achieves sales of £100 million, the purchases needed to generate that level of sales will be around £65 million. It follows that the quickest way to increase profits is to reduce the cost of purchases rather than to sell more products (important though that is). It is consequently something of a mystery why most purchasing managers are 'back-room boys' (or girls) on a mediocre salary. The strategic importance of the purchasing manager's spending is difficult to overstate.

The role of the purchasing manager

The *purchasing manager*, as we have seen, is an important person in an organisation. The job includes a number of distinct activities:

- Administering and organising all material inputs into the organisation.
- Acting as a 'window on the world' by monitoring changes in the supply industries, such as new products, price changes, etc.
- Visiting suppliers to check on quality and the reliability of suppliers to meet the company's input needs.
- Negotiating supply contracts with suppliers.
- 'Shopping around' for cheaper prices, better service or more reliable supply.
- Meeting with suppliers' representatives to find out about new products and any changes in the terms of supply and cultivating good relationships with suppliers.
- Inspecting and examining suppliers' sales information to establish the most appropriate products to buy and the optimal order quantity.

Goods inward and materials management

The goods inward part of operations is important for three reasons:

- It manages the RMs, thus ensuring that they are properly kept so they do not go off, decay, rust or become obsolescent in any way.
- It issues RMs to production when requested in precisely the right quantities so that the production process has just what it needs, when it is needed.
- It monitors stock levels of RMs so that there are no excess stocks or that no under stocking occurs (although in many cases, this part of the job has been replaced by computerised stock management systems).

The actual level of RM stocks held and how they are held will in part be determined by the type of operational philosophy used by the organisation (see Chapter 24). Some operational systems, for example, just-in-time (JIT), favour no stocks of RMs, in which case, the goods inward stage will assume a different role to that discussed above.

26.4 Manufacturing processes

The manufacturing part of operations is when RMs become WIP. The conversion (or processing) of materials results in the output of FG from the organisation. Of course the actual process of conversion will depend entirely upon the nature of the business; it might be assembly, reaction, transformation, mixing or any number of other mechanisms of conversion. Similarly, the scale of production varies enormously, from the one-person back-shed business making trout flies to the multinational company producing cars in 40 different manufacturing plants in as many countries.

Added value: the aim of manufacturing

The essential purpose of manufacturing is to *add value*. This means that by working on stocks, a business increases the value of the stocks and thus enables a profit to be made. When RMs are bought in, they are just that – RMs. A tonne of sheet metal is of little use to a customer who wishes to drive to Norwich. By taking the sheet metal, some plastic and some rubber, and transforming it, a motorcar manufacturer can turn such unlikely materials costing a few hundred pounds into a magnificent motorcar valued at many thousands of pounds.

Each stage of manufacturing that the materials pass through adds more value to the stocks. When a sheet of metal is pressed and cut into the front wing of a car, its value is increased as a front wing is worth more than a sheet of metal. When it is painted, it is worth even more and when it is bolted or welded onto an assembled car body, its value is maximised.

It follows from this principle that value is only being added to stocks when they are actually being worked on. If, at any time, the stocks are sitting idle or are waiting to be worked on, value is not being added and thus costs are being incurred (we have already identified the costs of stock). One of the aims of manufacturing is thus to keep stocks moving through the process. Stock queuing is thus the enemy of added value (see Figure 26.3).

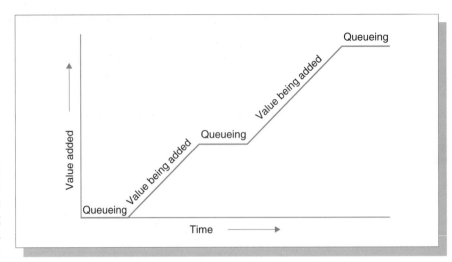

Figure 26.3
Progress of added
value in a
manufacturing
process with stock
queueing.

As we discuss the various types of production, we will see that some add value more rapidly than others.

Types of production

There are five generalised forms of production in manufacturing business:

- project manufacture,
- job manufacture,
- batch manufacture,
- flow and line manufacture,
- continuous manufacture.

The method chosen will depend in large part on the nature of the product being made. Some products can only be made by one method whereas for others, more than one method may be possible. We will briefly examine each in turn.

Project manufacture

As its name suggests, project manufacture is concerned with making 'one-off' jobs.

Projects are characterised by a number of features:

- In most cases, each project undertaken is unique and is made to a design explicitly specified by the customer.
- Projects are usually large objects which means that once they are built, they cannot be moved (although there are exceptions).

- Orders are won, not on the quality of the product produced (although this becomes important), but on the capabilities of the business – its track record at carrying out similar projects.
- Value is added continually as the project is being worked on all the time until it is finished. The entire operations function of the business is brought to bear on the project.

Examples of products which are made by project manufacturers include:

- civil engineering projects, such as buildings, roads, railways and special projects, such as the channel tunnel;
- building refurbishments and modifications, such as the building of extensions;
- shipping;
- off-shore installations, such as oil-rigs.

Job manufacture

Job manufacture is like project in that it involves making one-offs, but jobs tend to be on a much smaller scale – they are jobs rather than grander projects. The two approaches have other things in common as well:

- They both add value more-or-less continuously in that the product is being worked on all of the time until it is finished.
- They both produce products which are built according to customers' specifications (i.e. they are not standard 'off-the-shelf' products).
- They both employ relatively skilled workers who are specialised in a specific part of the manufacturing process (e.g. bricklayers, welders).
- They both suffer from relatively low machine utilisation. This means that a machine is used for one part of the manufacturing process only. It is thus quite possible for an expensive piece of equipment to sit idle for most of the time. Sometimes, manufacturers 'get round' this drawback by renting machines as needed, but this is not always possible.
- They both rely on the competencies of the business and its track record as the key qualifier in winning an order.
- They both rely on a relatively steady flow of orders. If the business enters a period with no orders, it is not possible for project or job manufacturers to make for stock as none of their goods are standard stock products.

In this respect, it is difficult to say where projects end and jobbing starts. Whilst we may agree that a large oil tanker taking over a year to make is a project, we may be less sure about a small fishing boat (i.e. we may say the fishing boat is a job). Examples of products which are usually seen as jobs rather than projects include:

- smaller engineering jobs (e.g. one-off prototypes);
- works of art, sculptures, etc.;
- tradespeople's jobs (e.g. plastering a wall, repairing a washing machine);
- car repairs.

Batch manufacture

Some types of product can be made in 'lots' rather than separately or individually. Batch manufacture thus results in the manufacture of 'lots' of identical products – a feature which contrasts sharply with the unique nature of each project or job. Whereas a job or project manufacturer will produce one ship, one motorway, etc. a batch process may produce 10,000 gallons of beer, 5000 bolts or 45 tins of paint.

Features of batch manufacture include:

- An ability to cope with much higher production volumes than project or batch processes.
- Products typically pass through several distinct stages in the batch process, as is also the case in project and job processes. Each stage may be based at a separate location or work-station and so there is the possibility of time being wasted in non-added-value activities, such as stock moving from place to place and in waiting to be worked on.
- The equipment and plant used in batch manufacturing is modified each time a new batch goes through the plant. This is because each batch is different and requires different settings or material inputs. After each batch, the work-station must be *tooled down* in order to be *tooled up* to run a different batch (this may of course be a washing or purging process or similar). Such modifications represent time delays which prevent value being added to stocks.
- The focus of a batch manufacturing business is on its products and customer's buying decisions are based upon the products rather than on the organisation's competence – the opposite of project and job.

■ The fact that batch operations are based in factories rather than out 'on-site' means that an increased emphasis is placed on maintaining factory volumes and in keeping machines busy.

Batch manufacture is very widely used in manufacturing industry owing to its flexibility. Products made by this method include:

■ beer, often in very large batches of several thousand gallons;
■ paints, in batches of anything from 5 litres to 20,000 litres;
■ pharmaceuticals, where batches run to millions of individual pills. Products like inhalers and vials are made in batches of up to 200,000 units;
■ nuts, bolts and other engineering products, such as car parts (e.g. a batch of 'patterned' exhausts for a Vauxhall Astra).

The advantages of a batch process include its ability to cope with variations in product and volume demand, its higher utilisation of equipment (compared to project and job processes), and the fact that it enables personnel in the factory to become specialised in the operation of their particular process.

Batch manufacturing's disadvantages include the difficulties in organising and scheduling batches through the factory. The fact that different products take different times to produce and that customers require products on different dates means that decisions on what to make where and on what machine can be a headache. In addition, the flexibility of batch manufacturing usually necessitates the holding of relatively high RM stocks as well as higher WIP stocks when queues between stages are involved.

Flow and line manufacture

Flow manufacture – balancing production stages

If you can imagine a batch manufacturing facility in which stocks never queue between workstations, then you have an idea of what flow manufacture is about. Imagine that the manufacture of a product involves three separate processes – A, B and C. Now suppose that due to the nature of the three processes, they take different times periods:

■ process A at workstation A takes 1 hour;
■ process B at workstation B takes half an hour;
■ process C at workstation C takes 2 hours.

The passage of stocks through this facility thus runs as follows. Stock for batch 1 enters process A and is completed after 1 hour. After it is finished, process B can begin work on the stock immediately as process A receives more RM stock to begin another job (batch 2). After another half an hour, process B has finished working on the batch 1 stock and upon passing the WIP onto process C, must sit idle for half an hour until the next consignment of WIP (batch 2) arrives from process A. Process C begins work on the batch 1 stock immediately, thus ensuring that batch 1 passes through all stages without queuing.

After sitting idle for half an hour, process B eventually receives the WIP for batch 2, which it then works on for the requisite half an hour. However, once batch 2 has finished at process B, the WIP itself must wait (or queue) for half an hour before it can pass to process C which requires 2 hours to finish working on batch 1. Once several batches have begun in the factory, the result is a frustrating scenario in which process B sits idle for half the time whilst large queues build up waiting to enter process C. Both of these things; machines not being used and stocks sitting idle, cost money.

Both of these problems can be sorted by 'line balancing'. If we install two machines at process A then there will be a delivery of WIP from process A once every half hour – perfect for process B. Process C must then be modified so that it can accept WIP from process B every half hour. As process C takes two hours, we will need four process C machines. The line is now balanced: there is no queuing and all the machines are fully utilised.

With the bottleneck between processes B and C removed, stock now *flows* through the factory. We have thus turned batch manufacture into flow manufacture.

Line manufacture

Line processes go one step further than flow processes. When a factory is geared up to run higher volumes than most batches through a range of processes, the 'line' of stages can be designed so that are literally in a line, thus making the passage of stock through the processes as simple as possible. Furthermore, if higher volumes of the same product are being produced, the times between tooling up and tooling down are much longer. Lines can thus be dedicated to making a standard product in high volume. Of course, such 'dedication' of a line to one product means that we lose the flexibility of a batch process – we lose the ability to just tool up to run a different product through the process.

Features of line production are therefore:

- a higher investment in plant than batch production;
- high volume production;
- dedicated lines which are inflexible to changes in the product being made;
- a given line produces just one product;
- very high machine utilisation (constant usage in most cases);
- workers on the line become very specialised in just one process along its length – work can be tedious and repetitive.

Products which are usually made on line processes include:

- motorcars,
- electronic consumer goods, such as televisions, video recorders, microcomputers,
- consumer kitchen appliances, such as washing machines, cookers, etc.

Continuous manufacture

The final type of general manufacturing system we will consider is continuous manufacturing. Just as line is an extension of batch, continuous is an extension of line. As its name suggests, a continuous process is one that never stops – rather like a line process for which demand is ongoing and where the product is never subject to fluctuations in demand due to changing fashions or consumer preferences. Continuous processes often run continually for years or even decades without being switched off.

It follows from this that continuous processes produce far higher volumes of output than any of the other production methods we have discussed. The nature of the products produced by this method also means that usually, the cost of setting up a continuous process is huge – usually dwarfing investments in any of the other methods. The size of the investment alone means that production must run constantly in order to generate sales that will pay for the large investment.

Continuous processes are usually controlled rather than worked on (all the other methods of production need at least some people to work on products as they pass through the plant). This means that whilst the continuous process is running, staff monitor production from a separate control room rather from the 'factory floor'.

Clearly then, continuous manufacture is a suitable production method for products which have a high and relatively predicable demand, such as:

- energy (e.g. power stations);
- petrochemicals (e.g. oil refineries producing petrol, diesel, etc.);
- steel (where iron is produced by smelting iron ore and converted into steel in the same production process);
- gas.

26.5 Distribution and outbound logistics

FG stock

Once the operational stock has passed through all of the stages of manufacturing, including any quality control filters that may be in place (see Chapter 24), it becomes FG stock. FG stock attracts the same costs as RM or WIP inventory and so it usually the case that a business wishes to distribute it to customers as soon as possible. In some cases, however, a reasonable FG stock is useful as it enables unexpected customer orders to be met rapidly. The alternative – to make to order – usually incurs a longer lead time than supplying directly from FG stock.

The optimum time of FG stock storage depends upon the value of the stock and the nature of the product. FG stocks in which a large amount of money is invested, such as shipping or defence orders, must be delivered immediately upon completion to gain payment. Other products need to be quickly distributed because they are perishable, such as fresh fruit, cooked food (e.g. chips) or bakery products.

Distribution

The process of distribution is the procedure by which FG stocks leave their point of manufacture and arrive at the point of consumption (e.g. the next stage in the supply chain or the end consumer). The nature of distribution systems varies from the very complex, such as the distribution of petrochemical products across the world, to the very simple, such as the distribution of fish and chips from the local chippy.

The distribution of goods – the science of logistics – is a complex subject in its own right. Academics study it at length and many companies earn revenues from it by means of road, rail, air and shipping haulage. We have probably all seen the ubiquitous Eddie Stobart lorries on UK roads – just one example of a medium-to-large business involved in this area of activity.

The method of distribution chosen by a given business will be guided by such things as the nature of the product and the requirements of the customer. Some products are delivered little-and-often, whilst others are distributed on a batch-at-a-time basis. In both cases, the same criteria for a good distribution system apply. A suitable system will ensure that:

- product *actually arrives* at the point of consumption, that is, the distribution company is reliable;
- deliveries will be *on time*, that is, within the time scale as determined by the customer;
- product *will not be damaged* in transit;
- deliveries will be *cost effective*, meaning that the cost of distribution does not make the selling of the product uneconomical at normal market prices.

The operational process is completed when the goods finally and successfully arrive at the customer.

Assignment 26.1

The purchasing manager of a small engineering company is attracted by a proposal from a components supplier to give a 15% price discount on bulk orders, with a minimum ordering limit. To obtain the discount, the company would have to make a contractual commitment for regular monthly deliveries rather than their current '*ad hoc*' system, which is flexible and dependent upon demand. It is estimated over the next financial year that the company would be required to buy 25% more RMs than the average for the last 3 years. The finance manager has initially been supportive of a move towards cost reduction, and the sales manger reckons that any cost reduction would make the products more price competitive and he could therefore sell more products. However, others in the company are less convinced that it is a suitable deal for them. In particular the production and distribution managers are greatly concerned about their manufacturing capacity.

With reference to the value chain:

- discuss the potential advantages and disadvantages of such a deal;
- recommend a course of action for the company.

Reference

1   Porter, M. (1985). *Competitive Advantage*. New York: Free Press.

Further reading

Anderson, E. (1994). *The Management of Manufacturing Models and Analysis.* London: Addison Wesley.

Baily, P., *et al.* (1998). *Purchasing, Principles and Management,* 8th edn. London: Pitman.

Campbell, D., *et al.* (1999). *Business Strategy an Introduction.* Oxford: Butterworth Heinemann.

Christopher, M. (1998). *Logistics and Supply Chain Management,* 2nd edn. London: FT Prentice Hall.

Dilworth, J. (1999). *Operations Management: Providing Value in Goods and Services.* London: Thomson Learning.

Gattorna, J.L. and Walters, D. (1996). *Managing the Supply Chain. A Strategic Perspective.* London: Palgrave Macmillan.

Hill, T. (1995). *Manufacturing Strategy. Text and Cases,* 3rd edn. London: Irwin.

Johnson, R. (1998). *Operations Management.* Oxford: Butterworth Heinemann.

Muhlemann, A.P. and Oakland, *et al.* (1992). *Production and Operations Management,* 6th edn. London: FT Prentice Hall.

Slack, N. *et al.* (2003). *Operations Management,* 4th edn. London: FT Prentice Hall.

Stevenson, W.J. (2004). *Operations Management,* 8th edn. London: McGraw-Hill.

Useful web sites

Institute of Operations Management: www.iomnet.org.uk

UK government manufacturing strategy: www.dti.gov.uk/manufacturing/

Human resource management: employee relations and people issues

After studying this chapter, students should be able to describe:

- the importance of human resources (HR) to organisations;
- the nature and evolution of human resource management (HRM);
- the significance of people policies, the HR department and people management;
- the role and functions of the HR department;
- the essentials of 'good practice' in key HR tasks, especially appointments, training and development and rewarding employees;
- the features of the two 'sides' of the employee–employer relationship with a focus on trade unions;
- the major theories of human motivation.

27.1 The importance of human resources in organisations

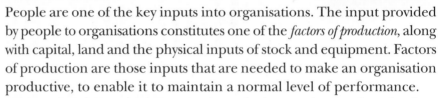

People are one of the key inputs into organisations. The input provided by people to organisations constitutes one of the *factors of production*, along with capital, land and the physical inputs of stock and equipment. Factors of production are those inputs that are needed to make an organisation productive, to enable it to maintain a normal level of performance.

There is, however, uniqueness about the human factor of production, unlike the others, people think and are able to make their own decisions, to withhold their input, to argue and disagree and to make costly mistakes. Of course, it is equally true that this factor of production is also able to make a unique contribution to an organisation's success by generating ideas, by working productively, by managing others and by contributing intellectual and creative power for the benefit of the organisation.

It is a simple fact that all organisations need people. It is an organisation's human resources (HR) that are the key to added value (the adding of value to goods and services as they are produced). People design the processes and attend work environments in which stocks are increased in value by a process of transformation. Without this resource, or with an insufficient level of it, an organisation could not make the most productive use of its other factors of production. Indeed, if we wish to get beyond the often quoted cliché of '*people are our most important asset*' then we might consider that the key to competitive advantage is to employ better people than your competitors. The challenge for organisations, therefore, is how to attract, develop and retain the best employees.

As with the other organisational inputs, HR cost money. It follows from this that an organisation has a need to make a return on its outlay. This need is the nub of human resource management (HRM), that is, to extract the optimum productivity from its investment in HR. Apart from those organisations which exist primarily for the benefit of their members (such as Handy's person cultures, see Chapter 22), all organisations use their HR for productive purposes. All of the areas we will consider in this chapter are designed to maximise human productivity for the organisation. It is a happy coincidence if this also entails satisfaction and fulfilment for the HR themselves.

27.2 Evolution of personnel and HRM

The origins of what became known as *personnel management* can be traced to the Nineteenth century with the philanthropic and paternalistic work of social reformers, such as Robert Owen at New Lanark in Scotland, who recognised that optimum performance and commitment by workers was not possible in the environment of poor working conditions and exploitation that were common in free enterprise system at that time. A radical perspective of employee relations in such societies is found in the *Marxist* philosophy that all work is exploitative of the workforce (and conflict is therefore unavoidable), but by the early Twentieth century the paternalistic style of managing the workforce had evolved into the 'welfare phase' of personnel management with some of the more enlightened firms, notably Cadbury's and Lever Brothers, providing employee benefits, such as sick pay and subsidised housing. The ethical and moral arguments that employers should adopt responsible attitudes towards the *welfare* of their workers, by providing reasonable facilities and benefits, are supported by the view that such business practices encourage productive and loyal employees. Against this background we can see the early stages of personnel specialist activities in the policy and procedural aspects of managing employees' welfare, although it has to be stressed that the *unitarist* perspective of employee relations was still the dominant philosophy. The unitarist approach indicates that work organisation is purposeful to the entire workforce and everybody has the same interest in achieving high efficiency levels. In other words, 'we are all one team' and success for the organisation means success for the individual, although the command structure does not permit challenges to orders from above; any conflict is viewed as some sort of failure which can be eliminated by management and there is no need for bargaining mechanisms.

The next stage in the evolution of personnel management followed the work of such social scientists as *Henri Fayol* and *F.W. Taylor* (see Chapter 1). In attempts to maximise organisational efficiency, personnel specialists applied analytical principles to the design of organisation structures and deployment of their workforces. However, the rigid application of scientific management techniques was seen by many as counterproductive, in that the psychological and sociological needs of workers were often ignored with consequential adverse effects on production and the creation of potential for industrial conflict. This led to the adoption of the *human relations* approach which built upon the works of people, such as Elton Mayo (see Chapter 1) and recognised the need for specialist personnel management skills to provide policies and practices that would promote the importance of social relationships and employee morale in the workplace in the pursuit of greater productivity.

The *industrial relations* era for personnel management originates from the years following the Second World War when the UK experienced a time of 'full' employment with a resultant scarcity of labour and a rapid growth of trade union membership. The changing industrial environment, growing bargaining power of the trades unions and the statutory obligation for collective bargaining in the newly nationalised industries, encouraged many of the largest UK companies to adopt a *pluralist* perspective in their employee relations. The pluralist perspective rests on the assumption that Society consists of various groups with their own interests and decisions are reached by a process of negotiation, compromise and concession. Conflict in organisations is seen as not only inevitable, but a necessity that can actually stimulate the productive process, and therefore the aim should not be to eliminate it but manage it via joint consultation, collective bargaining, arbitration, conciliation, etc. (see Section 27.8 below). Also, the balance of power had shifted with educated and organised trade unionists, strengthened by new employment rights legislation. As a consequence, organisations were obliged to develop personnel specialists with the relevant employee-relation skills to effectively manage the collective institutions.

By the early 1970s, the personnel specialist role had progressed from the generally reactive administration of employee contracts to a more pro-active and organisationally integrated management function, with an emphasis on focussed recruitment, development and retention of employees. The evolution continued with the arrival of the *manpower planning* era where information technology (IT) enabled personnel specialists to develop techniques of planning future workforce requirements. The purpose of manpower planning is to ensure that the organisation has the right number of people with the right skills in the right place at the right time. It is essentially comprised of three main elements:

- The forecast demand aims to assess the numbers of employees and their respective skills that will be required by the organisation in short, medium and long terms.
- The supply plan identifies the future supply sources labour based on current trends, planned changes in the organisation's strategic direction and trends in the external environment.
- Action plans to match demand with supply when required.

HRM, what's in a name?

The term *HRM* began to appear in management literature in the 1980s and, although claimed by some management scholars to represent a significant change of direction and emphasis for personnel specialists, a clear consensus of its meaning has proved to be elusive and still continues provide a good stimulus for debate.

At one level, the term 'HRM' is seen to be no more than a modern label for the activities of 'traditional' personnel management which is *workforce centred* and responsible for the recruitment, retention and release of employees plus the maintenance of contracts of employment. The latter function can place personnel managers in a mediation role between the needs of the workforce and the organisational management. On the other hand, HRM is seen to be *resource centred* and directed at the provision and deployment of HR, who may or may not be actual employees of the organisation (e.g. agency staff, consultants, etc.). It can also be argued that traditional personnel management is not directly involved in business strategy and is essentially task or activity based, whereas HRM is a strategic, coherent approach to the people assets of a business.

Personnel management versus HRM

There has, over recent years, been something of a debate with some resultant development of thought within the 'people' area of business. At the centre of the debate is the view that the organisation takes of its employees. According to proponents of the newer 'HR' ideology, traditional personnel management took the view that employees were a cost to the organisation. Like all costs, cash spent on the recruitment, reward and development of employees should thus be kept to a minimum. In contrast, HR theory views employees as key organisational inputs or *resources*. Accordingly, employees, like all other resources (e.g. financial, plant and equipment, etc.) should be cultivated, invested in and improved.

Although the above view of 'old' personnel management is something of a caricature (i.e. it is not as bad as some HR theorists suggest), there have been a number of changes in the way that people are managed in the workplace. The changes are driven by the underlying conviction that employees are a vital resource rather than an inconvenient cost. It is important to understand, therefore, that HRM is a *philosophy* rather than a *style* of management. Torrington and Hall (2002)[1] describe the philosophy of HRM (updated, in title only, from their 1995 description of 'personnel management') as follows: '*a series of activities which: first enables working people and the organisation which uses their skills to agree about the objectives and nature of their working relationship and, secondly, ensures that the agreement is fulfilled.*'

The 'infection' of modern organisations with HR ideas has signalled the introduction of a number or practices, such as involving employees in decision-making, increased staff development and a heightened sense of employees' 'comfort' at work. These changes do not, by themselves, mean that an organisation has adopted HRM. Most writers in this area contend that the adoption of HRM involves a change in the culture of the entire organisation, rather more than a simple change in practice. Many organisations have espoused HRM, but to varying degrees. Some organisations have implemented HRM in full accompanied by a significant change in corporate culture. Others have, perhaps a little cynically, merely changed the name of their personnel department to the HR department. To a certain extent, HRM is fashionable, but its full implementation has proved to be problematic in many cases.

Karen Legge (1995)[2] concluded that there are little, but important, differences between personnel management and HRM:

- HRM concentrates more on what is done to managers rather than on what is done to other employees;
- there is a more proactive role for line managers;
- there is a top management responsibility for managing culture.

Table 27.1 provides a comparative view of personnel management and HRM.

Table 27.1

Comparison of personnel management and HRM

	Personnel management	**HRM**
Time and planning perspective	Short-term, *ad hoc*, reactive, marginal	Long-term, strategic, proactive, integrated
Psychological contract	Compliance	Commitment
Control systems	External controls	Self-control
Employee relations perspective	Pluralist, collective, low trust	Unitarist, individual, high trust
Preferred structures/ systems	Bureaucratic/mechanistic, centralised, formal defined roles	Organic, devolved, flexible roles
Roles	Specialist/professional	Largely integrated into line management
Evaluation criteria	Cost minimisation	Maximum utilisation (human asset accounting)

Key purpose of HRM

According to the Chartered Institute of Personnel and Development (CIPD), *the key purpose of the personnel function is to enable management to enhance the individual and collective contributions to the short- and long-term success of the enterprise*[2]. The specialist knowledge and skills for such a range of tasks necessitates that the senior staff in the department are suitably qualified for the job. The CIPD is the professional body for those involved in the management and development of people, and the HR managers who run the department, will typically hold professional qualifications, recognised by the CIPD or will be qualified 'by experience.' Either way, the range of manpower activities into which he or she will have an input makes the jobholder a highly influential person in the success or failure of the organisation.

It follows that the range and scope of activities of the HR department is quite extensive and covers the following areas.

Employee resourcing

- HR planning.
- Identification of vacancies (or surpluses).
- Job analysis/job description/person specification.
- Recruitment and selection.
- Contracts of employment.
- Induction.
- Relocation and redeployment.
- Termination of employment.

Organisational development

- planning and implementing programmes to improve organisational effectiveness;
- advice on organisation structures and job design;
- support change management programmes.

Performance management

- managing and measuring performance;
- administering performance appraisal schemes;
- administering personal development plans.

Employee development

- developing organisational learning;
- systematic planning and developing of activities to enhance employee skills and competencies;

- training and development;
- planning and advising management development and career paths.

Employee reward and recognition

- developing and administering fair and appropriate reward systems;
- job evaluation;
- recognition schemes;
- employee benefits.

Employee relations

- management and maintenance of formal and informal relations with individuals, trade unions or staff representatives;
- communications of organisational matters of interest to all employees;
- administering equal opportunities;
- provide specialist advice on employment law to line managers.

Health, safety and welfare

- developing and administering health and safety programmes;
- developing and administering employee assistance (welfare) schemes;
- administering discipline and grievance systems.

27.3 HRM and people management

HRM takes place throughout an organisation, not just within a specific department, and in one sense, every manager who has subordinate staff has a HR role to his or her job, inasmuch as people management is a part of it. In addition, though, many organisations have a separate HRM (or personnel) department which contains people who are specialised in this function.

We have therefore encountered two key concepts:

- *People management* is the management of individuals in their jobs and is carried out by line managers throughout the organisation;
- *The HR department* is the part of an organisation that contains specialists in all matters of people management. It performs a

supporting role to line managers in their jobs, advising them and helping to administer matters like appointments, training and reward systems.

Both the HR department and employees' line mangers are concerned with *HR policies and procedures*. These are statements of the manner in which HR affairs in the organisation are conducted. Designed to ensure that employees are treated and dealt with equally and fairly, HR policies and procedures apply uniformly throughout all parts of the organisation. Typically, organisations will have a HR policy to cover each part of the job of people management.

HR policies and procedures: the University of Northumbria at Newcastle

The University of Northumbria is similar to most other large organisations in that it has HR policies and procedures to cover each area of the people management process. They are strictly applied to ensure fairness and equality.

Examples include policies on:

- recruitment and selection of staff,
- reward systems,
- equal opportunities,
- flexible working,
- health and safety,
- staff training and development,
- staff disciplinary procedures,
- trade union recognition,
- individual grievance procedures,
- appraisal and development,
- redundancy and redeployment.

The actual work that is undertaken by the HR department falls into two categories. Some work is concerned with *administering* the day-to-day functioning of the business, that is, the maintenance of 'good order' in relation to 'people' activities. This category includes issues such as salaries, routine problems, advising managers and negotiating with trade unions. Other work in the HR department is more *strategic* in nature as demonstrated by University of Northumbria at Newcastle (UNN):

- To ensure that innovative and flexible HR policies, procedures and processes are developed and sustained to support the University's business strategy, ensuring that high standards of HR practice are achieved by all managers in the University.

- To recruit, retain and appropriately reward a motivated, skilled and flexible workforce committed to the goals and mission of the university.
- To develop a performance management framework to ensure the appropriate development of employees to facilitate their maximum contribution to the achievement of the University's business objectives.

27.4 Functions of the HR department

The functions of HR (or personnel) departments vary from organisation to organisation; some organisations have large and elaborate HR departments, whilst others have no such designated specialist function (e.g. where all of the personnel management jobs are entirely carried out by line managers). We can consider the work carried out by the HR department by looking at the 'passage' of an employee through the organisation: from when the vacancy is identified to when the employee finally leaves. The HR department is therefore involved, to a greater or lesser degree (depending on the organisation in question), with the following activities:

- identification of a vacancy;
- job analysis;
- job description;
- person specification;
- recruitment;
- selection;
- induction;
- training and development;
- relocation and redeployment;
- termination of employment (by means of resignation, retirement, redundancy, dismissal or death).

27.5 The appointments process

The importance of appointments

Appointing new people to work in an organisation is perhaps the most important part of the HR function's role. This is for four reasons:

- the right person can make a strong positive effect on the organisation;

- appointing the wrong person can be potentially devastating for the organisation;
- it can be very difficult to 'get rid' of a less-than-perfect employee once he or she has been engaged;
- a new employee may stay with the organisation for as long as 50 years.

The stages in the appointments process

The general procedure followed in an appointment is as follows:

Identification of vacancy
↓
Job analysis
↓
Job description
↓
Person specification
↓
Recruitment
↓
Selection

Identification of vacancy

The process of appointing a new employee to an organisation begins with the identification of a vacancy that must be filled. There are a number of ways in which vacancies are identified:

- *Replacement* of staff that have left the organisation.
- *Organic growth* that requires extra employees to cope with expansion.
- Particular staff or *skill shortages* in a department or function (e.g. a company may decide to appoint an advertising specialist, a gardener, a specialist in a particular computer package, etc.).
- Some appointments are made on the basis on *ratios*. For example, Academic staff in a university faculty are typically appointed on an approximately ratio-based approach. Most staff members are required to teach a specific number of hours so the number of staff is arrived at by dividing the total number of lecture hours in the faculty by the required lecturing load of each staff member.

Job analysis and job description

Once it has been established that a vacancy exists, the personnel department is responsible for carrying out a job analysis. When the job is analysed, the personnel specialist is concerned with examining the tasks involved in performing the job. This sometimes involves a procedure called *work study*, the examination of a job to establish the tasks involved, the hours required and the best place (in the structure) to perform the job within the organisation.

Once the job has been analysed, the next step is to generate a job description, which is a document which records the component parts of the job. Job descriptions will differ in scope and detail between jobs and organisations but typical areas covered by a job description include:

- job title;
- location in organisation structure, function of department;
- purpose of the job;
- reporting relationships (upwards to immediate superior + downwards for number and job titles of direct subordinates;
- key objectives of the job;
- main duties and responsibilities;
- authority levels (e.g. financial budgets);
- circumstances of job (e.g. shift work, travelling, etc.).

There are some arguments against the use of job descriptions, particularly for senior management positions which are constantly changing in nature. Arguably, they can also be seen as promoting demarcation (e.g. 'that's not my job') and create barriers to the progress of teamwork in organisations. However, such arguments should not detract from the potential value of having definitive descriptions of job requirements as an aid to the recruitment and selection process. Job descriptions should therefore be appropriate to the needs of individual organisations and, for example, it may be more relevant to have job descriptions written in terms of key result areas rather than duties and responsibilities. Whatever format the job description takes, it is important that it reflects the current position, and regular reviews should be held to ensure its validity to the post in question.

An example of a 'live' job description is shown below at Figure 27.1

Person specification

Following the issue of a job description, the personnel specialist will use it as the basis for a *person specification*. The person specification is a document that describes the 'ideal' person to carry out the duties listed

EXAMPLE OF A JOB DESCRIPTION

Lecturer: School of the Built Environment
University of Northumbria at Newcastle

JOB TITLE: Lecturer in construction management
SCHOOL: Built Environment
GRADE: Lecturer
CATEGORY: Permanent

1 PURPOSE OF THE POST
To teach and manage the student experience within the Construction Group and to support the Group and School with scholarship and research activity.

2 RESPONSIBLE TO
The Subject Director.

3 GENERAL DUTIES
- Maintain and further the work and reputation of the school.
- Contribute to all forms of pedagogic work including classroom teaching, tutorial work and associated outreach work, preparation and support of distance learning materials and student placements, together with associated organisational and administrative work, cover for staff absence where necessary, preparation and marking.
- Contribute to the achievement of corporate and business objectives of the School.

4 MAIN DUTIES
- Develop a culture of personal excellence combined with innovation, in teaching and learning, consultancy and research development.
- Contribute in conjunction with other colleagues to the strategic development of the subject area, including curriculum development in the context of the Programmes offered and to be offered by the School.
- Support other academic and administrative in quality control of programmes including their validation and accreditation.
- Ensure the effective collection and review of student feedback within personal areas of responsibility.
- Meet targets set for personal activity within agreed timescales.
- Support the effective day to day operation of the programmes.

5 KEY ATTRIBUTES
The following is taken from the School Learning and Teaching Policy:

The key attributes of a *Northumbria Built Environment tutor* are that they will:
- Provide resource based teaching and encourage guided and independent learning.
- Encourage and support students in using the 'live laboratory' which is the built environment.
- Engage in scholarly activity and research linked to their teaching.
- Foster multi and inter disciplinary activity.
- Involve themselves and students with professional validation.
- Encourage students to engage with career and professional development.
- See students as the primary focus.

Figure 27.1
Example of a job description.

in the job description, and is a profile of the personal skills and characteristics to be used in the recruitment and selection process. It is thus important that the person for a job is not under or over specified. Under specification will result in the appointment of a person who may not be competent in all aspects of the job. Over specification will result in the appointment of a person who is overqualified and who may become bored or disillusioned in a short period of time.

Person specifications can vary enormously, compare the different skills that might comprise the person specifications for a factory's cleaner or its operations manager, and it is therefore essential that organisations 'customise' their person specifications to match their specific needs and the variety of jobs within the organisation.

Two systems of designing person specifications have been used by many organisations for a number of years and continue to serve (at least) as templates for customised versions:

John Munro Fraser's 'fivefold grading structure'[3]

- Impact on others
- Qualifications or acquired knowledge
- Innate abilities
- Motivation
- Adjustment or emotional balance.

Alec Rodger's 'seven-point plan'[4]

Attributes	Essential	Desirable
Physical features (e.g. appearance, manner, etc.)		
Attainment (e.g. education, minimum qualifications)		
General intelligence (e.g. quick on uptake)		
Special aptitudes (e.g. numerate, articulate)		
Interests (e.g. practical, intellectual applications)		
Disposition (e.g. keen, patient)		
Circumstances (e.g. able to meet to particular job requirements, such as travel, shifts, etc.)		

Note: The essential criteria indicate the minimum acceptable requirement levels, so that any candidate who does not meet that standard will not be further considered. The desirable elements form a significant part of the decision-making process by helping to identify the most suitable candidates.

If the field of applicants contains nobody with the essential criteria, it is unlikely that the organisation will make the appointment at all (it may then be re-advertised).

An example of a 'live' person specification is shown below at Figure 27.2.

EXAMPLE OF A PERSON SPECIFICATION

Lecturer: School of the Built Environment
University of Northumbria at Newcastle

JOB TITLE: Lecturer in construction management
SCHOOL: Built Environment
GRADE: Lecturer
CATEGORY: Permanent

CRITERIA CATEGORIES	ESSENTIAL	DESIRABLE
1 Specific Knowledge		
Awareness of the skills and process involved in producing buildings and current developments in Construction Management.	X	
2 Skills and Abilities		
Good communication and interpersonal skills.	X	
Ability to contribute to work in teams in a dynamic, changing environment.	X	
Familiar with current Construction Management practice.	X	
Ability to teach a range of Construction Management subjects.		X
Ability to manage a programme of teaching and assessment.	X	
A commitment to scholarship within the subject area.	X	
3 Experience		
Relevant industry experience in construction, specifically related to the management of projects.		X
Teaching experience at higher education level.		X
4 Education/Training		
A degree in a Construction Management discipline.	X	
Membership or eligibility for membership of the CIOB.	X	
5 Other requirements		
Potential to contribute to the School's research and consultancy portfolio, specifically in areas relevant to Construction Management and arising from the Constructing Excellence Agenda		X

Figure 27.2
Example of a person specification.

Assignment 27.1

Attempt to generate person specifications for the following jobs. Divide the contents of your specification into essential and desirable criteria:

1   Management accountant
2   Quantity surveyor
3   Nursery nurse
4   Part-time sales assistant (music store)
5   Driving instructor
6   Hotel receptionist
7   Vending equipment service engineer
8   Educational psychologist.

Recruitment and selection

Once the person specification has been finalised, the HR function turns its attention to finding and appointing an appropriate person to the post. This involves two further stages: recruitment and selection (R&S).

Recruitment is the process by which an organisation generates a pool of applicants for a vacancy. At this stage of the process, the organisation is seeking to generate the largest possible number of suitable applicants to give itself the widest possible choice. The need to attract applicants is usually reflected in the personnel policies on personnel recruitment. Such policies may, for example, state that:

- all vacancies will be advertised in the appropriate press media;
- all vacancies will be advertised internally;
- the company operates an equal opportunities policy;
- the company encourages applications from all sectors of the community.

The means by which organisations attract applicants are many and varied. The channel chosen will depend upon the nature of the vacancy and the media can be segmented for jobs in the same way as it can for marketing promotions. For senior positions, it is likely that the organisation will decide to advertise in the national newspapers whereas specialists tend to be attracted through their own specialist press (e.g. *Accountancy Age, Chemistry in Britain, The Engineer*). Jobs requiring a less specific level of skill or expertise are more likely to be advertised through Jobcentres or the local press. For particularly important positions, organisations sometimes employ *recruitment consultants*. These are private businesses with expertise in seeking out and attracting applications from appropriate people and then interviewing them in accordance with the organisation's person specification before sending a short list to the company for selection.

As the purpose of recruitment is to attract applicants, job adverts tend to take the form of 'selling' the organisation to its potential applicants. For senior positions, job adverts attempt to attract high calibre applicants by using 'attractive' statements, examples of which can be found every week in the appointments' sections of broadsheet newspapers such as *Sunday Times* or *The Guardian*. It is interesting to interpret the messages conveyed via the size, style and language of the advertisements.

Once the pool of applicants has been generated, applications are filtered according to the criteria of the person specification. This 'whittling down' process results in a *short list* of the few applicants who best match the essential and desirable criteria in the person specification. Note that the short list does not necessarily contain the best people as such, but the people who best match the person specification. Once the short list has been generated, the unsuccessful applicants are rejected and the short list goes forward to the selection stage.

Selection is the process that takes the short list generated by the recruitment stage and from it, selects the single person (or more if there are multiple vacancies) who most closely matches the person specification. Picking out the best person from the short list involves the use of a range of selection techniques. The selection techniques chosen will depend upon the nature of the appointment and the nature of the skills and aptitudes stated on the person specification.

Common selection techniques include:

- interviews;
- the examination of application forms and curriculum vitas (CVs);
- presentations or skill demonstrations by applicants;
- psychometric testing (the testing of personality, intelligence, team-working ability, etc. by means of complex written tests);
- observation of applicants manner, appearance, demeanour, confidence in social situations, etc.;
- 'assessment centre' activities (the testing of applicants in intensive situations in which candidates can undertake a range of social, skill and psychometric tests relevant to the job).

Owing to the diversity of criteria on the person specification, most selections involve more than one of these techniques. For matters of qualifications and experience, an examination of an application form or CV will usually suffice. For testing aptitudes and competencies, it is common to ask candidates to demonstrate the skills to the selectors. Secretaries, for examples, are often required to perform typing demonstrations to show their speed and accuracy of typing or their command of word-processing packages. Applicants to the position of university lecturer are often required to give a brief lecture as part of their selection to demonstrate their competence in coherent 'public' speaking.

Once the selection process has been completed, the selectors will have narrowed the short list down to the one candidate who most closely matches the person specification. It is then the task of the HR manager to persuade (in some cases) the most suitable candidate to accept the offer of a job. This is not as straightforward as it might appear. The fact that a candidate has applied and undergone selection for a job does not necessarily mean that he or she will accept the offer. The personnel function must design an appropriate rewards package that will swing the individual in favour of accepting the offer. Failure to persuade the successful candidate to accept may require going to the candidate who is the second closest to the person specification and this may involve some degree of compromise on such things as the desirable criteria.

The R&S process at the University of Northumbria

The UNN employs around 2200 individuals and is therefore a relatively large employer. Any organisation of this size will necessarily have a turnover of staff requiring a more-or-less ongoing need to appoint new staff members. In consequence, the university's HR department is well practised in all aspects of R&S. In its recruitment documentation, the university states its aim in R&S is to '*attract highly qualified and highly motivated teachers, administrators and service staff*'.

The procedure followed arises from the HR policy that is relevant to the task. The stages are as follows:

■ identification of vacancy;
■ job description is drawn up;
■ person specification is generated from job description;
■ decision on where to place advertisement for the vacancy;
■ advertisement is written/designed;
■ advertisement appears in relevant newspaper/magazine;
■ applicants respond to advertisement;
■ short list is made up from applicants;
■ short list are called for interview;
■ interview using a range of selection techniques, depending upon nature of appointment;

- verbal offer is made and this is accepted or declined;
- health check on successful candidate;
- references are checked;
- formal letter of offer is sent (returned by successful candidate);
- new employee starts work.

27.6 Induction, training and development

Once the successful applicant has been appointed, he or she joins the organisation as a new member of staff, and may then undergo procedures, overseen by the HR function, to improve performance at work and make the employee better at serving the organisation's needs. One of these procedures takes place when the employee joins the organisation and the others can take place at any time during the employee's service.

Induction

Induction is the process whereby a new employee is welcomed and acclimatised into the organisation. The complexity of the induction process varies greatly from organisation to organisation. Larger organisations tend to have more elaborated induction procedures than smaller ones who frequently have no formal induction at all.

The issues covered in induction include:

- 'welcome' to the organisation;
- meeting new colleagues and finding out 'who does what;'
- learning about the organisation's history and culture;
- learning where things are located, such as canteens, different departments, etc.;
- 'any questions' to managers about the organisation;
- explanations of company policy on such things as health and safety, fire procedures, grievances, etc.;
- receiving initial training and brief.

Training and development

These two activities are quite different in nature but share the same essential objectives: to improve an employee's performance at work. Both can be undertaken either 'on-the-job' or 'off-the-job.' The requirements for an employee's training and development are arrived at by the training and development 'equation':

Training and development needs = what the employee needs to do the job (including any future needs)
− what the employee can do now.

Training and development needs are often arrived at during an *appraisal*. Some organisations have formalised appraisals in their personnel policies and these typically take place annually. During an appraisal interview, the employee meets with his or her immediate line manager and the two parties discuss the employee's performance in the job, together with any problems and ideas that either party has for improvement. Appraisal interviews are usually designed to be open and 'stress-free' occasions where the manager and the employee can discuss areas for improvement as well as giving due credit and praise where appropriate. The terms can be defined as follows:

Training is the instruction of employees in specific techniques that are used in the working environment. Employees may be trained, for example:

- to use a piece of equipment such as a new lathe or similar machine tool;
- to operate a new computer application such as a word-processing package;
- how to escape in the event of fire or how to use a fire extinguisher;
- how to chair a meeting;
- how to engage in public speaking;
- how to 'close' a sale (for salespeople);
- in improving telephone technique, etc.

A systematic approach to training can be seen in the '*training cycle*' shown below at Figure 27.3. The process starts with identification of a deviation between actual performance and the desired standard. Of course, the root cause of the deficiency needs to be clearly established as there may be other factors, such as negligence or poor supervision causing the shortfall. A *Training Needs Analysis* (TNA) can confirm that a training solution is appropriate to fill the '*training gap*'. Clear objective for the training leads to the actual design and implementation of the training for the appropriate employees. Following the training, a validation exercise will confirm if the objectives have been achieved, for example, can the employee now do what was taught? Evaluation tests the

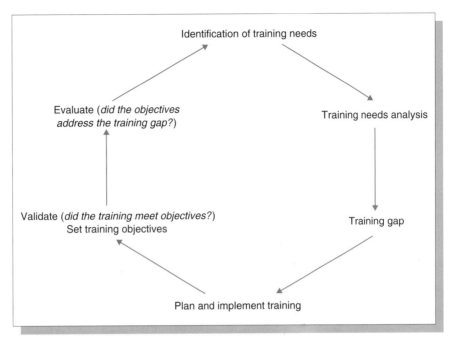

Figure 27.3
The training
cycle.

effects of the training on improvement of performance and in the cycle continues with the process of ongoing improvements for organisational effectiveness.

Development refers to activities that are designed to help employees realise their full potential on present jobs and, where appropriate, develop capabilities for future jobs. Ideally, development plans will aim to match future company requirements with those of the individual employees. It follows that development programmes are intended to broaden and deepen an employee's ability to cope with a wider range of working situations, and the approach taken to develop employees takes a different approach to those taken in training.

Some examples include:

- *Coaching*: close relationship between individual and an experienced person (usually the immediate line manager) that facilitates the individual learning from experience on an increasing range of tasks.
- *Delegation*: the authority to conduct specified higher level duties (dual responsibility in that the subordinate experiences the actual activities but ultimate responsibility remains with the delegating).
- *Educational development*: by allowing staff to attend day-release classes or by secondment to attend.

- *Universities or colleges*: for example, to undertake HNCs, HNDs or degrees.
- *Management development*: by sending staff on postgraduate degrees such as MBAs.
- *Mentoring*: the practice of a junior employee being 'taken under the wing' of a more senior and experienced colleague;
- *Job rotation/enlargement*: to enable staff to gain from a broader experience of working environments;
- *Conference attendance*: for specialist staff to exchange ideas with peers from outside the organisation.

Advantages of training and development

Organisations tend to view training and development in a similar way to any other investments. Both training and development cost money, whether it is by giving staff time-off work, course fees, or accepting a longer learning curve by such things as staff rotation. It follows that the organisation expects a return on its investment. Some of the returns are readily quantifiable in financial terms, but the majority are not. Benefits include:

- a more highly skilled workforce;
- increased competence in the working environment;
- higher productivity;
- greater staff confidence in their work;
- the possibility of higher staff morale, if staff appreciate that the organisation values them sufficiently to invest in their improvement;
- the possibility of lower staff turnover and greater staff loyalty as a result of the potentially higher staff morale;
- lower waste and higher quality;
- a more flexible workforce that is more able to accept change;
- a workforce that is more culturally homogeneous (i.e. one that thinks and 'does things' in a similar way).

27.7 HR and rewards

Since the abolition of slavery, an important consideration of personnel management has been the concept of reward or compensation. A key feature of the labour market is that suppliers of labour (employees) *sell* their labour to buyers of labour (employers). The process of selling necessarily involves an exchange. In exchange for the supply of labour, the buyer (the employer) provides a number of rewards to the employees.

Types of reward

A reward can be defined as *any form of gratification that an employee gains from his or her employment with an employer.* With such a broad definition, we would rightly expect there to be a wide range of rewards that organisations can use. There are two broad categories of reward: intrinsic and extrinsic.

Intrinsic rewards are those that arise from the nature of the job and of actually *doing* the job. Intrinsic rewards include:

- job satisfaction;
- working conditions;
- social relationships at work;
- job security;
- recognition and appreciation at work.

Extrinsic rewards are those that are tangible or that can be enjoyed outside of the work environment. Examples include:

- pay or salary;
- fringe benefits (e.g. company car, company pension, health insurance, etc.);
- holiday entitlements;
- commission on sales or productivity bonuses;
- status and social standing as a result of holding the job or the specific job title (e.g. '… and what do you do?' 'I'm a professor,' or, 'I am the UK manager for …').

The purposes of reward

There are a number of purposes of rewards. Examples include:

- to reward and recognise different levels of performance;
- to recognise seniority and 'wisdom;'
- to motivate;
- to reduce dissatisfaction and disquiet in the workplace;
- to retain staff and prevent them from seeking employment elsewhere;

> ■ to maintain and encourage employee loyalty;
>
> ■ to attract staff into the organisation.

27.8 Employer–employee relations

The two 'sides'

The two 'sides' of the employment system (employers and employees) inter-relate with each other in the work environment. In most situations, they are in agreement (i.e. they work together) but on occasions, the two can be in conflict. Such conflicts arise due to the two sides seeking essentially different objectives in the working environment:

■ Employers aim to extract the maximum amount of useful labour from the employees at the minimum reasonable cost to the organisation (this is not to say that the employer wished to exploit labour, but rather that it wants to obtain value for money from it).

■ Employees aim to achieve security of employment together with rewards commensurate with an acceptable standard of living.

As the nature of the relationship, it is generally assumed that the employer is the most powerful 'side.' Individual employees have little influence over the terms and conditions under which they work for an employer, so in order to further their aims with respect to employers, employees sometimes organise themselves into collectives called unions or trade unions.

Types of trade unions

A trade union (in the UK) is defined by the *Trade Union and Labour Relations Act (TULRA), 1974* as an organisation whose principal purpose is the regulation of relations between union members and their employers (the definition of a trade union was narrowed further by *The TULRA (Consolidation) Act, 1992*). The Advisory, Conciliation and Arbitration Service (ACAS) defines a trade union as *an organisation of workers created to protect and advance the interests of its members by negotiating agreements with employers on pay and conditions of work. Unions may also provide legal advice, financial assistance, sickness benefits and education facilities. An independent trade union* is one which is not under the domination or control of an employer and is independent from the employer financially. The *Certification Officer* at the *Department of Trade and Industry (DTI)* maintains a list of trade unions and is responsible for determining whether a trade union or staff association is 'independent'. Only independent trade unions can make statutory claims for recognition under the Schedule A1, TULRA (Consolidation) Act 1992. Independent trade unions are financed entirely by the contributions of their members (to ensure that they exist only for the benefit of the membership) and must submit annual accounts in a similar way to limited companies.

There are six broad types of unions:

- *Craft unions* are unions whose membership comprises specialists in a particular craft or skill. To join, one must have served an apprenticeship or have other recognised training in the craft. An example of a craft union is the Amalgamated Electrical and Engineering Union (AEEU) which represents engineers and electrical workers across a wide variety of industries.
- *General unions* do not require any qualifications for membership, and members can consequently be skilled, semi-skilled or unskilled. UNISON is the UK's biggest trade union with over 1.3 million members working in the public services, for private contractors providing public service and the essential utilities.
- *Industrial unions* comprise members from specific industries only. Within the industry, members can be drawn from all levels of employee from unskilled workers through to managers. Examples of industrial unions include the National Union of Mineworkers (NUM) which represents all types of employees in the mining industry.
- *Professional or 'white-collar' unions* represent exclusively staff, clerical and professional workers. An example of a staff union is NATFHE, The University and College Lecturers Union;
- *Company unions* are rare in the UK but more common in other parts of the world, such as the USA. A company union is formed when the employees of a specific employer organise themselves into a union to increase their bargaining power over the employer.
- *Professional associations* are the final type of workers' collective. In most cases, professional associations would not describe themselves as trade unions, but they are unions in that they occasionally represent their members with employers and provide representation (see later for a discussion of this) as necessary. Examples of professional associations include the British

Medical Association, the Royal Society of Chemistry and the Inns of Court which represent barristers.

Why do employees form and join unions?

The simple fact that union membership requires the payment of a subscription means that members will naturally expect some benefits in return. The benefits of membership arise from two angles.

Firstly, members benefit from the collective action of the union. The fact that members are organised into a single collective increases the employees' ability to influence the employer in their favour (in comparison with the weak bargaining power of a single employee). The commonest form of collective action is *collective bargaining*. This is the practice of the union negotiating contract terms (such as pay rises) with the employer on behalf of all members of the union.

Secondly, members benefit from *union representation*. This includes such things as legal representation by the union solicitor in the event of unfortunate occurrences, such as an industrial injury or an employer's claim against a member for improper conduct at work.

Forms of union action

Employees, by acting together under their trade union, can increase the power of their case against an employer. They do this by using a number of 'weapons' or forms of *industrial action*. Such measures may be used (usually after a ballot) when the union membership feels it has a legitimate case against the employer, such as when a desired level of wage increase has not been forthcoming or when the employer has imposed adverse changes to the work environment.

The most radical form of action is the *strike*. This involves two things:

■ A withdrawal of labour for a period of time, thus causing gross inconvenience to the employer.

■ The picketing of the employer's premises with the aim of discouraging other employees from going to work and to prevent supplies from arriving or leaving. Pickets are also designed to draw media attention to the strikers' case against the employer.

Secondly, the union may introduce a *work-to-rule*. This is the practice of employees conforming exactly to their job descriptions and refusing to go beyond the strict 'rule-book.' Whereas normally, employees would be relatively flexible in their relationship with the employer, work-to-rules exclude all flexibility in the work-place, a measure designed to inconvenience the employer and increase production costs.

Thirdly, and linked to the work-to-rule, is the *slowdown*. This is when employees deliberately perform work tasks more slowly than they normally would. Such a practice has obvious effects on production costs.

The fourth form of union action is the *overtime ban*. Overtime is frequently offered to and accepted by employees to help the employer to meet such things as production deadlines. A refusal on the part of employees to accept it can mean that deadlines are unmet. This potentially causes harm to the employer through such things as a loss of customer goodwill.

In practice, trade unions are reluctant to implement measures, such as those above and only do so when they feel that their aspirations cannot be met through normal negotiations. This is for two reasons:

- Some forms of industrial action *cost union members money* through lost earnings. Strikes are accompanied by the employer withholding pay for the time that the strike is in progress. In some cases, the union itself makes good the loss of earnings from its own financial reserves. Overtime bans also reduce employee earnings.
- All forms of industrial action, by definition, are designed to cause inconvenience and loss to the employer. Trade union members are usually aware that if they take industrial action 'too far' industrial action may ultimately *threaten their own jobs.*

Mediation and arbitration

When unions and employers are in dispute, the first means of resolving the disagreement is to meet to attempt to reach an acceptable compromise. The management is represented by a suitably briefed member of the senior management team (e.g. the personnel director) whilst the union is represented by a union member appointed by the other members to negotiate on their behalf (e.g. the works convenor). If, however, agreement cannot be reached, the two sides in the dispute may elect to appoint an independent mediator or an arbitrator.

- A *mediator* acts simply as a communicator between two sides when normal communication has become difficult or impossible.
- An *arbitrator* is empowered to determine a settlement between the two parties, an outcome which is binding on both parties

and which may be a compromise between the two positions. An arbitrator is only engaged in a dispute at the invitation and with the agreement of both parties.

In 1974, the UK government established the ACAS. ACAS is managed by a council of nine members:

- three from the Confederation of British Industry (CBI) representing the employers;
- three from the Trades Union Congress (TUC) representing the unions;
- three independent members.

The role which ACAS performs in negotiations is dependent upon the invitation of the two sides. In some cases, ACAS is engaged purely as a mediator whereas in other cases, the two sides agree that ACAS should perform an arbitration role.

Recent trends in the world of trade unions

Declining membership

Figure 27.4 shows the trend in total trade union density (membership compared to total workforce) between 1995 and 2003. We can see from the graph that there has been a marked decline in membership, but particularly in the years 1995 and 1998, and levels are much lower

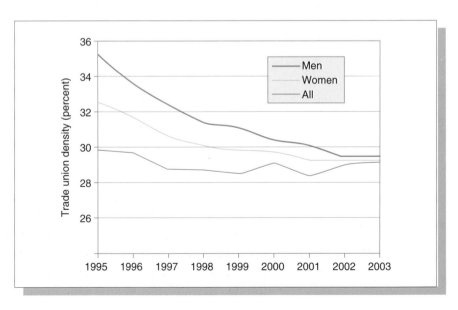

Figure 27.4
Trends in trade union density in the UK (i.e. union membership as a percentage of all workers)
Source: Office of National Statistics, 2003.

than the mid 1970s when the levels were averaged 52%. There are a number of reasons for this phenomenon.

1   The change in political power occurred in 1979. When Margaret Thatcher's Conservatives took over from James Callaghan's Labour Party, a number of laws were introduced that increased the regulation of trade unions. This is considered in more detail in Chapter 8. The laws that were introduced had the effect of imposing restrictions on both trade union activity and the ways in which they should be operated. The effect of these laws was to reduce union power with respect to employers.

2   A marked decline occurred in industries that were hitherto highly unionised. The reduction in size of industries like coal-mining, steel and shipbuilding has meant that union membership in these key industries has declined.

3   A growing belief that union membership does not bring the benefits with it that once it did. A number of key union defeats (e.g. the miners in 1984) and the changing nature of the job market in favour of employers have brought with them a heightened perception that unions have become increasingly impotent.

Mergers between unions

The decline in membership and the problems of lower bargaining power over employers brought about by increased regulation has triggered a spate of inter-union mergers. This means that two unions which have suffered from declining membership join forces to create a new, merged union. The larger size of the merged union brings two benefits:

- an increased ability to influence employers in favour of union members;
- increased financial stability of the union itself (resulting from economies of scale), thus providing continued support for its members.

Recent union mergers have brought about a slight blurring in the types of union we learned about above. There have, for example, been mergers between white collar and industrial unions. Such mergers, whilst not necessarily being what the union officials would have ideally wanted, were thought to be necessary as a means of gaining the benefits that a merger engenders.

Some of the more reported recent union mergers include:

- the Graphical, Paper and Media Union (GPMU) in 1991, from the merger of Society of Graphical and Allied Trades (SOGAT) and the National Graphical Association (NGA) to become the world's largest media, trade union with a membership in excess of 200,000;
- UNISON (1993) from a merger of three public sector unions – National Association of Local Government Officers (NALGO), National Union of Public Employees (NUPE) and Confederation of Health Service Employees (COHSE);
- the AEEU, completed in 1996, from two craft unions, the Amalgamated Union of Engineering Workers (AUEW) and the Electrical, Electronic, Telecommunications and Plumbing Union (EETPU).

27.9 Motivation

Given that personnel (or HR) management is concerned with maximising the economic return on the organisation's investment in its HR, the matter of how best to motivate the workforce is naturally a matter of concern. The problem is that an understanding of the ways in which humans are motivated is very complicated and this is mainly because people are very complicated.

The fact that there are several major theories on human motivation is testimony to the fact that none of them is sufficient in itself. Each theory adds to the total body of knowledge in this area, but we need to acknowledge each one to gain an overall picture of this issue. A number of writers have added their theories to the debate:

- Abraham Maslow,
- Frederick Herzberg,
- Clayton Alderfer,
- D.C. McClelland,
- Victor Vroom.

Abraham Maslow's hierarchy of human needs

Maslow's theory of motivation was first published in 1943 and remained the most influential for many years. His theory rests upon the premise that humans are motivated by the satisfaction of needs. Furthermore, human needs can be categorised into 'layers' or 'levels', some are very

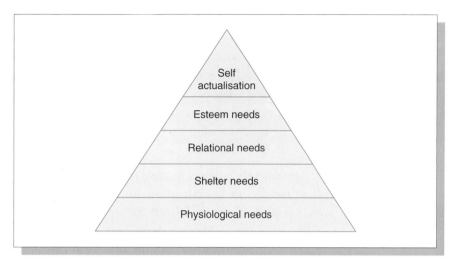

Figure 27.5
Maslow's hierarchy
of human needs.

basic and others are more advanced. The various levels can therefore be expressed as a hierarchy (Figure 27.5).[5]

Once one level of need has been satisfied, the individual is motivated to satisfy needs in the next level. This pattern continues upwards until the individual is motivated to meet the needs of self-actualisation. If, however, an individual seeking to satisfy higher needs experiences a threat to lower level needs, his or her attention is drawn back to the fulfilment of the threatened lower level needs. An individual who has his or her needs met up to the point of self-actualisation will, if drowning, be more motivated to meet immediate physiological needs, that is, the need for air. In such a circumstance, the unfortunate person will care little for his or her shelter, relational or esteem needs, such as the motivation to simply stay alive.

The levels of need in the hierarchy are explained below:

- *Physiological needs* are those which are essential to the simple continuance of life. Such needs include the needs for air, water, food, good health, etc. Some have argued that this category of needs also includes more basic 'quality of life' issues such as sleep, maternal or paternal fulfilment and the satisfaction of sexual appetites.
- *Shelter and protection needs* refer to an individual's need for a sense of personal security, freedom from danger, the need for order and predictability and in most cases, the need for a shelter or 'nest.'
- *Love and relational needs* are sometimes called social needs. They refer to an individual's need for human interrelationships such as friendship, a sense of belonging, affection, etc.
- *Esteem needs* refer to the individual's need to be held in esteem by oneself and by others. Such needs include the need for some

degree of status, prestige, recognition and appreciation from others.

- *Self actualisation* is the final level of needs fulfilment. These needs are consequently addressed only when all others have been satisfied. An individual's need to self actualise is connected with the desire to 'find yourself,' to be creative, to compose, to invent and to do things for their sake alone, and not as a means to other ends.

Maslow's theory is attractive in its simplicity but has a number of flaws. It is clearly an oversimplification of the complexities of the human makeup. Whilst it may hold for some people that they follow the hierarchy upwards as Maslow described, others seem to be a little different. Some individuals, for example, may be motivated to self-actualise (e.g. by painting, writing, etc.) with only the most modest means of shelter and with little or no apparent need for affectionate interaction. Indeed, Maslow later modified his theory to acknowledge an exception to the rule in respect of self-actualisation needs. So the work of Maslow, albeit a valuable contribution to the debate, cannot be considered to be a watertight and all-encompassing description of human motivation.

Frederick Herzberg's motivation-hygiene theory

Whereas Maslow's work attempted to describe the totality of an individual's motivation in all parts of life, Herzberg's writings focused on human motivation at work.[6] In examining the various features of a person's working environment, he concluded that some features served to motivate an employee to greater performance, whereas other features served to prevent the employee from becoming dissatisfied with his or her work. He attached names to these groups of features:

- *hygiene factors* are those features of work that prevent employees from becoming dissatisfied with their work. They do not motivate, but serve to maintain the employee's co-operation and loyalty;
- *motivating factors* are those features which motivate employees in their work.

Both hygiene and motivating factors are important if the employee is to be satisfied *and* motivated in his or her work.

Hygiene factors include:

- salary and remuneration;
- the quality and level of supervision in the working environment;

- the working conditions;
- company policy and administration;
- the interpersonal relationships that the employee enjoys (or does not enjoy) in the working environment.

Motivating factors include:

- the opportunity to achieve worthwhile goals at work;
- recognition of good work;
- the status attached to a job;
- the level of responsibility and authority attached to a job;
- opportunities for growth, development and promotion afforded by the job.

Herzberg's theory has been influential in management thinking and in job design. By using Herzberg's ideas, the features of a given job can be adjusted to meet an employee's particular circumstances, that is, hygiene or motivating factors can be addressed according the employee's needs. One of the oft criticised parts of Herzberg's theory is the inclusion of pay as a hygiene factor and not a motivating factor. By doing this, Herzberg is arguing the money in itself doesnot motivate, but this is not to say that money as a part of recognition or higher achievement is not in part motivating. Salary, Herzberg argues, prevents employees from becoming dissatisfied with their work. In simple terms, Herzberg's theory says that when hygiene factors are less than satisfactory, they can be demotivating but even if they are acceptable they will not actually provide motivational impetus. An analogy can perhaps be drawn with purified water which ensures that people will not become ill by drinking it, but they will not become healthier no matter how much purified water is drunk.

Clayton Alderfer's ERG theory

Alderfer published his theory in 1972 which post-dates both Maslow and Herzberg by a number of years. In his ERG theory, Alderfer contends that motivation can be expressed as a continuum containing three interconnecting zones:[7]

- *Existence* (E): motivations relating to simple matters pertaining to the continuance and simple enjoyment of life;
- *Relatedness* (R): motivations relating to the need to be personally connected through meaningful personal relationships, friendships, networks and intimacy;
- *Growth* (G): motivations pertaining to the need to develop oneself, to grow and improve oneself.

There is an apparent link between Alderfer's theory and that of Maslow and the ERG needs can be mapped to Maslow's theory as follows:

- *Existence*: physiological and safety needs;
- *Relatedness*: social and external esteem needs;
- *Growth*: internal esteem needs and self-actualisation.

The differences arise in that the ERG theory allows for different levels of needs to be pursued simultaneously and for the order of the needs to be different for different people. The ERG theory also acknowledges if a higher level need remains unfulfilled, the person may regress to lower level needs that appear easier to satisfy. This is known as the *frustration–regression principle*. Rather than a rigid hierarchy, the flexibility of ERG theory is best demonstrated as a continuum which allows the mapping of motivational up or down the continuum at different stages of an individual's life-cycle or career path (see Figure 27.6).

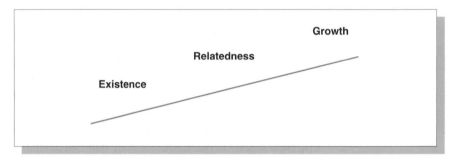

Figure 27.6
ERG continuum.

It is possible to be seeking fulfilment of both existence and relatedness needs simultaneously if an individual is on the part of the continuum between the two zones. Similarly, once existence needs have been satisfied, the individual moves onto the stages of relatedness and growth and may be motivated to fulfil both needs simultaneously. Hence, the ERG theory accounts for a more complex model of human psychology that the simple hierarchy proposed by Maslow.

D C McClelland's achievement motivation theory

D C McClelland and his colleagues worked at Harvard University in the early 1960s. He suggested that humans are motivated by four main arousal-based motives[8]

- the *achievement* motive (which McClelland called *n-Ach*);
- the *affiliation* motive (*n-Aff*);

- the *power* motive (*n-Pow*);
- the *avoidance* motive.

According to McClelland, different people show one of these motivations above the others. Some are primarily motivated by the need for achievement, some by the need for affiliation (relational needs) and others by a need for power and influence. Still others are seemingly motivated by indolence and a desire to avoid work altogether.

McClelland's study focused on just one of these motivating forces, the need for achievement (n-Ach). This is because this factor is apparently more important than the other factors in the workplace. The *achievement motivation theory* states that individuals with a highly pronounced n-Ach factor demonstrate:

- a constant need for achievement;
- an eagerness to accept positions of responsibility;
- a desire to set themselves realistic goals (i.e. they are 'self-starters');
- a willingness to positively respond to feedback on their performance;
- the trait that achievement is more important to them than affiliation needs.

McClelland contended that those with a pronounced n-Ach factor would make ideal managers. Such individuals, in seeking achievement above all other goals (e.g. affiliation needs), would be conscientious workers and effective managers. However, individuals with high n-Ach are likely to be task oriented and less concerned with relationships which can be a major disadvantage in getting results through other people (i.e. managers and supervisors). Nevertheless the theory has been influential inasmuch as HR specialists frequently seek n-Ach characteristics when appointing key managers in an organisation.

Victor Vroom's valence theory

Vroom's contribution to motivation theory is his valence (or expectancy) theory.[9] Like Herzberg, Vroom's theory concentrates mainly upon motivation in the workplace. The valence theory asserts that the degree of motivation that an individual feels towards a particular course of action depends of the strength of two variables, namely valence and expectancy:

$$motivation = valence \times expectancy.$$

The two variables are defined below.

Valence expresses the degree of satisfaction that an individual thinks will be enjoyed as a result of pursuing the course of action in question. It is thus future oriented and refers to the individual's *anticipated* satisfaction from the course of action, Vroom describes this as *instrumentality* which is the extent to which the individual perceives that effective performance will lead to desired rewards. Put crudely, valence refers to the intensity of desire that an individual feels towards an outcome or, 'how badly' it is desired.

Expectancy refers to the strength of belief that the action will lead to the particularly favourable outcome. It follows that expectancy is usually subjective in nature and depends upon the individual's perception of the probability of the successful outcome. It is possible that an individual may have an inaccurate perception of the probability (i.e. an unrealistically high expectancy), but the important things is the expectancy from the point of view of the individual, not the objective truth.

High motivation results, according to Vroom, when both valence and expectancy are at their highest. If either is weakened, either by uncertain desire (lower-valence) or by a lack of certainty (lower-expectancy), then overall motivation, which Vroom called *force*, will be reduced. He also distinguishes 'valence' from 'value' by defining the former as anticipated satisfaction and the latter in terms of actual satisfaction.

We can understand this better by constructing a simple example. Suppose a company's marketing director is due to retire in 12 months time and you, as an employee in the marketing department, are one of the people who may be considered to replace the director.

The motivation you have towards your work will depend upon two variables:

1   The *anticipated value* you attach to the benefits you believe will accrue as a result of the being appointed as the new marketing director (e.g. high salary, power, status, company car, etc.). This is the valence.

2   The *strength* of your belief in the possibility of actually getting the job. If you think there is a high probability of getting the job, you will have a higher expectancy than if there is a front-runner ahead of you.

The possible outcomes using Vroom's two variables are shown in Figure 27.7.

Your motivation at work over the 12 months until the present marketing director retires will depend upon these two factors. If you place a high value on the benefits of holding the marketing director's position

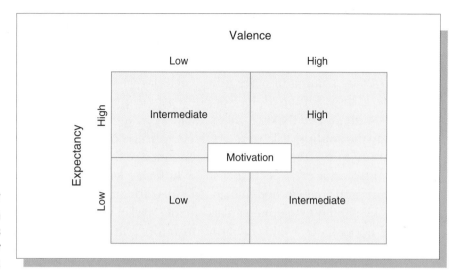

Figure 27.7
A representation of Vroom's valence–expectancy theory.

(high valence) *and* you believe you have the best chance of being appointed, then your motivation is maximised. If, however you do not value the rewards of a directorship (such as an indifference to increased financial reward, status, etc.) or you do not believe you are in a strong position to get the job, your motivation will be reduced accordingly.

Edwin Locke's goal theory

Unlike expectancy theory, where a satisfactory outcome is the prime motivator, *goal theory* suggests that the *goal* itself is the driving force.[10] Aiming at specific targets appears to be more effective than general exhortations to 'do the best you can'. Other important aspects of the theory are that of *goal-commitment* by individuals and their perceptions of ability to actually achieve the goals (i.e. *self-efficacy*, which aligns with the qualities at the heart of McClelland's n-Ach individuals). Feedback on performance is a vital element to individual motivation in the achievement of specific goals.

Assignment 27.2

Margaret Welsh has recently been recruited to the position of office manager for the post-graduate administration office at Newtown University. She has a support team of three administrators, two of whom have less than a year's experience in their present roles. The other member of the team has been with the university for more than 10 years, but for the last 18 months has been working on a part-time basis of 3 days per week because of domestic reasons. Margaret is aware that the work is cyclical in nature and has its peaks and troughs, particularly at the present time when a new semester is about to start. However, following a recently successful advertising campaign for new students, dozens of enquiries are coming into the office each day (+answer machine messages over the weekends). This is adding to the work of registering new students, processing marks for last year's students and making the graduation arrangements for the exiting students, in addition to the routine tasks of the office. Overtime of 3-hours per person per week has been authorised for 4 weeks but the attendance of one of the team members is unpredictable and Margaret suspects that she is suffering from stress connected with the pressure of work, and is concerned that an extended absence would have a serious detrimental effect on their ability to maintain an acceptable level of service. She is certain that the office workload necessitates additional administrators and has asked the HR department to supply at least one (and preferably two) additional administrators.

You are the assistant HR manager and your director has asked you to take charge of the situation, to investigate if Margaret Welsh has sound business case and, if a new post (or posts) can be justified and approved, then to manage the recruitment and selection process from start to finish.

Questions

- What steps might you take to establish whether Margaret Welsh has a legitimate case for a new member of staff?
- Given that the vacancy is approved, discuss the type of steps you would take to appoint a new person to the job.
- Suggest what might comprise the contents for a job description and person specification for the new post.
- Explain how you would carry out the recruitment and selection stages for the new administrator.
- What ongoing training and development might benefit an administrator and the university?

References

1   Torrington, D., Hall, L. and Taylor, S. (2002). *Human Resource Management*, 5th edn. London: Prentice Hall.
2   Legge, K. (1995). *Human Resource Management: Rhetorics and Realities*. London: MacMillan.
3   Fraser, J.M. (1978). *Employment Interviewing*, 5th edn. London: Macdonald and Evans.

4   Rodger, A. (1985). *Seven Point Plan.* London: NFER – Nelson Publishing.

5   Maslow, A. (1998). *Toward a Psychology of Being,* 3rd edn. London: John Wiley.

6   Herzberg, F. (1968). *Work and the Nature of Man,* London: Harper Collins.

7   Alderfer, C. (1973). *Existence, Relatedness and Growth: Human Needs in Organizational Settings,* USA: Free Press.

8   McClelland, D. (1985). *The Achieving Society,* London: Free Press.

9   Vroom, V. (1964). *Work and Motivation,* Chichester: John Wiley.

10   Locke, E. and Latham, G. (1990). *A Theory of Goal Setting and Task Performance.* London: Prentice Hall.

Further reading

Adair, J. (1996). *Effective Motivation.* London: Pan.

Armstrong, M. (2003). *A Handbook of Human Resource Management,* 9th edn. London: Kogan Page.

Beardwell, I. and Holden, L. *et al.* (2003). *Human Resource Management. A Contemporary Perspective,* 4th edn. London: FT Prentice Hall.

Bratton, J. and Gold, J. (1994). *Human Resource Management, Theory and Practice,* 3rd edn. London: Palgrave Macmillan.

Cole, G.A. (2004). *Management Theory and Practice.* 6th edn. London: Thomson.

Gennard, J. and Judge, G. (2002). *Employee Relations (People and Organizations),* 3rd edn. London: CIPD.

Hollinshead, G., Nicholls, P. and Tailby, S. (2002). *Employee Relations,* 2nd edn. London: Prentice Hall.

Miner, J.B. and Crane, D. (1995). *Human Resource Management. The Strategic Perspective.* London: Longman.

Torrington, D., Hall, L. and Taylor, S. (2002). *Human Resource Management,* 5th edn. Harlow: Prentice Hall.

Tyson, S. and York, A. (2000). *Essentials of HRM,* 4th edn. Oxford: Butterworth Heinemann.

Useful web sites

Advisory Conciliation and Arbitration Service (ACAS): www.acas.org.uk

Chartered Institute of Personnel Management: www.cipd.org.uk

Department of Trade and Industry: www.dti.giv.uk

Trades Union Congress: www.tuc.org.uk

CHAPTER 28

Marketing and business products

Learning objectives

After studying this chapter, students should be able to describe:

- the marketing concept;
- the role of the marketing function and the nature of the marketing mix;
- the nature of business products and the stages of the product life cycle;
- pricing strategies in marketing;
- market segmentation and distribution channels;
- the major methods of marketing communication and product promotion.

28.1 Marketing

Marketing has been interpreted in many different ways, and we should dispense at once with the notion it is simply about advertising and issuing press statements – it is much more. In the modern environment, marketing can be seen as the process of matching the abilities of the organisation to the existing and future needs of its customers, to achieve the greatest benefits for both parties. The result is an *exchange* in which the organisation receives income through meeting customers' needs, and the customers receive benefits that satisfy, or perhaps even exceed, their expectations. The term *exchange* refers to the act of giving something in return for receiving something, which may be in the form of a tangible or intangible product or service.

Consider the following two definitions of marketing:

Marketing is the management process which identifies, anticipates and supplies customer requirements efficiently and profitably.

The Chartered Institute of Marketing – CIM.[1]

Marketing is not only much broader than selling ... It encompasses the entire business. It is the whole business seen from the point of view of its final result, that is, from the customers' point of view.

Peter Drucker (1999).[2]

These two definitions show us two complementary approaches to marketing. Firstly, the Chartered Institute of Marketing (CIM) see it as a *management process*, that is, something that management does. A management process involves procedures and systems put in place to implement marketing within the organisation. Secondly, Drucker proposes a wider definition than the CIM in that it encompasses the entire business and we can see marketing as a *philosophy of business*. The marketing philosophy is one that is geared to doing everything with the benefit of the customer in mind.

Organisations that adopt *marketing* as an underlying philosophy of business are said to be *marketing-oriented* organisations. Such organisations focus on customer needs and, by establishing and maintaining close customer relations, are able to understand their current and future requirements. They are therefore prepared to make the necessary adaptations to their operations to meet changing market opportunities. This is in contrast to organisations which are based primarily around a different functional competence of the business. A heavy engineering facility (e.g. a shipyard or a steel-milling business), for example, will often be oriented towards its operations department and said to be *production oriented*. This is because of the nature of the products produced and the imperatives to maintain operational quality and reduce costs. Other organisations may be described as *sales-* or *financially oriented*, and we cannot say that one approach is right or wrong – we can simply say that the orientation should be chosen as that which most appropriate for the organisation and its products.

The marketing concept

The *marketing concept* signifies that the customer is of paramount importance to the organisation, and that corporate goals can only be achieved by meeting and exceeding customer expectations better than the competition. This philosophy requires an integrated approach where all of the organisation's policies and activities are focussed to that end, and all of the employees assume responsibility for the creation and maintenance of first class customer service. In other words, the belief that the customer is central to the well-being of the organisation must run through all departments irrespective of their specific functions. The role of the marketing department in such an organisation is that of product or service champion and co-ordinator of activities. The marketing concept is very much in line with the philosophies of *Total Quality Management* and *Six Sigma*, which are explained in more detail in Chapter 24.

28.2 The marketing function

The role of the marketing department varies according to the needs and situation of the organisation. Some are very large and elaborate whilst others have none at all or perhaps just one marketing person. Furthermore, the responsibilities of the marketing function also vary greatly. Some marketing functions include research and development (R&D) and sales whilst other merely look after any press releases or promotional activities undertaken. In one respect, therefore, it is impossible to generalise as to the precise activities of a marketing department. This chapter deals with what may be considered to be an idealised marketing department, or one which carries out all of the activities assigned to it by noted theorists and academics who specialise in the marketing field.

Marketing intelligence and research

Marketing intelligence has been described by Philip Kotler (1993)[3] as 'the collection of *everyday information about developments in the market*'. He emphasised that the nature of such information is generally patchy and frequently late; forcing forces managers into reactive decisions. While it is fair to say that in small (localised) organisations, a degree of useful information can be obtained through a range of casual routes, such as discussions with customers, visits to trade fairs and general knowledge of competitor activities, the need to have a more structured, *marketing research*, approach becomes apparent as organisations grow in size and complexity.

Marketing research is a planned, comprehensive and systematic method of information gathering and analysis. The essential need for organisations to employ a planned system of marketing research is underlined by the recent trend in marketing that shows that the geographical spread of customer bases is rapidly changing from familiar and local market places to unfamiliar national and international markets. Also, changes in buyer behaviour and competitive strategies emphasise the need for organisations to have sound, reliable and timely information to facilitate effective marketing decision-making.

Marketing planning

This activity is central to the marketing function and follows the analyses of market research information, ideally via a marketing information system (MIS), which, according to Kotler and Armstrong (2003), is '*an organised way of continually gathering and analysing data to provide marketing managers with the information they need to make decisions*'.[4] Marketing planning managers are concerned with the identification of market opportunities, the selection of target markets, and the preparation of plans for market, product or service development. They may also be involved with the preparation of action plans for achieving sales targets.

The marketing mix

With an understanding of its customers, an organisation can effectively develop its *marketing mix*, which is the term used to describe the framework for the tactical management of customer relationships. It comprises the set of controllable variable activities that can be blended to provide competitive advantage and influence the desired responses of the buyers in the target markets.

To enable a simpler understanding of the role of marketing in a business, writers in this field have traditionally used the '*4 Ps*' *model* to describe the marketing mix:

- *Product*: The product's distinguishing features (e.g. quality, brand name, uniqueness, packaging, etc.).
- *Price*: The amount of money to be paid for the product (and its perceived value to the customer), credit terms, discounts, etc.
- *Place*: The distribution channels and transportation, or how the goods will actually get to the customer.
- *Promotion*: The means of raising product awareness (e.g. publicity, advertising, sponsorship, etc.).

A criticism of the 4 Ps model is that oversimplifies the reality of marketing management and ignores the need for long-term customer relationship marketing, particularly with industrial customers. Also, the growing service sector prompts the need for an extension of a further 3 Ps to the model:

- *People:* The employees may be in effect the personification of the 'service' (e.g. waiters, hotel receptionists, etc.).
- *Process:* A key part of the service may be how it is delivered to the customer (e.g. demonstrating professionalism, courtesy, understanding, etc.).
- *Physical evidence:* The environment in which the service is delivered (e.g. clean and tidy, hygienic, appropriate décor for the nature of business, etc.).

The congruence of the elements of the marketing mix

An essential feature of good marketing is that each part of the process 'matches' all of the others. When a product is developed, it is usually with a certain place in mind. The price must also make the product attractive to the target market. Promotions must be geared to effectively communicate the benefits of the product to the target market.

Mis-matches can occur when any of the elements of the mix do not match the others. It may be, for example, that an organisation develops a good product aimed at a particular segment of the market, but then attaches too high a price to it and promotes it in an inappropriate way.

Marketing directs the R&D function

In an organisation which employs the marketing philosophy, it is the marketing people who 'have their finger on the pulse' of what the market wants. It therefore makes sense that is should be the marketing people who ultimately decide on the R&D function's agenda. This may take the form of regular meetings between the marketing manager and the R&D (or design) manager, or it may be the case that a marketing specialist actually oversees the activities of the product development staff.

Marketing sets prices

The ways in which businesses attach prices are complicated. The price that a product is given by its producer has a number of determining factors:

- the cost of production;
- the price of competitive products;
- the customer's expectations of what the price should be (the *utility* the customer attaches to the product);
- temporary tactics to influence the volume of sales (e.g. short-term price reductions to shift slow-moving stock);
- the elasticity of demand of the product.

With such a complex set of determinants, the price attached to a product depends in large part on the stage of the product on the product life cycle and the product's price elasticity of demand (i.e. how responsive the quantity demanded is to changes in the product's price, see Chapter 17).

Part of the marketing process is to attach a price to products sold. Usually working alongside an accountant, the marketing specialists will be aware of the prices that the target market will be willing to pay for the product. Careful marketing research will tell the marketing department the price that will yield the maximum long-term profit for the product and the price chargeable will almost certainly inform the design function as it produces the product at its inception. It may be, for example, that the price chargeable for a small family car, mainly targeted as a 'second' vehicle, is around £8000–9000. Working backwards, the price will guide the design function as it designs the car.

Pricing strategies

Pricing decisions at the point of a *new product* launch are a little more complicated than pricing existing products. On the one hand, there is good reason to attach a high price to the product to start recovering the new product's development costs. On the other hand, a high price may deter consumers from trying the product and so a lower price may help the product to become established.

The approach taken will depend in large part on the number of consumers that are expected to buy the product, its distinctiveness or uniqueness, and its price elasticity of demand (i.e. how responsive demand is to price). There are two broad introduction pricing strategies.

Price skimming involves attaching a relatively high price to the product at its launch. It is an appropriate when the early buyers of the product comprise a small part of the total market and who are prepared to pay the high price to enjoy the product's benefits (i.e. it has a price inelastic demand). It also relies on the presupposition that there are few competitors to match the product's benefits. Price skimming is used in sectors, such as pharmaceuticals and military equipment. If appropriate, new consumers are encouraged to buy the product with phased price reductions as time passes.

Price penetration involves the attachment of a relatively low price to the new product with a view to attracting a broad customer base early in the product's life. Price increases may then be applied as a loyal customer base is established. Penetration is appropriate when the product's demand is responsive to price (*price elasticity*) or when the product is entering a competitive market and market share is consequently a major consideration.

Marketing decides upon target population

Apart from the necessities of life, no single product can be aimed at *everybody*. The product and price will usually be designed to appeal to only part of the total market. Marketing specialists have ingenious ways of dividing people up according to their ability or willingness to buy certain products. They can predict who a new product will appeal to and where such customers can be found.

Marketing sells and promotes the product

This part of the marketing department's job is the best known, but as we have seen, is only part of the total workload. After all of the other parts of the mix have been carried out, the marketing department will work out how best to communicate the benefits of the product to the target market. The style of communication will be carefully chosen to appeal to the target market. For technical products, such as industrial products, promotions will often be restricted simply to a statement of the product's technical specification – this is all the buyer requires to make a decision. For many consumer products, communications are aimed at a 'mass market' and the promotion reflects this by including a persuasive element in the promotion.

28.3 Business products

What is a product?

The first misconception we must immediately dispense with is the notion that a product is merely something physical. A product can be a physical object, but need not necessarily be.

Consider the following definition: *A product is any organisational output which satisfies a consumer's wants or needs.*

Output

The output of an organisation falls into two broad categories: goods and services. Goods are tangible, physical products which can be touched and seen. Services are intangible. Goods are things you own, services are things done to you or things done on your behalf. A service may involve the use of goods in the course of imparting the benefit or the product. Similarly, the impartation of the benefits of a good may involve an element of service (such as when a petrol pump attendant dispenses petrol into your car).

Cars, chemicals and the book you are holding are all examples of goods. You take advantage of service products when, for example, you visit the hairdresser, when you employ a mechanic to repair your car or when you enrol at a university.

Wants and needs

Individuals are motivated to take advantage of an organisation's output when they believe it will be of some benefit to them. The distinction between needs and wants is rather blurred. A consumer will tend to be prepared to pay a higher price for a product which fulfils a felt or real need.

The economic nature of organisations means that the output must be paid for in some way. It is not, however, always the case that the individual enjoying the benefit of a product is the same person who pays for it. Whilst this is the norm, some organisations operate in such a way as to provide a product which is not necessarily aimed at those who pay. Government organisations provide services which every tax-payer pays for even although only those in need benefit from the output. Similarly, charities provide benefits which, in most cases, the beneficiaries do not directly pay for.

Types of product

There are several ways in which products can be subdivided. We have seen that the first way of dividing products is according to whether they are goods or services. We can also divide products according to the general types of customers that consume them. One such mechanism is the industrial–consumer goods distinction.

Industrial products are those used by businesses rather than individual people. They are rarely in their finished form and tend to undergo further processing by the business. A manufacturing business buys in raw materials and parts which it uses in its manufacturing processes. Service industries may purchase products which enable them to carry out the services. A plasterer will use plaster (an industrial product) as an essential input to his service business (Figure 28.1).

Figure 28.1
Types of product.

Consumer products are goods and services which are purchased by the end user. It is usually the case that little or no further transformation is performed on consumer products – they are consumed. Consumption, in this context, does not necessarily mean eaten, but rather used in the product's existing form. A consumer is unlikely to make modifications to his or her washing machine – it is simply used. The two major categories of consumer products are *consumer durables*, such as electrical goods, cars, etc. and *fast-moving consumer goods* (FMCGs) which are products we tend to buy little-and-often, such as food products.

Features of a product

Marketing specialists, when describing a product, see it as having two 'dimensions'. It is these two dimensions which define the totality of the product.

Generic product

The generic or *core* product comprise the features of the product which meet the basic needs of the customer. It is totally basic and has no embellishments at all.

The generic car would be a totally basic vehicle which meets minimum legal standards but has no 'add-on' features at all. It may, for example, have hard vinyl seats, floppy plastic steering wheel and a 750-cubic centimetre engine. It meets the basic needs of a car in that:

- it goes,
- it stops when brakes are applied,
- it prevents the ingress of rain.

The generic food product is one which fulfils the essential purpose of volume, sustenance and bulk for the body. It may possess little in the way of flavour, texture or convenience.

Question 28.1

Describe the *core* features of the following product types:

- a digital video disk (DVD) player,
- a digital camera,
- a mobile phone,
- a pair of spectacles.

Whilst most products contain the benefits of the core product, we can readily appreciate that most products we use have 'extra' benefits as well.

Augmented product

The augmented product comprises the totality of features of a product. It includes the core benefits and any number of 'add-on' or *premium* benefits, which make the product more acceptable to certain segments of the market.

Premium features are included to appeal to the senses of the consumer, and increase sales and profits to the business. The nature of premium features added to a product will obviously vary. For food products, premium features may include taste, texture, convenience, 'healthy image', etc. For our basic car, we could add premium features, such as appearance, metallic paint, engine size or design, leather seats, increased reliability, fuel economy, etc.

The presence of augmented features can significantly increase the cost (and hence the price) of a product. It is possible, for example, to pay £5000 or £500,000 for a new car. Both provide the core benefits, but the more expensive models contain much more in the way of augmentation. Not all premium benefits are tangible. Some are perceptual in nature – the image that the consumer associates with the use of certain products. In the case of an expensive car, almost all of the price goes towards paying for premium or augmented benefits.

A great deal of emphasis is placed on premium features in the process of marketing communications. Advertisements for cars, for example, are usually concerned with communicating premium benefits, such as style, utility, reliability, etc. We can imagine the response to an advertisement which only communicated the core benefits. ('Here is a car. It goes, it stops and it keeps the rain out! Buy it'.)

Question 28.2

For the following products describe some of the *premium* features which apply to each one:

- a DVD player,
- a digital camera,
- a mobile phone,
- a pair of spectacles.

The product life cycle

An essential feature of almost all products is that of its life cycle. The position of a product on its life cycle will have a large bearing upon its marketing. It may determine its design and will be relevant to its pricing and promotion. As shown in Figure 28.2, there are four distinct phases in the product life cycle.

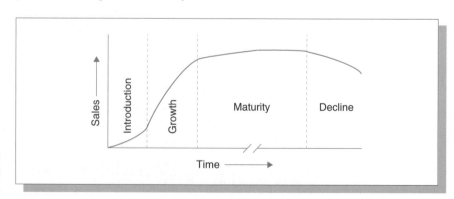

Figure 28.2
The product life cycle.

Introduction of a product

The introduction stage of a product follows its design, although as it is introduced to the market, it is not uncommon for further 'tweaking' to be made to render the product more acceptable to customers. If the product is unique (i.e. it is not a 'me too' product), it will benefit from a lack of competitors, although it risks early failure if the market does not take to it quickly. The company usually incurs extra costs at this stage due to promotional expenditure and in consequence, failure during introduction, before the company makes any meaningful sales, is especially costly.

The percentage failure rate varies according to the product type and the amount of market research that precedes the launch. New processed food products have a success rate of approximately 1 in 10. For more capital-intensive products like electronic and defence equipment, the success rate is more favourable. There have been some very expensive and notable 'flops' at the introduction stage. Certain products have become almost infamous at their well-publicised failure: the videodisk, the V2000 video and the Sinclair C5 electric car are good examples.

Growth

Products that successfully emerge from introduction enter the growth stage. Growth is characterised by several features, particularly rising sales and the appearance of profits which can initially be used to offset the development and introduction costs. If the product type is one which is readily 'copyable', then competitor products may come on-stream and threaten the rate of growth.

As demand for a product rises, the business can take advantage of this by increasing the product's price and thus enjoy higher profits. Much of the promotional activity will be geared to establishing the product as a leader in its product or market sector. However, as the product becomes better known due to increased usage, the business will usually reduce its promotional costs as a percentage of sales to allow higher returns to be made. The company will also pay great attention during growth to the product's distribution in order to ensure the optimal exposure of the product to the target market.

Maturity

In the same way that the majority of people are in maturity (aged between about 14 and 65 years), so are the majority of products.

Maturity is characterised by:

- static or slowly increasing growth in sales,
- a lot of competitive products,
- manoeuvring by competitors to 'steal' market share,
- lower prices than in the growth stage (and hence lower profits).

The fact that sales have stopped growing by any significant amount means that sales increases can only be achieved by taking a competitor's market share. For this reason, the mature phase is the most competitive. Companies go to great lengths to buy brand loyalty from customers. The product may be adjusted or 'tweaked' to make it more attractive to customers. For consumer products, such adjustments may take the form of new premium features or more attractive packaging. Advertising is widely used by companies seeking to promote mature products (e.g. coffee, washing powder, etc.). If the product's demand is elastic (see Chapter 16), market share can be increased by reducing the price, but this has obvious implications for profitability.

Decline

Decline occurs when customer preferences change away from the product. Whilst decline can be postponed by adroit product redesign, it cannot be avoided. It is characterised by:

- falling sales for all producers of the product,
- price cuts to maintain sales for as long as possible,
- declining profits,
- competitors abandoning the market.

When products begin to decline, the key decision is to when to discontinue production. Most companies producing declining products attempt to 'milk' sales for as long as possible. No investment would be made under such circumstances (i.e. no further development or marketing funds would be committed to the product).

Question 28.3

1   Which stage of the life cycle do you think the following products are in?
- liquefied petroleum (LPG) motorcars,
- iPods,
- de-caffeinated instant coffee,
- electric food processors,

- analogue televisions (TV),
- music compact disks.

2 Apart from the examples listed above, give three examples of product types that are currently in each stage of the product life cycle.

Life cycle – a metaphor from life

The concept of life cycle does not just apply to products; it applies to you and me. Human beings undergo a life cycle that has a huge bearing, not just on our biological changes, but on behaviour.

We undergo *introduction* when we are conceived and grow inside our mothers. After birth, we begin to *grow* – a process that continues until, after puberty, we reach our full height and weight. Our *maturity* phase is the longest. For most people, it will last from our mid-teens until the time when our faculties begin to fail us – perhaps in our sixties or seventies. When we reach old age, we begin to *decline*. Our eyesight may begin to deteriorate, we slow down and we may lose some of our intellectual sharpness. Finally, when decline has run its course, life is no longer viable, and we *die*.

The duration of the product life cycle

Just like the spans of human life, not all product life cycles are of the same duration. Some products go through the life cycle very quickly whereas others last for centuries.

History is littered with many examples of 'must have' products, such as *Hula-hoops* or *the Rubik's cube*, that experienced extremely strong sales in the short term, until the novelty waned or they were overtaken by some other popular fad. In particular, products which are subject to fashion – perhaps favoured by a popular football hero or associated with a blockbuster film – tend to have relatively short life cycles. For example, products linked to a tour by the latest rock superstar, and aggressively promoted, can experience phenomenal sales growth for a short period while the star is in the ascendancy. However, this can soon be followed by a rapid collapse in sales as the next pretender to the throne captures the public's attention. Also, consider the actual musical product itself, where the vast majority of popular records have an extremely short life cycle, as witnessed in the number of 'one-hit wonders' reported in the 2004 edition of the *Guinness Book of Hit Singles*.[5]

On the other hand, some products have impressive pedigrees of longevity in the mature stage. For example, many popular brands of confectionery have sold well over several generations of the population, with perhaps only minor changes in presentation (and size!). For staple food products, such as rice and grain, it is difficult to imagine them leaving the mature phase although brand competition with processed ingredients can see some individual producers or distributors unable to survive.

An example of a successful product with a long run at a mature level before coming to a sudden change can be found in the *Hoover* brand name. Hoover has produced upright vacuum carpet cleaners for more than 60 years, selling millions of units worldwide, and arguably becoming the generic title for all vacuum carpet cleaners. Over the years, Hoover and a few rivals, such as Electrolux and Panasonic, enjoyed a very mature market and, allowing for a few cosmetic adaptations, their models remained basically unchanged over that time. However, in 1993 James Dyson revolutionised the vacuum cleaner market when he launched his bagless *Dual Cyclone vacuum* cleaner which was both innovative in its technology and design. The buying public liked the new machine and in a short period of time it dominated the market and had become the *industry standard*, with the long-established manufacturers having to cut the life span of their traditional models and move quickly to introduce new competitive products.

Question 28.4

Apart from those products mentioned above, list five products which have had a short life cycle and five others which have enjoyed a very long life cycle.

28.4 Place the product

The *place* element of the marketing mix begins with an attempt to describe the type of customers who may be most interested in buying the product. This is done by the use of 'dividing tools' that can separate people from each other. These are the distinguishing features that circumscribe a *market segment* (see below). Following this, the next marketing decisions concern the establishment of *distribution channels, locations of outlets, stock levels* and *transportation methods,* which should be designed to ensure that products and services will be available in the right quantities, at the right time and in the right place to meet customer requirements.

Distribution channels

Distribution channels are the routes by which goods pass from the producer to the customers and may be through wholesalers or retailers. Some products benefit from a very short distribution channel in that they pass directly from the producer to the consumer. You may, for example, buy a dozen eggs direct from a farmer near your house. In this case the producer is in direct communication with the consumer. In other cases, the product may pass through several stages from the producer (e.g. a factory or a farm) to the end user. If you buy an imported motorcar, it is likely that the vehicle will have passed through a relatively lengthy channel before you take delivery.

The method of distribution chosen for a product will depend on two important considerations:

▪ the required level of market exposure,
▪ the costs associated with each stage of the channel.

Market exposure concerns the percentage of the target market that will have ready access to the product. It is usually the case that the longer the channel length, the higher the market exposure. It will typically be the case, for example, that a FMCG manufacturer will use the major national retailers (e.g. Tesco, Asda, etc.) to provide a high level of market exposure. This naturally necessitates a lengthening of the distribution channel.

The *costs* associated with channel length are said to be *proportional*. A longer channel means that more businesses are involved, each of whom will wish to make a profit on its handling of the goods. All of these costs will eventually be paid for by the consumer in the final price. This feature explains why it is usually the case that the nearer the producer a good is purchased, the cheaper it will be. You may, for example, save money by buying from a factory shop, from a wholesaler (e.g. a 'cash and carry') or even direct from an importer.

Some of the more commonly observed channels are shown in Figure 28.3. Note that the length and complexity of the channel becomes successively longer.

It follows that any distribution decision involves a trade-off or compromise. A producer will obviously want to increase its market exposure, but in doing so, it must accept that its products will eventually be sold at prices that reflect the profit margins of each stage in the channel. *Note:* This element of the marketing mix should not be confused with *product placement* which is a promotional activity (see Section 28.5).

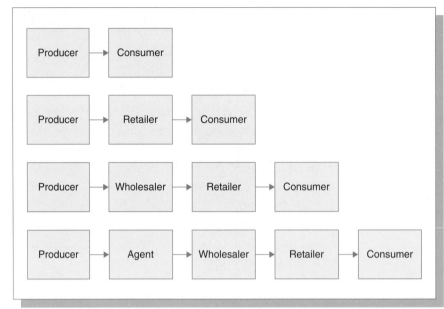

Figure 28.3
Basic models of
distribution
channel.

Market segmentation

Customers have different needs and wants, and should not be therefore be seen as part of some massively homogeneous market, but rather as numerous small islands of distinctiveness, each of which requires its own unique strategies in product policy, promotional strategy, pricing, distribution methods and direct selling techniques (Levitt, 1974).[6]

Market segmentation refers to the process of dividing the overall market into distinct groups (or segments) of buyers who are likely to respond favourably to different product and service offerings and market mixes. Such segments are used as the basis for *product targeting*, which is the process whereby identified market segments are evaluated and selected for specific product ranges.

For industrial products, market segments are almost self-suggesting, with clearer demarcation of sectors. For example, if a product is a part for an aircraft, the producer will target aircraft manufacturers in its marketing activities. On the other hand, the picture is a little more complicated for consumer products, where consumer products are aimed at the end user (the consumer). Consumer buyer behaviour is much less rational than that of industrial buyers and involves a variable range of economical, psychological and sociological elements. To enable a business to deploy its resources for optimum impact across the customer bases, the marketing people must find ways of dividing up the total population into relevant and meaningful segments. A common way of starting this process is by taking advantage of *demographic variables*, which works from the recognition that people are different and it is these differences which make some products appeal to some people but not to others.

Demographic segmentation bases

This part of marketing examines the ways in which people differ. The reasonable assumption underlying market segmentation is that different people will have different demands for products. Also, of customers' circumstances change over time (e.g. raising families, changing jobs, etc.) and businesses need to understand how different stages of people's life cycles affect their needs and wants. While it is true that people of any age may purchase any type of product or service, consider the predominant age groups that would be the principal customers for products, such as baby clothes, school uniforms, teenage fashions, houses or funeral plans.

The most frequently used segmentation bases ('people dividers') are:

- age,
- gender,
- stage in the family life cycle,
- occupation and income,
- type and place of residence,
- level of education.

Demographic variables

The most widely used demographic variables are described below.

Age

The period of life that a person is at will have a large influence upon both their spending power and their preferences. Broadly speaking, early attempts at age segmentation were relatively straightforward in that the population, in marketing terms, comprised babies, school-children, young adults and the elderly. However, in recent years, we have witnessed a rapid evolution in the formation of distinctive subsets of age-related segments, perhaps starting with at the arrival of the teenagers in the 1950s. This, of course, coincided with the rock 'n' roll era when for the first time young people in their teen years acquired an identity quite distinct from children (i.e. under 12 years) and adults (i.e. over 20 years). They established their own needs and wants in areas, such as fashion, music, food, etc. The trend in subdividing the age segments has continued apace, and today we can readily identify groupings, such as the 10–12-year old (or 'tweenies') who have their own fashions and music quite different from big sister or brother. The increase in life expectancy has seen growth of the older population, with relatively high levels of disposable incomes and active lifestyles – giving rise to the descriptions, such as *well-off older persons* (*WOOPS*) and the '*grey £*' as a symbol of the significant economic strength of this segment of the population. The period of life that a person is at will have a large influence upon both their spending power and prefer-ences, and organisations will factor age-related elements into their marketing mixes. For example, it is typical for magazines to have an age-related target market. The editorial styles employed and the contents of magazines are designed to appeal to differing levels of maturity – compare the readerships of *The Economist* with that of *Cosmopolitan* or *Hello*.

Gender

Like segmentation by age, gender differences allow for an obvious type of market segmentation (e.g. in the cases of clothes, shavers, fra-grances, hygiene products, etc.) and some less obvious examples. It is believed that one's gender creates certain product preferences as a result or male and female psychology rather than physical differences. Some alcoholic beverages are predominantly aimed at just one sex, as is also the case with some food products and cars.

Question 28.6

How many products or types of product can you think of that are generally aimed at one sex or the other?

Stage in the family life cycle

As people pass through the various stages of their family life, their preferences and spending power will change. Consider the case of a young newly married couple with no progeny, both working and with high disposable income, who may be heavy spenders on leisure activities, holidays or cars. However, after a few years when they have two children and probably a consequential reduction in their disposable income, their spending patterns will be more focussed on domestic items and child-related products. Also, a family with young children will tend to purchase less expensive furniture, not only because of their restricted spending power, but because of the higher probability that it will have to endure a higher level of wear and tear. At the other end of the life cycle, the older couple, whose children have 'flown the nest' are likely to have more spending power (mortgage paid off, higher income, etc.). Such people will tend to be more discerning in their preferences, opting for higher quality furniture and holidays as well as having more time for engaging in leisure or learning activities and hobbies.

Family life cycle

A commonly used classification of family types is as follows:

- Young single people, not living with parents.
- Young couples together with no children.
- Young couples, divorced with children or without children.
- Full nest 1 – youngest child under 6 years.
- Full nest 2 – youngest child aged 6 years or more.
- Full nest 3 – older couples with dependent children.
- Middle aged single or divorced people – living alone with or without dependent children.
- Empty nest 1 – older couples, employed and no children at home.
- Empty nest 2 – older couples, retired and no children at home.
- Solitary survivor – employed.
- Solitary survivor – retired.

Source: Based on the work of William Wells and George Gubar, 1966.[7]

Occupation and income

Segmenting people according to their jobs is one of the most powerful and most widely used 'dividers' of people. The underlying assumption of this approach is that a person's job will not only say something about their income and hence spending power, but also indicate certain preferences in taste.

Marketing specialists band people together into socio-economic groups according to the occupation of the major wage earner in a household. They use letters to describe each group:

Social grade	Percentage of UK population (adults over 15-year old)	Social status	Occupation (chief income earner in household)
A	3.2	Upper middle class	Higher managerial, senior administrative 'true' professional (e.g. doctors, lawyers)
B	20.5	Middle class	Intermediate managerial and administrative, other professionals
C1	23	Lower middle class	Supervisory, junior managerial, clerical (some professionals, e.g. nurses, policemen, teachers)
C2	32	Skilled working class	Skilled manual workers (e.g. electricians, plumbers and other trades people)
D	19	Working class	Semi- and unskilled manual workers (e.g. labourers, factory operatives)
E	10	Subsistence class	State pensioners, unemployed lowest grade or casual workers

Source: National Readership Survey, June 2002.

Type of residence and neighbourhood

Some products can be targeted at people according to the type and size of house they live in and the area in which the house is located. It would be appropriate, for example, to target lawn mowers at those who live in houses with gardens, but not those who live in tower blocks. Security systems (for properties) may well be most efficiently targeted at residents in inner city areas when the demand for such systems may be less in sleepy rural villages. Other variables, such as family size, occupation and ethnic background can be used for grouping small geographical areas (or *enumeration areas*) into distinct segments.

The ACORN classification (A Classification of Residential Neighbourhoods)[8] is a popular method used by marketing people for analysing different neighbourhood characteristics. It is a *geodemographic* (i.e. combined geographical and demographics analysis) classification of British social classes, used by marketing professionals when targeting products according to neighbourhood – they can select the most appropriate ACORN categories to focus the promotional activities for their products with a greater chance of success.

The most commonly used ACORN classification groups are listed:

A Agricultural areas
B Modern family housing, higher income
C Older housing of intermediate status
D Poor quality older terraced housing
E Better-off council estates
F Less well-off council estates
G Poorest council estates
H Multiracial areas
I High status non-family areas
J Affluent suburban housing
K Better-off retirement areas.

Level of education

The population as a whole has a very wide range of educational standards. The assumption underlying the use of education level as a basis of market segmentation is the belief that the level of education a person had enjoyed will influence buyer behaviour and determine certain preferences. It is probable that most graduates and professionals have a more enhanced 'intellectual appetite' than less well-educated people. This preference determines many things including the newspaper they read and their choice of TV programmes and radio stations. Among newspaper readerships, more highly educated people tend to prefer 'broadsheets', such as *The Times* and *The Daily Telegraph* due to their more thorough coverage and discussion. The 'tabloids', such as *The Sun* and *The Daily Star* tend to be read by those with a lesser appetite for detail – often those with lower educational accomplishments.

Special interests

In addition to the demographic variables hitherto discussed, an important 'divider' of people is the fact that some people are distinguished by their uniqueness or special interests. Some products are clearly targeted at highly specialised segments, such as railway modelling enthusiasts, motorcyclists, evangelical Christians or sufferers of a disease like diabetes. Such people will have specialised product requirements by virtue of their special interest, for example, diabetic chocolate is probably of little interest to anybody except diabetics.

Assignment 28.1

Ross–Whitson Kindergartens Limited is a company that provides child care for children aged between 6 weeks and 5 years. The original nursery was opened in a large converted house in 1999 by Gemma Ross, the current chief executive, and her business partner, Lewis Whitson, both of whom are qualified nurses with business degrees. Since then, they have opened four more nurseries in towns along the south coast of England, and Gemma's sister Fiona, a qualified primary school teacher has joined the management team with specific responsibility for the education of the 3–5-year old.

The nurseries are all designed to a template that provides separate accommodation for different age groups of children (i.e. 6 weeks to 1-year old, 1–2 years, 2–3 years and 3–5 years). There is a high nurse to child ratio and each specific group of children has dedicated staff, who comprise specialist qualified nurses for the under 2-year old, and staff with primary school experience for the three to five groups. The nurseries are open from 8.00 a.m. till 6.00 p.m., Monday to Friday all the year round with very flexible attendance arrangements. As a result, they are very popular and all of them are working to capacity, with waiting lists for vacancies. The overall quality of the organisation ensures that premium rates can be charged.

The company maintains high standards and each nursery has been recently given a first class report by Her Majesty's Inspectorate. The company has decided to expand with the purchase and conversion of another 10 nurseries over the next few years with the first of the new establishments to open in 3 years time. The management team have been discussing the possibility of locations for the new developments in attractive towns outside the south east, such as Bath, Harrogate and, perhaps Wales and Scotland.

Questions

- ▣ Explain the core and premium features of the product that a nursery school business like Ross–Whitson provides.
- ▣ Explain the purpose of the premium price that Ross–Whitson charges for its services.
- ▣ Given that Ross–Whitson will welcome the first guests into its new homes in 3 years time, define the market segment limits that should form the basis of any proposed marketing promotions.
- ▣ Discuss the range of options that the company could consider in seeking to promote the new nurseries to prospective clients. What might be the content of such promotions?

28.5 Promoting the product

Once the product has been designed, priced and the target market segment identified, marketing turns its attention to promoting the product to the market segment. Promotions are more correctly called *marketing communications*, so called because it is concerned with communicating the benefits of the product to the segment in question.

There are four commonly used techniques or vehicles for marketing communications:

- above-the-line promotions,
- below-the-line promotions,
- direct selling,
- public relations (PR), press and community involvement.

Above-the-line promotions

The term 'above-the-line' is a marketing jargon term for promotions using various types of media advertising. A business takes advantage of several media upon which to communicate its marketing messages. The one chosen will depend upon the nature of the product, target segment, budget available, etc. The most commonly used formats are as follows:

- commercial TV,
- commercial radio,
- magazines and newspapers,
- buses and other transport,
- posters,
- leaflets and handouts.

The need to gain optimal exposure to a target segment means that advertising campaigns tend to be carefully planned within budget constraints. The different media available also each offer their distinctive pros and cons. Whilst TV exposure offers the opportunity to convey a complex message owing to the ability to combine images and speech, it is the most expensive. Other media, such as posters and press are much cheaper, but only allow for a simple message, possibly only a single picture and a slogan.

The choice of media will partly depend upon the type of product. It would be inappropriate, for example, for industrial products to be promoted on TV, but instead, it would make sense to promote such products in the specialist industrial press, where a highly targeted readership could be addressed. Advertising specialists work upon the assumption that certain TV programmes, radio stations, papers and magazines attract different demographic profiles. Further refinement can be found in the targeting of specific demographic groupings at different times, time of day. Examine TV schedules and note the correlation between types of programmes, their time slots and the associated advertising.

Question 28.7

Try to describe the demographic profile that would be most likely to watch, listen or read the following:

- CBeebies – BBC TV
- Breakfast with Frost – BBC 1 TV
- The Independent newspaper
- Wake up with Wogan – BBC Radio 2
- The Simpsons – Sky one TV
- The Sun newspaper
- Q magazine
- Friends – Channel 4 TV
- The World Today – BBC World Service

1 Use the market segmentation demographic variables to describe each one (e.g. the readership of *Mother and Baby* might be sex: female, socio-economic group: ABC1, age: 20–40, stage of family life cycle: married with young children). Some productions may have a highly specific audience (e.g. the profile for *Songs of Praise* might include the description 'religious' or 'church-goer').
2 For each one, suggest a product that might be successfully advertised in it (i.e. one which is aimed at the profile in question).

The message conveyed will also vary according to product and target segment. Consumer product promotions may contain an element of emotional appeal whilst industrial products, such as chemicals, will tend to simply communicate their technical specification (because this is what the buyer cares about). Promotional communication messages are designed to convey the product's benefits to the target segment. This task is made easier if the product is in some way differentiated from its competitors. If it has a *unique selling proposition* (USP) and can be readily distinguished from others, then it makes sense to centre the marketing message on the unique features.

There is an interesting recent history of the use of innovative messages and ideas in advertising. Cigarette manufacturers, who must abide by strict guidelines in their advertising, have used the restrictions to their advantage. Readers may remember the 'Reg' campaign for Embassy Regal, or the ongoing images in Silk Cut press and poster adverts. A successful and memorable symbol or slogan can embed the brand image into consumers' consciousness – a very valuable asset in maintaining and increasing market share.

Question 28.8

How successful is TV advertising? Test your recall – which companies or brands are associated with the following slogans?

- … reassuringly expensive,
- the sweets you can eat between meals,
- the appliance of science,
- and all because the lady loves …,
- vorsprung durch technik,
- just do it,
- probably the best lager in the world,
- targeted relief for pain,
- have a break, have a …

Brands and Logos

Brands are the distinctive tangible identifiers of products that companies use to distinguish their products from those of competitors. There are many world famous brand names, such as '*Coke*' and '*Pepsi*', that are jealously guarded by the brand owners – the very colour schemes and shape of the product ranges also fall into a *family branding* theme. Often, brand names are supported by clearly identifiable *logos*, such as the large yellow '*M*' for *McDonalds* or '*KFC*', and its picture of '*Colonel Saunders*'.

The perception of a brand can have significant impact upon sales and the marketing function will be keen to establish and promote positive associations of brand and product.

Product placement

Product placement is the deliberate placing of products or their logos in films or TV by brand owners, in the expectation that a successful entertainment vehicle will bring related extensive exposure for their brands.

This can be a very expensive promotional investment but the returns from hugely popular productions can be substantial. Examples can be found in many films and TV shows, such as the use of *Aston Martin* cars in the James Bond film series or background neon signs and billboards for brands like *Sony*, *Coca Cola* and *Nokia* in films like '*Bladerunner*' or '*Minority Report*'. At a more localised level, the placement of items like *Kelloggs' Cornflakes* or *HP sauce* in a TV 'soap' can prove to be quite significant. Of course, there is always the possibility of poor investment decisions when, perhaps, the chosen film is unsuccessful or lack of control may reduce the effectiveness of the placement with the action overshadowing the product.

Below-the-line promotions

Below-the-line promotions are marketing communications which do not use the media. The fact that they can be very highly targeted means that they have grown in importance over recent years such that in some sectors, below-the-line expenditure exceeds above-the-line spending. The nature of this type of promotion means that they are especially suited to activity in the consumer goods retail sector, although they can also be used for industrial products.

As a category, below-the-line promotions can be conveniently divided into two types:

- *Push promotions* are incentives for salespeople to increase their sales of products.
- *Pull promotions* are those which encourage customers to increase their weight of purchase.

Unlike above-the-line promotions, which tend by their nature to be relatively unfocused, below-the-line communications can be very closely targeted to gain a high exposure to the target market segment. Efforts can be focused upon a single product or market at relatively modest cost.

Push promotions can be centred upon one product which a business wishes to particularly promote or they can apply generally. Examples include:

- commission on sales for sales staff;
- increases in dealer margins (i.e. price reductions to distributors);
- trade or shop demonstrations or exhibitions;
- 'best salesperson of the year' award.

Pull promotions include:

- Short-term price decreases (e.g. a *loss leader* – a price reduction on a selected item designed to get customers 'through the door' in the belief that additional sales will recoup the profit reduction in the loss leader).
- More favourable credit terms (e.g. lower interest rates, longer credit periods or both).
- 'Buy one get one free' offers.
- Coupons and trading stamps.
- Improved guarantees (e.g. extended guarantees – some car companies offer up to 3 years 'free' servicing, etc.).
- Point of sale displays (features in a shop designed to attract customers' attention).
- Checkout savers (where the 'ringing through' of one item through a supermarket till will automatically trigger a money-off voucher for a direct competitor brand – paid for by the competitor).

Pull promotions assume great importance in some sectors. A notable example is petrol retailing where competitors are expected by customers to offer a range of vouchers, etc. Customers may remain brand loyal to a particular brand purely because of a below-the-line promotion.

Direct selling

Direct selling, in most instances, is the most closely targeted marketing promotion. Sales representatives and salespeople in shops generally do not find themselves discussing the benefits of a product unless the potential customer has at least a reasonable interest in buying it.

The way in which a company carries out direct selling again depends upon the nature of the product and the characteristics of the customer. Typical formats used include:

- retail outlets employing salespeople as opposed to check outs (e.g. for electrical goods, motorcars, etc.);
- trade counters and factory shops;
- showrooms and warehouses;
- travelling sales representatives (reps). Usually involved in the sale of industrial goods;
- telephone sales (the practice of telephoning potential customers of a certain product, often by the use of an ACORN based segmentation).

The thing which all direct selling approaches have in common is that they involve a person-to-person communication. This affords the business the opportunity to closely understand the needs and motivations of the customer and to fashion the sales presentation accordingly.

Public Relations (PR) and community involvement

PR is that part of marketing communication activity which is usually geared to cultivate a favourable impression of the organisation, rather than a product, in the eyes of its various stakeholders (see Chapter 2). In consequence, PR tends to be less focused than other forms of marketing communication. An organisation may have many reasons to enhance its public perception. Common motivations include:

- to stimulate investors' interest in the company's shares;
- to enhance the organisation's reputation for quality, service, etc.;
- to answer criticism or scepticism about certain commercial activities;
- to enhance the organisation's reputation as a good employer to encourage good people to apply for jobs;
- to make the organisation appear to be caring, environmentally responsible, etc.;
- to influence the opinions of politicians;
- to counteract unfavourable publicity.

Organisations use several vehicles for PR:

- 'open days', where stakeholders are invited to visit and see the organisation in action;
- press and PR departments, where staff are happy to answer queries from any interested stakeholders;
- press statements – items written by the company for publication in newspapers, etc.;
- 'roadshows', such as visits to local schools, exhibitions at conferences, etc.;
- videos issued to stakeholder groups;
- charitable donations and sponsorship of community projects;
- visitor centres, where interested people can come and learn about company activities (such as the elaborate visitor centre at the Sellafield nuclear reprocessing centre in Cumbria);
- sponsorship of sports events, football teams, etc.

References

1   The Chartered Institute of Marketing website: www.cim.co.uk
2   Drucker, P. (1999). *The Practice of Management.* London: Heinemann.
3   Kotler, P. (1993). *Marketing Management & Analysis – Planning and Control*, 8th edn. US imports & PHIPEs.
4   Kotler, P. and Armstrong, G. (eds) (2003). *Principles of Marketing*, 10th edn. London: Prentice-Hall.
5   Roberts, D. (ed.) (2004). *Guinness World Records: British Hit Singles and Albums.* London: Guinness World Records Ltd.
6   Levitt, T. (1974). *Marketing for Business Growth.* New York: McGraw Hill.
7   Wells, W. and Gubar, G. (1966). *Life cycle concept in marketing research. Journal of Marketing Research*, **3** (November): pp. 355–363.
8   ACORN is the registered trademark of CACI limited; reproduced with permission.

Further reading

Adcock, D., Bradfield, R., Halborg, A. and Ross, C. (1998). *Marketing. Principles and Practice*, 3rd edn. London: Financial Times Prentice Hall.

Baker, M.J. (1996). *Marketing: An Introductory Text*, 6th edn. London: Macmillan Press.

Fletcher, A.C. and Jones, N. (1997). *Value Pricing. How to Price Products and Services.* London: Kogan Page.

Gregory, A. (ed.) (2003). *Public Relations in Practice.* London: Kogan Page.

Hart, N. (ed.) (1995). *Strategic Public Relations.* London: Macmillan.

Hutchings, A. (1995). *Marketing. A Resource Book.* London: Pitman.

Jobber, D. (2004). *Principles and Practice of Marketing*, 4th edn. Maidenhead: McGraw Hill.

Kinnear, T.C., Bernhardt, K.I. and Krentler, K.A. (1995). *Principles of Marketing*, 4th edn. London: Longman.

Lancaster, G.A. and Reynolds, P. (1995). *Marketing.* Oxford: Butterworth Heinemann.

Stone, N. (1995). *The Management and Practice of Public Relations.* London: Macmillan Press.

Useful web sites

The Chartered Institute of Marketing website: www.cim.co.uk

Corporate finance and accounting

After studying this chapter, students should be able to describe:

- why a business needs money;
- the sources of money;
- the types of accountants and their roles;
- the structure and content of the legally-required financial statements;
- the principal methods of analysing financial performance of organisations.

29.1 Money and business

Why does a business need money?

Essentially, business can be said to be all about money – acquiring it, managing it, investing it and spending it. It follows that the management of money in an organisation is a job of great importance. In most organisations, this responsibility rests with the accounting function (sometimes called the finance function).

At the beginning of a chapter on accounting and finance, it seems appropriate to ask the question: why does a business need money?

Firstly, *a business needs money to meet its operating costs*. In the course of normal business activities, a business incurs costs through having to pay for such things as:

- wages and salaries;
- rent and local authority taxation;
- raw materials and purchased items;
- insurance;
- energy (e.g. fuels).

Secondly, money is needed *to purchase new capital items* to enable the business to grow and develop. Included in this category are such things as:

- new land and buildings,
- new plant and equipment,
- new technologies.

Thirdly, money is sometimes needed *to make good short-term cash deficits* that arise from overspends on operating or capital costs. From time to time, a business runs out of money for a short period of time, in much the same way that you or I might in the week before pay-day or at the end of term. Money must be found to enable the business to continue through such periods.

Where does money come from?

Having discussed why a business needs money, we now turn to the sources of money open to a business.

The first and most important source of money is *from sales of goods and services*. Businesses in the 'for-profit' sector produce outputs which they exchange for money. This type of money is called *revenue* or *income*.

Secondly, business can obtain money *from loans*. Loans take many forms depending upon the size of the loan and the body that lends it. Money can be obtained from banks, building societies and other financial institutions, but also from private individuals.

Thirdly, business can obtain money *from its retained profits* or *reserves*. This is money earned in previous years from the sales of goods and services which can be accessed to use as and when appropriate (in the same way that you and I might use our savings).

Fourthly, money can be obtained *from donations, gifts or non-repayable grants*. Charities and political organisations make use of gifts whilst public sector organisations make use of funding from central government, such as the funding a university receives indirectly from central government to operate its courses, research, etc. Grants are sometimes paid by government agencies to attract businesses to set up in areas of high unemployment.

Fifthly, money can be raised *by selling shares*. When a limited company begins in business, it raises its money through selling shares. However, the same method of money raising can be used later in the company's life in a *rights issue*. This approach is not often used as it can exert a downward pressure on the market price of existing shares.

29.2 People and roles in the accounting function

The importance of the management of financial resources means that in most organisations, the responsibility is entrusted to a professionally qualified individual called an accountant.

Accountants and accounting technicians

An accountant is a person who has gained a professional qualification from one of the main accountancy bodies. Entry to such bodies is by examination and passing all of the papers for a given body can take several years (the Association of Chartered Certified Accountant, e.g. currently requires that each candidate passes 14 papers to gain admission as a professional member). The bodies recognised in the various parts of the UK are as follows (brackets indicate designatory letters of professional members):

- Association of Chartered Certified Accountants (ACCA)
- Chartered Institute of Management Accountants (CIMA)
- Chartered Institute of Public Finance and Accountancy (CIPFA)
- Institute of Chartered Accountants in England and Wales (ICAEW)
- Institute of Chartered Accountants in Scotland (ICAS)
- Institute of Chartered Accountants in Ireland (ICAI).

A second important type of employee in the accounting department is the accounting technician. These are people who have qualified as members of the *Association of Accounting Technicians* (AAT), a body that qualifies people to work closely with accountants and to assist them in managing the accounting function. Accounting technicians form an important part of the administration in many accounting departments.

The diversity of the jobs that are performed in the accounting function means that both accountants and accounting technicians are usually assisted by other administrative and clerical staff.

Types of accountant

Accountants are found in all sectors of business and governmental activity. Any organisation that uses money (i.e. all but a tiny minority) have a potential need for accounting professionals. Generally speaking, accountants do one or more of four things:

- they *report* on the financial performance or financial state of an organisation;
- they *manage* finance and financial information and they advise non-financial managers based on their knowledge;
- they *audit* (check and approve) financial information by carrying out procedures to ensure the veracity of financial statements;
- they *advise* on business and money-related matters, such as investments, taxation and forecasting.

Accordingly, there are four broad types of accounting:

- *financial accounting*, producing financial reports;
- *management accounting*, assisting with the management of the organisation;
- *auditing*, checking the financial statements and accounting systems of an organisation;
- *consultancy* and specialist accounting.

The majority of accountants work in the first three areas. These are the 'bread and butter' accountancy areas. A minority act as advisers or consultants in specialised areas. In addition to specialism in such things as tax, some accountants work in accounting law or in mergers and acquisitions whilst others work in areas, such as international finance, banking and insurance. This chapter cannot possibly be exhaustive in its discussion, but it hoped that the discussion acts as an overview of the subject. Readers should bear in mind that although the accounting areas are considered separately, the tasks may be performed by the same person in smaller companies.

Financial accountants

Financial accountants produce accounting reports and may also assist in the organisation's financial management. In practice, this means three things.

Firstly, financial accountants oversee the process of *financial recording*. This involves logging all transactions onto documents called ledgers. Whereas at one time the accounting office in a business was lined with ledger books, all but a minority have now installed computerised systems. Although the financial accountant is unlikely to enter the transactions himself, he will oversee the administrators and clerks as they enter the details of each sale, purchase, expense claim, bank deposit and withdrawal, etc.

Secondly, financial accountants ensure the business has sufficient finance available at any one time to operate normally and to invest when necessary. In consequence, they are often skilled at raising finance in the various ways we considered at the beginning of this chapter. They work out the most cost-effective way of *financing* the business and ensuring that cash is available when required. It is thus the financial accountant that organises such things as bank loans and rights issues. He or she oversees the recording of all the financial transactions of the business such as sales and purchases.

The third area in which the financial accountant is involved is in the *reporting* of the financial position of the business in accordance with the law and agreed accounting standards. This means preparing accounts for publication at timely intervals (typically at the financial year end and at half year intervals). One of the conditions placed upon limited companies is the requirement to file an audited '*Annual Report and Accounts*'.

There are five compulsory components to this document, as set out in the UK in the *Companies Act, 1985 (amended)*:

- the chairman's statement;
- the auditor's report;
- the profit and loss (P&L) account;
- the balance sheet;
- the cash-flow statement (CFS).

The accounting rules by which they are constructed are prescribed in *Financial Reporting Standards* (FRSs), to ensure that all companies mean the same thing when they make an entry in one of the statements. When they are completed (following the company's financial year end), they become publicly available – each shareholder receives a copy, and a copy is lodged at *Companies House*.

Later in this chapter, we will examine the elements and uses of the P&L, the balance sheet and the CFS.

Management accountants

As their title suggests, management accountants are engaged in accounting as it relates to helping to manage the business. Their task extends to the preparation of information that helps other (non-accountant) managers perform their jobs with the maximum possible information 'at their fingertips'. In consequence, it will be the management accountant that managers approach to receive advice of such things as investment (e.g. in new machinery), staffing levels, marketing spending, and the funding of research and development programmes. In most companies, all senior managers will consult or be consulted by the management accountant on a regular basis.

As a professional who understands the company's financial affairs and who is also in possession of a wide range of planning and forecasting skills, a management accountant can carry out several management tasks for or on behalf of other managers. The most common are described below:

- *Management accounts*: The issuing of financial information on (usually) a monthly basis to inform managers on the financial state of the business to facilitate understanding and to promote intelligent decision-making.
- *Costing*: The process of determining the costs associated with the organisation's products and services. There are a number of approaches to costing; the approach adopted depends upon the type of information wanted by the management. It may be that a manager wants to know the cost of materials in a product or it may be that the full cost is required including the share of fixed costs attributable to the product's production.
- *Cash-flow forecasting*: The setting of revenue and payments estimates on a monthly basis for a forthcoming period of time (typically a year). By doing this, a business can see how cash balances vary from month to month and also highlight any months where there is a net cash outflow, in which case a way must be found for making good the shortfall.
- *Budgeting*: The practice of setting income and expenditure expectations for a forthcoming period of time. A spending or *expenditure budget* represents an expectation or a limit at which

spending departments, such as operations, should aim towards. An *income budget* applies to those departments that raise money for the organisation. Hence, there may be a sales budget or a fund-raising budget (for charities). Budgets are set internally as a means of control where the value of a budget is set (usually) in negotiation with the departmental manager to whom it applies.

- *Variance analysis*: This provides a means of comparison of actual performance against budget. Variances against budget are typically calculated monthly and can be good or bad news to the management accountant.
  - *Adverse variances* are those which are unfavourable to the business, that is, expenditure above budget or income below budget.
  - *Favourable variances* are those which are good news, that is, expenditure below budget or income above budget.
- *Investment appraisal*: This appraisal is the responsibility of the management accountant and involves evaluating the financial viability of investments proposed by departmental managers. It may be, for example, that the manufacturing director wishes to purchase some extra factory space or a new machine. The management accountant will calculate the returns from the investment (in increased sales or reduced costs as a result of the purchase) and compare this against the price of the investment. If the price of the investment can be repaid within an acceptable time period, the accountant will probably approve the investment and release the cash. If, however, it looks like the investment will not give significant benefits to the business, it is likely that the accountant will recommend that it is not approved.
- *Competitor analysis*: This analysis involves gaining intelligence on a company's competitors by analysing financial information in competitors' published accounts. Whilst this task could theoretically be done by anybody, the management accountant is often best suited for the task. He or she will usually 'pick through' competitors' accounts to see how the competitor looks against his own business. In a management technique called *benchmarking*, accountants analyse the performance of the leading competitor in an industry (e.g. the most profitable) and seek to learn how the superior performance has been brought about. This can help to inform the practice of departmental managers in the business as they

seek to improve the efficiency of their particular specialist areas.

29.3 Financial statements

When accountants (usually financial accountants) report on a company's performance, they must do so using strictly defined formats. The three mandatory reporting statements are, as we have seen, the profit and loss statement, the balance sheet and the CFS. The law requires that each statement be constructed using specific rules so that observers know that they are making a meaningful comparison when they study the accounts of more than one business. The old *Statements of Standard Accounting Practice* (SSAPs) are being replaced with instruments called FRSs. Companies are thus bound to work within the provisions of these standards when reporting on financial matters.

Profit and loss statement

What is the P&L account?

The *P&L*, is essentially a *trading account* for a period, usually a year, but also can be monthly and cumulative. It shows profit performance, and often has little to do with cash, stocks and assets which must viewed from a separate perspective using the balance sheet and CFS. Basically, the P + L serves to demonstrate how the company has performed in its trading activities.

The P&L typically shows:

- sales revenues;
- cost of sales/cost of goods sold (COGS);
- gross profit margin (sometimes called the contribution);
- fixed overheads and/or operating expenses;
- profit before interest and tax (PBIT).

A fully detailed P&L can be quite complex dependent on the size and nature of the company, and the policies and conventions in use. However for demonstration purposes, an example of a simplified P&L

account is shown below:

Company Name

Trading profit and loss account for the year to dd/mm/yy

£

Sales

Income from sold goods

Cost of goods sold

Opening finished goods in stock

Add: Cost of finished goods manufactured

Less: Closing finished goods in stock

Gross profit

Less:

Expenses

Distribution costs

Selling costs

Administration costs

Other income + expenditure

Net profit before interest and tax

In practice, of course, company accounts are not as simple as the above general form. An example of the complexities of a real company P&L are shown below in the summary of the P&L for British Telecommunications (BT) plc, as at 31 March, 2004 for the financial year 2003–2004. It should be noted that this P&L refers to BT Group plc, which is the listed *holding company* for an integrated group of businesses in the UK and worldwide (i.e. BT Retail, BT Wholesale, BT Global Services, BT Openworld and BT Exact). There are individual trading accounts for each of these businesses.

British Telecommunications plc

Profit and loss statement for year ended 31 March 2004

	£ millions
Group turnover	18,519
Group operating profit (loss)	2892
Group's share of operating profit (loss) of associates and joint ventures	(8)
Total operating profit (loss)	2884
Profit on sale of fixed asset investments and group undertakings	4
Profit on sale of property fixed assets	14

Amounts written off investments	–
Net interest payable	(886)
Profit (loss) before taxation	2016
Tax	(568)
Profit (loss) after taxation	1448
Minority interests	8
Profit (loss) for the financial year	1456
Net goodwill amortisation and exceptional items	(39)
Dividends	(732)
Retained profit	685
Earnings per share (after amortisation and exceptional items)	16.4p
Dividends per share	8.5p

Source: Reproduced courtesy of British Telecommunications plc, Annual Report 2004.

Items in the P&L statement

- *Group turnover* refers to total sales of products and services from all of the holding company's businesses.
- *Operating costs* refer to the total cost of running the business. This can be divided into the various types of cost: purchases of stocks for resale, labour, administration and distribution, which are the *operating costs*. As PBIT represents the surplus made on normal operating and trading activities, this figure is sometimes referred to as *operating profit*. Before the business can consider the profit its own, it must pay the appropriate proportion to the Inland Revenue in taxation and interest on any outstanding loans.
- *COGS* refers to the value.
- *Profit after interest and tax* (PAIT), or earnings refers to the money that a company realises after all costs, expenses and taxes have been paid. It is calculated by subtracting business, depreciation, interest and tax costs from revenues. It is this money that is available to the management and shareholders of a company to use at their discretion. There are three possible uses for PAIT:
  1 part of it can be paid to shareholders as *dividends*, thus providing the shareholders with a *return on their investment*;

2 it can be *retained* by the business in the bank for future investment and expansion;

3 it can offset *losses* made in previous years by paying off *long-term debts*.

Note: *Profit*, is the overarching mission in private sector companies, whereas *governmental* or *non-profit organisations* either operate at a loss or attempt to achieve a zero profit as their overarching mission is a charter for service, or a goal to be achieved. Therefore there is a basic distinction in measures of strategic success between profit and non-profit or governmental organisations.)

- *Amortisation* is the repayment of the capital, or principal of a loan. It is the accounting process where an interest bearing liability (such as a mortgage) is paid off over time through regular installments that comprise both principal and interest. The term is also used to describe the writing-down of the book value of assets.

- *Dividends* are payments a corporation makes when it distributes earnings to shareholders in proportion to the number of shares they hold. A preferred dividend is usually for a fixed amount, while a common dividend may fluctuate with the profits of the company. A company is under no legal obligation to pay either preferred or common dividends.

- *Earnings per share* (EPS) is the profit for the financial year divide by the average number of shares in issue during the period.

Balance sheet

What is a balance sheet?

The balance sheet is a statement which lists the assets, liabilities and equity of a business at any specified time. In simple terms it is a 'snapshot' of the financial health of the business at that point in time and most companies will prepare a balance sheet every 6 or 12 months.

The term 'balance sheet' derives from the two-way process of detailing the sources of finance on one side of the balance sheet and how it has been used on the other side. Every entry for an item of incoming finance must have a corresponding entry for usage, hence the term '*double entry*'. It must always balance.

British Telecommunications plc

Balance sheet at 31 March 2004

A look at a real-life example will show us how this looks. The example is that of BT Group plc for the financial year 2003–2004, simplified for the purposes of this demonstration:

	£ millions
Fixed assets	16,068
Current assets	10,550
Creditors: amounts falling due within one year	(8548)
Net current assets	2002
Total assets fixed and current less current liabilities	**18,070**
Creditors: amounts falling due after one year	2426
Provisions for liabilities and charges	2504
Minority interests	46
Capital and reserves	3094
	18,070

Source. Reproduced courtesy of British Telecommunications plc, Annual Report 2004.

Items in the balance sheet: assets side

- *Fixed assets* include '*tangible assets*' that is, the value of money invested in plant, machinery, buildings, fittings, vehicles and land. They also include the value of longer-term investments.
- *Current assets* refer to the value of money tied in things which enable the business to operate in the relatively short term. There are three categories of current asset:
  - *stocks* are items stored by the business to be processed or to sold,
  - *debtors* refer to the amount of money owed to the company,
  - *investments* refer to the value of short-term investments,
  - *cash* is simply money which is immediately available either in a bank account or in literal notes and coins.
- *Current liabilities* refer to the value of money that the business owes to its suppliers for goods supplied or for services rendered. These are sometimes called *creditors* and fit into two categories:
  - '*due within one year*' are loans or debts due for repayment with a year;
  - '*due after one year*' are loans and debts due for repayment over the longer term.

Items in the balance sheet: 'funded by' side

- *Share capital* is the money that the company has made use of from its shareholders.
- *Reserves* are the accumulated and retained difference between profits and losses year on year. They can come from the sale of assets (e.g. subsidiary businesses) or from retained profits (money put aside from previous successful years' trading).
- *P&L* is earnings from the P&L account transferred across to the balance sheet. This is a form of 'reserves' in itself.

Cash-flow statement

The CFS is the third compulsory financial statement. The CFS is unique in that examines only movements of cash in and out of the company over the course of the financial year. In this respect, it is different from the balance sheet in that the balance sheet refers to just the last day of the financial year and that it records the value of assets as well as cash on the day in question.

It follows from the statement's *raison d'être*, that it should be structured in such a way as to show each area of inward and outward cash movement. This is indeed the case. The general form of the CFS is as follows:

	£
Cash generated from operating activities	XXX
Returns on investments and servicing of finance	XXX
Taxation paid	XXX
Cash generated from investing activities	XXX
Net cash inflow/outflow before financing	XXX
Payments to the sources of finance	XXX
Net cash flow for the year	**XXX**

CFS: British Telecommunications plc

The following statement is simplified from the BT Group plc accounts for the year to 31 March 2004.

	£ millions
Net cash flow from operating activities	5,389
Dividends from associates and joint ventures	3
Returns on investments and servicing of finance	(527)
Taxation paid	(317)
Capital expenditure and financial investment	(2477)
Free cash flow	2071
Acquisitions and disposals	(60)
Equity dividends paid	(645)
Cash inflow before management of liquid resources and financing	1366
Management of liquid resources	1123
Financing	(2445)
Increase (decrease) in cash in the year	44
Decrease in net debt in the year resulting from cash flows	1222

Source: Reproduced courtesy of British Telecommunications plc, Annual Report 2004

Items in the CFS

- *Net cash inflow from operating activities* shows cash injections from normal trading. This is often simply the cash gained from profits after all outgoing costs (e.g. dividends) have been paid.
- *Returns on investment and servicing of finance* shows the amount of cash gained or lost as a result of investments and debts. The company pays servicing costs on its debts (rather like a mortgage-holder pays a monthly instalment on a mortgage), but it receives income from any investments it has made, such as bank deposits.
- *Free cash flow* refers to cash receipts less payments from trading activities before corporate transactions, dividend payments and financing.
- *Financing* concerns the provision of cash to the business for use over the longer term and can include such things as new long-term loans (cash income), loan repayment (cash outgoing) or proceeds from the sale of new shares in the company (cash income – a process known as a *rights issue*).
- *Taxation* is cash paid on all of the company's taxable income. This includes tax on profits and on income from investments.

The completed CFS shows a net inflow or outflow of cash over the course of the financial year in question. It follows that a positive figure is significantly more favourable than a negative figure.

29.4 Financial management

An analysis of a company's financial position is an indispensable part of any strategic review. Decision-makers need to know whether or not the company has the level of funding required to finance their strategies and, if not, financial resource will have to be raised.

It is usually important to know where a company has obtained its capital and the cost of the capital. Both share capital and loan capital have their advantages and disadvantages for use in strategic development. It is important to note whether or not current levels of profitability are sufficient to service the costs of capital.

In the next section, we will examine a range of the main analytical tools that can be used to make sense of a company's financial statements.

29.5 Analysing financial statements

Financial information, at its simplest, is essentially a set of numbers. In order to make sense of it and to make it useful, we must analyse it. We do this by employing a few simple techniques:

- by examining trends in financial numbers;
- by calculating ratios comparing one financial figure with another;
- by comparing one company's financial information with another's.

Financial trends

Accounting numbers are made more meaningful when they are compared to the same numbers over previous years. For example, in the year ended 31 March 2003, the total sales for J Sainsbury plc, the supermarket chain amounted to £18,495 – a substantial sum but, in itself, it is only a number. We will be able to say much more about what this tells us about the company's performance if we compare it with the sales volume in previous years, and particularly the percentage growth of 'like for like' sales, year on year. The data in Figure 29.1 shows us a fluctuating picture of sales performance over a 5-year period. We can see that the company recovered from a very low position in 2000 to a relatively much improved position by 2002, before 2003 saw a return to a level similar to that in 1999.

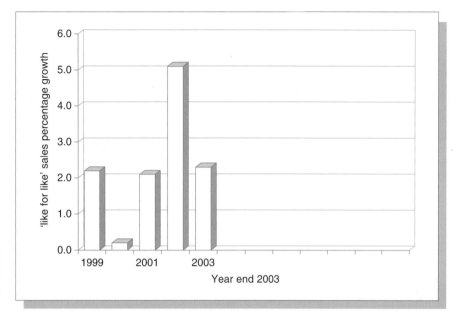

Figure 29.1
J Sainsbury plc:
annual percentage
sales growth,
1999–2003.

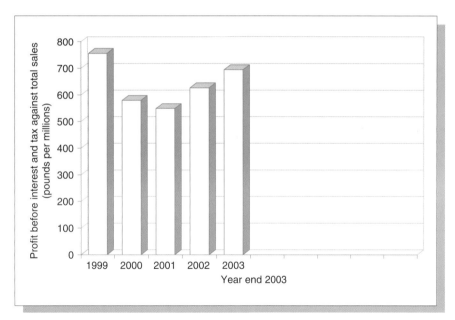

Figure 29.2
J Sainsbury plc:
trend in
profitability,
1999–2003.

There are many other accounting numbers we can examine in addition to trends in sales. We may also construct a graph to show how the company's profitability has grown or shrunk over a number of years (Figure 29.2).

The lesson to be drawn from the use of trends is that figures are much more meaningful when they are placed into the context of previous years' results and by examining the numbers from Figures 29.1 and 29.2

we can see that, against a backdrop of fluctuating sales, there is an upward trend in profit levels for the 3 years to 2003. While this provides useful information, we need to analyse a wider range of financial data in order to fully appreciate the trading and financial health of the company. We can use any of the figures in the P&L or balance sheet to construct a trend – or use any of the ratios we will consider in the next section.

Financial ratios

The figures that appear in company accounts are not, in themselves, very meaningful. A number in an account is simply that, a number. In order to make the analysis of accounts more meaningful, numbers are compared against each other in the form of ratios.

A ratio is arrived at by dividing one number by another. We can appreciate the value of ratios by looking at a simple example. Suppose you hear of the weight of two people: person A weighs 15 stone weight and person B weighs 10 stone weight. You might then conclude that person A is fatter and therefore less healthy than person B. Such a conclusion would be unwise because the body weight itself is meaningless unless you also know the person's height. This is because the 'fatness' of a person is defined by the ratio between height and weight. If the two people are the same height then it is clearly obvious the person A is the fatter. If, however, person A at 15 stone is 8 feet tall, it is likely that he or she will actually be thin.

The lesson is clear: figures must be placed within a meaningful context to make them significant. Two companies each with a turnover of £100 million might appear at first glance to be similar, but until we know about their respective profits, capital employed, etc. we cannot make an intelligent comment about the two companies' performance.

In accountancy, financial ratios are used to analyse the financial features of accounts (usually annual accounts). For the purposes of our discussion, we can say that the most useful ratios fall into five broad categories:

- performance ratios,
- efficiency ratios,
- working capital ratios,
- financial structure ratios,
- investors' ratios.

The following discussion focuses upon some of the most widely used accounting ratios. Readers should be aware that many more than these can be calculated.

Performance ratios

Performance ratios, as their name suggests, are those which are used to determine how well the company has performed in business terms. The crux of performance is *return*. A return is a financial profit compared to either the company's sales or the company's capital employed. There is, however, as we have seen, more than one definition of profit. We might think of profit in terms of *PBIT*, or *earnings* (PAIT). We must consequently specify which one we refer to in any performance ratio:

- *Return on Capital Employed* (ROCE) is a measure of how effectively the company has used the shareholders' investment. For a business to make effective use of this investment, ROCE must at least be greater than the current rate of interest – the rate or return that the shareholder could get by investing his or her money in the local building society:

$$\text{ROCE} = \frac{\text{PBIT}}{\text{net capital employed}} \times 100.$$

  Note: Capital Employed is usually taken to mean shareholders equity.

- *Return on Sales* (RoS) – sometimes called the profit margin – gives an indication of how successfully the company has managed to control its costs in relation to sales income generated:

$$\text{RoS} = \frac{\text{PBIT}}{\text{total sales}}.$$

- *Return on Investment* (RoI) is a measure of how much a company earns on the money the company itself has invested. It is calculated by dividing the company's net income by its net assets.

Efficiency ratios

Efficiency ratios record how well the company has used its factor inputs. Given that the company pays for inputs such as land, machinery and personnel, efficiency ratios attempt to assess how well the company has used these inputs in its business activities. Examples of efficiency ratios include:

$$\text{sales per employee} = \frac{\text{total sales}}{\text{number of employees}}.$$

$$\text{profit per employee} = \frac{\text{PBIT}}{\text{number of employees}}.$$

Both of these ratios measure how efficiently the company has turned its labour inputs into money – either in terms of sales or profits. In some industries such as retailing, efficiency can be measured by comparing sales or profits with the floor area of a shop.

$$\text{sales per square metre} = \frac{\text{total sales}}{\text{floor area of shop in square metres}}.$$

This ratio tells us how well the retail company uses its limited floor space. Efficient retailers will produce higher sales per square metre that inefficient ones. We can apply efficiency ratios to any of the factors of production.

Working capital ratios

Working capital is the amount of money that a company has tied up in the normal operation of its business. Working capital comprises money tied up in stocks, in debtors (money owed to the business), creditors (money the company owes) and in actual cash or current bank deposits. A company's objective is thus to either minimise this figure or at least to make efficient use of it.

To test how well a company uses working capital, a number of ratios can be used. For example:

$$\text{days-debtors} = \frac{\text{value of debtors}}{\text{total sales}} \times 365.$$

$$\text{days-creditors} = \frac{\text{value of creditors}}{\text{total sales}} \times 365.$$

These two ratios tell us two things. Days-creditors tell us how effective the company is in delaying its payments to creditors. The larger the number, the longer the company takes to pay its creditors and thus the better the company uses its working capital. Conversely, days-debtors tell us how many days the company takes, on average, to collect its money owed. Good working capital management would usually be indicated by a low days-debtors.

The effectiveness of a company's stock management can be measured by its stock turn:

$$\text{rate of stock turnover} = \frac{\text{total sales}}{\text{value of stock}}.$$

We measure stock in the number of times the stock is turned over in the course of the financial year. If, for example a company's total sales is £2 million and its balance sheet value of stocks is £500,000, then the company turns its stock over four times. A high ratio indicates that a company is efficient in managing its stock levels whereas a low result would indicate inefficiency with the company carrying dead or slow moving stock.

Liquidity

An important area of working capital management is to monitor the company's liquidity. *Liquidity ratios* test the company's ability to meet its short-term cash needs by measuring the relationship between current assets (i.e. those which can be turned into cash relatively quickly) against the short-term debt value (current assets/current liabilities), also referred to as the *current ratio*. A company may be vulnerable to *insolvency* (running out of money) if its liquidity ratios are unfavourable.

We saw above that current liabilities comprise those items in the balance sheet which the company must be paid in the short-term. Conversely, current assets represent cash items that the company can 'count on' either because it is money owed or in cash form. To calculate liquidity, stock is subtracted from current assets because they are deemed to be slower to turn into cash than other current assets (because they have to be worked on and/or sold first):

$$\text{The current ratio} = \frac{\text{current assets}}{\text{current liabilities}}$$

If a low result is produced, it would indicate that the company has cash problems and would have difficulty paying any creditors, whereas a high figure could indicate that there is surplus cash available which should be put to work for the company, perhaps by way of investment elsewhere. A ratio of 2:1 would be the optimum for most companies.

$$\text{The quick ratio (acid test)} = \frac{\text{current assets} - \text{stock inventory} + \text{prepaid expenses}}{\text{current liabilities}}$$

> *Note.* This ratio is sometimes shown as: $\dfrac{\text{liquid assets}}{\text{current liabilities}}$.

This is a stern measure of a company's ability to pay its short-term debts, in that stock is excluded from asset value. The ideal ratio for this would be 1:1, and if the ratio is lower it may indicate that the company is currently having difficulty paying its current bills or financing its activities in the not too distant future.

Financial structure ratios

Financial structure refers to the way in which the company finances itself. We learned earlier that a company can use two broad methods of financing capital investment (quite a different thing to working capital which finances normal operations). Firstly, it can use shareholders funds which includes any retained profits which obviously also belong to the shareholders. Secondly, it can use debt from a bank or from another lender.

The ratio between these two is called the company's *debt/equity ratio (gearing)* – *equity* in this case means shareholders funds.

There are two common ways of calculating gearing:

$$\dfrac{\text{debt/equity}}{\text{(gearing)}} = \dfrac{\text{long-term borrowings}}{\text{borrowings} + \text{shareholders funds}}.$$

This ratio gives borrowings as a percentage of the company's total long-term capital.

$$\dfrac{\text{debt/equity}}{\text{(gearing)}} = \dfrac{\text{long-term borrowings}}{\text{shareholders funds}}.$$

This ratio tells us simply the ratio of the two. A figure greater than one means the company has more borrowings than equity; less than one, the converse.

Whilst it is common for businesses to make extensive use of debt to fund investment, being in too much debt increases the company's vulnerability to increases in the interest rate (see Chapter 9). A high gearing is also an indication that the company must eventually find the money to repay its debts. It is not a good indicator of future business performance. Debt has the advantage, however, of enabling the company to retain its equity for other purposes.

Investors' ratios

Investors are those people who inject their own money into a company, mainly shareholders, although banks and other lenders can also be considered as investors. Shareholders have three essential interests in a company. Firstly, they want to be sure that their investment is safe and that the company will survive, which they can gauge from ratios such as liquidity. Secondly, they want to receive dividends on their shares of meaningful value against the value of their investment. Thirdly, shareholders want to see the value of the share increase (*capital growth*) so that they can sell at a personal profit (the value of *performance ratios* will have an influence on this). *Investors' ratios* are those which inform shareholders of the state of their investment or which guide potential investors in a company as to the attractiveness of the company as an investment target. It follows that shareholders will potentially be interested in all ratios, although they may be particularly keen to analyse performance ratios.

Some ratios, however, are designed to give information which concerns various aspects of unique interest to shareholders and other investors. The EPS ratio takes the profit figure from the P&L account and tells us how much of the figure is attributable to each share:

$$EPS \text{ ratio} = \frac{\text{PAIT (in most recent annual accounts)}}{\text{number of shares issued (i.e. share volume)}}.$$

The EPS allows a shareholder to know how much profit is attributable to him or her on the basis of how many shares are owned. It should be borne in mind, however that only a part of the EPS will be payable as dividend.

Price per earnings

This is an important indicator as to how the market views the health, performance, prospects and investment risk of a public company listed on the stock market. The price per earnings (P/E) ratio is a highly complex concept that should not be taken as an absolute measure in itself but should be used in conjunction with other indicators. As EPS are a yearly total, the P/E ratio is also an expression of how many years it will take for earnings to cover the share price investment. P/E ratios are best viewed over a long period of time so that trends can be identified. A steadily increasing P/E ratio would be seen as speculatively high risk as it would take longer for earnings to cover the share price. The P/E ratio is an indication of the confidence that the investment community has in a company's shares:

$$\text{P/E ratio} = \frac{\text{current price of share}}{\text{EPS at last declaration of results}}.$$

Dividend yield is a ratio informing investors of the current return on the share as a percentage. Dividends are paid to shareholders as a return on their investment and are usually paid as a percentage of the earnings (PAIT). The company's directors recommend that some of the earnings exist kept in the company to reinvest as retained profits:

$$\text{dividend yield} = \frac{\text{gross dividend per share}}{\text{current price of share}} \times 100.$$

The yield is measured in percentage terms, and gives the investor an indication of the attractiveness of the share as a means of providing an economic return on his or her investment. Bearing in mind that the top of the ratio is *gross* dividend (i.e. before tax is paid on it by the recipient of the dividend), an investor would be looking to see that the yield is greater than the current rate of interest – the return that could be gained simply be placing the investment in the local building society or bank.

Cross-sectional (or comparison) analysis

To gauge a realistic assessment of the performance of a company, it is useful to make a comparative analysis with its competitors or companies in other industries. For example, if we were to identify a sales growth trend of 10% per annum over a number of years, we might be tempted to think that the company was performing well. However, if we compared this company with its competitors and found that the *industry average* rate of growth was 15% we might wish to modify our initial assessment of its performance. It is for the purposes of comparisons that *cross-sectional analyses* are important. As well as comparing accounting numbers like turnover, it is often helpful to compare two or more companies' ratios such as RoS or one of the *working capital ratios*.

Financial benchmarking

Inter-company comparison or *benchmarking* is a variation on cross-sectional analysis. It usually involves an analysis of 'like' companies, typically in the same industry though it can occasionally be an inter-industry analysis.

In order to make the benchmarking analysis meaningful, the company selection should normally be guided by similarity:

- Company size (i.e. comparable in terms of turnover, market value etc.);
- Industry (i.e. in that the companies produce similar products);
- Market (i.e. the companies share a similar customer base).

In practice, sample selection for a benchmarking study always involves some compromise because no two companies are in all respects directly comparable. Many companies, for example, operate in more than one industry and this may render problematic any comparisons with another company that operates in only one industry.

The practice of cross-sectional analysis using financial data has been undertaken by accountants for many years. Benchmarking, however, can be used to compare financial and, importantly, non-financial information between two or more companies.

Benchmarking is now used to compare the effectiveness of various processes, products and procedures against others. The objective is to identify where superior performance is found in whatever variable that is being used for comparison. Once the company with the highest performance is identified, the exercise becomes the exploration of the reasons behind the superior performance.

The benchmarking process therefore involves decisions on:

- what are we going to benchmark (financial and/or non-financial data)?
- who are we going to benchmark against (sample selection)?
- how will we get the information?
- how will analyse the information?
- how will we use the information?

The value of benchmarking is in identifying not only which company has the superior performance in a sector but also *why* this is the case. If, for example, our analysis throws up the fact that Company X enjoys a RoS significantly higher than the other companies in the sector, then Company X occupies the profitability benchmark in that sector.

The other companies may then wish to examine the practices within Company X that give rise to this level of performance.

For non-financial indicators, our analysis may highlight the fact that Company Y is able to attract the best-qualified people within a key category of personnel (e.g. the best scientists or computer programmers). In this case, Company Y demonstrates the benchmark in successful recruitment. Other companies who are unable to attract the best personnel would usually wish to examine Company Y to see why it is so successful in this regard.

Assignment 29.1

Obtain the financial accounts of a public limited company of your choice for the past 5 years (published accounts often contain 5- or 10-year trends whilst databases like FAME have 5 years' results as standard).

You are required to do the following:

- For the company in question, record or calculate, for the 5-year period: the turnover, the ROCE and the operating profit margin.
- Comment on the trend in each ratio. Do they show an optimistic or pessimistic outlook for the company? Give reasons for your conclusions.
- By checking the company's current share price (in the financial pages of a broadsheet newspaper), calculate the current price earnings ratio.
- From the P/E ratio, comment on the market's confidence in the company's shares.
- Prepare a short report on the company, its activities and recent performance to a potential investor. Would you recommend purchasing the shares?

Further reading

Atrill, P. (2002). *Management Accounting for Non-specialists*, 2nd edn. London: Prentice Hall.

Atrill, P., Harvey. D. and McLaney, E. (1994). *Accounting for Business*. Oxford: Butterworth Heinemann.

Bendrey, M., Hussey, R. and West, C. (1996). *Accounting and Finance for Business*, 4th edn. London: DP Publications.

Hussey, J. and R. (1994). *Essential Elements of Management Accounting*. London: DP Publications.

Millichamp, A.H. (1995). *Finance for Non-financial Managers*, 2nd edn. London: DP Publications.

Oldcorn, R. (1996). *Company Accounts*, 3rd edn. London: Macmillan Press.

Useful web sites

Chartered Institute of Management Accountants: www.cima.org.uk
Chartered Institute of Public Finance and Accountancy: www.cipfa.org.uk
Chartered Institute of Bankers: www.cib.org.uk
Institute of Chartered Accountants of England and Wales: www.icaew.co.uk
Institute of Chartered Accountants in Ireland: www.icai.co.uk
Institute of Chartered Accountants of Scotland: www.icas.org.uk
Institute of Cost and Executive Accountants: www.icea.enta.net
Institute of Financial Accountants: www.ifa.org.uk

Index